Ordnance Survey

STREET ATLAS
East Essex

Contents

IV *Key to maps*

VI *Administrative boundaries*

1 *Street maps*

206 *Index explanation and abbreviations*

207 *Index of towns, villages and rural localities*

208 *Index of street names*

PHILIP'S

First edition published 1990
Second edition published 1994
Reprinted 1997, 1998 by

Ordnance Survey®   and George Philip Ltd.
Romsey Road   an imprint of Reed Books Ltd
Maybush   Michelin House, 81 Fulham Road, London, SW3 6RB
Southampton SO16 4GU   and Auckland and Melbourne

ISBN 0-540-05848-3 (hardback)
ISBN 0-540-05866-1 (softback)

To the best of the Publishers' knowledge, the information in this atlas was correct at
the time of going to press. No responsibility can be accepted for any errors or their
consequences.

The representation in this atlas of a road, track or path is no evidence of the
existence of a right of way.

**The mapping between pages 1 and 204 (inclusive) in this atlas is derived from
Ordnance Survey® Land-Line® data and Landranger® mapping.**

Ordnance Survey, Land-Line and Landranger are registered trade marks of
Ordnance Survey, the National Mapping Agency of Great Britain.

Printed and bound in Great Britain by Bath Press, Bath

Key to map symbols

⇌	British Rail Station
⊖	London Transport station
🚂	Private railway station
●━●	Bus or coach station
Ⓗ	Heliport
◆	Police station (may not be open 24 hours)
✚	Hospital with casualty facilities (may not be open 24 hours)
☐	Post office
+	Place of worship
▄▟	Important building
P	Parking
120	Adjoining page indicator
≣	Motorway or dual carriageway
A27(T)	Main or through road (with Department of Transport number)
┬	Gate or obstruction to traffic (restrictions may not apply at all times or to all vehicles)
- - - - -	Footpath
— — —	Bridleway
– – –	Path
═══	Track

The representation in this atlas of a road, track or path is no evidence of the existence of a right of way

AmbSta	Ambulance station	LC	Level crossing
Coll	College	Liby	Library
FB	Footbridge	Mus	Museum
FSta	Fire station	Sch	School
Hospl	Hospital	TH	Town Hall

0	¼	½	¾	1 mile
0	250m	500m	750m	1 kilometre

The scale of the maps is 3½ inches to 1 mile (1:18103)

The small numbers around the edges of the maps
identify the 1 kilometre National Grid lines

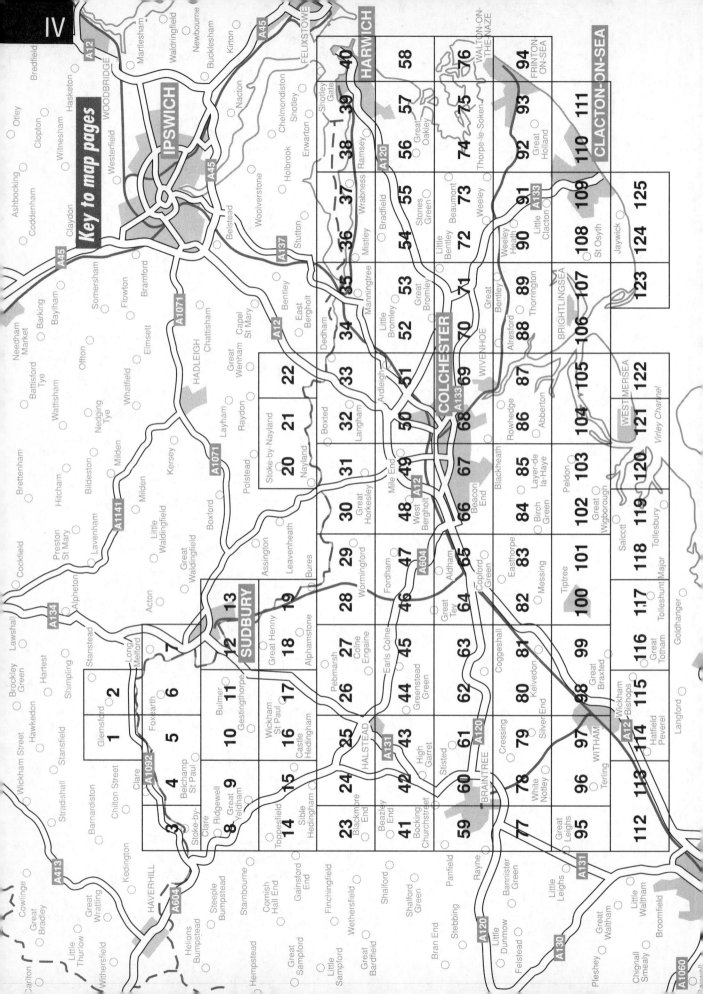

V

NORTH SEA

Virley Channel

126 **127** Little Waltham Broomfield
128 **129** CHELMSFORD
130 **131** Langford
Hatfield Peverel
132 **133** Tolleshunt Major Goldhanger Great Totham
134 **135** River Blackwater Tollesbury
136 **137** **138** Bradwell-on-Sea
Woodham Walter
MALDON

139 **140** **141** Galleywood Writtle Roxwell A1060 A414
142 **143** Danbury Bicknacre A414
144 **145** Mundon
146 **147** Steeple
148 **149** Tillingham Ramsey Island
150 **151**

A12 Ingatestone Loves Green

152 **153** West Hanningfield East Hanningfield A130
154 **155** Cold Norton South Woodham Ferrers A132
156 **157** Latchingdon
158 **159** Southminster Mayland
160 **161** Asheldham
162

BILLERICAY Stock South Hanningfield

163 Runwell
164 **165** Hullbridge A132
166 **167** South Fambridge North Fambridge
168 **169** Althorne Canewdon Ostend
170 **171** BURNHAM-ON-CROUCH
172 **173** River Crouch

Little Burstead A127 A129

174 **175** A127
176 **177** Hockley RAYLEIGH
178 **179** Ashingdon Rochford
180 **181** Paglesham Churchend
182 **183** Churchend FOULNESS ISLAND
184 Courtsend

Laindon A13

185 BASILDON **186** **187** **188** A13 SOUTH BENFLEET A13
189 **190** **191**
192 **193** Great Wakering
194

Horndon on the Hill A128 A130

195 **196** **197** CANVEY ISLAND A130
198 **199** SOUTHEND-ON-SEA
200 **201** **202** SHOEBURYNESS

Corringham Stanford-le-Hope A1014 A13

203 Thames Haven **204**

Chadwell St Mary

TILBURY

Yantlet Dredged Channel

SHEERNESS

Grain

Allhallows

Cooling Cliffe Woods Cliffe

Chalk

GRAVESEND A226 A227 A2 ROCHESTER A228

Higham St Werburgh Hoo Kingsnorth A228 A278 GILLINGHAM A2 A249

Queenborough Queensborough Minster Eastchurch ISLE OF SHEPPEY Leysdown on Sea

ISLE OF SHEPPEY

WHITSTABLE HERN BAY A291 A299

Chestfield Herne Broomfield Marshside A229 A2

0 1 2 3 4 5 6 7 8 km
0 1 2 3 4 5 miles

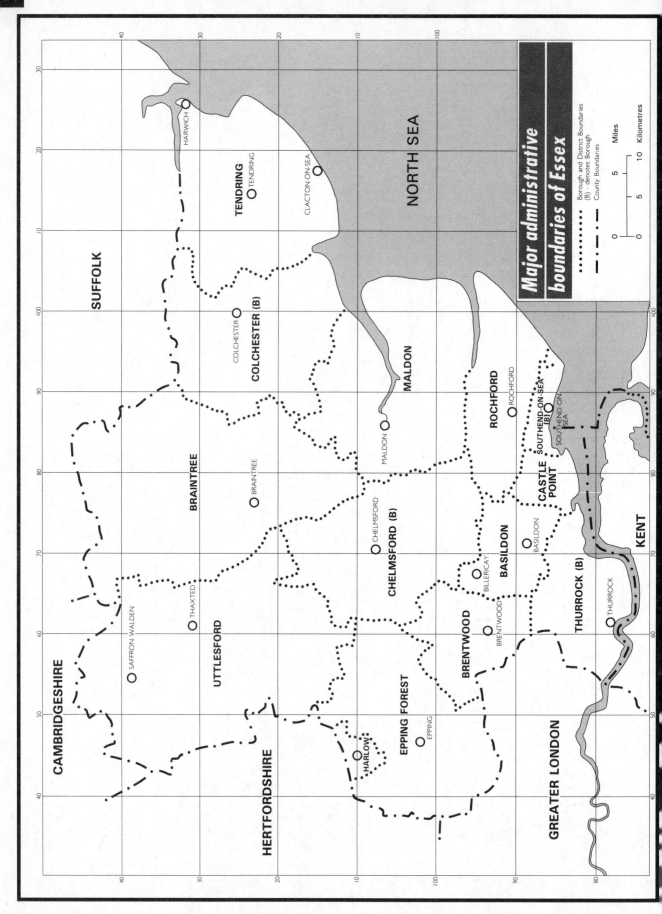

Major administrative boundaries of Essex

1

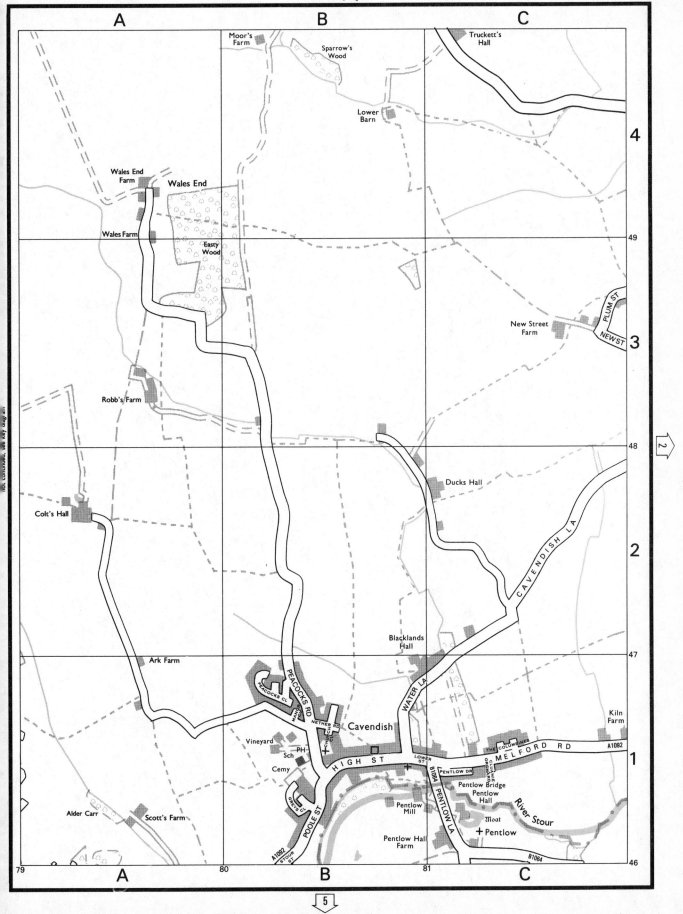

A   B   C

Moor's Farm

Sparrow's Wood

Truckett's Hall

Lower Barn

4

Wales End Farm

Wales End

Wales Farm

Easty Wood

49

PLUM ST

New Street Farm

NEW ST

3

Robb's Farm

Colt's Hall

48

2

Ducks Hall

CAVENDISH LA

2

Ark Farm

Blacklands Hall

47

PEACOCKS RD

PEACOCKS CL

Cavendish

Kiln Farm

MANOR RD

NETHER RD

CHURCH CL

Vineyard

WATER LA

THE COLUMBINES

MELFORD RD

A1092

PH

LOWER ST

Sch

HIGH ST

Cemy

Pentlow Bridge

1

GREY'S CL

POOLE ST

B1064

PENTLOW DR

CLUANIE ORCHARD

Pentlow Hall

Alder Carr

Scott's Farm

A1092

STOUR ST

Pentlow Mill

PENTLOW LA

Pentlow Hall Farm

Moat

+ Pentlow

River Stour

B1064

46

79   A   80   B   81   C

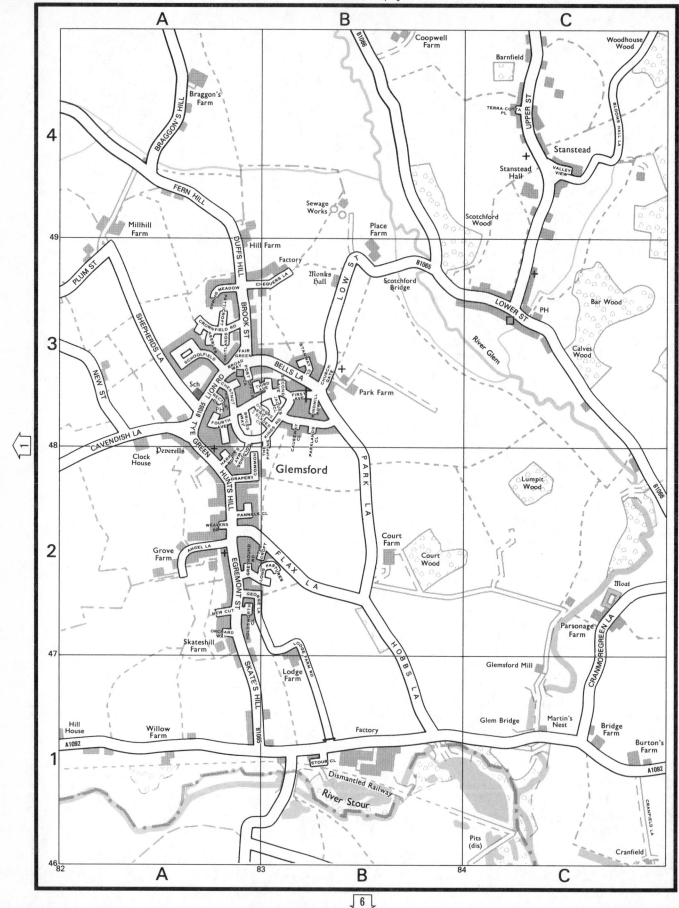

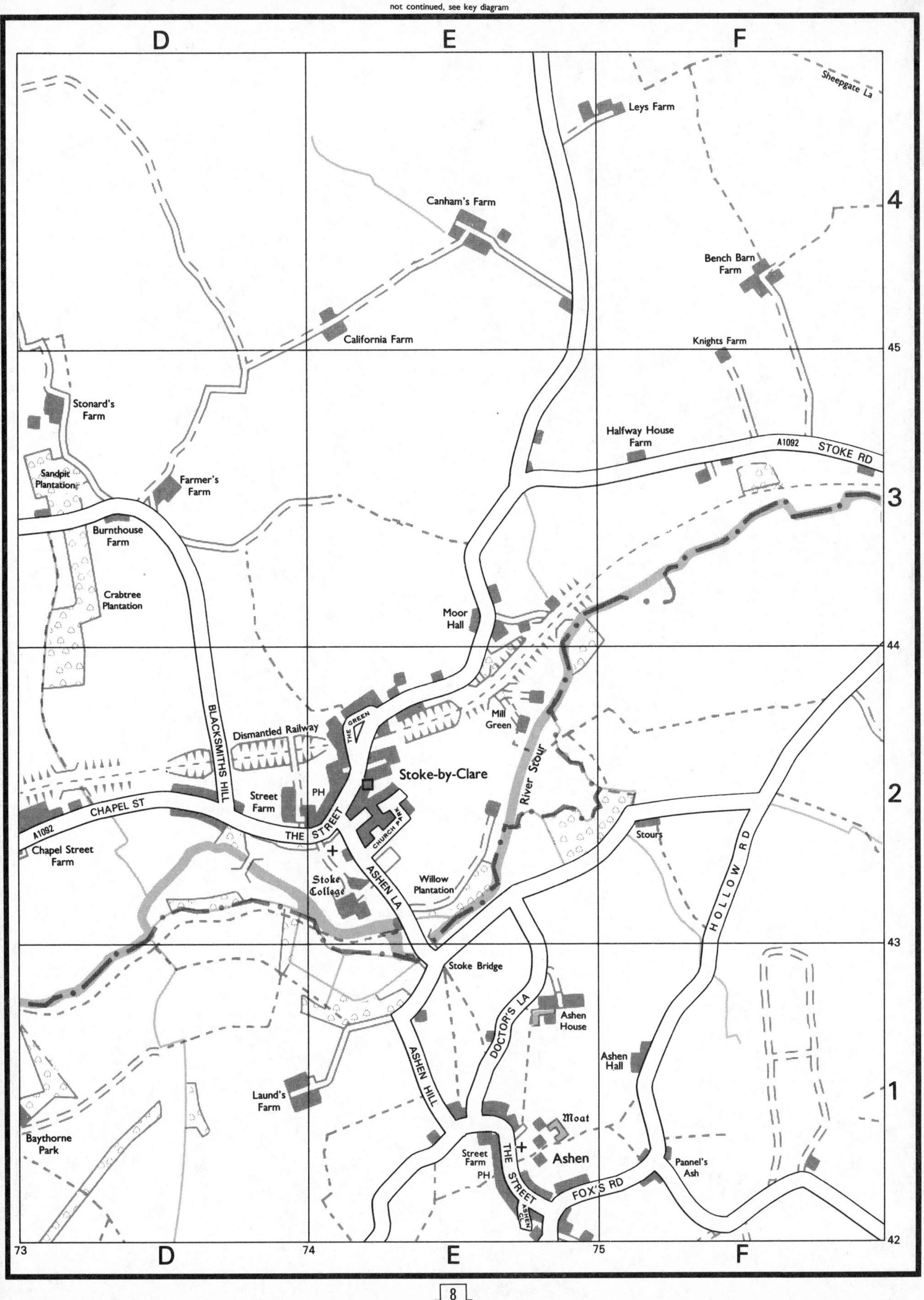

D
E
F

Sheepgate La

Leys Farm

4

Canham's Farm

Bench Barn
Farm

California Farm

Knights Farm

45

Stonard's
Farm

Halfway House
Farm

A1092 STOKE RD

Sandpit
Plantation

Farmer's
Farm

3

Burnthouse
Farm

Crabtree
Plantation

Moor
Hall

River Stour

44

4

Mill
Green

BLACKSMITHS HILL

Dismantled Railway

THE GREEN

Stoke-by-Clare

2

CHAPEL ST

Street
Farm

PH

THE STREET

Stours

HOLLOW RD

A1092

Chapel Street
Farm

CHURCH ST

ASHEN LA

Willow
Plantation

Stoke
College

43

Stoke Bridge

DOCTOR'S LA

Ashen
House

ASHEN HILL

Ashen
Hall

Laund's
Farm

1

Baythorne
Park

Moat

Ashen

Pannel's
Ash

Street
Farm

THE STREET

PH

ASHEN

Ashen

FOX'S RD

42

73
D
74
E
75
F

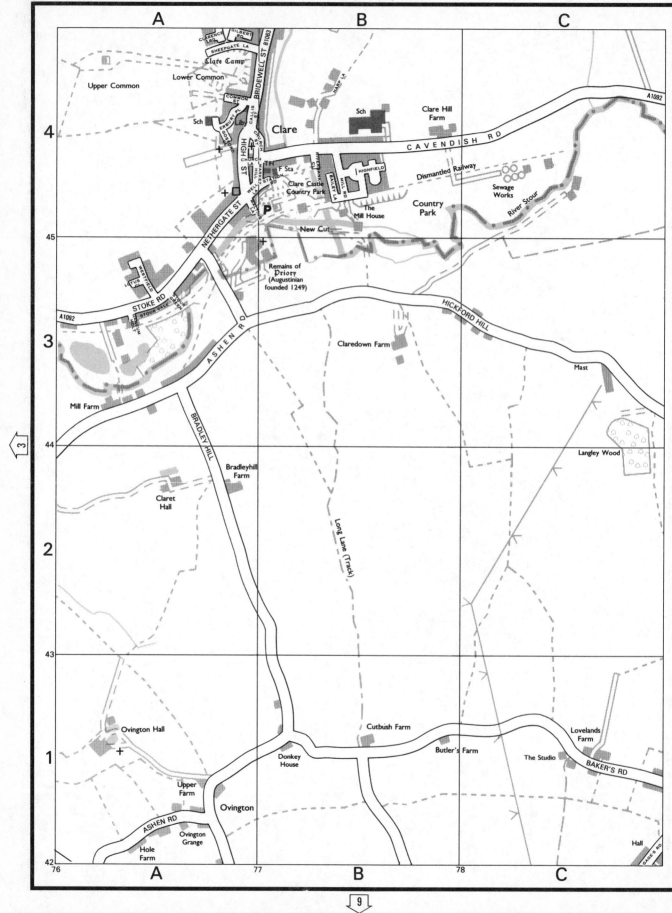

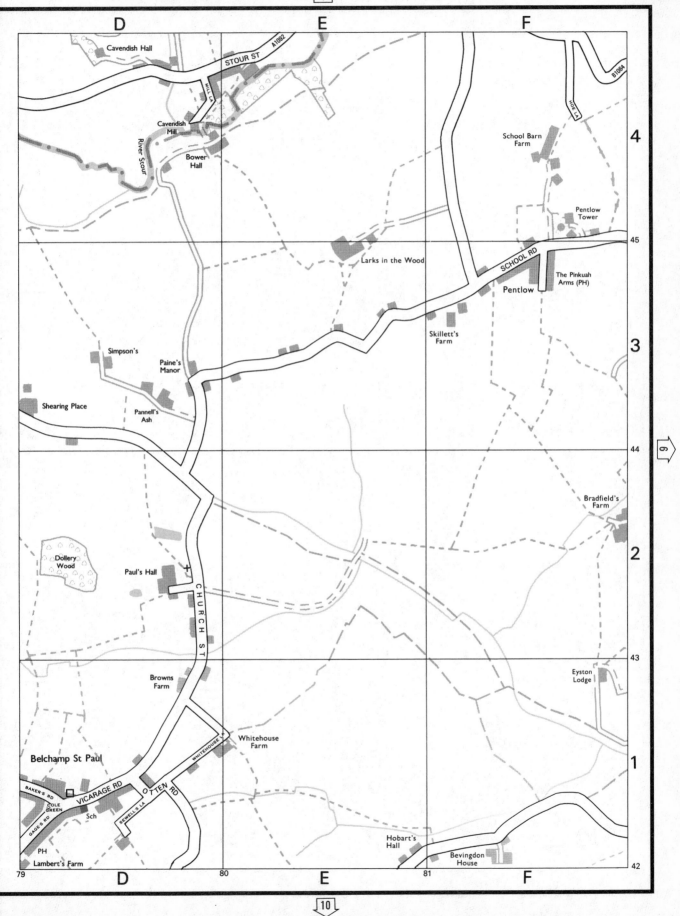

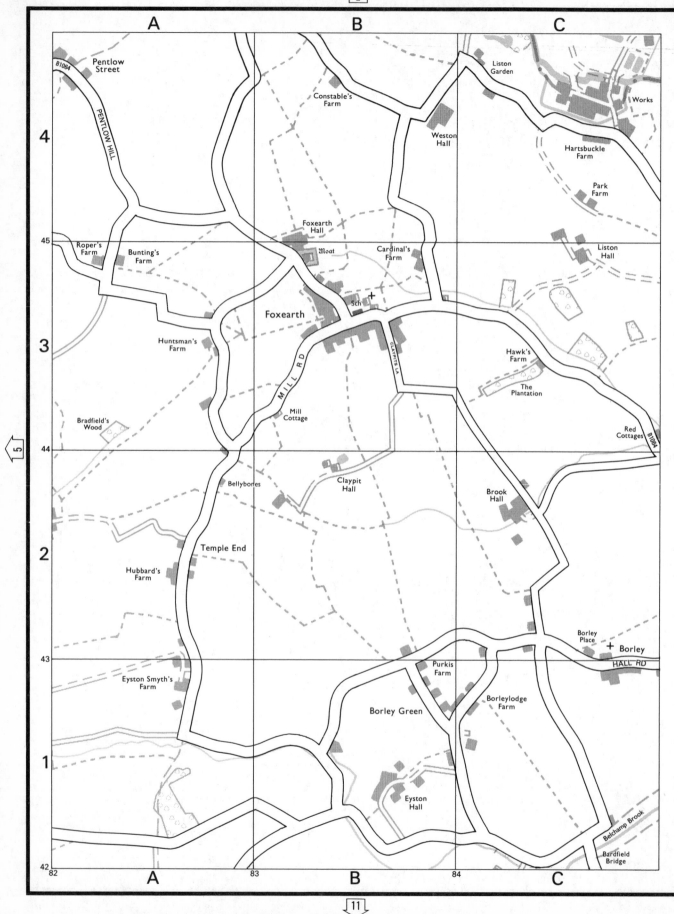

not continued, see key diagram

3

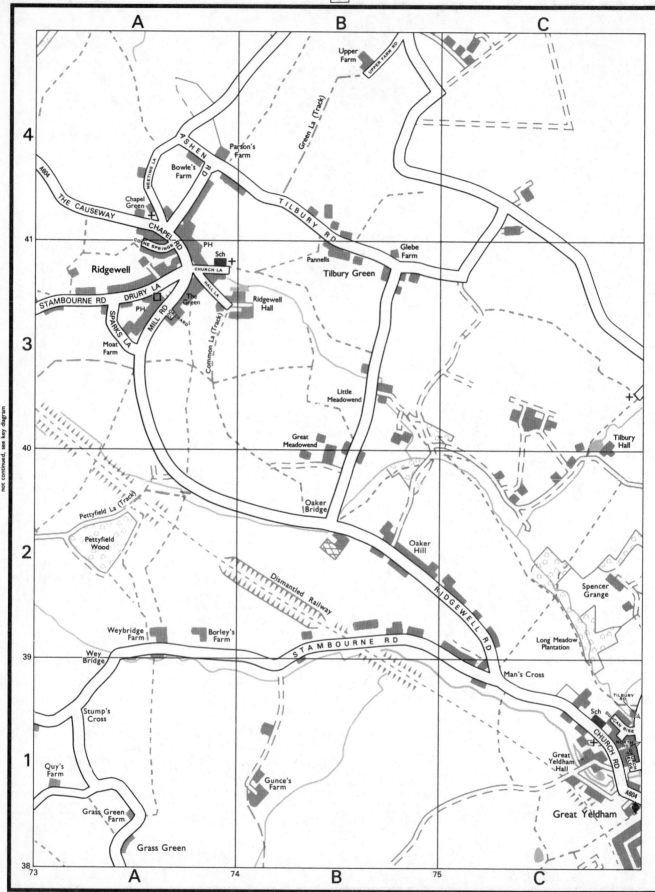

A   B   C

Upper Farm

UPPER FARM RD

Green La (Track)

ASHEN RD

Parson's Farm

Bowle's Farm

MEETING LA

THE CAUSEWAY

A604

Chapel Green

CHAPEL RD

COLNE SPRINGS RD

TILBURY RD

Pannells

Glebe Farm

4

PH

Sch

Ridgewell

CHURCH LA

Tilbury Green

STAMBOURNE RD

DRURY LA

PH

HALL LA

The Green

ORCHARD

MILL RD

SPARKS LA

Ridgewell Hall

41

Common La (Track)

Moat Farm

3

Little Meadowend

Tilbury Hall

Great Meadowend

Oaker Bridge

40

Pettyfield La (Track)

Pettyfield Wood

Oaker Hill

RIDGEWELL RD

Spencer Grange

2

Dismantled Railway

Long Meadow Plantation

Weybridge Farm

Borley's Farm

STAMBOURNE RD

Man's Cross

Wey Bridge

39

Stump's Cross

Sch

TILBURY RD

DUNCAN RISE

Quy's Farm

CHURCH RD

NORTH END RD

SOUTH END FIELDS

Great Yeldham Hall

Gunce's Farm

1

Grass Green Farm

A604

Grass Green

Great Yeldham

not continued, see key diagram

38

73   A   74   B   75   C

14

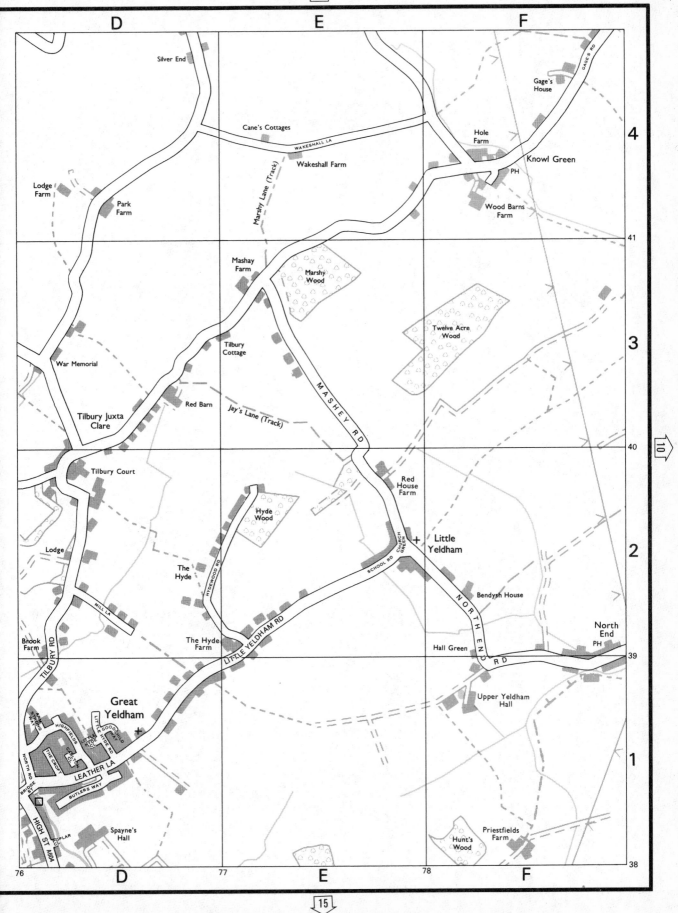

D   E   F

Silver End

GAGE'S RD

Gage's House

Cane's Cottages

Hole Farm

Knowl Green

4

WAKESHALL LA

Wakeshall Farm

PH

Lodge Farm

Park Farm

Wood Barns Farm

41

Marshy Lane (Track)

Mashay Farm

Marshy Wood

Twelve Acre Wood

3

Tilbury Cottage

War Memorial

MASHEY RD

Red Barn

Jay's Lane (Track)

Tilbury Juxta Clare

40

Tilbury Court

Red House Farm

Hyde Wood

Little Yeldham

2

HYDEWOOD RD

Lodge

The Hyde

SCHOOL RD

CHURCH GREEN

Bendysh House

NORTH END

MILL LA

North End

PH

Brook Farm

TILBURY RD

The Hyde Farm

LITTLE YELDHAM RD

Hall Green

RD

39

Upper Yeldham Hall

Great Yeldham

HIGHFIELDS

LITTLE HYDE RD

GOODCHILD WAY

LITTLE HYDE RD

1

NORTH RD

THE CROFT

LEATHER LA

BUTLERS WAY

BRIDGE ST

HIGH ST A604

POPLAR CT

Spayne's Hall

Hunt's Wood

Priestfields Farm

38

76   D   77   E   78   F

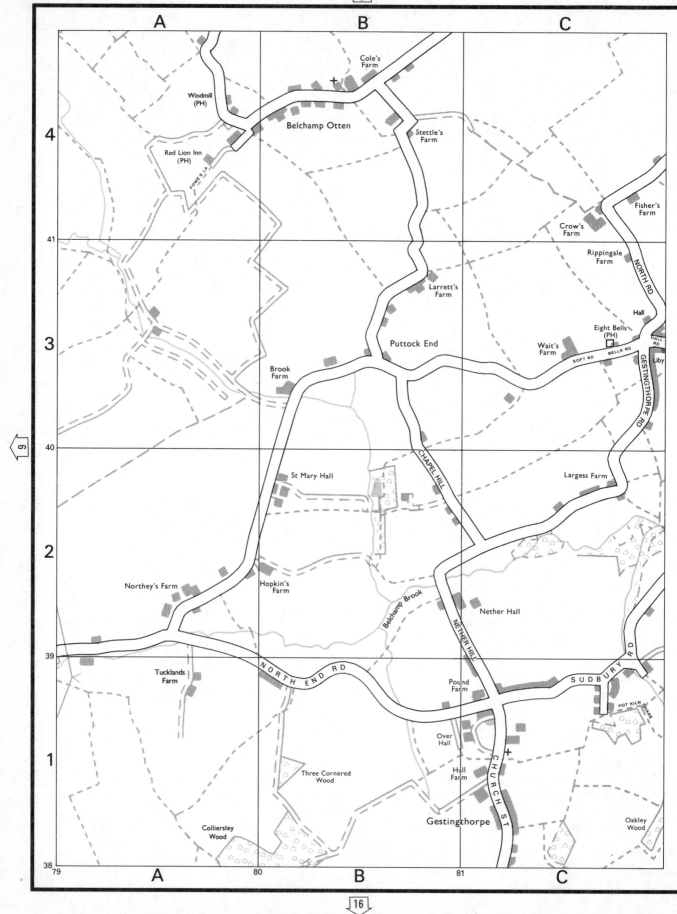

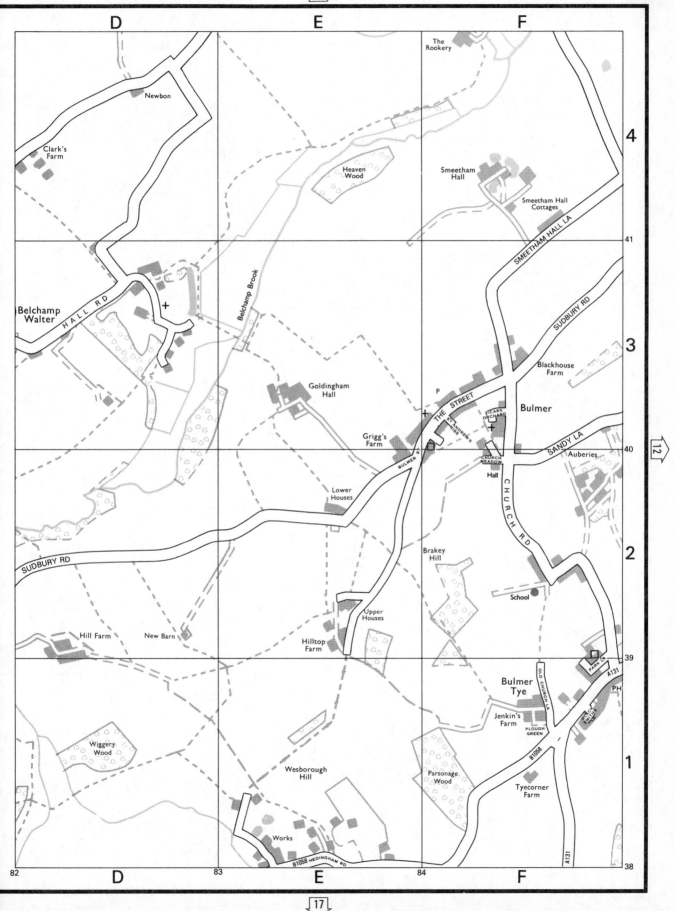

D   E   F

The
Rookery

Newbon

4

Clark's
Farm

Heaven
Wood

Smeetham
Hall

Smeetham Hall
Cottages

SMEETHAM HALL LA

41

Belchamp Brook

HALL RD

Belchamp
Walter

SUDBURY RD

3

Goldingham
Hall

Blackhouse
Farm

P

THE STREET

Bulmer

VICARS
ORCHARD

Grigg's
Farm

BULMER ST

ST ANDREW'S

SANDY LA

Auberies

40

12

CHURCH
MEADOW

Hall

Lower
Houses

CHURCH RD

Brakey
Hill

2

School

Sudbury Rd

SUDBURY RD

Upper
Houses

Hill Farm

New Barn

Hilltop
Farm

39

PARK LA

A131

Bulmer
Tye

OLD CHURCH LA

PH

Jenkin's
Farm

Wiggery
Wood

PLOUGH
GREEN

B1058

1

Wesborough
Hill

Parsonage
Wood

Tyecorner
Farm

Works

B1058 HEDINGHAM RD

A131

38

82   D   83   E   84   F

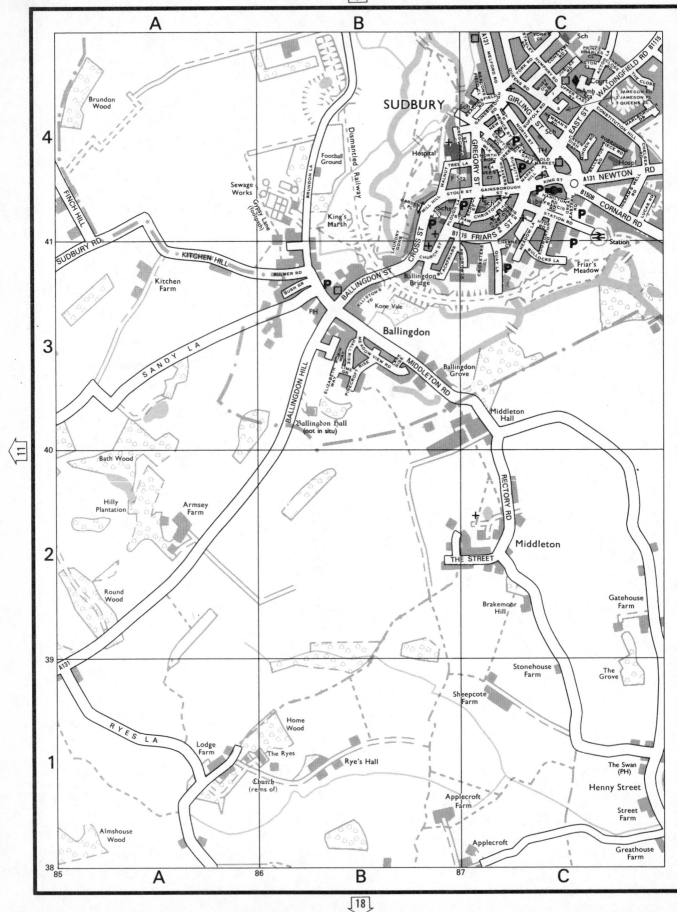

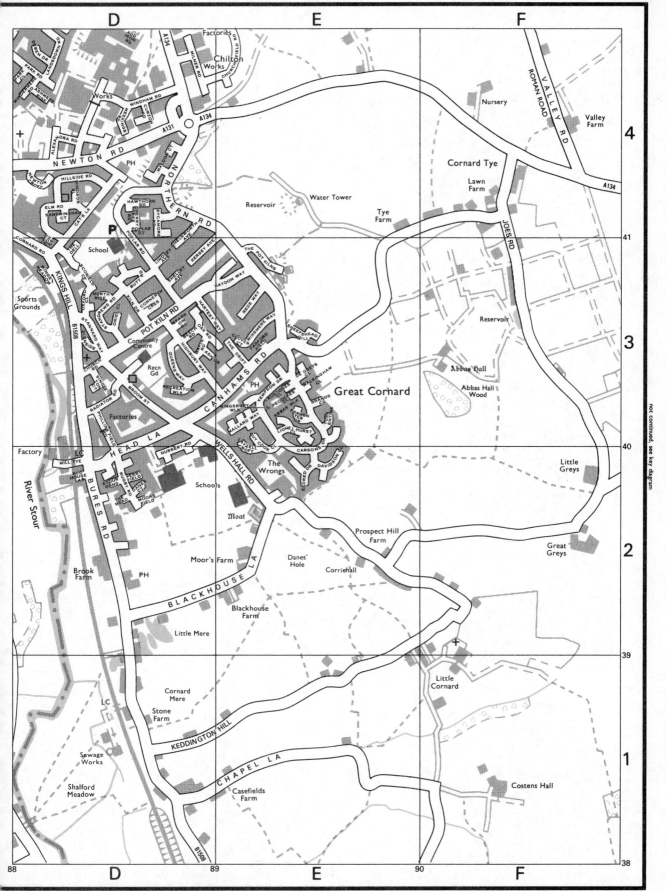

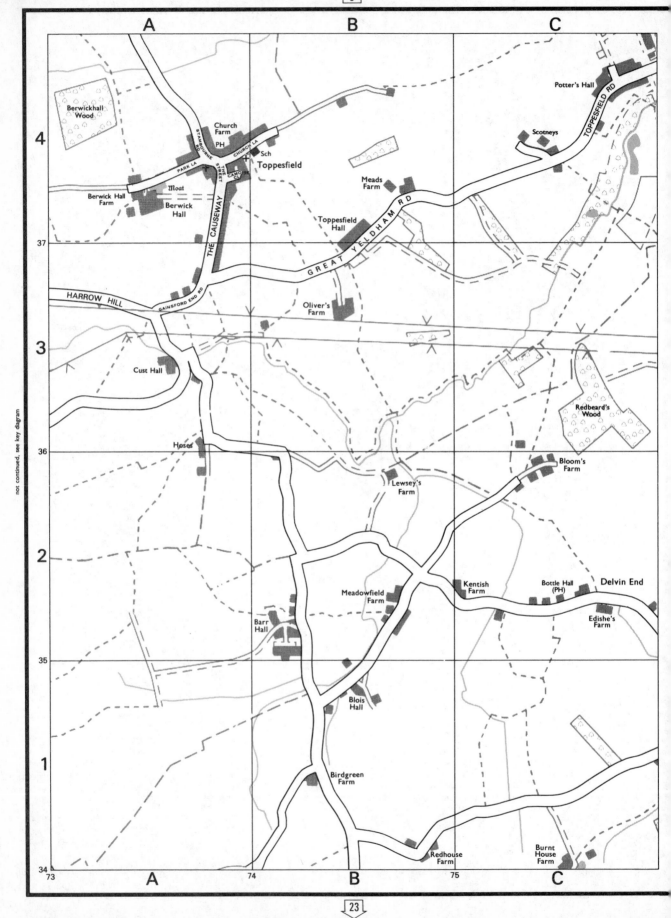

A	B	C

Berwickhall
Wood

4

Church
Farm
PH
Toppesfield
Sch
Moat
Berwick Hall
Farm
Berwick
Hall

STAMBOURNE RD
PARK LA
CHURCH LA
THE STREET
CAMOISE CL

THE CAUSEWAY

GAINSFORD END RD

37

HARROW HILL

Oliver's
Farm

Meads
Farm

Toppesfield
Hall

GREAT YELDHAM RD

Potter's Hall

Scotneys

TOPPESFIELD RD

3

Cust Hall

Redbeard's
Wood

36

Hoses

Lewsey's
Farm

Bloom's
Farm

2

Meadowfield
Farm

Kentish
Farm

Bottle Hall
(PH)

Delvin End

Barr
Hall

Edishe's
Farm

35

Blois
Hall

1

Birdgreen
Farm

Redhouse
Farm

Burnt
House
Farm

34
73	A	74	B	75	C

9

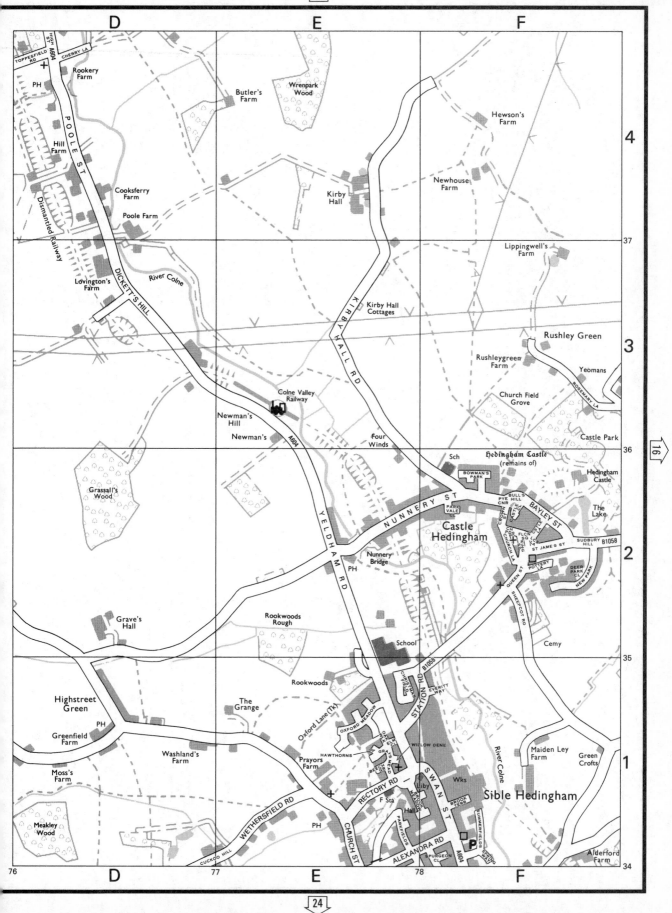

16
24

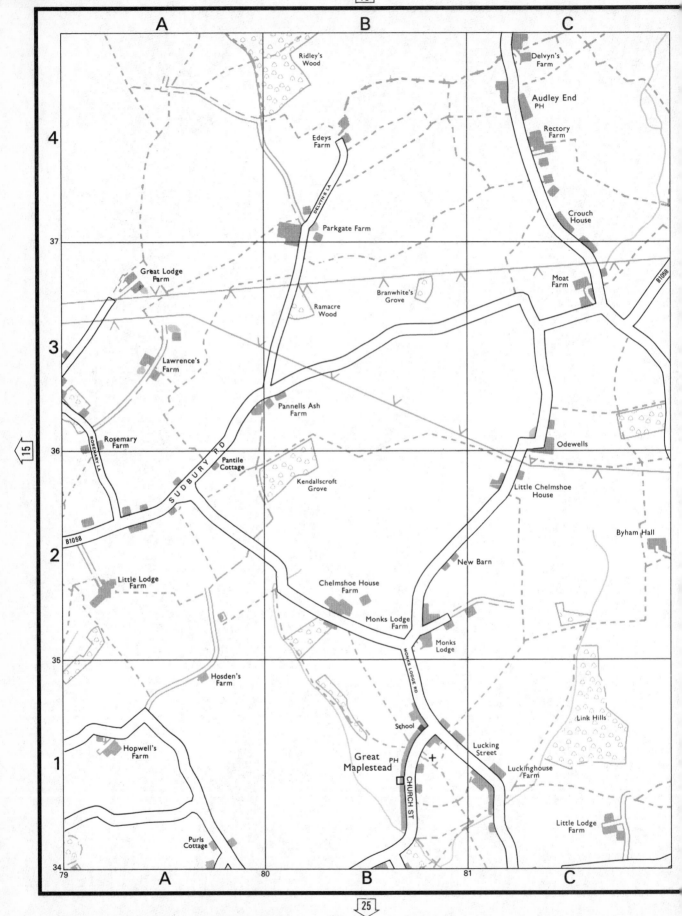

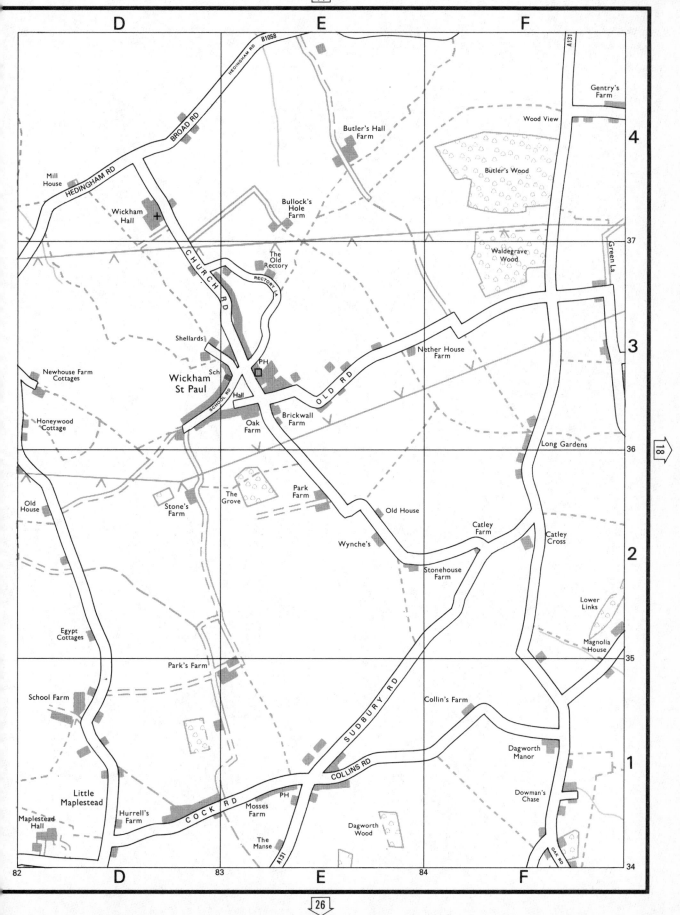

D E F

B1058

HEDINGHAM RD

A131

Gentry's Farm

Wood View

Butler's Hall Farm

4

Mill House

BROAD RD

HEDINGHAM RD

Wickham Hall

Bullock's Hole Farm

Butler's Wood

CHURCH RD

The Old Rectory

RECTORY LA

Waldegrave Wood

37

Green La

Shellards

Nether House Farm

3

Newhouse Farm Cottages

Wickham St Paul

Sch

PH

Hall

Honeywood Cottage

SCHOOL RD

Oak Farm

Brickwall Farm

OLD RD

Long Gardens

36

18

Old House

Stone's Farm

The Grove

Park Farm

Old House

Catley Farm

Catley Cross

2

Wynche's

Stonehouse Farm

Lower Links

Egypt Cottages

Magnolia House

35

Park's Farm

School Farm

SUDBURY RD

Collin's Farm

Dagworth Manor

1

Little Maplestead

COLLINS RD

Hurrell's Farm

COCK RD

Mosses Farm

PH

Dowman's Chase

Maplestead Hall

The Manse

A131

Dagworth Wood

OAK RD

34

82 D 83 E 84 F

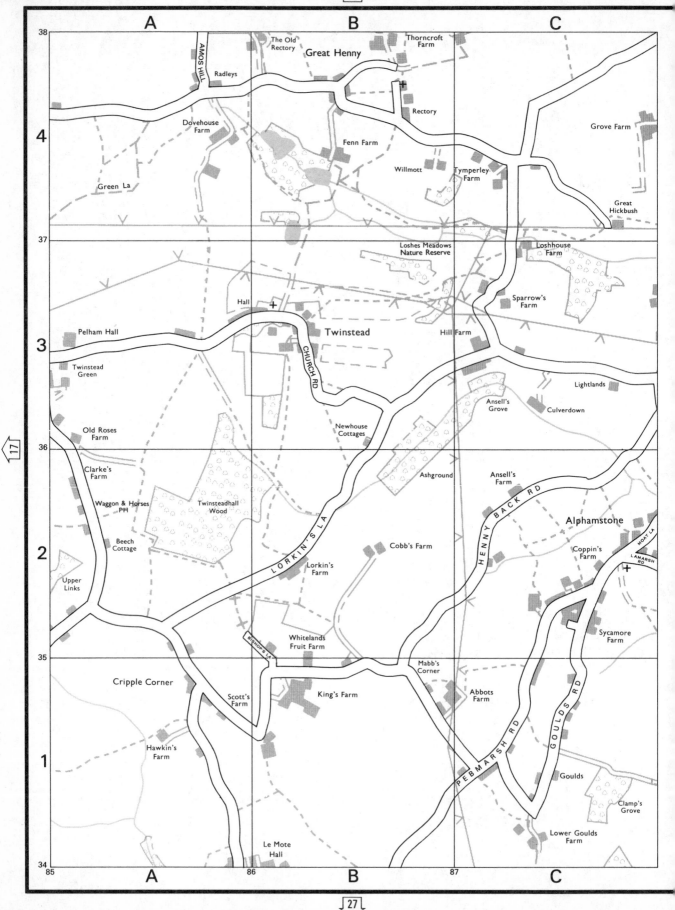

AMOS HILL

A **B** **C**

38

The Old
Rectory

Thorncroft
Farm

Great Henny

Radleys

+

Rectory

Grove Farm

Dovehouse
Farm

4

Fenn Farm

Willmott

Tymperley
Farm

Great
Hickbush

Green La

37

Loshes Meadows
Nature Reserve

Loshhouse
Farm

Hall

+

Sparrow's
Farm

Pelham Hall

3

Twinstead

Hill Farm

CHURCH RD

Twinstead
Green

Lightlands

Ansell's
Grove

Culverdown

Old Roses
Farm

Newhouse
Cottages

36

Clarke's
Farm

Ashground

Ansell's
Farm

HENNY BACK RD

Alphamstone

MOAT LA

Waggon & Horses
PH

Twinsteadhall
Wood

Coppin's
Farm

LAMARSH
RD

Beech
Cottage

2

Cobb's Farm

+

LORKIN'S LA

Upper
Links

Lorkin's
Farm

Sycamore
Farm

Whitelands
Fruit Farm

BISHOP'S LA

35

Mabb's
Corner

GOULDS RD

Cripple Corner

Scott's
Farm

King's Farm

Abbots
Farm

PEBMARSH RD

1

Hawkin's
Farm

Goulds

Clamp's
Grove

Le Mote
Hall

Lower Goulds
Farm

34

85 **A** 86 **B** 87 **C**

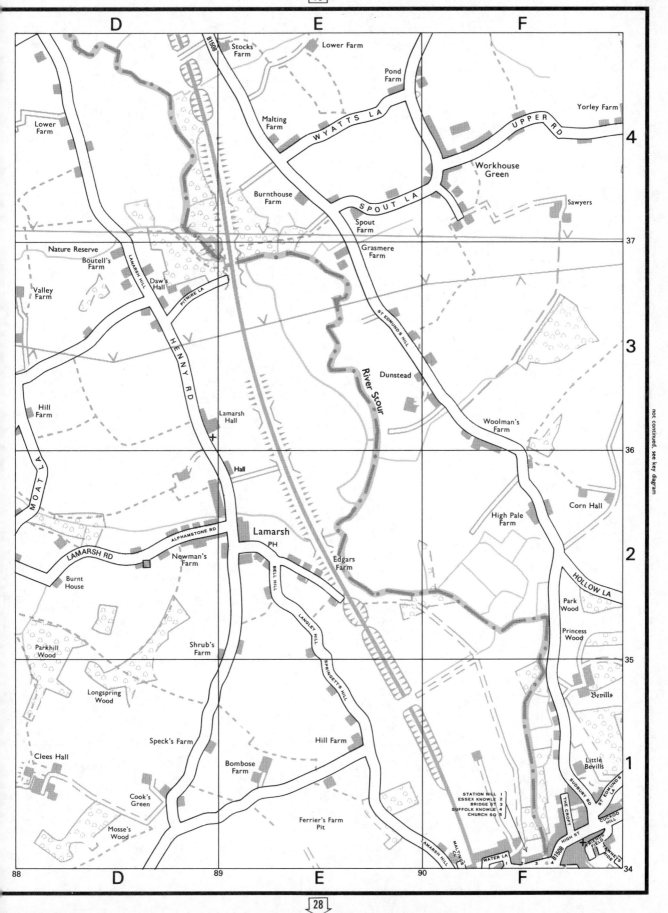

D   **E**   **F**

Stocks Farm

Lower Farm

Pond Farm

Yorley Farm

UPPER RD

WYATTS LA

Lower Farm

Malting Farm

Workhouse Green

SPOUT LA

Sawyers

Burnthouse Farm

Spout Farm

4

37

Nature Reserve

Boutell's Farm

Grasmere Farm

LAMARSH HILL

Daw's Hall

Valley Farm

PITMIRE LA

ST. EDMUND'S HILL

HENNY RD

Dunstead

River Stour

3

Hill Farm

Lamarsh Hall

Woolman's Farm

36

MOAT LA

Hall

High Pale Farm

Corn Hall

ALPHAMSTONE RD

Lamarsh

PH

Edgars Farm

LAMARSH RD

Newman's Farm

BELL HILL

HOLLOW LA

2

Burnt House

Park Wood

Princess Wood

Parkhill Wood

Shrub's Farm

LANGLEY HILL

SPRINGETT'S HILL

35

Longspring Wood

Bevills

Speck's Farm

Hill Farm

Clees Hall

Bombose Farm

Little Bevills

1

SUDBURY RD

ST. EDMUND'S HILL

Cook's Green

STATION HILL 1
ESSEX KNOWLE 2
BRIDGE ST 3
SUFFOLK KNOWLE 4
CHURCH SQ 5

THE CROFT

CUCKOO HILL

Mosse's Wood

Ferrier's Farm Pit

LAMARSH HILL

MALTINGS CL

WATER LA

HIGH ST

B1508

TAWNEY'S RIDE

34

88   **D**   89   **E**   90   **F**

not continued, see key diagram

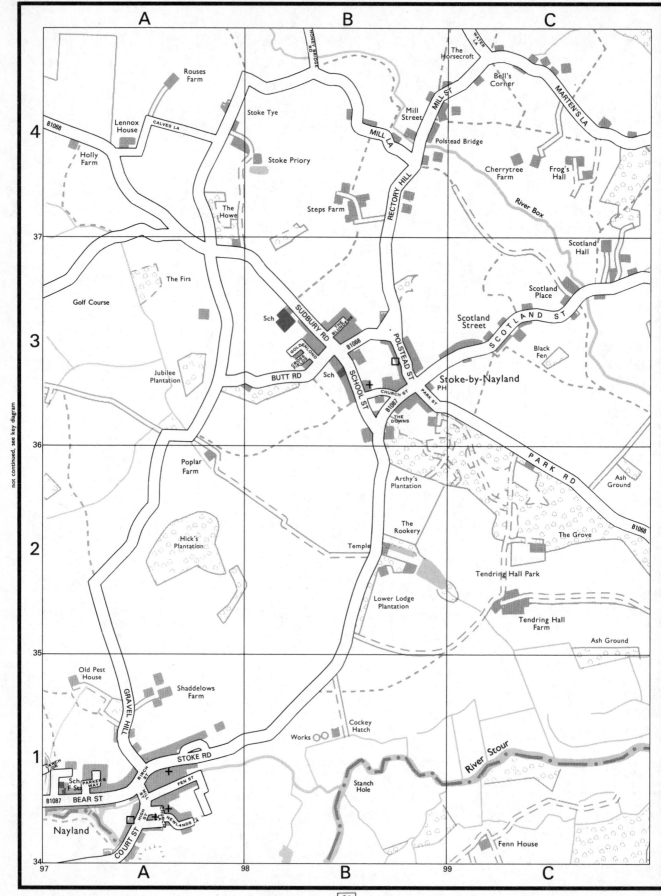

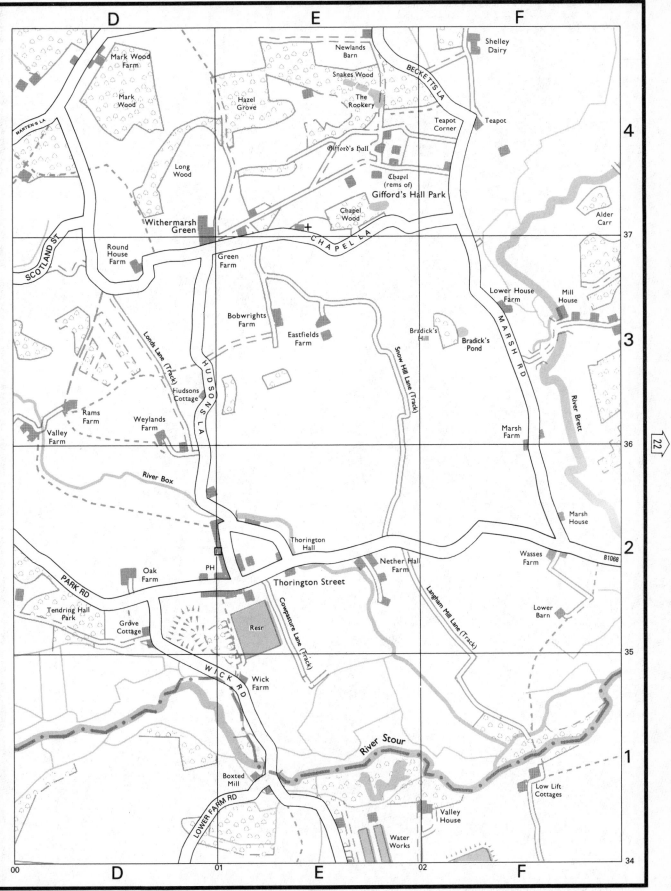

D

E

F

Mark Wood Farm

Mark Wood

MARTEN'S LA

Long Wood

Hazel Grove

Newlands Barn

Snakes Wood

The Rookery

Gifford's Hall

Shelley Dairy

BECKETTS LA

Teapot Corner

Teapot

4

Chapel (rems of)

Gifford's Hall Park

Chapel Wood

Alder Carr

Withermarsh Green

SCOTLAND ST

Round House Farm

Green Farm

CHAPEL LA

37

Bobwrights Farm

Eastfields Farm

Bradick's Hill

Bradick's Pond

Lower House Farm

Mill House

MARSH RD

3

Londs Lane (Track)

Hudsons Cottage

HUDSONS LA

Snow Hill Lane (Track)

River Brett

Rams Farm

Weylands Farm

Valley Farm

Marsh Farm

36

22

River Box

Marsh House

PARK RD

Oak Farm

PH

Thorington Hall

Nether Hall Farm

Wasses Farm

B1068

2

Tendring Hall Park

Grove Cottage

Resr

Thorington Street

Compasture Lane (Track)

Langham Mill Lane (Track)

Lower Barn

35

WICK RD

Wick Farm

1

River Stour

Low Lift Cottages

LOWER FARM RD

Boxted Mill

Valley House

Water Works

34

00

D

01

E

02

F

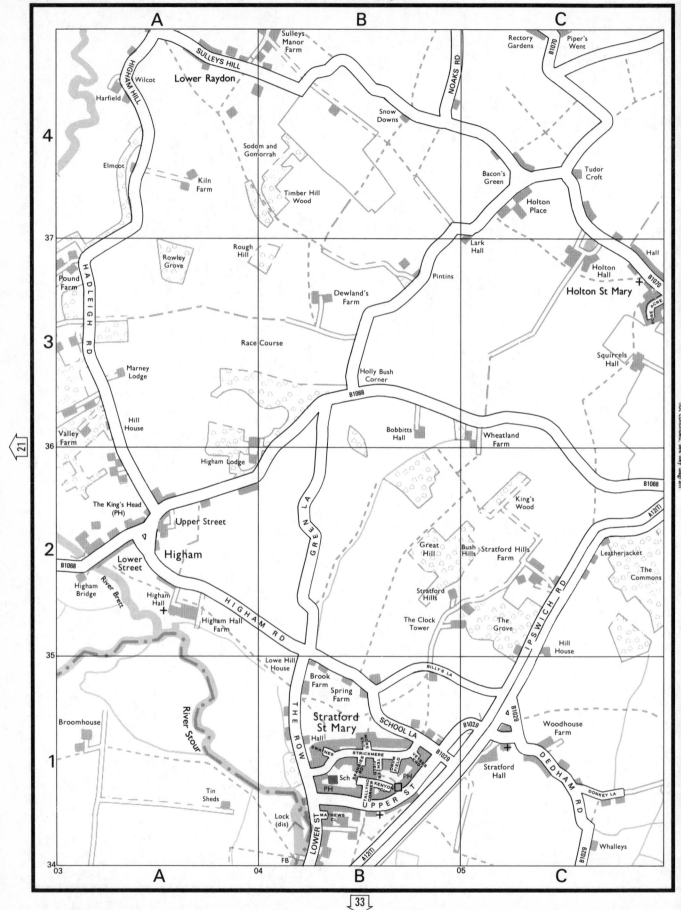

A   **B**   **C**

Sulleys Manor Farm

SULLEYS HILL

Lower Raydon

HIGHAM HILL

Wilcot

Harfield

Snow Downs

NOAKS RD

Rectory Gardens

B1070

Piper's Went

4

Elmcot

Sodom and Gomorrah

Timber Hill Wood

Bacon's Green

Tudor Croft

Kiln Farm

Holton Place

Holton Hall

Hall

37

HADLEIGH RD

Pound Farm

Rowley Grove

Rough Hill

Dewland's Farm

Pintins

Lark Hall

Holton St Mary

B1070

ROSE ACRE

3

Race Course

Holly Bush Corner

B1068

Squirrels Hall

Marney Lodge

21

Hill House

Bobbitts Hall

Wheatland Farm

36

Valley Farm

Higham Lodge

King's Wood

B1068

The King's Head (PH)

Upper Street

GREEN LA

Great Hill

Bush Hills

Stratford Hills Farm

Leatherjacket

A1271

2

Higham

Lower Street

Stratford Hills

The Commons

B1068

River Brett

Higham Bridge

HIGHAM RD

Higham Hall

The Clock Tower

The Grove

IPSWICH RD

Hill House

Higham Hall Farm

35

Lowe Hill House

Brook Farm

Spring Farm

BILLY'S LA

SCHOOL LA

B1029

B1029

Woodhouse Farm

Broomhouse

River Stour

THE ROW

Stratford St Mary

Hall

SWANES

STRICKMERE

DRUM FIELD

B1029

Stratford Hall

DEDHAM RD

1

Tin Sheds

LOWER ST

MATHEWS CL

Sch

KENYON CORNER

UPPER ST

PH

PH

DONKEY LA

Whalleys

34

Lock (dis)

FB

A1271

B1029

14

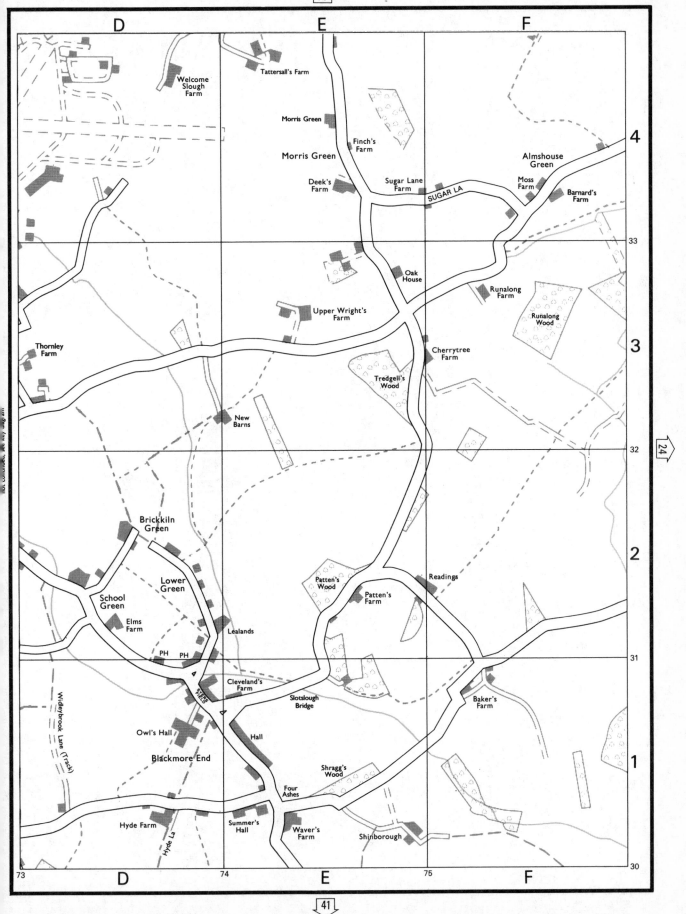

24

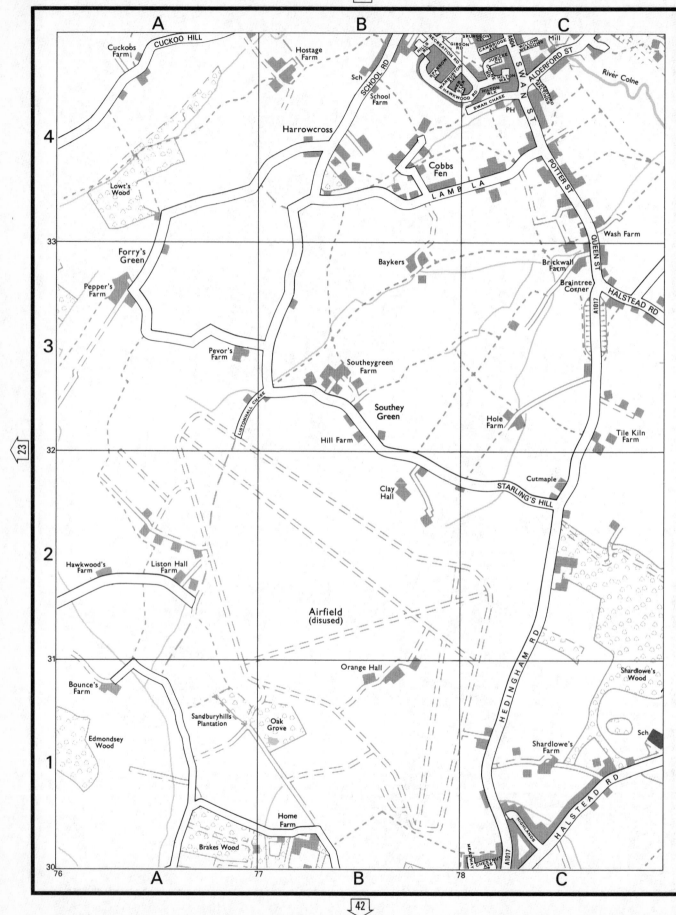

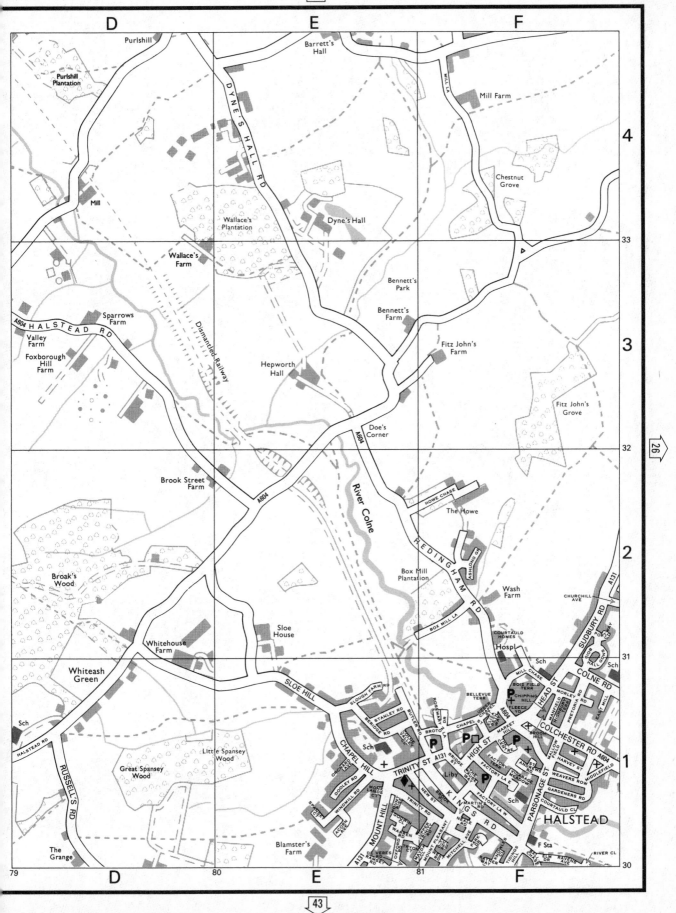

D E F

Purlshill

Purlshill
Plantation

Mill

BARRETT'S HALL

Mill Farm

Chestnut
Grove

Wallace's
Plantation

DYNE'S HALL RD

Dyne's Hall

4

33

Wallace's
Farm

Bennett's
Park

Bennett's
Farm

Fitz John's
Farm

A804 HALSTEAD RD

Sparrows
Farm

Valley
Farm

Foxborough
Hill
Farm

Dismantled Railway

Hepworth
Hall

Doe's
Corner

A604

Fitz John's
Grove

3

32

26

Brook Street
Farm

A804

River Colne

HOWE CHASE

The Howe

Broak's
Wood

Box Mill
Plantation

Wash
Farm

REDINGHAM RD

BOX MILL LA

CHURCHILL
AVE

A131

SUDBURY RD

2

31

Whitehouse
Farm

Sloe
House

COURTAULD
HOMES

Hospl

Sch

COLNE RD

Whiteash
Green

Sch

SLOE HILL

SLOUGH FARM RD

Sch

CHAPEL HILL

TRINITY ST

HIGH ST

COLCHESTER RD A604

Liby

Sch

HALSTEAD RD

Great Spansey Wood

Little Spansey
Wood

KINGS RD

PARSONAGE ST

HALSTEAD

1

RUSSELL'S RD

The
Grange

Blamster's
Farm

MOUNT HILL

A131

TRINITY RD

F Sta

RIVER CL

30

79 D 80 E 81 F

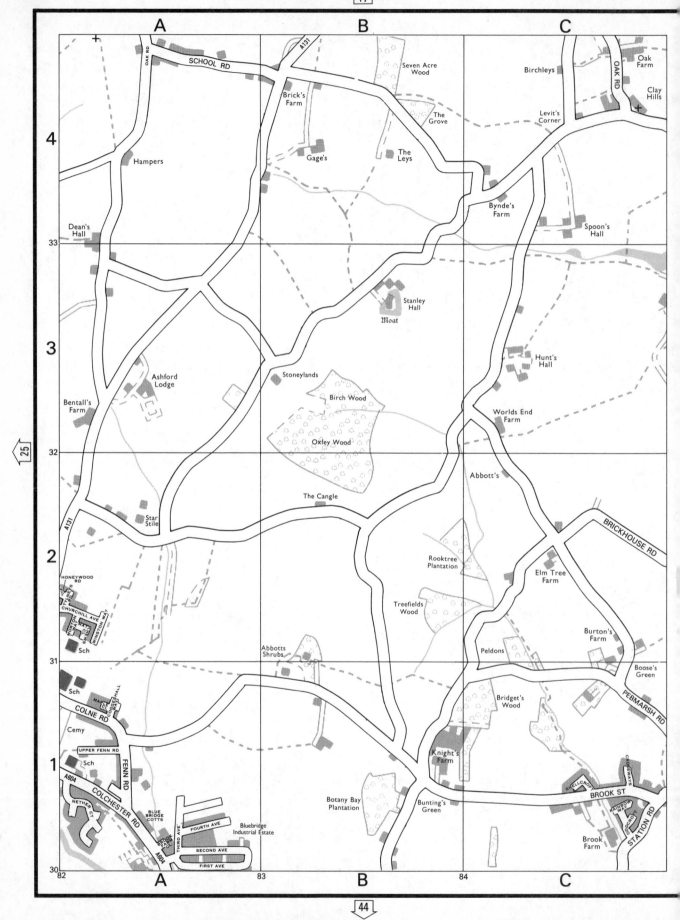

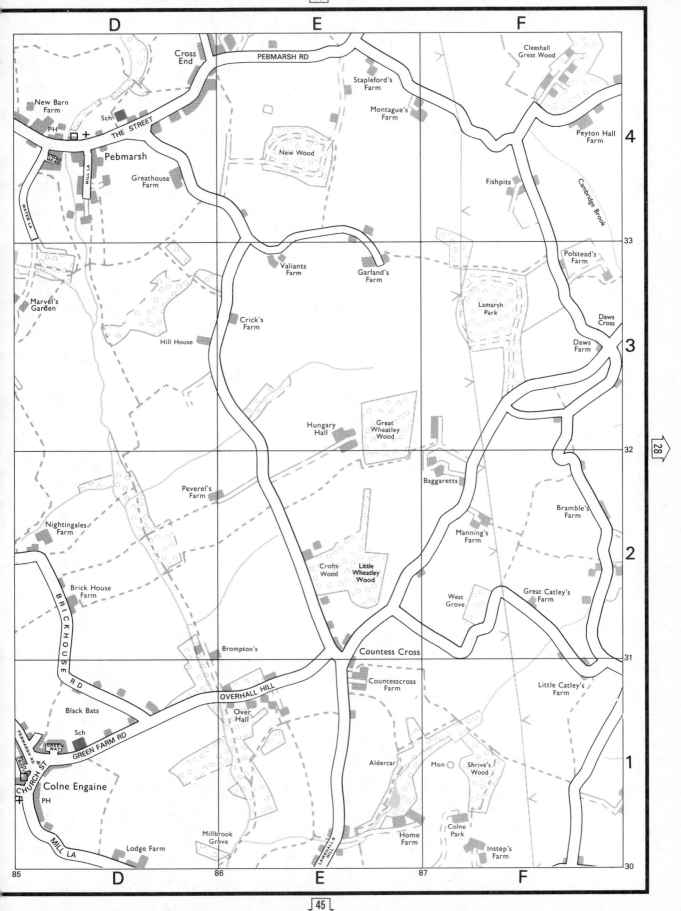

D   E   F

Cross
End

PEBMARSH RD

Stapleford's
Farm

Cleeshall
Great Wood

New Barn
Farm

Montague's
Farm

Peyton Hall
Farm

4

PH

Sch

THE STREET

New Wood

Fishpits

Cambridge Brook

Pebmarsh

KINGS
MEAD

MILL LA

Greathouse
Farm

WATER LA

33

Valiants
Farm

Garland's
Farm

Polstead's
Farm

Marvel's
Garden

Crick's
Farm

Lamarsh
Park

Daws
Cross

Hill House

Daws
Farm

3

Hungary
Hall

Great
Wheatley
Wood

Great
Wheatley
Wood

Peverel's
Farm

Baggaretts

32

28

Nightingales
Farm

Manning's
Farm

Bramble's
Farm

2

Brick House
Farm

Crofts
Wood

Little
Wheatley
Wood

West
Grove

Great Catley's
Farm

BRICKHOUSE RD

Brompton's

Countess Cross

31

OVERHALL HILL

Countesscross
Farm

Little Catley's
Farm

Black Bats

Over
Hall

Sch

GREEN
WAY

GREEN FARM RD

Aldercar

Mon

Shrive's
Wood

1

PEBMARSH RD

CHURCH ST

Colne Engaine

PH

Colne
Park

Instep's
Farm

MILL LA

Lodge Farm

Millbrook
Grove

LAWSHALL'S HILL

Home
Farm

85   D   86   E   87   F   30

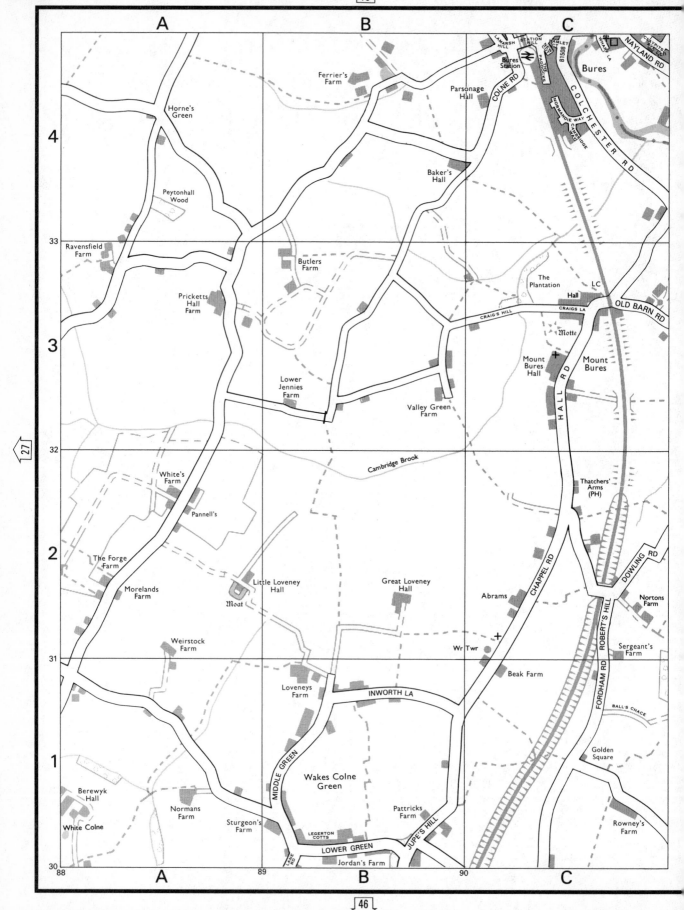

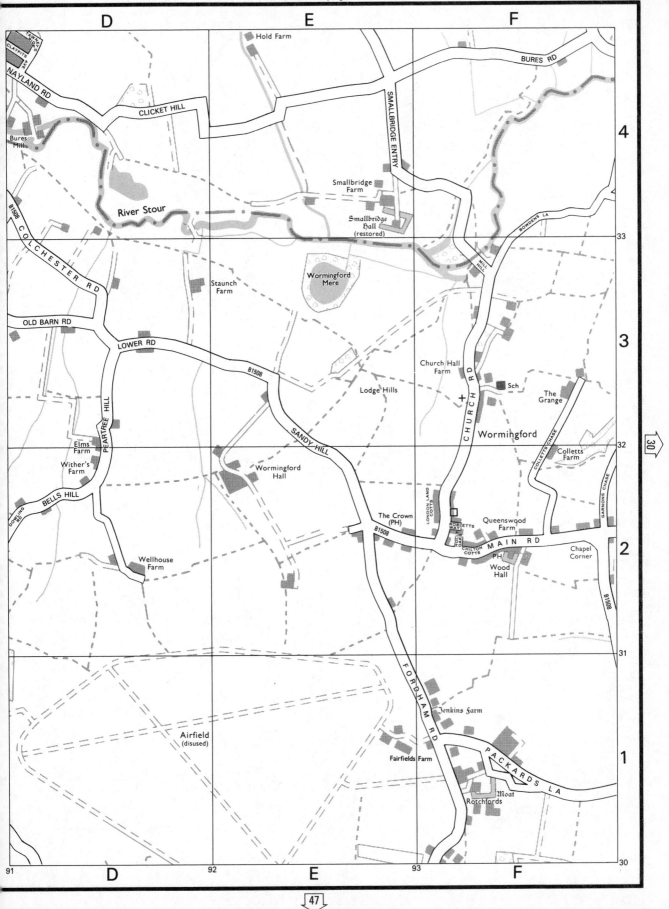

T⇒R. h. h.

D

E

F

Hold Farm

BURES RD

4

NAYLAND RD

CLICKET HILL

SMALLBRIDGE ENTRY

Bures
Mill

Smallbridge
Farm

BOWDENS LA

33

River Stour

Smallbridge
Hall
(restored)

B1508

COLCHESTER RD

Wormingford
Mere

MILL HILL

Staunch
Farm

OLD BARN RD

LOWER RD

3

B1508

Church Hall
Farm

CHURCH RD

Sch

The
Grange

Lodge Hills

+

PEARTREE HILL

Wormingford

Elms
Farm

32

Wither's
Farm

COLLETTS CHASE

Colletts
Farm

Wormingford
Hall

SANDY HILL

GARNONS CHASE

BELLS HILL

LODGE LAND
COTTS

Queenswood
Farm

The Crown
(PH)

HOBLETTS
WAY!

ROCK
ROCHILTON
COTTS

MAIN RD

Chapel
Corner

B1508

Wellhouse
Farm

PH

Wood
Hall

B1508

31

FORDHAM RD

Jenkins Farm

Airfield
(disused)

PACKARDS LA

1

Fairfields Farm

Moat
Rotchfords

30

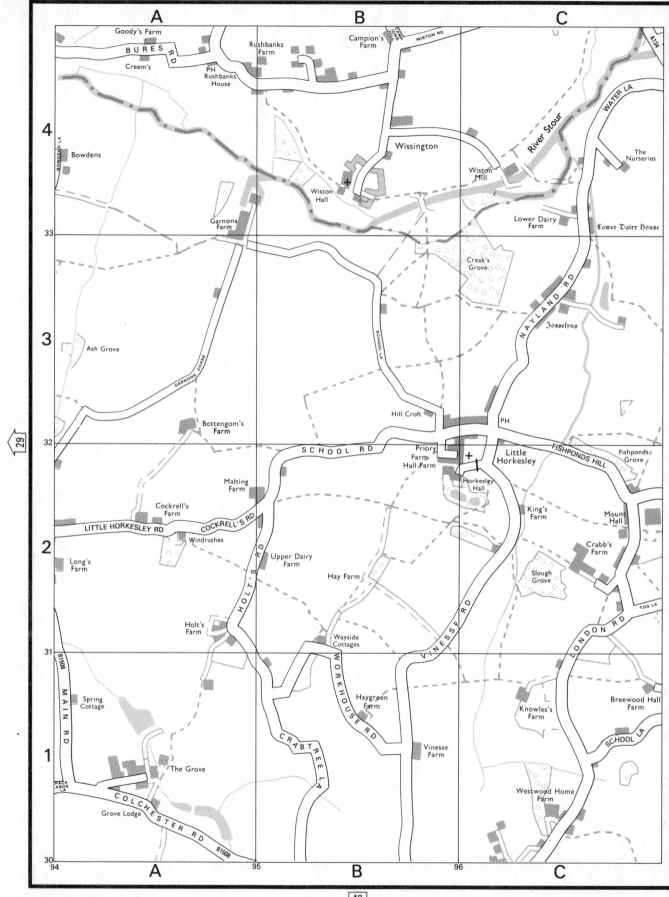

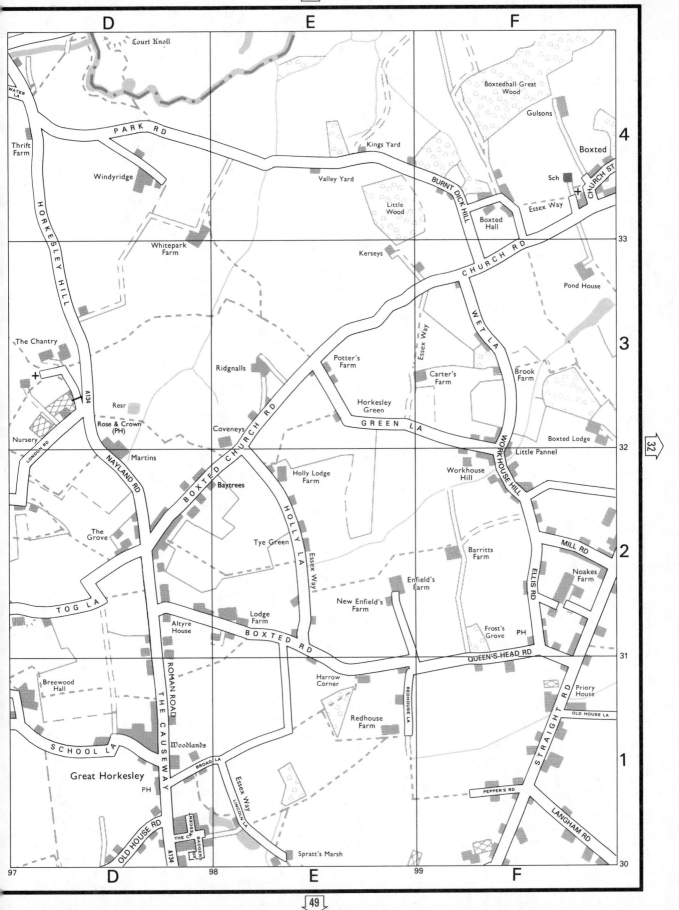

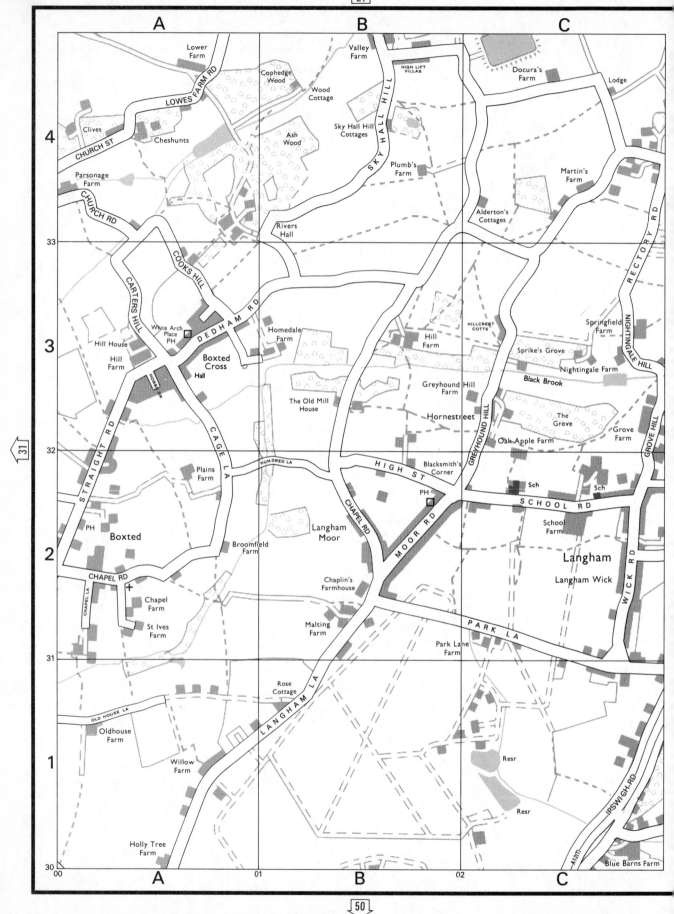

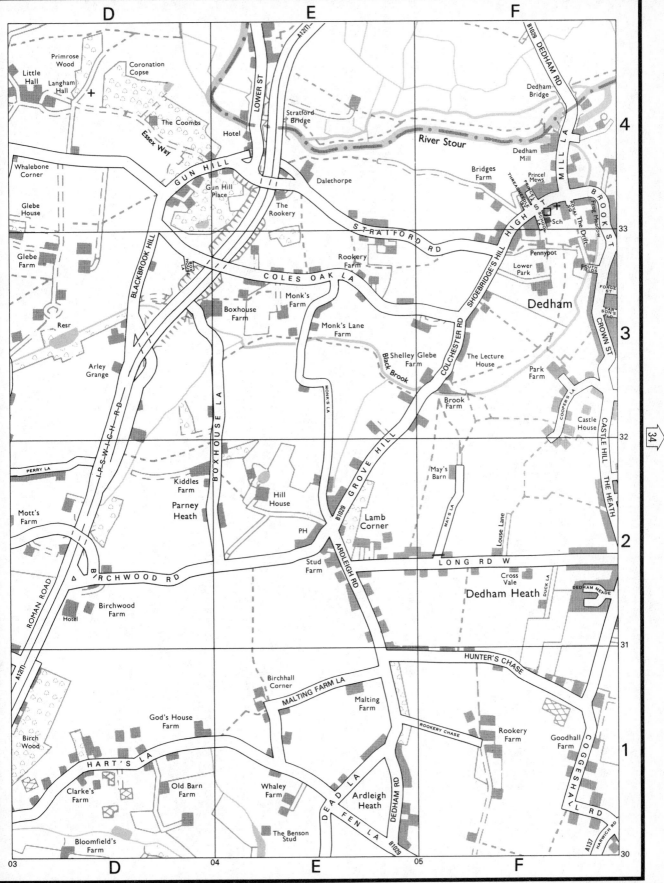

D   E   F

Primrose Wood
Coronation Copse
Little Hall
Langham Hall
The Coombs
Essex Way
Hotel
Lower St
Stratford Bridge
Gun Hill
Gun Hill Place
The Rookery
Dalethorpe
River Stour
Dedham Bridge
Dedham Mill
Bridges Farm
Princel Mews
Mill La
Brook St
4
Whalebone Corner
Glebe House
Blackbrook Hill
Boxhouse La
Stratford Rd
Shoebridge's Hill
High St
The Drift
Sch
Pennypot
Lower Park
Forge St
South Fields
33
Glebe Farm
Coles Oak La
Rookery Farm
Dedham
Park Son's La
Resr
Monk's Farm
Boxhouse Farm
Monk's Lane Farm
Shelley Glebe Farm
Colchester Rd
The Lecture House
Park Farm
3
Arley Grange
Black Brook
Brook Farm
Cooper's La
Castle House
Castle Hill
Ipswich Rd
Boxhouse La
Monk's La
Grove Hill
May's Barn
32
Perry La
Kiddles Farm
Parney Heath
Hill House
B1029
Lamb Corner
May's La
Louse Lane
The Heath
Mott's Farm
PH
Long Rd W
2
Birchwood Rd
Ardleigh Rd
Stud Farm
Cross Vale
Dedham Heath
Duck La
Dedham Meade
Roman Road
Hotel
Birchwood Farm
Hunter's Chase
31
Birch Wood
God's House Farm
Birchhall Corner
Malting Farm La
Malting Farm
Rookery Chase
Rookery Farm
Goodhall Farm
Coggeshall Rd
1
Hart's La
Clarke's Farm
Old Barn Farm
Whaley Farm
Dead La
Fen La
Ardleigh Heath
Dedham Rd
B1029
Bloomfield's Farm
The Benson Stud
A137
Harwich Rd
30

03   D   04   E   05   F

34

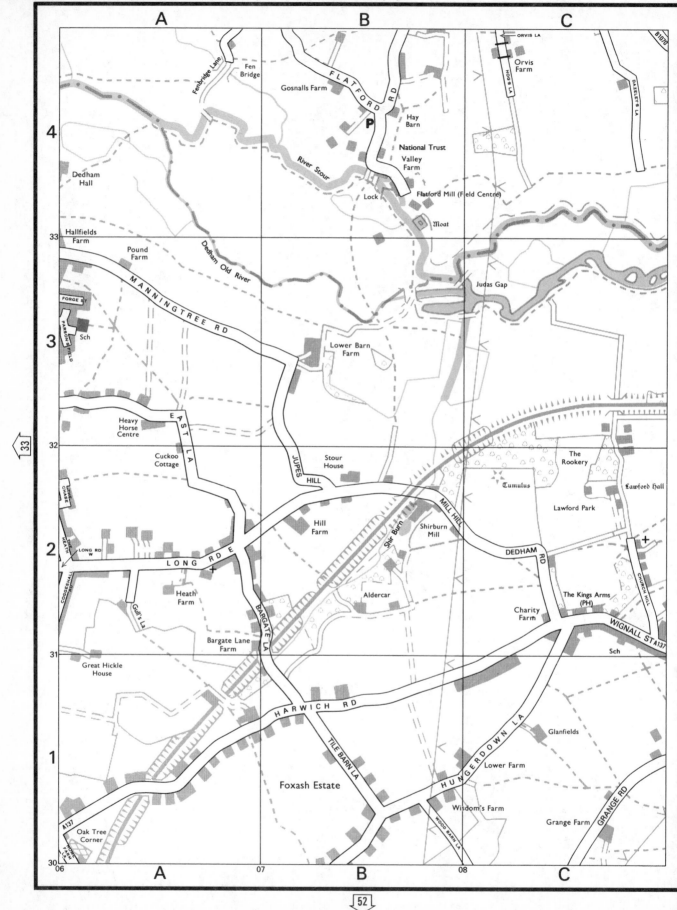

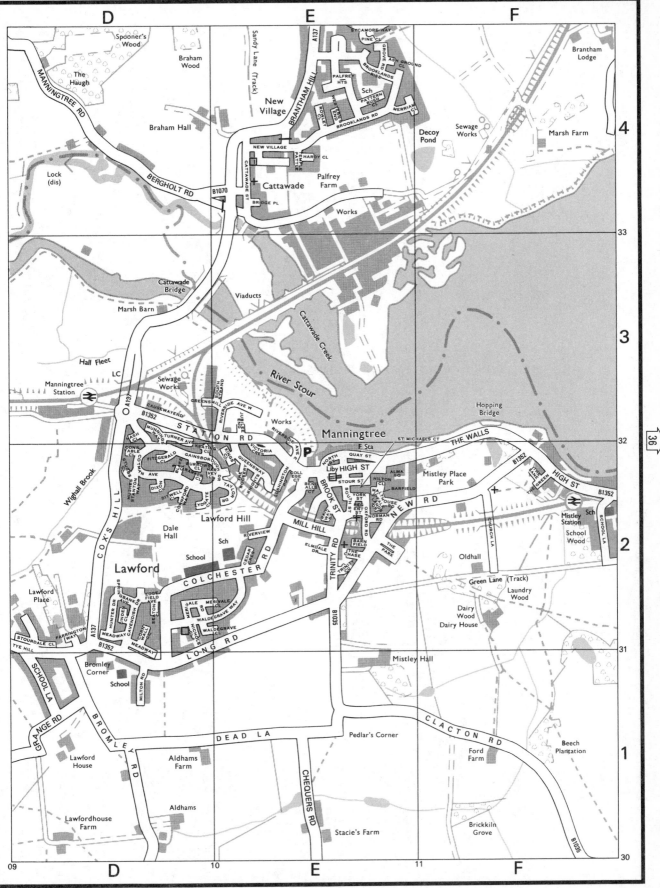

36

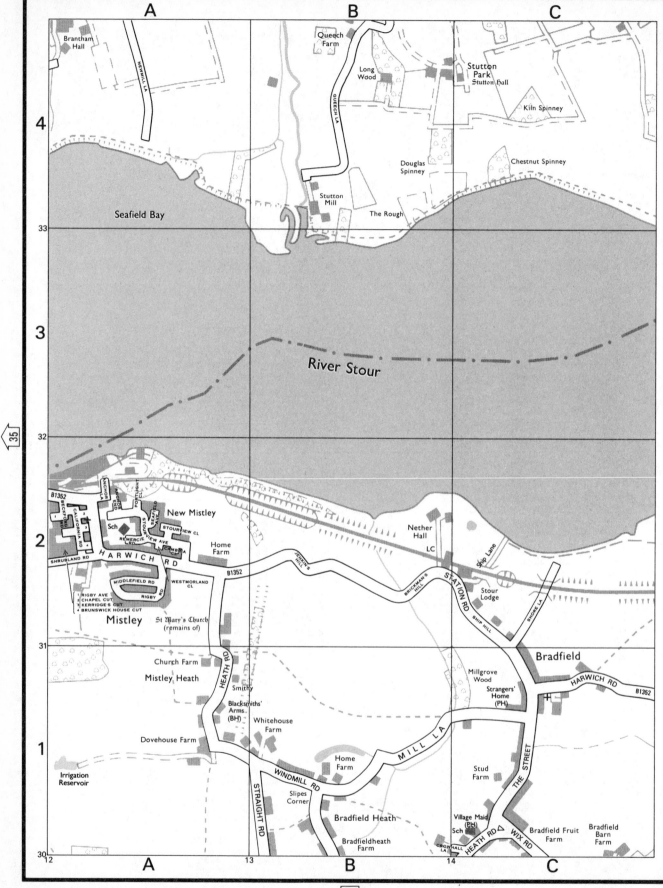

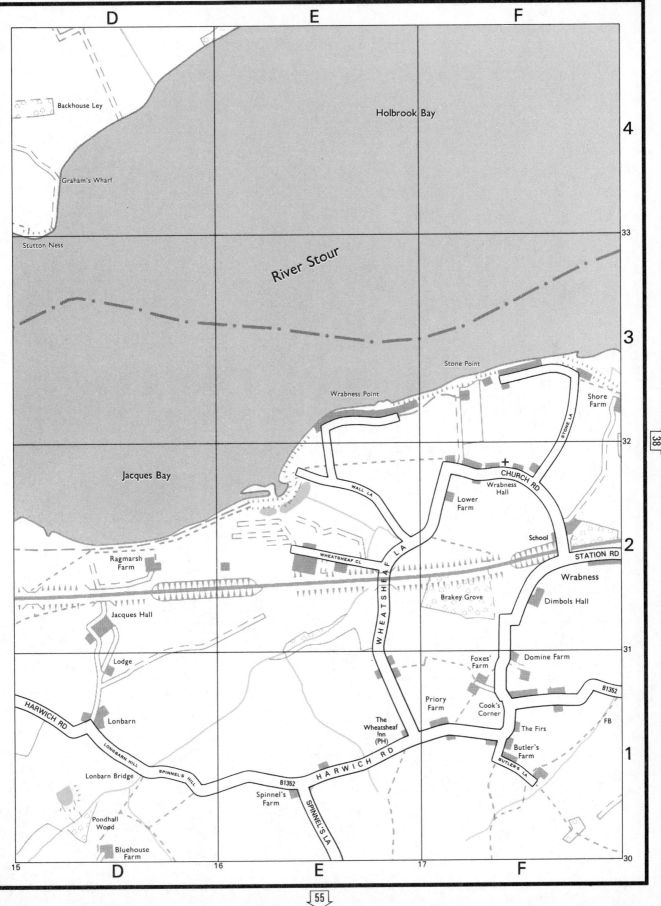

D

E

F

Backhouse Ley

Holbrook Bay

4

Graham's Wharf

Stutton Ness

33

River Stour

3

Stone Point

Wrabness Point

Shore Farm

32

38

Jacques Bay

Lower Farm

Wrabness Hall

CHURCH RD

WALL LA

WHEATSHEAF LA

STONE LA

School

STATION RD

2

Ragmarsh Farm

WHEATSHEAF CL

Wrabness

Brakey Grove

Dimbols Hall

Jacques Hall

31

Lodge

Foxes' Farm

Domine Farm

B1352

HARWICH RD

Lonbarn

Priory Farm

Cook's Corner

The Firs

FB

LONGBARN HILL

The Wheatsheaf Inn (PH)

Butler's Farm

1

Lonbarn Bridge

SPINNEL'S HILL

HARWICH RD

BUTLER'S LA

B1352

Spinnel's Farm

SPINNEL'S LA

Pondhall Wood

Bluehouse Farm

30

15

D

16

E

17

F

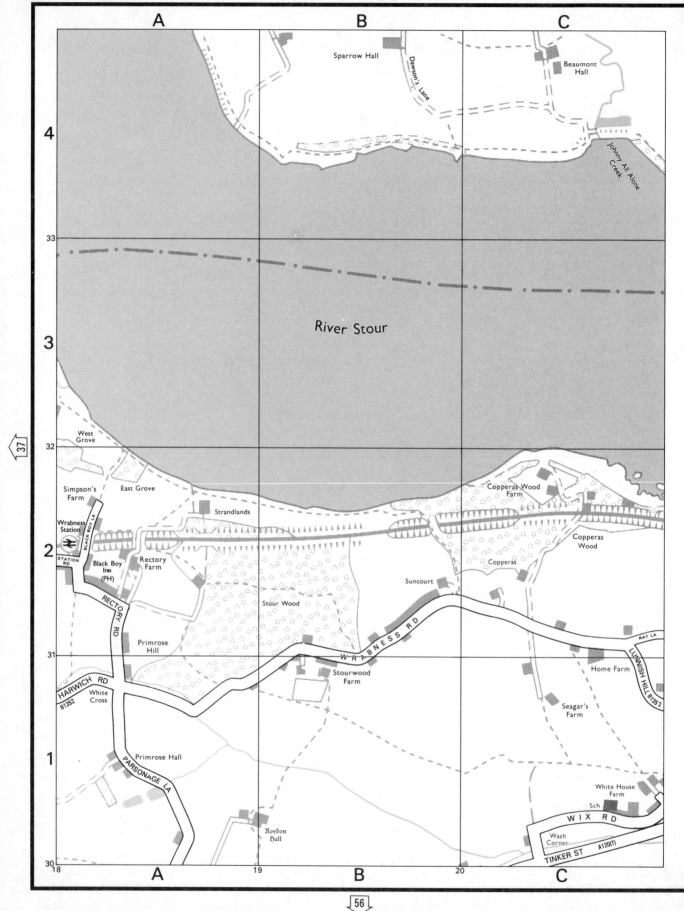

A
B
C

4

33

River Stour

3

37

32

West Grove

Simpson's Farm

East Grove

Copperas Wood Farm

Wrabness Station

Strandlands

Copperas Wood

Rectory Farm

Copperas

2

STATION RD

Black Boy Inn (PH)

Suncourt

Stour Wood

Primrose Hill

WRABNESS RD

RAY LA

Home Farm

31

HARWICH RD B1352

White Cross

Stourwood Farm

Seagar's Farm

LUNWISH HILL B1352

Primrose Hall

PARSONAGE LA

White House Farm

1

Sch

WIX RD

Roydon Hall

Wash Corner

TINKER ST A120(T)

30
18

A

19

B

20

C

Sparrow Hall

Dawson's Lane

Beaumont Hall

Johnny All Alone Creek

BLACK BOY LA

RECTORY RD

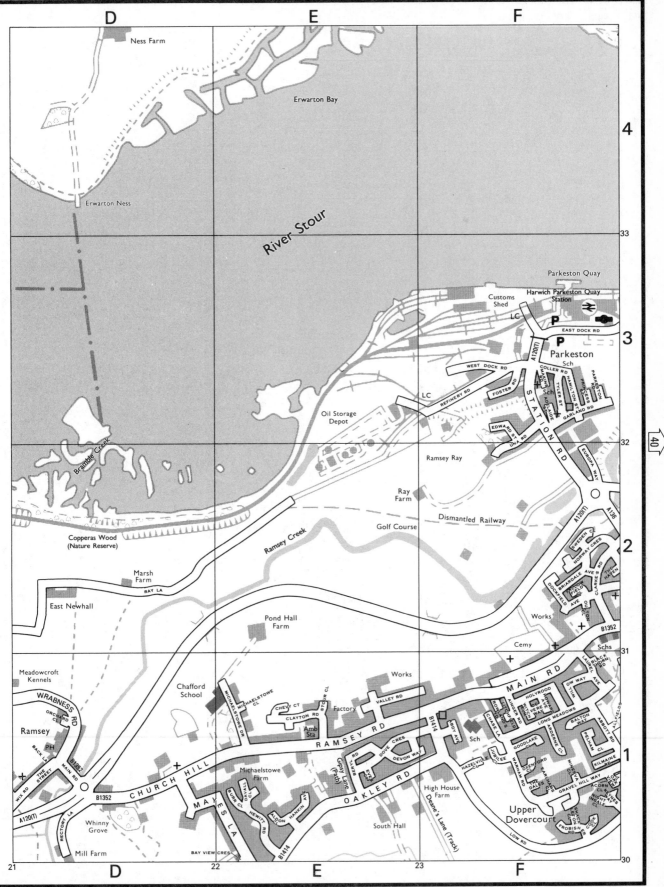

D

E

F

4

Ness Farm

Erwarton Bay

River Stour

Erwarton Ness

33

Parkeston Quay

Harwich Parkeston Quay Station

Customs Shed

LC

P East Dock Rd

P Parkeston

3

Sch

West Dock Rd

COLLER RD

LC

FOSTER RD

REFINERY RD

Sch

ADELAIDE

TYLER ST

HAMILTON ST

PRINCESS

PARKESTON

GARLAND RD

STATION RD

Oil Storage Depot

EDWARD ST

UNA RD

32

40

Bramble Creek

Ramsey Ray

EUROPA WAY

Copperas Wood (Nature Reserve)

Ramsey Creek

Ray Farm

Golf Course

Dismantled Railway

A120(T)

A136

SWEDEN CL

NORMAY CRES

2

Marsh Farm

RAY LA

BRIARDALE AVE

CLARKE RD

PASSON FIELD

STOUR HAVEN

DOCKFIELD AVE

East Newhall

Works

B1352

Pond Hall Farm

Cemy

Schs

31

Meadowcroft Kennels

Works

MAIN RD

LAUREL AVE

BLACKTHORN AVE

Chafford School

MICHAELSTOWE DR

MICHAELSTOWE CL

CHEVY CT

CLAYTON RD

STOUR CL

Factory

VALLEY RD

HOLYROOD

AINGER RD

OW WAY

WILL

WRABNESS RD

ORCHARD CL

Ramsey

PH

Amb Sta

RAMSEY RD

DOVE CRES

DEVON WAY

B1414

CHASE LA

CHASE RD

Sch

HAZELVILLE CL

JUBILEE

LONG MEADOWS

VEVERE WAY

ARDERNE CL

GOODLAKE

WARNAN RD

PELHAM

BALTON WAY

KILMAINE RD

1

BACK LA

THE STREET

MAIN RD

B1352

CHURCH HILL

MAYES LA

BURR CL

DAVALL CL

ALDON

HANKIN

GIPSY LANE (Path)

OAKLEY RD

B1414

IVY AVE

THE DALES

MINERVA

EARLGATE

GRAVEL HILL WAY

NIGHTACRES

ACORN

Upper Dovercourt

FROBISH

WIX RD

RECTORY LA

A120(T)

Whinny Grove

Michaelstowe Farm

HEWITT RD

High House Farm

Deane's Lane (Track)

LOW RD

COOK

Mill Farm

BAY VIEW CRES

South Hall

30

21

D

22

E

23

F

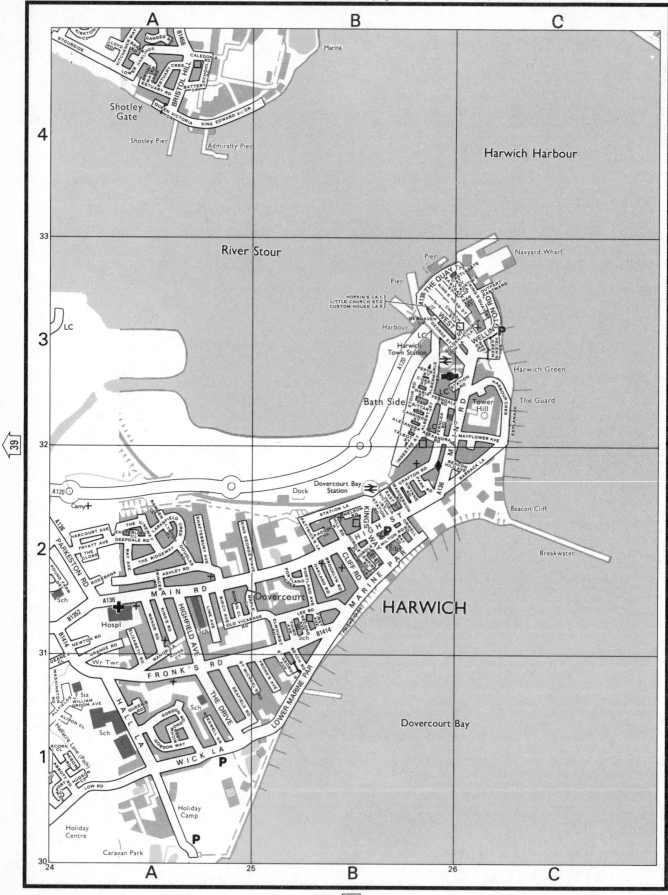

A   B   C

Harwich Harbour

33

River Stour

Shotley
Gate

Shotley Pier   Admiralty Pier

4

LC

3

HOPKIN'S LA 1
LITTLE CHURCH ST 2
CUSTOM HOUSE LA 3

Pier   Navyard Wharf

Pier

THE QUAY

WEST ST

WELLINGTON RD

Harbour

Newhaven

LC

Harwich
Town Station

Harwich Green

The Guard

Bath Side

Tower
Hill

32

Dovercourt Bay
Station

Dock

Beacon Cliff

A120

Cemy

A136

2

STATION LA

KINGSWAY

MARINE PAR

Breakwater

Dovercourt

HARWICH

PARKSTON RD

Sch

Hospl

MAIN RD

HIGHFIELD AVE

B1352

B1414

Newton

31

Grange Rd

FRONK'S RD

THE DRIVE

Dovercourt Bay

Wr Twr

F Sta

WILLIAM
GROOM AVE

Sch

HALL LA

WICK LA

LOWER MARINE PAR

P

1

Holiday
Camp

Holiday
Centre

P

Caravan Park

30
24   25   26

A   B   C

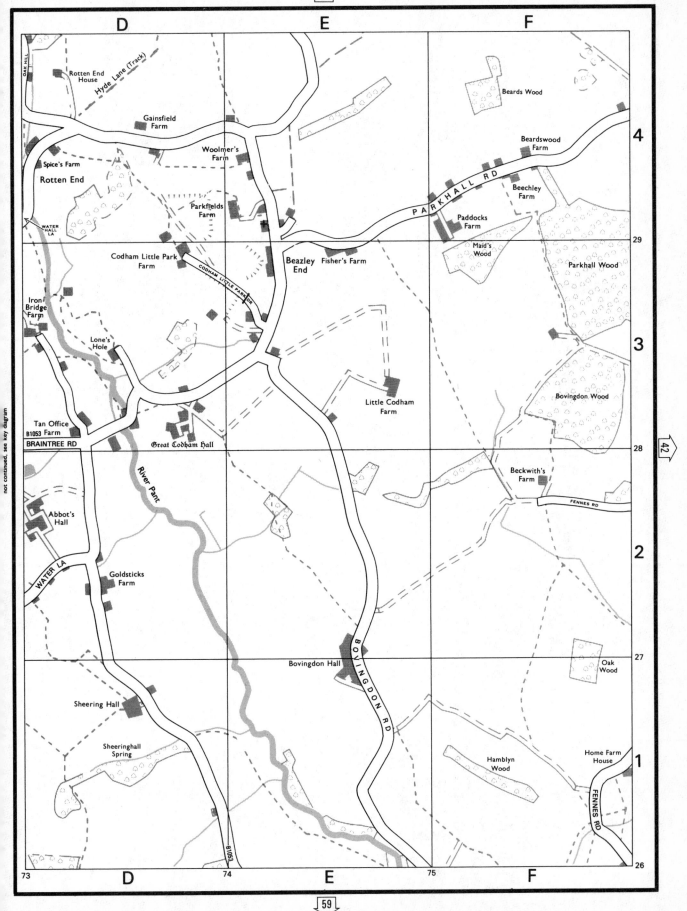

D E F

Oak Hill

Rotten End House

Hyde Lane (Track)

Beards Wood

Gainsfield Farm

Woolmer's Farm

4

Beardswood Farm

Spice's Farm

Rotten End

PARKHALL RD

Beechley Farm

Parkfields Farm

Paddocks Farm

29

WATER HALL LA

Codham Little Park Farm

CODHAM LITTLE PARK DR

Beazley End

Fisher's Farm

Maid's Wood

Parkhall Wood

Iron Bridge Farm

Lone's Hole

3

Little Codham Farm

Bovingdon Wood

Tan Office Farm

B1053

BRAINTREE RD

Great Codham Hall

28

42

Beckwith's Farm

FENNES RD

River Pant

Abbot's Hall

2

WATER LA

Goldsticks Farm

27

Oak Wood

Bovingdon Hall

BOVINGDON RD

Sheering Hall

Sheeringhall Spring

Hamblyn Wood

Home Farm House

1

FENNES RD

B1053

26

73 D 74 E 75 F

not continued, see key diagram

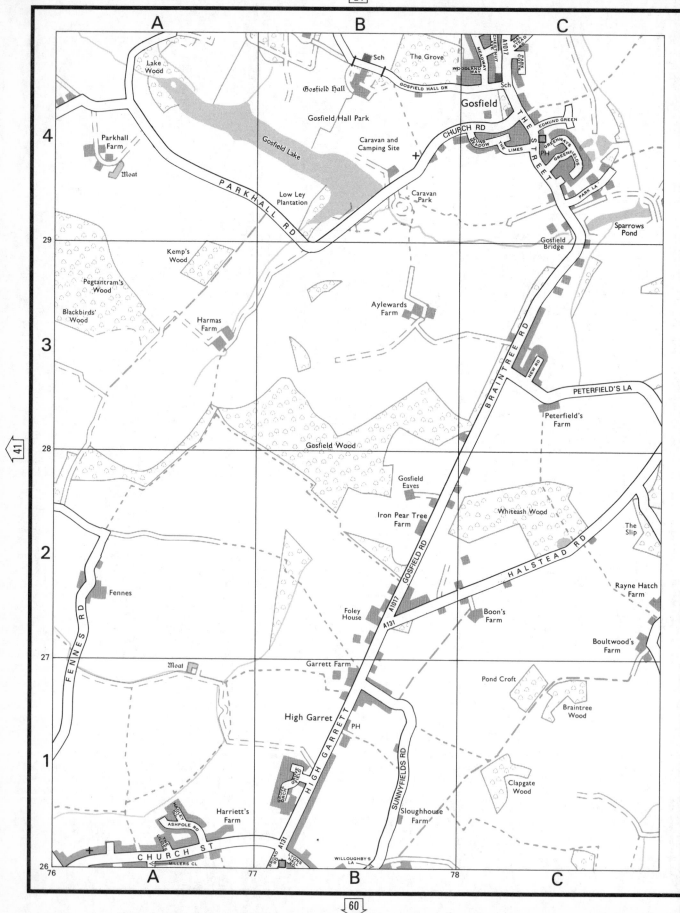

A   B   C

4

Lake
Wood

Sch

The Grove

WOODLAND WAY

CHESTNUT

MEADOW WAY

PARK WK

A1017

Gosfield Hall

GOSFIELD HALL DR

Sch

Gosfield

Gosfield Hall Park

Parkhall
Farm

Moat

Gosfield Lake

Caravan and
Camping Site

CHURCH RD

LONG MEADOW

EDMUND GREEN

THE LIMES

THE STREET

PH

GREENWAYS
GREENFIELDS
GREENFIELDS

PARK LA.

Sparrows
Pond

Low Ley
Plantation

Caravan
Park

Gosfield
Bridge

29

Kemp's
Wood

Pegtantram's
Wood

Blackbirds'
Wood

Harmas
Farm

Aylewards
Farm

BRAINTREE RD

NEW RD

PETERFIELD'S LA.

Peterfield's
Farm

3

Gosfield Wood

28

Gosfield
Eaves

Whiteash Wood

The
Slip

Iron Pear Tree
Farm

GOSFIELD RD

HALSTEAD RD

Rayne Hatch
Farm

2

Fennes

FENNES RD

Foley
House

A1017

A131

Boon's
Farm

Boultwood's
Farm

27

Moat

Garrett Farm

Pond Croft

Braintree
Wood

High Garret

HIGH GARRETT

PH

SUNNYFIELDS RD

Clapgate
Wood

1

BROAD GREEN
GREENS
ORCHARD

Harriett's
Farm

THE WILLOWS

ASHPOLE RD

CHURCH ST

MILLERS CL.

A131

BROAD GREEN
LYONS LA.

Sloughhouse
Farm

WILLOUGHBY'S
LA.

26
76   77   78

A   B   C

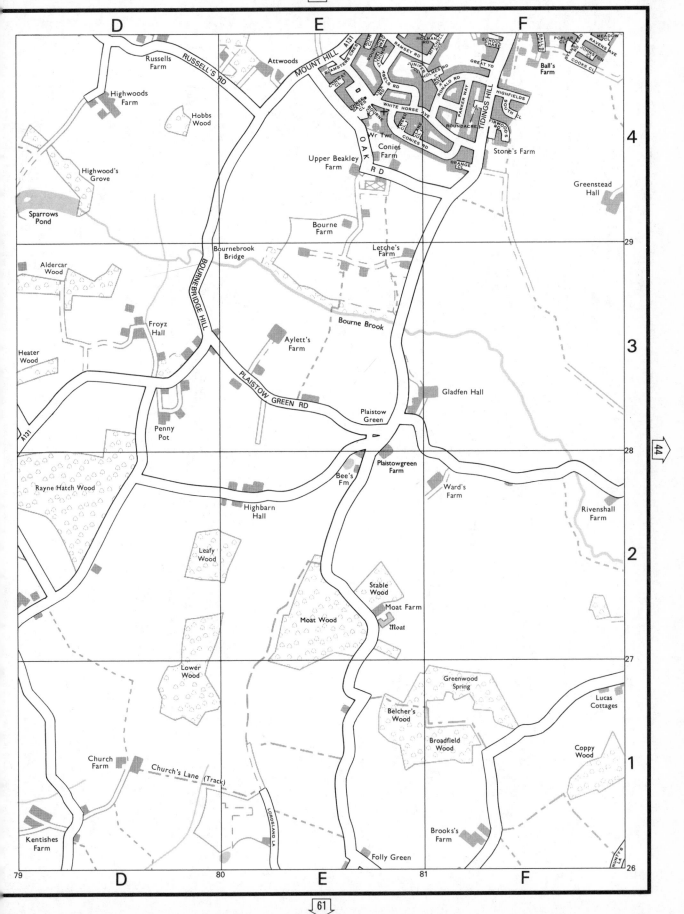

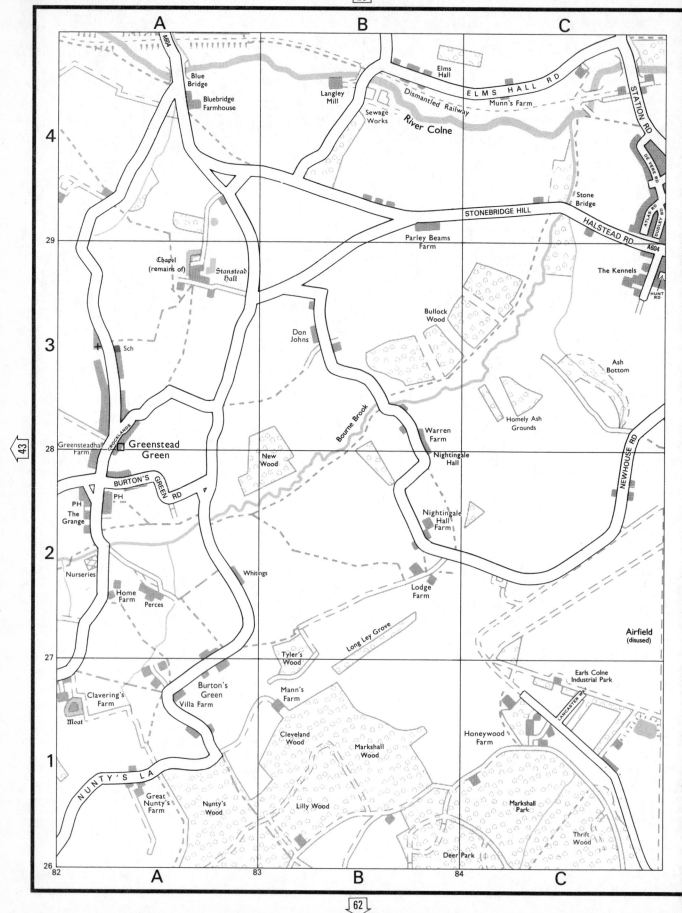

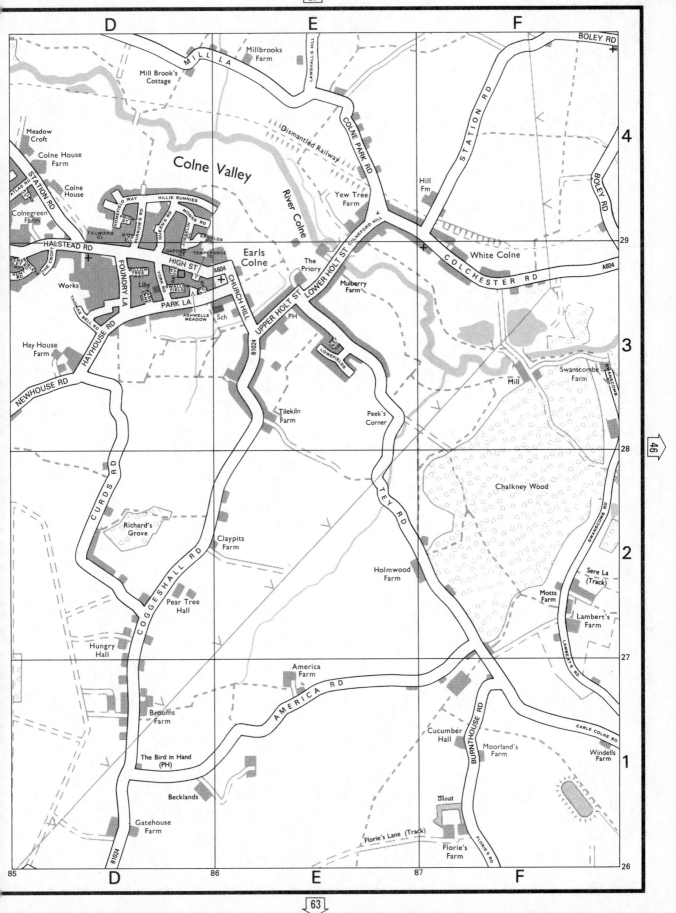

BOLEY RD

D   E   F

Millbrooks
Farm

Mill Brook's
Cottage

MILL LA

LAWSHALL'S HILL

4

Meadow
Croft

Colne House
Farm

Dismantled Railway

COLNE PARK RD

STATION RD

BOLEY RD

Colne
House

Colne Valley

Yew Tree
Farm

Hill
Fm

Colnegreen
Farm

STATION RD
ATLAS RD

HOMEFIELD WAY
HILLIE BUNNIES

PRIORY ST
BURROWS RD
QUEEN'S RD
MONKS RD
JOSSELIN
ERNALDS

River Colne

29

Halstead Rd

TILLWICKS CL

Earls
Colne

The
Priory

COLNEFORD HILL

White Colne

COLCHESTER RD

A604

Works

HIGH ST

OXFORD
TEMPERANCE
YD

Liby

WILLOW
TREE
SWAY

YORK RD

A604

LOWER HOLT ST

Mulberry
Farm

3

FOUNDRY LA

HAYHOUSE RD

PARK LA

SWALLOW
FIELD

CHURCH HILL

UPPER HOLT ST

PH

Mill

Swanscombe
Farm

ST SWANSCOMB

THOMAS BELL RD

ASHWELLS
MEADOW

Sch

B1024

LOWEFIELDS

Hay House
Farm

NEWHOUSE RD

Tilekiln
Farm

Peek's
Corner

TEY RD

28

46

CURDS RD

Richard's
Grove

Claypits
Farm

Chalkney Wood

SWANSCOMBE RD

2

COGGESHALL RD

Pear Tree
Hall

Holmwood
Farm

Sere La
(Track)

Motts
Farm

Lambert's
Farm

LAMBERT'S RD

Hungry
Hall

27

America
Farm

AMERICA RD

EARLS COLNE RD

Brooms
Farm

Cucumber
Hall

Moorland's
Farm

Windells
Farm

BURNTHOUSE RD

1

The Bird in Hand
(PH)

Becklands

Moat

Gatehouse
Farm

B1024

Florie's Lane (Track)

Florie's
Farm

FLORIES RD

26

85   D   86   E   87   F

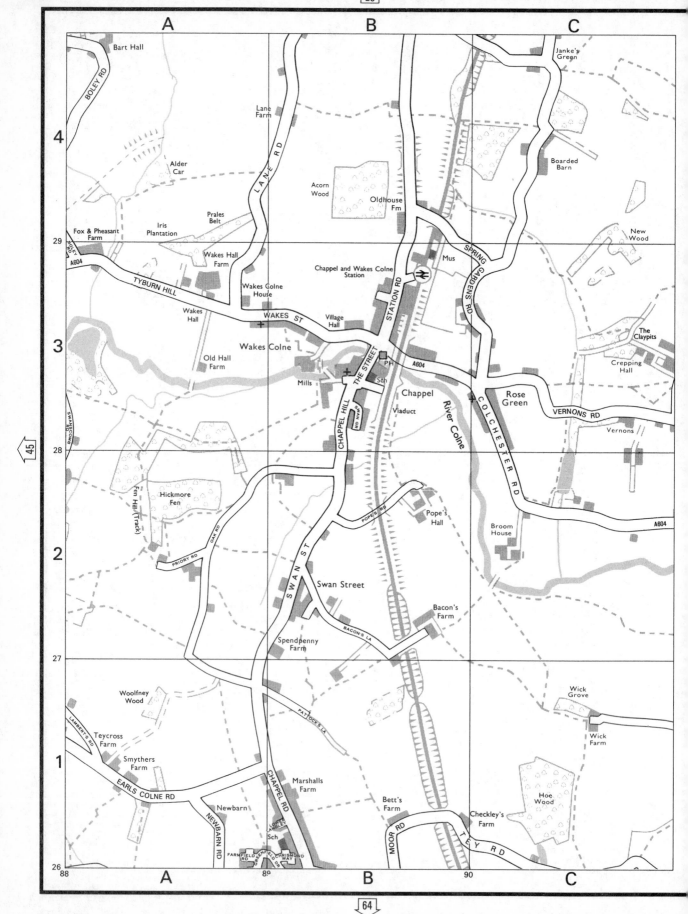

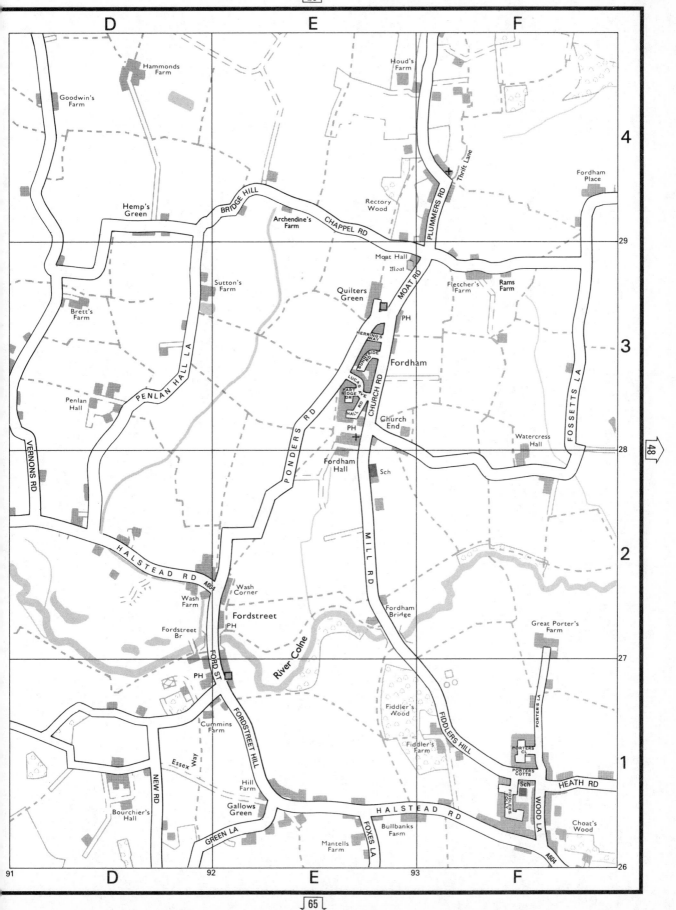

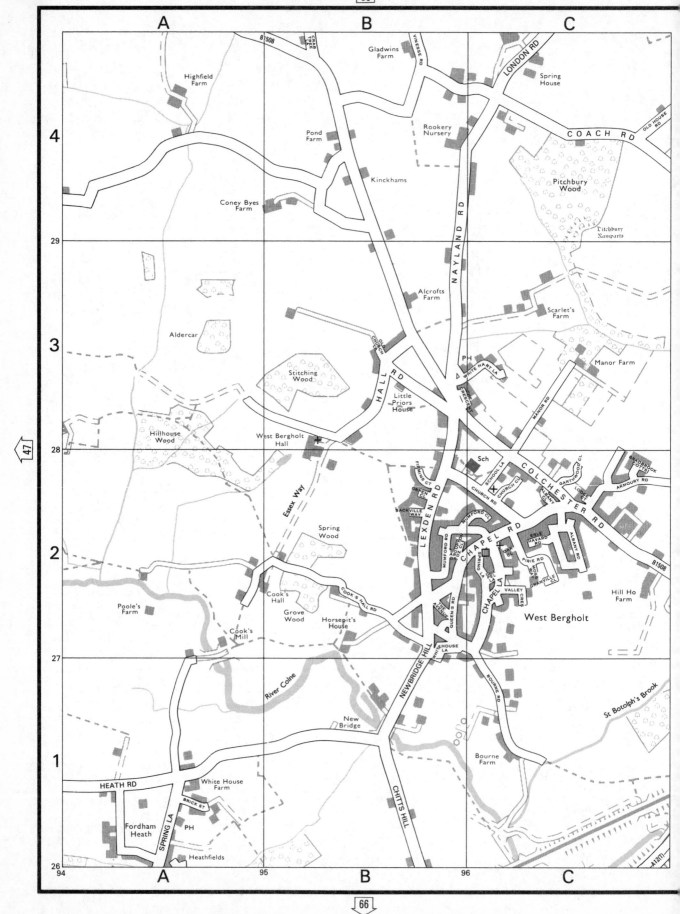

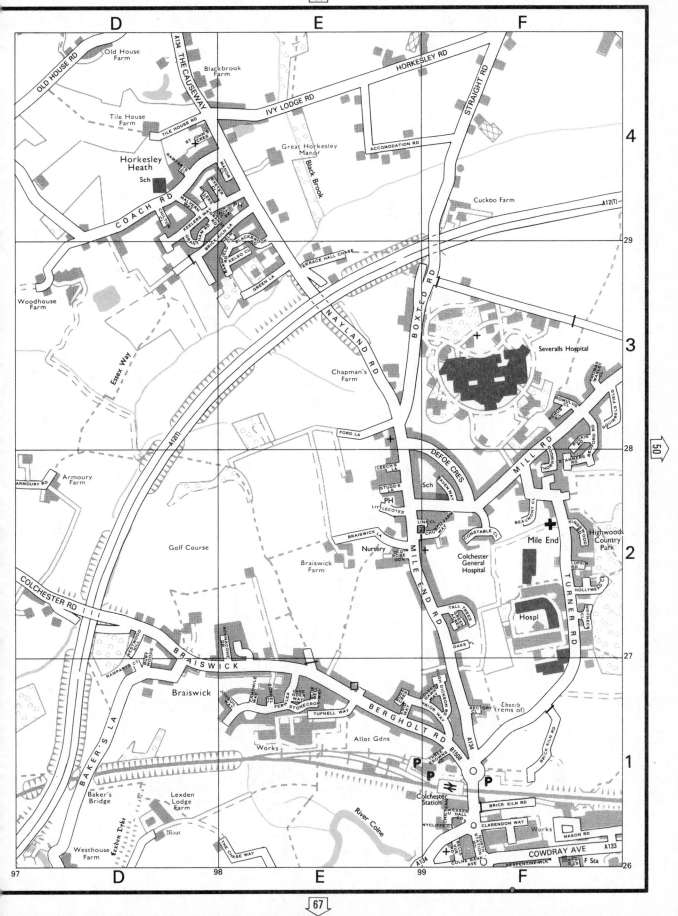

D E F

4

3

29

28

27

1

50

D E F

97 98 99

OLD HOUSE RD
Old House Farm
A134
THE CAUSEWAY
Blackbrook Farm
HORKESLEY RD
STRAIGHT RD
IVY LODGE RD
Tile House Farm
Tile House RD
ST JOHN'S CRES
Great Horkesley Manor
ACCOMODATION RD
Horkesley Heath
Sch
Black Brook
A12(T)
Cuckoo Farm
COACH RD
RAMPARTS
MANOR RD
MALVERN WAY
KEELERS WAY
CHITON
GRANT
OAKHAM RD
BRICK KILN LA
BRADFIELD
KELSO CL
BLACKBROOK
GREEN LA
TERRACE HALL CHASE
BOXTED RD
Severalls Hospital
THOMAS MANLEY
Woodhouse Farm
NAYLAND RD
Essex Way
A12(T)
Chapman's Farm
ROMULUS CL
REMUS CL
GOODWIN
RUDKIN RD
STAMMERS RD
BEDFORD RD
SQUIRRELS FIELD
MILL RD
THOR
FORD LA
DEFOE CRES
Armoury Farm
ARMOURY RD
LEECH'S LA
STUDD'S
Sch
RAVEN WAY
BEAUMONT CL
KINGSWOOD
Highwoods Country Park
PH
LITTLECOTES
BRAISWICK LA
Nursery
LINK CL
CHURCH FARM WAY
OLD ROSE GDN
CONSTABLE CL
Mile End
LUFKIN RD
HOLLYMEAD
Golf Course
Braiswick Farm
MILE END RD
Colchester General Hospital
Hospl
TURNER RD
HAYHOUSE
COLCHESTER RD
WESTWOOD
BIRCH WOODS
BRAISWICK
RAMPARTS CT
ACWASCONE DR
TALL TREES
OAK TREES ACRE
OAKS PL
BAKER'S LA
Braiswick
JONQUIL WAY
CHAMOMILE WAY
SORREL
FERN LEA
LAVENDER WAY
STONECROP
TUFNELL WAY
PRIORY WAY
BERGHOLT RD
DICKSON RD
PRIOR WAY
RECTORY CL
Church (rems of)
BRICK KILN RD
Works
Allot Gdns
THREE CROWNS RD
B1508
A134
P
P
Baker's Bridge
Lexden Lodge Farm
Lexden Dyke
Moat
River Colne
Colchester Station
P
Brick Kiln RD
ESSEX HALL RD
CLARENDON WAY
Works
MASON RD
A133
Westhouse Farm
THE CHASE WAY
WYCLIFFE CL
NORTH STATION RD
COLNE BANK AVE
COWDRAY AVE
SERPENTINE WLK
A134
F Sta
26

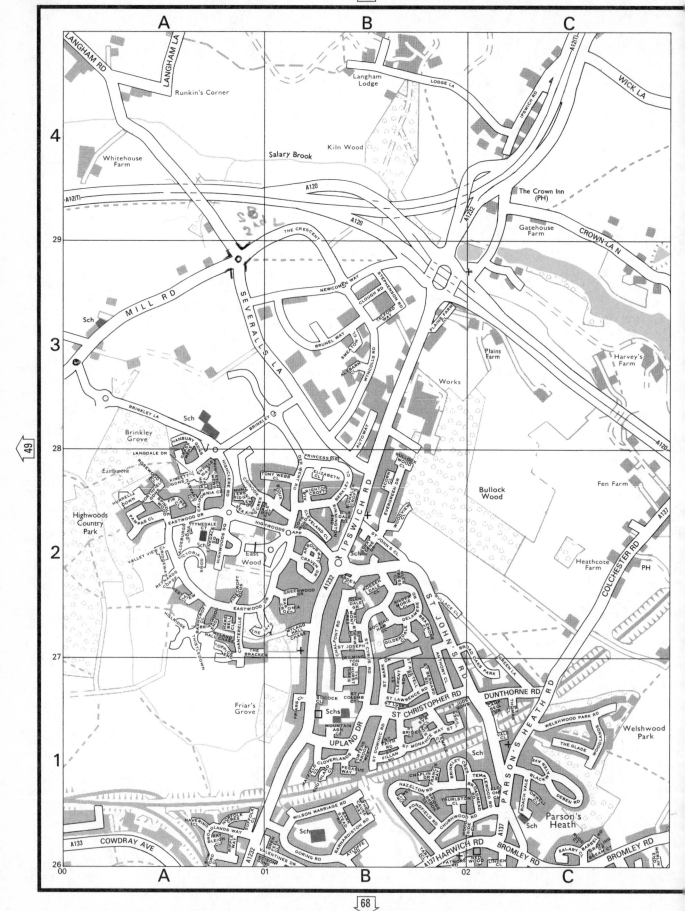

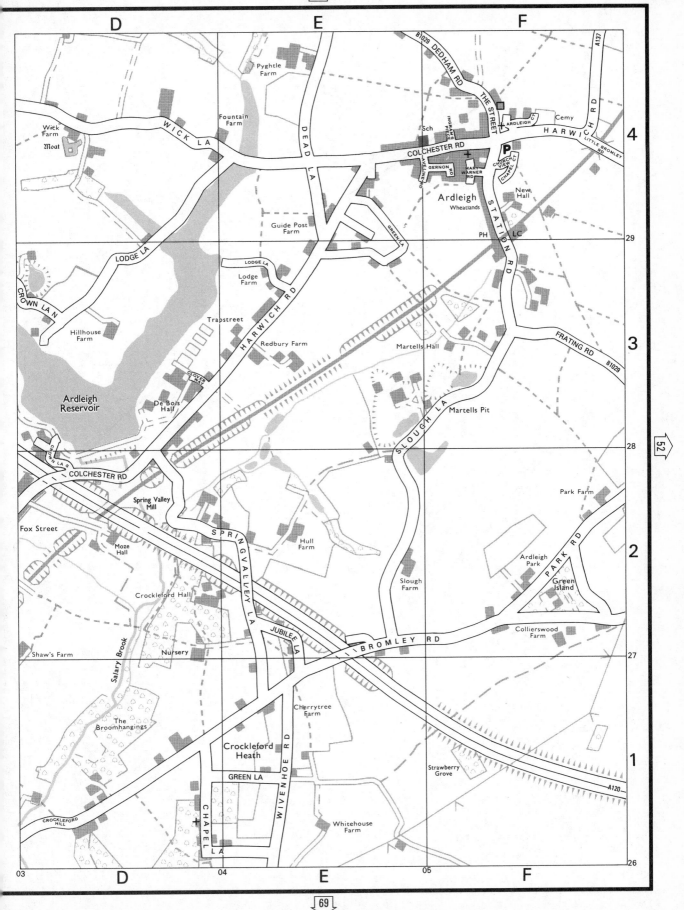

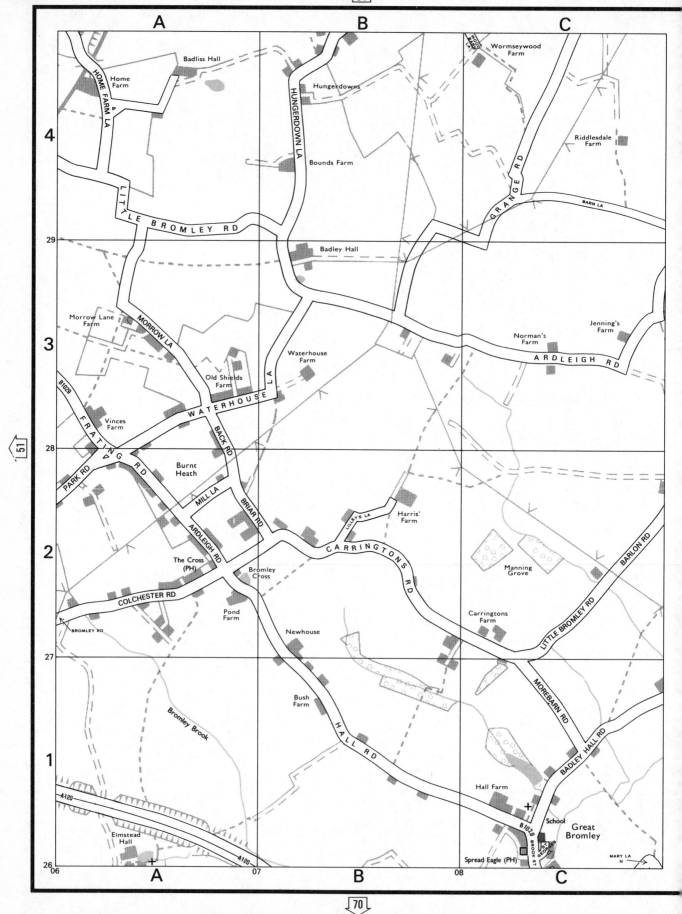

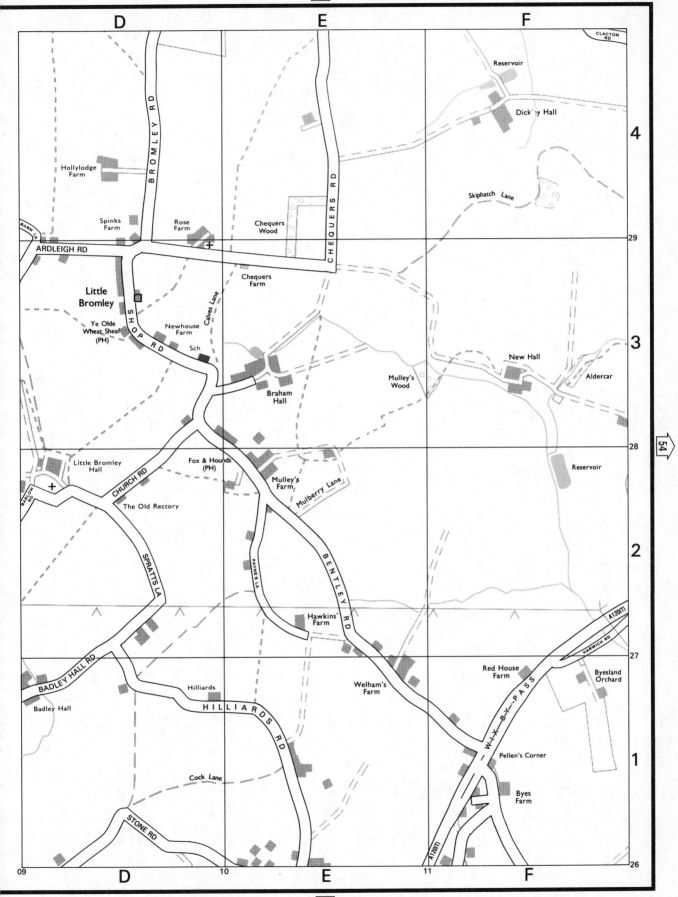

D

E

F

CLACTON RD

Reservoir

Dick'ey Hall

4

Hollylodge
Farm

BROMLEY RD

Skiphatch Lane

Spinks
Farm

Rose
Farm

Chequers
Wood

CHEQUERS RD

29

BARN LA

ARDLEIGH RD

Little
Bromley

Chequers
Farm

Calves Lane

New Hall

Ye Olde
Wheat Sheaf
(PH)

Newhouse
Farm

SHOP RD

Sch

Mulley's
Wood

Aldercar

3

Braham
Hall

Little Bromley
Hall

CHURCH RD

Fox & Hounds
(PH)

28

Reservoir

+

BARLOW RD

The Old Rectory

Mulley's
Farm

Mulberry Lane

SPRATTS LA

PAYNES LA

BENTLEY RD

2

A120(T)

Hawkins'
Farm

HARWICH RD

27

BADLEY HALL RD

Hilliards

Welham's
Farm

Red House
Farm

Byesland
Orchard

Badley Hall

HILLIARDS RD

W-I-X-B-Y-PASS

Pellen's Corner

1

Cock Lane

Byes
Farm

STONE RD

A120(T)

26

09

D

10

E

11

F

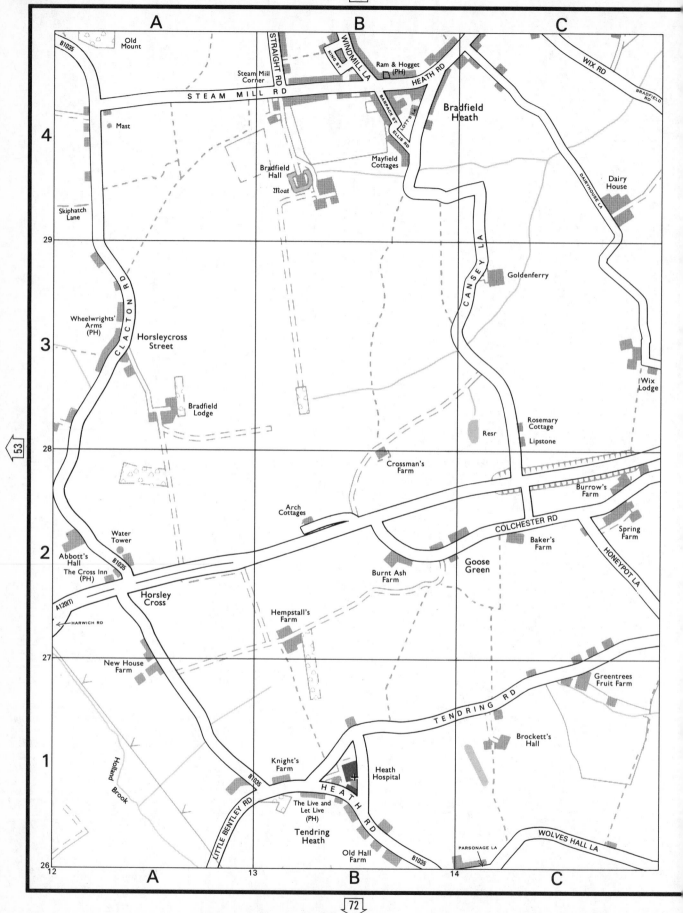

A   B   C

B1035
Old Mount

STRAIGHT RD

KING ST
WINDMILL LA
Ram & Hogget (PH)
HEATH RD

WIX RD
BRADFIELD RD

Steam Mill Corner

STEAM MILL RD

Mast

BARRACK ST
POTT'S LA
ELLIS RD
Bradfield Heath

Mayfield Cottages

Bradfield Hall
Moat

CANSEY LA

DAIRYHOUSE LA
Dairy House

Skiphatch Lane

29

Goldenferry

CLACTON RD

Wheelwrights' Arms (PH)
Horsleycross Street

3

Wix Lodge

Bradfield Lodge

Rosemary Cottage
Lipstone

Resr

28

Crossman's Farm

Burrow's Farm

Arch Cottages

COLCHESTER RD

Spring Farm

Water Tower

Baker's Farm

HONEYPOT LA

Abbott's Hall
The Cross Inn (PH)
B1035

2

Goose Green

Burnt Ash Farm

A120(T)
Horsley Cross

HARWICH RD

Hempstall's Farm

27

New House Farm

Greentrees Fruit Farm

TENDRING RD

Brockett's Hall

1

Knight's Farm

Heath Hospital

B1035

HEATH RD
Holland Brook

The Live and Let Live (PH)

LITTLE BENTLEY RD

Tendring Heath

Old Hall Farm
B1035

PARSONAGE LA
WOLVES HALL LA

26
12   A   13   B   14   C

53

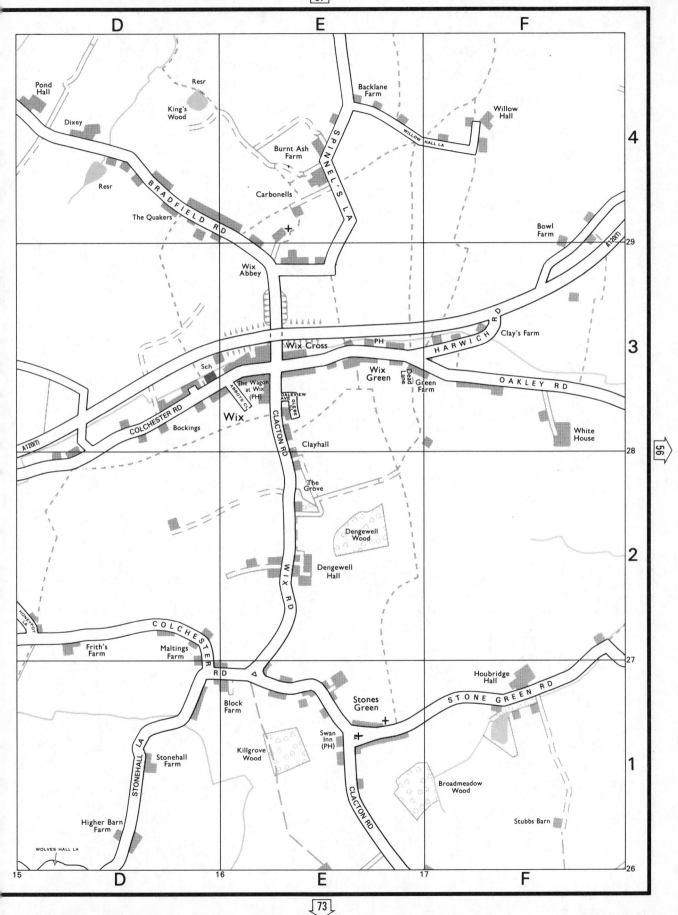

D E F

Pond Hall

Dixey

Resr

King's Wood

Resr

BRADFIELD RD

The Quakers

Burnt Ash Farm

Carbonells

SPINNEL'S LA

Backlane Farm

Willow Hall

WILLOW HALL LA

Bowl Farm

A120(T)

29

Wix Abbey

Wix Cross

PH

HARWICH RD

Clay's Farm

3

Sch

Wix Green

Dead Lane

Green Farm

OAKLEY RD

The Wagon at Wix (PH)

ABBOT'S CL

DALEVIEW AVE

GLEBE CL

Wix

COLCHESTER RD

Bockings

CLACTON RD

Clayhall

White House

A120(T)

28

56

The Grove

Dengewell Wood

2

Dengewell Hall

HONEYPOT LA

COLCHESTER RD

Frith's Farm

Maltings Farm

RD

27

Houbridge Hall

STONE GREEN RD

STONEHALL LA

Block Farm

Stones Green

Stonehall Farm

Killgrove Wood

Swan Inn (PH)

Broadmeadow Wood

1

Higher Barn Farm

CLACTON RD

Stubbs Barn

WOLVES HALL LA

26

15 D 16 E 17 F

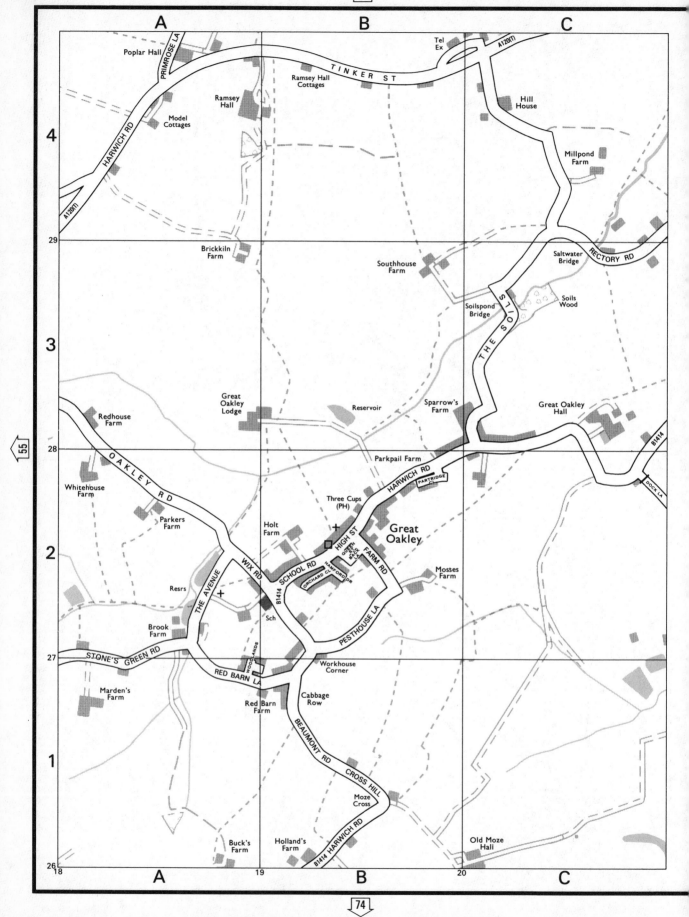

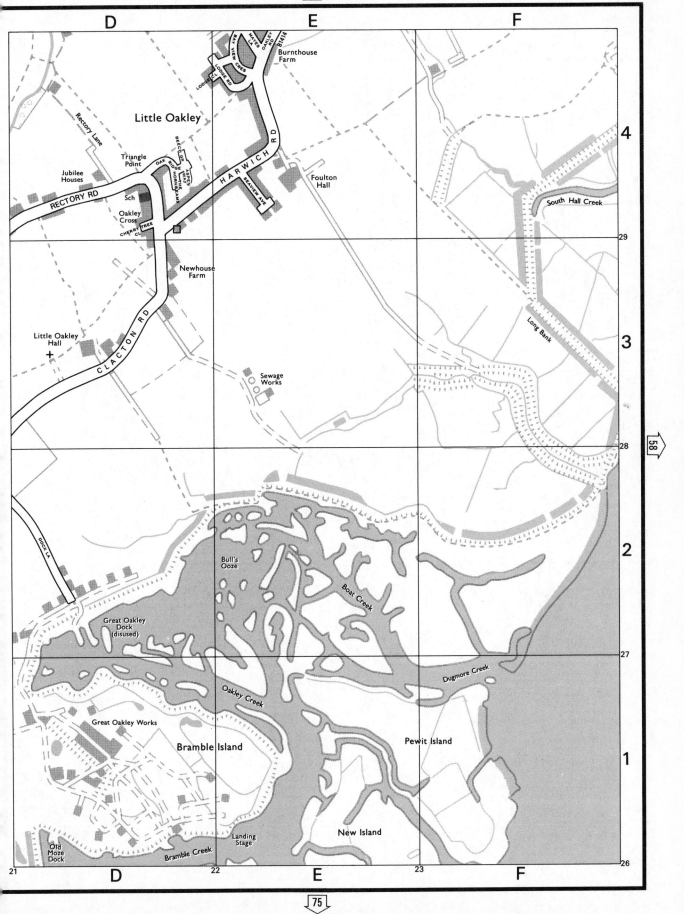

D   E   F

Burnthouse Farm

Little Oakley

4

Rectory Lane

Triangle Point

Jubilee Houses

Foulton Hall

South Hall Creek

RECTORY RD

Oakley Cross

29

Newhouse Farm

Long Bank

CLACTON RD

3

Little Oakley Hall

Sewage Works

58

28

2

Bull's Ooze

Boat Creek

DOCK LA

Great Oakley Dock (disused)

27

Dugmore Creek

Oakley Creek

Great Oakley Works

Bramble Island

Pewit Island

1

New Island

Old Moze Dock

Landing Stage

Bramble Creek

21 D   22 E   23 F 26

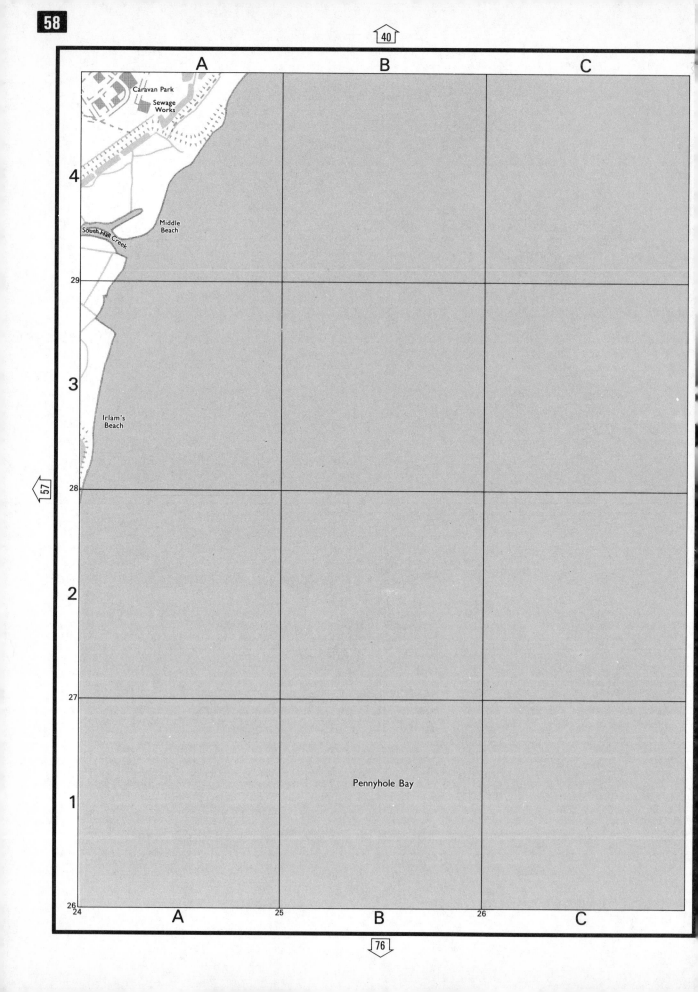

A

B

C

Caravan Park

Sewage
Works

4

Middle
Beach

South Hall Creek

29

3

Irlam's
Beach

28

2

27

Pennyhole Bay

1

26

24

A

25

B

26

C

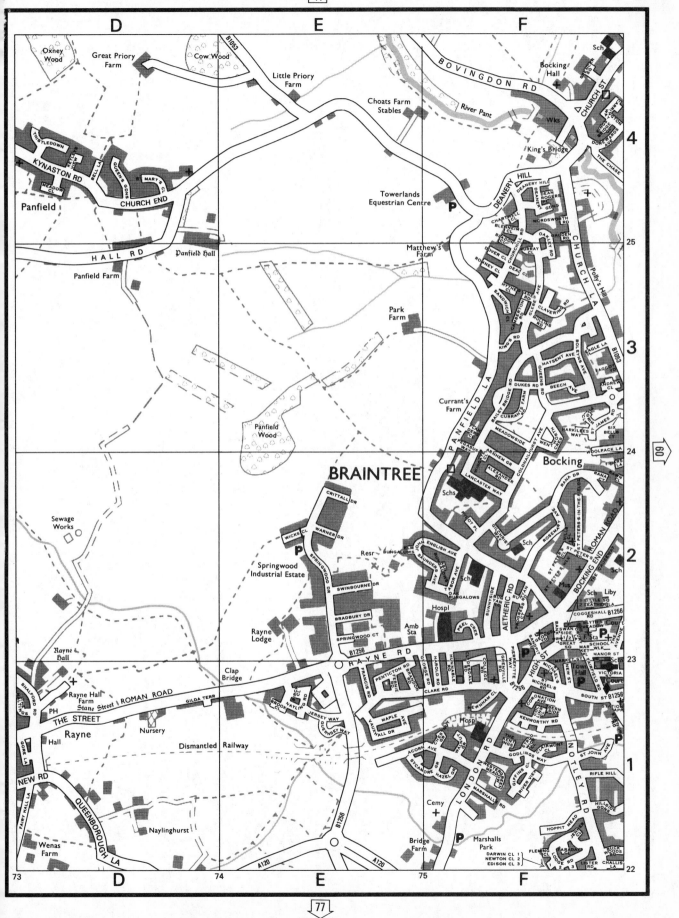

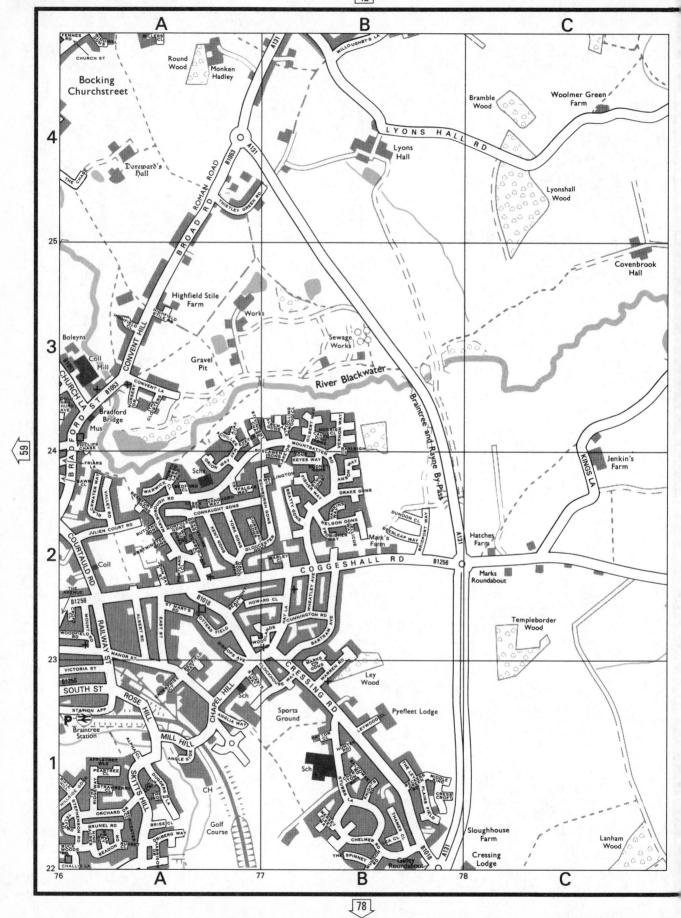

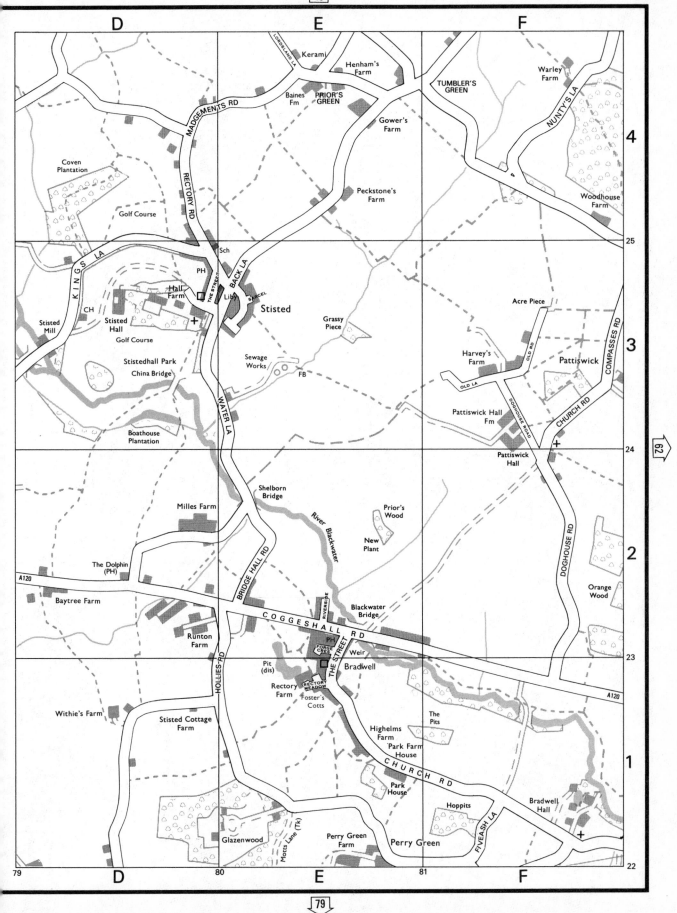

D

E

F

Kerami

LONGLAND LA

Henham's
Farm

TUMBLER'S
GREEN

Warley
Farm

NUNTY'S LA

4

MADGEMENTS RD

Baines
Fm

PRIOR'S
GREEN

Gower's
Farm

RECTORY RD

Coven
Plantation

Peckstone's
Farm

Woodhouse
Farm

Golf Course

25

Sch

KINGS LA

PH

BACK LA

THE STREET

Liby

SARCEL

Stisted

Grassy
Piece

Acre Piece

OLD RD

COMPASSES RD

3

Hall
Farm

CH

Stisted
Mill

+

Stisted
Hall

Golf Course

Sewage
Works

FB

Harvey's
Farm

OLD LA

Pattiswick

CHURCH RD

Stistedhall Park

China Bridge

Pattiswick Hall
Fm

DOGHOUSE ROAD

WATER LA

Boathouse
Plantation

Pattiswick
Hall

+

24

Shelborn
Bridge

Milles Farm

River Blackwater

Prior's
Wood

New
Plant

DOGHOUSE RD

Orange
Wood

2

BRIDGE HALL RD

The Dolphin
(PH)

A120

Baytree Farm

RIVERSIDE

Blackwater
Bridge

COGGESHALL RD

Runton
Farm

PH

FORGE
CRES

Weir

THE STREET

23

HOLLIES RD

Pit
(dis)

Bradwell

A120

Rectory
Farm

RECTORY
MEADOW

Foster's
Cotts

Withie's Farm

Stisted Cottage
Farm

Highelms
Farm

The
Pits

Park Farm
House

1

CHURCH RD

Park
House

Hoppits

Bradwell
Hall

FIVEASH LA

+

Glazenwood

Motts Lane (Tk)

Perry Green
Farm

Perry Green

79

D

80

E

81

F

22

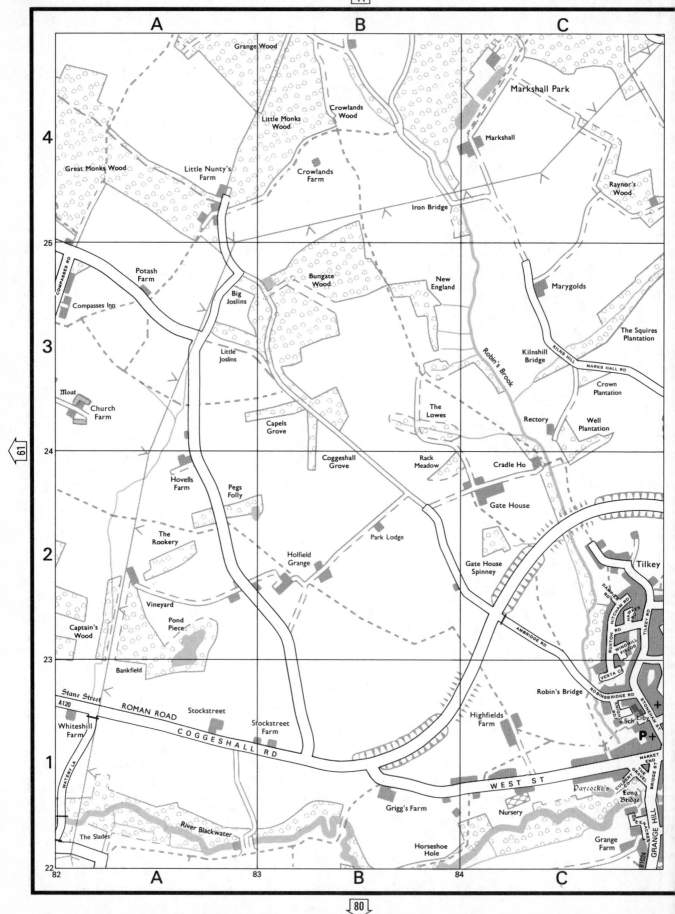

A B C

61

4

Grange Wood

Markshall Park

Little Monks Wood

Crowlands Wood

Markshall

Great Monks Wood

Little Nunty's Farm

Crowlands Farm

Raynor's Wood

Iron Bridge

25

New England

Marygolds

COMPASSES RD

Potash Farm

Bungate Wood

The Squires Plantation

Compasses Inn

Big Joslins

Robin's Brook

Kilnshill Bridge

KILNS HILL

MARKS HALL RD

3

Little Joslins

Crown Plantation

Moat

Church Farm

Capels Grove

The Lowes

Rectory

Well Plantation

24

Coggeshall Grove

Rack Meadow

Cradle Ho

Hovells Farm

Pegs Folly

Gate House

The Rookery

Park Lodge

Gate House Spinney

Tilkey

2

Holfield Grange

DAMNER RD

HITCHAM RD

HAWKES RD

TILKEY RD

Vineyard

Pond Piece

AMBRIDGE RD

BUXTON RD

WINDHILL FIELDS

Captain's Wood

VESTA CL

Bankfield

Robin's Bridge

ROBINSBRIDGE RD

KINGS RD

STONEHAM ST

23

Stane Street

Robin's Bridge

+

A120

ROMAN ROAD

Stockstreet

Sch

Liby RD

Whiteshill Farm

COGGESHALL RD

Stockstreet Farm

Highfields Farm

P +

MARKET END

1

WATERY LA

WEST ST

Paycocke's

CULVERT DRIVE

GRAVEL

Long Bridge

BRIDGE ST

Grigg's Farm

Nursery

GREEN

MACKAYS RD

GRANGE HILL

River Blackwater

Grange Farm

BT024

The Slades

Horseshoe Hole

22

82

A

83

B

84

C

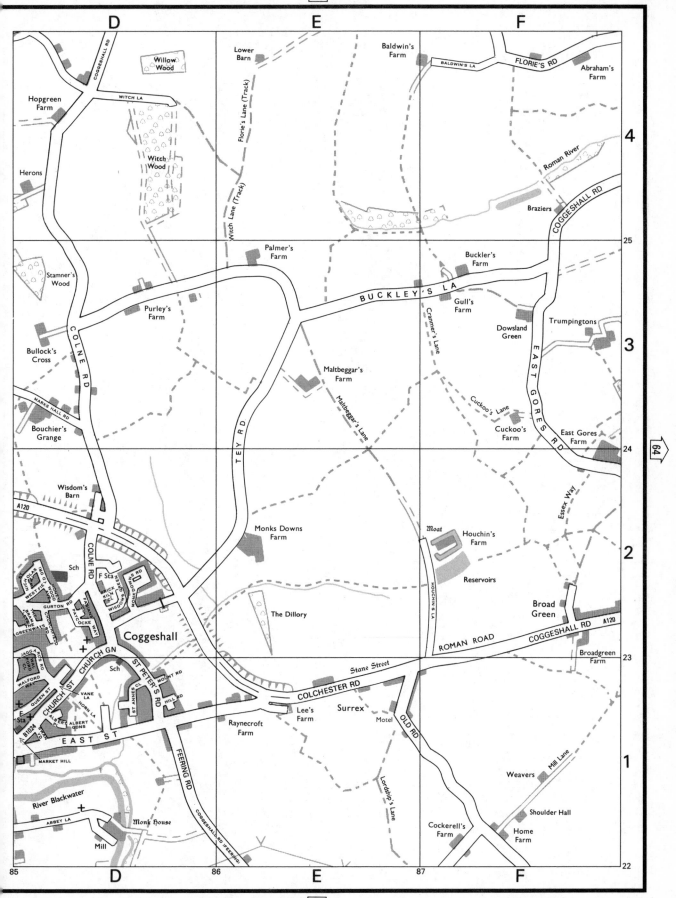

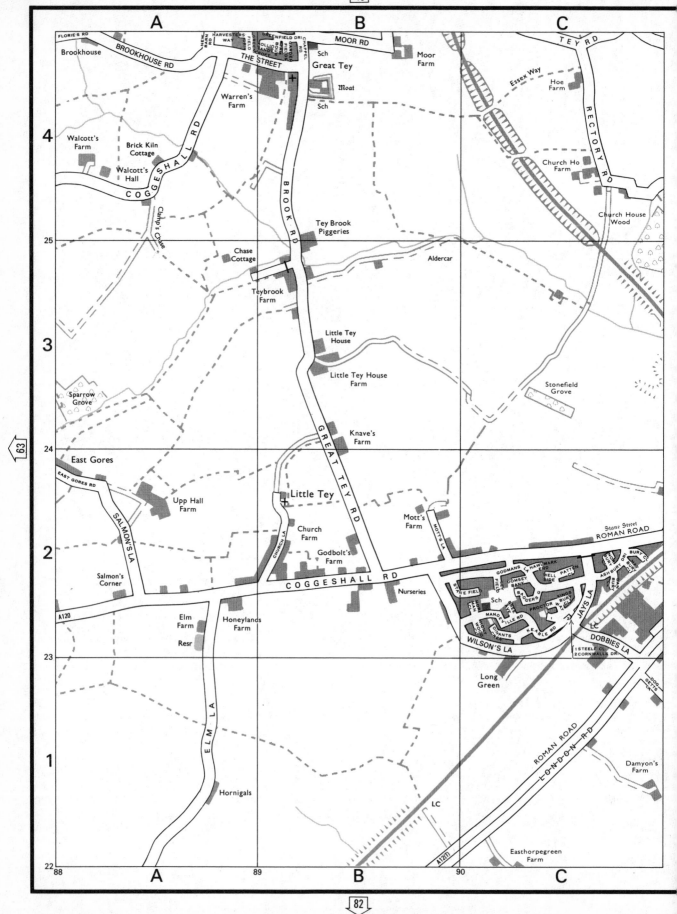

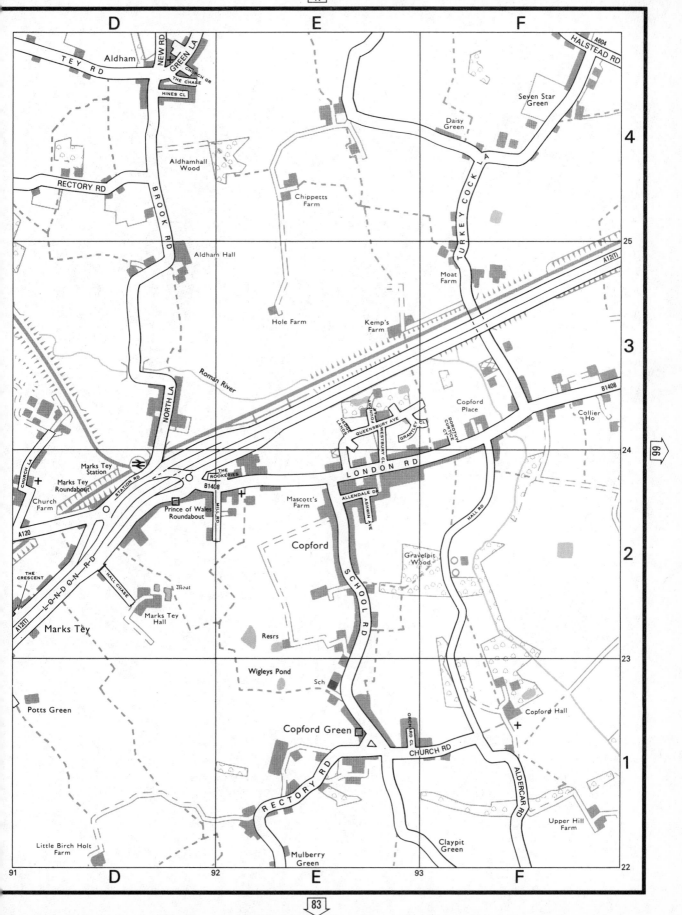

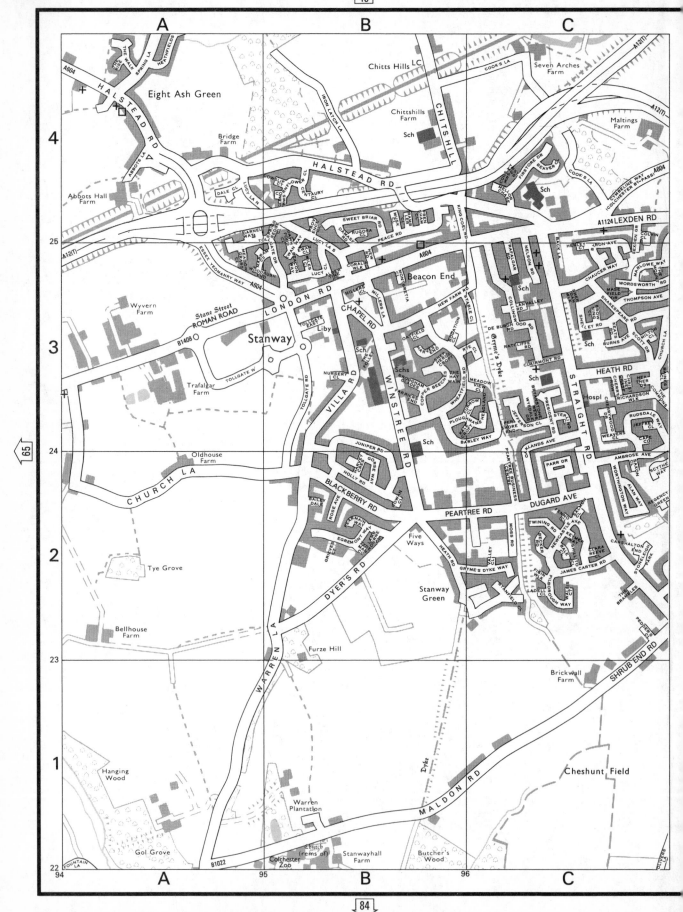

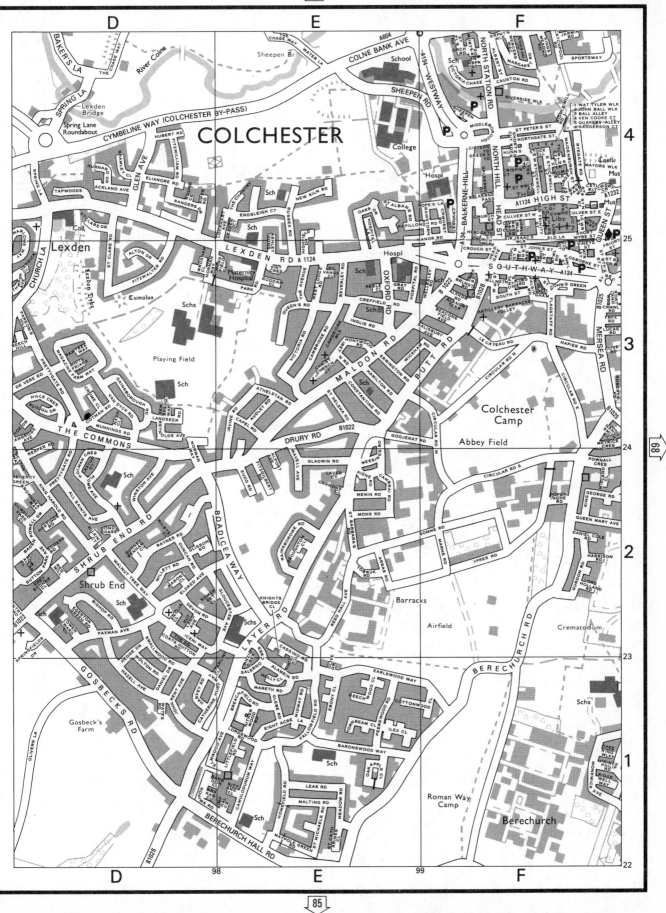

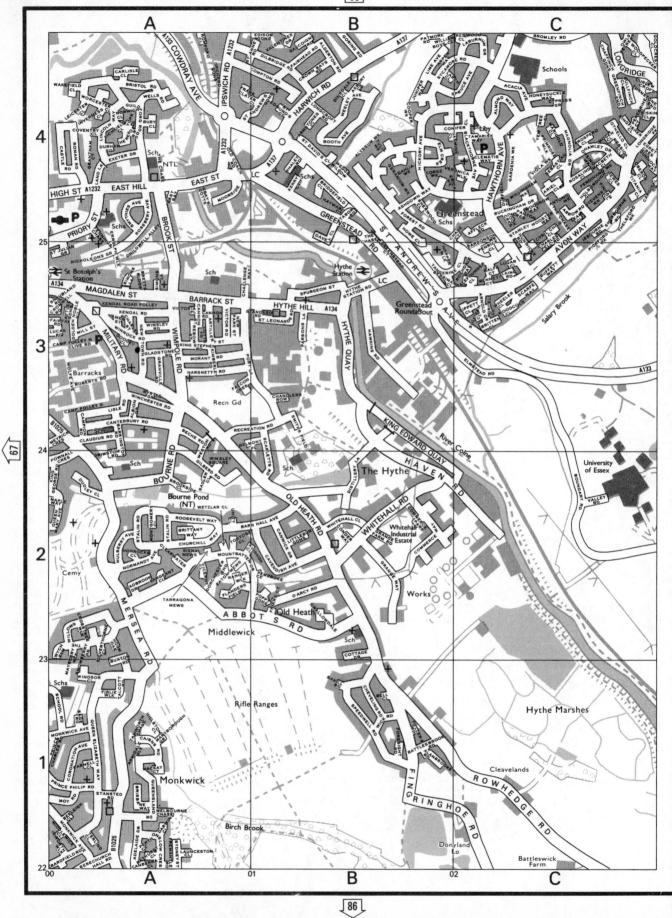

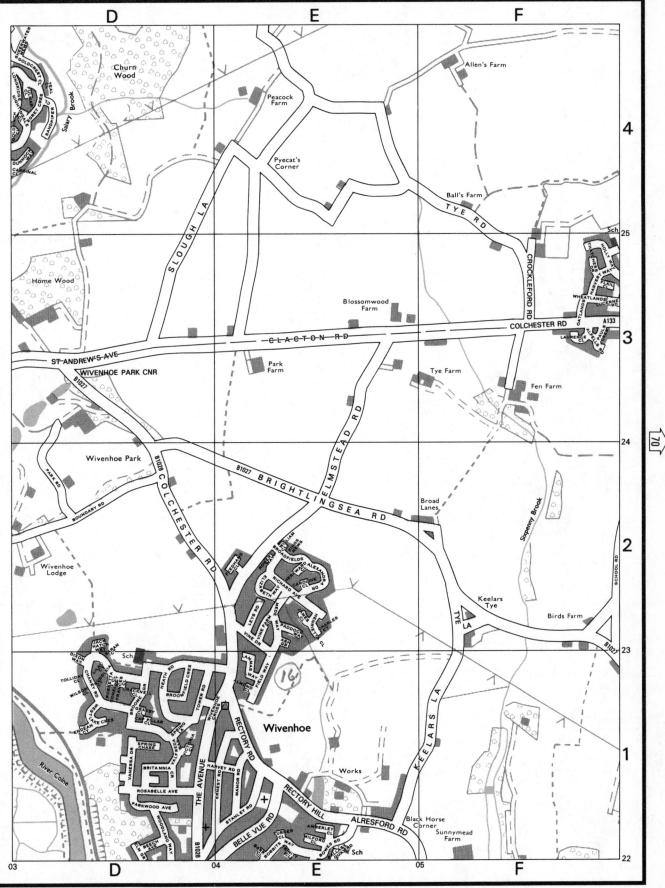

51

D   E   F

Churn Wood

Peacock Farm

Allen's Farm

Pyecat's Corner

Ball's Farm

TYE RD

4

25

Sch

Salary Brook

Home Wood

Blossomwood Farm

CROCKLEFORD RD

THATCHERS DR
HOLLY WAY
HARVEST WAY
FLAIL CL
WHEATLANDS
OATLANDS
LUCERNE RD

COLCHESTER RD

A133

LAURENCE CL
ALFELS
PAULS RD

3

CLACTON RD

ST ANDREW'S AVE

WIVENHOE PARK CNR

Park Farm

Tye Farm

Fen Farm

B1027

Wivenhoe Park

B1028 COLCHESTER RD

B1027 BRIGHTLINGSEA RD

ELMSTEAD RD

Broad Lanes

Sixpenny Brook

SCHOOL RD

24

70

PARK RD

BOUNDARY RD

Wivenhoe Lodge

Keelars Tye

Birds Farm

2

BLACK HATCH WAY
DITON WAY
TOLLIDAY CL
CHANEY RD
WILSON
ROBLETTS
BROOMFIELD CRES
BRACKNELL CL
HEATH RD
TOWER RD
BROOMFIELD CRES

FELDHAM
ROWAN
BROADFIELDS
WILLIAM
ALEXANDRA RD
RICHARD
CAROLINE AVE
LETTS RD
VINE DR
PADDOCK
CHARLES
VINE FARM WAY
MEDE WAY
CHARLES CL
ABBEY

Sch

TYE LA

B1027

23

RECTORY RD

Wivenhoe

16

SPRING CHASE
VANESSA DR
BRITANNIA
ROSABELLE AVE
PARKWOOD AVE
THE AVENUE
STANLEY RD
HARVEY RD
ERNEST RD
MANOR RD

Works

1

River Colne

BEECH AVE
WOODLAND WAY

BELLE VUE RD

B1028

RECTORY HILL

TURNER
WILFORD CL
AMBERLEY CL
BOWES RD
BOBBITTS WAY
QUARRY RD

ALRESFORD RD

Black Horse Corner

Sunnymead Farm

Sch

22

03   D   04   E   05   F

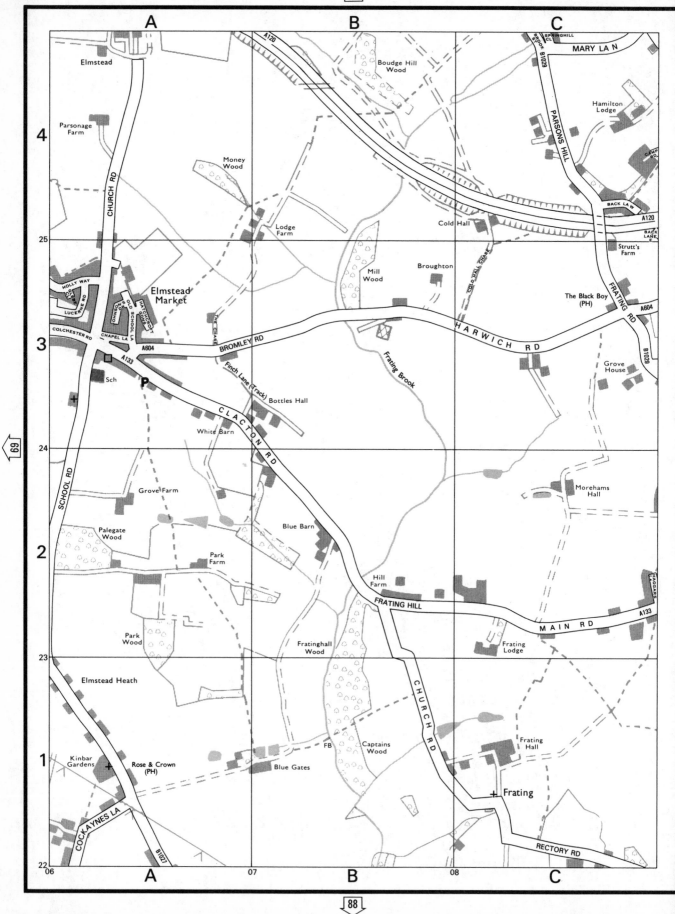

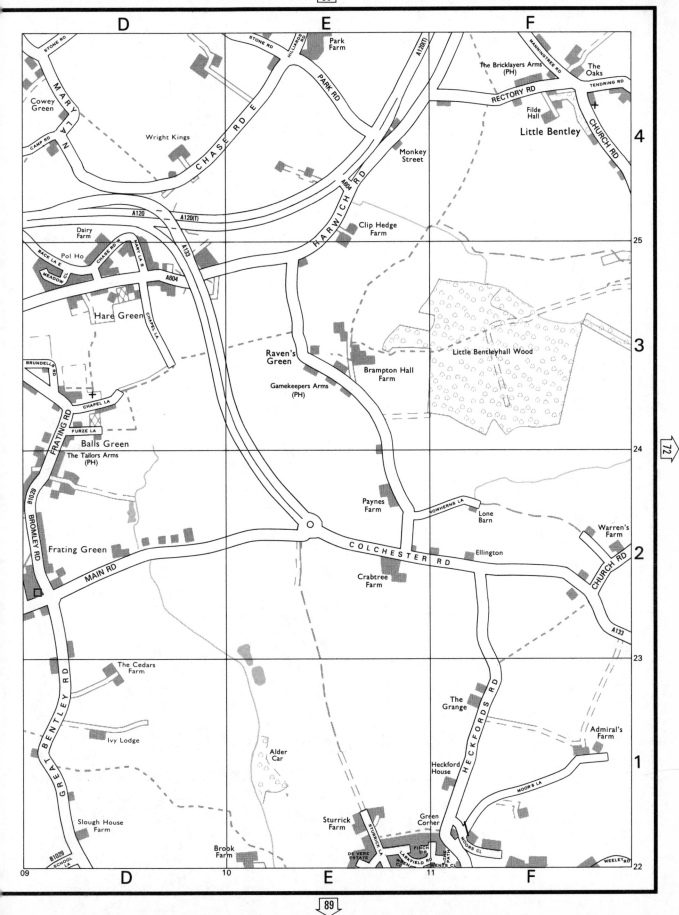

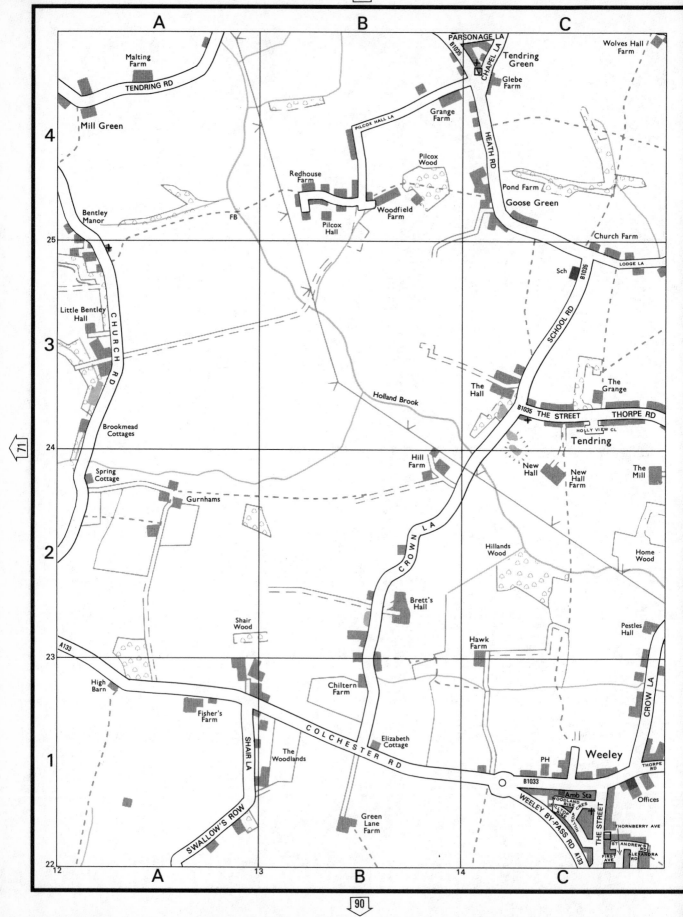

71

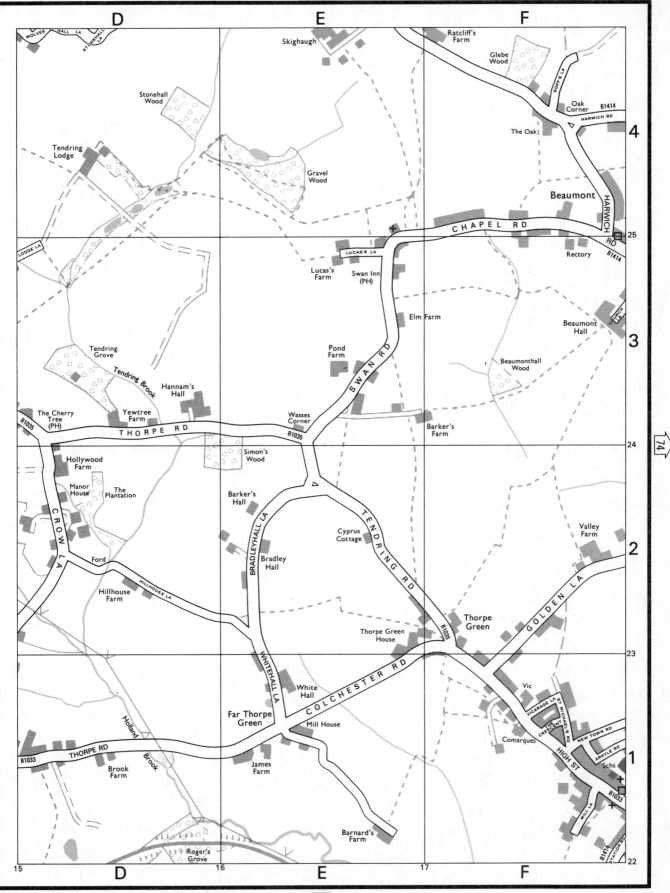

D   E   F

WOLVES HALL LA
STONEHALL LA

Skighaugh

Ratcliff's Farm

Glebe Wood

Stonehall Wood

GOFFS LA

Oak Corner

B1414

HARWICH RD

The Oak

4

Tendring Lodge

Gravel Wood

Beaumont

HARWICH RD

LODGE LA

CHAPEL RD

25

Lucas's LA

Rectory

B1414

Lucas's Farm

Swan Inn (PH)

Elm Farm

Beaumont Hall

CLIFF LA

3

Tendring Grove

Tendring Brook

Hannam's Hall

SWAN RD

Pond Farm

Beaumonthall Wood

The Cherry Tree (PH)

Yewtree Farm

Wasses Corner

B1035

Barker's Farm

B1035

THORPE RD

24

74

Hollywood Farm

Simon's Wood

Manor House

The Plantation

Barker's Hall

BRADLEYHALL LA

TENDRING RD

Cyprus Cottage

Valley Farm

CROW LA

Ford

Bradley Hall

GOLDEN LA

2

HILLHOUSE LA

Hillhouse Farm

Thorpe Green

B1035

Thorpe Green House

23

WHITEHALL LA

COLCHESTER RD

White Hall

Vic

VICARAGE LA

ST MICHAELS RD

NEW TOWN RD

Far Thorpe Green

Mill House

THE CRESCENT

Comarques

ARGYLE RD

Holland

B1033

THORPE RD

Brook

James Farm

HIGH ST

Schs

1

Brook Farm

MILL LA

B1033

Roger's Grove

Barnard's Farm

B1414

STATION RD

22

15   D   16   E   17   F

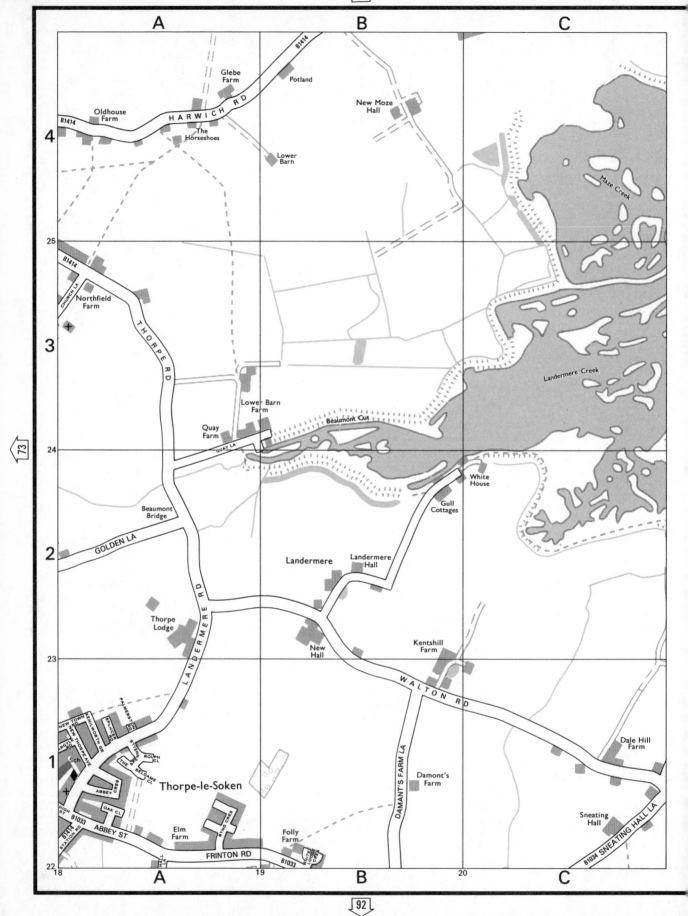

A   B   C

4

B1414

Glebe Farm

Potland

New Moze Hall

Oldhouse Farm

HARWICH RD

The Horseshoes

B1414

Lower Barn

Maze Creek

25

B1414

Northfield Farm

CHURCH LA

THORPE RD

3

Landermere Creek

Lower Barn Farm

Beaumont Cut

Quay Farm

QUAY LA

24

73

White House

Beaumont Bridge

Gull Cottages

GOLDEN LA

2

Landermere

Landermere Hall

LANDERMERE RD

Thorpe Lodge

Kentshill Farm

New Hall

23

WALTON RD

PALMERSTON RD

NEW TOWN RD

KENILWORTH DR

NEW THORPE AVE

ST DENNIS RD

ROLPH CL

THE BELDAMS CL

Dale Hill Farm

1

Sch

Thorpe-le-Soken

DAMANT'S FARM LA

Damont's Farm

ABBEY CRES

BING CRES

OAK CL

Sneating Hall

HIGH ST

B1033

STATION RD

ABBEY ST

Elm Farm

Folly Farm

B1034 SNEATING HALL LA

22

HALL LA

FRINTON RD

B1033

WHITE LODGES CL

18   A   19   B   20   C

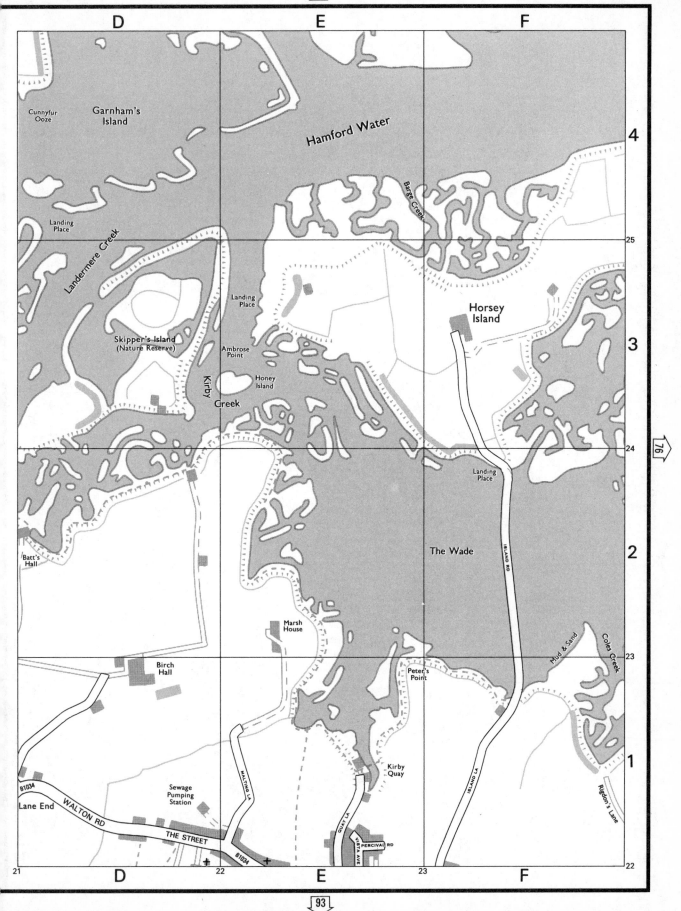

D　　　　　　　　E　　　　　　　　F

Cunnyfur
Ooze

Garnham's
Island

Hamford Water

Barge Creek

4

Landing
Place

Landermere Creek

25

Landing
Place

Horsey
Island

Skipper's Island
(Nature Reserve)

Ambrose
Point

3

Honey
Island

Kirby

Creek

ISLAND RD

24

Landing
Place

Batt's
Hall

The Wade

2

Marsh
House

Mud & Sand

Coles Creek

23

Birch
Hall

Peter's
Point

MALTING LA

Kirby
Quay

ISLAND LA

1

B1034

Sewage
Pumping
Station

QUAY LA

Rigdon's Lane

Lane End

WALTON RD

THE STREET

B1034

VISTA AVE

PERCIVAL RD

22

21　　　　　　D　　　　22　　　　E　　　　23　　　　F

76

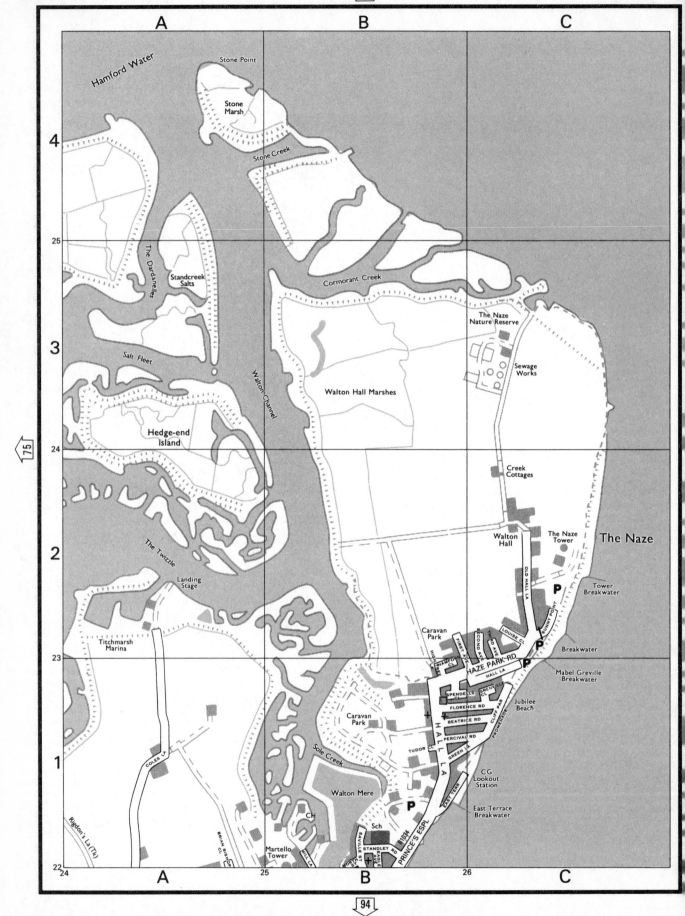

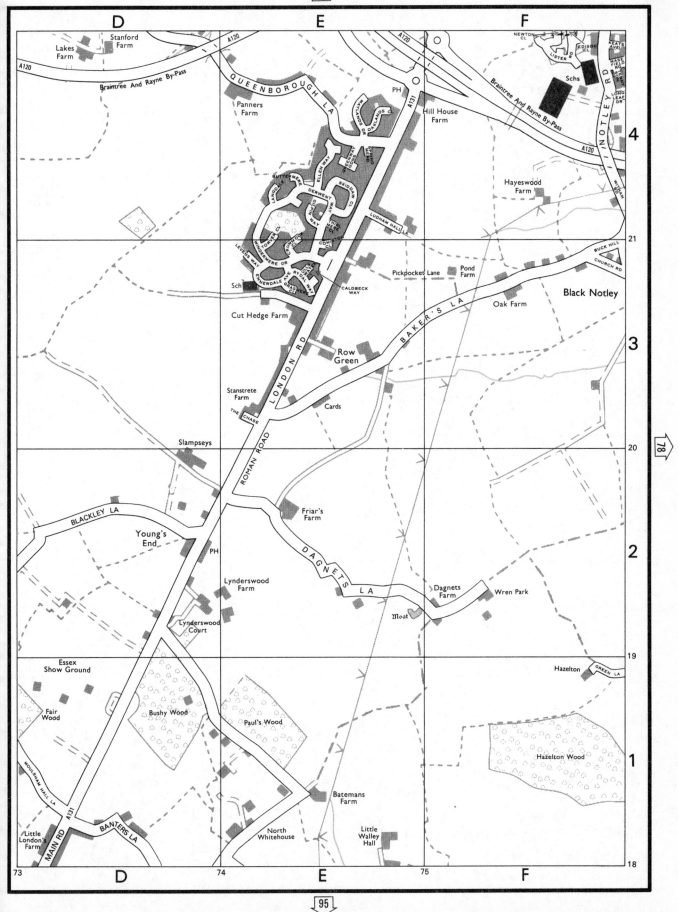

D   **E**   **F**

Stanford Farm

Lakes Farm

A120

Braintree And Rayne By-Pass

QUEENBOROUGH LA

A120

Panners Farm

PH

HAYLANDS DR

OAKLANDS CL

A131

Hill House Farm

Braintree And Rayne By-Pass

NEWTON CL

LISTER RD

EDISON CL

KEAT'S AVE

MASEFIELD RD

LONG LEAF DR

NOTLEY RD

Schs

Schs

A120

4

GREENWAY

CONWAY

ELLEN WAY

SKIDDAW CL

STRING MEAD

BUTTERMERE

DERWENT

WAY

LANGDALE

RYDAL

THIRL MERE CL

LUDHAM HALL LA

Hayeswood Farm

WITHAM RD

WINDERMERE DR

CRUMMOCK

GRANGE WAY

LEVELS WAY

ENNERDALE AVE

RYDAL WAY

GRASMERE CL

CONISTON

CALDBECK WAY

21

Sch

Cut Hedge Farm

Pickpocket Lane

Pond Farm

Oak Farm

BUCK HILL

CHURCH RD

Black Notley

3

Row Green

BAKER'S LA

Stanstrete Farm

LONDON RD

THE CHASE

Cards

Slampseys

ROMAN ROAD

20

BLACKLEY LA

Young's End

PH

Friar's Farm

DAGNETS

LA

Dagnets Farm

Wren Park

2

Lynderswood Farm

Lynderswood Court

Moat

19

Essex Show Ground

Hazelton

GREEN LA

Fair Wood

Bushy Wood

Paul's Wood

Hazelton Wood

1

MOULSHAM HALL LA

A131

MAIN RD

BANTERS LA

Little London's Farm

Batemans Farm

North Whitehouse

Little Walley Hall

18

73   **D**   74   **E**   75   **F**

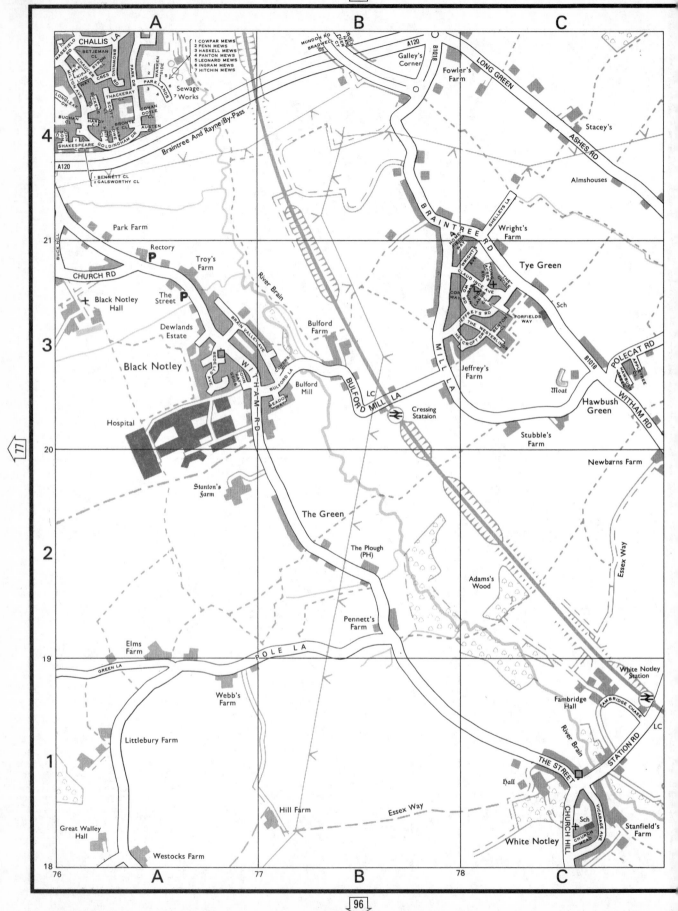

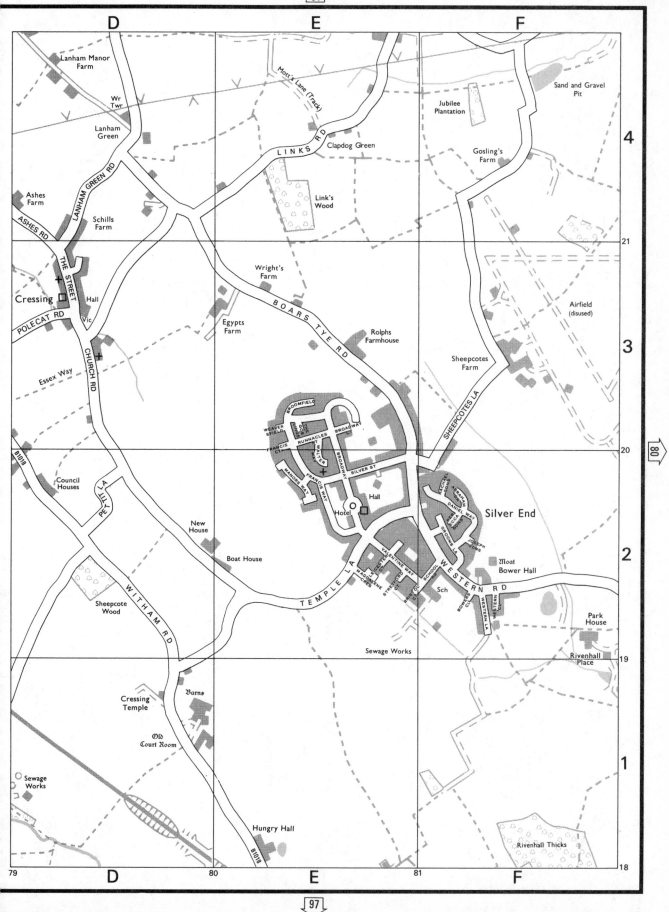

D E F

4

Lanham Manor Farm
Mott's Lane (Track)
Sand and Gravel Pit
Wr Twr
Jubilee Plantation
Lanham Green
LINKS RD
Clapdog Green
Gosling's Farm
Ashes Farm
Link's Wood
Schills Farm
LANHAM GREEN RD
ASHES RD

21

THE STREET
Wright's Farm
Airfield (disused)
Cressing
Hall
BOARS TYE RD
Vic
POLECAT RD
Egypts Farm
Rolphs Farmhouse
Sheepcotes Farm

3

CHURCH RD
Essex Way
SHEEPCOTES LA

BROOMFIELD
WEAVER SFIELD
BROADWAY
FRANCIS CT
RUNNACLES
ST WALTER
Council Houses
B1018
BROADWAY
Silver End
PETT LA
SILVER ST
MANORS WAY
FRANCIS WAY
Hall
BACH FACONS
ABRAHAM
DANIEL WAY
GROOMS LA
JOSEPH

20

New House
Hotel
Moat Bower Hall
WITHAM RD
Boat House
TEMPLE LA
VALENTINE WAY
SCHOOL
Sch
WESTERN RD
Park House

2

Sheepcote Wood
MAGDALENE CRES
STREPFORD
BOWERS CL
WESTERN LA
NELTER
Rivenhall Place

Sewage Works

19

Cressing Temple
Barns
Old Court Room

1

Sewage Works
Hungry Hall
B1018
Rivenhall Thicks

18

79 D 80 E 81 F

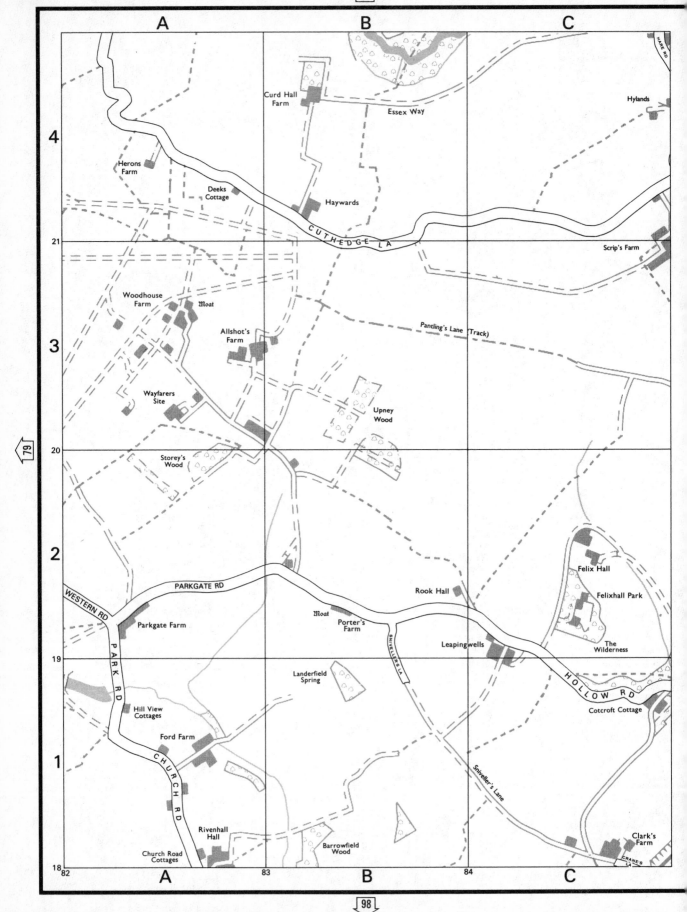

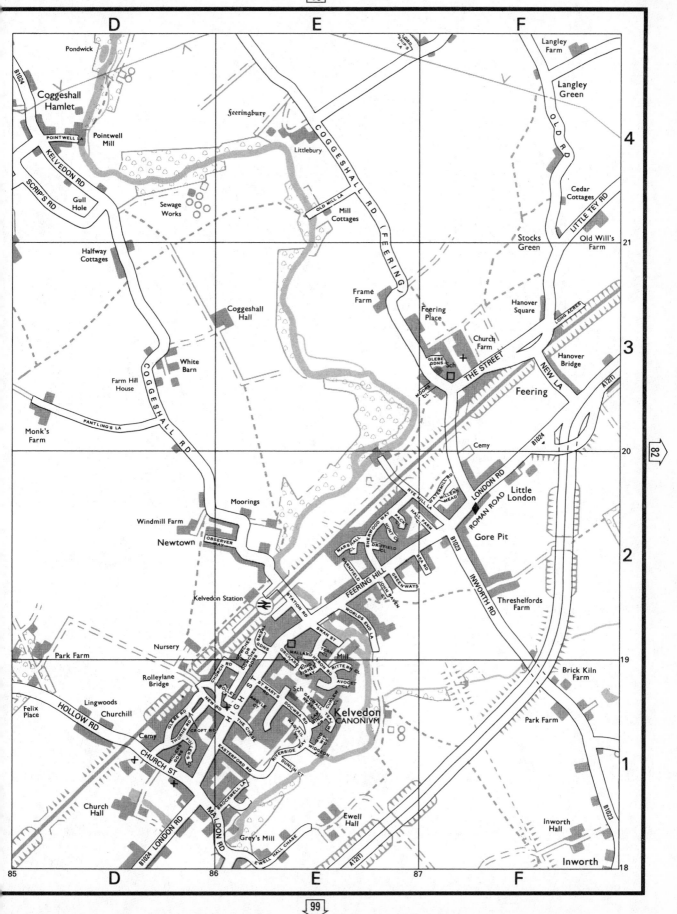

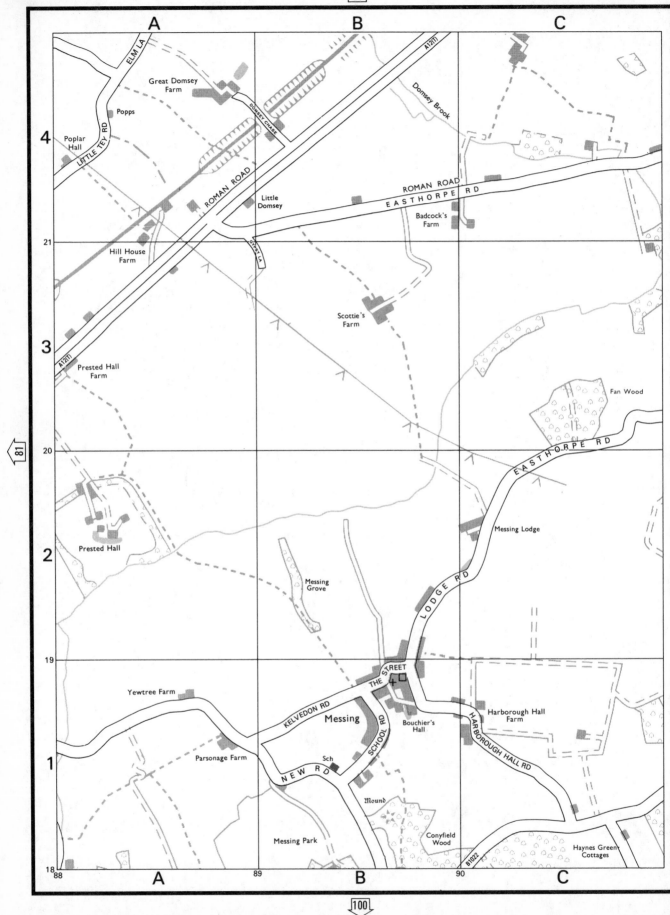

81

A　　　　　　　　　B　　　　　　　　　C

ELM LA

Great Domsey
Farm

Popps

LITTLE TEY RD

Poplar
Hall

DOMSEY CHASE

A12(T)

Domsey Brook

ROMAN ROAD

Little
Domsey

ROMAN ROAD

EASTHORPE RD

Badcock's
Farm

Hill House
Farm

GYPSY LA

A12(T)

Scottie's
Farm

Fan Wood

Prested Hall
Farm

EASTHORPE RD

Prested Hall

Messing Lodge

Messing
Grove

LODGE RD

THE STREET

Yewtree Farm

KELVEDON RD

Messing

SCHOOL RD

Bouchier's
Hall

Harborough Hall
Farm

HARBOROUGH HALL RD

Parsonage Farm

NEW RD

Sch

Mound

Messing Park

Conyfield
Wood

B1022

Haynes Green
Cottages

A　　　　　　　　　B　　　　　　　　　C

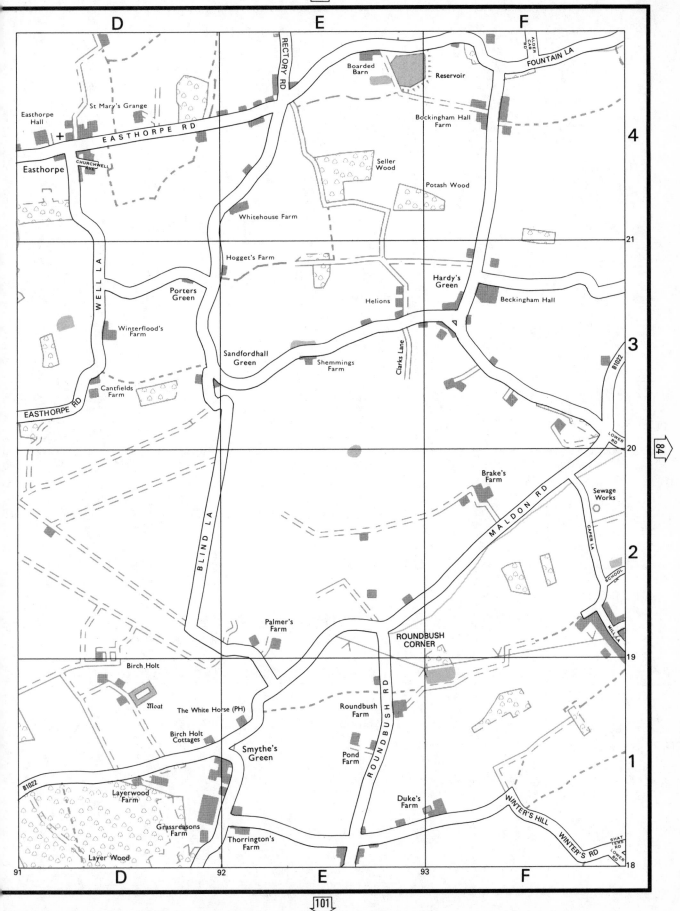

D   E   F

Boarded Barn

RECTORY RD

FOUNTAIN LA

ALDER CAR RD

Reservoir

St Mary's Grange

Easthorpe Hall

Bockingham Hall Farm

4

EASTHORPE RD

CHURCHWELL AVE

Easthorpe

Seller Wood

Potash Wood

Whitehouse Farm

21

WELL LA

Hogget's Farm

Porters Green

Hardy's Green

Beckingham Hall

Winterflood's Farm

Helions

Clarks Lane

3

B1022

Sandfordhall Green

Shemmings Farm

EASTHORPE RD

Cantfields Farm

LOWER RD

20

84

Brake's Farm

Sewage Works

BLIND LA

MALDON RD

CAPER LA

2

SCHOOL CH

MILL LA

Palmer's Farm

ROUNDBUSH CORNER

19

Birch Holt

ROUNDBUSH RD

Moat

The White Horse (PH)

Roundbush Farm

Birch Holt Cottages

Smythe's Green

Pond Farm

1

B1022

Layerwood Farm

Duke's Farm

WINTER'S HILL

Grassreasons Farm

Thorrington's Farm

WINTER'S RD

SHATTERS RD

LOWER RD

Layer Wood

18

91   D   92   E   93   F

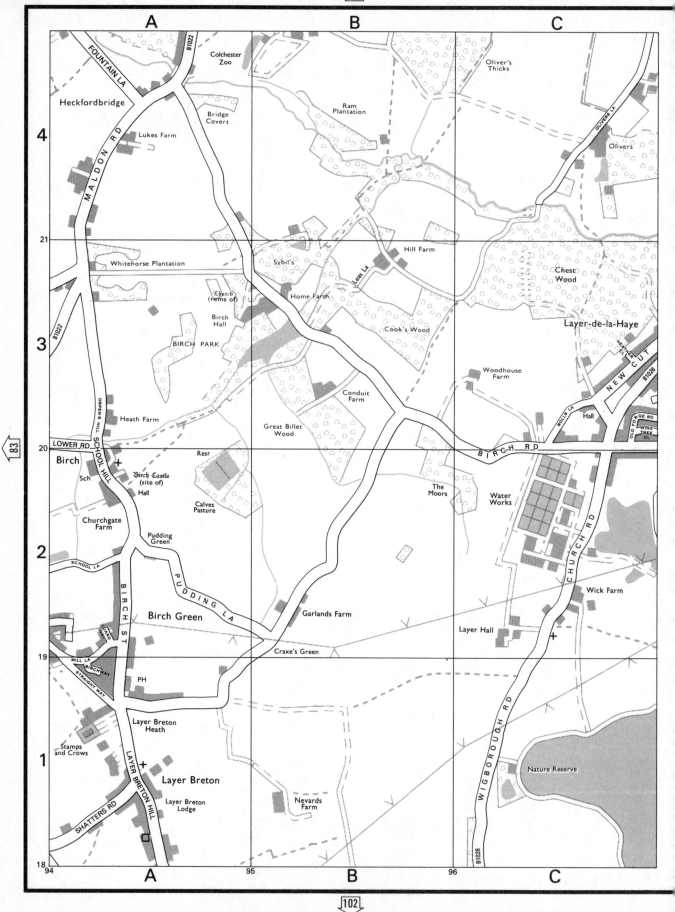

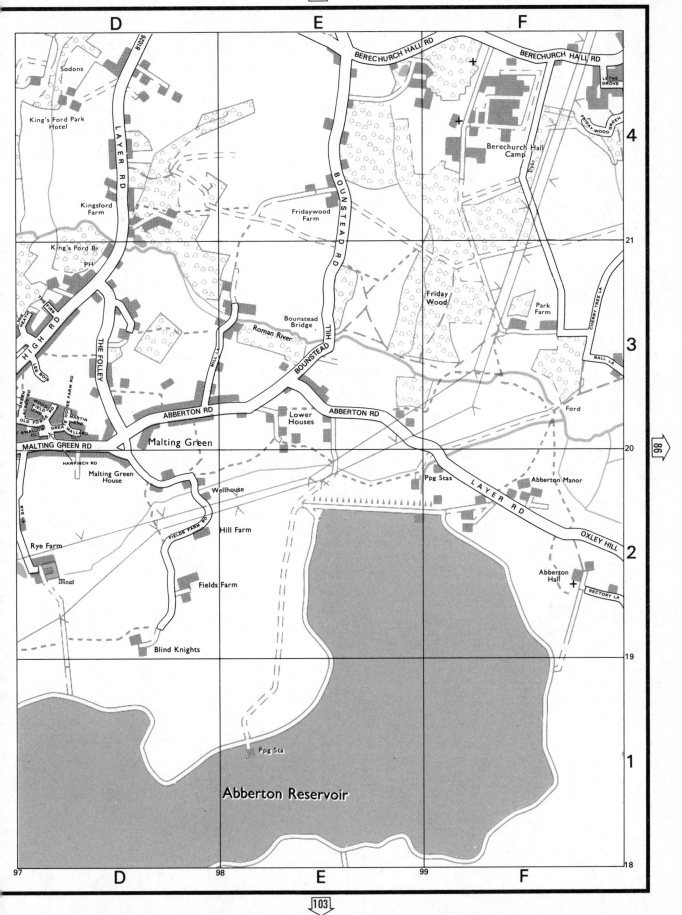

Abberton Reservoir

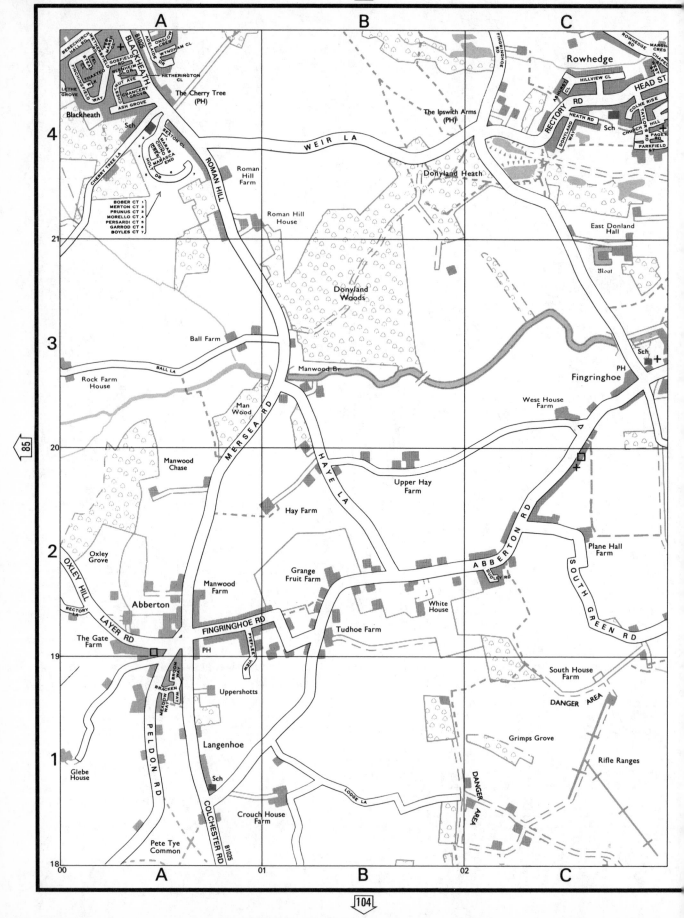

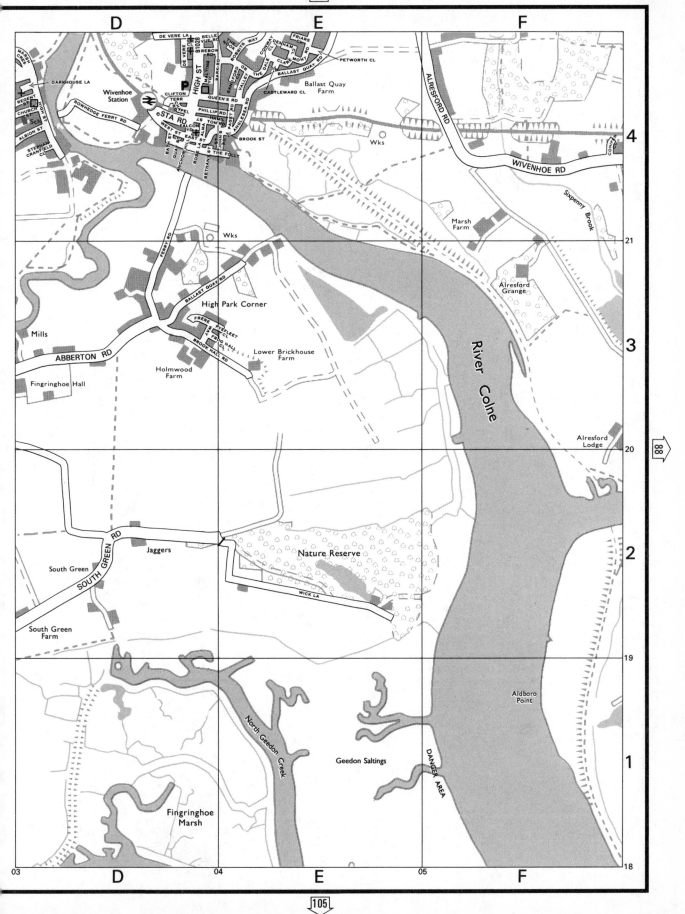

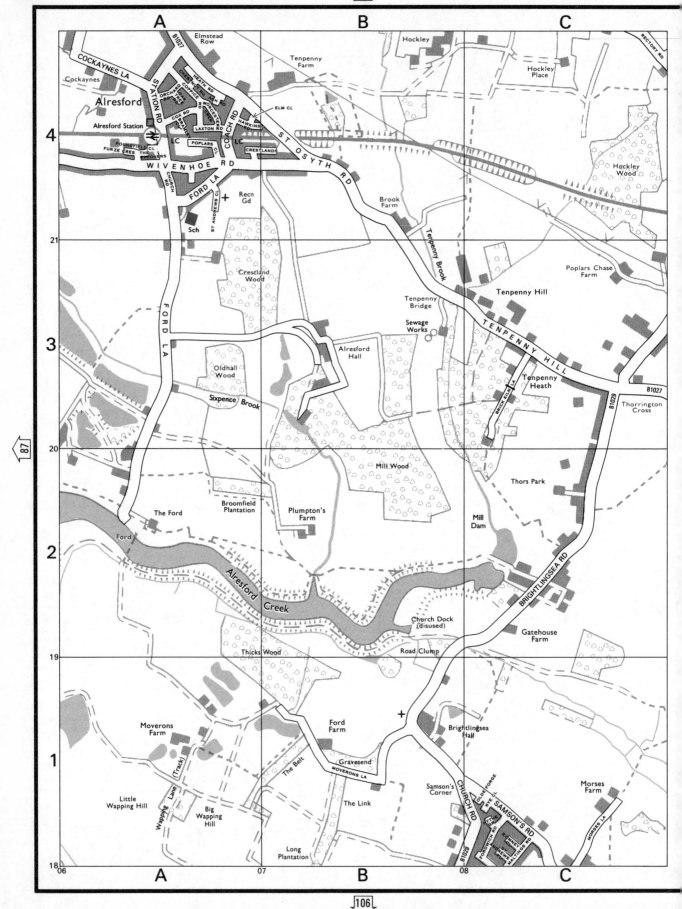

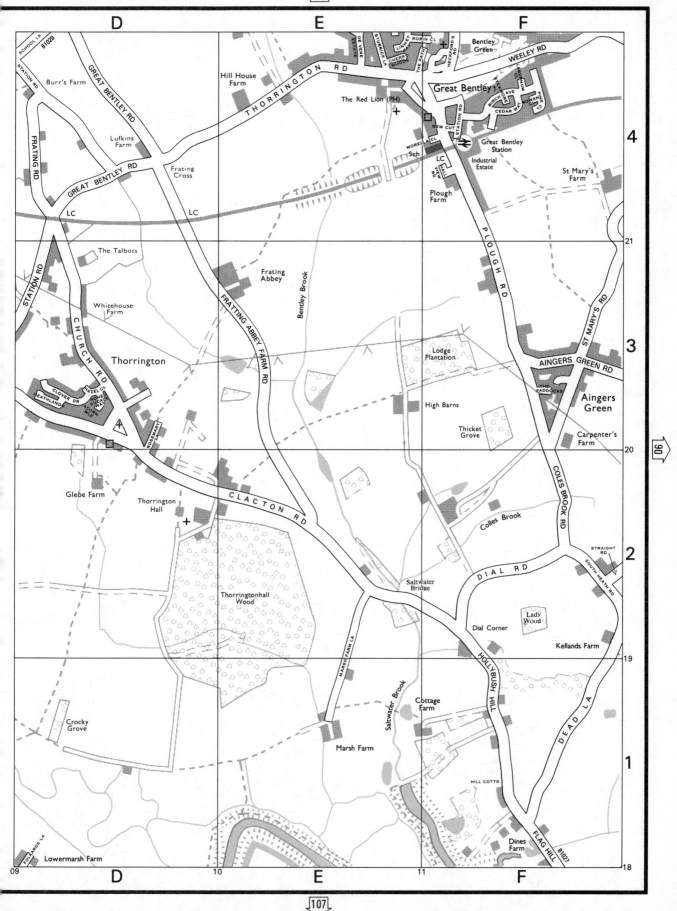

D   E   F

SCHOOL LA
B1029
STATION RD
Burr's Farm
GREAT BENTLEY RD
Hill House Farm
THORRINGTON RD
DE VERE ESTATE
STURRICK LA
LINNET
THE PATH
ROBIN CL
HECKFORD'S CL
CHERRY WOODS
Bentley Green
WEELEY RD

Great Bentley
BIRCH CAVE
LABURNUM CL
CEDAR WAY
ROMAN CL

FRATING RD
GREAT BENTLEY RD
Lufkins Farm
Frating Cross
The Red Lion (PH)
STATION RD
New Cut
MORELLA CL
Sch
LC
HALL VIEW RD
Great Bentley Station
Industrial Estate
St Mary's Farm

4

LC
LC
Plough Farm
PLOUGH RD

21

STATION RD
The Talbots
Frating Abbey
Bentley Brook
FRATTING ABBEY FARM RD
Lodge Plantation
ST MARY'S RD
AINGERS GREEN RD

3

Whitehouse Farm
CHURCH RD
Thorrington
High Barns
THE PADDOCKS
Aingers Green

HAZEL CL
CLOVER DR
HONEY SUCKLE WAY
HEATHLAND
ACORN WLK
Thicket Grove
Carpenter's Farm

20

ROSEMARY
Glebe Farm
Thorrington Hall
CLACTON RD
Colles Brook
COLES BROOK RD

STRAIGHT RD

2

Thorringtonhall Wood
Saltwater Bridge
DIAL RD
Lady Wood
SOUTH HEATH RD

MARSH FARM LA
Dial Corner
Kellands Farm

19

Crocky Grove
HOLLYBUSH HILL
DEAD LA

Saltwater Brook
Cottage Farm

Marsh Farm

1

FOXLARDS LA
Lowermarsh Farm
HILL COTTS
Dines Farm
FLAG HILL
B1027

18

09   D   10   E   11   F

90

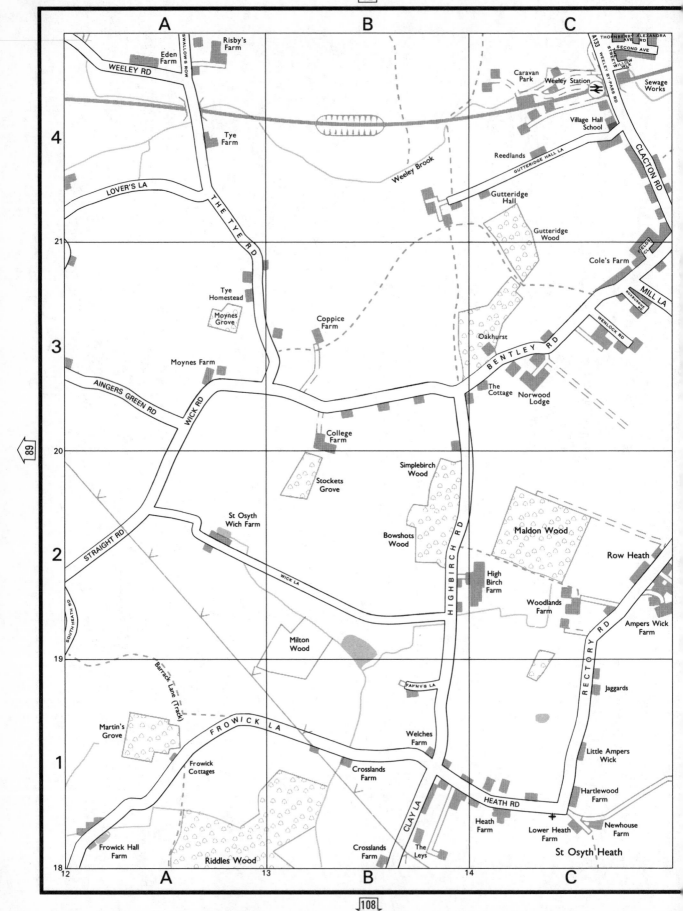

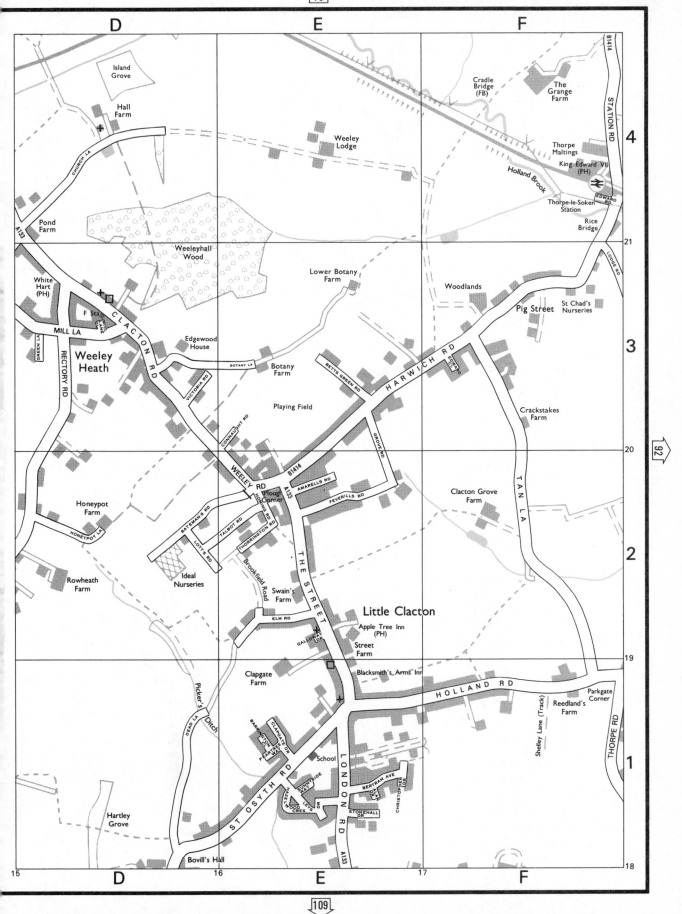

D   E   F

Island Grove

Hall Farm

Weeley Lodge

Cradle Bridge (FB)

The Grange Farm

STATION RD

B1414

Thorpe Maltings

King Edward VII (PH)

Holland Brook

Thorpe-le-Soken Station

Rice Bridge

CHURCH LA

Pond Farm

A133

White Hart (PH)

Weeleyhall Wood

Lower Botany Farm

Woodlands

LODGE RD

21

Pig Street

St Chad's Nurseries

MILL LA

F Sta

GREEN LA

CLACTON RD

Weeley Heath

Edgewood House

BOTANY LA

Botany Farm

BETTS GREEN RD

HARWICH RD

EDGE RD

Crackstakes Farm

3

RECTORY RD

VICTORIA RD

Playing Field

20

CONNAUGHT RD

GROVE RD

B1414

AMARELLS RD

FEVERILLS RD

Clacton Grove Farm

TAN LA

92

WEELEY RD

A133

Plough Corner

HUNT END RD

Honeypot Farm

BATEMAN'S RD

TALBOT RD

THORRINGTON RD

LOTT'S RD

Brookfield Road

THE STREET

2

HONEYPOT LA

Ideal Nurseries

Swain's Farm

Little Clacton

Rowheath Farm

ELM RD

GALLOWAY DR

Apple Tree Inn (PH)

Street Farm

19

Clapgate Farm

Blacksmith's Arms Inn

HOLLAND RD

Parkgate Corner

Picker's Ditch

DEAD LA

BARRINGTON RD

CLAPGATE DR

PART TREE WAY

School

ST OSYTH RD

LONDON RD

SUNNYSIDE

HAZELWOOD CRES

LETS DR

BERTRAM AVE

STONEHALL DR

CHRISTOPHER DR

Shelley Lane (Track)

Reedland's Farm

THORPE RD

1

Hartley Grove

Bovill's Hall

A133

18

15   D   16   E   17   F

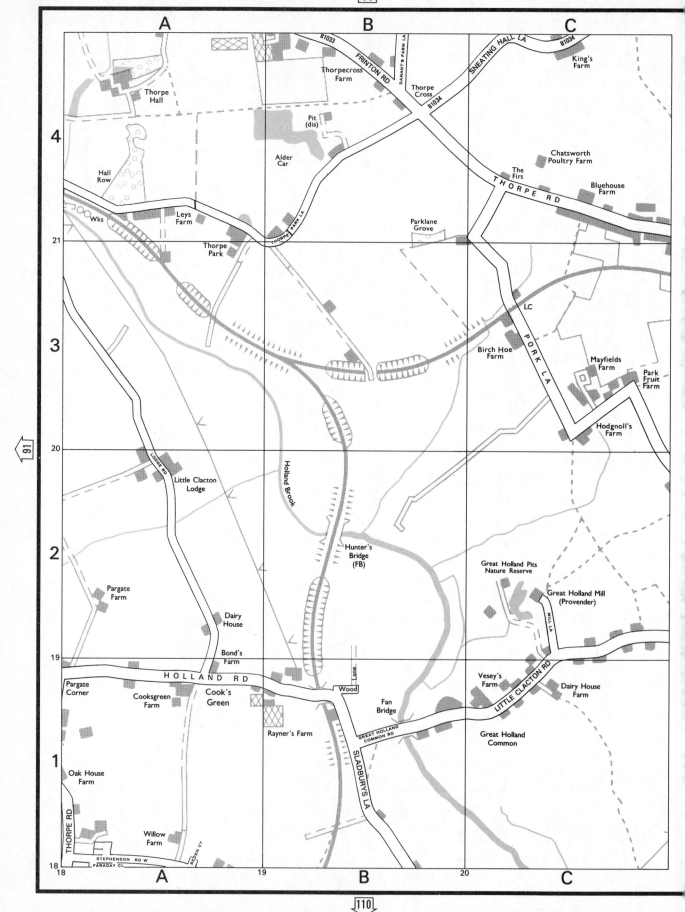

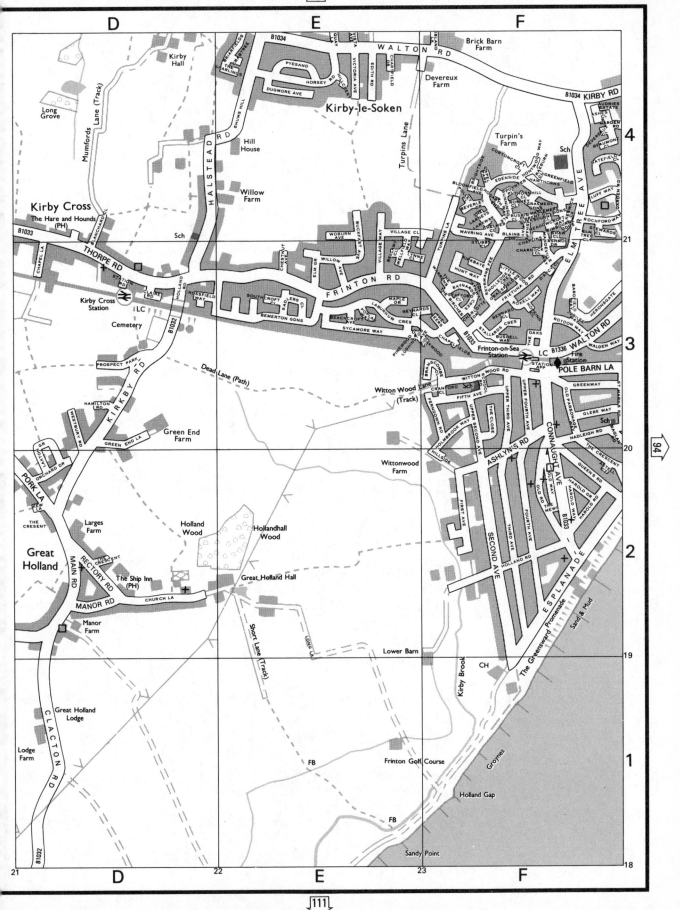

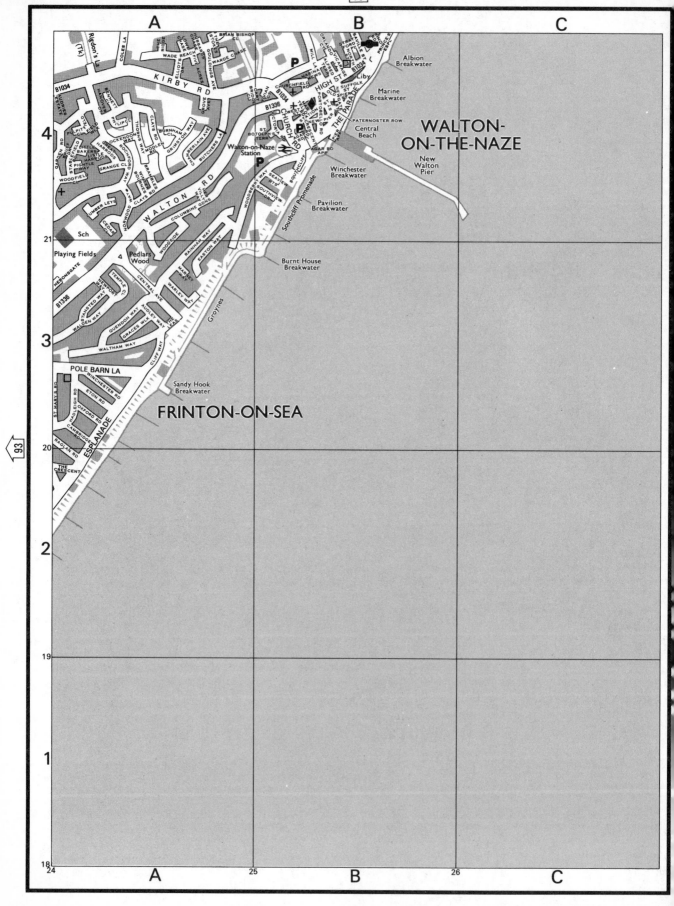

93

WALTON-
ON-THE-NAZE

Albion
Breakwater

Marine
Breakwater

PATERNOSTER ROW

Central
Beach

New
Walton
Pier

Winchester
Breakwater

Pavilion
Breakwater

Southcliff Promenade

Burnt House
Breakwater

Walton-on-Naze
Station

KIRBY RD

B1034

HIGH ST

CHURCH RD

B1336

WALTON RD

Playing Fields

Pedlars
Wood

HERONSGATE

B1336

Groynes

Sandy Hook
Breakwater

FRINTON-ON-SEA

POLE BARN LA

ESPLANADE

THE CRESCENT

A   B   C

4

21

3

20

2

19

1

18

24   25   26

A   B   C

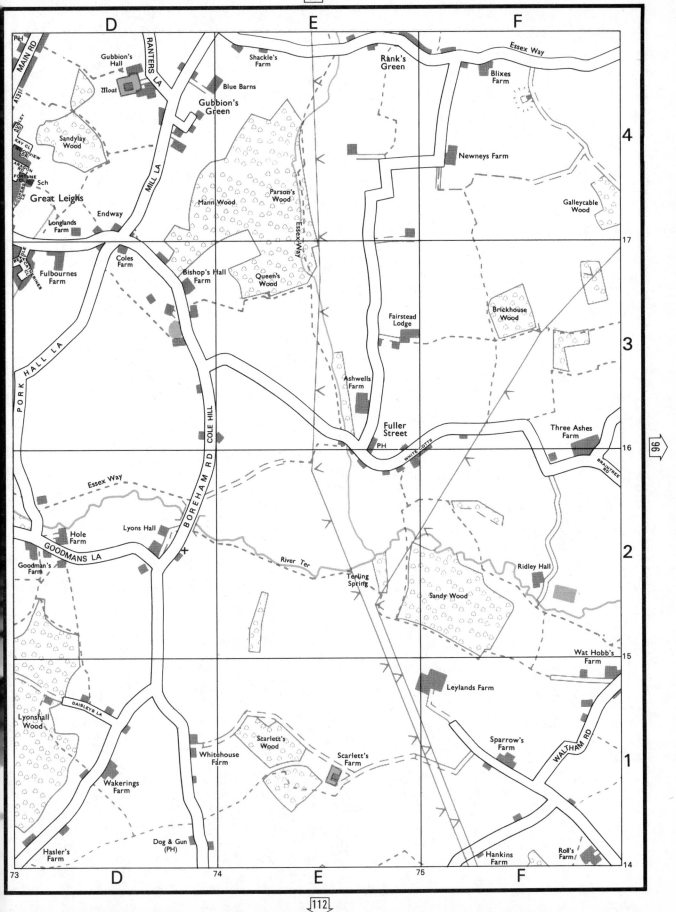

D E F

PH
MAIN RD
RANTERS LA
Gubbion's Hall
Moat
Blue Barns
Gubbion's Green
Shackle's Farm
Rank's Green
Essex Way
Blixes Farm

4

A1317
MILL LA
Sandylay Wood
Mann Wood
Parson's Wood
Newneys Farm
Galleycable Wood

Great Leighs
Sch
Endway
Longlands Farm
Coles Farm
Bishop's Hall Farm
Queen's Wood
Essex Way

17

BEADLE CHINNIES
Fulbournes Farm
Fairstead Lodge
Brickhouse Wood

3

PORK HALL LA
COLE HILL
BOREHAM RD
Ashwells Farm
Fuller Street
PH
WHITE COTTS
Three Ashes Farm
BRAINTREE RD

16

96

Essex Way
Hole Farm
Lyons Hall
GOODMANS LA
Goodman's Farm
River Ter
Terling Spring
Sandy Wood
Ridley Hall

2

Wat Hobb's Farm

15

DAISLEYS LA
Lyonshall Wood
Whitehouse Farm
Scarlett's Wood
Scarlett's Farm
Leylands Farm
Sparrow's Farm
WALTHAM RD

1

Wakerings Farm
Hasler's Farm
Dog & Gun (PH)
Hankins Farm
Roll's Farm

14

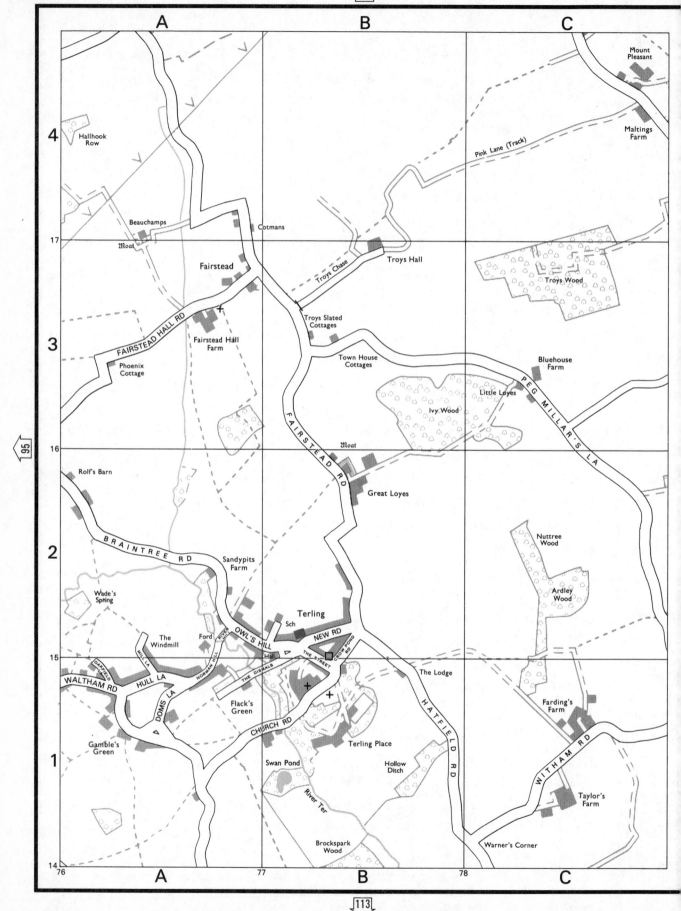

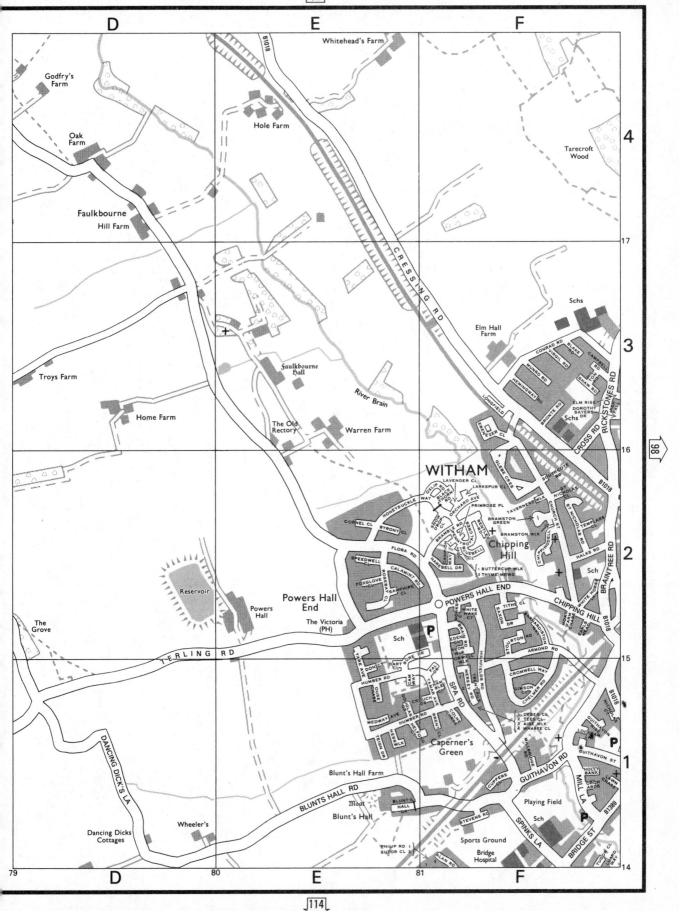

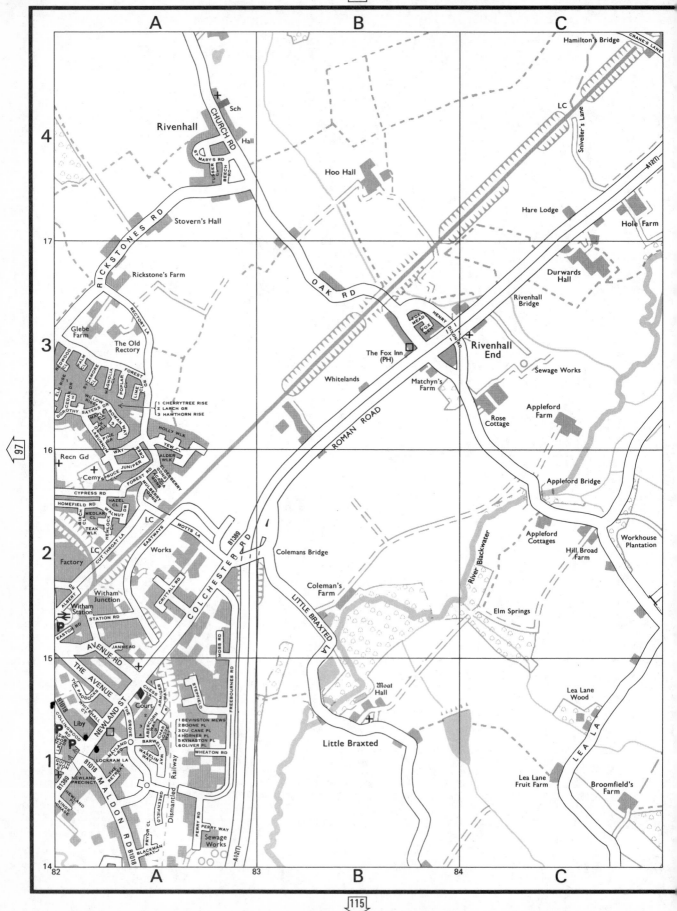

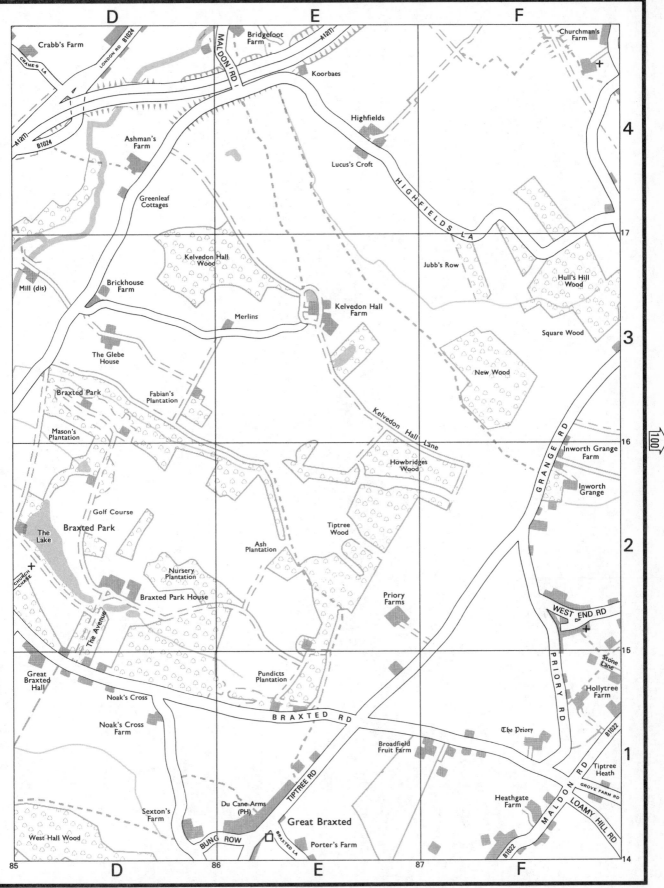

D   E   F

Crabb's Farm

CRANE'S LA

LONDON RD B1024

Bridgefoot Farm

MALDON RD

Koorbaes

A12(T)

Highfields

4

A12(T)

B1024

Ashman's Farm

Lucus's Croft

HIGHFIELDS LA

Churchman's Farm

Greenleaf Cottages

17

Mill (dis)

Kelvedon Hall Wood

Jubb's Row

Hull's Hill Wood

Brickhouse Farm

Merlins

Kelvedon Hall Farm

Square Wood

The Glebe House

New Wood

3

Braxted Park

Fabian's Plantation

Kelvedon Hall Lane

Mason's Plantation

Howbridges Wood

16

Inworth Grange Farm

GRANGE RD

100

Golf Course

Braxted Park

Tiptree Wood

Inworth Grange

The Lake

Ash Plantation

2

CHURCH CHASE

Nursery Plantation

Braxted Park House

Priory Farms

WEST END RD

The Avenue

Great Braxted Hall

15

Stone Lane

PRIORY RD

Hollytree Farm

Noak's Cross

Pundicts Plantation

BRAXTED RD

Noak's Cross Farm

The Priory

B1022

Broadfield Fruit Farm

1

MALDON RD

Tiptree Heath

TIPTREE RD

GROVE FARM RD

Sexton's Farm

Du Cane Arms (PH)

Heathgate Farm

LOAMY HILL RD

West Hall Wood

BUNG ROW

BRAXTED LA

Great Braxted

Porter's Farm

B1022

14

D   E   F

85   86   87

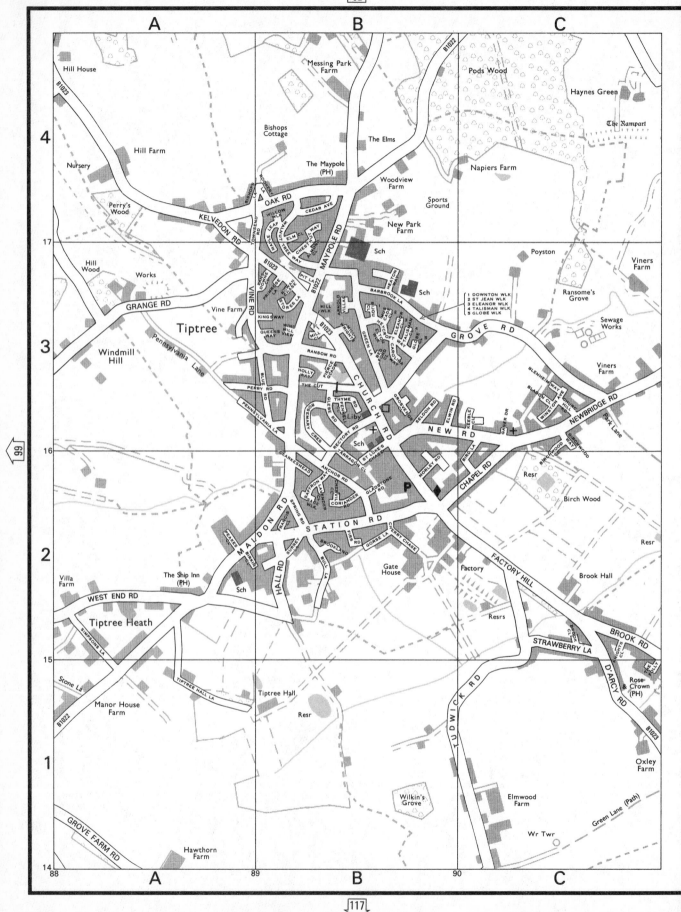

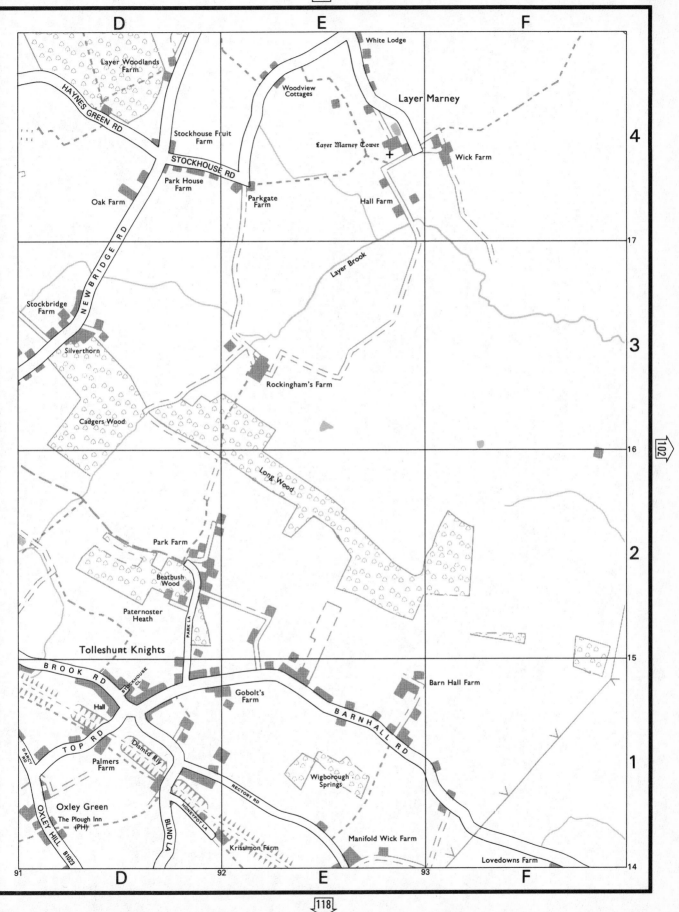

83

102

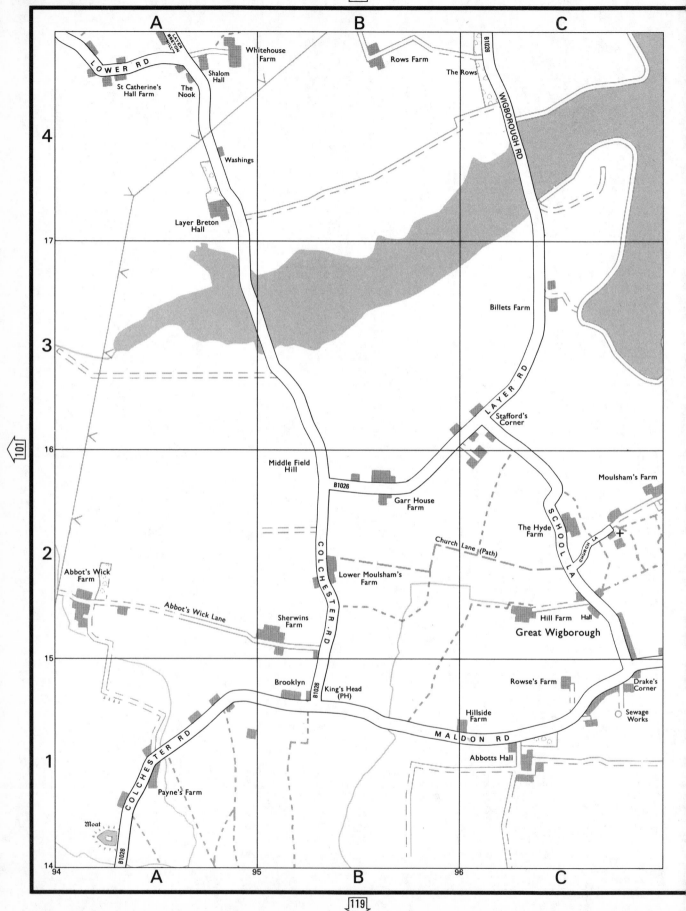

A · B · C

Lower Rd

Whitehouse Farm

Rows Farm

The Rows

St Catherine's Hall Farm

Shalom Hall

The Nook

LAYER BRETON HILL

WIGBOROUGH RD

B1026

Washings

Layer Breton Hall

Billets Farm

LAYER RD

Stafford's Corner

Middle Field Hill

B1026

Moulsham's Farm

Garr House Farm

Church Lane (Path)

The Hyde Farm

SCHOOL LA

CHURCH LA

Abbot's Wick Farm

COLCHESTER RD

Lower Moulsham's Farm

Abbot's Wick Lane

Sherwins Farm

Hill Farm

Hall

Great Wigborough

Brooklyn

King's Head (PH)

B1026

Rowse's Farm

Drake's Corner

MALDON RD

Hillside Farm

Sewage Works

COLCHESTER RD

Abbotts Hall

Payne's Farm

Moat

B1026

94 · 95 · 96

A · B · C

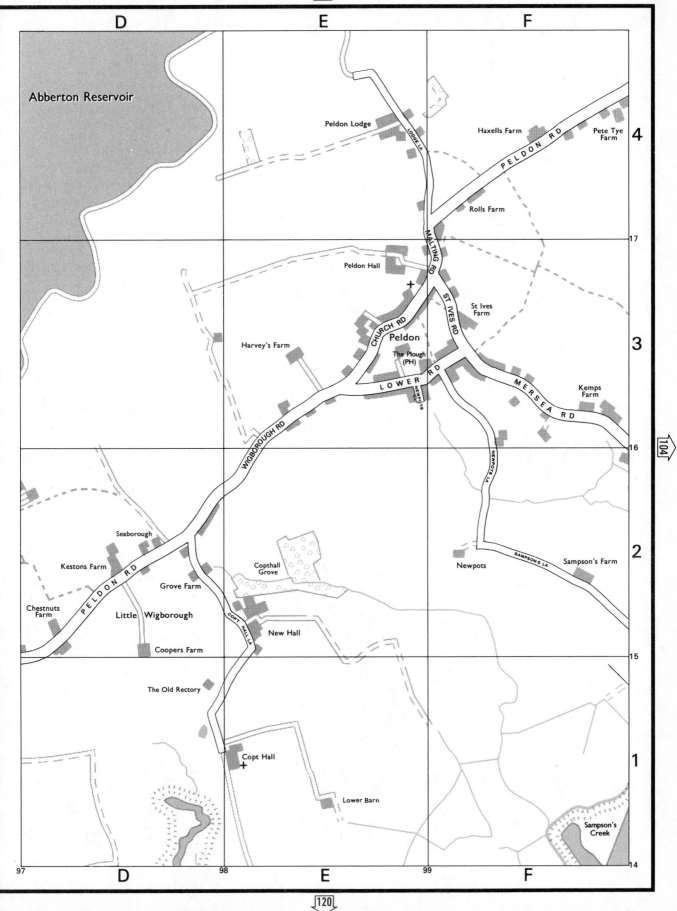

D E F

Abberton Reservoir

Peldon Lodge

LODGE LA

Haxells Farm

PELDON RD

Pete Tye Farm

4

Rolls Farm

MALTING RD

17

Peldon Hall

+

St Ives Farm

ST IVES RD

Harvey's Farm

CHURCH RD

Peldon

The Plough (PH)

LOWER RD

NEWPOTS CL

MERSEA RD

Kemps Farm

3

WIGBOROUGH RD

16

104

Seaborough

Kestons Farm

PELDON RD

Grove Farm

Copthall Grove

NEWPOTS LA

Newpots

SAMPSON'S LA

Sampson's Farm

2

Chestnuts Farm

Little Wigborough

Coopers Farm

COPT HALL LA

New Hall

15

The Old Rectory

Copt Hall

+

Lower Barn

Sampson's Creek

1

97 D 98 E 99 F 14

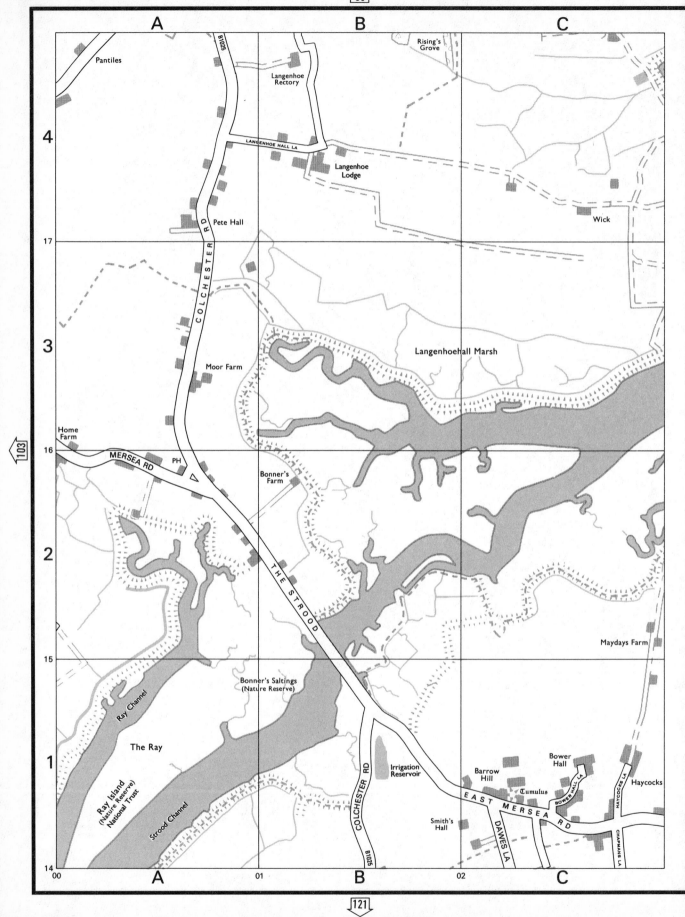

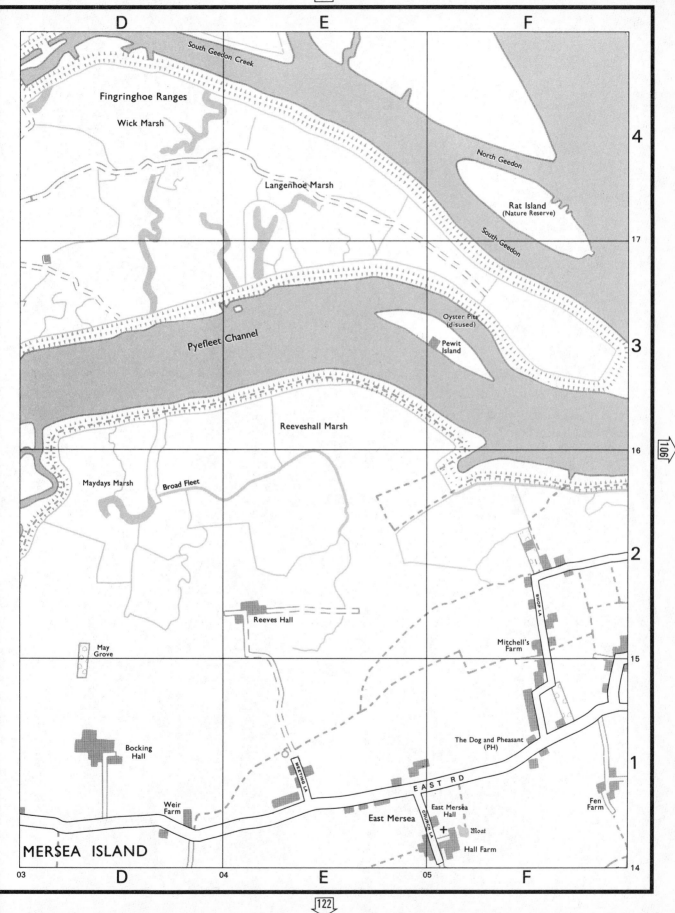

D E F

South Geedon Creek

Fingringhoe Ranges

Wick Marsh

North Geedon

4

Langenhoe Marsh

Rat Island
(Nature Reserve)

South Geedon

17

Oyster Pits
(disused)

Pewit
Island

Pyefleet Channel

3

Reeveshall Marsh

106

16

Maydays Marsh Broad Fleet

2

Reeves Hall

SHOP LA

Mitchell's
Farm

May
Grove

15

The Dog and Pheasant
(PH)

Bocking
Hall

MEETING LA

1

Fen
Farm

Weir
Farm

EAST RD

CHURCH LA

East Mersea Hall

East Mersea

Moat

+

Hall Farm

MERSEA ISLAND

03 D 04 E 05 F 14

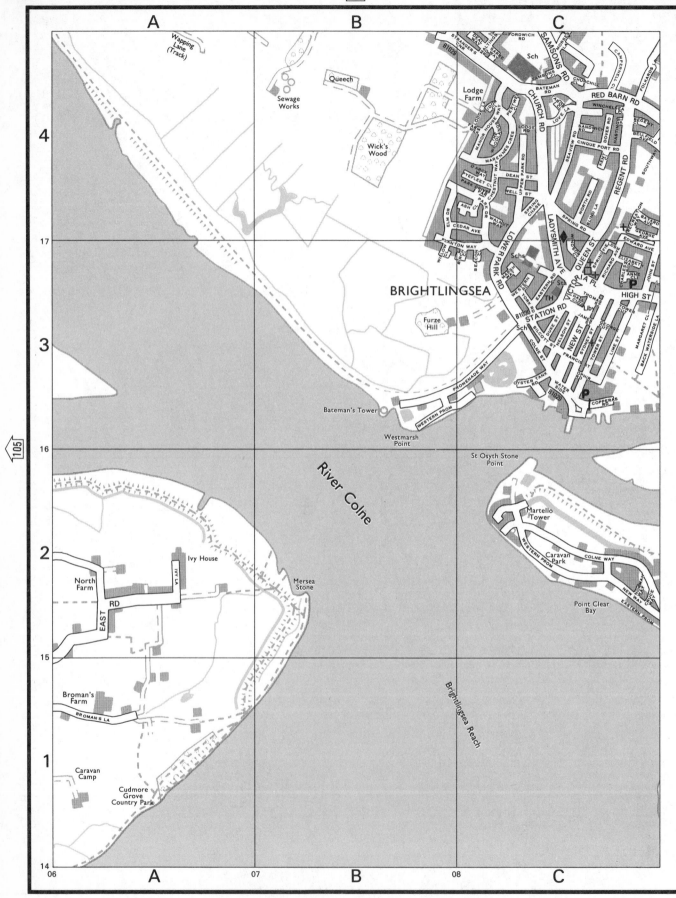

105

BRIGHTLINGSEA

River Colne

Brightlingsea Reach

Wapping Lane (Track)

Sewage Works

Queech

Wick's Wood

Lodge Farm

Furze Hill

Bateman's Tower

Westmarsh Point

St Osyth Stone Point

Martello Tower

Caravan Park

Western Prom

Point Clear Bay

Ivy House

Mersea Stone

North Farm

EAST RD

IVY LA

Broman's Farm

BROMAN'S LA

Caravan Camp

Cudmore Grove Country Park

RED BARN RD

SAMSONS RD

CHURCH RD

LOWER PARK RD

LADYSMITH AVE

QUEEN ST

VICTORIA PL

STATION RD

NEW ST

HIGH ST

89

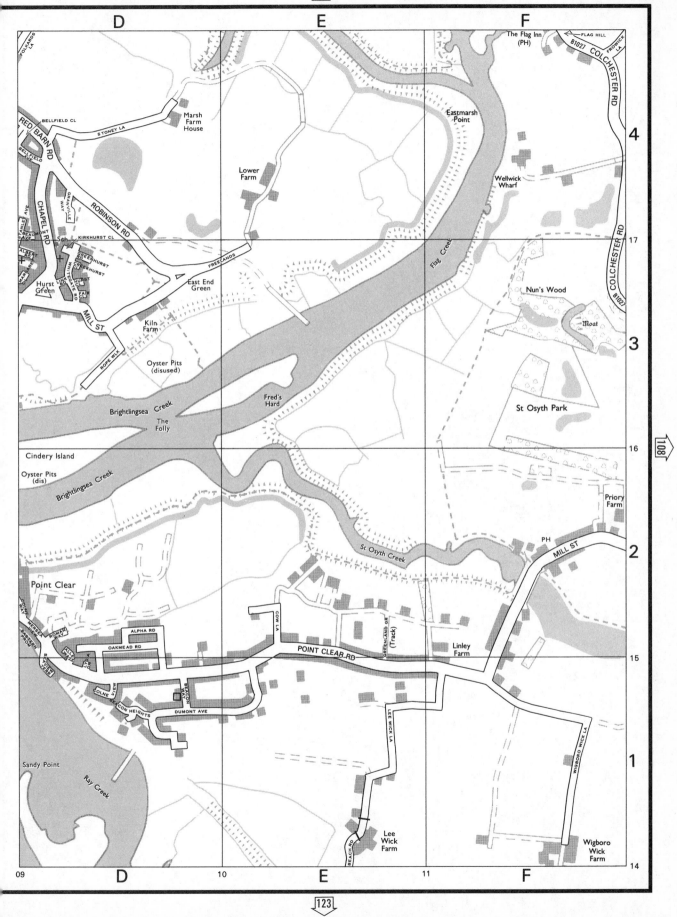

D   E   F

FLAG HILL

The Flag Inn
(PH)

B1027

COLCHESTER RD

FRONICK LA

Marsh
Farm
House

BELLFIELD CL

STONEY LA

Eastmarsh
Point

4

RED BARN RD

BELLFIELD

Lower
Farm

Wellwick
Wharf

CHAPEL RD

GRANVILLE WAY

ROBINSON RD

KIRKHURST CL

17

Flag Creek

COLCHESTER RD

B1027

BEAUMONT AVE

Sch

FREELANDS

Nun's Wood

GREENHURST
CREEKHURST

East End
Green

Moat

HURST GREEN

WHITEGATE RD

MILL ST

St Osyth Park

Kiln
Farm

3

ROPE WLK

Oyster Pits
(disused)

Brightlingsea Creek

Fred's
Hard

The Folly

Cindery Island

16

108

Oyster Pits
(dis)

Priory
Farm

Brightlingsea Creek

PH

MILL ST

St Osyth Creek

2

Point Clear

COW LA

GREENLAND GR (Track)

Linley
Farm

POINT WAY

MERSEA WAY

ROMAN WAY

ALPHA RD

OAKMEAD RD

POINT CLEAR RD

15

SAXON WAY

ALBA RD

COLNE VIEW

BEACON HEIGHTS

BEACON WAY

DUMONT AVE

LEE WICK LA

WIGBORO WICK LA

Sandy Point

1

Ray Creek

BEACH RD

Lee
Wick
Farm

Wigboro
Wick
Farm

14

09   D   10   E   11   F

123

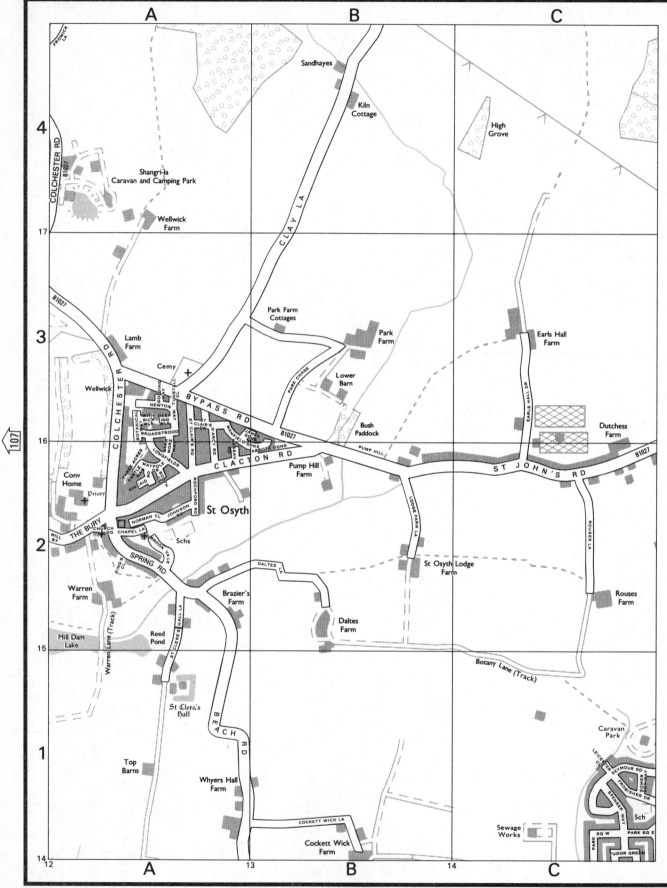

A   B   C

FROWICK LA

COLCHESTER RD
B1027

4

Shangri-la
Caravan and Camping Park

Wellwick
Farm

17

Sandhayes

Kiln
Cottage

CLAY LA

High
Grove

B1027

3

Lamb
Farm

Cemy

Wellwick

COLCHESTER RD

BYPASS RD

Park Farm
Cottages

PARK CHASE

Park
Farm

Lower
Barn

Earls Hall
Farm

EARLS HALL DR

Dutchess
Farm

16

Conv
Home

Priory

GOLDING WAY
BOTANICAL
WITH RICK WLK
BROADSTROOD
THREE ACRES
CASTLE
KINCAID
MAYPOLE CL

NEWTON
DEEPING WLK
TUNSTALL
ST CLAIR'S DR
D'ARCY RD
ST CLAIR'S RD
MANNIFIELD GDNS
BEACH RD
JAMES GDNS
ABBOTS GDNS
LONGFIELDS

B1027

Bush
Paddock

PUMP HILL

ST JOHN'S RD

B1027

CLACTON RD

Pump Hill
Farm

St Osyth

ROCHFORD RD

LODGE FARM LA

ROUSES LA

THE BURY
MILL ST
KING'S CL

CHURCH SQ
NORMAN CL
CHAPEL LA
JOHNSON RD
BROOK VALE
Schs

SPRING RD

2

Warren
Farm

Brazier's
Farm

DALTES LA

St Osyth Lodge
Farm

Rouses
Farm

ST CLERES HALL LA

Mill Dam
Lake

WARREN LANE (Track)

Reed
Pond

Daltes
Farm

15

Botany Lane (Track)

St Clere's
Hall

BEACH RD

Top
Barns

Caravan
Park

LEICESTER CL
SEYMOUR RD
FROBISHER DR
SPENSER WAY
Sch

1

Whyers Hall
Farm

Sewage
Works

PARK SQ W
PARK SQ E
TUDOR GREEN

COCKETT WICK LA

Cockett Wick
Farm

14

12   A   13   B   14   C

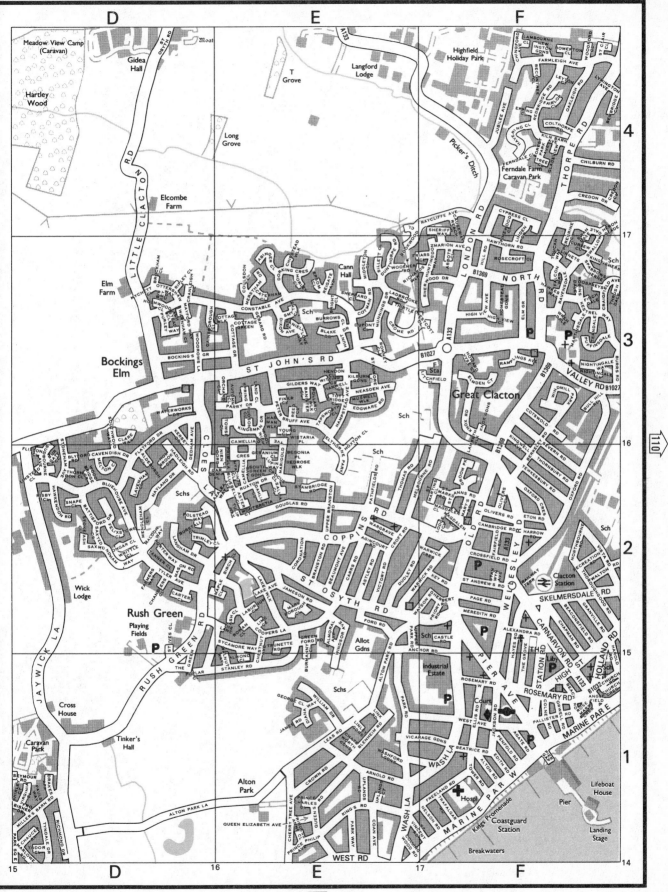

D   **E**   **F**

Meadow View Camp (Caravan)

Gidea Hall

Moat

Highfield Holiday Park

Langford Lodge

Hartley Wood

T Grove

Long Grove

Picker's Ditch

4

Ferndale Farm Caravan Park

Elcombe Farm

LITTLE CLACTON RD

Elm Farm

Cann Hall

NORTH RD

LONDON RD

17

Bockings Elm

ST JOHN'S RD

B1369

B1027

A133

Great Clacton

B1027

VALLEY RD

3

WATERWORKS

Sch

16

Sch

Sch

Rush Green

Playing Fields

COPPINS RD

ST OSYTH RD

Allot Gdns

Clacton Station

SKELMERSDALE RD

2

CARNARVON RD

HIGH ST

Cross House

RUSH GREEN RD

JAYWICK LA

Tinker's Hall

Schs

Industrial Estate

Courts

ROSEMARY RD

Liby

MARINE PAR E

15

Caravan Park

Alton Park

Vicarage Gdns

WASH LA

Hosp

1

Lifeboat House

Pier

ALTON PARK LA

QUEEN ELIZABETH AVE

WEST RD

Kings Promenade

Coastguard Station

MARINE PAR W

Breakwaters

Landing Stage

14

D   16   **E**   17   **F**

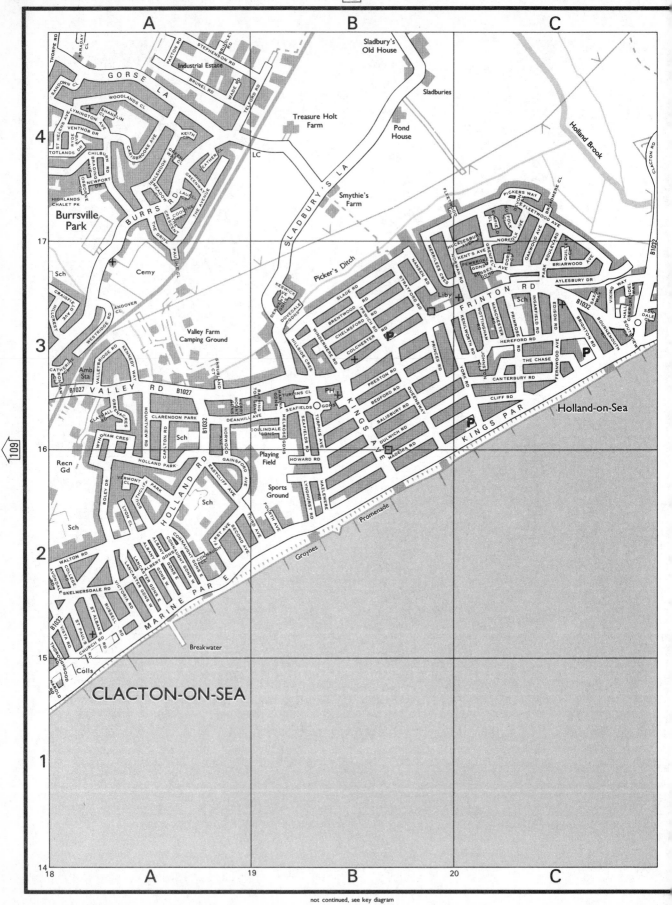

CLACTON-ON-SEA

Holland-on-Sea

Burrsville Park

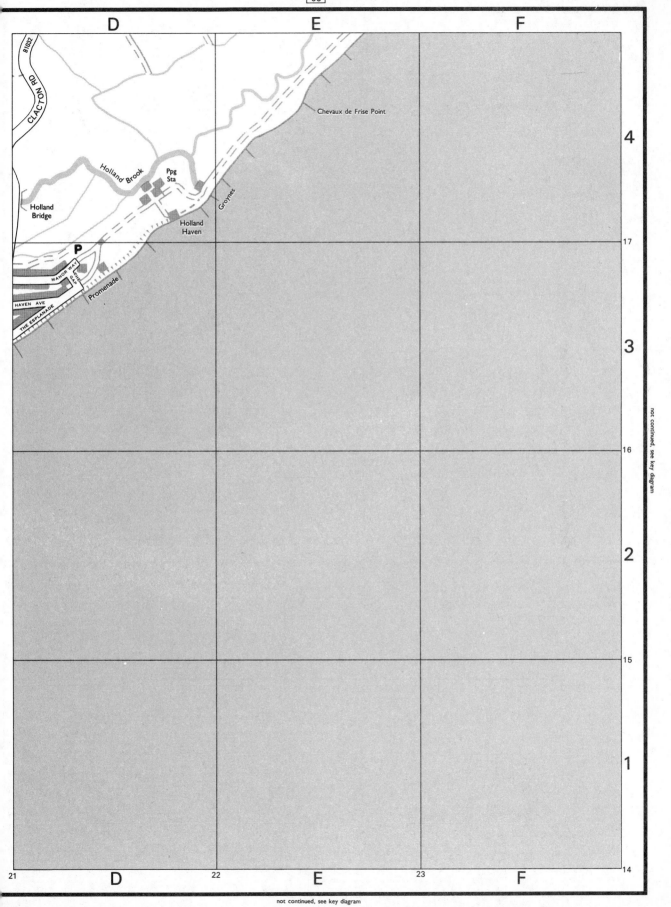

D E F

4

Chevaux de Frise Point

17

3

16

2

15

1

14

21 D 22 E 23 F

not continued, see key diagram

not continued, see key diagram

Clacton Rd
B1032
Holland Brook
Ppg Sta
Holland Bridge
Holland Haven
Groynes
P
Manor Way
Gap
Haven Ave
The Esplanade
Promenade

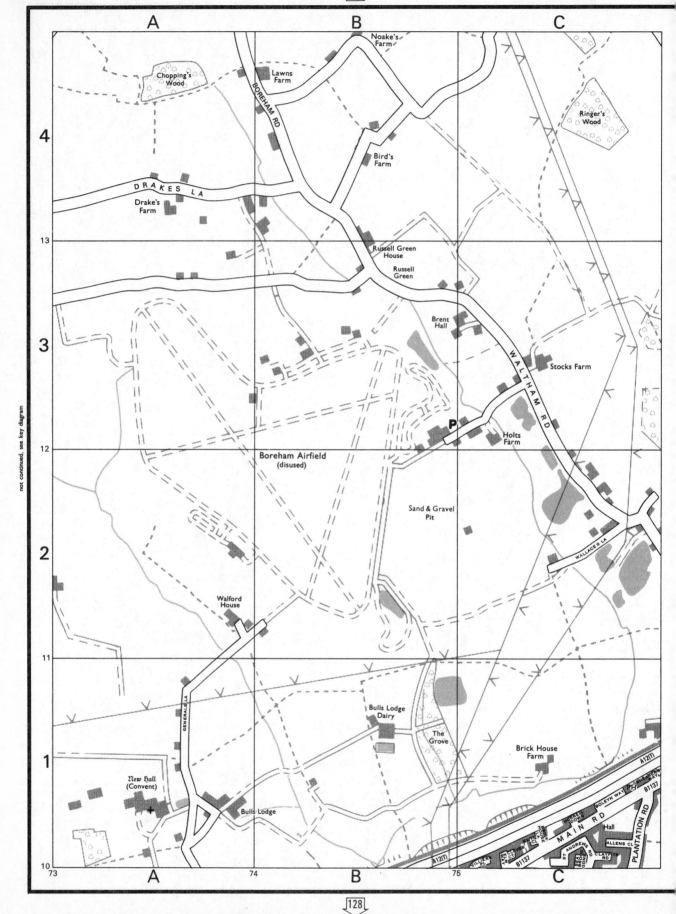

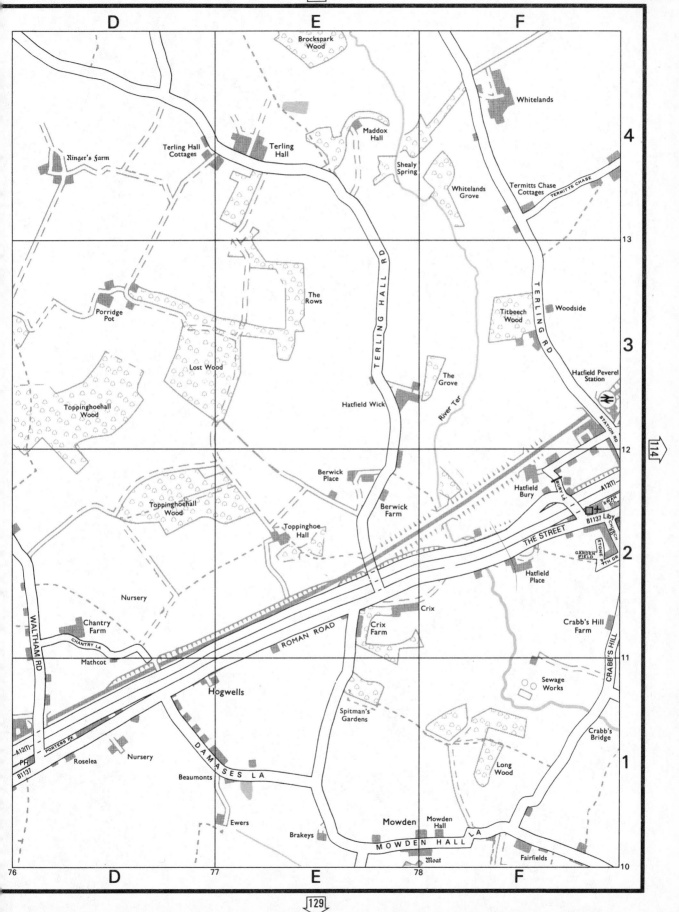

D　　　　　E　　　　　F

Brockspark
Wood

Whitelands

4

Maddox
Hall

Terling
Hall

Ringer's Farm

Terling Hall
Cottages

Shealy
Spring

Termitts Chase
Cottages

TERMITTS CHASE

Whitelands
Grove

13

TERLING HALL RD

TERLING RD

The
Rows

Porridge
Pot

Titbeech
Wood

Woodside

3

Lost Wood

Toppinghoehall
Wood

The
Grove

River Ter

Hatfield Wick

Hatfield Peverel
Station

STATION RD

12

Toppinghoehall
Wood

Berwick
Place

Berwick
Farm

Hatfield
Bury

BURY LA

A12(T)

SWAN

Hatfield
Place

Liby
CHURCH

B1137

STONE

4TH DR

GARDEN
FIELD

THE STREET

2

Toppinghoe
Hall

Nursery

Crix

Crix
Farm

Crabb's Hill
Farm

CRABB'S HILL

Chantry
Farm

ROMAN ROAD

CHANTRY LA

WALTHAM RD

Mathcot

11

Sewage
Works

Hogwells

DAMASES LA

Spitman's
Gardens

Crabb's
Bridge

PORTERS PK

A12(T)

PH

Roselea

Nursery

Long
Wood

1

B1137

Beaumonts

Ewers

Brakeys

Mowden

Mowden
Hall

LA

Fairfields

MOWDEN HALL

Moat

76　　　　　D　　　　　77　　　　　E　　　　　78　　　　　F　　　　　10

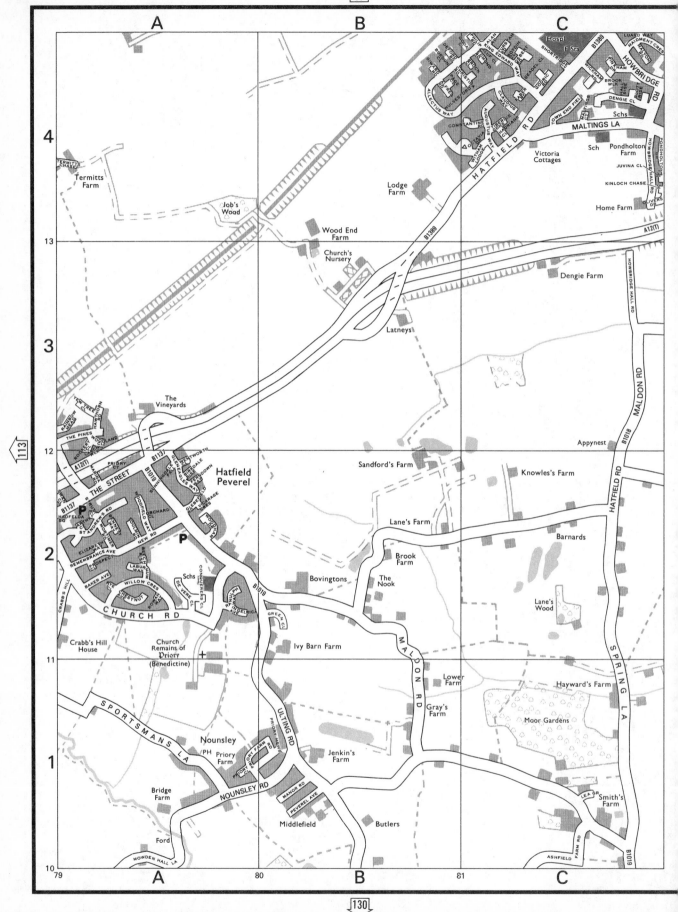

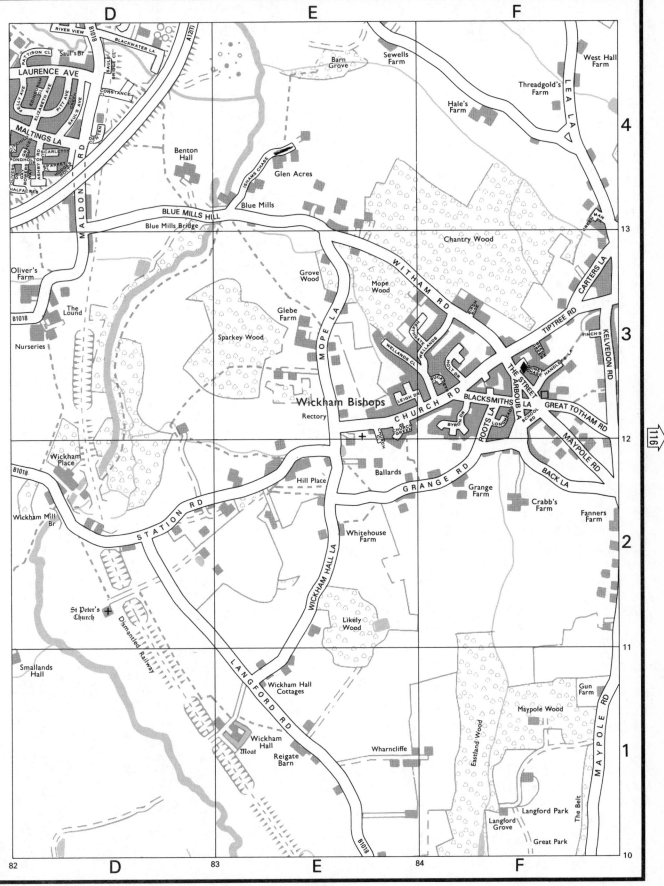

D
E
F

4

13

3

116

12

2

11

1

10

D 83 E 84 F

99

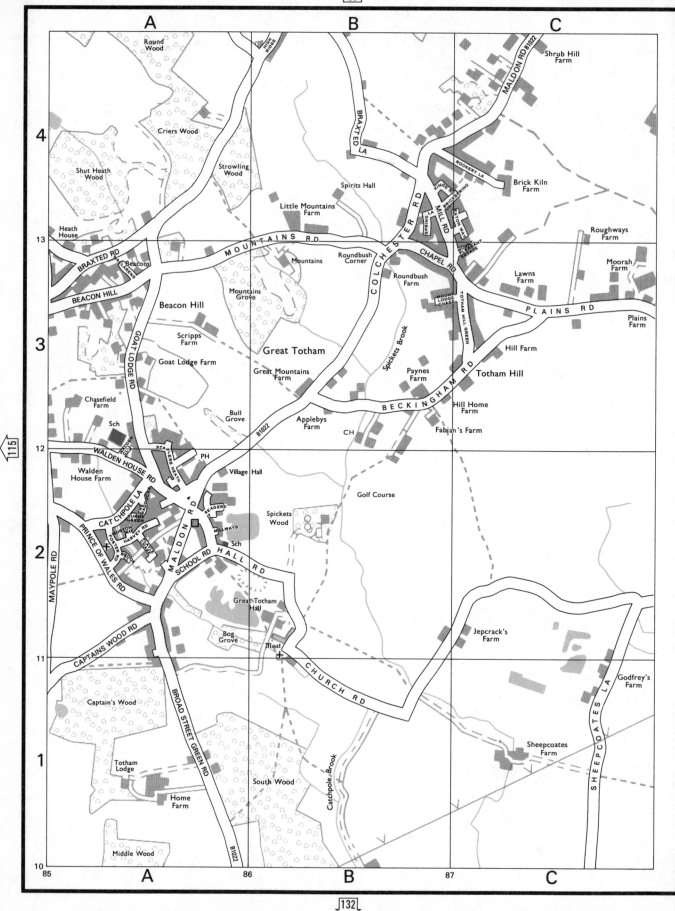

115

132

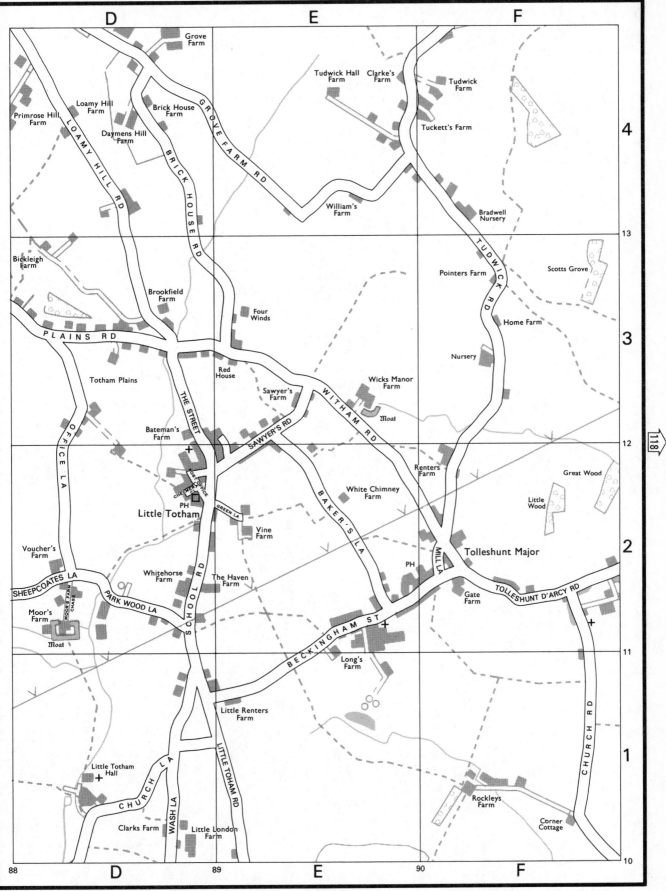

D

E

F

Grove Farm

Tudwick Hall Farm

Clarke's Farm

Tudwick Farm

Loamy Hill Farm

Brick House Farm

Primrose Hill Farm

Daymens Hill Farm

Tuckett's Farm

4

L O A M Y   H I L L   R D

B R I C K   H O U S E   R D

G R O V E   F A R M   R D

William's Farm

Bradwell Nursery

13

Bickleigh Farm

T U D W I C K   R D

Pointers Farm

Scotts Grove

Brookfield Farm

Four Winds

Home Farm

P L A I N S   R D

Totham Plains

Red House

Sawyer's Farm

Nursery

3

Wicks Manor Farm

W I T H A M   R D

Moat

Bateman's Farm

S A W Y E R ' S   R D

Renters Farm

12

T H E   S T R E E T

POST OFFICE

CHELMER D.C.

PH

Little Totham

GREEN LA

Vine Farm

White Chimney Farm

B A K E R ' S   L A

Great Wood

Little Wood

Voucher's Farm

M I L L   L A

Tolleshunt Major

2

Whitehorse Farm

The Haven Farm

PH

S H E E P C O A T E S   L A

P A R K   W O O D   L A

MOOR'S FARM CHASE

S C H O O L   R D

Gate Farm

T O L L E S H U N T   D ' A R C Y   R D

Moor's Farm

Moat

Long's Farm

Little Renters Farm

B E C K I N G H A M   S T

11

C H U R C H   R D

Little Totham Hall

C H U R C H   L A

L I T T L E   T O H A M   R D

Rockleys Farm

1

W A S H   L A

Clarks Farm

Little London Farm

Corner Cottage

10

88

D

89

E

90

F

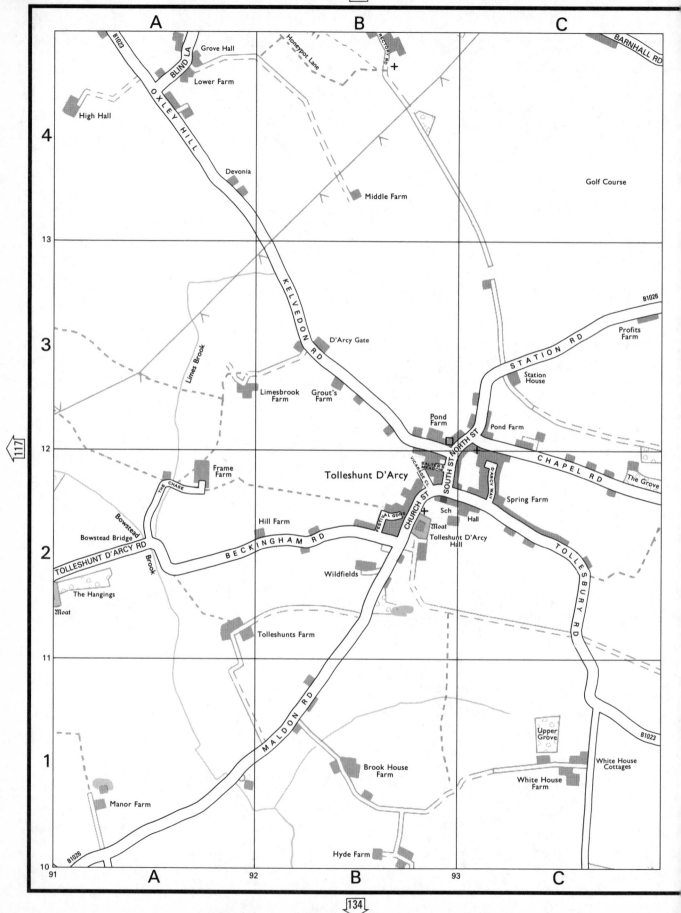

A   B   C

BARNHALL RD

Grove Hall

BLIND LA

Lower Farm

Honepot Lane

RECTORY RD

B1023

High Hall

OXLEY HILL

4

Devonia

Golf Course

Middle Farm

13

B1026

KELVEDON RD

D'Arcy Gate

STATION RD

Profits Farm

3

Limes Brook

Limesbrook Farm

Grout's Farm

Station House

Pond Farm

Pond Farm

12

Tolleshunt D'Arcy

Frame Farm

THE CHASE

VICARAGE CL

SALTERS MEADOW

NORTH ST

SOUTH ST

CHAPEL RD

The Grove

Hill Farm

FESTIVAL GDNS

CHURCH ST

DARCY WAY

Spring Farm

Bowstead

Bowstead Bridge

Sch

Hall

TOLLESBURY RD

TOLLESHUNT D'ARCY RD

BECKINGHAM RD

Moat

Tolleshunt D'Arcy Hall

2

Brook

Wildfields

The Hangings

Moat

Tolleshunts Farm

11

MALDON RD

Upper Grove

B1023

White House Cottages

1

Manor Farm

Brook House Farm

White House Farm

B1026

Hyde Farm

10

91   A   92   B   93   C

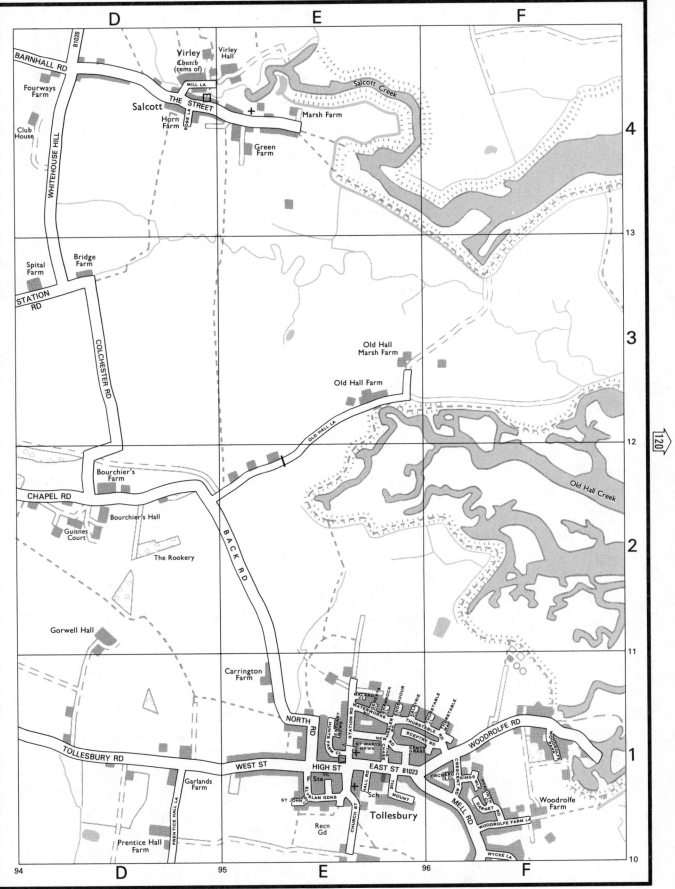

D   E   F

BARNHALL RD

B1026

Fourways
Farm

Virley
Hall

Virley
Church
(rems of)

MILL LA

THE STREET

Salcott

Club
House

Horn
Farm

ROSE LA

Marsh Farm

Salcott Creek

WHITEHOUSE HILL

Green
Farm

4

Spital
Farm

Bridge
Farm

STATION
RD

COLCHESTER RD

Old Hall
Marsh Farm

Old Hall Farm

3

OLD HALL LA

120

Bourchier's
Farm

CHAPEL RD

Bourchier's Hall

Guisnes
Court

The Rookery

BACK RD

Old Hall Creek

2

Gorwell Hall

Carrington
Farm

11

NORTH
RD

WOODROLFE RD

WOODROLFE

TOLLESBURY RD

WEST ST

HIGH ST

EAST ST B1023

MALARD
CL

WATERWORKS

HUNTS PARK CL

STATION RD

CHASE
ST
HADDOCK

ENDEAVOUR
VALKYRIE

THURSTABLE RD

THURSTABLE

SCEPTRE RD

NEW
CHASE

ST MARYS
MEWS

KENTS
GRASS

HUNTS PARK
MEWS

WESTBURY
MEWS

CRESCENT RD

KINGS
WLK

ORCHARD
CL

MELL RD

Woodrolfe
Farm

HORNET
RD

Garlands
Farm

F Sta

St JOHN'S

ELYSIAN GDNS

HALL RD

CHURCH ST

THE
MOUNT

Sch

Tollesbury

Recn
Gd

PRENTICE HALL LA

Prentice Hall
Farm

WOODROLFE FARM LA

WYCKE LA

94   D   95   E   96   F

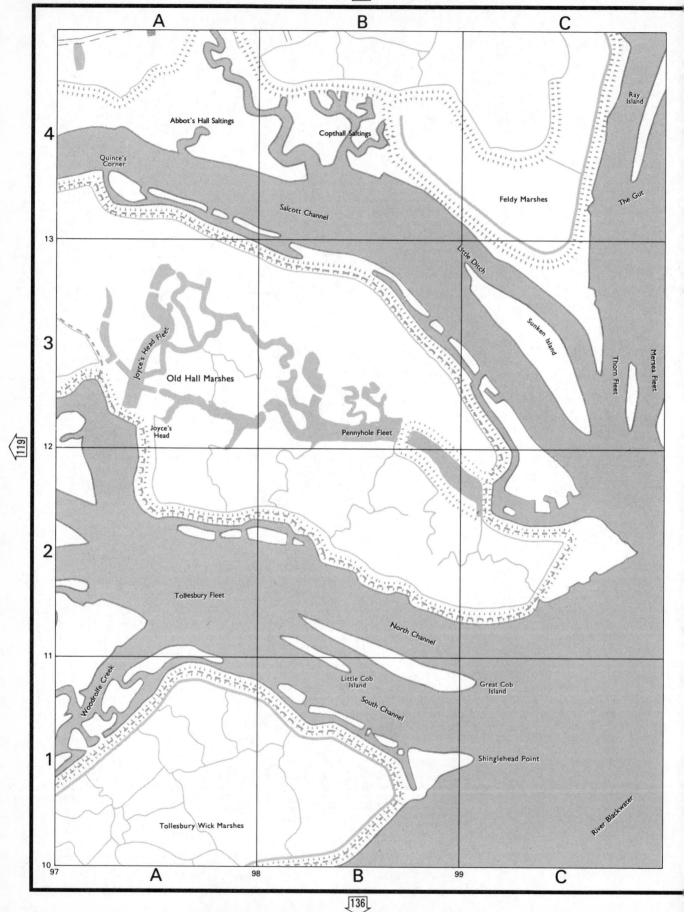

A B C

4
Abbot's Hall Saltings
Copthall Saltings
Ray Island
Quince's Corner
Feldy Marshes
The Gut
Salcott Channel

13

Little Ditch

3
Joyce's Head Fleet
Old Hall Marshes
Sunken Island
Thorn Fleet
Mersea Fleet

Joyce's Head
Pennyhole Fleet

12

2
Tollesbury Fleet

North Channel

11
Woodrolfe Creek
Little Cob Island
Great Cob Island
South Channel

1
Shinglehead Point

River Blackwater

Tollesbury Wick Marshes

10
97 A 98 B 99 C

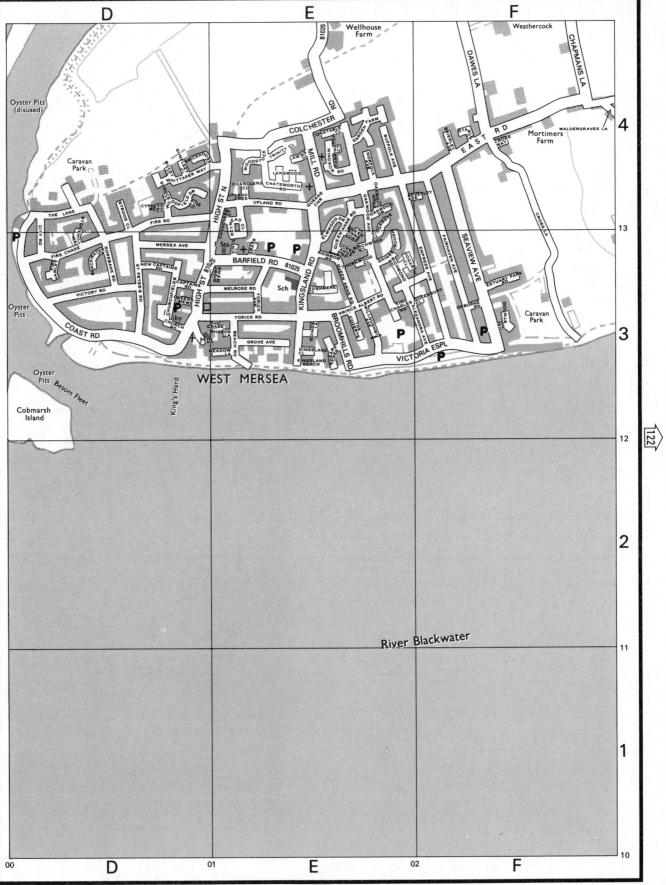

D   E   F

Wellhouse Farm

Weathercock

B1025

Oyster Pits (disused)

Caravan Park

COLCHESTER RD

CONSTABLE

GARDEN FARM

DAWES LA

CHAPMANS LA

EAST RD

Mortimers Farm

WALDERGRAVES LA

4

The Lane

Whittaker Way

CYPRESS MEWS

FIRS RD

HIGH ST N

CHANDLERS CL

UPLAND CRES

WOODSTOCK

TRINITY CL

LANGWOOD

CHATSWORTH

LAW

MILL RD

QUEENS CNR

BUFFOLK AVE

NORFOLK

TEVERLEY AVE

CROSS LA

CROSS WAY

City RD

STROOD CL

FIRS RD

UPLAND RD

MERSEA AVE

Sta

BARFIELD RD

B1025

KINGSLAND RD

RAINBOW

SEAVIEW AVE

13

FIRS CHASE

BLACKWATER DR

ROSEBANK RD

VICTORY RD

NEW CAPTAINS RD

CAPTAINS RD

ST PETERS RD

CHURCHFIELDS

HIGH ST B1025

QUEENS MEWS

MELROSE RD

YORICK

Sch

BUSHMERE

FAIRHAVEN AVE

ESTUARY PARK RD

Caravan Park

P

Oyster Pits

MALL

COAST RD

LIby CHURCH

THE CHASE PHAROS

BEACH RD

YORICK RD

GROVE AVE

PRINCE ALBERT RD

VICTORIA ESPL

OSBORNE RD

P

3

MEADOW LA

KINGSLAND LA

KINGSLAND BEACH

BROOMHILLS RD

P

Oyster Pits

Besom Fleet

King's Hard

WEST MERSEA

Cobmarsh Island

12

122

2

River Blackwater

11

1

00   D   01   E   02   F

10

105

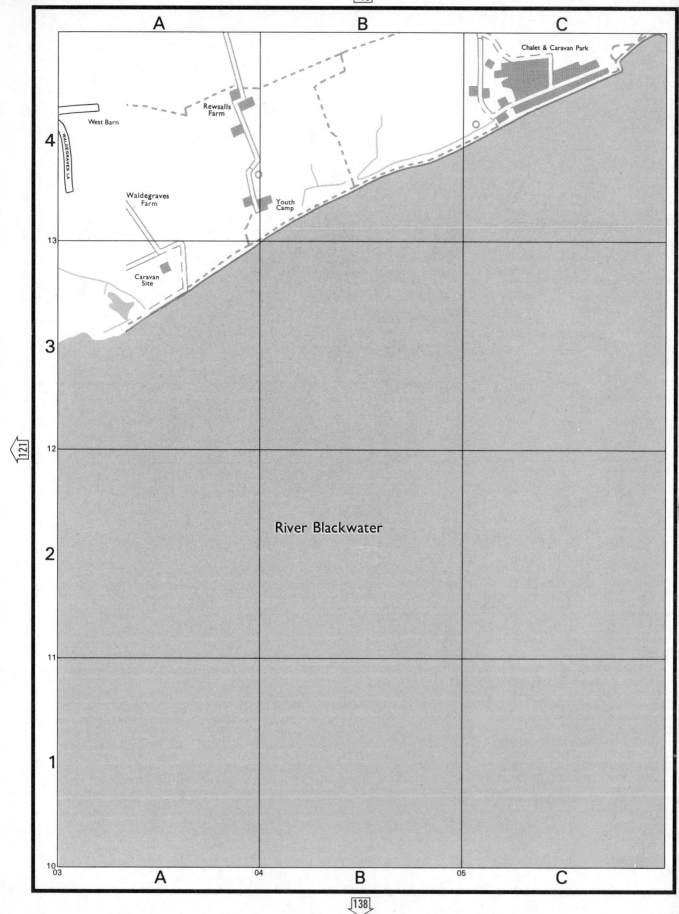

A

B

C

West Barn

WALDEGRAVES LA

Rewsalls
Farm

4

Waldegraves
Farm

Youth
Camp

Chalet & Caravan Park

13

Caravan
Site

3

121

12

River Blackwater

2

11

1

10

03   04   05

A   B   C

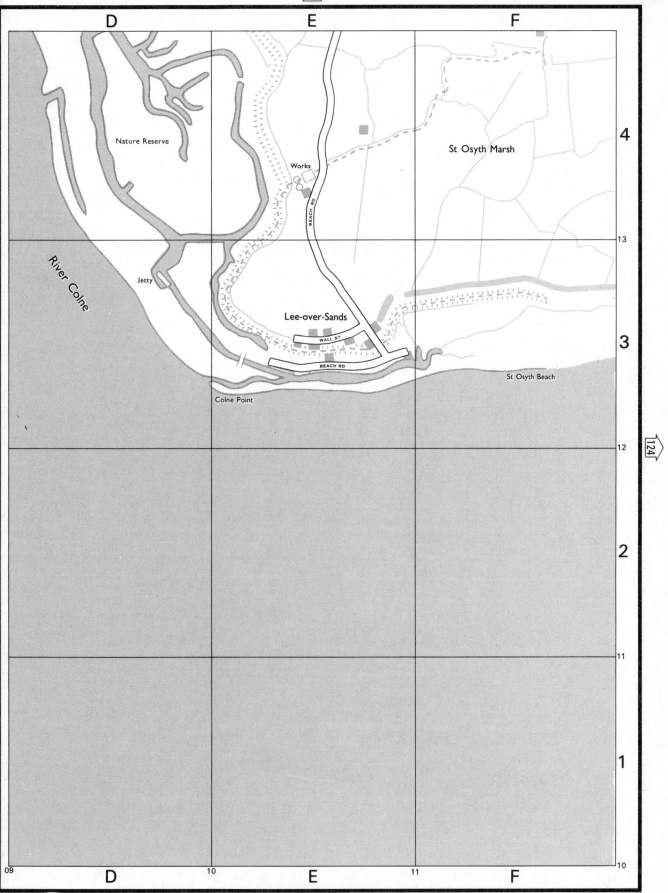

D

E

F

Nature Reserve

Works

St Osyth Marsh

4

River Colne

Jetty

13

Lee-over-Sands

WALL ST

BEACH RD

3

St Osyth Beach

Colne Point

124

12

2

11

1

09

D

10

E

11

F

10

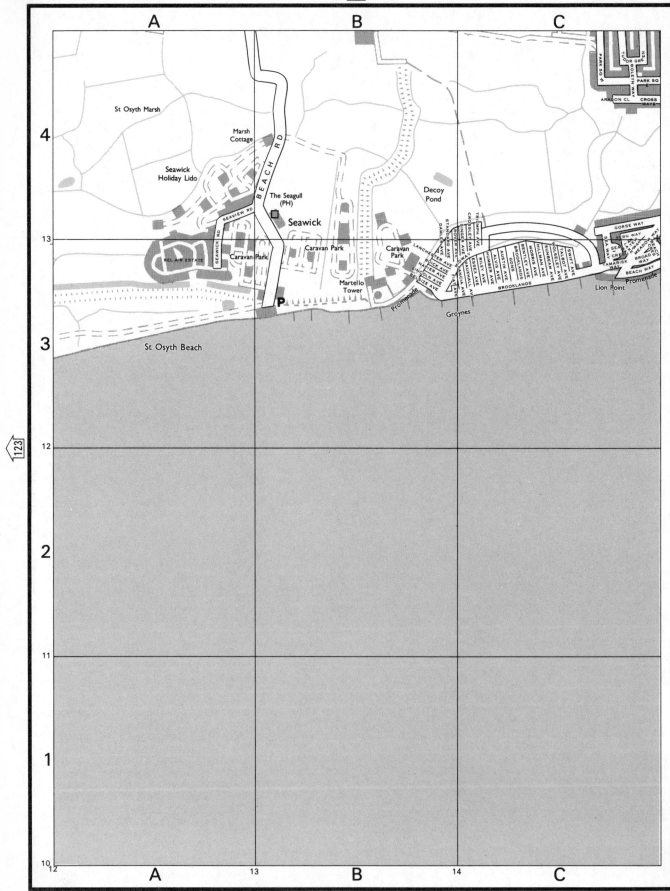

A B C

4

St Osyth Marsh

Marsh Cottage

Seawick Holiday Lido

BEACH RD

The Seagull (PH)

Decoy Pond

SEAVIEW RD

Seawick

13

SEAWICK RD

BEL-AIR ESTATE

Caravan Park

Caravan Park

Caravan Park

Martello Tower

LANCHESTER AVE
DARLEY AVE
BUICK AVE
NAPIER AVE
LINCOLN AVE
BELSIZE AVE

STANDARD AVE
SINGER AVE
ROVER AVE
HUMBER AVE
LANCIA AVE
VAUXHALL AVE
FIAT AVE

CROSSLEY AVE
TRIUMPH AVE
RILEY AVE
ESSEX AVE
ALVIS AVE

AUSTIN AVE
MORRIS AVE
BENTLEY AVE
GDNS
BROOKLANDS
HILLMAN AVE
WOLSELEY AVE
SUNBEAM AVE
TALBOT AVE
SWIFT AVE

BROOKLANDS

GORSE WAY
RN WAY
MEADOW
BROAD
BEACH WAY

Promenade

Lion Point

Promenade

Groynes

P

3

St Osyth Beach

12

2

11

1

10

A 13 B 14 C

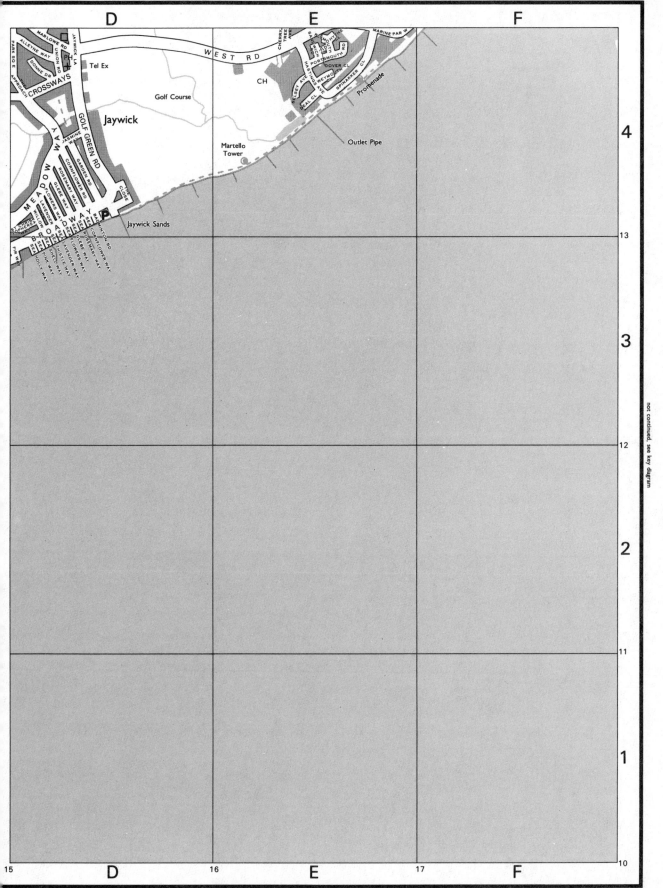

109

D   E   F

MARLOWE RD
ALLEYNE WAY
PARK SQ E
DONNE DR
UNION RD
JAYWICK LA
PH A
APPROACH
CROSSWAYS
Tel Ex
WEST RD
CHERRY TREE AVE
SANDWICH
PLYMOUTH TREE
PORTSMOUTH RD
MARINE PAR W
DOVER CL
CH
Golf Course
SELSEY AVE
HASTINGS AVE
REAL CL
WEYMOUTH
SPINAKER CL
Promenade
Jaywick

GOLF GREEN RD
JASMINE WAY
MEADOW WAY
CORNFLOWER RD
GARDEN RD
GLEBE WAY
LAVENDER
FLOWERS WAY
WILLOW
BROADWAY
ROSEMARY WAY
THE CLOSE

4

Martello
Tower

Outlet Pipe

Jaywick Sands

13

3

not continued, see key diagram

12

2

11

1

10

15   D   16   E   17   F

not continued, see key diagram

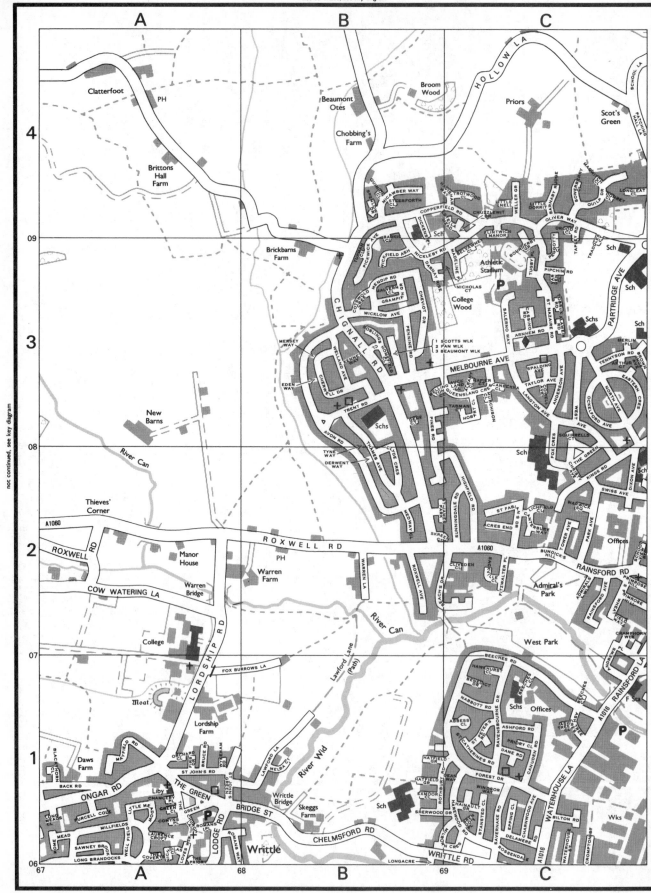

Clatterfoot

PH

Beaumont Otes

Broom Wood

Priors

Scot's Green

HOLLOW LA

Brittons Hall Farm

Chobbing's Farm

MICAWBER WAY
STEERFORTH
TROTWOOD
COPPERFIELD RD
CHUZZLEWIT
WELLER GR
LITTLE DORRIT
OLIVER WAY
BARNABY RUDGE
LONGLEAT
QUILP GR

DICKENS PL
DROOD
LINTWICK MANOR
PEGOTTY GR
TAPLY RD
TRADDLES
Sch

Brickbarns Farm

PICKWICK AVE
WICKFIELD ASH
NICKLEBY RD
DARNAY SER
MADELINE CT
BELVIGNE CL
Sch
BOUNDERBY GR
PIPCHIN RD
Sch

CHIGNALL RD
COTSWOLD
MENDIP RD
MALVERN CL
GRAMPN
WICKLOW AVE
CHEVIOT DR
NICHOLAS CT
College Wood
P
SALERNO WAY
CASSINO RD
ST NAZAIRE RD
Schs
Sch
PARTRIDGE AVE
MERLIN PL
ARTHUR

MERSEY WAY
KENNET WAY
WELLAND AVE
CHERWELL DR
EDEN WAY
OSLINGS HOMEFIELD
PENNINE RD
Athletic Stadium
1 SCOTTS WLK
2 FAN WLK
3 BEAUMONT WLK
MELBOURNE AVE
SPALDING AVE
TAYLOR AVE
ANDERSON AVE
LANGTON AVE
TENNYSON RD
EASTERN CRES
OCKELFORD AVE
NORTH AVE
WEST

New Barns

TRENT RD
Schs
DERE CL
PINES RD
TASMAN CT
RAPIER CL
QUEENSLAND CRES
CANBERRA CL
GARRISON
HOSP
SQUIRRELS CT
FOX CRES
Sch
THE GREEN

River Can

AVON RD
THAMES AVE
CLYDE CRES
TYNE WAY
DERWENT WAY
MEDWAY CL
HIGHFIELD RD
SUNNINGDALE RD
ST FABIAN
LICHFIELD CL
ACRES END
CANTERBURY WAY
WARWICK SQ
PARK AVE
SWISS AVE
DIXON AVE
KINGS RD
CHATS

Thieves' Corner

A1060

ROXWELL RD

ROXWELL RD
A1060
CLIVEDEN CL
MANOR
PLE
FITZWALTER PL
BUNDICK'S HILL
TOWER AVE
RAINSFORD RD
Offices

Manor House

Warren Farm

PH

WARREN LA
ROXWELL AVE
SACHS GR
SKREENS

ROXWELL RD

Admiral's Park
RAINSFORD AVE
ADMIRALS
PRIMROSE
FIELD WK
CRAWTHORN WEM

COW WATERING LA

Warren Bridge

River Can

West Park

BEECHES RD
ANDREWS PL

College

LORDSHIP RD

Lawford Lane (Path)

FOX BURROWS LA

HAWKHURST
BENEDICT DR
NABBOTT RD
Schs
Offices
ABBESS CL
ASHFORD RD
BEECHES
A1016 RAINSFORD LA
F Sch

Moat

Lordship Farm

LAWFORD LA
MELBA CT
River Wid
ST CATHERINES RD
PRIORY CL
DANE RD
RAVENSBOURNE DR
CANUDEN RD
FOREST DR
P

Daws Farm

MAYFIELD RD
ORCHARD
BRUCE RD
WYCKHAM
WYERHAM WD
ST JOHN'S RD
Writtle Bridge
Skeggs Farm
HATFIELD
HATFIELD
DEAN WAY
WINDSOR WAY
EXMOOR
HAINAULT CL
Sch
SHERWOOD DR
HARWOOD
STANSTED CL
EPPING CL
CHARNWOOD RD
WATERHOUSE LA
BILTON RD
Wks

BLACKTHORN RD
BACK RD
ONGAR RD
Liby
THE GREEN
CHANCERY PL
GREEN CL
The Green
BRIDGE ST

LONG MEADS
ROME MEAD
PURCELL COLE
MILLFIELDS
LAURENCE CROFT
LITTLE ME
MOOR
COYNES
WELL FIELD
NICOLAS
LOVES WK
COVERT
P
ROMANS PL
ROMANS WAY
THE PRIORY
Writtle
CHELMSFORD RD
SAWNEY BRO
LONG BRANDOCKS
LODGE RD
BRIDGE ST

SAVERNAKE RD
DELAHERE
ROSSENDALE
A1016
WATERHOUSE
CROMPTON ST

WRITTLE RD
LONGACRE
WRITTLE RD

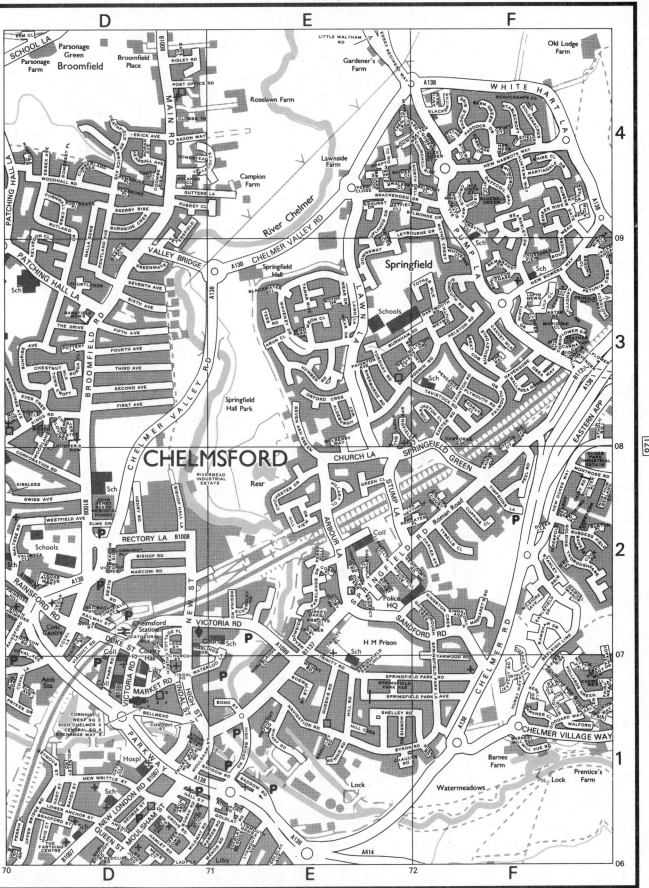

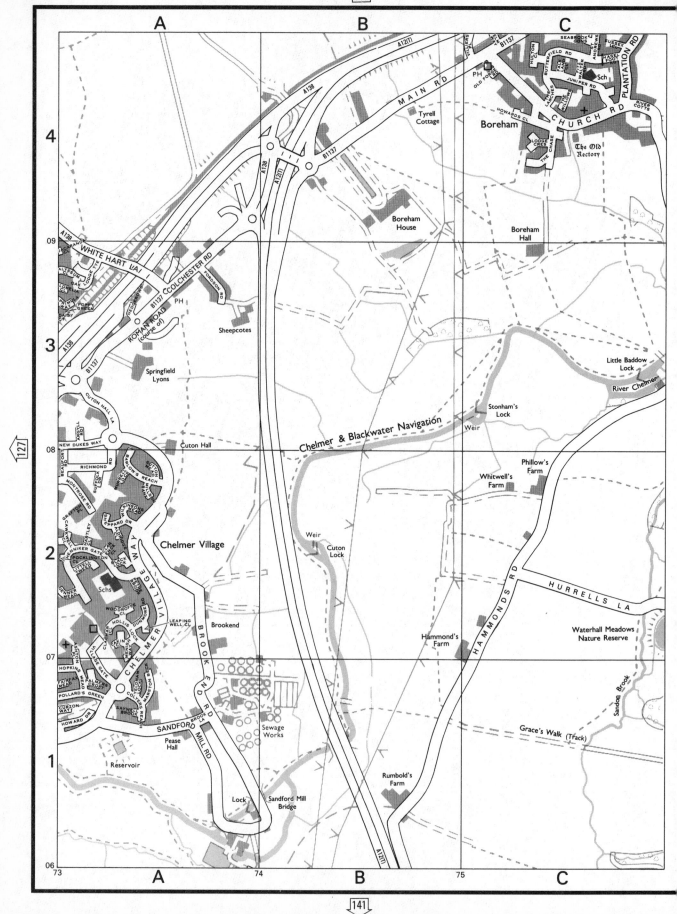

113

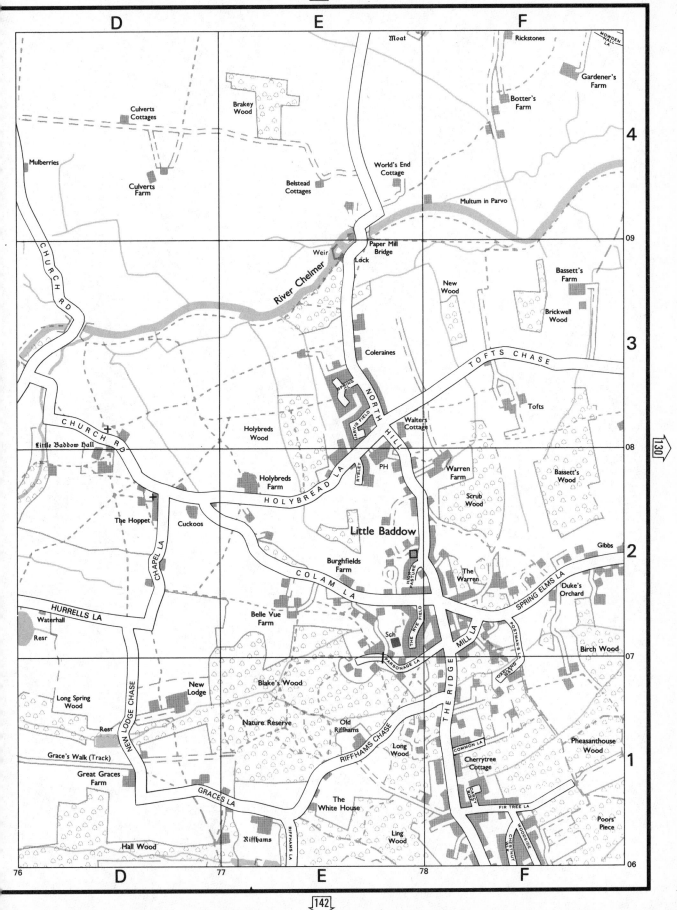

D   E   F

4

3

08

2

07

1

06

76   D   77   E   78   F

130

Moat
Rickstones
HOWDEN HALL LA
Gardener's Farm
Culverts Cottages
Brakey Wood
Botter's Farm
Mulberries
World's End Cottage
Belstead Cottages
Culverts Farm
Multum in Parvo
09
River Chelmer
Weir
Lock
Paper Mill Bridge
New Wood
Bassett's Farm
CHURCH RD
Brickwell Wood
TOFTS CHASE
Coleraines
SPRING
Tofts
NORTH HILL
Holybreds Wood
DARVIL FIELD
Walters Cottage
CHURCH RD
Little Baddow Hall
HOLYBREAD LA
RYSLEY
PH
Warren Farm
Bassett's Wood
Holybreds Farm
Scrub Wood
The Hoppet
Cuckoos
CHAPEL LA
Little Baddow
Gibbs
COLAM LA
Burghfields Farm
The Warren
SPRING ELMS LA
Duke's Orchard
HURRELLS LA
Waterhall
Resr
Belle Vue Farm
HIGHTREE PASTURE
Sch
THE RYE FIELD
MILL LA
POSTMAN'S LA
Birch Wood
PARSONAGE LA
Long Spring Wood
New Lodge
NEW LODGE CHASE
Blake's Wood
THE RIDGE
OAKLAND WY
Resr
Nature Reserve
Old Riffhams
Long Wood
COMMON LA
Pheasanthouse Wood
Grace's Walk (Track)
RIFFHAMS CHASE
Cherrytree Cottage
Great Graces Farm
GRACES LA
The White House
FIR TREE LA
DAIRY FM
WOODSIDE
Poors' Piece
Hall Wood
Riffhams
RIFFHAMS LA
Ling Wood
CHESTNUT MLL

114

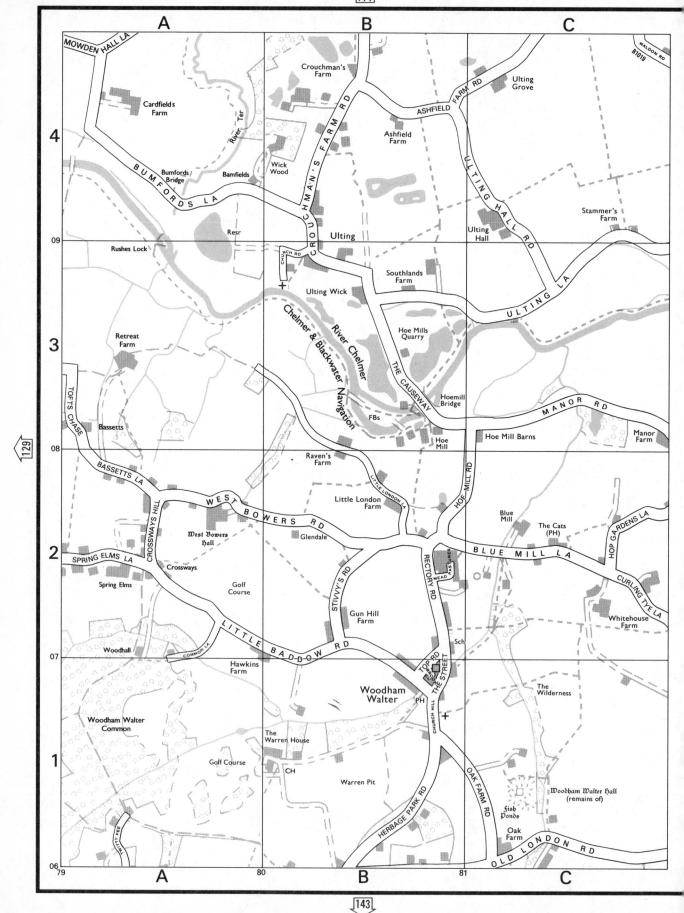

129

A

B

C

MOWDEN HALL LA

Cardfields
Farm

River Ter

BUMFORDS LA

Bumfords
Bridge

Bamfields

Resr

Rushes Lock

Crouchman's
Farm

CROUCHMAN'S FARM RD

Wick
Wood

ASHFIELD FARM RD

Ashfield
Farm

Ulting

MALDON RD
B1019

Ulting
Grove

ULTING HALL RD

Ulting
Hall

Stammer's
Farm

4

09

3

TOFTS CHASE

Retreat
Farm

Bassetts

08

BASSETTS LA

CROSSWAYS HILL

WEST BOWERS RD

West Bowers
Hall

Glendale

Little London
Farm

LITTLE LONDON LA

CHURCH RD

Ulting Wick

River Chelmer

Chelmer & Blackwater Navigation

Southlands
Farm

Hoe Mills
Quarry

THE CAUSEWAY

Hoemill
Bridge

FBs

Hoe
Mill

Hoe Mill Barns

ULTING LA

MANOR RD

Manor
Farm

Raven's
Farm

HOE-MILL RD

Blue
Mill

The Cats
(PH)

HOP GARDENS LA

2

SPRING ELMS LA

Spring Elms

Crossways

Golf
Course

STIVVY'S RD

Gun Hill
Farm

RECTORY RD

MEAD PASTURES

BLUE MILL LA

CURLING TYE LA

Whitehouse
Farm

07

Woodhall

COMMON LA

LITTLE BADDOW RD

Hawkins
Farm

TOP RD
THE STREET

Sch

PO

CHURCH HILL

The
Wilderness

1

Woodham Walter
Common

Golf Course

CH

The
Warren House

Warren Pit

HERBAGE PARK RD

Woodham
Walter

PH

OAK FARM RD

Fish
Ponds

Oak
Farm

Woodham Walter Hall
(remains of)

OLD LONDON RD

TRINITY FEE

06

79

A

80

B

81

C

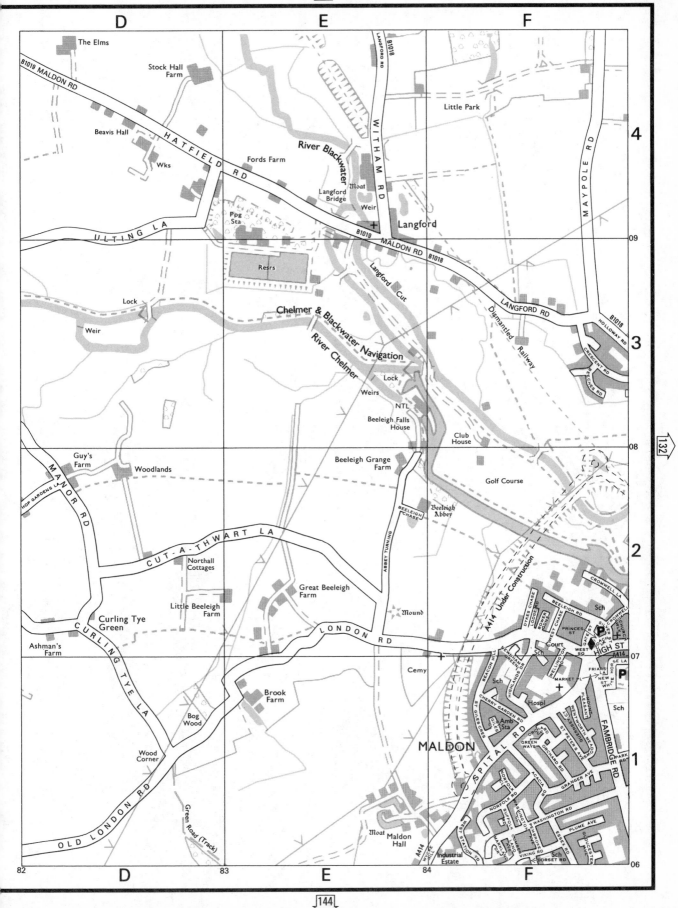

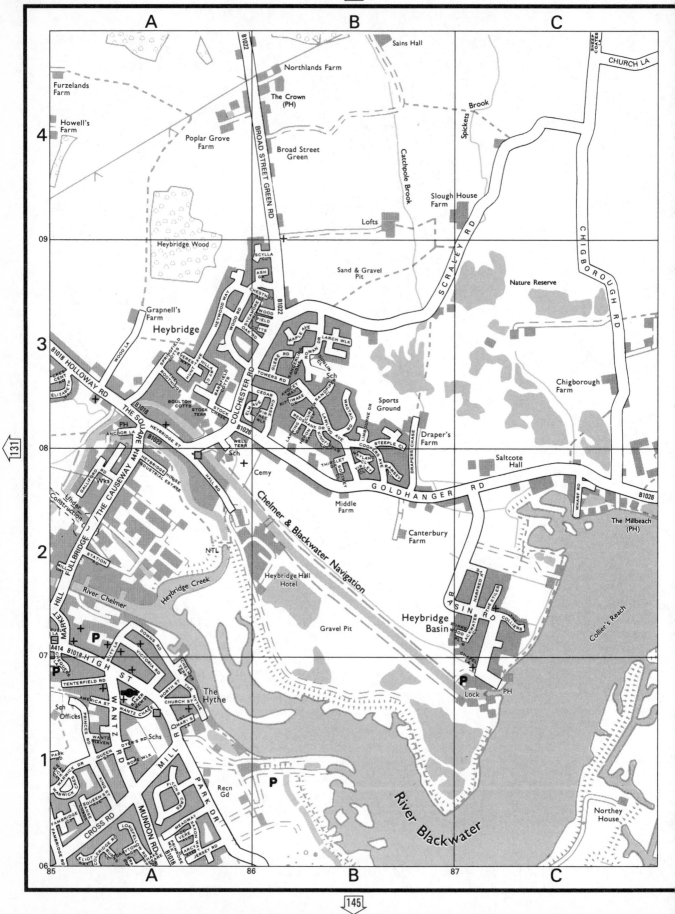

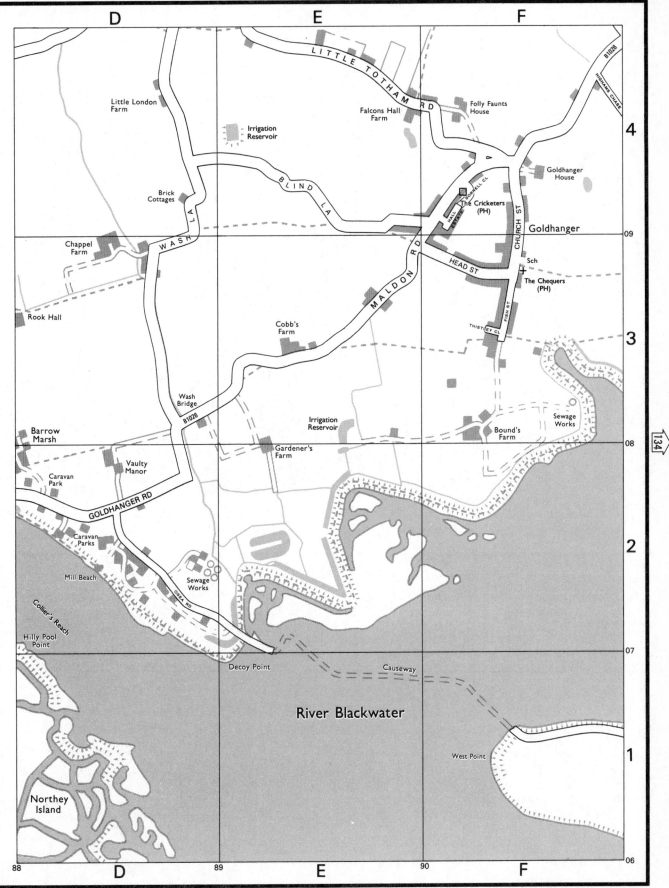

D   E   F

LITTLE TOTHAM RD

Little London Farm

Irrigation Reservoir

Falcons Hall Farm

Folly Faunts House

B1026

HIGHAM CHASE

Brick Cottages

BLIND LA

Goldhanger House

POWELL CL

The Cricketers (PH)

HALL ESTATE

CHURCH ST

Goldhanger

WASH LA

Chappel Farm

MALDON RD

HEAD ST

Sch

The Chequers (PH)

09

Rook Hall

Cobb's Farm

FISH ST

THISTLEY CL

3

Wash Bridge

B1026

Irrigation Reservoir

Sewage Works

Barrow Marsh

Bound's Farm

08

Vaulty Manor

Gardener's Farm

Caravan Park

134

GOLDHANGER RD

Caravan Parks

2

Mill Beach

OSEA RD

Sewage Works

Collier's Reach

Hilly Pool Point

07

Decoy Point

Causeway

West Point

River Blackwater

1

Northey Island

88   D   89   E   90   F   06

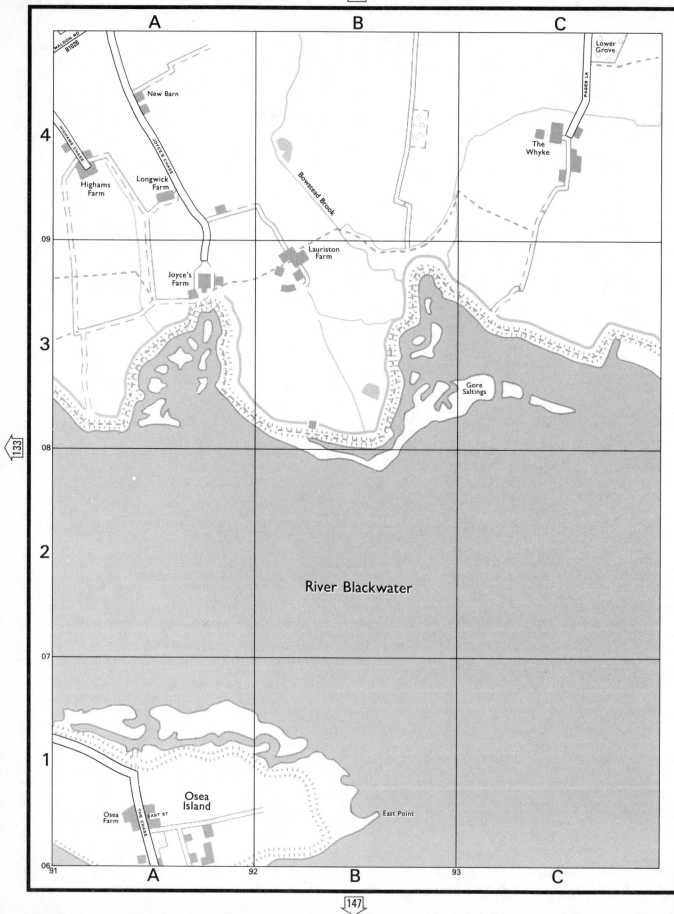

A B C

MALDON RD
B1026

New Barn

HIGHAMS CHASE

JOYCE'S CHASE

Highams
Farm

Longwick
Farm

Bowstead Brook

PAGES LA

Lower
Grove

The
Whyke

4

09

Lauriston
Farm

Joyce's
Farm

3

Gore
Saltings

08

2

River Blackwater

07

1

Osea Island

Osea
Farm

THE CHASE

EAST ST

East Point

06
91 92 93

A B C

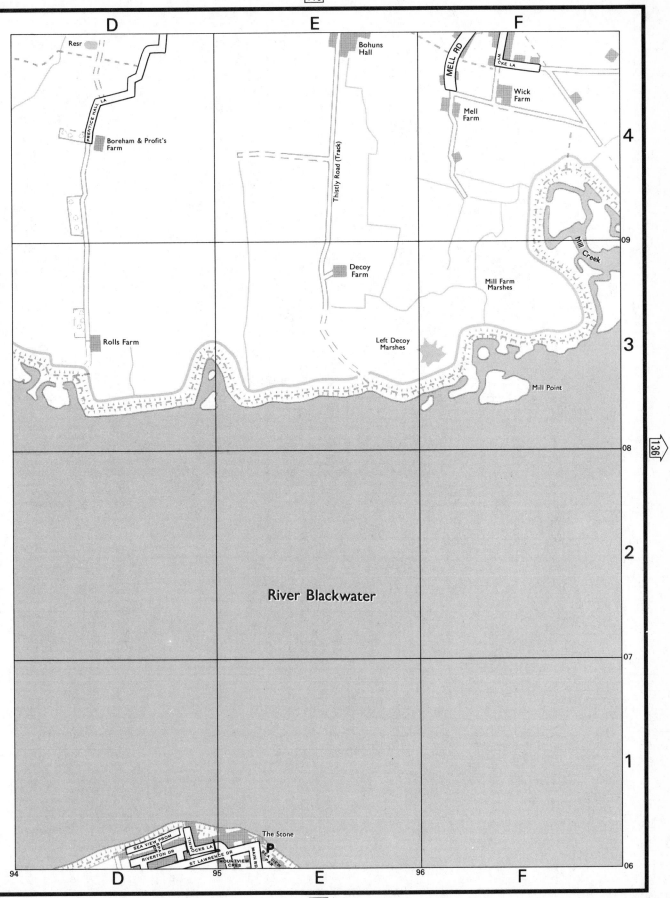

D   E   F

Resr

PRENTICE HALL LA

Boreham & Profit's
Farm

Bohuns
Hall

MELL RD

CKE LA

Wick
Farm

Mell
Farm

4

Thistly Road (Track)

09

Decoy
Farm

Mill Farm
Marshes

Mill Creek

136

Rolls Farm

Left Decoy
Marshes

Mill Point

3

08

2

River Blackwater

07

1

SEA VIEW PROM

RIVERTON DR

TINNOCKS LA

ST LAWRENCE DR

MOUNTVIEW
CRES

MAIN RD

SEA VIEW

The Stone

P

06

94   D   95   E   96   F

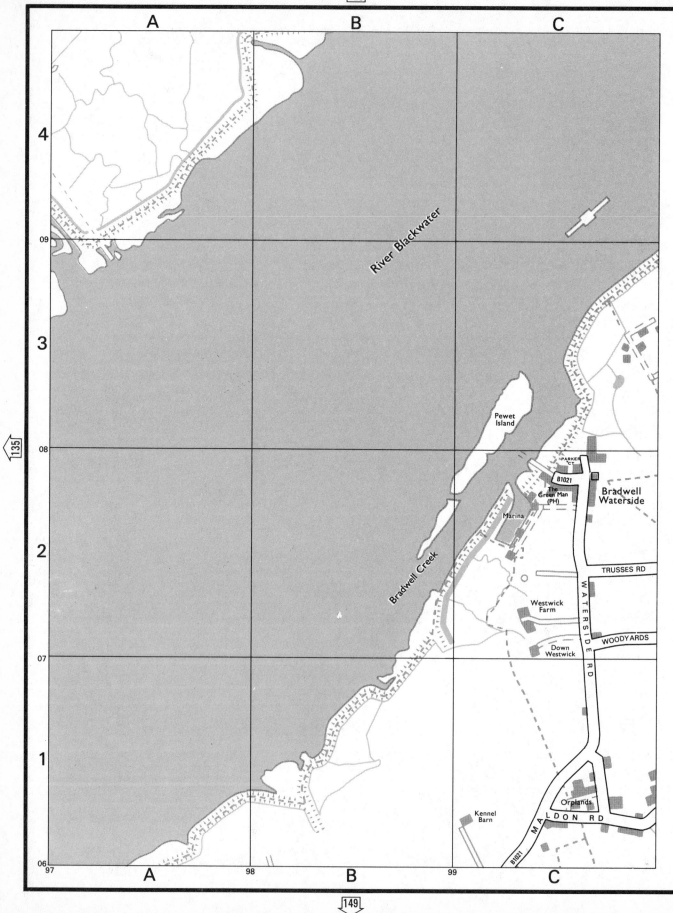

A
B
C

4

River Blackwater

09

3

Pewet
Island

135

08

PARKER
CT

B1021

The
Green Man
(PH)

Bradwell
Waterside

Marina

2

TRUSSES RD

Bradwell Creek

Westwick
Farm

W
A
T
E
R
S
I
D
E

R
D

WOODYARDS

07

Down
Westwick

1

Orplands

Kennel
Barn

M
A
L
D
O
N

R
D

B1021

06
97

A

98

B

99

C

138

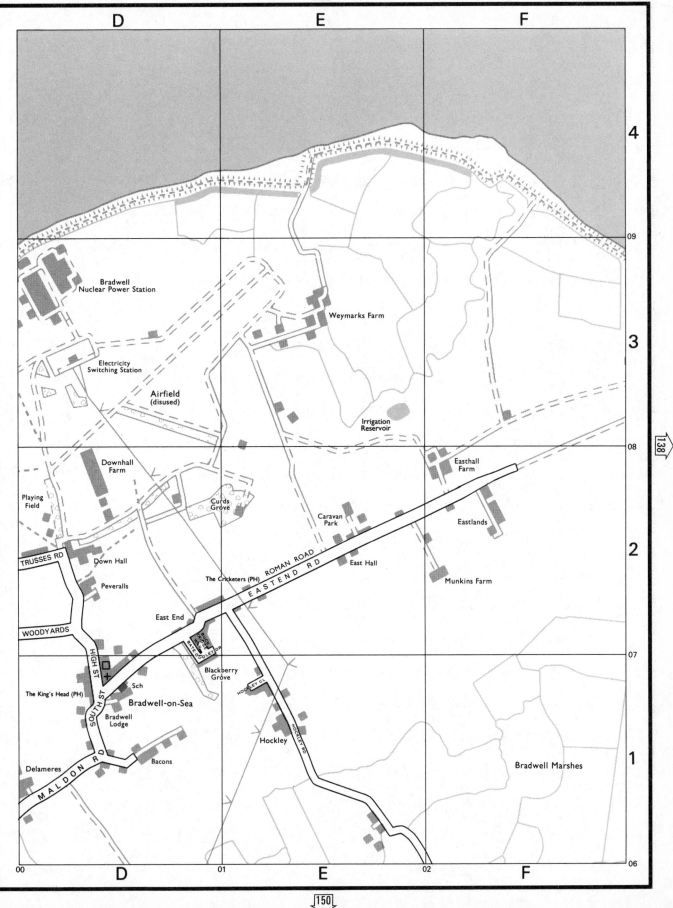

D   E   F

Bradwell
Nuclear Power Station

Weymarks Farm

Electricity
Switching Station

Airfield
(disused)

Irrigation
Reservoir

Downhall
Farm

Easthall
Farm

Playing
Field

Curds
Grove

Caravan
Park

Eastlands

TRUSSES RD

Down Hall

ROMAN ROAD

Munkins Farm

Peveralls

The Cricketers (PH)

East Hall

EASTEND RD

East End

WOODYARDS

HIGH ST

Blackberry
Grove

SOUTH ST

Sch

BATE DUDLEY DR

HOCKLEY CL

The King's Head (PH)

Bradwell-on-Sea

Bradwell
Lodge

HOCKLEY RD

Hockley

MALDON RD

Delameres

Bacons

Bradwell Marshes

4

3

2

1

00   D   01   E   02   F

09

08

07

06

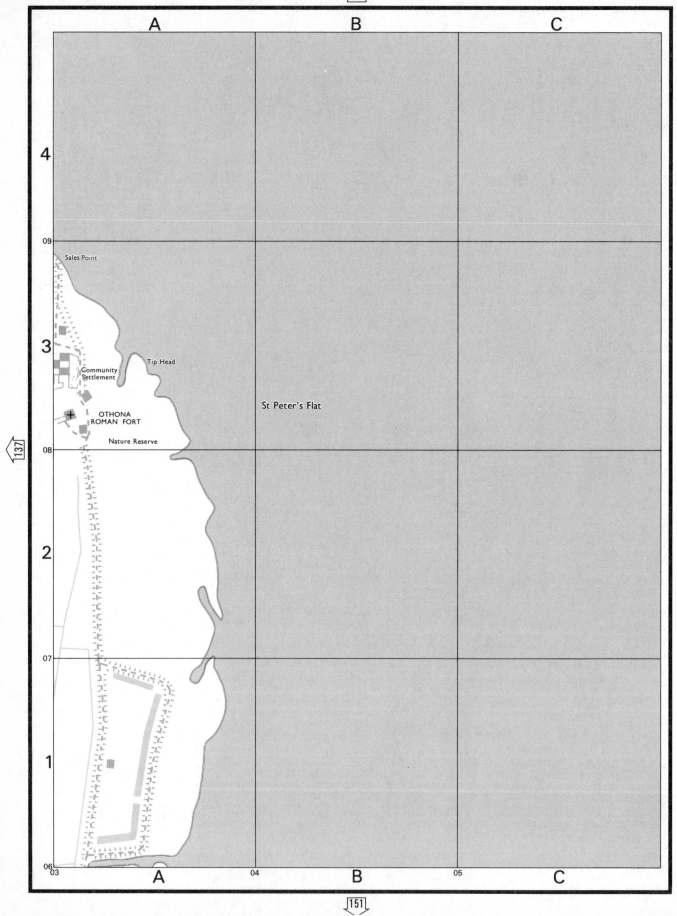

Sales Point

Tip Head

Community
Settlement

OTHONA
ROMAN FORT

Nature Reserve

St Peter's Flat

A

B

C

4

3

2

1

09

08

07

06

03

04

05

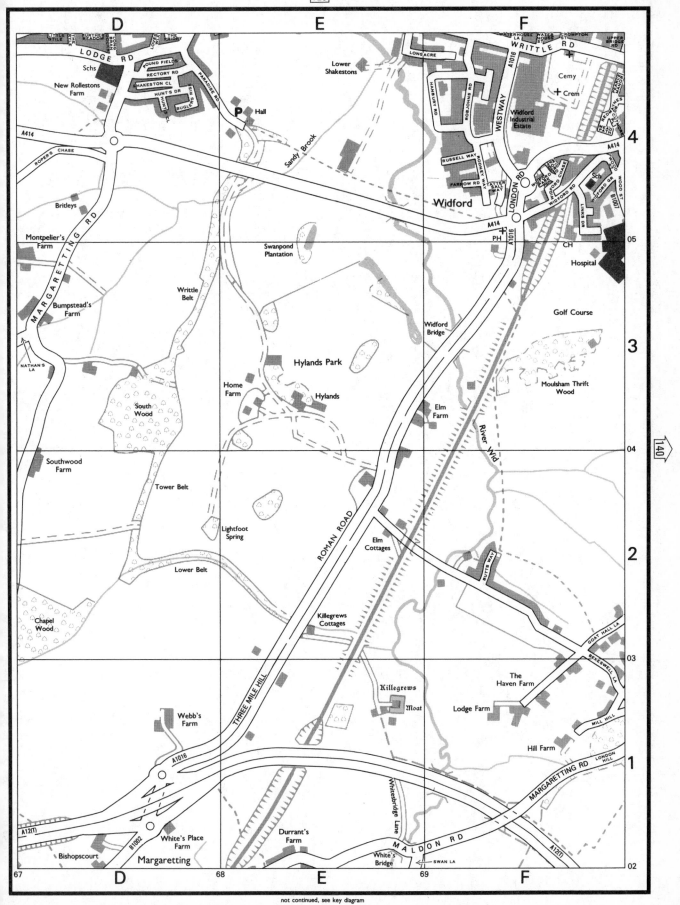

not continued, see key diagram

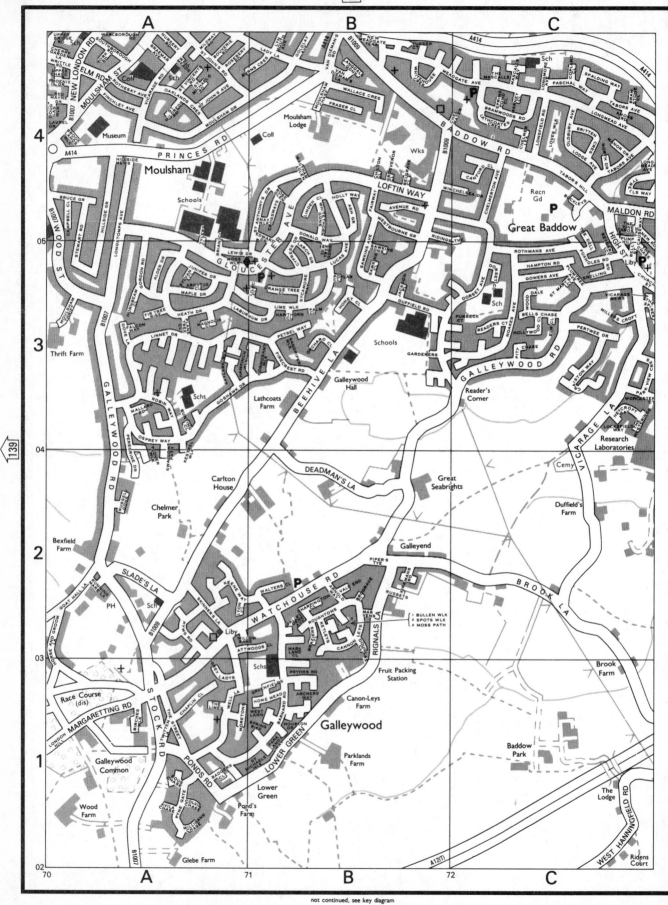

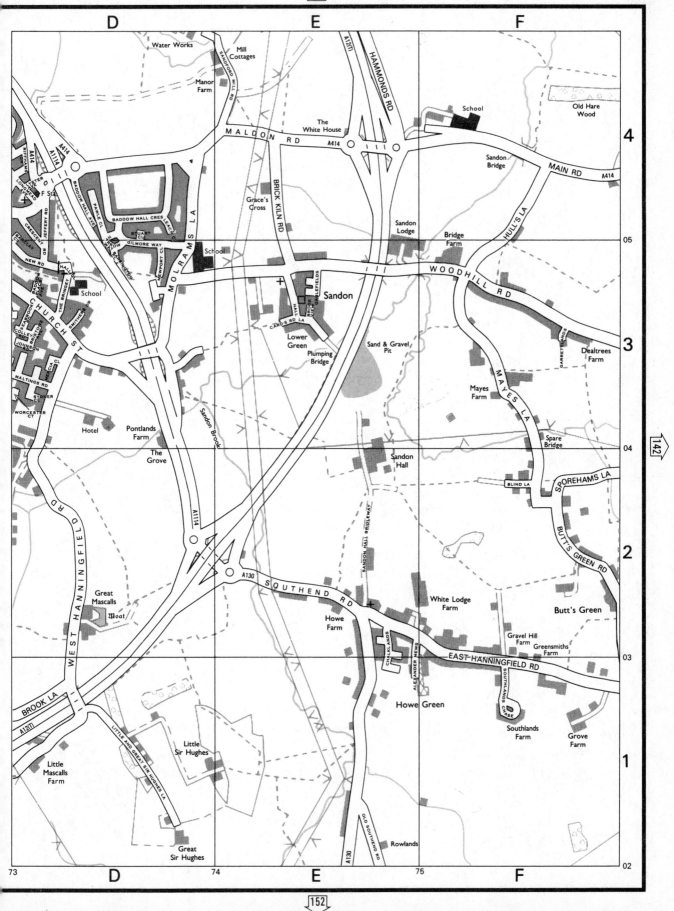

128

142

152

D E F

4

05

3

04

2

03

1

02

73 74 75

Water Works
Mill Cottages
Manor Farm
SANDFORD MILL RD
The White House
A12(T)
HAMMONDS RD
School
Old Hare Wood
M A L D O N R D
A414
Sandon Bridge
MAIN RD A414
A414
LESTER
RIFFHAMS
LONGMEAD
A1114
A414
F Sta
BADDOW HALL AVE
PANKLE CL
STUART CL
LEACH CL
BADDOW HALL CRES
Grace's Cross
BRICK KILN RD
Sandon Lodge
Bridge Farm
HULL'S LA
M O L R A M S L A
JEFFERY RD
CRESCENT
BARCLAY RD
NEW RD
GILMORE WAY
NEWPORT CL
BENNINGTON
School
Sandon
WOODHILL RD
HALL
THE BRINGEY
School
CHURCH ST
CARD'S RD LA
BROOK HALL
GABLEFIELDS
BROOK VIEW
Lower Green
Plumping Bridge
Sand & Gravel Pit
Mayes Farm
GARRETTLANDS
Dealtrees Farm
LEABROOK
COLLEY
JOHNSON
MEDGE CL
MALTINGS RD
SYDNER
WORCESTER CT
Hotel
Pontlands Farm
Sandon Brook
The Grove
A1114
M A Y E S L A
Spare Bridge
Sandon Hall
BLIND LA
SPOREHAMS LA
W E S T H A N N I N G F I E L D R D
A1114
SANDON HALL BRIDLEWAY
BUTT'S GREEN RD
Great Mascalls
Moat
A130
S O U T H E N D R D
Howe Farm
White Lodge Farm
Butt's Green
Gravel Hill Farm
Greensmiths Farm
CHALKLANDS
ALEXANDER MEWS
EAST HANNINGFIELD RD
BROOK LA
A12(T)
LITTLE AND GREAT SIR HUGHES LA
Little Sir Hughes
Howe Green
SOUTHLANDS CHASE
Southlands Farm
Grove Farm
Little Mascalls Farm
Great Sir Hughes
A130
OLD SOUTHEND RD
Rowlands

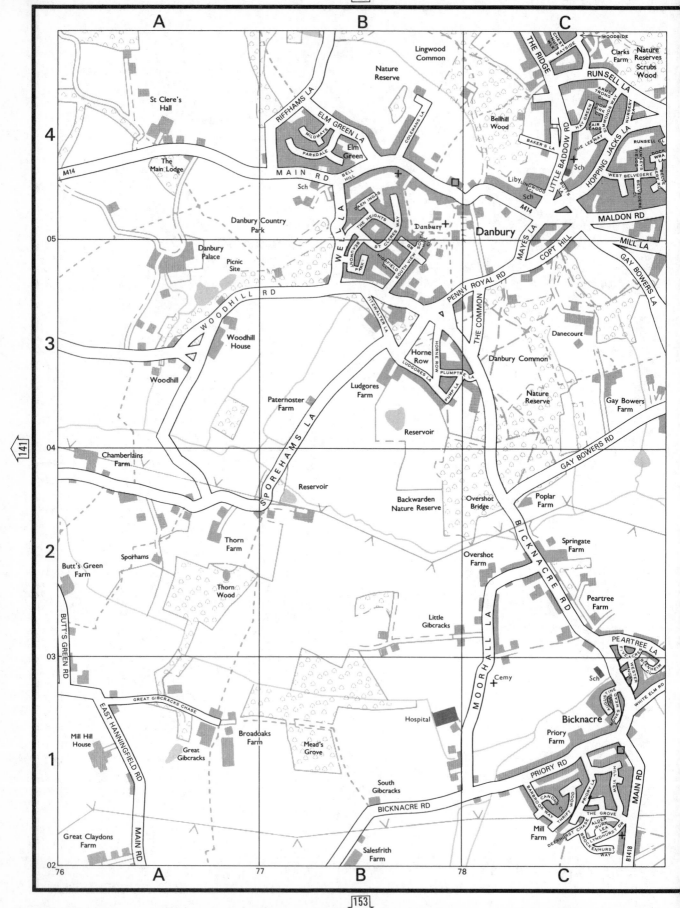

141

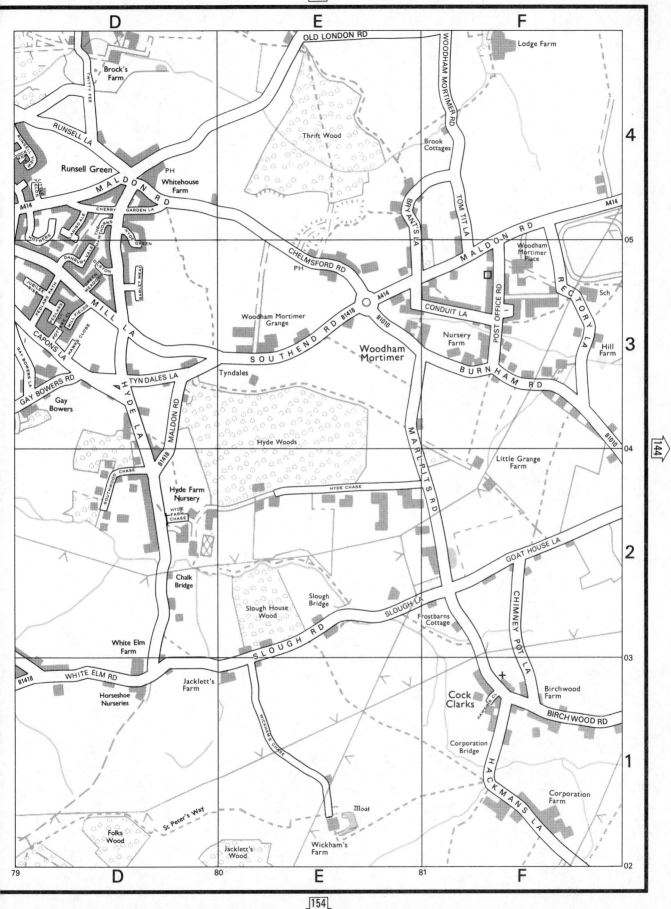

131

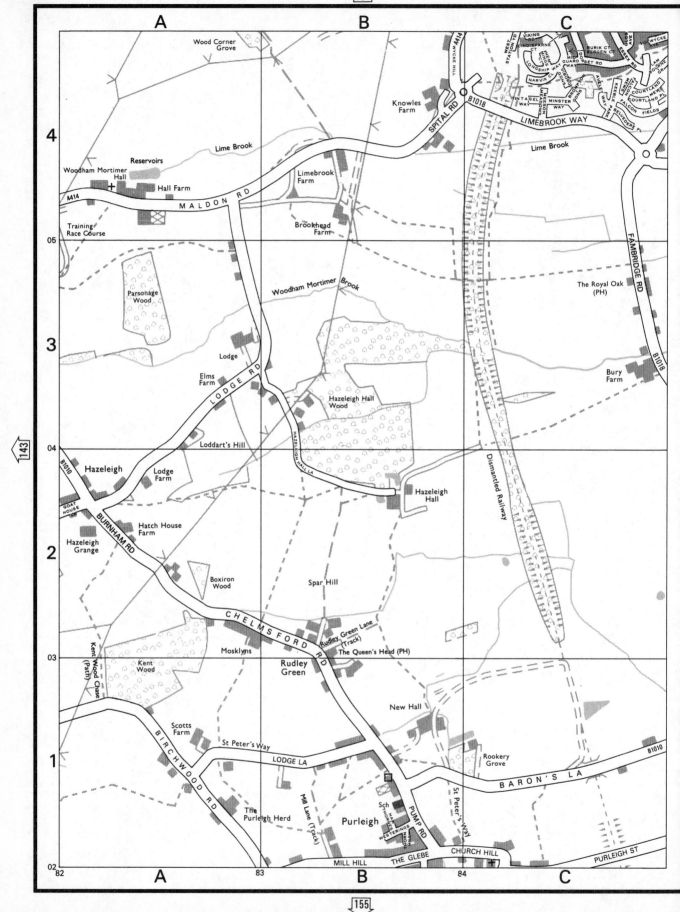

143

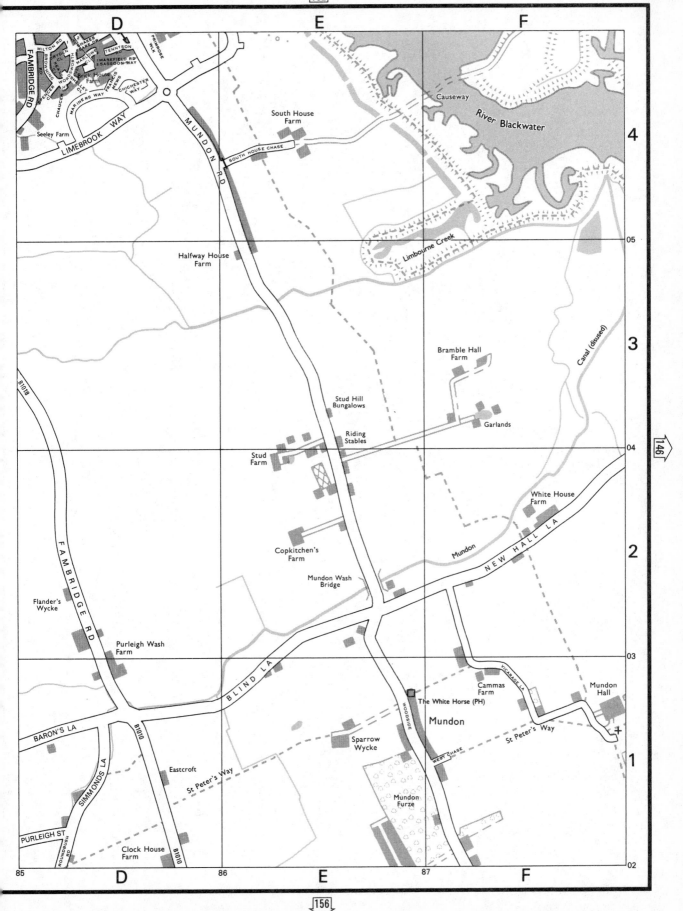

D   E   F

FAMBRIDGE RD

MILTON RD
COWPER
BROWNING
SPENCER CL
CHAUCER CL
WORDSWORTH
SHAKESPEARE DR
TENNYSON
MARLOWE
MASEFIELD RD
SASSOON WAY
FRANCIS MEWS
CHICHESTER WAY
MARINERS WAY
PRIMROSE WALK

Brick House Farm

Seeley Farm

LIMEBROOK WAY

MUNDON RD

South House Farm

SOUTH HOUSE CHASE

Causeway

River Blackwater

4

Halfway House Farm

Limbourne Creek

05

Bramble Hall Farm

Canal (disused)

3

B1018

Stud Hill Bungalows

Garlands

Riding Stables

146

Stud Farm

04

White House Farm

FAMBRIDGE RD

Copkitchen's Farm

Mundon

NEW HALL LA

2

Flander's Wycke

Mundon Wash Bridge

Purleigh Wash Farm

03

BLIND LA

Cammas Farm

VICARAGE LA

Mundon Hall

BARON'S LA

B1010

The White Horse (PH)

WOODSIDE

Mundon

St Peter's Way

+

1

SIMMONDS LA

Eastcroft

St Peter's Way

Sparrow Wycke

WEST CHASE

ROUNGBRUSH RD

PURLEIGH ST

Mundon Furze

B1010

Clock House Farm

02

85   D   86   E   87   F

133

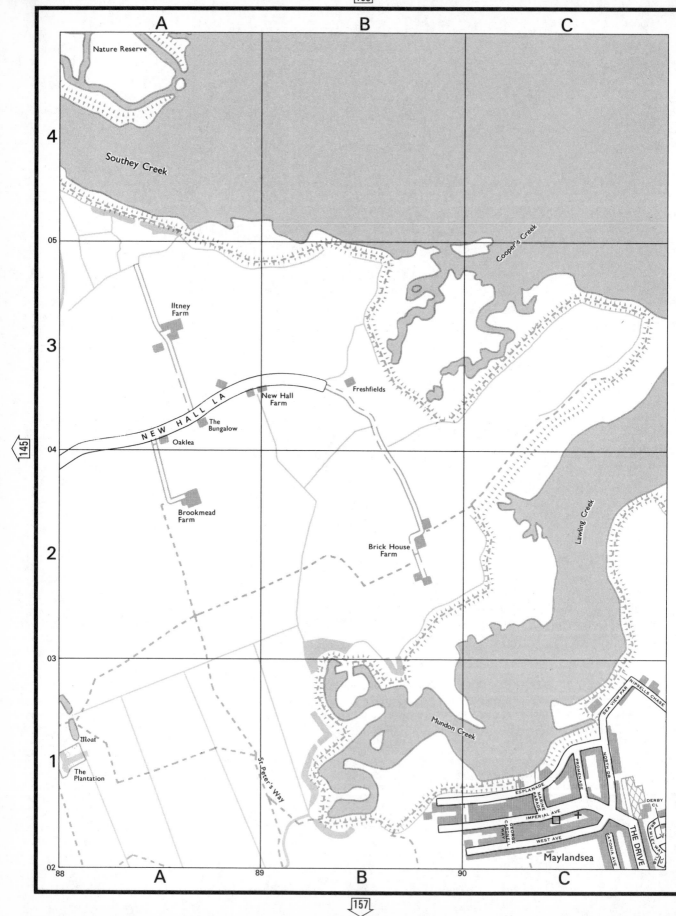

A   B   C

Nature Reserve

4

Southey Creek

Cooper's Creek

05

Iltney Farm

3

Freshfields

New Hall Farm

NEW HALL LA

The Bungalow

04

Oaklea

Lawling Creek

Brookmead Farm

2

Brick House Farm

03

Mundon Creek

Moat

1

The Plantation

St. Peter's Way

SEA VIEW PAR

NIPSELLS CHASE

PROMENADE

NORTH DR

DERBY CL

ESPLANADE

MARINE PARADE

IMPERIAL AVE

WEST AVE

GEORGE WAY

COCKRELL WAY

CATONIA AVE

THE DRIVE

Maylandsea

02
88   A   89   B   90   C

145

157

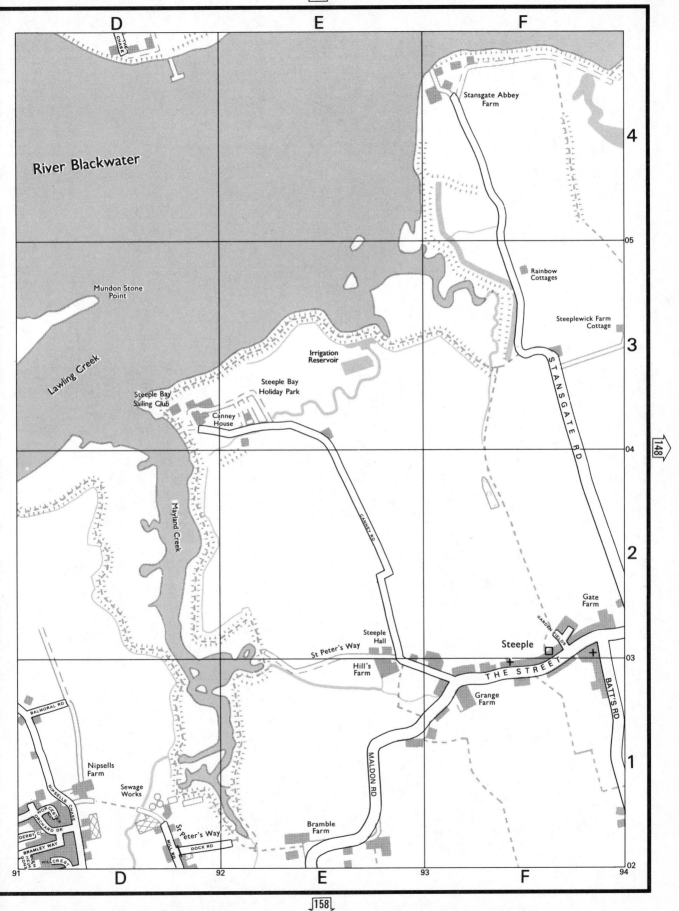

D E F

River Blackwater

Mundon Stone
Point

Lawling Creek

Stansgate Abbey
Farm

4

05

Rainbow
Cottages

Steeplewick Farm
Cottage

3

Irrigation
Reservoir

Steeple Bay
Holiday Park

Steeple Bay
Sailing Club

Canney
House

STANSGATE RD

04

Mayland Creek

CANNEY RD

2

Gate
Farm

GARDEN FIELDS

Steeple

Steeple
Hall

St Peter's Way

Hill's
Farm

THE STREET

03

BATT'S RD

Grange
Farm

Nipsells
Farm

BALMORAL RD

NIPSELLS CHASE

WORCESTER
ORCHARD DR

DERBY CL

BRAMLEY WAY

HILL CREST

HERON POND

Sewage
Works

St Peter's Way

MILL RD

DOCK RD

MALDON RD

Bramble
Farm

1

02

91 D 92 E 93 F 94

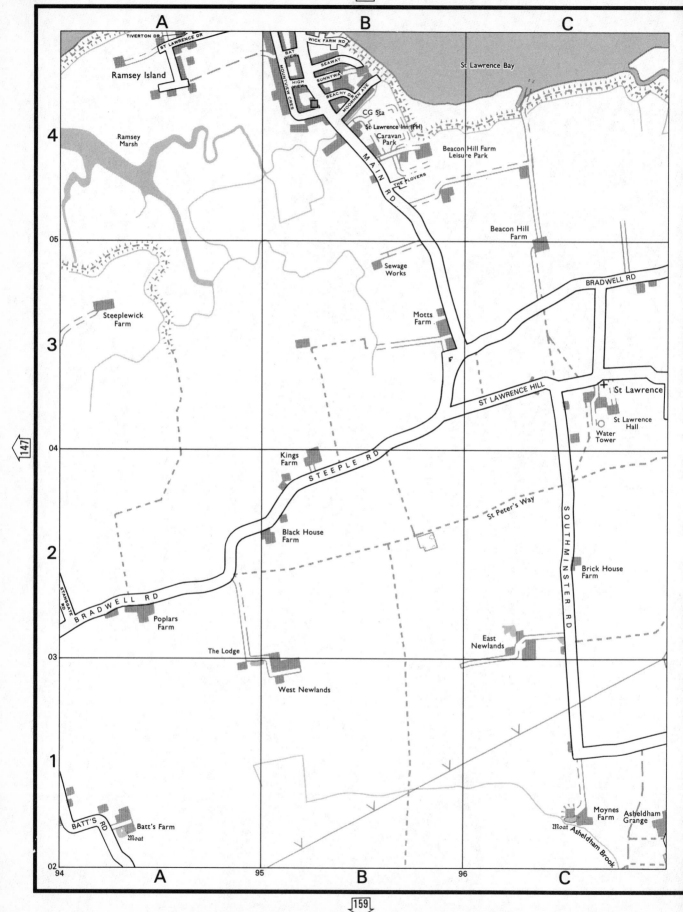

A

B

C

TIVERTON DR

ST LAWRENCE DR

Ramsey Island

BAT VIEW

WICK FARM RD

SEAWAY

St Lawrence Bay

HIGH VIEW

MOUNTVIEW CRES

SUNNYWAY

BEACHY DR

REN AVE

MOORHEN RD

CG Sta

4

Ramsey Marsh

St Lawrence Inn (PH)

Caravan Park

Beacon Hill Farm Leisure Park

MAIN RD

THE PLOVERS

Beacon Hill Farm

05

BRADWELL RD

Sewage Works

Steeplewick Farm

Motts Farm

3

St Lawrence Hill

St Lawrence

St Lawrence Hall

Water Tower

04

Kings Farm

STEEPLE RD

St Peter's Way

SOUTHMINSTER RD

Black House Farm

Brick House Farm

2

STANGATE RD

BRADWELL RD

Poplars Farm

East Newlands

The Lodge

03

West Newlands

1

BATT'S RD

Batt's Farm

Moat

Moynes Farm

Asheldham Grange

Moat Asheldham Brook

02

94

A

95

B

96

C

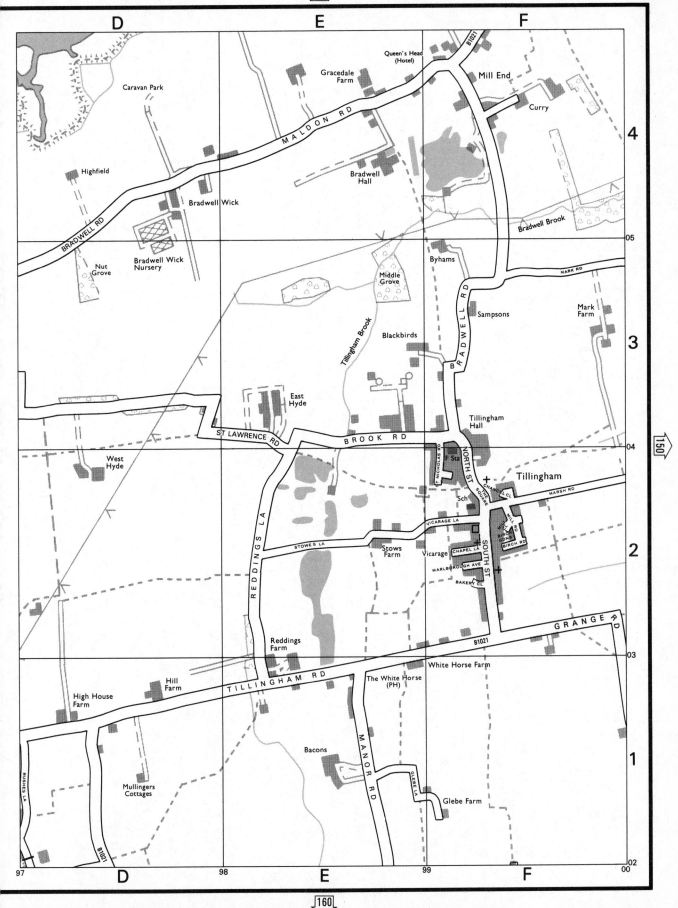

D

E

F

Caravan Park

Highfield

MALDON RD

Gracedale Farm

Queen's Head (Hotel)

Mill End

Curry

Bradwell Wick

Bradwell Hall

4

BRADWELL RD

Bradwell Brook

05

Nut Grove

Bradwell Wick Nursery

Byhams

MARK RD

Middle Grove

Sampsons

Mark Farm

Tillingham Brook

Blackbirds

BRADWELL RD

3

East Hyde

Tillingham Hall

West Hyde

ST LAWRENCE RD

BROOK RD

04

150

ST NICHOLAS RD

F Sta

NORTH ST

Tillingham

CHANCEL CL

MARSH RD

Sch

THE SQUARE

REDDINGS LA

MILL RD

BIRCH GDNS

BIRCH RD

STOWES LA

Stows Farm

VICARAGE LA

Vicarage

CHAPEL LA

SOUTH ST

2

MARLBOROUGH AVE

BAKERY CL

Reddings Farm

GRANGE RD

03

B1021

Hill Farm

TILLINGHAM RD

White Horse Farm

High House Farm

The White Horse (PH)

RUSHES LA

Bacons

MANOR RD

1

Mullingers Cottages

GLEBE LA

Glebe Farm

B1021

02

97

D

98

E

99

F

00

137

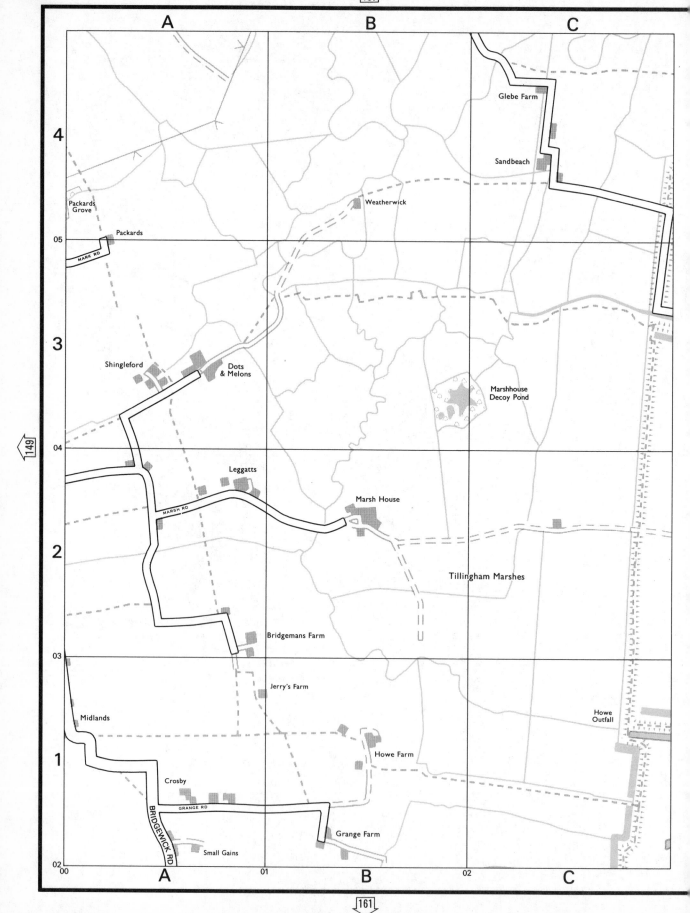

149

161

Packards
Grove

Packards

MARK RD

Weatherwick

Glebe Farm

Sandbeach

Shingleford

Dots
& Melons

Marshhouse
Decoy Pond

Leggatts

MARSH RD

Marsh House

Tillingham Marshes

Bridgemans Farm

Jerry's Farm

Midlands

Howe
Outfall

Howe Farm

Crosby

GRANGE RD

BRIDGEWICK RD

Small Gains

Grange Farm

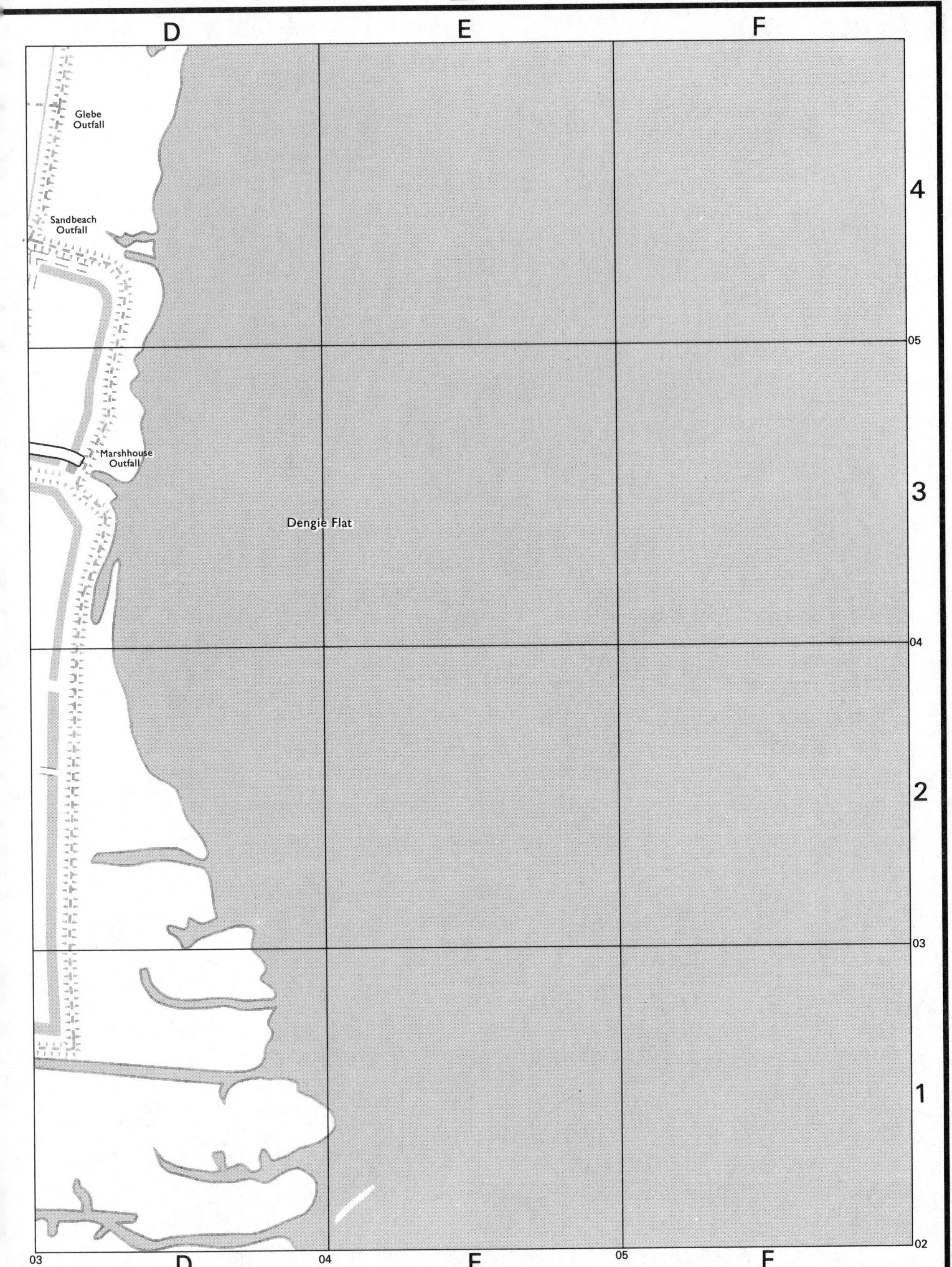

D

E

F

Glebe
Outfall

Sandbeach
Outfall

4

05

Marshhouse
Outfall

3

Dengie Flat

04

2

03

1

02

03

D

04

E

05

F

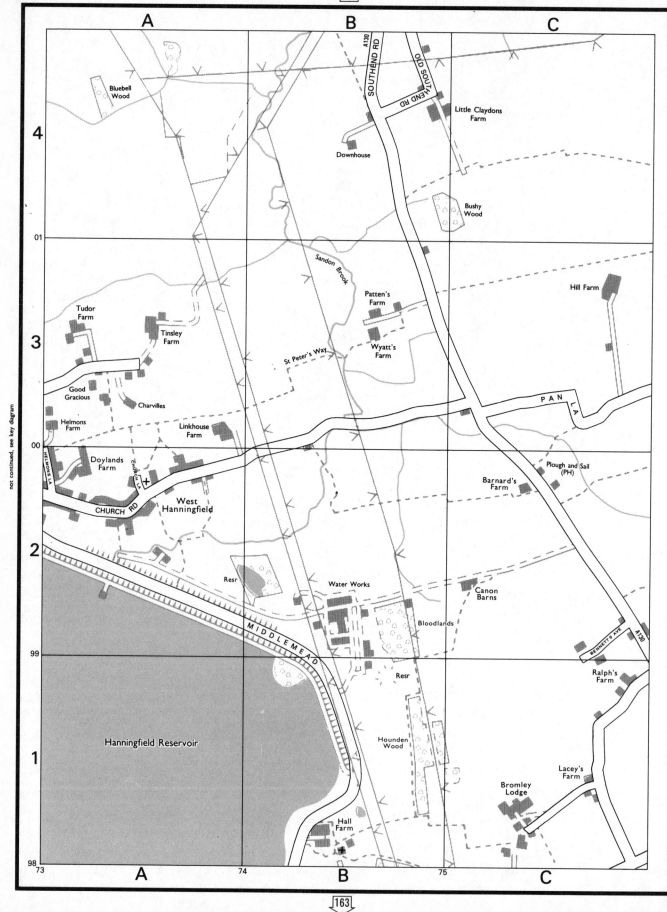

A   B   C

Bluebell Wood

Little Claydons Farm

SOUTHEND RD

OLD SOUTH RD

Downhouse

4

Bushy Wood

Sandon Brook

Patten's Farm

Hill Farm

Tudor Farm

Tinsley Farm

3

Wyatt's Farm

St Peter's Way

PAN LA

Good Gracious

Charvilles

Helmons Farm

Linkhouse Farm

Plough and Sail (PH)

00

Doylands Farm

Barnard's Farm

HELMONS LA

CHURCH LA

West Hanningfield

CHURCH RD

2

Resr

Water Works

Canon Barns

Bloodlands

BENNETT'S AVE

A130

99

Resr

Ralph's Farm

Hounden Wood

Hanningfield Reservoir

MIDDLEMEAD

1

Lacey's Farm

Bromley Lodge

98

Hall Farm

73   A   74   B   75   C

not continued, see key diagram

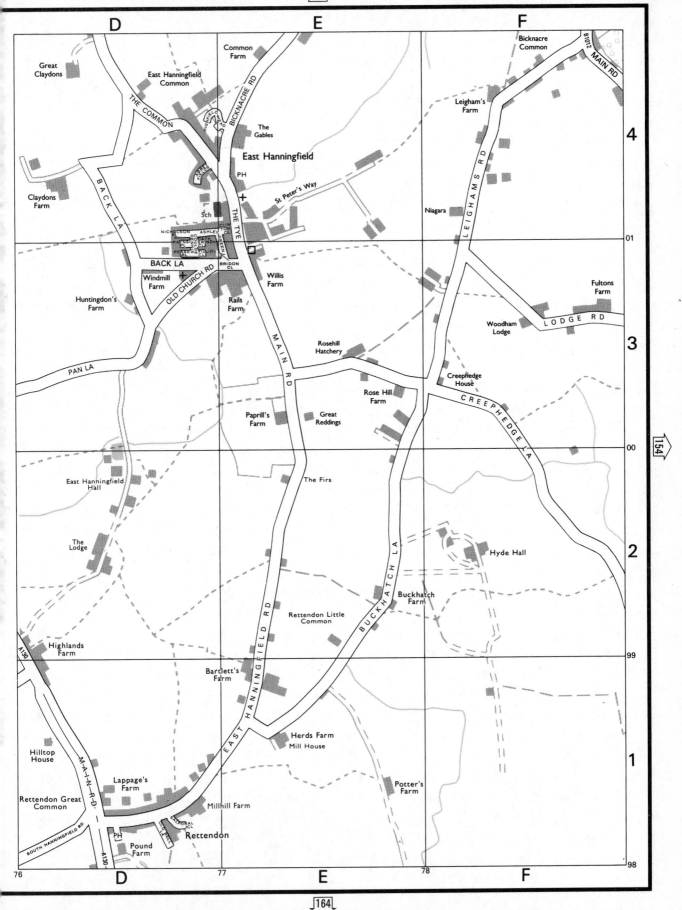

D

E

F

4

Great
Claydons

East Hanningfield
Common

Common
Farm

BICKNACRE RD

Bicknacre
Common

B1012

MAIN RD

THE COMMON

HIGHFIELD HEAD

The
Gables

Leigham's
Farm

East Hanningfield

BACK LA

Claydons
Farm

PYMER

PH

St Peter's Way

Niagara

LEIGHAMS RD

01

Sch

THE TYE

NICHOLSON ASHLEY

BACK LA

BRIDON CL

Willis
Farm

Fultons
Farm

Windmill
Farm

OLD CHURCH RD

Huntingdon's
Farm

Rails
Farm

Woodham
Lodge

LODGE RD

3

PAN LA

MAIN RD

Rosehill
Hatchery

Creephedge
House

CREEPHEDGE LA

Paprill's
Farm

Great
Reddings

Rose Hill
Farm

00

East Hanningfield
Hall

The Firs

The
Lodge

Hyde Hall

2

BUCKHATCH LA

Buckhatch
Farm

EAST HANNINGFIELD RD

Rettendon Little
Common

A130

Highlands
Farm

99

Bartlett's
Farm

Hilltop
House

MAIN RD

Herds Farm
Mill House

1

Lappage's
Farm

Potter's
Farm

Rettendon Great
Common

Millhill Farm

SOUTH HANNINGFIELD RD

A130

PH

Pound
Farm

Rettendon

98

76

D

77

E

78

F

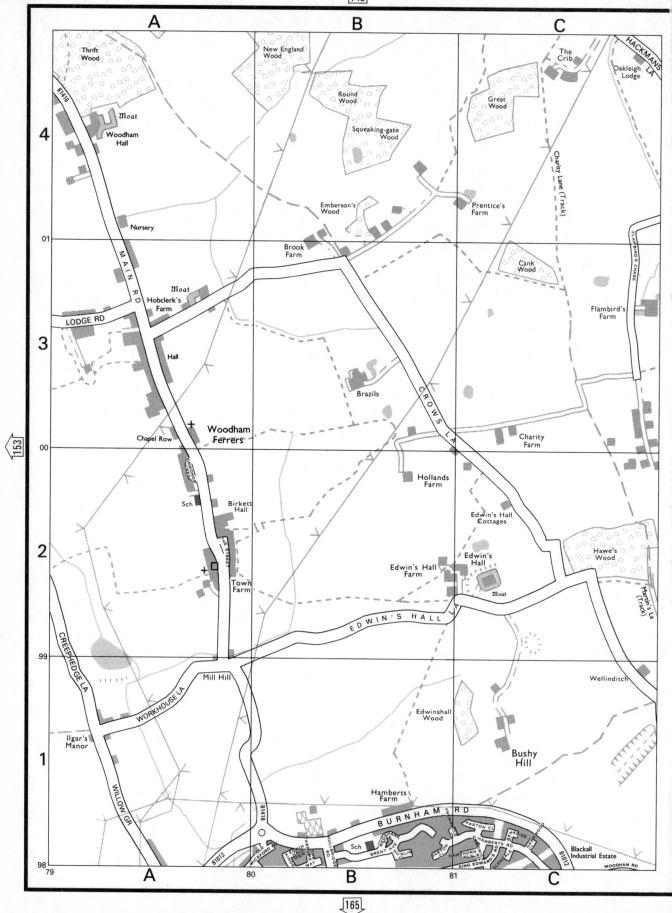

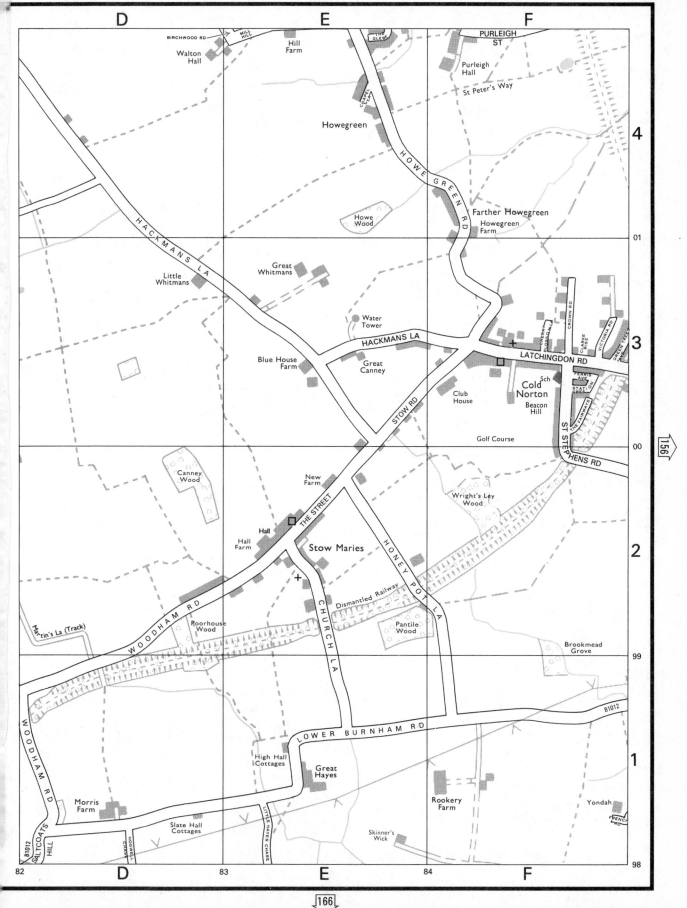

D E F

BIRCHWOOD RD
MILL HILL
Walton Hall
Hill Farm
THE GLEBE
PURLEIGH ST

CHAPEL LA
Purleigh Hall
St Peter's Way

Howegreen

4

HOWE GREEN RD
Farther Howegreen
Howegreen Farm

Howe Wood

01

Great Whitmans
Little Whitmans

HACKMANS LA
CROWN RD
CHERRY BLOSSOM LA
CLARKE RISE
VICTORIA RD
GREEN TREES

Water Tower
HACKMANS LA
LATCHINGDON RD

3

Blue House Farm
Great Canney

Sch
Cold Norton
Beacon Hill
FERRIS AVE
STATION GREE
THE FAIRWAYS

STOW RD
Club House
Golf Course

ST STEPHENS RD

00

156

Canney Wood
New Farm

Wright's Ley Wood

THE STREET
Hall
Hall Farm
Stow Maries

HONEY POT LA

2

Martin's La (Track)
Poorhouse Wood
Dismantled Railway
Pantile Wood

CHURCH LA

Brookmead Grove

99

WOODHAM RD

B1012

LOWER BURNHAM RD

High Hall Cottages
Great Hayes

Rookery Farm

Yondah

1

WOODHAM RD
Morris Farm
Slate Hall Cottages
Skinner's Wick
LITTLE HAYES CHASE
HOWELL CHASE
SALTCOATS
HILL
B1012
FRENCH RD

82 D 83 E 84 F 98

145

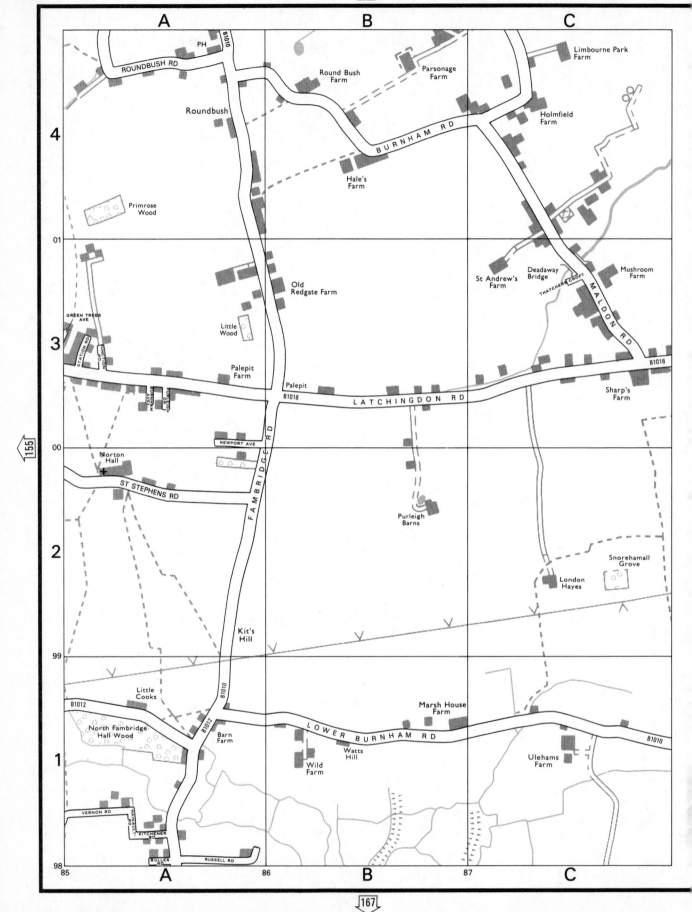

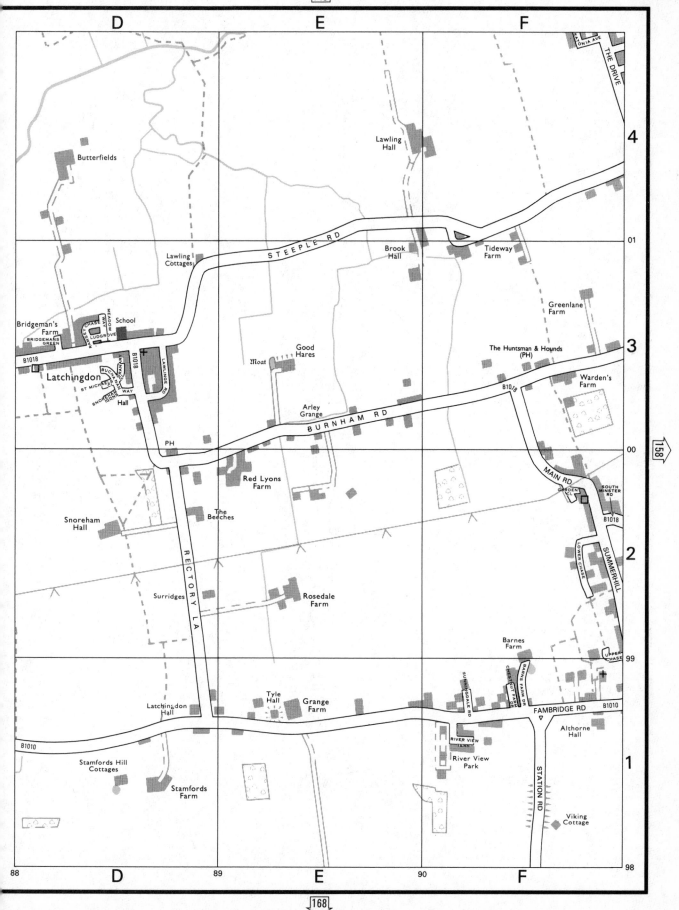

D E F

4

01

3

00

2

99

1

98

D E F

88 89 90

158

Butterfields

Lawling Hall

Lawling Cottages

STEEPLE RD

Brook Hall

Tideway Farm

Greenlane Farm

Bridgeman's Farm

School

MEADOW WAY

CHASE

LUDGROVE

BRIDGEMAN'S GREEN

B1018

Latchingdon

ST MICHAEL'S CL

SNOREHAM GDNS

Hall

BUCKINGHAM WAY

LAWLING RD

B1018

Moat

Good Hares

The Huntsman & Hounds (PH)

B1018

Warden's Farm

PH

Arley Grange

BURNHAM RD

Red Lyons Farm

MAIN RD

GARDEN CL

SOUTH MINSTER RD

B1018

Snoreham Hall

The Beeches

RECTORY LA

LOWER CHASE

SUMMERHILL

Surridges

Rosedale Farm

Barnes Farm

UPPER CHASE

Latchingdon Hall

Tyle Hall

Grange Farm

SUNNINGDALE RD

BARNS FARM DR

CHESTNUT FARM

FAMBRIDGE RD

B1010

Althorne Hall

B1010

Stamfords Hill Cottages

Stamfords Farm

RIVER VIEW TERR

River View Park

STATION RD

Viking Cottage

KATONIA AVE

THE DRIVE

147

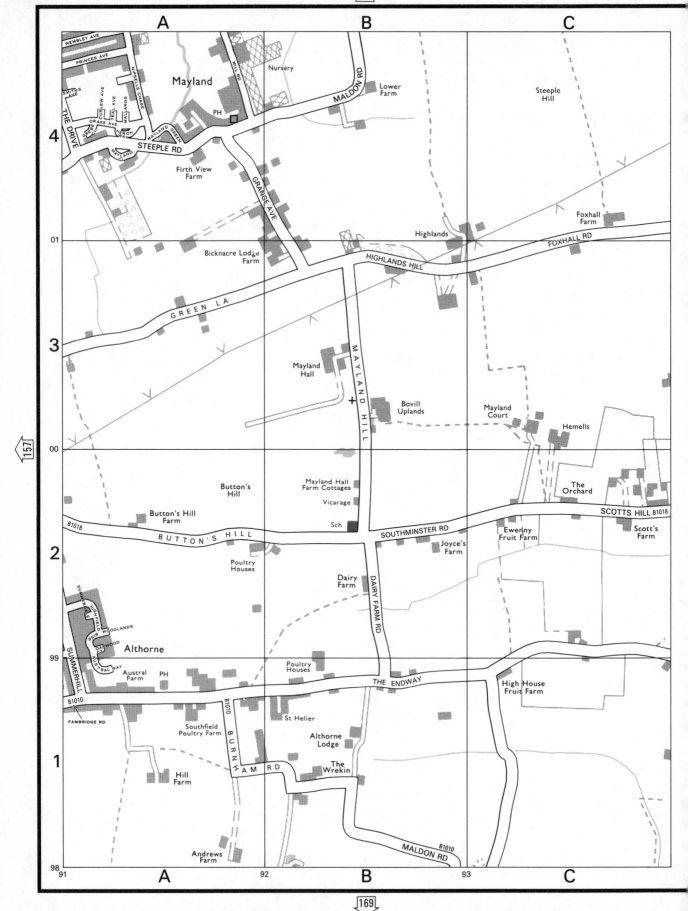

A   B   C

157
169

WEMBLEY AVE
PRINCES AVE
NIPSELLS CHASE
SMITHS AVE
CURLEW AVE
GREBE
DRAKE AVE
TEAL AVE
MALLARDS
HERON
WAY
MAYLAND
THE DRIVE
Mayland
MILL RD
Nursery
MALDON RD
Lower Farm
Steeple Hill
PH
MAYLAND GREEN
STEEPLE RD
Firth View Farm
GRANGE AVE
Highlands
Foxhall Farm
FOXHALL RD
01
Bicknacre Lodge Farm
HIGHLANDS HILL
GREEN LA
MAYLAND HILL
Mayland Hall
3
Bovill Uplands
Mayland Court
Hemells
00
Button's Hill
Mayland Hall Farm Cottages
The Orchard
Button's Hill Farm
Vicarage
SCOTTS HILL B1018
B1018
BUTTON'S HILL
Sch
SOUTHMINSTER RD
Ewenny Fruit Farm
Scott's Farm
2
Poultry Houses
Joyce's Farm
Dairy Farm
DAIRY FARM RD
SUMMERHILL
HIGHFIELD
B518 WOODLANDS
OAKWOOD
Althorne
99
Poultry Houses
High House Fruit Farm
SUMMERHILL
AUSTRAL WAY
Austral Farm
PH
THE ENDWAY
B1010
FAMBRIDGE RD
BURNHAM RD
Southfield Poultry Farm
St Helier
Althorne Lodge
1
Hill Farm
The Wrekin
Andrews Farm
MALDON RD
B1010
98
91   A   92   B   93   C

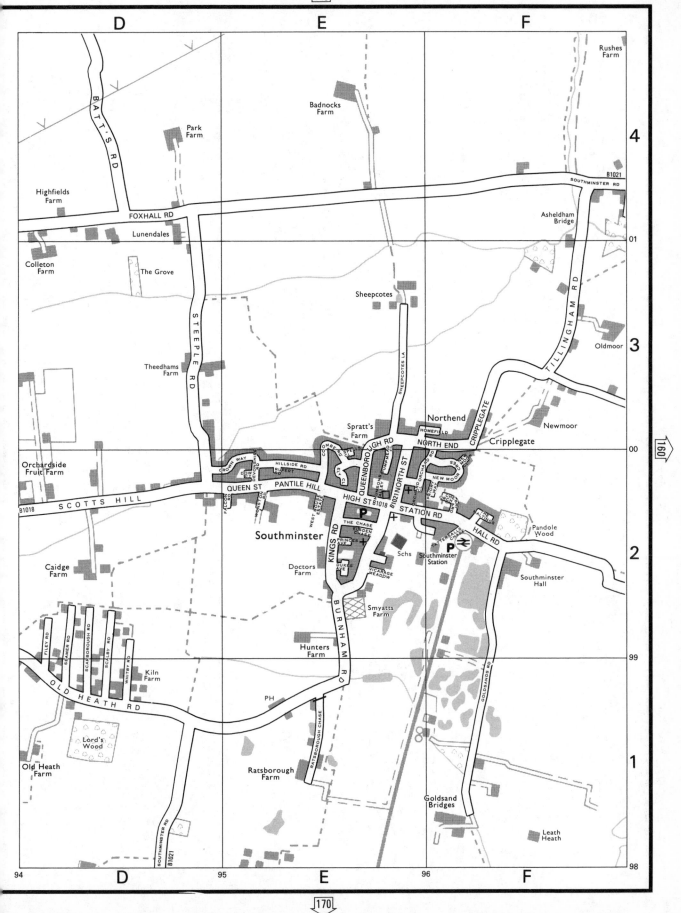

149

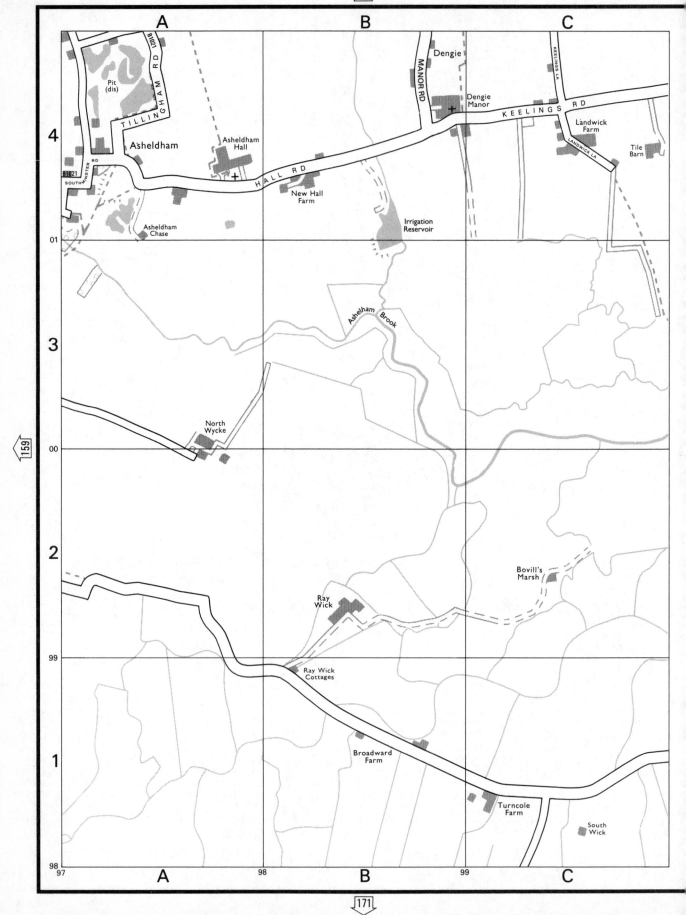

A

B

C

Dengie

MANOR RD

Dengie
Manor

KEELINGS RD

KEELINGS LA

Landwick
Farm

Tile
Barn

B1021

TILLINGHAM RD

Pit
(dis)

Asheldham

Asheldham
Hall

HALL RD

New Hall
Farm

LANDWICK LA

SOUTHMINSTER RD

B1021

Asheldham
Chase

Irrigation
Reservoir

4

01

Ashelham Brook

3

North
Wycke

00

2

Bovill's
Marsh

Ray
Wick

99

Ray Wick
Cottages

Broadward
Farm

1

Turncole
Farm

South
Wick

98

97

A

98

B

99

C

159

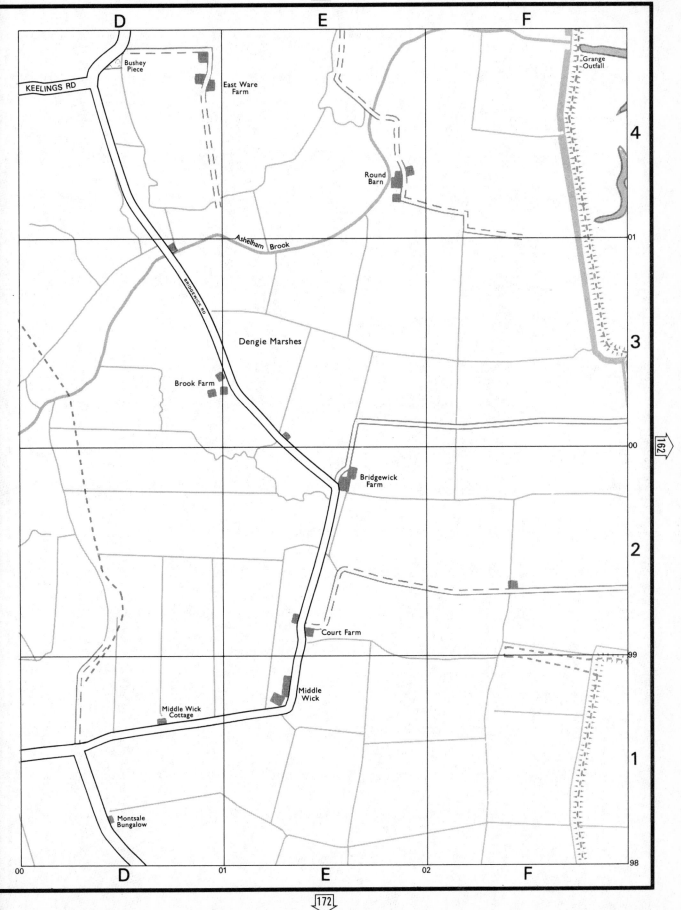

162

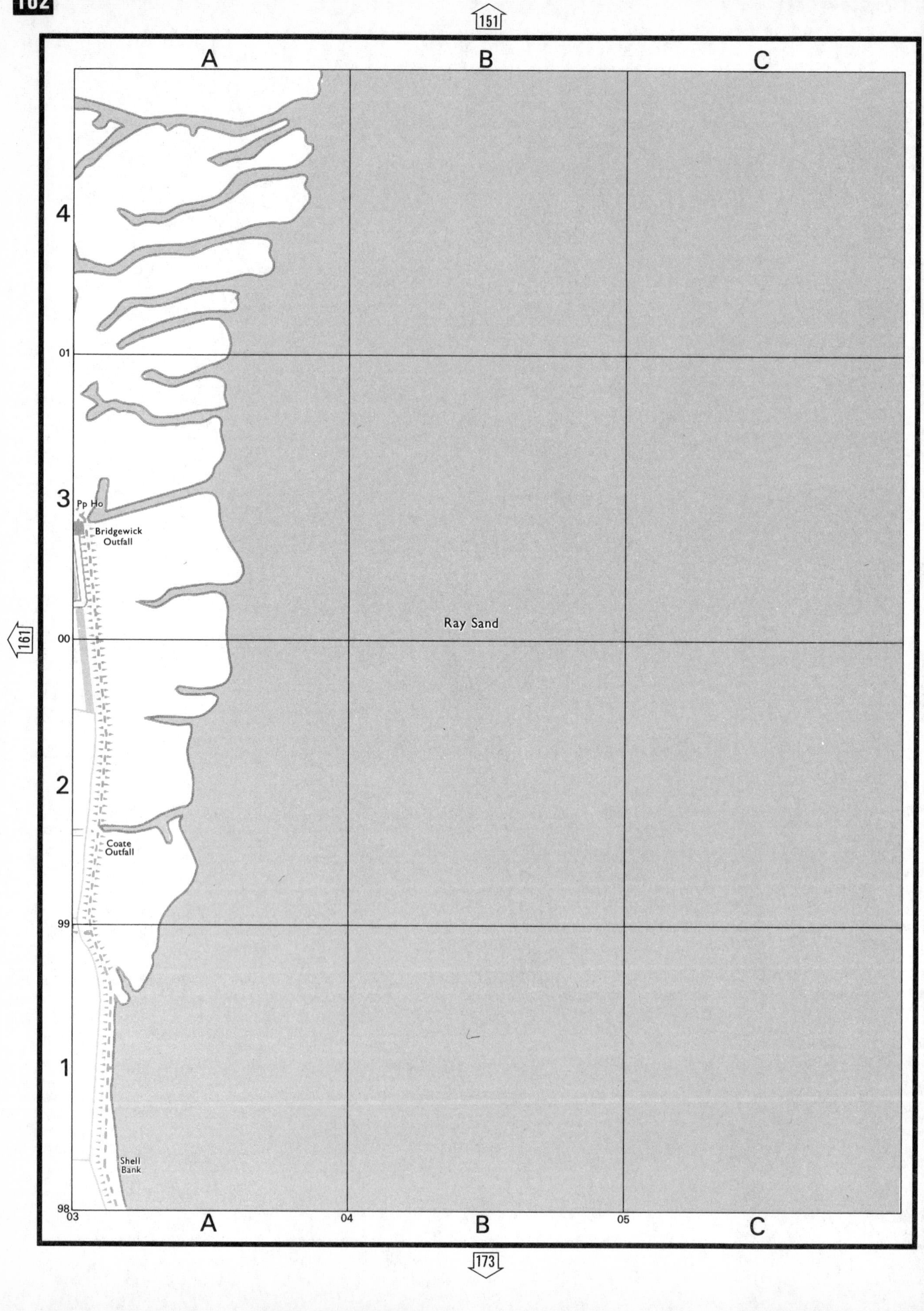

151

A   B   C

4

01

3   Pp Ho

Bridgewick
Outfall

161

00   Ray Sand

2

Coate
Outfall

99

1

Shell
Bank

98
03   A   04   B   05   C

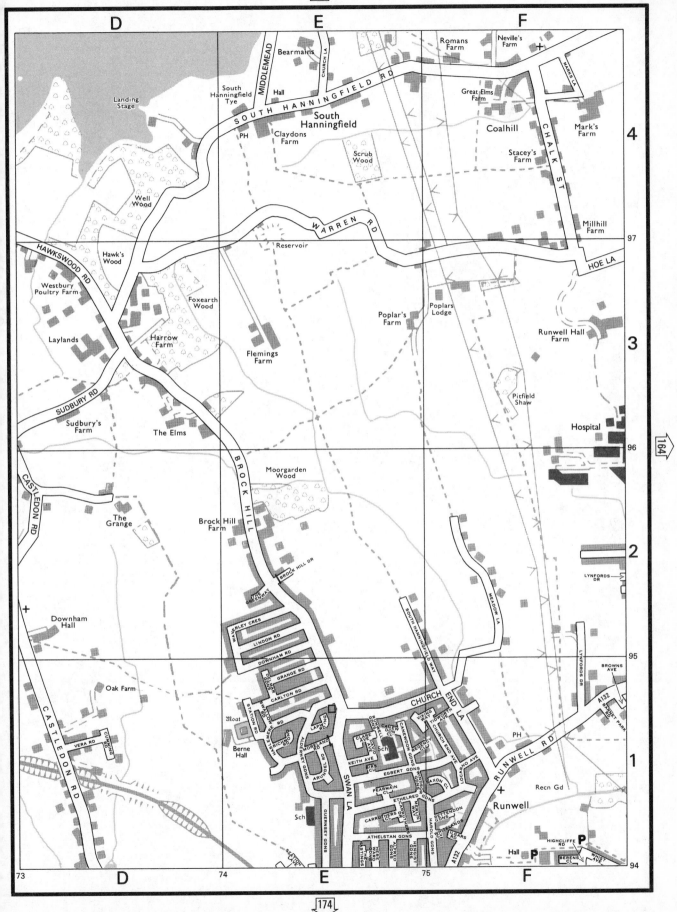

152

164

174

D | E | F

Landing Stage

Bearmans

South Hanningfield Tye

Hall

MIDDLEMEAD

CHURCH LA

SOUTH HANNINGFIELD RD

Romans Farm

Neville's Farm

Great Elms Farm

MARKS LA

South Hanningfield

PH

Claydons Farm

Scrub Wood

Coalhill

Mark's Farm

Stacey's Farm

CHALK ST

4

Well Wood

WARREN RD

Millhill Farm

Reservoir

97

HOE LA

HAWKSWOOD RD

Hawk's Wood

Westbury Poultry Farm

Foxearth Wood

Poplar's Farm

Poplars Lodge

Runwell Hall Farm

Laylands

Harrow Farm

Flemings Farm

3

Pitfield Shaw

SUDBURY RD

Sudbury's Farm

The Elms

Hospital

96

CASTLEDON RD

The Grange

Moorgarden Wood

BROCK HILL

Brock Hill Farm

LYNFORDS DR

2

BROCK HILL DR

MEADOW LA

Downham Hall

THE GREEN WAY

WAVERLEY CRES

LINDON RD

BROWNS AVE

95

Oak Farm

DOWNHAM RD

GRANGE RD

STATION RD

CARLTON RD

SOUTH HANNINGFIELD WAY

LYNFORDS DR

A132

BARRET PARK

CASTLEDON RD

VERA RD

CUMMING

Moat

HASLEMERE

RD

RICHMOND

MORELAND

ARDVOEL RD

LAPWING

CHURCH END LA

VIKING WAY

TOWER

CHURCH END AVE

REGENCY

PH

RUNWELL RD

1

Berne Hall

KEITH AVE

CLARE AVE

CARES DON GDNS

CANEWDON GDNS

HUDSON GDNS

CANO AVE

Sch

+

Recn Gd

Runwell

SWAN LA

PEARMAIN CL

EGBERT GDNS

ETHELRED GDNS

SAXON CL

MERLIN

RETTENDON GDNS

FRIARS RD

Sch

GUERNSEY GDNS

CARRUTHERS CL

CARDEN

HAROLD GDNS

WHITELANDS

HIGHCLIFFE RD

P

ATHELSTAN GDNS

STATION

HASTINGS

THE WARD

HERBERT

ALFRED RD

ERNEST RD

A132

Hall

P

BERENS CL

WHIT AVE

P

94

73 | D | 74 | E | 75 | F

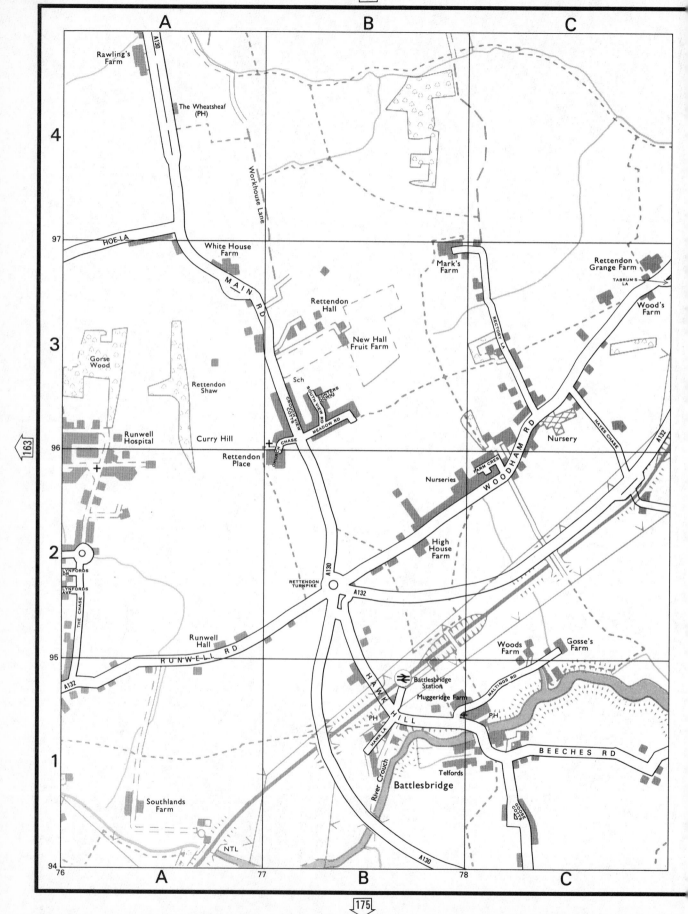

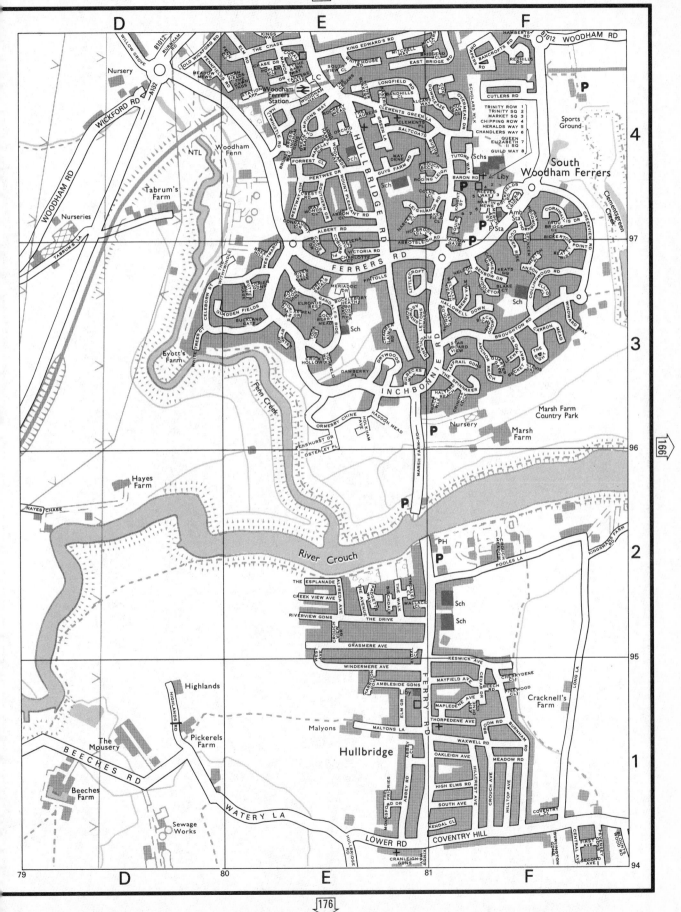

D   E   F

TRINITY ROW	1
TRINITY SQ	2
MARKET SQ	3
CHIPPING ROW	4
HERALDS WAY	5
CHANDLERS WAY	6
QUEEN ELIZABETH II SQ	7
GUILD WAY	8

South Woodham Ferrers

Sports Ground

Marsh Farm Country Park

Marsh Farm

River Crouch

Hullbridge

WICKFORD RD

WOODHAM RD

B1012 WOODHAM RD

BEECHES RD

WATERY LA

LOWER RD

COVENTRY HILL

Hayes Farm

HAYES CHASE

The Mousery

Highlands

Pickerels Farm

Beeches Farm

Sewage Works

Woodham Ferrers Station

Woodham Fenn

Tabrum's Farm

Nurseries

Nursery

Eyott's Farm

Fenn Creek

Cran'nell's Farm

Malyons

Clemensgreen Creek

166

97

96

95

94

3

2

1

4

79   80   81

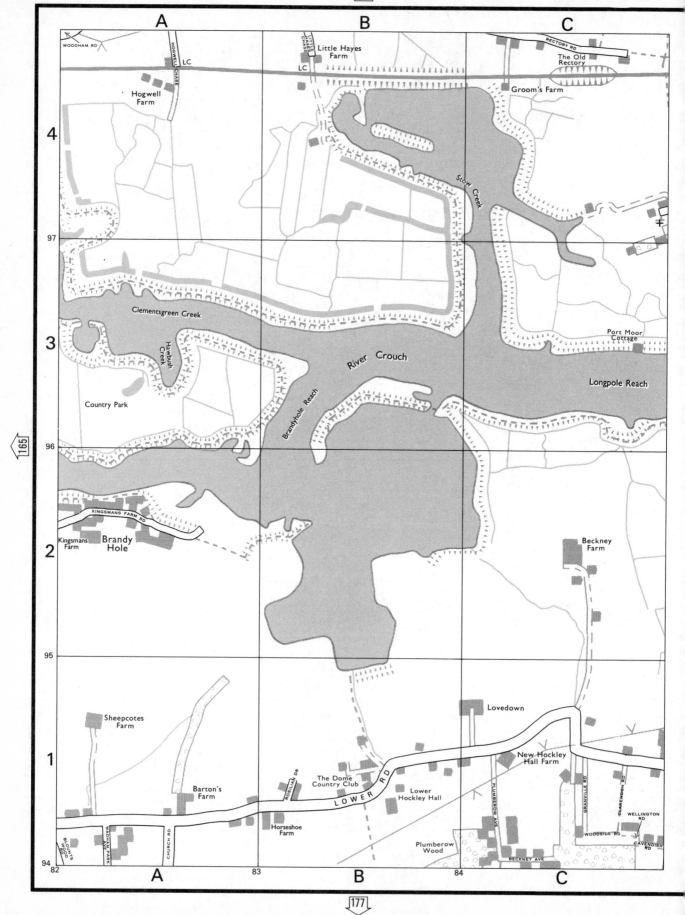

A   B   C

4

97

3

96

2

95

1

94

82   A   83   B   84   C

WOODHAM RD

Hogwell Farm

HOGWELL CHASE

LC

Little Hayes Farm

LITTLE HAYES CHASE

LC

RECTORY RD

The Old Rectory

Groom's Farm

Stow Creek

Clementsgreen Creek

Hawbush Creek

Country Park

River Crouch

Brandyhole Reach

Port Moor Cottage

Longpole Reach

Kingsmans Farm

Kingsmans Farm Rd

Brandy Hole

Beckney Farm

Sheepcotes Farm

Barton's Farm

Lovedown

New Hockley Hall Farm

ROSILIAN DR

The Dome Country Club

LOWER RD

Lower Hockley Hall

Horseshoe Farm

Plumberow Wood

PLUMBEROW AVE

GRANVILLE RD

CLARENDON RD

WELLINGTON RD

WOODSIDE RD

CAVENDISH RD

BECKNEY AVE

BLOUNTS WOOD

WADHAM PARK AVE

CHURCH RD

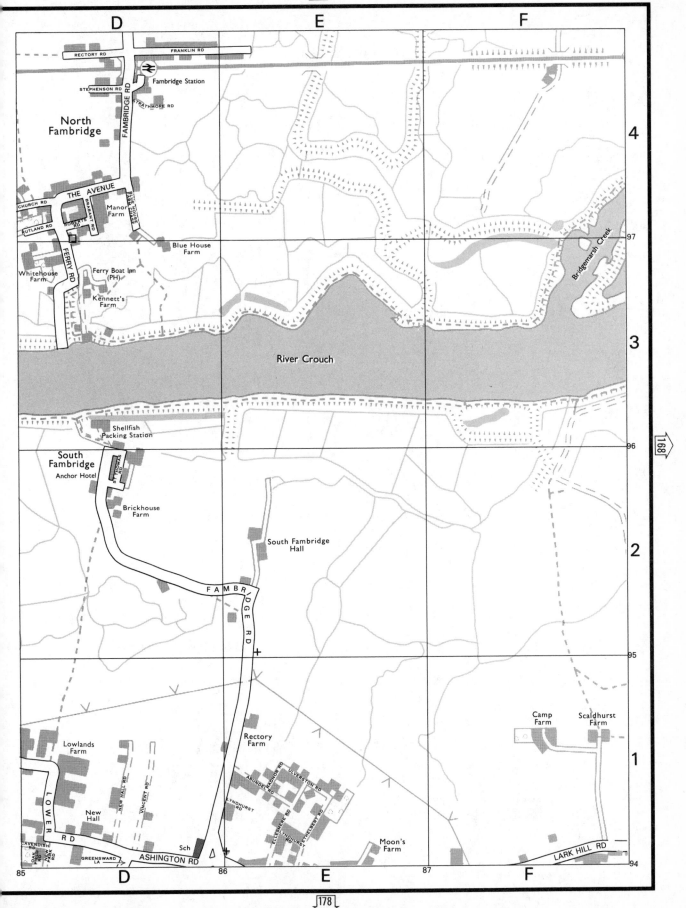

156
168
178

D E F

4
3
2
1

97
96
95
94

85 86 87

North
Fambridge

RECTORY RD
FRANKLIN RD
STEPHENSON RD
FAMBRIDGE RD
STRATHMORE RD
Fambridge Station

THE AVENUE
CHURCH RD
RUTLAND RD
ROBERTS RD
BRABANT RD
FERRY HOUSE RD
Manor
Farm
Blue House
Farm

FERRY RD
Whitehouse
Farm
Ferry Boat Inn
(PH)
Kennett's
Farm

River Crouch

Bridgemarsh Creek

Shellfish
Packing Station

South
Fambridge
Anchor Hotel
ST THOMAS RD
Brickhouse
Farm

South Fambridge
Hall

FAMBRIDGE RD

Lowlands
Farm
NEW HALL RD
VINCENT RD
New
Hall
LOWER RD
CAVENDISH RD
GREENSWARD LA
Sch
ASHINGTON RD

Rectory
Farm
ARUNDEL RD
RADNOR RD
ULVERSTON RD
LYNDHURST RD
ELLESMERE RD
LYNDHURST RD
ETHELWER RD

Moon's
Farm

Camp
Farm
Scaldhurst
Farm

LARK HILL RD

D E F

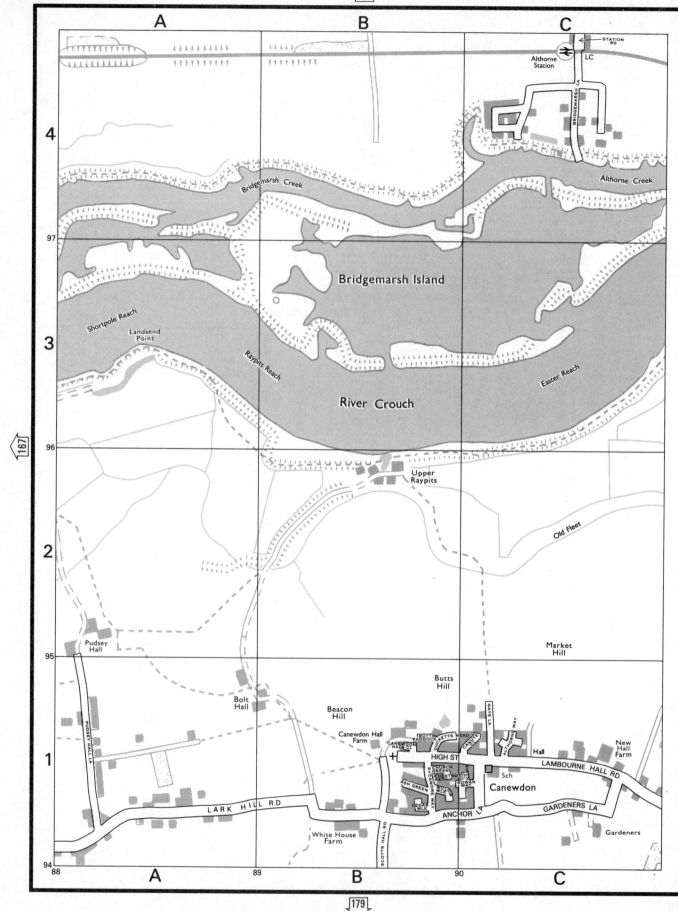

Althorne Station

STATION RD

LC

BRIDGEMARSH LA

Althorne Creek

Bridgemarsh Creek

Bridgemarsh Island

Shortpole Reach

Landsend Point

Raypits Reach

Easter Reach

River Crouch

Upper Raypits

Old Fleet

Pudsey Hall

Market Hill

Butts Hill

Bolt Hall

Beacon Hill

Canewdon Hall Farm

PUDSEY HALL LA

BUTTS PADDOCK

DUCKETTS MEAD

CANEWDON HALL RD

GAYS LA

CANUTE

ALTHORNE WAY

New Hall Farm

HIGH ST

Hall

CHURCH GREEN

CHESTNUT WLK

ROWAN WAY

SYCAMORE WAY

WILLOW WLK

ASH GREEN RD

CEDAR WLK

Sch

Canewdon

LAMBOURNE HALL RD

LARK HILL RD

SCOTTS HALL RD

ANCHOR LA

GARDENERS LA

Gardeners

White House Farm

167

88   A   89   B   90   C

94
95
96
97

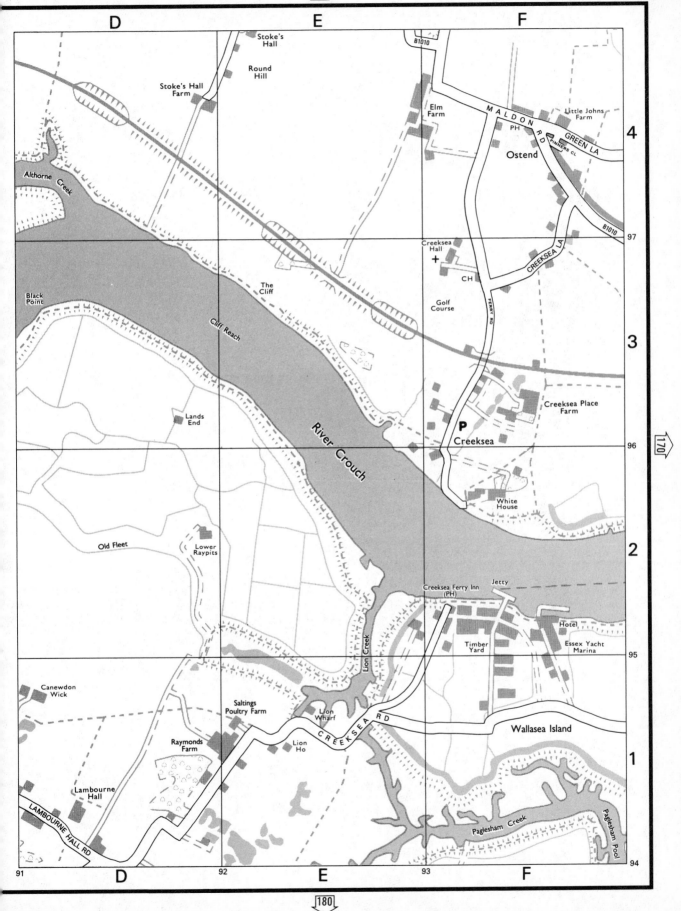

D
E
F

Stoke's
Hall

Round
Hill

Stoke's Hall
Farm

B1010

MALDON RD

Little Johns
Farm

Elm
Farm

PH

GREEN LA

PINNERS CL

4

Ostend

Althorne Creek

Creeksea
Hall

97

CH

CREEKSEA LA

B1010

Black
Point

The
Cliff

Golf
Course

FERRY RD

Cliff Reach

Lands
End

Creeksea Place
Farm

3

River Crouch

P

Creeksea

96

White
House

Old Fleet

Lower
Raypits

2

Creeksea Ferry Inn
(PH)

Jetty

Lion Creek

Hotel

Essex Yacht
Marina

Timber
Yard

95

Canewdon
Wick

Saltings
Poultry Farm

Lion
Wharf

CREEKSEA RD

Wallasea Island

Raymonds
Farm

Lion
Ho

1

Lambourne
Hall

Paglesham Creek

Paglesham Pool

LAMBOURNE HALL RD

91
D
92
E
93
F
94

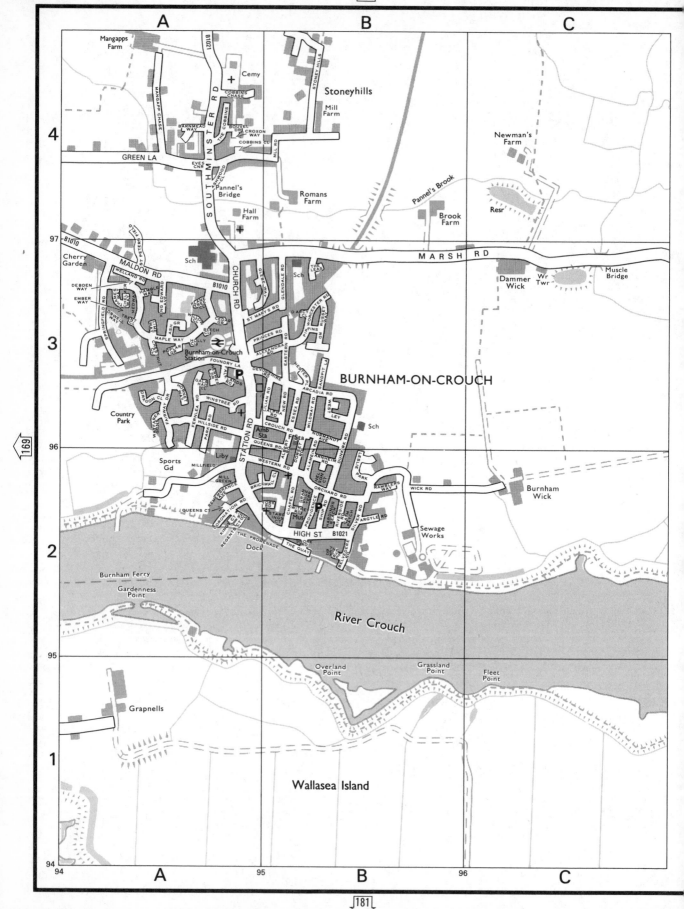

169

Map labels

A   B   C

Mangapps Farm

Cemy

Stoneyhills

Mill Farm

MANGAPP CHASE

B1021

SOUTHMINSTER RD

COBBINS CHASE

BARNMEAD WAY

THE COBBINS

BOUVEL DRI

CROXON WAY

COBBINS CL

STONEY HILLS

Newman's Farm

GREEN LA

EVES CNR

LINWOOD CL

MILL RD

Pannel's Bridge

Romans Farm

Pannel's Brook

Brook Farm

Resr

Hall Farm

97 B1010

MARSH RD

Muscle Bridge

Cherry Garden

MALDON RD

WELLAND RD

ST PETER'S FIELD

Sch

THE LEAS

Sch

GLEN WAY

GLENDALE RD

Dammer Wick

Wr Twr

DEBDEN WAY

EMBER WAY

HAMBRO

KING EDWARD AVE

ST MARY'S RD

D'ARCY RD

WORCESTER RD

RUSSET WAY

SPRINGFIELD RD

ORWELL WAY

ASH

MAPLE WAY

POPLAR

BEECH

HOLLY

CEDAR

PRINCES RD

ALEXANDRA RD

EASTERN RD

PIPPINS RD

CHESTER

B1010

CHURCH RD

GR

3 Burnham-on-Crouch Station

FOUNDRY LA

DEVONSHIRE RD

BURNHAM-ON-CROUCH

P

ORCHID CL

GABLE

HALL RD

FAIRWAY DRI

FERNLEA RD

WINSTREE RD

HILLSIDE RD

PARK

LILIAN RD

NEW RD

CROUCH RD

ESSEX RD

ARCADIA RD

MILDMAY RD

WEST LEY

NORMANDY AVE

Sch

Country Park

WALFARE RD

STATION RD

AmB Sta

QUEENS RD

F Sta

DUNKIRK RD

96 Sports Gd

Liby

MILLFIELD

MILL GREEN

Millfield

BRICKWAY

WESTERN RD

CHAPEL RD

GRANVILLE RD

DORSET RD

SHIRE

ALAMEIN RD

NEW CON CL

ORCHARD RD

ARNHEM RD

LESLIE

PARK

RAMBLERS WALK

WICK RD

Burnham Wick

QUEENS CT

REMEMBRANCE WAY

CORONATION RD

KING

REGENTS

THE PROMENADE

STABLINGS

YORK

SHORE

Mus

PROVIDENCE

SHIPYARD

MAUNDS

RIVERSIDE

THE CATCH

SILVER RD

ARGYLE RD

Sewage Works

HIGH ST

B1021

Dock

THE QUAY

THE BORROWS

DEBEN

2 Burnham Ferry

Gardenness Point

River Crouch

95

Overland Point

Grassland Point

Fleet Point

Grapnells

1 Wallasea Island

94   A   95   B   96   C

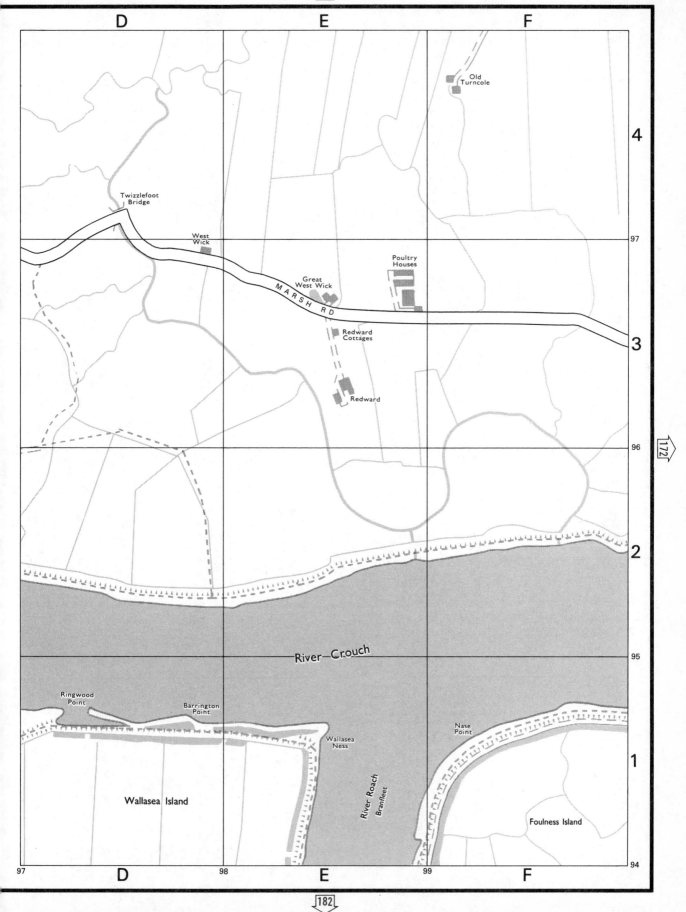

D   E   F

Old
Turncole

4

Twizzlefoot
Bridge

West
Wick

97

Poultry
Houses

Great
West Wick

MARSH RD

Redward
Cottages

3

Redward

96

172

2

River–Crouch

95

Ringwood
Point

Barrington
Point

Nase
Point

Wallasea
Ness

1

Wallasea Island

River Roach

Branfleet

Foulness Island

94

97   D   98   E   99   F

161

171

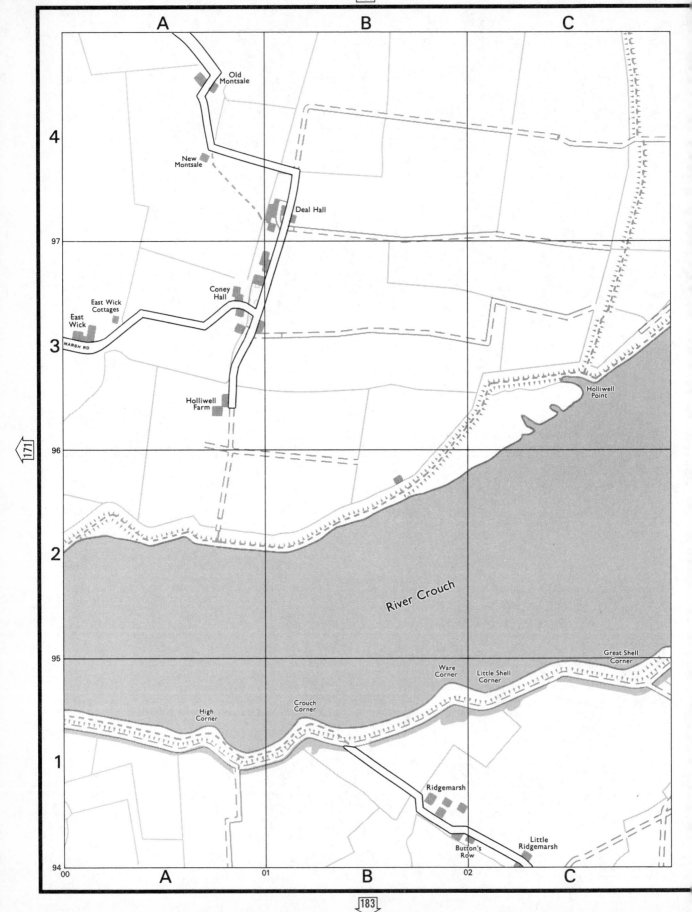

A   B   C

4

Old Montsale

New Montsale

Deal Hall

97

Coney Hall

East Wick Cottages

East Wick

MARSH RD

3

Holliwell Point

Holliwell Farm

96

River Crouch

2

95

Great Shell Corner

Ware Corner

Little Shell Corner

High Corner

Crouch Corner

1

Ridgemarsh

Little Ridgemarsh

Button's Row

94

00   A   01   B   02   C

183

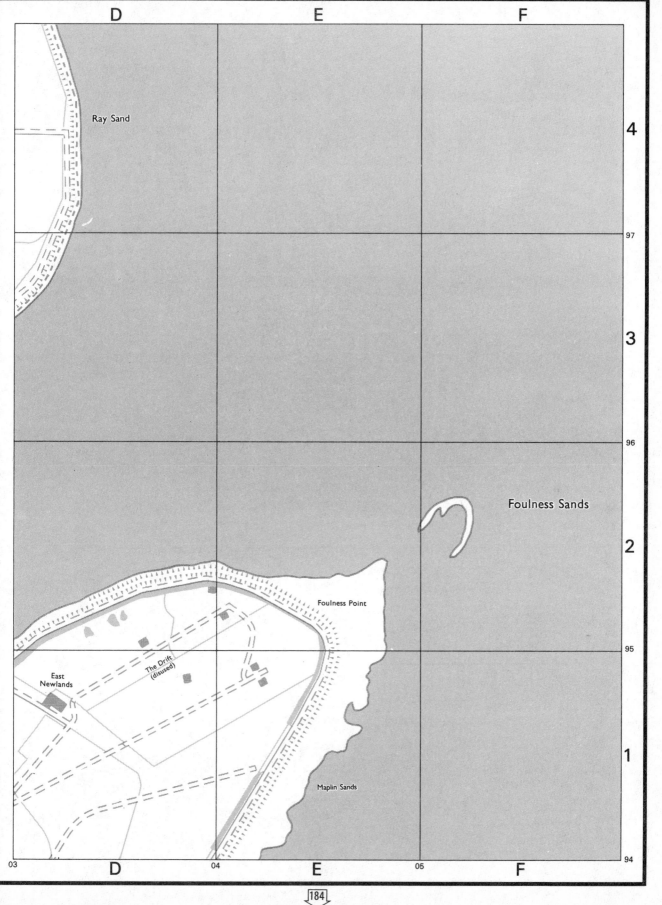

Ray Sand

Foulness Sands

Foulness Point

The Drift
(disused)

East
Newlands

Maplin Sands

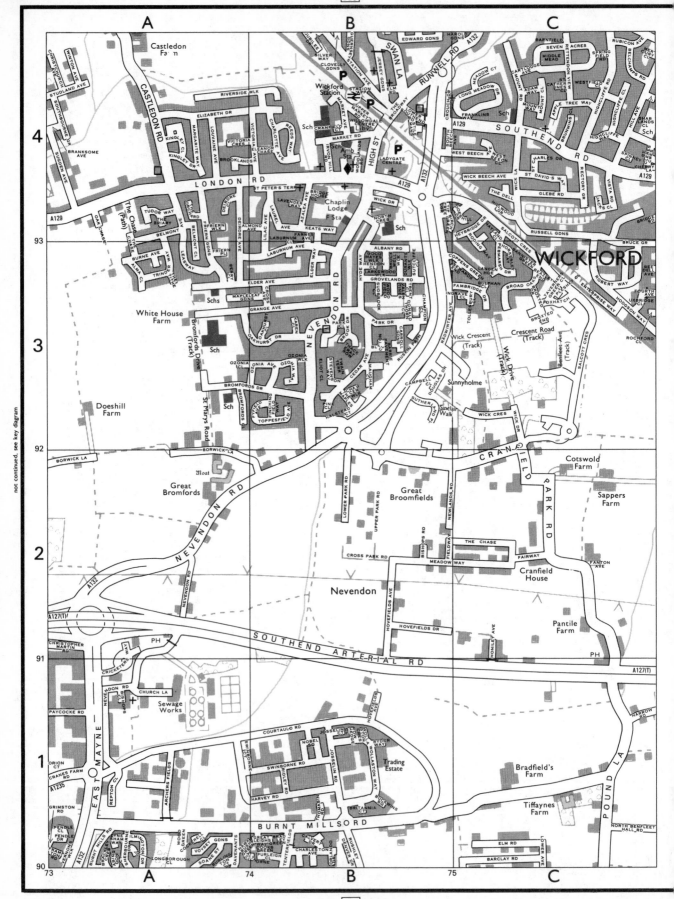

not continued, see key diagram

WICKFORD

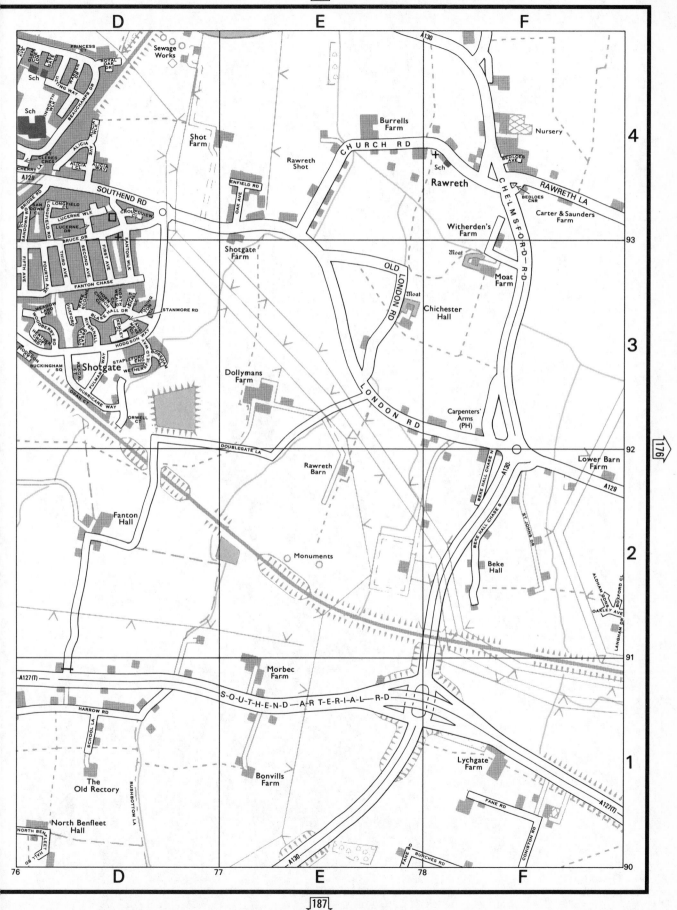

175

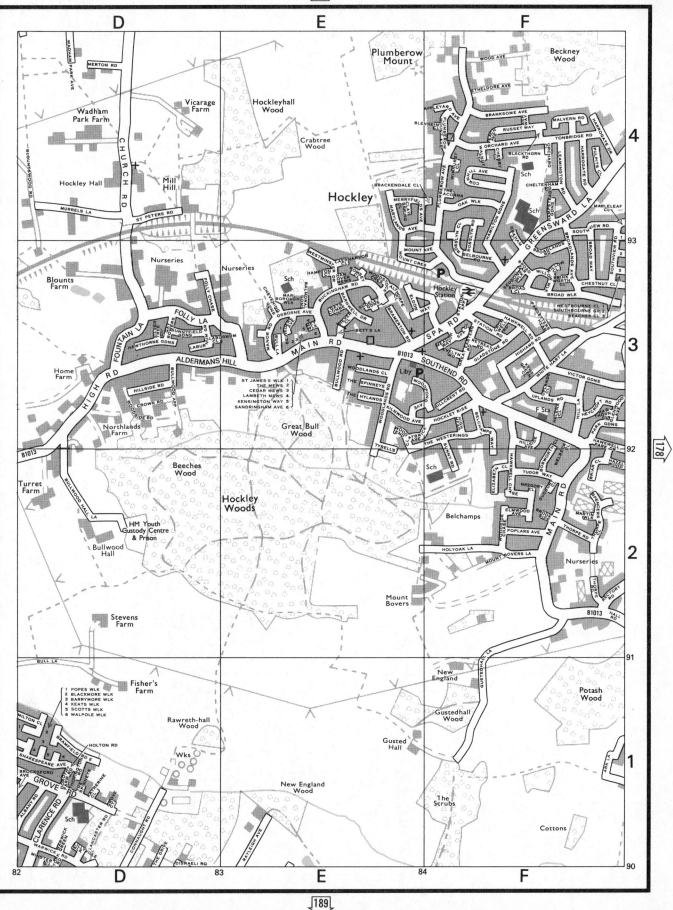

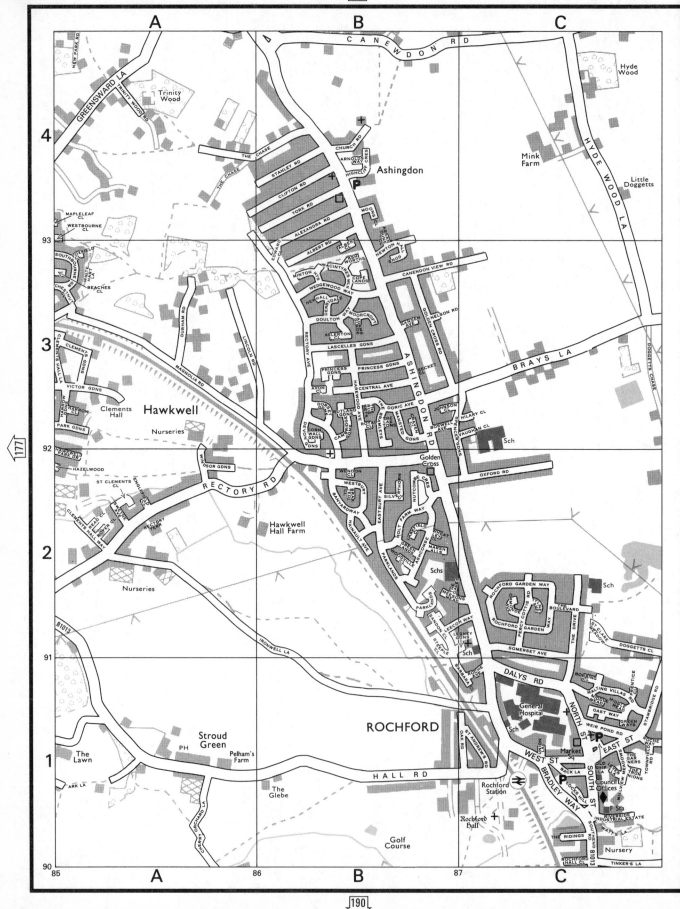

168

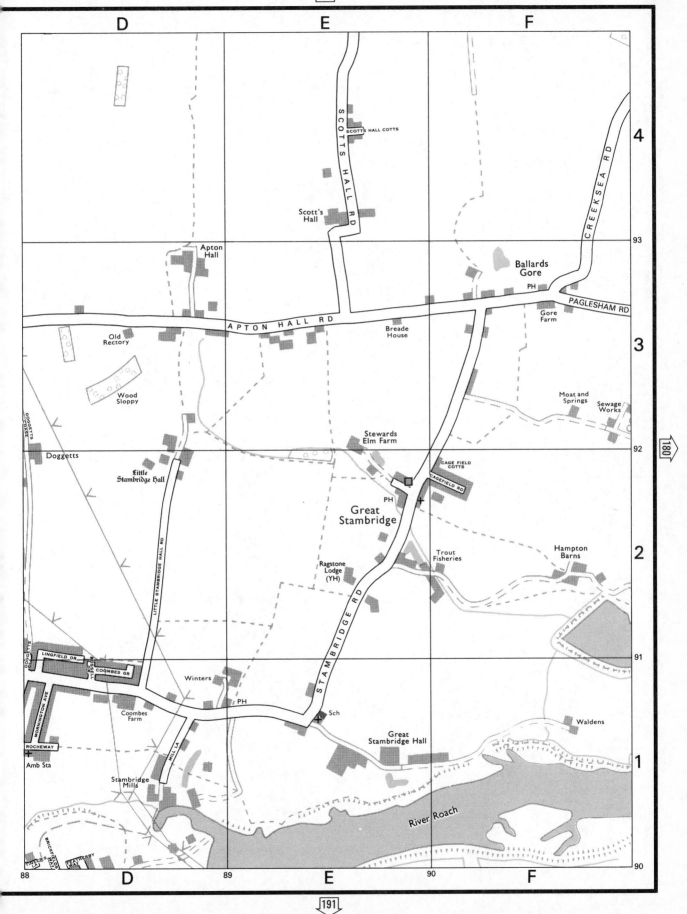

180

D E F

4
93
3
92
2
91
1
90

88 89 90

SCOTTS HALL RD

SCOTTS HALL COTTS

Scott's
Hall

CREEKSEA RD

Apton
Hall

Ballards
Gore

PH

PAGLESHAM RD

Old
Rectory

APTON HALL RD

Breade
House

Gore
Farm

Wood
Sloppy

Moat and
Springs

Sewage
Works

Doggetts

Stewards
Elm Farm

CAGE FIELD
COTTS

Little
Stambridge Hall

Great
Stambridge

PH

CAGEFIELD RD

DOGGETTS CHASE

LITTLE STAMBRIDGE HALL RD

Ragstone
Lodge
(YH)

STAMBRIDGE RD

Trout
Fisheries

Hampton
Barns

DOGGETTS

LINGFIELD DR

COOMBES GR

BRAESIDE

Winters

PH

Waldens

MORNINGTON AVE

Coombes
Farm

Sch

Great
Stambridge Hall

ROCHEWAY

MILL LA

Amb Sta

Stambridge
Mills

River Roach

BRICKFIELD RD

TINKERS LA

HEATHERBY WAY

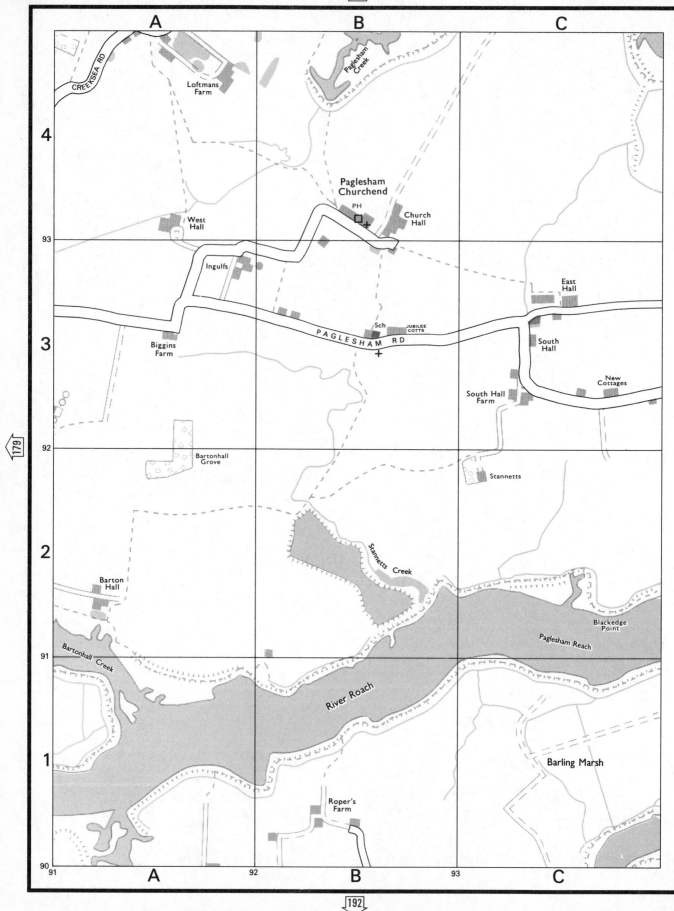

A B C

CREEKSEA RD

Loftmans
Farm

Paglesham
Creek

4

Paglesham
Churchend

West
Hall

PH

Church
Hall

93

Ingulfs

East
Hall

PAGLESHAM RD

Sch

JUBILEE
COTTS

South
Hall

3

Biggins
Farm

South Hall
Farm

New
Cottages

92

Bartonhall
Grove

Stannetts

2

Stannetts Creek

Barton
Hall

Blackedge
Point

Paglesham Reach

91

Bartonhall Creek

River Roach

Barling Marsh

1

Roper's
Farm

90

91 A 92 B 93 C

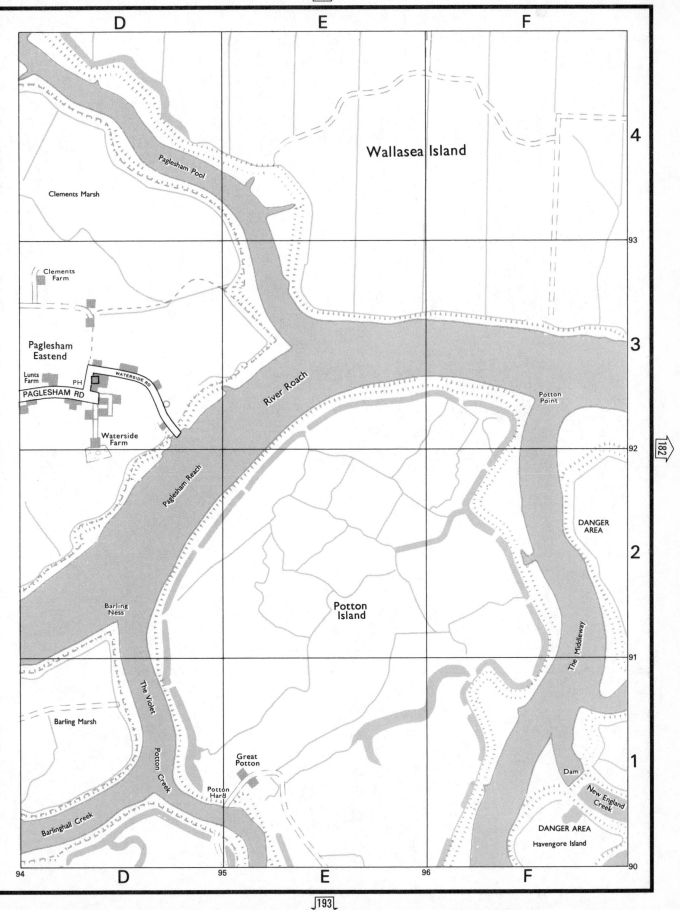

D E F

Wallasea Island

4

Paglesham Pool

Clements Marsh

93

Clements Farm

3

Paglesham Eastend

WATERSIDE RD

Lunts Farm

PH

PAGLESHAM RD

River Roach

Potton Point

Waterside Farm

Paglesham Reach

92

182

DANGER AREA

2

Barling Ness

Potton Island

The Middleway

91

The Violet

Barling Marsh

Potton Creek

1

Great Potton

Dam

New England Creek

Potton Hard

Barlinghall Creek

DANGER AREA

Havengore Island

90

94 D 95 E 96 F

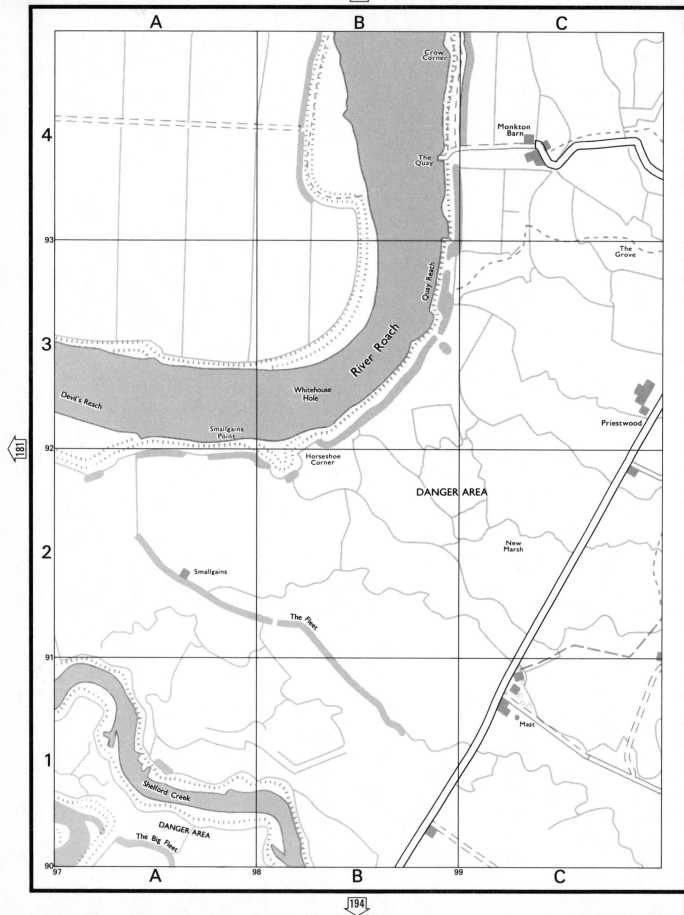

181

A B C

4

93

3

92

2

91

1

90

97 A 98 B 99 C

Crow
Corner

Monkton
Barn

The Quay

The
Grove

Quay Reach

River Roach

Whitehouse
Hole

Devil's Reach

Smallgains
Point

Priestwood

Horseshoe
Corner

DANGER AREA

New
Marsh

Smallgains

The Fleet

Mast

Shelford Creek

DANGER AREA

The Big Fleet

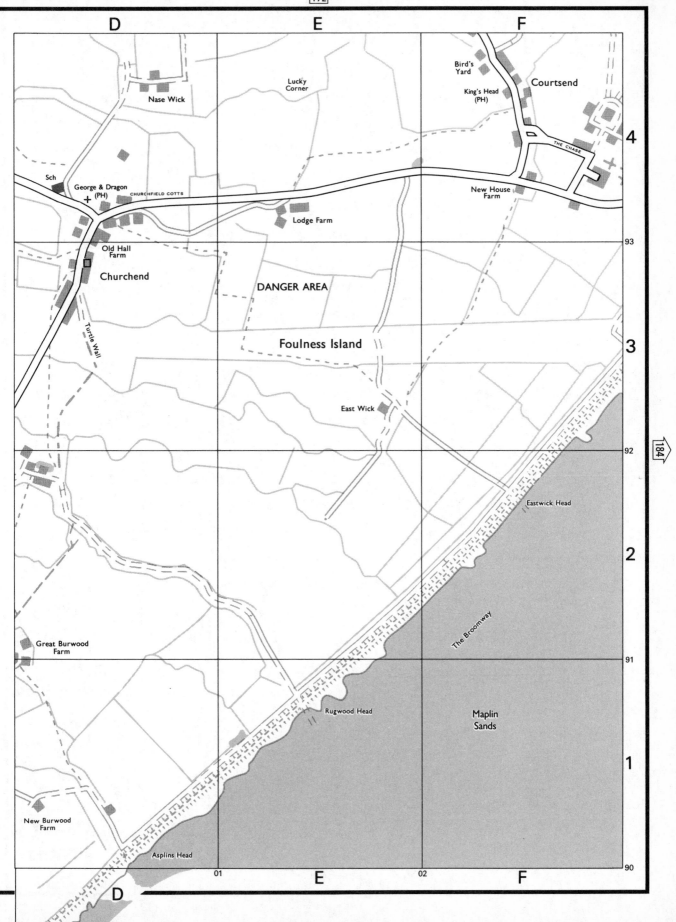

D   E   F

Nase Wick

Lucky
Corner

Bird's
Yard

King's Head
(PH)

Courtsend

THE CHASE

4

Sch

George & Dragon
(PH)

CHURCHFIELD COTTS

Lodge Farm

New House
Farm

Old Hall
Farm

Churchend

93

DANGER AREA

Turtle Wall

Foulness Island

3

East Wick

92

184

Eastwick Head

2

The Broomway

Great Burwood
Farm

91

Rugwood Head

Maplin
Sands

1

New Burwood
Farm

Asplins Head

00

01   E   02   F

90

D

173

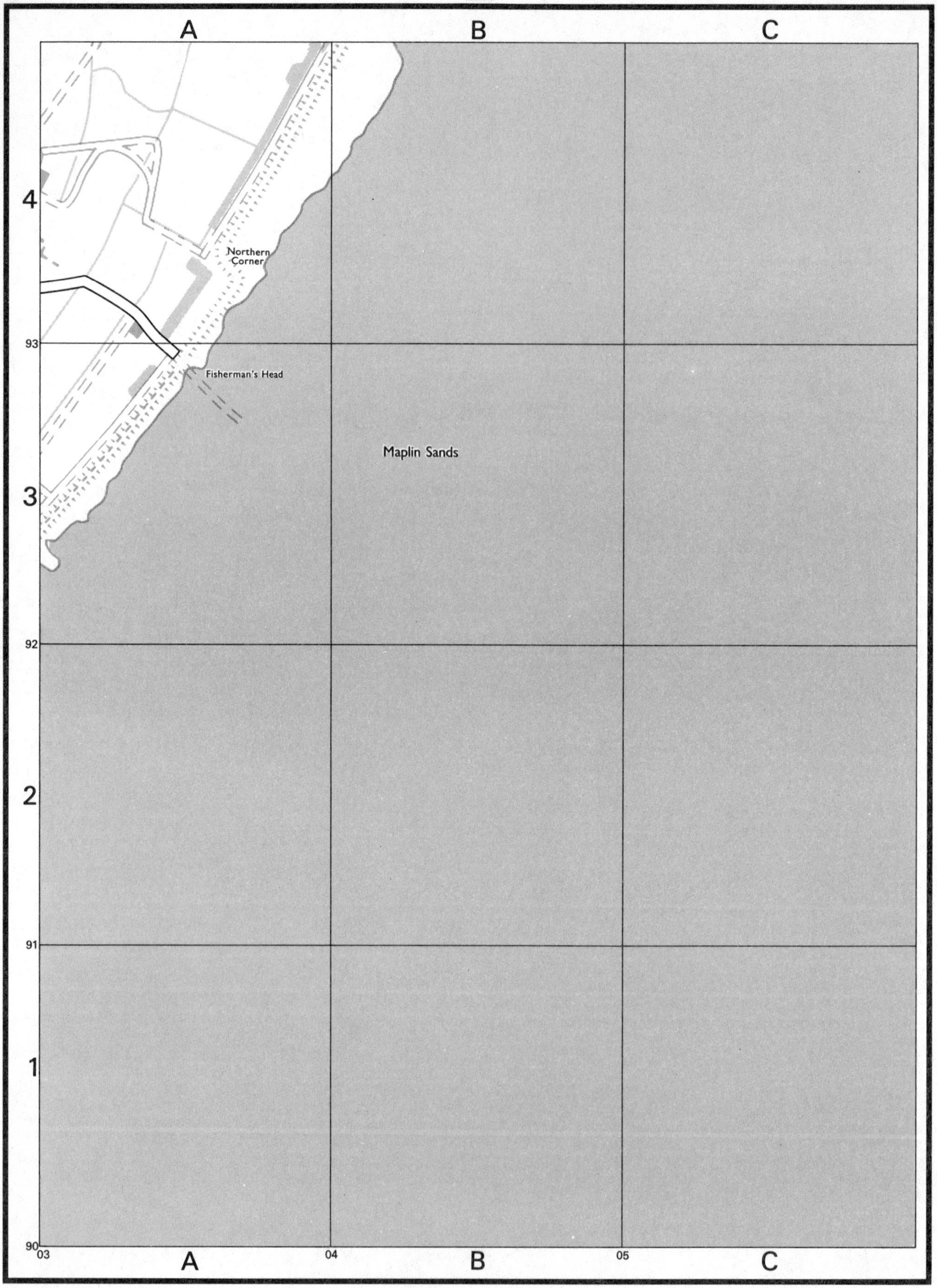

183

A   B   C

4

Northern
Corner

93

Fisherman's Head

Maplin Sands

3

92

2

91

1

90
03   04   05

A   B   C

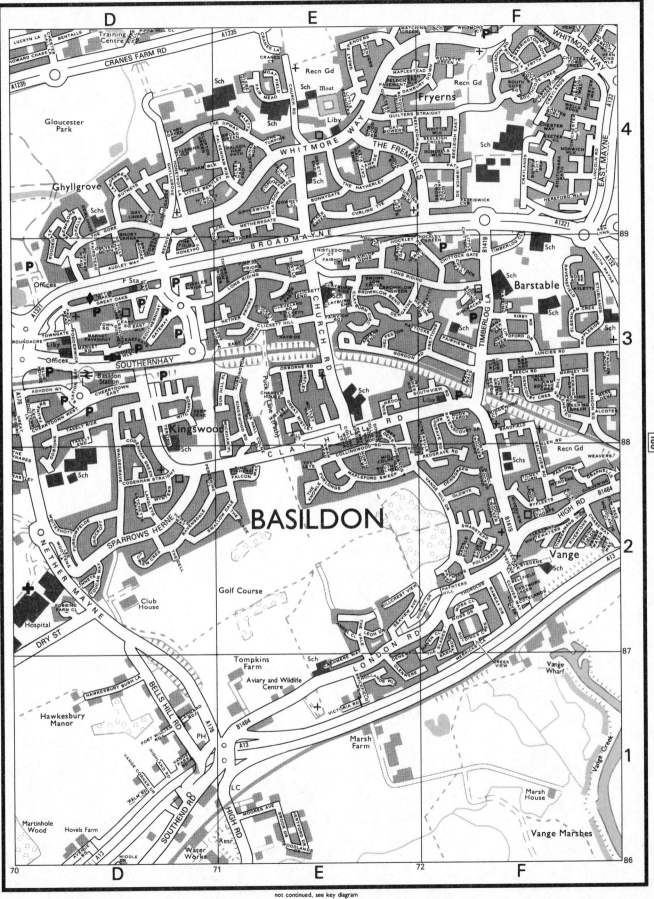

BASILDON

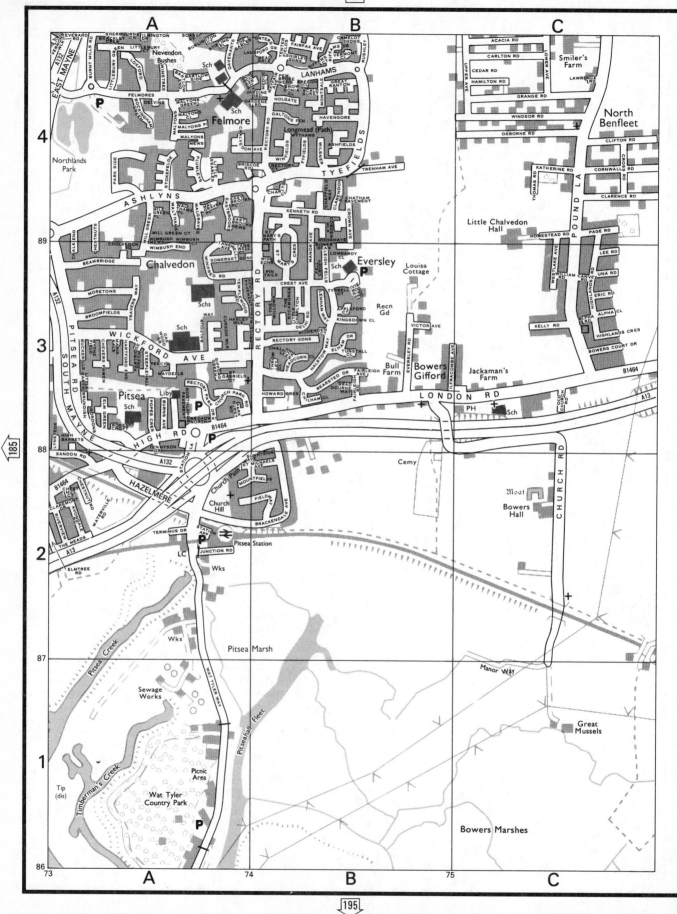

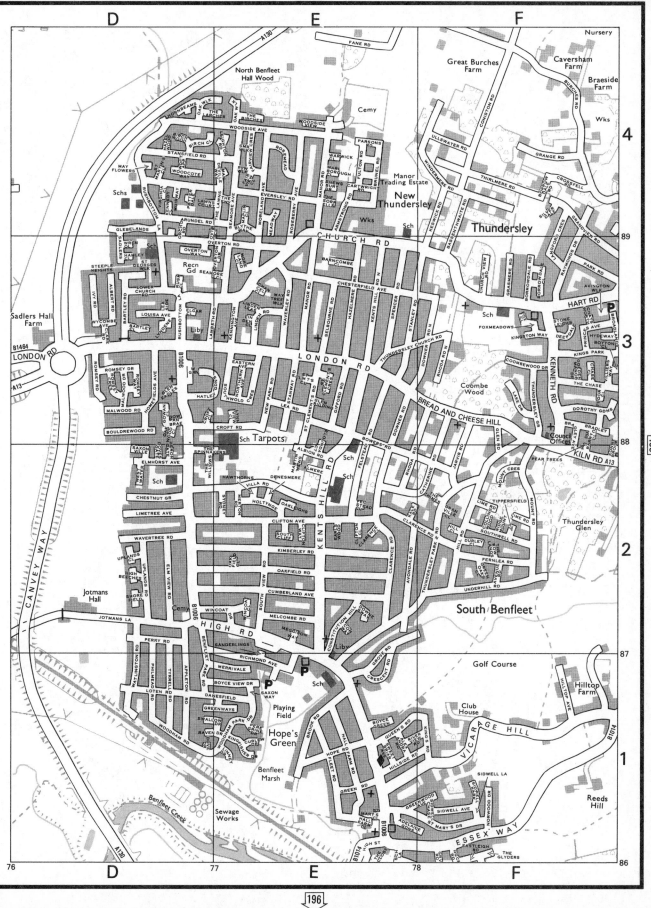

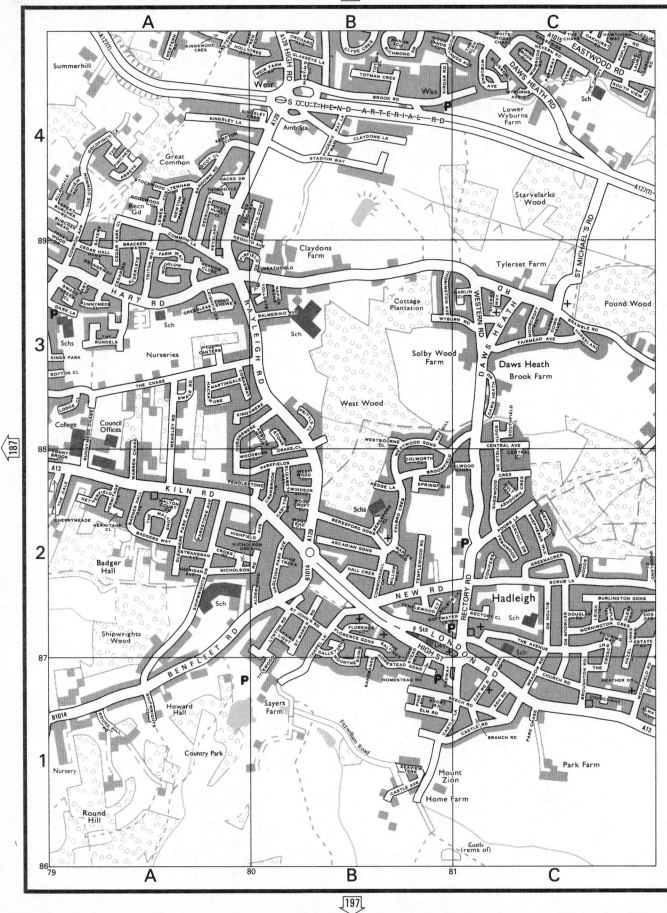

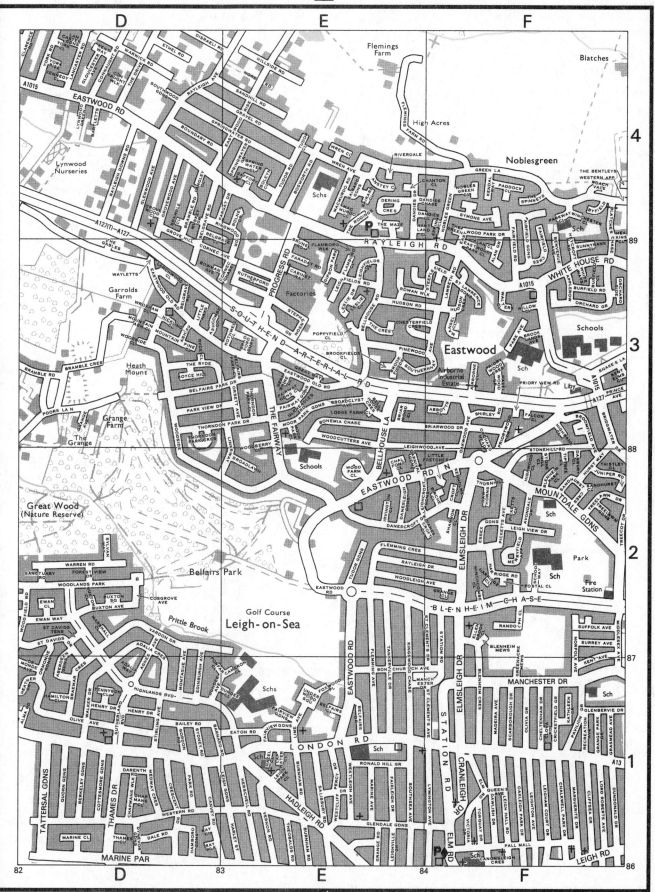

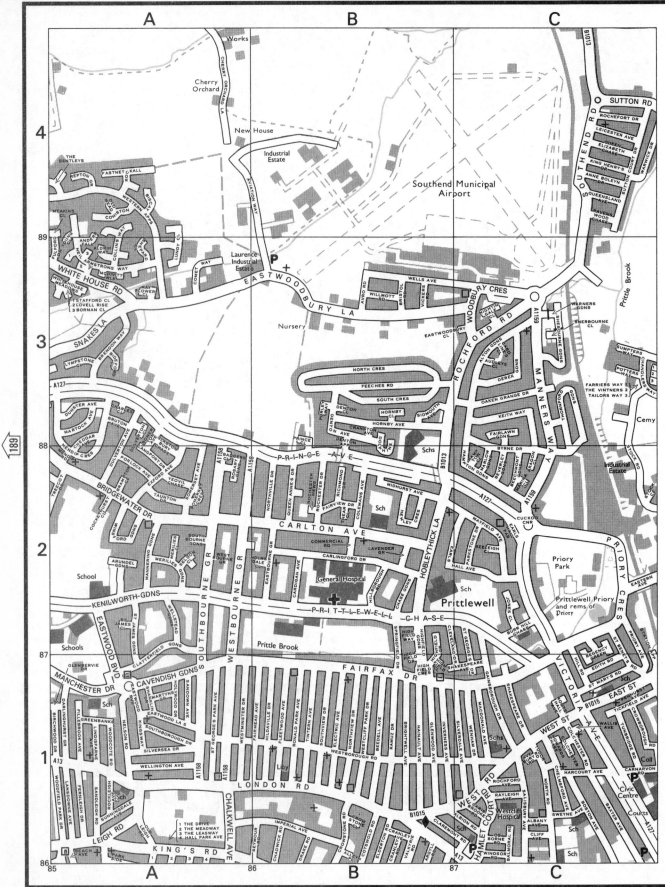

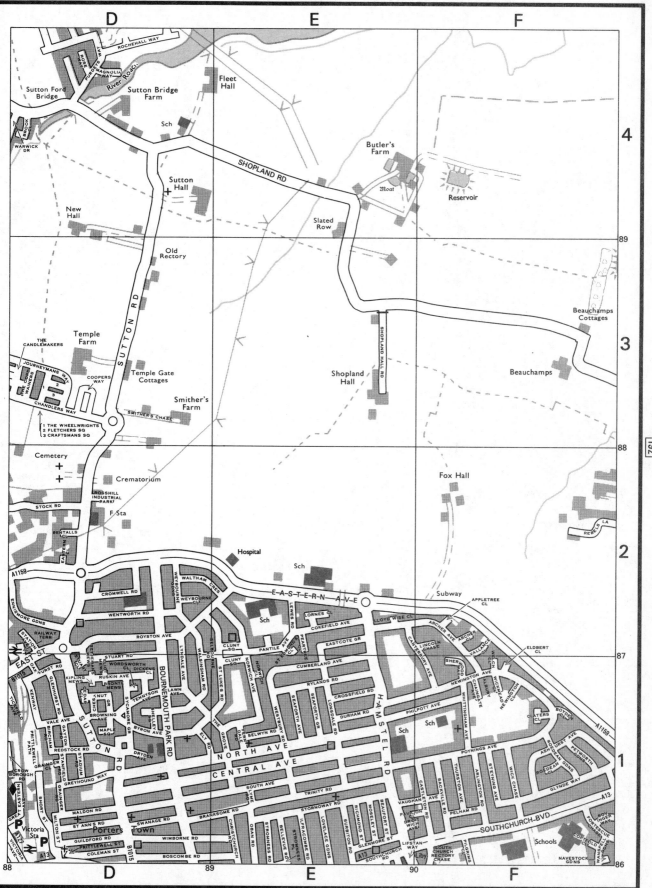

192

D E F

4

89

3

88

2

87

1

86

ROCHEHALL WAY
ROSE
FURORS
MAGNOLIA WAY
River Road
Sutton Ford Bridge
Sutton Bridge Farm
Fleet Hall
BROOK
WARWICK DR
Sch
SHOPLAND RD
Butler's Farm
Moat
Reservoir
Sutton Hall
New Hall
Slated Row
Old Rectory
SUTTON RD
Beauchamps Cottages
THE CANDLEMAKERS
JOURNEYMANS WAY
FYFE COURT
WAINERS
CHANDLERS WAY
COOPERS WAY
Temple Farm
Temple Gate Cottages
Smither's Farm
SMITHER'S CHASE
Shopland Hall
SHOPLAND HALL RD
Beauchamps
1 THE WHEELWRIGHTS
2 FLETCHERS SQ
3 CRAFTSMANS SQ
Cemetery
Crematorium
CROSSHILL INDUSTRIAL PARK
STOCK RD
F Sta
BENTALLS CL
EASTERN CL
A1159
Fox Hall
LA REBELS
Hospital
Sch
EASTERN AVE
Subway
APPLETREE CL
CROMWELL RD
WALTHAM CRES
WEYBOURNE
WEYBOURNE CL
WENTWORTH RD
ROYSTON AVE
RAILWAY TERR
STATION
EAST ST
ENNISMORE GDNS
Sch
LEWES RD
CLUNY SQ
PANTILE AVE
ST THOMAS RD
LORNES CL
COKEFIELD AVE
PEARTREE
EASTCOTE GR
LLOYD WISE CL
ARCHER AVE
ARCHER
LINCOLN CHASE
CANTERBURY AVE
VALLANCE
ELDBERT CL
STUART RD
OAK
HURST RD
KIPLING MEWS
DICKENS CL
WORDSWORTH CL
RUSKIN AVE
BRIGHTS MEWS
CLUNY SQ
ST LUKE'S RD
NORWICH AVE
NORWICH CL
CUMBERLAND AVE
RYLANDS RD
CROSSFIELD RD
PHILPOTT AVE
SHERWOOD
NEWINGTON AVE
CHAINS GATE
ALBURY
WICKHAM
NEW RD
WICKFORD
CLATERS CL
BOLDEN
A1159
B1013
KENWAY
VALE AVE
BIRCHAM
GORDON
REDSTOCK RD
SYCAMORE GR
NUT
COAL
SHELLEY
TENNYSON AVE
LAWN AVE
THE GROVE
WALSINGHAM RD
LYNDALE AVE
BROWNING AVE
MAPLE
BYRON AVE
DRYDEN AVE
SELWYN RD
WESTBURY RD
SEAFORTH AVE
BEANORTH AVE
SEAPORTH GR
LONSDALE RD
DURHAM RD
HAMSTEL RD
Sch
Sch
POYNINGS AVE
THURSTON AVE
STEYNING AVE
ARLINGTON RD
WICK CHASE
ASHBURST RD
ROEDEAN GDNS
ROGDEAN AVE
GLYNDE WAY
PETWORTH
PRITTLEWELL PATH
GRAINGER CL
STANFIELD
GRAINGER
STADIUM RD
GREYHOUND WAY
SUTTON RD
NORTH AVE
CENTRAL AVE
SOUTH AVE
LYME RD
BRANKSOME RD
CHRISTCHURCH
TRINITY RD
STORNAWAY RD
RICHMOND ST
MOSELEY ST
GLENMORE ST
SURBITON RD
CASTLETON RD
SACKVILLE RD
VAUGHAN
PAVILION DR
ORT WICH AVE
PELHAM RD
ROEHURST
FORTESCUE
SOPEFIELD
BOYINGER RD
WANSTEAD
VICTORIA STA
GREAT EASTERN
CROW BOROUGH
SHORT ST
MALDON RD
ST ANN'S RD
SWANAGE RD
WIMBORNE RD
MILTON ST
GUILDFORD RD
PRITTLEWELL ST
COLEMAN ST
BOSCOMBE RD
Porters Town
OBAN RD
STRONNESS RD
BELLEVUE RD
STRONNESS RD
ILFRACOMBE GDNS
LOVELACE GDNS
BEAUFORT ST
BOURNEMOUTH PARK RD
SOUTHCHURCH
A13
LIFSTAN WAY
SOUTH CHURCH RECTORY CHASE
PILGRIMS
SOUTHCHURCH BVD
Schools
NAVESTOCK GDNS
Liby
A13
A1011
VICTORIA
A127

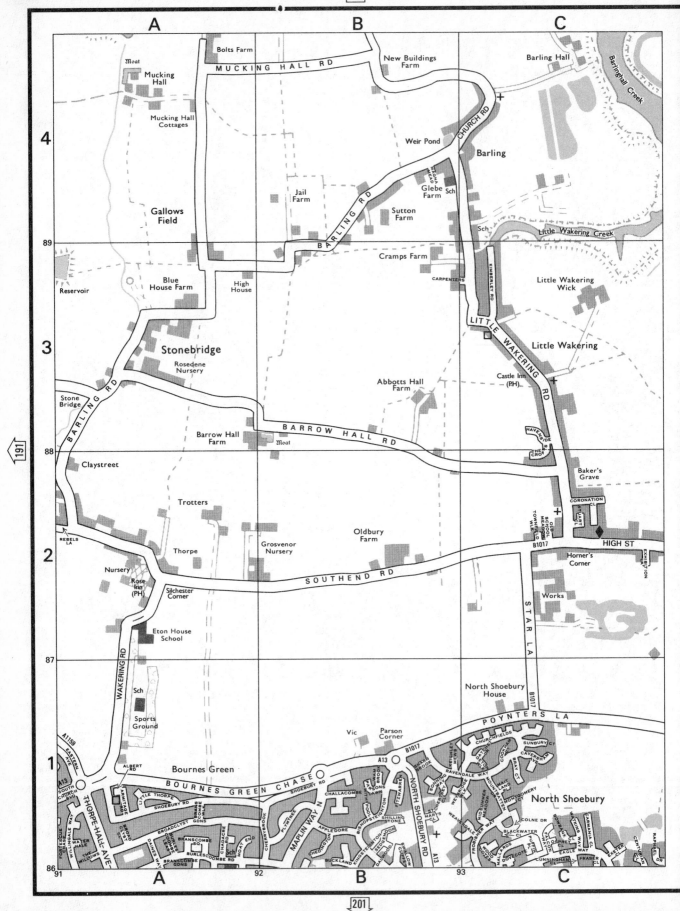

A   B   C

Bolts Farm

MUCKING HALL RD

New Buildings Farm

Barling Hall

Moat

Mucking Hall

Barlinghall Creek

CHURCH RD

4

Mucking Hall Cottages

Weir Pond

Barling

Jail Farm

Sch

BARLING RD

Sutton Farm

Glebe Farm

MEAD HEAD

Gallows Field

Sch

Little Wakering Creek

89

Cramps Farm

Little Wakering Wick

CARPENTERS

Reservoir

Blue House Farm

High House

KIMBERLEY RD

Little Wakering

3

Stonebridge

LITTLE WAKERING RD

Rosedene Nursery

Abbotts Hall Farm

Castle Inn (PH)

BARLING RD

Stone Bridge

HAVENGORE

Barrow Hall Farm

BARROW HALL RD

CHERRY CROFT

88

Moat

Baker's Grave

Claystreet

CORONATION CL

Trotters

SCHOOL MEADOWS

TOWNFIELD WK

Oldbury Farm

REBELS LA

2

Thorpe

Grosvenor Nursery

HIGH ST

Horner's Corner

Nursery

STUART CL

EXHIBITION

Rose Inn (PH)

Silchester Corner

SOUTHEND RD

Works

B1017

Eton House School

STAR LA

87

North Shoebury House

WAKERING RD

B1017

Sch

POYNTERS LA

Sports Ground

Vic

Parson Corner

CHURCHFIELDS

SUNBURY CT

EASTERN AVE

A1159

Bournes Green

A13

CAVERSHAM

1

BOURNES GREEN CHASE

Shoebury Rd

Challacombe

RAVENDALE WAY

BRAY CT

North Shoebury

ALBERT RD

Little Thorpe

Shoebury Rd

MAPLIN WAY

NORTH SHOEBURY RD

A13

THORPE HALL AVE

Colne Dr

BLACKWATER

86

91   A   **92**   B   **93**   C

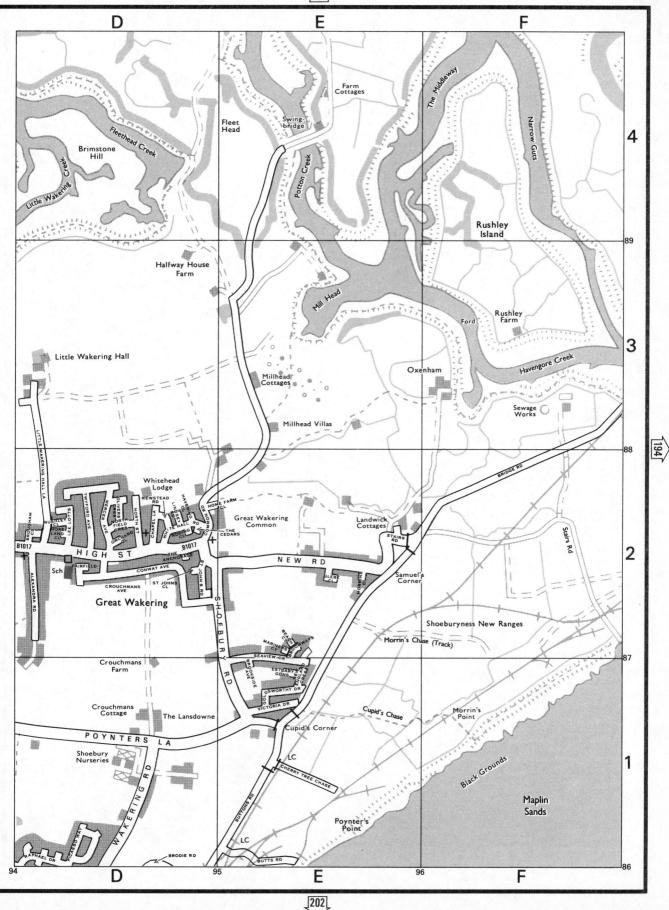

D   E   F

Brimstone
Hill

Fleethead Creek

Little Wakering Creek

Fleet
Head

Swing-
bridge

Farm
Cottages

The Middleway

Narrow Guts

4

Potton Creek

Rushley
Island

89

Halfway House
Farm

Mill Head

Ford

Rushley
Farm

3

Little Wakering Hall

Millhead
Cottages

Oxenham

Havengore Creek

Millhead Villas

Sewage
Works

88

194

Whitehead
Lodge

NEWSTEAD RD

HOME FARM CL

Great Wakering
Common

Landwick
Cottages

BRIDGE RD

LITTLE WAKERING HALL LA

WYBURN RD

RUSHLEY CL

TWYFORD AVE

MERCER AVE

NORTH ST

CHAPEL LA

LINDSEY RD

WHITE HALL RD

HOOKING LA

THE CEDARS

STAIRS
RD

Stairs Rd

2

B1017

OAK RD

OVERCLIFF

FIELD

ORCHARD

B1017

THE
ANCHORAGE

NEW RD

Samuel's
Corner

HIGH ST

+

Sch

FAIRFIELD

CONWAY AVE

ST JOHNS CL

ST JOHNS RD

GLEBE CL

NORTH ST

ALEXANDRA RD

CROUCHMANS
AVE

Great Wakering

SHOEBURY RD

Shoeburyness New Ranges

Crouchmans
Farm

BEACH CL

MARINERS
CT

SEAVIEW DR

BROADWAYS

Morrin's Chase (Track)

87

Crouchmans
Cottage

The Lansdowne

BROOKSIDE
AVE

ESTUARY
GDNS

ELDON WAY

Cupid's Chase

Morrin's
Point

OSWORTHY DR

VICTORIA DR

POYNTERS LA

WAKERING RD

Cupid's Corner

Cupid's Corner

Shoebury
Nurseries

LC

Black Grounds

1

SUTTONS RD

CHERRY TREE CHASE

Maplin
Sands

RAPHAEL DR

PICASSO WAY

LC

Poynter's
Point

BRODIE RD

BUTTS RD

94   D   95   E   96   F   86

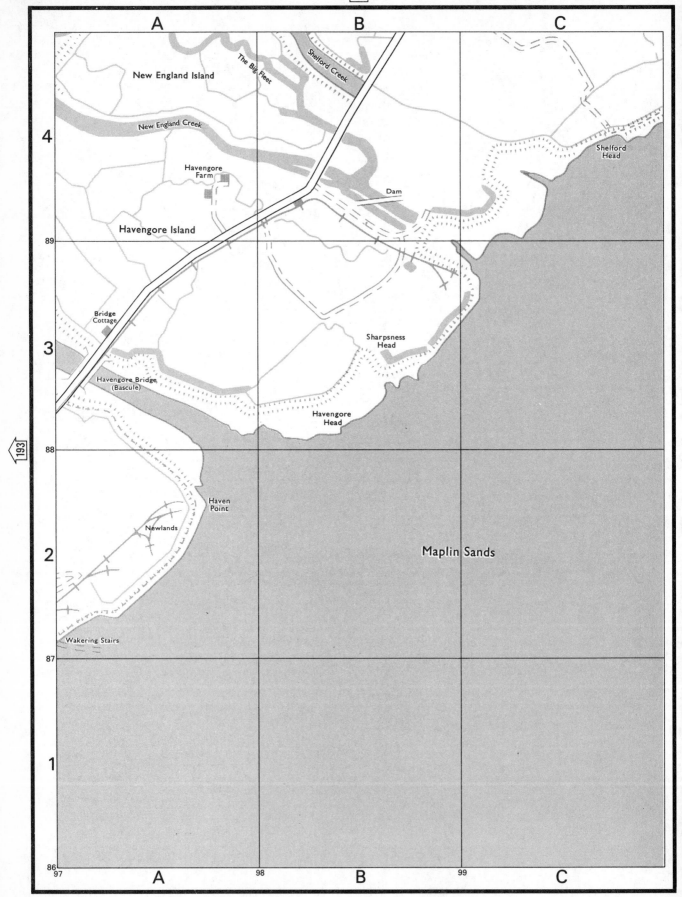

A B C

4

89

3

88

2

87

1

86
97 A 98 B 99 C

New England Island

The Big Fleet

Shelford Creek

New England Creek

Havengore Farm

Dam

Shelford Head

Havengore Island

Bridge Cottage

Sharpsness Head

Havengore Bridge (Bascule)

Havengore Head

Haven Point

Newlands

Maplin Sands

Wakering Stairs

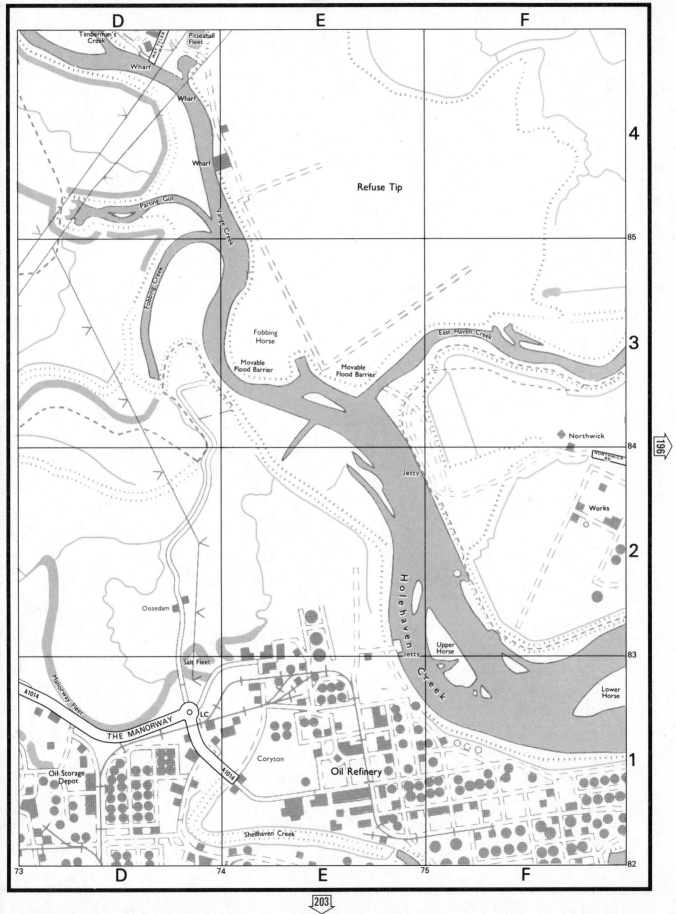

196

D   E   F

Timberman's Creek

Pitseahall Fleet

WAT TYLER WAY

Wharf

Wharf

Wharf

Parting Gut

Vange Creek

Fobbing Creek

Refuse Tip

4

85

Fobbing Horse

Movable Flood Barrier

Movable Flood Barrier

East Haven Creek

3

Northwick

84

NORTHWICK RD

Jetty

Works

Holehaven Creek

2

Oozedam

Upper Horse

Jetty

83

Salt Fleet

Lower Horse

A1014

Manorway Fleet

THE MANORWAY

LC

A1014

Coryton

Oil Refinery

1

Oil Storage Depot

Shellhaven Creek

73   D   74   E   75   F   82

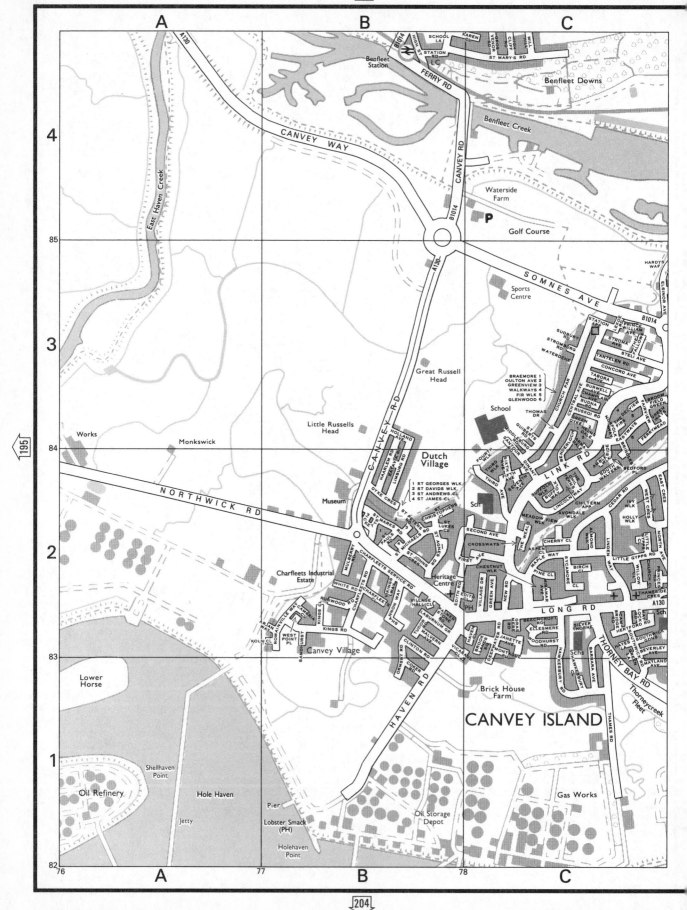

CANVEY ISLAND

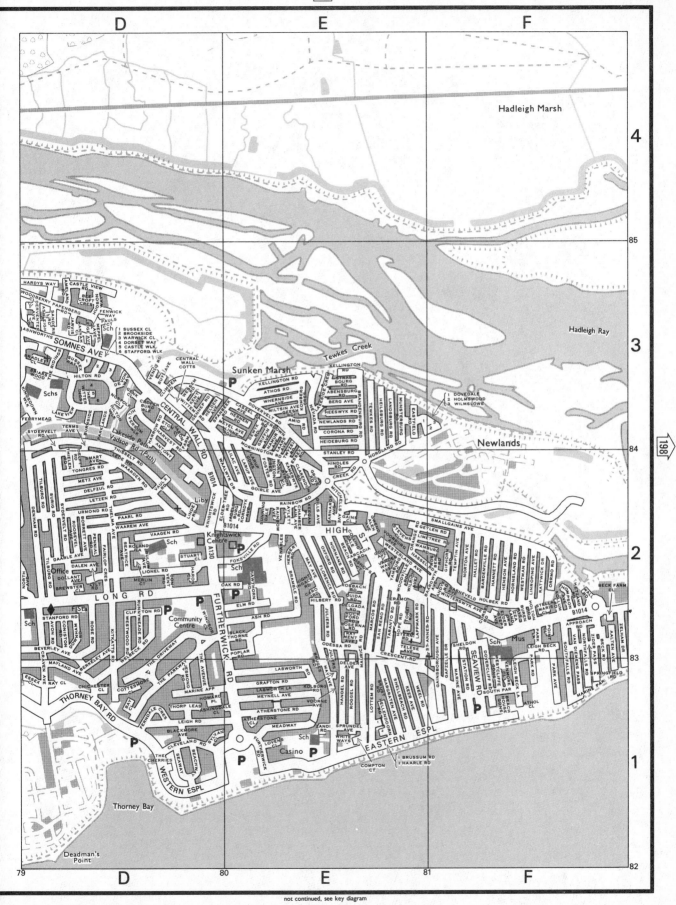

188

198

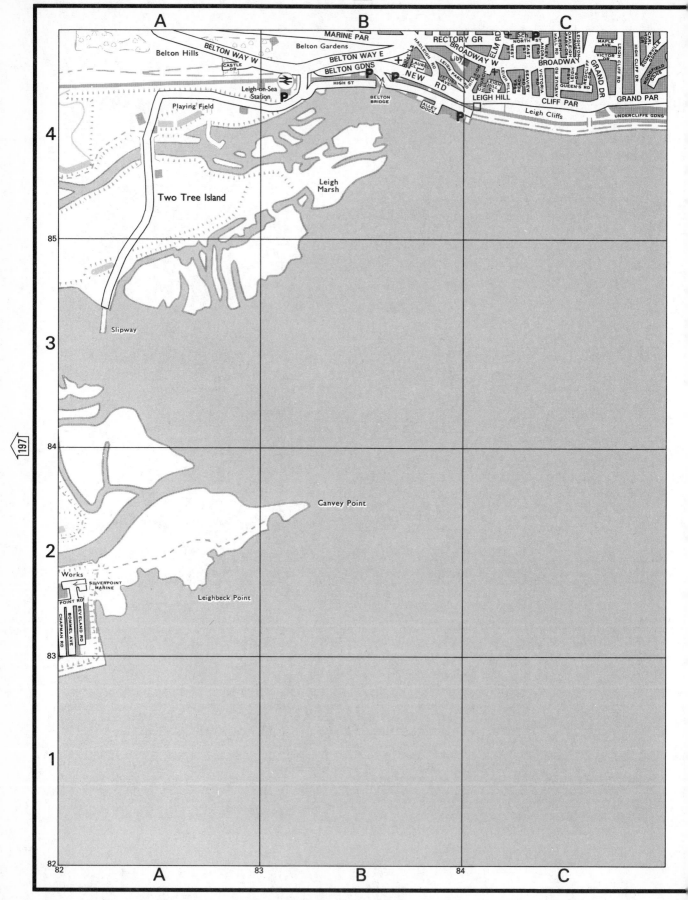

197

A   **B**   **C**

MARINE PAR

BELTON WAY W

Belton Hills

Belton Gardens

BELTON WAY E

CASTLE DR

BELTON GDNS

HIGH ST

RECTORY GR

BROADWAY W

Sch

NORTH

Leigh-on-Sea Station

Playing Field

Two Tree Island

Leigh Marsh

Billet La

Hadleigh Rd

Leigh Park

New Rd

Belton Bridge

Alley Dock

Leigh Hill

Cliff Par

Leigh Cliffs

Undercliffe Gdns

Broadway

Grand Par

Grand Dr

Slipway

Canvey Point

Works

Silverpoint Marine

Leighbeck Point

Point Rd

Beveland Rd

Bommel Ave

Chapman Rd

4

85

3

84

2

83

1

82

82

83

84

A   **B**   **C**

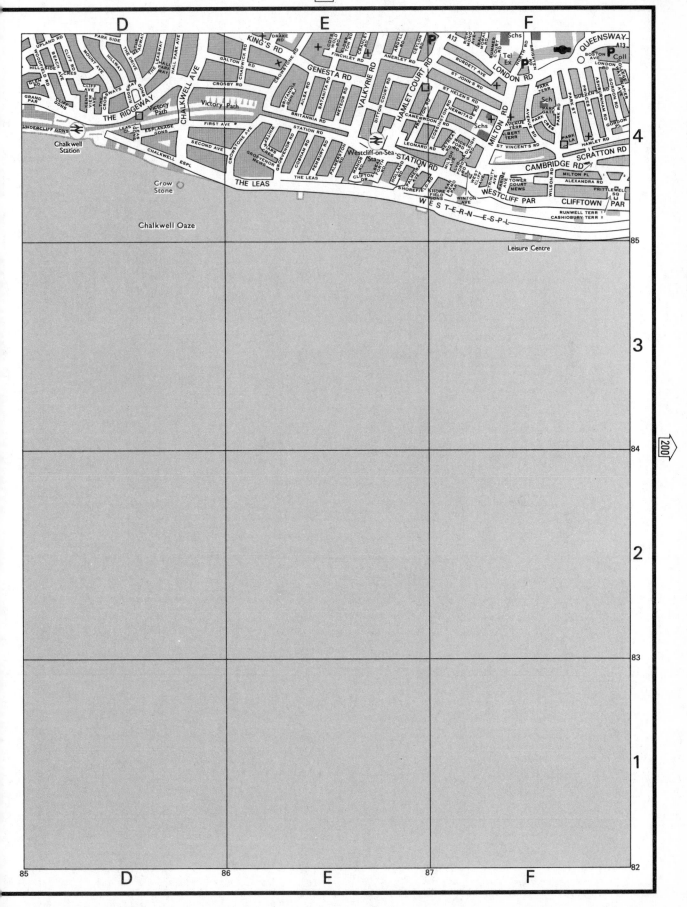

D   E   F

UPLAND RD PARK SIDE
WOODFIELD RD THE DRIVE
HILL-SIDE RD BEACH AVE MOUNT AVE HILLWAY THE LEASWAY
GLEN RD CLIFF RD HALL PARK AVE
GRAND PAR CLIFF AVE THE CROSSWAYS RIDDESDALE RD
CLIFF GDNS THE RIDGEWAY

KING'S RD DRAKE RD
GALTON RD CHADWICK RD GOLD WD RD FINCHLEY RD CRANLEY RD
CROSBY RD CROWSTONE RD GENESTA RD VALKYRIE RD ANERLEY RD ARGYLL RD CEFLON RD
Victory Path BRITANNIA ALSA RD SATANITA RD METEOR RD A13 BURDETT AVE
FIRST AVE BRITANNIA RD ST JOHN'S RD
Victory Path CHALKWELL AVE
SECOND AVE CROWSTONE AVE STATION RD ST HELEN'S RD
Underctiff Gdns Chalkwell Station CHALKWELL ESPL GROSVENOR MEWS Westcliff-on-Sea LEONARD CANEWDON HERMITAG Schs
Crow Stone THE LEAS GROSVENOR RD COBHAM RD RAMBURY RD PALMERSTON Manor Sta. STATION RD ST VINCENT'S RD
THE LEAS CLIFTON DR CRES MANOR RD HOLLAND PALM SHOREFIL WINTON AVE TOWER COURT MEWS
Chalkwell Oaze SHOREFIELD GDNS WESTCLIFF PAR MILTON PL ALEXANDRA RD

Schs Schs QUEENSWAY A13 Coll
LONDON RD Tel Ex Boston Ave LONDON RD
PARK TERR Sch PARK GATE PARK CRES QUINCE ST PRINCE ST ASHBURNHAM RD GORDON RD
MILTON RD AVENUE TERR AVENUE RD WILSON RD PARK LA HAMLET RD
CAMBRIDGE RD SCRATTON RD
RUNWELL TERR 1 CLIFFTOWN PRITTLEWELL SQU PAR
CASHIOBURY TERR 2

WESTERN ESPL

Leisure Centre

85 D 86 E 87 F 82

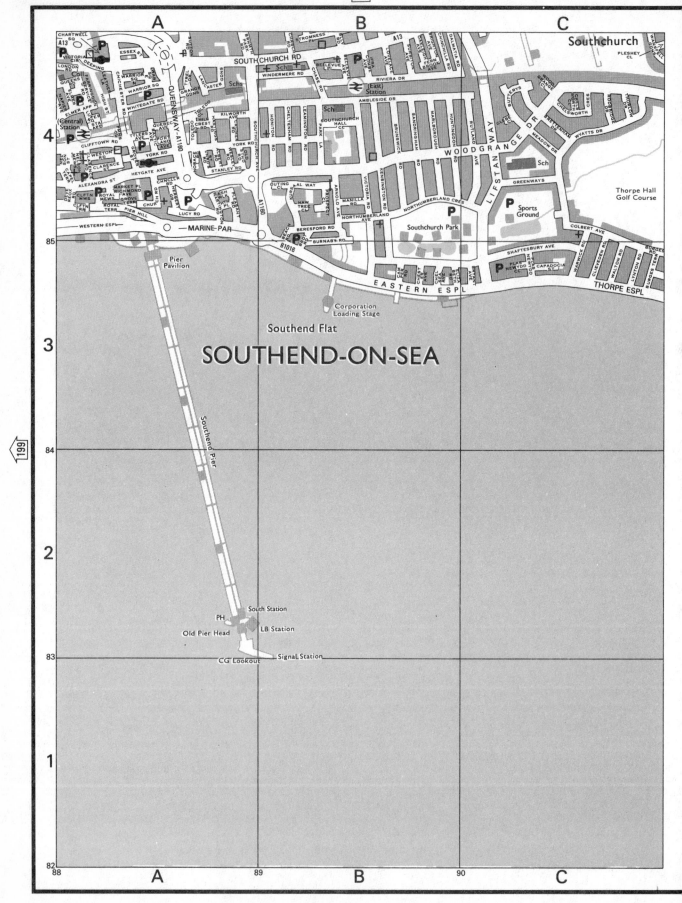

SOUTHEND-ON-SEA

Southchurch

Thorpe Hall
Golf Course

Southend Flat

Southend Pier

Pier
Pavilion

Corporation
Loading Stage

Southchurch Park

Sports
Ground

Old Pier Head

PH

South Station

LB Station

CG Lookout

Signal Station

WESTERN ESPL — MARINE-PAR

EASTERN ESPL

THORPE ESPL

SOUTHCHURCH RD

Coll

(Central)
Station

Schs

Sch

(East)
Station

WOODGRANGE RD

LIFSTANE WAY

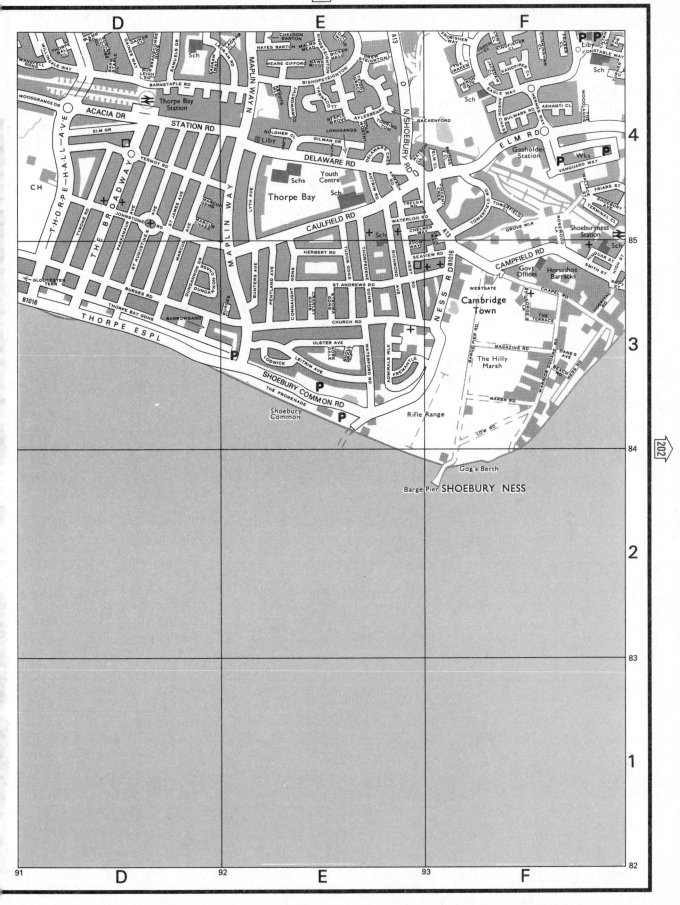

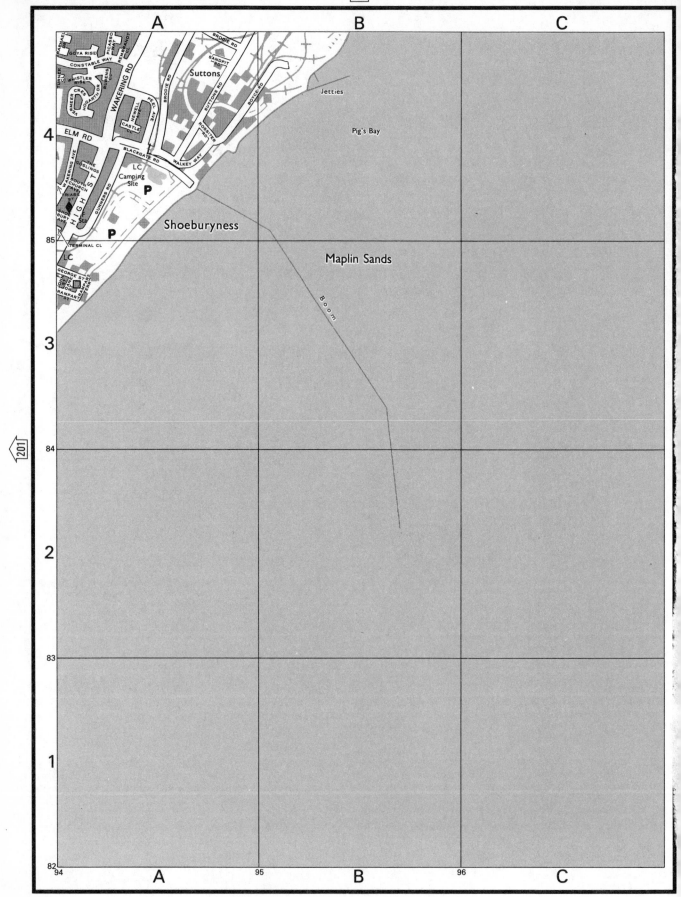

193

201

A B C

GOYA RISE
RAPHAEL DR
CONSTABLE WAY
TURNER CLSE
WHISTLER RISE
VERMEER CRES
HOGARTH DR
PICASSO WAY
REMBRANDT CL
WAKERING RD
BRODIE RD
SANDPIT RD
BRODIE RD
Suttons
SUTTONS RD
BOYCE RD
PEEL AVE
CASTLE CL
NEWELL
ROSSITER RD
Jetties
Pig's Bay

ELM RD
WAKERING AVE
THE GOSLINGS
SOUTH WAY
CHURCH
BLACKGATE RD
WALKEY WAY
GUNNERS RD
LC
Camping
Site
P

HIGH ST
FRIARS ST
SHOE-
BURY
AVE
F Sta
P
Shoeburyness
85

TERMINAL CL
LC
Maplin Sands
GEORGE ST
RAMPART ST
RAMPART TERR

Boom

84

83

82
94 95 96

A B C

4

3

2

1

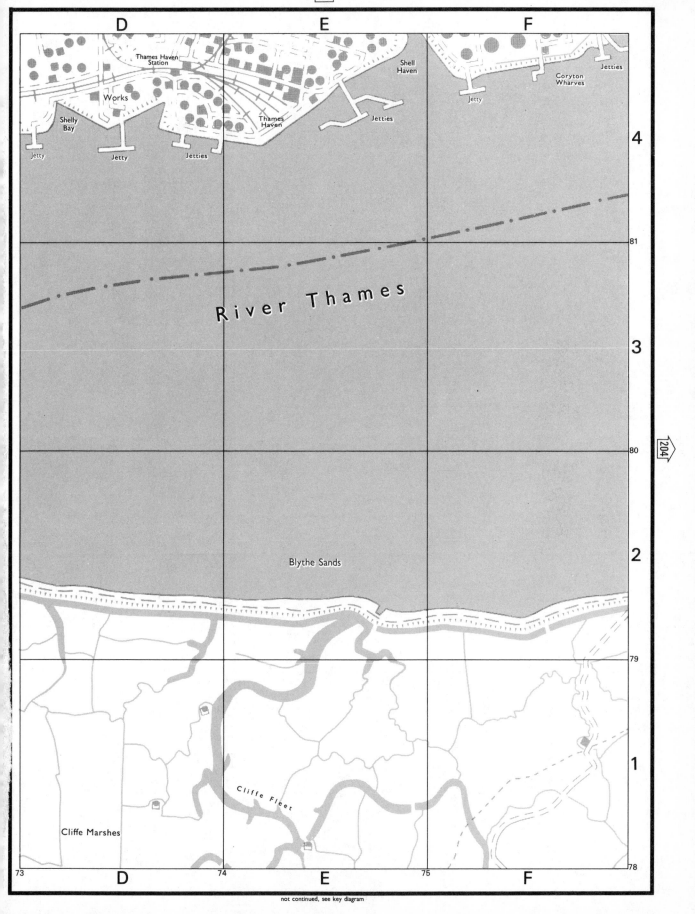

D

E

F

Thames Haven
Station

Shell
Haven

Coryton
Wharves

Jetties

Works

Jetty

Shelly
Bay

Thames
Haven

Jetties

Jetty

Jetty

Jetties

4

River Thames

81

3

204

80

Blythe Sands

2

79

1

Cliffe Fleet

Cliffe Marshes

78

73

D

74

E

75

F

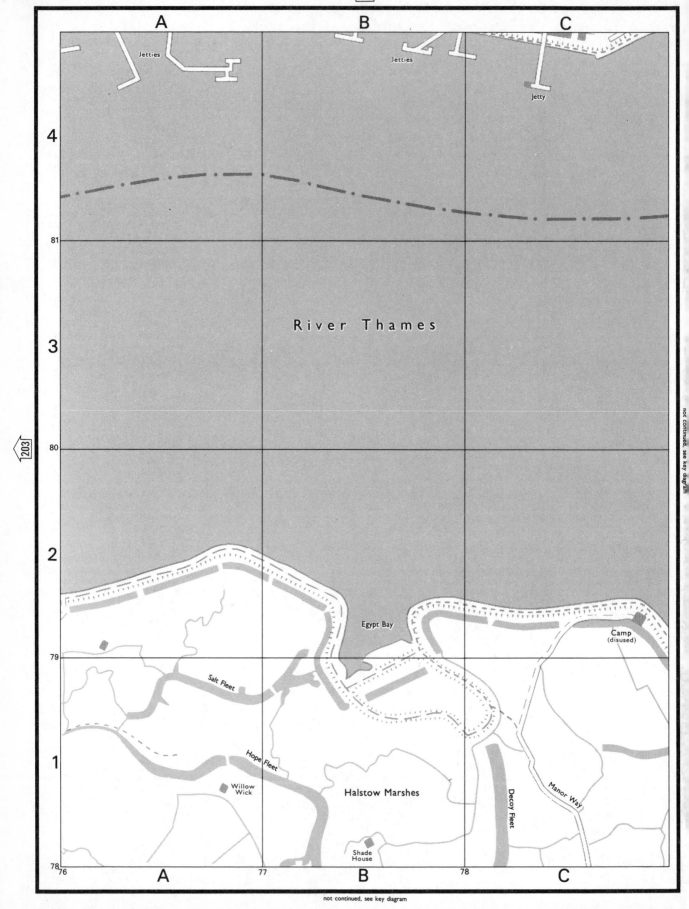

203

not continued, see key diagram

A   B   C

Jetties

Jetties

Jetty

4

81

River Thames

3

80

2

Egypt Bay

Camp
(disused)

79

Salt Fleet

Hope Fleet

1

Willow
Wick

Halstow Marshes

Decoy Fleet

Manor Way

Shade
House

78

76   A   77   B   78   C

USER'S NOTES

EXPLANATION OF THE STREET INDEX REFERENCE SYSTEM

Street names are listed alphabetically and show the locality, the page number and a reference to the square in which the name falls on the map page.

Example:	Cedar Way. Gt Ben..89 F4

Cedar Way	This is the full street name, which may have been abbreviated on the map.

Gt Ben	This is the abbreviation for the town, village or locality in which the street falls.

89	This is the page number of the map on which the street name appears.

F4	The letter and figure indicate the square on the map in which the centre of the street falls. The square can be found at the junction of the vertical column carrying the appropriate letter and the horizontal row carrying the appropriate figure.

ABBREVIATIONS USED IN THE INDEX
Road Names

Approach	App	Lane	La
Avenue	Ave	North	N
Boulevard	Bvd	Orchard	Orch
Broadway	Bwy	Parade	Par
By-Pass	By-Ps	Passage	Pas
Causeway	Cswy	Place	Pl
Common	Comm	Pleasant	Plea
Corner	Cnr	Precinct	Prec
Cottages	Cotts	Promenade	Prom
Court	Ct	Road	Rd
Crescent	Cres	South	S
Drive	Dr	Square	Sq
Drove	Dro	Street,Saint	St
East	E	Terrace	Terr
Gardens	Gdns	Walk	Wlk
Grove	Gr	West	W
Heights	Hts	Yard	Yd

Towns, Villages and Rural Localities

Place	Abbr.	No.	Grid
Aldham	Ald	65	D4
Alphamstone	Alph	18	C2
Alresford	Alres	88	A4
Althorne	Alth	158	A2
Ardleigh	Ard	51	F4
Asheldham	Ashe	160	A4
Ashen	Ashe	3	E1
Ashington	Ashi	178	B4
Barling	Barl	192	C4
Basildon	Basil	185	E2
Beaumont	Beau	73	F4
Belchamp Otten	Bel O	10	B4
Belchamp St Paul	Bel S P	5	D1
Belchamp Walter	Bel W	11	D3
Birch	Birch	84	A2
Black Notley	Bl Not	78	A3
Boreham	Bore	128	C4
Boxted	Box	31	F4
Bradfield	Brad	36	C1
Bradwell	Bradw	61	E1
Bradwell-on-Sea	Brad O S	137	D1
Braintree	Brain	59	E2
Brightlingsea	Brigh	106	B3
Broomfield	Broom	127	D4
Bulmer	Bul	11	F3
Bures	Bures	28	C4
Burnham-On-Crouch	Burn	170	B3
Canewdon	Cane	168	C1
Canvey Island	Canv	196	C1
Castle Hedingham	Ca Hed	15	F2
Cattawade	Catt	35	E4
Cavendish	Cav	1	B1
Chelmsford	Chelm	127	D2
Churchend	Church	183	D3
Clacton-on-Sea	Clact	110	A1
Clare	Cla	4	B4
Coggeshall	Cogg	63	D2
Colchester	Colch	67	E4
Cold Norton	Col N	155	F3
Colne Engaine	Col En	27	D1
Copford	Copf	65	E2
Corringham	Corr	185	D1
Danbury	Dan	142	C4
Dedham	Ded	33	F3
Dengie	Deng	160	B4
Earls Colne	Ea Col	45	E3
East Hanningfield	E Han	153	E4
East Mersea	E Mers	105	E1
Eight Ash Green	E A Gr	66	A4
Elmstead Market	Elmst M	70	A3
Fairstead	Fair	96	A3
Faulkbourne	Faulk	97	D4
Feering	Fee	81	F3
Fingringhoe	Fing	86	C3
Fordham	Ford	47	E3
Foxearth	Fox	6	B3
Frating	Frat	70	C1
Frinton-on-Sea	Frin	96	A3
Gestingthorpe	Gest	10	B1
Glemsford	Glems	2	B2
Goldhanger	Gold	133	F4
Gosfield	Gos	42	C4
Great Baddow	Gt Bad	140	C4
Great Bentley	Gt Ben	89	F4
Great Braxted	Gt Brx	99	E1
Great Bromley	Gt Bro	52	C1
Great Henny	Gt H	18	B4
Great Horkesley	Gt Hor	31	D1
Great Leighs	Gt Le	95	D4
Great Maplestead	Gt Map	16	B1
Great Oakley	Gt Oak	56	B2
Great Stambridge	Gt Stam	179	E2
Great Tey	Gt T	64	B4
Great Totham	Gt Tot	116	B3
Great Wakering	Gt Wak	193	D2
Great Wigborough	Gt Wig	102	C2
Great Yeldham	Gt Y	9	D1
Hadleigh	Hadl	188	C2
Halstead	Hals	25	E1
Harwich	Harw	40	B2
Hatfield Peverel	Hat Per	114	A2
Hawkwell	Hawk	178	A3
Hazeleigh	Haze	144	A2
Higham	High	22	A2
Hockley	Hock	177	E4
Hullbridge	Hull	165	E1
Kelveden	Kelv	81	E1
Lamarsh	Lam	19	E2
Langenhoe	Lang	86	A1
Langford	Langf	131	E4
Langham	Langh	32	C2
Latchingdon	Latch	157	D3
Lawford	Lawf	35	d2
Layer Breton	Lay Br	84	A1
Layer Marney	Lay M	101	E4
Layer-de-la-Haye	Lay H	84	C3
Little Baddow	Lit Bad	129	E2
Little Bentley	Lit Ben	71	F4
Little Braxted	Lit Brx	98	B1
Little Bromley	Lit Bro	53	D3
Little Clacton	Lit Cla	91	E2
Little Horkesley	Lit Hor	30	C2
Little Maplestead	Lit Map	17	D1
Little Oakley	Lit Oak	57	D4
Little Totham	Lit Tot	117	D2
Little Waltham	Lit Wal	112	A4
Little Yeldam	Lit Y	9	F2
Long Melford	L Mel	7	E4
Maldon	Mald	131	F1
Manningtree	Mann	35	E3
Margaretting	Marg	139	D1
Marks Tey	Mks T	65	D2
Mayland	May	158	A4
Messing	Mess	82	B1
Middleton	Midd	12	C2
Mistley	Mist	36	A2
Mount Bures	M Bure	29	C3
Mundon	Mund	145	F1
Nayland	Nay	20	A1
North Fambridge	N Fam	167	D4
Ovington	Ovi	4	A1
Paglesham Churchend	Pag Ch	180	B4
Panfield	Pan	59	D4
Pebmarsh	Peb	27	D4
Peldon	Peld	103	E3
Pentlow	Pent	5	F3
Purleigh	Purl	144	B1
Ramsey	Rams	39	D1
Rayleigh	Rayl	176	A1
Rayne	Ray	59	D1
Rettendon	Rett	153	D1
Ridgewell	Ridge	8	A3
Rivenhall	Rive	98	A4
Rochford	Roch	178	B1
Rowhedge	Rowh	86	C4
Runwell	Runw	163	F1
Sandon	Sand	141	E3
Shotley Gate	Sho G	40	A4
Sible Hedingham	Si Hed	15	F1
Silver End	Silv E	79	F2
South Benfleet	S Ben	188	F2
South Hanningfield	S Han	163	E4
South Woodham Ferrers	S Woo F	165	F4
Southend-On-Sea	South	200	B3
Southminster	Soum	159	E2
Springfield	Sprin	127	F3
St Lawrence	St L	148	C3
St Osyth	St O	108	A2
Stanway	Stanw	66	B3
Steeple	Steep	147	F2
Stisted	Stis	61	E3
Stonebridge	Stobr	192	A3
Stow Maries	Stow M	155	E2
Stratford St Mary	Str S M	22	B1
Sudbury	Sud	12	B4
Tendring	Tend	72	C3
Terling	Terl	96	B2
Thorpe-le-Soken	Th L S	74	A1
Thorrington	Thor	89	D3
Thundersley	Thund	187	F4
Tillingham	Till	149	F2
Tiptree	Tipt	100	A3
Tollesbury	Tolle	119	E1
Tolleshunt D'Arcy	Toll D	118	B2
Tolleshunt Knights	Toll K	101	D2
Tolleshunt Major	Toll M	117	F2
Toppesfield	Topp	14	B4
Twinstead	Twin	18	B3
Tye Green	T Gr	78	C3
Ulting	Ult	130	B4
Virley	Virl	119	D4
Wakes Colne	Wa Col	46	B3
Walton on the Naze	Walt	94	B4
Weeley	Weel	72	C1
West Bergholt	W Berg	48	C2
West Hanningfield	W Han	152	A2
West Mersea	W Mers	121	E3
Wethersfield	Weth	23	D1
White Notley	Wh Not	78	C1
Wickford	Wick	174	C3
Wickham Bishops	Wic Bis	115	E3
Wickham St Paul	Wic S P	17	D3
Witham	With	97	F2
Wivenhoe	Wiv	69	E1
Wix	Wix	55	E3
Woodham Mortimer	Woo Mor	143	E3
Woodham Walter	Woo Wa	130	B1
Wormingford	Worm	29	F3
Wrabness	Wrab	37	E3
Writtle	Writ	126	B1

Aalten Ave. Canv 197 F2
Abbas Wlk. Sud 13 E3
Abberton Rd. Fing 86 C2
Abberton Rd. Lay H 85 D3
Abbess Cl. Chelm 126 C1
Abbey Cl. Hull 165 E1
Abbey Cres. Th L S 74 A1
Abbey Fields. E Han 153 D4
Abbey La. Cogg 63 D1
Abbey Rd. Hull 165 E1
Abbey Rd. Sud 7 F1
Abbey St. Th L S 74 A1
Abbey Turning. Mald 131 E2
Abbeygate St. Colch 67 F3
Abbot's Rd. Colch 68 A2
Abbots Cl. Clact 109 F3
Abbots Cl. Wix 55 E3
Abbots Gdns. St O 108 B2
Abbots La. E A Gr 66 A4
Abbots Wlk. South 201 E4
Abbotsleigh Rd. S Woo F 165 F3
Abbotswood. Thund 188 B3
Abbott Rd. Harw 39 F1
Abbotts Cl. Chelm 127 E2
Abbotts Cl. South 189 F3
Abdy Ave. Harw 39 F1
Abels Rd. Hals 43 E4
Abensburg Rd. Canv 197 E3
Abercorn Way. With 98 A1
Aberdeen Gdns. Hadl 189 D1
Abingdon Ct. Basil 174 A1
Abinger Cl. Clact 109 E3
Abraham Dr. Silv E 79 F2
Abreys. Thund 188 A4
Acacia Ave. Colch 68 C4
Acacia Dr. Mald 131 F1
Acacia Dr. South 201 D4
Acacia Gdns. With 98 A2
Acacia Rd. Basil 186 C4
Accomodation Rd. Box 49 E4
Achilles Way. Brain 60 A3
Achnacone Dr. Colch 49 E2
Ackland Ave. Colch 67 D4
Acorn Ave. Brain 59 E1
Acorn Ave. Hals 25 E1
Acorn Cl. Colch 50 B2
Acorn Cl. Harw 40 A1
Acorn Wlk. Thor 89 D3
Acorns The. Hock 177 F4
Acres End. Chelm 126 C2
Acton Cl. Sud 12 C4
Acton Green. Sud 12 C4
Acton La. Sud 7 F1
Adalia Cres. Hadl 189 D2
Adalia Way. Hadl 189 D1
Adam Way. Wick 174 C4
Adams Glade. Hawk 178 B3
Addison Pavement. Basil ... 186 A3
Addison Rd. Sud 13 D4
Adelaide Dr. Colch 68 A1
Adelaide Gdns. S Ben 187 E1
Adelaide St. Rams 39 F3
Adelsburg Rd. Canv 197 E2
Admirals Wlk. Chelm 126 C2
Admirals Wlk. South 201 E3
Aetheric Rd. Brain 59 F2
Affleck Rd. Colch 68 C4
Agar Rd App. Walt 94 B4
Agate Rd. Clact 109 F1
Agincourt Rd. Clact 109 E2
Agnes Ave. Hadl 189 D2
Ailsa Rd. South 199 E4
Ainger Rd. Harw 39 F1
Aingers Green Rd. Gt Ben ... 90 A3
Airborne Cl. South 189 F3
Aire Wlk. With 97 F1
Aisne Rd. Colch 67 E2
Ajax Cl. Brain 60 A3
Akenfield Cl. S Woo F 165 F4
Alamein Rd. Brain 170 B2
Alamein Rd. Chelm 126 C3
Alamein Rd. Colch 67 E1
Alan Cl. South 189 F3
Alan Dr. Lit Cla 91 E1
Alan Gr. South 189 F3
Alan Rd. With 97 F1
Alan Way. Colch 66 C2
Alanbrooke Rd. Colch 68 B1
Albany Ave. South 190 C1
Albany Cl. Chelm 126 C3
Albany Cl. W Berg 48 C2
Albany Gdns E. Clact 110 A2
Albany Gdns W. Clact 110 A2
Albany Rd. Rayl 177 D1
Albany Rd. W Berg 48 C2
Albany Rd. Wick 174 B3
Albemarle Gdns. Brain 60 B3
Albermarle St. Harw 40 B3
Albert Cl. Ashi 178 B3
Albert Cl. Rayl 176 C2
Albert Gdns. Clact 110 A2
Albert Gdns. Cogg 63 D1
Albert Pl. Cogg 63 D1
Albert Rd. Ashi 178 B3
Albert Rd. Brain 60 A2
Albert Rd. Brigh 107 D3
Albert Rd. Burn 170 B2
Albert Rd. Rayl 176 C2
Albert Rd. S Woo F 165 E4

Albert Rd. South 192 A1
Albert Rd. South 200 A4
Albert Rd. Thund 187 D3
Albert Rd. With 98 A2
Albert St. Colch 67 F4
Albert St. Harw 40 B3
Albert Terr. South 199 F4
Albertine Cl. Stanw 66 B3
Albion Gr. Colch 68 A3
Albion Rd. S Ben 187 E2
Albion Rd. South 190 C1
Albion St. Rowh 87 D4
Albrighton Croft. Colch 50 B2
Albury. South 191 F1
Alcotes. Basil 185 F3
Aldeburgh Cl. Clact 109 D2
Aldeburgh Gdns. Colch 50 A2
Aldeburgh Way. Sprin 127 E3
Alder Dr. Chelm 140 A3
Alder Wlk. With 98 A2
Alderbury Lea. S Woo F 142 C1
Aldercar Rd. Copf 65 F1
Alderford Maltings. Si Hed ... 24 C4
Alderford St. Si Hed 24 C4
Alderleys. Thund 188 A3
Aldermans Hill. Hock 177 D3
Alderney Gdns. Runw 163 E1
Alderton Rd. Colch 68 B4
Alderwood Way. S Ben 188 B2
Aldham Gdns. Rayl 175 F2
Aldon Cl. Harw 39 E1
Aldridge Cl. Sprin 128 A2
Aldrin Way. South 190 A3
Alefounder Rd. Colch 68 C3
Alexander Ct. Sprin 127 F4
Alexander Mews. Sand 141 E1
Alexander Rd. Brain 59 F2
Alexandra Ave. W Mers 121 F3
Alexandra Dr. Wiv 69 E2
Alexandra Rd. Ashi 178 B4
Alexandra Rd. Burn 170 B3
Alexandra Rd. Clact 109 F2
Alexandra Rd. Colch 67 F3
Alexandra Rd. Gt Wak 193 D2
Alexandra Rd. Harw 40 B3
Alexandra Rd. Rayl 176 C2
Alexandra Rd. S Ben 187 E1
Alexandra Rd. Si Hed 15 E1
Alexandra Rd. South 198 C4
Alexandra Rd. South 199 F4
Alexandra Rd. Sud 13 D4
Alexandra Rd. Weel 72 C1
Alexandra St. South 200 A4
Alexandra Terr. Colch 67 F3
Alexandria Dr. Rayl 176 A2
Alfells Rd. Elmst M 69 F3
Alfred Gdns. Runw 163 E1
Alfred Terr. Walt 94 B4
Alfreda Ave. Hull 165 E2
Alfreg Rd. With 114 B4
Algars Way. S Woo F 165 E4
Alicia Ave. Wick 175 D4
Alicia Cl. Wick 175 D4
Alicia Way. Wick 175 D4
Alicia Wlk. Wick 175 D4
Alison Cl. Harw 40 A1
All Saints Ave. Colch 67 D2
All Saints Cl. Sprin 127 F2
Allandale. Thund 188 A4
Allectus Way. With 114 B4
Allen Way. St O 107 D2
Allendale Dr. Copf 65 E2
Allens Cl. Bore 112 C1
Allerton Cl. Hawk 178 B3
Alley Dock. South 198 B4
Alleyn Pl. South 190 B1
Alleyne Way. Clact 125 D4
Allfields. Harw 39 F1
Allfields. Harw 40 A1
Alma Cl. Hadl 189 E1
Alma Cl. Wick 174 A3
Alma Dr. Chelm 127 D1
Alma Rd. Hadl 189 D1
Alma Sq. Mann 35 E2
Alma St. Wiv 87 D4
Almere. S Ben 187 E2
Almond Ave. Wick 174 B4
Almond Cl. Clact 109 E2
Almond Cl. Tipt 100 B3
Almond Cl. Wiv 69 E1
Almond Way. Colch 68 C4
Almond Wlk. Canv 196 C2
Alpha Cl. Basil 186 C3
Alpha Cl. Brain 60 A1
Alpha Rd. Basil 186 C3
Alpha Rd. Burn 170 B3
Alpha Rd. St O 107 D2
Alphamstone Rd. Lam 19 D2
Alport Ave. Colch 67 E2
Alresford Rd. Elmst M 87 F4
Altbarn Cl. Colch 50 B3
Althorne Cl. Basil 174 A1
Althorne Way. Cane 168 C1
Althorpe Cl. Hock 177 E3
Alton Dr. Colch 67 D3
Alton Gdns. South 190 C3
Alton Park La. Clact 109 D1
Alton Park Rd. Clact 109 E1

Alton Rd. Clact 109 F1
Aluf Cl. With 114 C4
Alvis Ave. Clact 124 C3
Alyssum Cl. Bore 128 A3
Alyssum Wlk. Colch 68 B4
Amarells Rd. Lit Cla 91 E2
Amberley Cl. Elmst M 69 E1
Ambleside Dr. South 200 B4
Ambleside Gdns. Hull 165 E1
Ambleside Wlk. Canv 196 C2
Ambrose Ave. Colch 66 C2
Ameland Rd. Canv 197 D3
America Rd. Ea Col 45 E1
America St. Mald 132 A1
Amid Rd. Canv 197 E3
Amos Hill. Gt H 18 A4
Amoss Rd. Gt Bad 140 C4
Ampers End. Basil 185 E3
Anchor End. Mist 36 A2
Anchor Hill. Wiv 87 D4
Anchor La. Cane 168 B1
Anchor La. Mald 132 A3
Anchor La. Mist 36 A2
Anchor Rd. Clact 109 F2
Anchor Rd. Tipt 100 B2
Anchor Reach. S Woo F 165 F3
Anchor St. Chelm 127 D1
Anchorage The. Gt Wak 193 D2
Anders Fall. South 190 A3
Anderson Ave. Chelm 126 C3
Andover Cl. Clact 110 A3
Andrew Cl. Brain 59 F3
Andrews Pl. Chelm 126 C2
Andyk Rd. Canv 197 F2
Anerley Rd. South 199 E4
Angel Cl. Basil 185 E3
Angel La. Glems 2 A2
Angle Side. Brain 60 A1
Anglefield. Clact 109 F1
Anglesea Rd. Wiv 87 E4
Anglia Cl. Colch 67 D2
Anglia Way. Brain 60 A1
Anne Boleyn Dr. Roch 190 C4
Anne Cl. Brigh 106 C3
Anson Chase. South 201 F4
Anson Cl. S Woo F 165 F3
Anson Way. Brain 60 B2
Anstey Cl. South 189 E4
Anthony Cl. Colch 50 B1
Antonio Wlk. Colch 68 C4
Antony Cl. Canv 197 D3
Antrim Rd. South 201 E4
Anvil Way. Sprin 127 F4
Anzio Cres. Colch 67 E2
Apple Tree Way. Wick 174 C4
Appledore. South 192 B1
Appleford Ct. Basil 186 B3
Applerow. South 189 F3
Appleton Rd. S Ben 187 D1
Appletree Cl. South 191 F2
Appletree Cl. T Gr 78 C3
Appletree Wlk. Brain 60 A1
Appleyard Ave. Hock 177 F4
Approach Rd. Canv 197 F2
Approach The. Clact 125 D4
Approach The. Rayl 176 B2
Apton Hall Rd. Gt Stam 179 E3
Apton Hall Rd. Roch 179 E3
Aragon Cl. Clact 124 C4
Aragon Cl. South 190 C2
Arakan Cl. Colch 67 D1
Arbour La. Wic Bis 115 F3
Arbour La. Sprin 127 E2
Arbour Way. Colch 50 B2
Arbutus Cl. Chelm 140 A3
Arcadia Rd. Burn 170 B3
Arcadia Rd. Canv 197 E2
Arcadian Gdns. Hadl 188 B2
Archer Ave. South 191 F2
Archer Cl. South 191 F2
Archers Fields. Basil 174 A1
Archers Way. Chelm 140 B1
Arden Cl. Colch 50 B2
Arderne Cl. Harw 39 F1
Ardleigh Ct. Ard 51 F4
Ardleigh Rd. Ded 33 E2
Ardleigh Rd. Gt Bro 52 A2
Ardleigh Rd. Lit Bro 52 C3
Ardleyway. Rayl 176 B2
Argyle Cl. South 190 C2
Argyle Rd. Burn 170 B2
Argyle Rd. Th L S 73 F1
Argyll Rd. Bore 128 A3
Argyll Rd. South 199 E4
Ariel Cl. Colch 68 C4
Arjan Way. Canv 196 B2
Ark La. Roch 178 A1
Arlington Rd. South 191 F1
Armadale. Canv 196 C3
Armagh Rd. South 201 E4
Armidale Wlk. Colch 68 A1
Armiger Way. With 98 A1
Armitage Rd. South 192 A1
Armond Rd. With 97 F2
Armoury Rd. W Berg 48 C2
Armstrong Cl. Dan 142 C4
Armstrong Rd. Thund 187 E4
Armstrong Way. Gt Y 9 D1

Arnheim Rd. Burn 170 B2
Arnhem Gr. Brain 59 F2
Arnhem Rd. Chelm 126 C3
Arnold Ave. South 200 B4
Arnold Dr. Colch 68 C3
Arnold Rd. Clact 109 E1
Arnold Villas. Tipt 100 B3
Arnold Way. Chelm 140 B2
Arnolds Way. Ashi 178 B4
Arnstones Cl. Colch 68 B4
Arras Rd. Colch 67 E2
Arrow Rd. Colch 68 C4
Arthur Ct. Chelm 126 C3
Arthur St. Colch 67 F3
Arthy Cl. Hat Pev 114 A2
Artillery Barracks Folley. Colch 67 F3
Artillery St. Colch 68 A3
Arun Cl. Sprin 127 E3
Arundel Gdns. South 190 A2
Arundel Rd. Ashi 167 E1
Arundel Rd. Runw 163 E1
Arundel Rd. Thund 187 D4
Arwen Gr. S Woo F 165 E3
Asbury Cl. Colch 68 B4
Ascot Cl. Thund 188 A4
Ash Bungalows. Brain 59 F2
Ash Cl. Brigh 106 C4
Ash Cl. Clact 109 E2
Ash Fall. With 97 F3
Ash Gr. Burn 170 A3
Ash Gr. Chelm 140 B4
Ash Gr. Mald 132 B3
Ash Gr. Sud 13 E3
Ash Gr. Wiv 69 E2
Ash Green. Cane 168 B1
Ash Ground Cl. Catt 35 E4
Ash Grove. Colch 86 A4
Ash Rd. Alres 88 A4
Ash Rd. Canv 197 E2
Ash Rd. Hadl 188 C1
Ash Tree Cl. Chelm 126 C1
Ash Tree Cres. Chelm 126 C1
Ash Tree Wlk. Basil 185 F3
Ash Way. Hock 177 F4
Ash Wlk. South 200 A4
Ashanti Cl. South 201 F4
Ashburnham Rd. South 199 F4
Ashbury Dri. Mks T 64 C2
Ashby Rd. With 115 D4
Ashcombe Cl. South 189 D3
Ashcombe Way. Rayl 176 C1
Ashcombe. Rayl 178 B2
Ashdene Cl. Hull 165 F1
Ashdon Way. Basil 185 D3
Ashdown Cres. Hadl 188 C2
Ashdown Way. Colch 68 B4
Ashen Cl. Ashe 3 E1
Ashen Hill. Ashe 3 E1
Ashen La. Ashe 3 E2
Ashen Rd. Ashe 8 A4
Ashen Rd. Bel S P 4 A3
Ashen Rd. Ovi 4 A1
Ashes Cl. Walt 93 F4
Ashes Rd. T Gr 78 C4
Ashfield Farm Rd. Ult 130 B4
Ashfields. Basil 186 B4
Ashford Rd. Chelm 126 C1
Ashingdale Cl. Canv 197 E1
Ashingdon Rd. Ashi 178 B3
Ashingdon Rd. Roch 178 B3
Ashleigh Cl. Canv 197 D3
Ashleigh Dr. South 198 C4
Ashley Gdns. Colch 67 E4
Ashley Green. E Han 153 D4
Ashley Rd. Harw 40 A2
Ashlong Gr. Hals 25 F2
Ashlyn's Rd. Frin 93 F2
Ashlyns. Basil 186 A4
Ashmans Row. S Woo F 165 E3
Ashmere Rise. Sud 13 D4
Ashmole Dr. Walt 93 F3
Ashpole Rd. Brain 42 A1
Ashstead Cl. Clact 109 D3
Ashton Pl. Sprin 128 A2
Ashurst Ave. South 191 F1
Ashurst Cl. Rowh 86 C4
Ashurst Dr. Sprin 127 E4
Ashwells Meadow. Ea Col ... 45 D3
Ashwin Ave. Copf 65 E2
Ashwood Cl. Burn 170 A4
Ashworths. Canv 197 D3
Ashworths. Hawk 178 B3
Aspen Cl. Canv 196 C2
Aspen Cl. Colch 68 B4
Aspen Way. Lit Oak 57 D4
Asquith Ave. Thund 188 B3
Assandune Cl. Ashi 178 B4
Astell Ct. Frin 93 F2
Aster Cl. Clact 109 E2
Aster Cl. Sprin 127 F3
Astley Rd. Clact 109 E2
Athelstan Gdns. Runw 163 E1
Athelstan Rd. Colch 67 E3
Atherstone Cl. Canv 197 E1
Atherstone Rd. Canv 197 E1
Athol Cl. Canv 197 F1
Athol Rd. Sprin 127 F3
Athos Rd. Canv 197 E3

Atlas Ct. Ea Col 45 D4
Atlas Rd. Ea Col 44 C4
Attlee Gdns. Colch 68 A3
Attwoods Cl. Chelm 140 B2
Aubrey Cl. Chelm 127 D4
Auckland Cl. Chelm 126 C3
Audley Cl. Colch 67 E3
Audley Way. Basil 185 D3
Audley Way. Frin 94 A3
Audleys Cl. South 190 C3
Audries Estate. Walt 94 A4
Augustine Way. S Woo F ... 142 C1
Augustus Way. With 114 C4
Austen Cl. Brain 78 A4
Austin Ave. Clact 124 C3
Autoway. Colch 50 B3
Autumn Cl. Clact 109 E3
Avebury Rd. South 190 C1
Aveley Way. Mald 144 C4
Aveline Rd. Ard 51 F4
Avenue Rd. Corr 185 D1
Avenue Rd. Gt Bad 140 B4
Avenue Rd. S Ben 187 F2
Avenue Rd. South 198 C4
Avenue Rd. South 199 F4
Avenue Rd. With 98 A2
Avenue Terr. South 199 F4
Avenue The. Brain 59 F2
Avenue The. Canv 197 D1
Avenue The. Clact 110 A4
Avenue The. Colch 67 E3
Avenue The. Gt Oak 56 A2
Avenue The. Hadl 188 C2
Avenue The. Hull 165 E2
Avenue The. N Fam 167 D4
Avenue The. W Berg 48 B2
Avenue The. With 98 A1
Avenue The. Wiv 69 D1
Aviation Way. Roch 190 B4
Avignon Cl. Colch 68 A2
Avila Chase. Chelm 140 A1
Avington Wlk. Thund 187 F3
Avocet Cl. Kelv 81 E1
Avocet Way. Mald 132 B3
Avon Cl. Hawk 178 B3
Avon Rd. Canv 197 D2
Avon Rd. Chelm 126 B3
Avon Way. Colch 68 C3
Avon Way. South 201 E4
Avon Wlk. With 97 F2
Avondale Cl. Rayl 176 C1
Avondale Dr. South 189 F2
Avondale Rd. Basil 186 A4
Avondale Rd. Clact 110 A2
Avondale Rd. Rayl 176 C1
Avondale Rd. S Ben 187 E2
Avondale Wlk. Canv 196 C2
Avro Rd. South 190 B3
Aylesbeare. South 201 E4
Aylesbury Dr. Clact 110 A3
Aylett Cl. Canv 197 E2
Ayletts. Basil 185 F3
Ayloffe Rd. Colch 50 B1
Azalea Ave. Wick 174 B4
Azalea Way. Clact 109 E2

Baardwyk Ave. Canv 197 F2
Back La E. Gt Bro 71 D3
Back La W. Gt Bro 70 C4
Back La. Colch 66 C4
Back La. E Han 153 D4
Back La. Gt Oak 56 B2
Back La. Lt Tot 115 F2
Back La. Rams 39 D1
Back La. Roch 178 C1
Back La. Stis 61 E3
Back Rd. Ard 52 A3
Back Rd. Tolle 119 E2
Back Rd. Writ 126 A1
Back Waterside La. Brigh .. 106 C3
Bacon's La. Wa Col 46 B2
Baddow Hall Ave. Gt Bad .. 141 D4
Baddow Hall Cres. Gt Bad . 141 D4
Baddow Place Ave. Gt Bad . 141 D3
Baddow Rd. Chelm 127 E1
Baddow Rd. Chelm 140 C4
Baddow Rd. Gt Bad 140 C4
Baden Powell Dr. Colch 67 D2
Badger Hall Ave. S Ben 188 A2
Badgers Cl. Chelm 140 A1
Badgers Cl. South 190 A2
Badgers Gr. Gt Hor 31 D1
Badgers Way. S Ben 188 A2
Badley Hall Rd. Gt Bro 52 C4
Badminton Rd. Clact 125 D4
Bailey Bridge Rd. Brain 59 F3
Bailey Dale. Stanw 66 B2
Bailey La. Cla 4 B4
Bailey Rd. Hadl 189 D1
Bailey The. Rayl 176 B1
Baines Cl. Colch 66 C3
Baker Ave. Hat Pev 114 A2
Baker Mews. Mald 132 A1
Baker Rd. Sho G 40 A4
Baker St. Chelm 127 D1
Baker's La. Bl Not 77 E3
Baker's La. Colch 49 D1
Baker's La. Dan 142 C4

Baker's La. Toll M 117 E2
Baker's Rd. Bel S P 4 C1
Bakers Cl. S Woo F 165 E4
Bakery Cl. Till 149 F2
Baldwin's La. Gt T 63 D4
Bale Cl. Colch 66 C2
Balfe Ct. Colch 68 C3
Balfour Way. Basil 186 A3
Balkerne Cl. Colch 67 F4
Balkerne Hill. Colch 67 F4
Balkerne Pass. Colch 67 F4
Ball Alley. Colch 67 F4
Ball La. Rowh 86 A3
Ball's Chace. M Bure 28 C1
Ball's Chase. Hals 25 F1
Ballast Quay Rd. Elmst M 69 E1
Ballast Quay Rd. Elmst M 87 E4
Ballast Quay Rd. Fing 87 D3
Ballingdon Hill. Sud 12 B3
Ballingdon St. Sud 12 B3
Balmerino Ave. Thund 188 B3
Balmoral Ave. Clact 109 E2
Balmoral Gdns. Hock 177 E3
Balmoral Rd. South 190 C1
Balmoral Rd. Steep 147 D1
Baltic Ave. South 200 A4
Balton Way. Harw 39 F1
Bancrofts Rd. S Woo F 165 E4
Bandhills Cl. S Woo F 165 E4
Banister Cl. Clact 109 E3
Bank Pass. Colch 67 F4
Bank St. Brain 59 F2
Bankart La. Sprin 127 F2
Bankside Cl. S Woo F 154 C1
Bannister Green. Wick 174 C3
Banters La. Gt Le 77 D1
Banyardway. Hawk 178 B2
Barbara Ave. Canv 196 C1
Barbara Cl. Hawk 178 C1
Barbel Rd. Colch 50 C1
Barbrook La. Tipt 100 B3
Barbrook Way. S Woo F 142 C1
Barclay Cl. Gt Bad 141 D3
Barclay Rd. Basil 174 C1
Bardenville Rd. Canv 197 F2
Bardfield Rd. Colch 68 A1
Bardfield Way. Rayl 176 A2
Bardfield Way. Walt 93 F3
Bardfield. Basil 185 F3
Barfield Rd. W Mers 121 F4
Barfield. Mann 35 E2
Bargate La. Ded 34 A2
Barge Pier Rd. South 201 F3
Barker Cl. Lawf 35 D2
Barkis Cl. Chelm 126 B4
Barkstead Rd. Colch 50 B1
Barley Mead. Dan 143 D3
Barley Way. Colch 66 C3
Barling Rd. Barl 192 B4
Barling Rd. Stobr 192 A3
Barlon Rd. Lit Bro 52 C2
Barlow's Reach. Sprin 128 A2
Barn Green. Sprin 127 F4
Barn Hall Ave. Colch 68 B2
Barn La. Lawf 52 C4
Barnaby Rudge. Chelm 126 C4
Barnard Cl. Basil 185 F1
Barnard Rd. Chelm 140 B1
Barnard Rd. Hadl 189 E1
Barnardiston Rd. Colch 50 B1
Barnardiston Way. With 97 F2
Barnards Ave. Canv 197 E2
Barncombe Cl. Thund 187 E3
Barncroft Cl. Colch 50 A2
Barnes Mill Rd. Sprin 127 F1
Barnet Park Rd. Runw 163 F1
Barneveld Ave. Canv 197 F2
Barnfield Cotts. Mald 132 A4
Barnfield Mews. Chelm 127 D3
Barnfield Rd. Gt Hor 49 E3
Barnfield. Fee 81 E2
Barnfield. Mann 35 E2
Barnfield. Wick 174 C4
Barnhall Rd. Toll K 101 E1
Barnmead Way. Burn 170 A4
Barns Farm Dr. Alth 157 F1
Barnstaple Rd. South 201 D4
Barnstaple Rd. South 201 D4
Barnwell Dr. Hock 177 E3
Baron Rd. S Woo F 165 F4
Baron's La. Purl 144 C1
Baronia Croft. Colch 50 B2
Barons Court Rd. Rayl 176 B3
Baronswood Way. Colch 67 E1
Barpack St. Brad 54 B4
Barr Cl. Wiv 69 E1
Barrack La. Harw 40 C2
Barrack Sq. Chelm 127 D1
Barrack St. Colch 68 A4
Barrie Pavement. Wick 174 B3
Barrington Cl. Basil 185 F4
Barrington Cl. Gt Bad 141 D3
Barrington Cl. Lit Cla 91 E1
Barrington Gdns. Basil 185 F4
Barrington Gdns. Colch 110 B3
Barrington Rd. Colch 68 A3
Barringtons Cl. Rayl 176 B2
Barrow Hall Rd. Barl 192 B3
Barrow Hall Rd. Stobr 192 B3

Barrowsand. South 201 D3
Barrymore Wlk. Rayl 177 D1
Bartlett Cl. May 146 C1
Bartletts. Rayl 189 D4
Bartley Cl. Thund 187 D3
Bartley Rd. Thund 187 D3
Bartlow End. Basil 186 A4
Bartlow Side. Basil 186 A4
Barton Cl. S Woo F 154 B1
Bartram Ave. Brain 60 B2
Barwell Way. With 98 A1
Basin Rd. Mald 132 C2
Bassenthwaite Rd. Thund .. 187 F4
Bassetts La. Lit Bad 130 A2
Bat View. St L 148 B4
Batavia Rd. Canv 196 B2
Bate-Dudley Dr. Brad O S .. 137 D2
Bateman Rd. Brigh 106 C4
Bateman's Rd. Clact 91 D2
Bath St. Wiv 87 D4
Bathurst Cl. Colch 68 A1
Batt Hall. Bul 12 A3
Batt's Rd. Steep 148 A1
Battery La. Sho G 40 A4
Battisford Dr. Clact 109 D2
Battlesbrook Rd. Colch 68 B1
Bawn Cl. Brain 60 A2
Bawtree Way. Colch 67 D3
Baxter Ave. South 190 C1
Bay Cl. Canv 197 D1
Bay Rd. Harw 40 B2
Bay View Cres. Lit Oak 57 E4
Bayard Ave. Brigh 106 C4
Bayley St. Ca Hed 15 F2
Baynards Cres. Walt 93 F3
Beach Ave. South 199 D4
Beach Cres. Clact 124 C3
Beach Ct. Gt Wak 193 E2
Beach House Gdns. Canv ... 197 F1
Beach Rd. Canv 197 E2
Beach Rd. Clact 109 F1
Beach Rd. Harw 40 B1
Beach Rd. South 200 B4
Beach Rd. South 201 F3
Beach Rd. St O 108 A1
Beach Rd. St O 123 E4
Beach Rd. W Mers 121 E3
Beach Way. Clact 124 C3
Beach's Dr. Chelm 126 B2
Beachcroft Ave. Walt 93 E3
Beaches Cl. Hock 178 A3
Beachway. Canv 197 D1
Beachy Dr. St L 148 B4
Beacon Cl. Brigh 106 C3
Beacon Hill Ave. Harw 40 C2
Beacon Hill. Gt Tot 116 A3
Beacon Hill. Mald 131 F1
Beacon Hts. St O 107 D1
Beacon Way. St O 107 D1
Beaconsfield Ave. Colch 67 F3
Beaconsfield Cl. Sud 12 C4
Beaconsfield Rd. Clact 109 F2
Beaconsfield Rd. Sud 12 C4
Beadle Way. Gt Le 95 D3
Beadon Dr. Brain 60 A1
Beambridge. Basil 186 A3
Bear St. Nay 20 A1
Beardsley Dr. Sprin 127 F4
Bearsted Dr. Basil 186 B3
Beatrice Ave. Canv 197 D2
Beatrice Rd. Clact 109 F1
Beatrice Rd. Walt 76 C1
Beatty Gdns. Brain 60 B2
Beatty La. Basil 185 F3
Beatty Rise. S Woo F 165 F3
Beauchamps Cl. Sprin 127 F4
Beauchamps Dr. Wick 175 D4
Beaufort Gdns. Brain 60 A2
Beaufort Rd. Sprin 128 A2
Beaufort St. South 191 E1
Beaumont Ave. Brigh 107 D4
Beaumont Ave. Clact 109 E2
Beaumont Cl. Colch 49 F2
Beaumont Cl. Walt 93 F4
Beaumont Park. Dan 142 B3
Beaumont Pl. Brain 60 A2
Beaumont Rd. Gt Oak 56 B1
Beaumont Wlk. Chelm 126 B3
Beaver Cl. Colch 66 C4
Beazley End. Wick 174 C3
Beche Rd. Colch 68 A3
Beck Farm Cl. Canv 197 F2
Beck Rd. Canv 197 D2
Becker Rd. Colch 66 C2
Beckers Green Rd. Brain 60 B1
Becket Cl. Ashi 178 B3
Becket Way. S Woo F 165 F3
Becketts La. High 21 F4
Beckford Rd. Mist 36 A2
Beckingham Rd. Gt Tot 116 B3
Beckingham Rd. Toll D 118 B2
Beckingham St. Toll M 117 E2
Beckney Ave. Hock 166 C1
Becontree Cl. Clact 109 F4
Bedells Ave. Bl Not 78 A3
Bedford Cl. Brain 60 A2
Bedford Cl. Rayl 176 B1
Bedford Cl. Tipt 100 B3

Bedford Pl. Canv 196 C2
Bedford Rd. Clact 110 B3
Bedford Rd. Colch 49 F3
Bedloes Ave. Rayl 175 F4
Bedloes Cnr. Rayl 175 F4
Beech Ave. Brain 59 F3
Beech Ave. Rayl 176 B2
Beech Ave. Wiv 69 D1
Beech Cl. Burn 170 A3
Beech Ct. Basil 185 F3
Beech Gr. Lit Oak 57 D4
Beech Gr. Si Hed 15 E1
Beech Green. Lit Brx 115 F3
Beech Hill. Colch 67 D3
Beech Rd. Basil 185 F3
Beech Rd. Hadl 188 C1
Beech Rd. Hull 165 F1
Beech Rd. Sud 13 D3
Beech Rd. With 98 A4
Beech Rise. Hat Pev 114 A2
Beechcroft Rd. Canv 196 C2
Beeches Cl. Chelm 126 C1
Beeches Ct. Chelm 126 C1
Beeches Rd. Chelm 126 C1
Beeches Rd. Mald 131 F3
Beeches Rd. Rayl 164 C1
Beechmont Gdns. South ... 190 C2
Beechwood Cl. Colch 67 E1
Beecroft Cres. Canv 197 D3
Beedell Ave. South 190 B1
Beedell Ave. Wick 174 C1
Beehive La. Basil 185 D3
Beehive La. Chelm 140 B3
Beehive La. Gt Bad 140 B3
Beeleigh Chase. Mald 131 E2
Beeleigh Cl. Colch 68 A1
Beeleigh Cl. South 190 C2
Beeleigh Cross. Basil 185 F4
Beeleigh East. Basil 185 F4
Beeleigh Link. Sprin 127 F2
Beeleigh Rd. Mald 131 F2
Beeleigh West. Basil 185 E4
Begonia Cl. Sprin 127 F3
Begonia Pl. Clact 109 E2
Beke Hall Chase N. Rayl ... 175 F2
Beke Hall Chase S. Rayl ... 175 F2
Bekeswell La. Chelm 139 F1
Bel-Air Estate. St O 124 A3
Belchamps Rd. Wick 174 C4
Belchamps Way. Hawk 177 F3
Beldams Cl. Th L S 74 A1
Beldowes. Basil 185 E3
Belfairs Cl. Hadl 189 E1
Belfairs Dr. South 189 E1
Belfairs Park Cl. Hadl 189 E3
Belfairs Park Dr. Hadl 189 D3
Belgrave Cl. Gt Bad 140 B4
Belgrave Cl. Rayl 189 D4
Belgrave Rd. Rayl 189 D4
Bell Cl. Colch 68 B1
Bell Hill. Dan 142 B4
Bell Hill. Lam 19 E2
Bell La. Pan 59 D4
Bell St. Gt Bad 140 C3
Bellamy St. Walt 93 E3
Belle Vue Rd. Colch 49 F1
Belle Vue Rd. Sud 12 C4
Belle Vue. Wiv 69 E1
Belle Vue. Chelm 127 D1
Bellevue Ave. South 200 B4
Bellevue Pl. South 200 B4
Bellevue Rd. South 191 E1
Bellevue Terr. Hals 25 F1
Bellfield Ave. Brigh 107 D4
Bellfield Cl. Brigh 107 D4
Bellfield. Basil 185 F2
Bellhouse Cres. South 189 E3
Bellhouse La. South 189 E3
Bellhouse Rd. South 189 E3
Bellingham La. Rayl 176 B1
Bellmead. Chelm 127 D1
Bells Chase. Gt Bad 140 C3
Bells Hill Rd. Basil 185 D1
Bells Hill. M Bure 29 D2
Bells La. Glems 2 B3
Bells Rd. Bel W 10 C3
Belmonde Dr. Sprin 127 F4
Belton Bridge. Hadl 198 B4
Belton Gdns. Hadl 198 B4
Belton Way E. Hadl 198 B4
Belton Way W. Hadl 198 A4
Belvawney Cl. Chelm 126 C3
Belvedere Ave. Hock 177 E3
Belvedere Cl. Dan 142 C4
Belvedere Pl. Mald 144 C4
Belvedere Rd. Burn 170 B2
Belvedere Rd. Dan 142 C4
Belvedere The. Burn 170 B2
Bembridge Cl. Clact 109 F4
Bemerton Gdns. Walt 93 E3
Benbow Dr. S Woo F 165 F3
Bendalls Ct. Lawf 35 E2
Benderloch. Canv 196 C3

Benedict Dr. Chelm 126 C1
Benfield Way. Brain 60 A1
Benfleet Park Rd. S Ben 187 D1
Benfleet Rd. S Ben 188 A2
Bennett Cl. Brain 78 A4
Bennett Cl. Walt 94 A4
Bennett Ct. Colch 68 C3
Bennett Way. Hat Pev 114 A2
Bennett's Ave. E Han 152 C2
Bentalls Cl. South 191 D2
Bentley Ave. Clact 124 C3
Bentley Rd. Lit Bro 53 E2
Bentley Rd. St O 90 B3
Bentley Rd. Weel 90 B3
Bentley Rd. With 97 F2
Bentleys The. South 190 A4
Benton Cl. T Gr 78 C3
Benvenue Ave. South 189 F3
Berdens. Basil 185 E3
Berechurch Hall Rd. Colch .. 85 F4
Berechurch Rd. Colch 67 F1
Berens Cl. Runw 163 F1
Beresford Cl. Hadl 188 B2
Beresford Gdns. Hadl 188 B2
Beresford Rd. South 200 B4
Berg Ave. Canv 197 E3
Bergen Ct. Mald 144 C4
Bergholt Rd. Colch 49 E1
Bergholt Rd. Str S M 35 D4
Beridge Rd. Hals 25 E1
Berkeley Ave. Canv 197 D2
Berkeley Gdns. Hadl 189 D1
Berkeley Rd. Clact 109 F3
Berkshire Cl. South 189 E3
Bernard Cl. Walt 93 F3
Berners Wlk. Basil 185 E4
Bernside. Brain 59 F1
Berrimans Cl. Colch 68 B3
Berry Cl. Wick 174 A3
Berry Vale. S Woo F 165 F3
Bertram Ave. Lit Cla 91 E1
Berwick Ave. Chelm 127 D4
Beryl Rd. Harw 39 E1
Bethany St. Wiv 87 D4
Betjeman Cl. Brain 78 A4
Betjeman Cl. Rayl 176 C2
Betjemens Mews. South ... 191 D1
Bett's La. Hock 177 E3
Betts Green Rd. Lit Cla 91 E3
Beveland Rd. South 198 A2
Beverley Ave. Canv 197 D2
Beverley Ave. W Mers 121 F4
Beverley Dr. Walt 93 F4
Beverley Gdns. South 190 C2
Beverley Rd. Colch 67 E3
Bevington Mews. With 98 A1
Bickenhall. South 201 E4
Bickerton Point. S Woo F .. 165 F3
Bicknacre Rd. Dan 142 C2
Bicknacre Rd. E Han 153 E4
Bicknacre Rd. S Woo F 142 C2
Biddenden Ct. Basil 186 B3
Bideford Cl. South 190 A3
Bight The. S Woo F 165 F3
Bignalls Croft. Colch 50 B2
Bijou Cl. Tipt 100 B3
Billy's La. Str S M 22 B1
Bilsdale Cl. Colch 50 B2
Bilton Rd. Chelm 126 C1
Bilton Rd. Hadl 188 C2
Binley Rd. Sprin 127 F1
Birch Ave. Gt Ben 89 F4
Birch Ave. Harw 40 A2
Birch Cl. Brain 59 E1
Birch Cl. Brigh 106 C3
Birch Cl. Cane 168 C1
Birch Cl. Canv 196 C1
Birch Cl. Clact 109 E2
Birch Cl. Rayl 176 B2
Birch Cl. Thund 187 D4
Birch Cl. With 98 A2
Birch Gdns. Till 149 F2
Birch Green. Wick 174 B4
Birch Rd. Lay H 84 C3
Birch Rd. Till 149 F2
Birch Rise. Lit Brx 115 F3
Birch St. Birch 84 A2
Birch St. Nay 20 A1
Bircham Rd. South 191 D1
Birchdale. Hull 165 E2
Birche Cl. South 189 F2
Birches The. Thund 187 E4
Birches The. Walt 93 F3
Birches Wlk. Chelm 140 A1
Birchway. Birch 84 A1
Birchwood Cl. Tipt 100 C3
Birchwood Cl. W Mers 121 E3
Birchwood Dr. South 190 A1
Birchwood Rd. Ded 33 D2
Birchwood Rd. Purl 144 A1
Birchwood Way. Tipt 100 C3
Birchwood. Thund 187 D4
Bird La. Mess 100 C2
Birdkale Rise. Hat Pev 114 A2
Birkin Cl. Tipt 100 A2
Birs Cl. Runw 163 E1
Biscay. South 190 A4
Bishop Hall La. Chelm 127 D2

Bishop Rd. Chelm 127 D2
Bishop Rd. Colch 67 D2
Bishop's Ct. Canv 197 E2
Bishop's La. Twin 18 B2
Bishops Ave. Brain 60 A2
Bishops Cl. Basil 174 A1
Bishops La. Gt Le 100 B4
Bishops Rd. Wick 174 B2
Bishopscourt Gdns. Sprin .. 127 F2
Bishopsteignton. South 192 B1
Bisley Cl. Clact 109 D3
Bittern Cl. Kelv 81 E1
Black Boy La. Wrab 38 A2
Blackberry Rd. Stanw 66 B2
Blackbrook Hill. Langh 33 D3
Blackbrook Rd. Gt Hor 49 E4
Blackfriars. Sud 12 B3
Blackgate Rd. South 202 A4
Blackheath. Colch 86 A4
Blackhouse La. Sud 13 E2
Blackley La. Gt Le 77 D2
Blacklock. Sprin 128 A2
Blackman Way. With 98 A1
Blackmore Ave. Canv 197 D1
Blackmore Wlk. Rayl 177 D1
Blacksmith Cl. Sprin 127 F4
Blacksmiths Hill. Cla 3 D2
Blacksmiths La. Bul 11 F1
Blacksmiths La. Wic Bis 115 F3
Blackthorn Cl. Writ 126 A1
Blackthorn Rd. Harw 39 F1
Blackthorn Rd. Hock 177 F4
Blackthorn Rd. With 97 F2
Blackthorne Ave. Colch 68 C4
Blackthorne Rd. Canv 197 E2
Blackwater Ave. Colch 50 C1
Blackwater Cl. Mald 132 C2
Blackwater Cl. South 192 C1
Blackwater Cl. Sprin 127 E3
Blackwater Dr. W Mer 121 D3
Blackwater La. With 115 D4
Blackwater Way. Brain 60 A2
Blackwood Chine. S Woo F. 165 F3
Bladon Cl. Brain 59 F4
Bladon Cl. Tipt 100 C3
Blaine Dr. Walt 93 F4
Blake Cl. Lawf 35 D2
Blake Ct. S Woo F 165 F3
Blake Dr. Brain 60 B2
Blake Dr. Clact 109 E3
Blake Hall Dr. Wick 175 D3
Blake Rd. With 97 F3
Blamsters Cres. Hals 43 E4
Blanchard Cl. Walt 93 F3
Blatches Chase. South 189 F4
Blenheim Chase. South 189 F2
Blenheim Cl. S Woo F 142 C1
Blenheim Cres. South 189 F1
Blenheim Dr. Colch 86 A4
Blenheim Gdns. Steep 147 D1
Blenheim Mews. South 189 F2
Blenheim Park Rd. South .. 189 F2
Blenheim Rd. Clact 109 E1
Blenheim Way. Tipt 100 C3
Blennein Cl. Brain 59 F4
Blind La. Birch 83 D2
Blind La. Brigh 106 C4
Blind La. Gold 133 E4
Blind La. Purl 145 E1
Blind La. Sand 141 F2
Blind La. Toll K 101 D1
Bloomfield Ave. Walt 93 F4
Blooms Hall La. Glems 2 C4
Blott Rise. With 114 C4
Blountswood Rd. Hull 177 D4
Blower Cl. Rayl 176 C2
Blue Bridge Cotts. Hals 26 A1
Blue House Ave. Clact 109 D2
Blue House Fm Chase. N Fam167 D4
Blue Mill La. Woo Wa 130 C2
Blue Mills Hill. With 115 E4
Blue Rd. Tipt 100 B3
Bluebell Ave. Clact 109 E2
Bluebell Cl. With 97 F2
Bluebell Green. Sprin 127 F4
Bluebell Way. Colch 49 E1
Bluehouse. Basil 185 D3
Blundens The. Nay 20 B3
Blunt's Hall Dr. With 97 E1
Blunts Hall Rd. With 97 E1
Blyford Rd. Clact 109 D2
Blyth's Meadow. Brain 59 F2
Blythe Way. Thund 187 E4
Blyton Cl. Wick 174 B3
Boadicea Way. Colch 67 E2
Boars Tye Rd. Silv E 79 E3
Bobbing Cl. Roch 178 C1
Bobbits Way. Wiv 87 E4
Bober Ct. Rowh 86 A4
Bocking End. Brain 59 F2
Bocking's Gr. Clact 109 D3
Bockingham Green. Basil .. 186 A4
Bodmin Rd. Sprin 127 F3
Bohemia Chase. South 189 E3
Bois Field Terr. Hals 25 F1
Bois Hall Gdns. Hals 25 F2
Boley Dr. Clact 110 A2
Boley Rd. Wa Col 46 A4
Boleyn Cl. Rayl 189 E4

Boleyn Way. Bore 112 C1
Boleyn Way. Clact 124 C4
Boleyns Ave. Brain 59 F3
Bolls La. Lay H 84 C3
Bolney Dr. Rayl 189 E4
Bommel Ave. South 198 A2
Bonchurch Ave. South 189 E1
Bond St. Chelm 127 E1
Bonham Cl. Clact 110 A3
Bonington Chase. Sprin 127 F3
Bonnygate. Basil 185 E4
Boone Pl. With 98 A1
Borda Cl. Chelm 127 D3
Boreham Cl. Wick 175 D3
Boreham Rd. Gt Le 95 D2
Borley Rd. L Mel 7 D2
Borman Cl. South 190 A3
Borrett Ave. Canv 197 D2
Borrowdale Cl. Thund 187 F3
Borrowdale Rd. Thund 187 F3
Boscawen Gdns. Brain 60 B2
Boscombe Rd. South 191 D1
Boston Ave. Rayl 176 A2
Boston Ave. South 190 C1
Boswell Ave. Roch 178 B3
Boswells Dr. Chelm 127 E1
Bosworth Cl. Hawk 177 F2
Bosworth Rd. Rayl 189 E4
Botanical Way. St O 108 A3
Botany La. Weel 91 E3
Bouchers Mead. Sprin 127 F4
Bouldrewood Rd. S Ben 187 D3
Boulevard The. Roch 178 C2
Boulton Cotts. Mald 132 A3
Boundary Rd. Colch 68 C2
Boundary Rd. Rayl 189 D4
Bounderby Gr. Chelm 126 C3
Bounstead Hill. Lay H 85 E3
Bounstead Rd. Colch 85 E4
Bourchier Way. Hals 43 E4
Bourne Cl. Hals 43 E4
Bourne Rd. Colch 68 A2
Bourne Rd. W Berg 48 C1
Bournebridge Hill. Hals 43 D3
Bournemouth Park Rd. South 191 D1
Bournemouth Rd. Clact 110 C3
Bournes Green Chase. South 192 A1
Bouvel Dr. Burn 170 A4
Bouverie Rd. Chelm 140 A4
Bovingdon Rd. Brain 41 E1
Bovinger Way. South 191 F1
Bowbank Cl. South 192 C1
Bowdens La. Worm 29 F4
Bower Gdns. Mald 131 F2
Bower Hall La. W Mers 104 C1
Bower La. Basil 185 F4
Bowers Cl. Silv E 79 F2
Bowers Court Dr. Basil 186 C3
Bowers Rd. S Ben 187 E3
Bowes Rd. Elmst M 69 E1
Bowman Ave. Rayl 189 D3
Bowman's Park. Ca Hed 15 F2
Box Mill La. Hals 25 F2
Boxford Cl. Rayl 175 F2
Boxhouse La. Ded 33 E3
Boxted Church Rd. Gt Hor 31 E2
Boxted Rd. Colch 49 F3
Boxted Rd. Gt Hor 31 E2
Boyce Green. S Ben 187 E1
Boyce Hill Cl. Hadl 189 D3
Boyce Rd. South 202 A4
Boyce View Dr. S Ben 187 E1
Boyden Cl. South 191 F1
Boydin Cl. With 114 C4
Boyles Ct. Rowh 86 A4
Boyne Dr. Sprin 127 E3
Boyton Cl. Thund 187 F3
Brabant Rd. N Fam 167 D4
Brace Wlk. S Woo F 165 F3
Bracken Dell. Rayl 176 C1
Bracken The. Colch 50 A2
Bracken Way. Lang 86 A1
Bracken Way. Thund 188 A3
Brackendale Ave. Basil 186 B2
Brackendale Cl. Hock 177 F4
Brackenden Dr. Sprin 127 E4
Brackley Cres. Basil 174 A1
Bradbourne Way. Basil 186 B3
Bradbrook Cotts. W Berg 48 C2
Bradbury Dr. Brain 59 E2
Bradfield Rd. Wix 55 D4
Bradford St. Brain 60 A3
Bradford St. Chelm 127 D1
Bradfordbury. Hadl 189 E3
Brading Ave. Clact 110 A4
Bradley Ave. Thund 187 F3
Bradley Cl. Canv 197 D3
Bradley Cl. Thund 187 F3
Bradley Green. Basil 174 B1
Bradley Hill. Ovi 4 A3
Bradley Way. Roch 178 C1
Bradleyhall La. Th L S 73 E2
Bradwell Cl. Brain 78 B4
Bradwell Rd. Brad O S 149 D4
Bradwell Rd. St L 148 C3
Bradwell Rd. Steep 148 A2
Bradwell Rd. Till 149 F3
Braemar Ave. Chelm 140 A4

Braemar Cres. Hadl 189 D1
Braemore Cl. Colch 50 B2
Braemore. Canv 196 C3
Braggon's Hill. Glems 2 A4
Brain Rd. With 97 F2
Brain Valley Ave. Bl Not 78 A3
Braintree Rd. Gos 42 C3
Braintree Rd. T Gr 78 C4
Braintree Rd. Terl 96 A2
Braintree Rd. With 97 F2
Braiswick La. Colch 49 E1
Braiswick. Colch 49 D1
Bramble Cl. Rayl 189 D4
Bramble Cres. Hadl 189 D3
Bramble Rd. Canv 197 E2
Bramble Rd. Hadl 188 D3
Bramble Rd. Rayl 189 D4
Bramble Rd. With 97 F2
Brambles The. Colch 66 C2
Brambles. Walt 94 A4
Bramerton Rd. Hock 177 E3
Bramfield Rd E. Rayl 177 D1
Bramfield Rd W. Rayl 176 C1
Bramley Cl. Alres 88 A4
Bramley Cl. Brain 60 A1
Bramley Cl. Colch 67 D4
Bramley Way. May 146 C1
Bramleys The. Cogg 63 D2
Bramleys The. Hawk 178 B3
Brampton Cl. South 190 A2
Bramston Green. With 97 F2
Bramston Wlk. With 97 F2
Bramstone Cl. Gt Bad 140 C4
Bramwoods Rd. Gt Bad 140 C4
Branch Rd. Hadl 188 C1
Brandenburg Rd. Canv 197 E3
Brandon Rd. Brain 59 E1
Brands Cl. Sud 13 E3
Branksome Ave. Hock 177 F4
Branksome Rd. South 191 E1
Branscombe Cl. Frin 93 F3
Branscombe South 201 D4
Branscombe Sq. South 201 D4
Branscombe Wlk. South 192 A1
Branston Rd. Clact 109 E2
Brantham Hill. Catt 35 E4
Braxted Cl. Hawk 178 B2
Braxted La. Gt Tot 116 B4
Braxted Rd. Gt Brx 99 E1
Braxted Rd. Lit Brx 116 A3
Bray Ct. South 192 C1
Braybrooke. Basil 185 D3
Brays La. Roch 178 C3
Braziers Cl. Chelm 140 B2
Breachfield Rd. Colch 67 E1
Bread and Cheese Hill. Thund187 F3
Bream Ct. South 192 C1
Brecon Cl. Basil 186 B4
Bree Ave. Mks T 64 C2
Bree Hill. S Woo F 165 E4
Brempsons. Basil 185 D4
Brendon Pl. Chelm 126 C1
Brendon Way. South 190 A3
Brent Ave. S Woo F 154 B1
Brent Cl. Walt 93 F4
Brent Cl. With 97 F1
Brentwood Rd. Clact 110 B3
Bressingham Gdns. S Woo F 165 E4
Brettenham Dr. South 200 C4
Bretts Bldgs. Colch 68 A3
Brewster Cl. Canv 197 D2
Brian Bishop Cl. Walt 76 B2
Brian Cl. Chelm 140 A3
Briar Cl. Hawk 177 F2
Briar Rd. Gt Bro 52 A2
Briardale Ave. Harw 39 F2
Briarfields. Walt 93 E4
Briarswood. Canv 197 D3
Briarswood. Sprin 127 E4
Briarwood Ave. Clact 110 C3
Briarwood Dr. South 189 F3
Briarwood End. Colch 50 A2
Briary The. Wick 174 A4
Brices Way. Glems 2 A3
Brick House La. Bore 112 C1
Brick House Rd. Toll M 117 D4
Brick Kiln Cl. Cogg 63 D2
Brick Kiln La. Alres 88 C3
Brick Kiln La. Gt Hor 49 E4
Brick Kiln Rd. Colch 49 F1
Brick Kiln Rd. Sand 141 E4
Brick St. E A Gr 48 A1
Brickfield Rd. Basil 185 E1
Brickfields Rd. S Woo F 165 F4
Brickfields Way. Roch 179 D1
Brickhouse Cl. W Mers 121 D4
Brickhouse Rd. Col En 27 D2
Brickman's Hill. Brad 36 B2
Brickspring La. Gt Tot 116 B4
Brickwall Cl. Burn 170 A2
Bridewell St. Cla 4 A4
Bridge Cl. South 201 F4
Bridge Hall Rd. Bradw 61 E2
Bridge Hill. Ford 47 E4
Bridge House Cl. Wick 174 B4
Bridge Pl. Catt 35 E4
Bridge Rd. Wick 175 D4
Bridge St. Bures 19 F1

Bridge St. Cogg 62 C1
Bridge St. Gt Y 9 D1
Bridge St. Hals 25 F1
Bridge St. With 97 F1
Bridge St. Writ 126 B1
Bridgebrook Cl. Colch 50 B1
Bridgefield Cl. Colch 68 B4
Bridgemans Green. Latch 157 D3
Bridgemarsh La. Alth 168 C4
Bridgend Cl. S Woo F 165 F4
Bridgewater Dr. South 190 A2
Bridgewick Rd. Deng 161 D3
Bridon Cl. E Han 153 D3
Bridport Rd. Sprin 127 E3
Bridport Way. Brain 60 B2
Brierley Ave. W Mers 121 F4
Bright Cl. Clact 109 E3
Brighten Rd. South 199 F4
Brightlingsea Rd. Thor 88 C2
Brightlingsea Rd. Wiv 69 E2
Brighton Ave. South 200 B4
Brighton Rd. Clact 110 C3
Brightside. Walt 93 F4
Brightwell Ave. South 190 B1
Brindles. Canv 196 C3
Brindley Rd. Clact 110 A4
Bringey The. Gt Bad 141 D3
Brinkley Cres. Colch 50 B1
Brinkley La. Colch 50 B3
Brinkworth Cl. Hock 177 F3
Brisbane Way. Colch 68 A1
Briscoe Rd. Basil 186 A4
Brise Cl. Brain 60 A1
Bristol Cl. Rayl 176 B3
Bristol Cl. Silv E 79 F2
Bristol Hill. Sho G 40 A4
Bristol Rd. Colch 68 A4
Bristol Rd. South 190 B3
Bristowe Ave. Gt Bad 141 D3
Britannia Cr. Wiv 69 D1
Britannia Ct. Basil 174 B1
Britannia Gdns. South 199 E4
Britannia Rd. South 199 E4
Brittany Way. Colch 68 A2
Britten Cl. Colch 68 C3
Britten Cres. Gt Bad 140 C4
Brixham Cl. Rayl 176 B3
Broad Cl. Hock 177 F3
Broad Green. Basil 185 E4
Broad La. Gt Hor 31 D1
Broad Oak Way. Rayl 176 C1
Broad Oaks Park. Colch 50 C1
Broad Oaks. Wick 174 C3
Broad Par. Hock 177 F3
Broad Rd. Brain 60 A4
Broad Rd. Wic S P 17 D4
Broad Street Green Rd. Gt Tot116 A1
Broad Street Green Rd. Mald 132 B4
Broad Way. Hock 177 F3
Broad Wlk. Hock 177 F3
Broadclyst Ave. South 189 E3
Broadclyst Cl. South 192 A1
Broadclyst Gdns. South 192 A1
Broadfields. Wiv 69 E2
Broadlands Ave. Hock 177 F3
Broadlands Ave. Rayl 176 B2
Broadlands Rd. Hock 177 F3
Broadlands Way. Colch 50 A1
Broadlands. Thund 187 F3
Broadlawn. Hadl 189 D2
Broadmayne. Basil 185 E3
Broadmead Rd. Colch 50 C1
Broadmere Cl. Clact 110 C4
Broadstrood. St O 108 A3
Broadwater Gdns. Sho G 40 A4
Broadway. Silv E 79 E3
Broadway North. Basil 186 A3
Broadway The. Runw 174 B4
Broadway W. South 198 B4
Broadway. Clact 125 D4
Broadway. Glems 2 A3
Broadway. Silv E 79 E2
Broadway. South 198 B4
Brock Cl. With 114 C4
Brock Hill Dr. Runw 163 E2
Brock Hill. Runw 163 E2
Brockenhurst Way. S Woo F . 142 C1
Brockham Cl. Clact 109 D3
Brockley Rd. Chelm 127 E1
Brocksford Ave. Rayl 176 C1
Brockwell La. Kelv 81 E1
Brockwell Wlk. Wick 174 B3
Brodie Rd. South 202 A4
Brograve Cl. Chelm 140 B2
Broman's La. E Mers 106 A1
Bromfords Cl. Wick 174 A3
Bromfords Dr. Wick 174 B3
Bromley Rd. Ard 51 E2
Bromley Rd. Colch 50 C1
Bromley Rd. Elmst M 70 A3
Bromley Rd. Frat 71 D2
Bromley Rd. Lawf 35 D1
Brompton Gdns. Mald 144 C4
Bronte Cl. Brain 78 A4
Bronte Mews. South 191 D1
Bronte Rd. With 97 F3
Brook Cl. Brain 59 E1
Brook Cl. Gt Tot 116 A2

Brook Cl. Roch 191 D4
Brook Cl. Tipt 100 C2
Brook Cl. Woo Wa 130 B1
Brook Dr. Basil 185 E1
Brook Dr. Wick 174 B3
Brook End Rd. Sprin 128 A2
Brook Farm Cl. Hals 26 A1
Brook Hall Rd. Fing 87 D3
Brook La. Chelm 140 C2
Brook La. Sprin 128 A1
Brook La. W Han 140 C2
Brook Meadow. Si Hed 15 E1
Brook Pl. Hals 25 F1
Brook Rd. Ald 65 D4
Brook Rd. Gt T 64 B4
Brook Rd. Rayl 188 B4
Brook Rd. S Ben 187 E1
Brook Rd. Till 149 E3
Brook Rd. Toll K 101 D1
Brook St. Col En 26 C1
Brook St. Colch 68 A4
Brook St. Ded 33 F4
Brook St. Glems 2 A3
Brook St. Gt Bro 52 C1
Brook St. Mann 35 E2
Brook St. Wiv 87 D4
Brook Terr. Si Hed 15 F1
Brook Vale. St O 108 A2
Brook View. Sand 141 E3
Brook Wlk. With 114 C4
Brooke Sq. Mald 132 A1
Brookfields Cl. South 189 E3
Brookfields. South 189 E3
Brookhouse Rd. Gt T 64 A4
Brookhurst Cl. Sprin 127 E2
Brookland. Tipt 100 B2
Brooklands Ave. South 189 F3
Brooklands Gdns. Clact 124 C3
Brooklands Rd. Catt 35 E4
Brooklands Rise. Catt 35 E4
Brooklands Sq. Canv 196 C2
Brooklands Wlk. Chelm 140 A4
Brooklands. Clact 124 C3
Brooklands. Wick 174 A4
Brooklyn Dr. Rayl 176 B3
Brooklyn Rd. Harw 40 B2
Brookside Ave. Gt Wak 193 E1
Brookside Cl. Colch 68 A2
Brookside. Canv 197 D3
Brookside. Hawk 177 F2
Broom Hill. Hals 25 F1
Broom Rd. Hull 165 F1
Broom St. Sud 13 D3
Broom Way. Lang 86 A1
Broome Gr. Wiv 69 D1
Broomfield Ave. Rayl 176 A2
Broomfield Ave. South 189 F3
Broomfield Cres. Wiv 69 D1
Broomfield Green. Canv 196 C3
Broomfield Rd. Chelm 127 D3
Broomfield. Hadl 188 B2
Broomfield. Silv E 79 E3
Broomfields. Basil 186 A3
Broomhills Rd. W Mers 121 E3
Broomways. Gt Wak 193 E2
Broton Dr. Hals 25 F1
Brougham Cl. Gt Wak 193 D2
Brougham Glades. Stanw 66 B3
Broughton Cl. Colch 67 E2
Broughton Rd. Hadl 188 C1
Broughton Rd. S Woo F 165 F3
Browning Ave. South 191 D1
Browning Cl. Colch 66 C3
Browning Rd. Brain 78 A4
Browning Rd. Mald 145 D4
Brownings Ave. Chelm 127 D3
Brownlow Bend. Basil 185 E3
Brownlow Cross. Basil 185 E3
Brownlow Green. Basil 185 E3
Browns Ave. Runw 163 F1
Brownsea Way. Colch 67 D2
Broxted Dr. Wick 174 C3
Broxted End. Wick 174 C3
Bruce Gr. Chelm 140 A4
Bruce Gr. Wick 175 D4
Bruce Rd. Writ 126 A1
Bruff Dr. Walt 94 A4
Bruges Rd. Canv 197 E1
Brundells Rd. Gt Bro 71 D3
Brundish. Basil 186 A3
Brundon La. Sud 12 B4
Brunel Rd. Brain 60 A1
Brunel Rd. Clact 110 A4
Brunel Rd. South 189 E3
Brunel Rd. Thund 187 E4
Brunel Way. Colch 50 B3
Brunel Way. S Woo F 165 E4
Brunswick House Cut. Mist .. 36 A2
Brunswick Rd. South 200 B4
Brunwins Cl. Wick 174 C4
Brussum Rd. Canv 197 E1
Brust Rd. Canv 197 E1
Bruton Ave. South 190 A3
Bryanstone Mews. Colch 66 C3
Bryant Ave. South 200 C3
Bryant's La. Woo Mor 143 E4
Bryce Way. Basil 186 B3
Buchan Cl. Brain 78 A4
Buchanan Way. Latch 157 D3

Buck Hill. Bl Not 77 F3
Buckeridge Way. Brad O S ... 137 D2
Buckerills. Basil 186 A3
Buckfast Ave. Walt 93 E3
Buckhatch La. Rett 153 E2
Buckingham Dr. Colch 68 C4
Buckingham Rd. Hock 177 E3
Buckingham Sq. Wick 175 D3
Buckland Gate. S Woo F 165 E3
Buckland. South 192 B1
Bucklebury Heath. S Woo F . 165 E3
Buckley's La. Gt T 63 E3
Buckleys Cl. Wic Bis 115 F3
Buckleys. Gt Bad 140 C4
Buckwins Sq. Basil 174 B1
Buckwoods Rd. Brain 60 A1
Buddleia Ct. Wiv 69 D1
Budna Rd. Canv 196 C3
Buffett Way. Colch 68 C3
Buglers Rise. Writ 139 D4
Buick Ave. Clact 124 B3
Bulbecks Wlk. S Woo F 165 E3
Bulford La. Bl Not 78 B3
Bulford Mill La. T Gr 78 B3
Bull Hill Rd. Clact 109 F3
Bull La. Hock 177 E3
Bull La. L Mel 7 E4
Bull La. Mald 132 A2
Bull La. Rayl 176 C1
Bull La. Tipt 100 B2
Bull's Hill. Ca Hed 15 F2
Bullace Cl. Colch 50 B2
Bullen Wlk. Chelm 140 B2
Buller Rd. N Fam 156 A1
Bullfinch Cl. Colch 68 C4
Bullock Wood Cl. Colch 50 B2
Bullocks La. Sud 12 C3
Bullwood App. Hock 177 D3
Bullwood Hall La. Rayl 177 D2
Bullwood Rd. Hock 177 E3
Bulmer Rd. Sud 12 B3
Bulmer St. Bul 11 E2
Bulow Ave. Canv 197 D2
Bulphan Cl. Wick 174 C3
Bulwark Rd. South 201 F4
Bumfords La. Hat Per 130 A4
Bumfords La. Ult 130 A4
Bundick's Hill. Chelm 126 C2
Bung Row. Gt Brx 99 E1
Bunters Ave. South 201 E3
Bunting Cl. Chelm 140 A3
Bunyan Rd. Brain 59 F2
Burches Mead. Thund 188 A3
Burches Rd. Thund 187 F4
Burdett Ave. South 199 F4
Burdett Rd. South 200 B4
Burdun Cl. With 114 B4
Bure Dr. With 97 E2
Buren Ave. Canv 197 F2
Bures Ave. Canv 197 E2
Bures Rd. Bures 30 A4
Bures Rd. Sud 13 D2
Burfield Cl. South 189 E3
Burfield Rd. South 189 F3
Burgate Cl. Clact 109 D2
Burges Cl. South 201 E3
Burges Rd. South 201 D3
Burges Terr. South 200 C3
Burgess Field. Sprin 127 F2
Burgundy Gdns. Basil 186 A4
Burkitts La. Sud 12 C4
Burleigh Sq. South 201 D4
Burlescoombe Cl. South 201 D4
Burlescoombe Leas. South ... 192 A1
Burlescoombe Rd. South 192 A1
Burlington Ct. Basil 174 A1
Burlington Gdns. Hadl 188 C2
Burlington Gdns. Hull 176 C4
Burlington Rd. Colch 67 F3
Burmanny Cl. Clact 109 E2
Burnaby Rd. South 200 B4
Burne Ave. Wick 174 A3
Burnham Ave. Col N 156 A3
Burnham Cl. Walt 94 A4
Burnham Rd. Alth 158 A1
Burnham Rd. Hull 165 F1
Burnham Rd. Latch 157 E3
Burnham Rd. Mund 156 B4
Burnham Rd. S Woo F 154 B1
Burnham Rd. Soum 159 E1
Burnham Rd. South 189 E1
Burnham Rd. Sprin 127 E3
Burnham Rd. Woo Mor 143 F3
Burns Ave. Basil 186 A3
Burns Ave. Colch 66 C3
Burns Cl. Mald 132 A4
Burns Cres. Chelm 140 B4
Burnside Cres. Chelm 127 D4
Burnside. Canv 197 D3
Burnt Dick Hill. Box 31 F4
Burnt Mills Rd. Basil 174 B1
Burnthouse Rd. Ea Col 45 F1
Burr Cl. Lit Oak 39 E1
Burr Hill Chase. South 190 C2
Burroughs Piece Rd. Sud 12 C4
Burrow's Rd. Ea Col 45 D4
Burrows Cl. Clact 109 E3
Burrows Cl. Lawf 35 D2
Burrows Way. Rayl 176 B1

Burrs Rd. Clact 110 A4
Burrswood Pl. Mald 132 C2
Burstall Cl. Clact 109 D2
Burton Pl. Sprin 127 F2
Burton's Green Rd. Hals 44 A2
Burwell Ave. Canv 196 C3
Bury Cl. Colch 68 A4
Bury Cl. Mks T 64 C2
Bury La. Hat Pev 113 F2
Bury The. St O 108 A2
Burywoods. Colch 49 D2
Bush Gr. Sud 12 B3
Bushell Way. Walt 93 F3
Bushey Cl. S Woo F 165 F4
Butchers La. Walt 94 A4
Butler Rd. Hals 25 E1
Butler's La. Wrab 37 F1
Butlers Way. Gt Y 9 D1
Butneys. Basil 185 D4
Butt La. Mald 132 A2
Butt Rd. Colch 67 F3
Butt Rd. Nay 20 B3
Butt Rd. Sud 13 D3
Butt's Green Rd. Dan 142 A2
Butt's Green Rd. Sand 141 F2
Butterbur Chase. S Woo F 165 E4
Buttercup Wlk. With 97 F2
Buttercup Wlk. With 97 F2
Butterfield Rd. Bore 128 C4
Buttermere. Bl Not 77 E4
Butterys. South 200 C4
Button's Hill. Alth 158 A2
Butts La. Dan 142 C4
Butts Paddock. Cane 168 B1
Butts Rd. South 193 E1
Butts Way. Chelm 139 F2
Buxey Cl. W Mers 121 E4
Buxton Ave. Hadl 189 D2
Buxton Cl. Hadl 189 D2
Buxton Rd. Cogg 62 C2
Buxton Rd. Colch 68 A2
Buxton Sq. Hadl 189 D2
Buyl Ave. Canv 197 D3
Byfield. South 189 F4
Byfleets. Basil 185 F2
Byford Cl. Rayl 176 C2
Byng Cres. Th L S 74 A1
Byng Gdns. Brain 60 B2
Bypass Rd. St O 108 A3
Byrne Dr. South 190 C2
Byron Ave. Colch 66 C4
Byron Ave. South 191 D1
Byron Cl. Brain 78 A4
Byron Cl. Canv 197 E4
Byron Dr. Wic Bis 115 F3
Byron Rd. Chelm 127 E1
Byrony Cl. With 97 E2
Bywater Rd. S Woo F 165 E3

Cabinet Way. South 189 E3
Cadenhouse Mews. Colch 66 C4
Caernarvon Cl. Hock 177 E3
Cage Field Cotts. Gt Stam 179 F2
Cage Rd. Box 32 A3
Cagefield Rd. Gt Stam 179 F2
Cairns Rd. Colch 68 A1
Calamint Rd. With 97 E2
Caldbeck Way. Bl Not 77 E4
Caledonia Rd. Sho G 40 A4
California Cl. Colch 50 A4
California Rd. Mist 36 A2
Callis St. Cla 4 A4
Calm Patch. Burn 170 B2
Calvert Dr. Basil 174 B1
Calves La. Nay 20 A4
Cam Way. With 97 E1
Camberton Rd. Brain 59 F3
Camborne Cl. Sprin 127 F3
Cambrai Rd. Colch 67 E2
Cambria Cl. Canv 196 B2
Cambria Cl. Mist 36 A2
Cambridge Gdns. Hawk 178 B3
Cambridge Rd. Canv 196 C2
Cambridge Rd. Clact 109 F2
Cambridge Rd. Colch 67 E3
Cambridge Rd. Frin 94 A3
Cambridge Rd. South 199 F4
Cambridge Way. Bures 28 C4
Cambridge Wlk. Colch 67 E3
Camellia Ave. Clact 109 E2
Camellia Cl. Sprin 127 F3
Camellia Cres. Clact 109 E2
Camelot Gdns. Basil 186 B4
Cameron Cl. Hadl 189 E1
Camoise Cl. Topp 14 A4
Camomile Way. Colch 49 E1
Camp Folley N. Colch 68 A3
Camp Folley S. Colch 68 A3
Camp Rd. Gt Bro 71 D4
Campbell Cl. Chelm 140 A4
Campbell Cl. Wick 174 B3
Campbell Dr. Colch 50 C1
Campbell Rd. With 97 F3
Camper Rd. South 200 B3
Camperdown Rd. Canv 197 E3
Campernell. Brigh 106 C4
Campfield Rd. South 201 F3
Campion Rd. Colch 68 A3
Campion Way. With 97 F2

Campions Hill. Bures 30 B4
Camulodunum Way. Colch 67 E1
Canberra Cl. Chelm 126 C3
Canberra Cl. Colch 68 A1
Candlemakers The. South 191 D3
Candytuft Rd. Sprin 127 F3
Canendon View Rd. Ashi 178 B3
Canewdon Cl. Runw 163 E1
Canewdon Gdns. Runw 163 E1
Canewdon Hall Cl. Cane 168 B3
Canewdon Rd. Ashi 178 B4
Canewdon Rd. South 199 F4
Canford Cl. Gt Bad 140 C4
Canhams Rd. Sud 13 E3
Canney Rd. Steep 147 E2
Canning St. Harw 40 B3
Cannon Leys. Chelm 140 B2
Cannon Rd. Colch 68 A3
Cannon St. Colch 68 A3
Cannons Cl. Colch 67 E2
Canons Cl. S Woo F 142 C1
Canonsleigh Cres. South 189 F1
Cansey La. Brad 54 C3
Canterbury Ave. South 191 F2
Canterbury Cl. Basil 185 F4
Canterbury Rd. Clact 110 C3
Canterbury Rd. Colch 68 A3
Canterbury Rd. Sud 7 E1
Canterbury Way. Chelm 126 C2
Canters The. Thund 188 A3
Canuden Rd. Chelm 126 C1
Canute Cl. Cane 168 C1
Canvey Rd. Basil 186 C3
Canvey Rd. Canv 196 B2
Canvey Rd. Hadl 189 D1
Canvey Way. S Ben 187 D2
Canvey Wlk. Sprin 127 F3
Canwick Gr. Colch 68 B3
Cap Pillar Cl. Wiv 69 D1
Capadocia St. South 200 C3
Cape Cl. Colch 66 C3
Capel Cl. Chelm 127 D4
Capel Park. Walt 93 F3
Capel Rd. Colch 67 E3
Capel Terr. South 200 A4
Caper La. Birch 83 F2
Capons La. Dan 143 D3
Captains Rd. W Mers 121 D3
Captains Wood Rd. Gt Tot 116 A2
Card's Rd. Sand 141 E3
Cardigan Ave. South 190 B2
Cardinal Cl. Colch 69 D4
Carisbrooke Ave. Clact 110 A4
Carisbrooke Dr. S Woo F 165 E4
Carisbrooke Rd. South 190 C1
Carlingford Dr. South 190 B2
Carlisle Cl. Colch 68 A4
Carlton Ave. South 190 B2
Carlton Cl. Gt Y 9 D1
Carlton Dr. South 198 C4
Carlton Dr. Thund 188 B2
Carlton Rd. Basil 186 A4
Carlton Rd. Clact 110 A3
Carlton Rd. Runw 163 E1
Carmania Cl. South 192 C1
Carnarvon Rd. Clact 109 F2
Carnarvon Rd. South 190 C1
Carnation Cl. Sprin 127 F3
Carnival Gdns. South 189 E2
Caro Rd. Canv 197 E2
Carolina Way. Tipt 100 B3
Caroline Cl. Wiv 69 E2
Caroline's Cl. South 190 C1
Carpenters. Barl 192 C3
Carraways. With 115 D4
Carriage Dr. Sprin 127 F4
Carrington Ct. W Mers 121 E4
Carrington Way. Brain 59 F4
Carringtons Rd. Gt Bro 52 B2
Carroll Gdns. Wick 174 B3
Carron Mead. S Woo F 165 F3
Carrs Rd. Clact 109 E2
Carruthers Cl. Runw 163 E1
Carruthers Dr. Runw 163 E1
Carshalton End. Colch 66 C2
Carsons Dr. Sud 13 E3
Cartbridge Cl. Walt 94 A4
Carters Cl. Clact 109 D2
Carters Hill. Box 32 A3
Carters La. Lit Brx 115 F3
Cartlodge Ave. Wick 174 C4
Cartwright Dr. Thund 187 E4
Cartwright Wlk. Sprin 127 F1
Cashiobury Terr. South 199 F4
Cashmere Way. Basil 185 E1
Cassel Ave. Canv 197 E3
Cassino Rd. Chelm 126 C3
Cassino Rd. Colch 67 E2
Castle Ave. Hadl 188 B1
Castle Bailey. Colch 67 F4
Castle Cl. Ca Hed 15 F2
Castle Cl. Rayl 176 B1
Castle Cl. South 202 A4
Castle Dr. Hadl 198 A4
Castle Dr. Rayl 176 B2
Castle Hill. Ded 33 F3
Castle La. Ca Hed 15 F2
Castle La. Hadl 188 C1
Castle Rd. Clact 109 F2

Castle Rd. Colch 68 A4
Castle Rd. Hadl 188 C1
Castle Rd. Rayl 176 B1
Castle Terr. Rayl 176 B1
Castle View Rd. Canv 197 D3
Castle Way. St O 108 A2
Castle Wlk. Canv 197 D3
Castlegate St. Harw 40 B3
Castleton Rd. South 191 F1
Castleward Cl. Elmst M 87 E4
Caswell Mews. Sprin 127 F1
Cat's La. Sud 13 D4
Catchpole La. Gt Tot 116 A2
Catchpool Rd. Colch 67 F4
Caterham Cl. Clact 109 E3
Cathedral Wlk. Chelm 127 D2
Catherine Cl. Clact 110 A3
Catherine Cl. E Han 153 D3
Catherine Hunt Way. Colch 67 E1
Catherine Rd. S Ben 187 F2
Catherines Cl. Gt Le 95 D3
Cattawade End. Basil 185 E4
Cattawade Link. Basil 185 E4
Cattawade St. Catt 35 E4
Caulfield Rd. South 201 E4
Causeway Cl. Glems 2 B3
Causeway Reach. Clact 109 F4
Causeway The. Brain 59 F2
Causeway The. Colch 50 B1
Causeway The. Gt Bad 140 C4
Causeway The. Gt Hor 31 D1
Causeway The. Hals 25 F1
Causeway The. Mald 132 A2
Causeway The. Ridge 8 A4
Causeway The. Topp 14 A4
Causeway The. Ult 130 B3
Causewayend. Lawf 35 D3
Causton Rd. Colch 67 F4
Caustones Cl. Sud 13 E3
Caustonway. Rayl 176 B2
Cavendish Ave. Colch 68 B2
Cavendish Dr. Clact 109 D2
Cavendish Dr. Lawf 35 D2
Cavendish Gdns. Brain 60 B3
Cavendish Gdns. South 190 A1
Cavendish La. Cav 1 C2
Cavendish La. Glems 2 A3
Cavendish Rd. Ashi 166 C1
Cavendish Rd. Cla 4 B4
Cavendish Way. Sud 12 C4
Caversham Ave. South 190 B2
Caversham Park Ave. Rayl 176 B3
Cawkwell Cl. Sprin 128 A2
Cecil Way. Rayl 176 C1
Cedar Ave. Brigh 106 C4
Cedar Ave. Chelm 127 D2
Cedar Ave. Tipt 100 B4
Cedar Ave. Walt 174 B3
Cedar Avenue W. Chelm 127 D2
Cedar Chase. Mald 132 B3
Cedar Cl. Rayl 188 C4
Cedar Cl. South 191 D1
Cedar Cl. Walt 94 A4
Cedar Cres. Lawf 35 E2
Cedar Dr. Hull 165 F1
Cedar Dr. With 98 A3
Cedar Gr. Burn 170 A3
Cedar Hall Gdns. Thund 188 A3
Cedar Mews. Hock 177 E3
Cedar Park Cl. Thund 188 A4
Cedar Rd. Basil 186 C4
Cedar Rd. Canv 196 C2
Cedar Rd. Thund 188 A3
Cedar Way. Gt Ben 89 F4
Cedar Wlk. Cane 168 B3
Cedars Rd. Colch 67 F3
Cedars The. Gt Wak 193 D2
Cedars The. S Woo F 165 E4
Celeborn St. S Woo F 165 D3
Centaury Cl. Stanw 66 B4
Central Ave. Canv 196 C3
Central Ave. Frin 94 A4
Central Ave. Hadl 188 C3
Central Ave. Hawk 178 B3
Central Ave. Hull 176 C4
Central Ave. South 191 E1
Central Ave. Walt 94 A3
Central Cl. Hadl 188 C2
Central Sq. Chelm 127 D1
Central Wall Cotts. Canv 197 D3
Central Wall Rd. Canv 197 D3
Central Wall. Canv 197 D3
Centre The. Hals 25 F1
Centurion Cl. South 201 F4
Ceylon Rd. South 199 E4
Chadacre Rd. South 192 A1
Chadburn Rd. L Mel 7 E4
Chadwick Rd. S Woo F 154 C1
Chadwick Rd. South 199 E4
Chaffinch Cl. South 201 F4
Chaffinch Gdns. Colch 68 C4
Chaingate Ave. South 191 F1
Chalfont Cl. South 189 E2
Chalfont Rd. Colch 50 B2
Chalk End. Basil 186 A3
Chalk St. Rett 163 F4
Chalklands. Sand 141 E2
Chalkwell Ave. South 199 D4
Chalkwell Espl. South 199 D4

Chalkwell Park Dr. South 189 F1
Challacombe. South 192 B1
Challenge Way. Colch 68 A3
Challis La. Brain 59 F1
Challis Rd. Brain 78 A4
Challock Lees. Basil 186 B3
Chalvedon Ave. Basil 186 A4
Chamberlain Ave. Canv 197 E2
Chamberlain Ave. Walt 94 A4
Chamberlains Rd. S Woo F 165 E3
Champion Cl. Wick 174 B3
Champions Way. S Woo F 165 E4
Champlain Ave. Canv 196 C3
Chancel Cl. Thund 187 E3
Chancel Cl. Till 149 F2
Chancellor Rd. South 200 A4
Chancery Grove. Colch 86 A4
Chancery Pl. Writ 126 A1
Chandlers Cl. Clact 109 D2
Chandlers Cl. W Mers 121 E4
Chandlers Ct. W Mers 121 E4
Chandlers Row. Colch 68 B3
Chandlers Way. S Woo F 165 F4
Chandlers Way. South 191 D3
Chandos Par. Hadl 188 C2
Chaney Rd. Wiv 69 D1
Chanterelle. Colch 50 A2
Chanton Cl. South 189 E4
Chantry La. Bore 113 D2
Chantry The. Colch 67 E4
Chapel Ct. Ard 51 F4
Chapel Cut. Mist 36 A2
Chapel Hill. Bel W 10 B2
Chapel Hill. Brain 60 A1
Chapel Hill. Hals 25 E1
Chapel La. Ard 51 D1
Chapel La. Box 32 A2
Chapel La. Elmst M 70 A3
Chapel La. Gt Bro 71 D3
Chapel La. Gt Wak 193 D2
Chapel La. High 21 E3
Chapel La. Lit Bad 129 D2
Chapel La. Mald 132 C1
Chapel La. Purl 155 E4
Chapel La. S Ben 188 B2
Chapel La. St O 108 A2
Chapel La. Sud 13 E1
Chapel La. Tend 72 C4
Chapel La. Thor 89 D3
Chapel La. Till 149 F2
Chapel La. W Berg 48 C2
Chapel La. Walt 93 D3
Chapel Rd. Beau 73 F4
Chapel Rd. Box 32 A2
Chapel Rd. Brigh 107 D4
Chapel Rd. Burn 170 B2
Chapel Rd. Gt Tot 116 B3
Chapel Rd. Ridge 8 A4
Chapel Rd. South 201 F3
Chapel Rd. Stanw 66 B3
Chapel Rd. Tipt 100 C2
Chapel Rd. Toll D 118 C2
Chapel Rd. Tolle 118 C2
Chapel Rd. W Berg 48 C2
Chapel Rd. Wiv 87 D4
Chapel St N. Colch 67 F3
Chapel St S. Colch 67 F3
Chapel St. Cla 3 D2
Chapel St. Hals 25 F1
Chapel St. Wiv 87 D4
Chapelfields. Walt 93 F3
Chaplin Cl. Chelm 140 A1
Chaplin Dr. Colch 50 B1
Chaplins. Walt 93 F4
Chapman Rd. Clact 109 F2
Chapman Rd. South 198 A2
Chapmans Cl. Hadl 189 D1
Chapmans La. W Mers 121 E4
Chapmans Wlk. Hadl 189 D1
Chappel Hill. Wa Col 46 B3
Chappel Rd. Ford 47 E4
Chappel Rd. Gt T 46 B1
Chappel Rd. M Bure 28 C2
Charfleets Cl. Canv 196 B2
Charfleets Rd. Canv 196 B2
Charfleets Service Rd. Canv 196 B2
Charles Cl. South 190 A3
Charles Ct. Wiv 69 E2
Charles Pell Rd. Colch 68 C4
Charles Rd. Brigh 106 C3
Charles St. Colch 68 A3
Charleston Ave. Basil 174 B1
Charlotte Ave. Wick 174 B4
Charlotte Ct. S Woo F 165 E4
Charlotte Dr. Walt 93 F3
Charlotte Way. With 98 A1
Charlton Cl. Basil 186 B4
Charnock Cl. Walt 93 F3
Charnwood Ave. Chelm 126 C1
Charterhouse. Basil 185 E3
Chartfield Dr. Walt 93 E4
Chartwell Cl. Brain 59 F4
Chartwell Sq. South 200 A4
Chase Cl. Thund 187 F3
Chase Ct. Colch 68 C4
Chase Dr. S Woo F 165 E4
Chase End. Rayl 176 C1
Chase Gdns. South 190 B2

Chase La. Harw 39 F1
Chase Rd E. Gt Bro 71 E4
Chase Rd W. Gt Bro 71 D3
Chase Rd. South 200 B3
Chase The. Ald 65 D4
Chase The. Ashi 178 B4
Chase The. Bl Not 77 E3
Chase The. Bore 128 C4
Chase The. Brain 59 F4
Chase The. Church 183 F4
Chase The. Clact 110 C3
Chase The. Colch 68 A4
Chase The. Colch 68 B4
Chase The. Colch 68 C4
Chase The. Ded 34 A2
Chase The. Elmst M 70 A3
Chase The. Gold 134 A1
Chase The. Gt Bad 140 C3
Chase The. Kelv 81 E1
Chase The. Rayl 176 C1
Chase The. Runw 164 A2
Chase The. S Woo F 165 E4
Chase The. Soum 159 E2
Chase The. Thund 188 A4
Chase The. Toll D 118 A2
Chase The. Tolle 119 E1
Chase The. W Mers 121 E3
Chase The. Wick 174 A3
Chase The. Wick 174 C4
Chase Way The. Colch 49 E1
Chaseside. Rayl 188 C4
Chaseway. Basil 185 F2
Chatfield Way. Basil 186 B4
Chatham Pavement. Basil 186 B4
Chatsworth Gdns. Clact 109 E1
Chatsworth Rd. W Mers 121 E4
Chatsworth. Thund 187 F3
Chaucer Cl. Clact 109 D1
Chaucer Cl. Mald 145 E4
Chaucer Cres. Brain 78 A4
Chaucer Rd. Chelm 127 E1
Chaucer Rd. Sud 7 E1
Chaucer Way. Colch 66 C2
Chaucer Wlk. Wick 174 B3
Cheapside E. Rayl 176 B1
Cheapside W. Rayl 176 A2
Cheddar Ave. South 190 A3
Chedington. South 192 B1
Cheldon Barton. South 201 E4
Chelmer Ave. Rayl 176 B1
Chelmer Cl. Lit Tot 117 D2
Chelmer Cl. Walt 93 F4
Chelmer Lea. Gt Bad 140 C4
Chelmer Pl. Chelm 127 E2
Chelmer Rd. Brain 60 B1
Chelmer Rd. Sprin 127 F2
Chelmer Rd. With 97 F1
Chelmer Terr. Mald 132 A1
Chelmer Valley Rd. Chelm 127 E3
Chelmer Village Way. Sprin 128 A2
Chelmer Way. Burn 170 A3
Chelmer Way. South 201 E4
Chelmerton Ave. Gt Bad 140 C4
Chelmsford Ave. South 190 C1
Chelmsford Rd. Chelm 126 B1
Chelmsford Rd. Clact 110 B3
Chelmsford Rd. Rayl 164 C1
Chelmsford Rd. Rayl 175 F4
Chelmsford Rd. Woo Mor 143 E3
Chelsea Ave. South 200 B3
Chelsea Rd. Sud 12 C4
Chelsworth Ave. Sud 13 D4
Chelsworth Cl. South 200 A4
Chelsworth Cres. South 200 C4
Cheltenham Dr. South 189 F1
Cheltenham dr. Thund 188 A4
Cheltenham Rd. Hock 177 E4
Cheltenham Rd. South 200 B4
Chelwater. Gt Bad 140 B4
Chequers La. Glems 2 B3
Chequers La. Mald 132 A1
Chequers Rd. Lit Bro 53 E4
Chequers The. Alres 88 A4
Cheriton Rd. Brain 60 B1
Cherries The. Canv 197 D1
Cherry Blossom La. Col N 155 F3
Cherry Chase. Tipt 100 B2
Cherry Cl. Canv 196 C2
Cherry Cl. Hock 177 F4
Cherry Garden La. Dan 143 D4
Cherry Garden Rd. Mald 131 F1
Cherry La. Gt Y 15 D4
Cherry La. Wick 175 D4
Cherry Orchard La. Roch 178 A1
Cherry Orchard. Soum 159 F2
Cherry Row. Colch 66 C3
Cherry Tree Ave. Clact 109 E1
Cherry Tree Chase. Gt Wak 193 E1
Cherry Tree Ct. Lit Oak 57 D4
Cherry Tree La. Colch 86 A4
Cherrybrook. South 192 B1
Cherrydene Cl. Hull 165 F1
Cherrydown East. Basil 185 D3
Cherrydown West. Basil 185 D3
Cherrydown. Rayl 176 B2
Cherrygarden La. Chelm 140 A4
Cherrymeade. S Ben 188 C2
Cherrytree Rd. Sud 13 D4

Cherrytree Rise. With 98 A3
Cherrywood Dr. Colch 66 C3
Cherrywoods. Gt Ben 89 E4
Chertsey Cl. South 192 B1
Chervil Cl. Tipt 100 B2
Cherwell Dr. Chelm 126 B3
Cheshunt Dr. Rayl 176 A3
Chess La. With 98 A1
Chester Ave. South 200 B3
Chester Pl. Chelm 127 D3
Chester Way. Basil 185 F4
Chesterfield Ave. Thund 187 F3
Chesterfield Cres. South 189 E3
Chesterford Gdns. Basil 185 F4
Chesterford Green. Basil 185 F4
Chestnut Ave. Clact 109 E2
Chestnut Ave. Colch 86 A4
Chestnut Ave. Gos 42 C4
Chestnut Ave. Hat Pev 114 A2
Chestnut Ave. Mald 132 B3
Chestnut Ave. Walt 93 E3
Chestnut Cl. Burn 170 A3
Chestnut Cl. Hock 177 F3
Chestnut Ct. Basil 186 A2
Chestnut Farm Dr. Alth 157 F1
Chestnut Gr. Brain 59 F1
Chestnut Gr. S Ben 187 D2
Chestnut Gr. South 191 D1
Chestnut Path. Cane 168 B1
Chestnut Rd. Alres 88 A4
Chestnut Rd. Basil 186 A2
Chestnut Rd. Glems 2 A3
Chestnut Way. Brigh 106 C4
Chestnut Way. Tipt 100 B4
Chestnut Wlk. Canv 196 C2
Chestnut Wlk. Chelm 127 D3
Chestnut Wlk. Lit Bad 129 F1
Chestnuts The. Rayl 176 C2
Chestnuts. Basil 186 A4
Cheveling Rd. Colch 68 B1
Chevening Gdns. Hock 177 E3
Chevers Pawen. Basil 186 A3
Cheviot Dr. Chelm 126 B3
Chevy Ct. Harw 39 E1
Cheyne Ct. Sud 12 C3
Chichester Cl. Basil 185 F4
Chichester Cl. Canv 197 D1
Chichester Dr. Sprin 127 E2
Chichester Rd. South 200 A4
Chichester Way. Mald 145 D4
Chigborough Rd. Gt Tot 132 C3
Chignall Rd. Chelm 126 B3
Chilburn Rd. Clact 110 A4
Childwell Alley. Colch 68 A4
Chilham Cl. Basil 186 A3
Chiltern App. Canv 196 C2
Chiltern Cl. Colch 49 F1
Chiltern Cl. Rayl 176 B2
Chilterns The. Canv 196 C2
Chilton Cl. Gt Bad 140 B4
Chilton Cl. Gt Hor 49 D4
Chilton Cotts. Worm 29 F2
Chilton Ct. Sud 13 D4
Chimes The. S Ben 187 E2
Chimney Pot La. Purl 143 F2
Chinchilla Rd. South 200 B4
Chingford Ave. Clact 109 F4
Chinook. Colch 50 B2
Chipping Hill. Hals 25 F1
Chipping Hill. With 97 F2
Chipping Row. S Woo F 165 F4
Chippingdell. With 97 F2
Chipstead Wlk. Clact 109 E3
Chittock Gate. Basil 185 F3
Chittock Mead. Basil 185 F3
Chitts Hill. E A Gr 48 B1
Chitts Hill. Stanw 66 B4
Cholvedon Sq. Basil 186 A3
Chrismund Way. Gt T 46 B1
Christ Church Ct. Colch 67 E3
Christchurch Ave. Wick 174 A4
Christchurch Rd. South 191 E1
Christina Rd. With 114 C4
Christine Chase. Colch 66 C3
Christmas Field. Si Hed 15 E1
Christopher Cl. Sud 12 C4
Christopher Dr. Lit Cla 91 E1
Christopher La. Sud 12 C4
Christy Ave. Chelm 126 C2
Church Chase. Gt Brx 99 D2
Church Chase. Rett 164 B3
Church Cl. Canv 196 C2
Church Cl. Cav 1 B1
Church Cl. W Berg 48 C2
Church Cl. Wic Bis 115 E3
Church Cres. Clact 109 F1
Church End Ave. Runw 163 F1
Church End La. Runw 163 F1
Church End. Pan 59 D4
Church Farm Way. Colch 49 F2
Church Field Rd. Sud 13 E4
Church Fields. Gt Y 8 C1
Church Gate. Glems 2 B3
Church Gr. Ald 65 D4
Church Green. Cane 168 B1
Church Green. Cogg 63 D2
Church Green. Lit Y 9 E2
Church Green. Wic Bis 115 E3
Church Hill. Ea Col 45 E3

Church Hill. Lawf 34 C2
Church Hill. Purl 144 C1
Church Hill. Rams 39 D1
Church Hill. Rowh 86 C4
Church Hill. South 198 C4
Church Hill. Wh Not 78 C1
Church Hill. Woo Wa 130 B1
Church La. Ald 64 B2
Church La. Basil 174 A1
Church La. Beau 74 A3
Church La. Brain 59 F3
Church La. Ca Hed 15 F2
Church La. Chelm 127 D1
Church La. Cla 4 A4
Church La. Colch 67 F4
Church La. E Mers 105 F1
Church La. Frin 93 D2
Church La. Gt Wig 102 C2
Church La. Harw 40 C3
Church La. Lit Tot 117 D1
Church La. Mist 35 F2
Church La. Mks T 64 B2
Church La. Mks T 65 D2
Church La. Nay 20 A1
Church La. Ridge 8 A3
Church La. S Han 163 E4
Church La. Sprin 127 E2
Church La. Stanw 66 A2
Church La. Stow M 155 E2
Church La. Topp 14 A4
Church La. W Han 152 A2
Church La. Weel 91 D4
Church La. Writ 126 A1
Church Mead. Wh Not 78 C1
Church Meadow. Bul 11 F2
Church Par. Canv 196 C3
Church Park Rd. Basil 186 A3
Church Park. Cla 3 E2
Church Rd. Alres 88 A4
Church Rd. Ashi 178 B4
Church Rd. Barl 192 C4
Church Rd. Basil 185 E3
Church Rd. Basil 186 C2
Church Rd. Bl Not 78 A3
Church Rd. Bore 129 D3
Church Rd. Box 31 F3
Church Rd. Bradw 61 E1
Church Rd. Bradw 61 F3
Church Rd. Brigh 106 C4
Church Rd. Bul 11 F2
Church Rd. Burn 170 A3
Church Rd. Clact 110 A2
Church Rd. Copf 65 F1
Church Rd. Elmst M 70 A4
Church Rd. Ford 47 E3
Church Rd. Frat 70 B1
Church Rd. Gos 42 C4
Church Rd. Gt Tot 116 B1
Church Rd. Gt Y 8 C1
Church Rd. Hadl 188 C1
Church Rd. Hat Pev 114 A2
Church Rd. Hock 177 D4
Church Rd. Kelv 81 E1
Church Rd. Lay H 84 C2
Church Rd. Lit Bad 129 D3
Church Rd. Lit Bro 53 D2
Church Rd. N Fam 167 D4
Church Rd. Peld 103 E3
Church Rd. Rayl 175 E4
Church Rd. Rayl 176 C1
Church Rd. South 200 A4
Church Rd. South 201 E3
Church Rd. Sud 13 D3
Church Rd. T Gr 79 D3
Church Rd. Tend 72 A3
Church Rd. Terl 96 B1
Church Rd. Thor 89 D3
Church Rd. Thund 187 E3
Church Rd. Tipt 100 B3
Church Rd. Toll M 117 F1
Church Rd. Twin 18 B3
Church Rd. Ult 130 B3
Church Rd. W Berg 48 C2
Church Rd. W Han 152 A2
Church Rd. W Mers 121 D3
Church Rd. Walt 94 B4
Church Rd. Wic Bis 115 F3
Church Rd. Wic S P 17 D3
Church Rd. With 80 A1
Church Rd. Worm 29 F3
Church Rd. Wrab 37 F2
Church Sq. Bures 19 F1
Church Sq. St O 108 A2
Church St. Bel S P 5 D2
Church St. Box 32 A4
Church St. Chelm 127 D1
Church St. Cla 4 A4
Church St. Cogg 63 D1
Church St. Col En 27 D1
Church St. Colch 67 F4
Church St. Fee 81 D1
Church St. Gest 10 C1
Church St. Gold 133 F4
Church St. Gt Bad 141 D3
Church St. Gt Map 16 B1
Church St. Harw 40 C3
Church St. Mald 132 A1
Church St. Nay 20 B3
Church St. Pan 59 F4

Church St. Rayl 176 B1
Church St. Rowh 87 D4
Church St. Si Hed 15 E1
Church St. Sud 12 B3
Church St. Toll D 118 B2
Church St. Tolle 119 E1
Church St. With 97 F2
Church View Rd. Thund 187 F3
Church View. Ard 51 F4
Church Wlk. Colch 67 F4
Church Wlk. Mald 131 F2
Church Wlk. Sud 12 C4
Churchfield Cotts. Church 183 D4
Churchfield Rd. Cogg 63 D2
Churchfield Rd. Walt 94 B4
Churchfields. South 192 C1
Churchfields. W Mers 121 D3
Churchill Ave. Hals 26 A2
Churchill Cl. Brigh 106 C4
Churchill Dr. Sud 7 F1
Churchill Rd. Brain 59 F4
Churchill Rd. Tipt 100 C3
Churchill Rise. Sprin 127 F4
Churchill W. South 200 A4
Churchill Way. Colch 68 A2
Churchponds. Ca Hed 15 F2
Churchway. Hadl 188 C1
Churchwell Ave. Copf 83 D4
Churnwood Rd. Colch 50 B1
Chuzzlewit Dr. Chelm 126 C4
Cimarron Cl. S Woo F 165 E4
Cinque Port Rd. Brigh 106 C4
Circular Rd E. Colch 67 F3
Circular Rd N. Colch 67 F3
Circular Rd S. Colch 67 F2
Cistern Yd. Colch 67 F4
City Rd. W Mers 121 D3
Clachar Cl. Sprin 128 A2
Clacton Rd. Elmst M 70 B2
Clacton Rd. Frin 93 D1
Clacton Rd. Gt Oak 55 E1
Clacton Rd. Lit Oak 57 D3
Clacton Rd. Mist 54 A3
Clacton Rd. St O 108 A2
Clacton Rd. Thor 89 E2
Clacton Rd. Weel 91 D3
Clacton Rd. Wiv 69 E3
Clacton Rd. Wix 55 E3
Claire Cotts. Birch 83 F3
Claire Rd. Walt 93 D3
Clairmont Cl. Brain 59 F1
Clairmont Rd. Colch 66 C3
Clapgate Dr. Lit Cla 91 E1
Clara Reeve Cl. Colch 66 C2
Clare Ave. Runw 163 E1
Clare Cl. Hals 43 E4
Clare Rd. Brain 59 F1
Clare Rd. Thund 187 D3
Clare Way. Clact 109 D3
Claremont Dr. Basil 186 A2
Claremont Rd. Elmst M 87 E4
Claremont Rd. South 190 C1
Clarence Cl. S Ben 187 E2
Clarence Cl. Sprin 128 A2
Clarence Rd N. S Ben 187 F2
Clarence Rd. Basil 186 C4
Clarence Rd. Cla 4 A4
Clarence Rd. Rayl 177 D1
Clarence Rd. S Ben 187 E2
Clarence Rd. South 200 A4
Clarence Rd. Sud 7 F1
Clarence St. South 200 A4
Clarendon Park. Clact 110 A3
Clarendon Rd. Ashi 166 C1
Clarendon Rd. Basil 186 B4
Clarendon Rd. Canv 197 E2
Clarendon Way. Colch 49 F1
Clarke Rise. Col N 155 F3
Clarke's Rd. Harw 39 F2
Clarkesmead. Tipt 100 B2
Claters Cl. South 191 F1
Clatterfield Gdns. South 190 A1
Claud Ince Ave. T Gr 78 C3
Claudius Rd. Colch 68 A3
Claudius Way. With 114 C4
Clavering Rd. Brain 59 F3
Clavering. Basil 185 F2
Clay Hill Rd. Basil 185 E3
Clay La. St O 108 B4
Clay Lane Gr. Colch 50 B2
Claybrick Ave. Hawk 177 E3
Clayburn Circ. Basil 185 E3
Clayburn End. Basil 185 E3
Clayburn Side. Basil 185 E3
Claydon Cres. Basil 185 E4
Claydons La. Hadl 188 B4
Clayhall Rd. Clact 110 A3
Claypits Ave. Bures 29 D4
Claypits La. Fox 6 B3
Claypits Rd. Bore 112 C1
Clays Rd. Walt 94 A4
Clayspring Cl. Hock 177 E4
Clayton Rd. Harw 39 E1
Clearwater. Colch 68 A2
Clematis Tye. Sprin 127 F4
Clematis Way. Colch 68 C4
Clements Gdns. Hawk 178 A3
Clements Green La. S Woo F 165 E4
Clements Hall La. Hawk 178 A3

Clements Hall Way. Hawk 178 A2
Clements Pl. S Woo F 165 E4
Cleveland Cl. Colch 50 B2
Cleveland Dr. South 190 B2
Cleveland Rd. Basil 185 E3
Cleveland Rd. Canv 197 D1
Cleves Ct. Bore 112 C1
Clevis Dr. S Woo F 165 F3
Clickett End. Basil 185 E3
Clickett Hill. Basil 185 E3
Clickett Side. Basil 185 E3
Clieveden Rd. South 200 C3
Cliff Ave. South 190 C1
Cliff Ave. South 199 D4
Cliff Gdns. South 199 D4
Cliff Par. South 198 B4
Cliff Par. Walt 76 C1
Cliff Rd. Clact 110 C3
Cliff Rd. Harw 40 B2
Cliff Rd. South 199 D4
Cliff Way. Frin 94 A3
Cliffsea Gr. South 189 F1
Clifftown Par. South 199 F4
Clifftown Rd. South 200 A4
Clifton Ave. S Ben 187 E2
Clifton Cl. S Ben 187 E2
Clifton Dr. South 199 E4
Clifton Mews. South 200 A4
Clifton Rd. Ashi 178 B4
Clifton Rd. Basil 186 C4
Clifton Rd. Canv 197 D2
Clifton Terr. South 200 A4
Clifton Terr. Wiv 87 D4
Clifton Way. S Ben 187 E2
Climmen Rd. Canv 197 D3
Clinton Cl. E Han 153 E4
Clinton Rd. Canv 196 B2
Clive Rd. Colch 68 A3
Cliveden Cl. Chelm 126 C2
Clobbs Yd. Chelm 127 D4
Clockhouse Way. Brain 60 B1
Cloes La. Clact 109 D2
Cloisters The. Brain 60 A3
Clopton Dr. L Mel 7 E3
Clopton Green. Basil 185 D4
Close The. Clact 125 D4
Close The. Frin 93 D2
Close The. Frin 93 F3
Close The. Harw 40 A2
Close The. S Ben 187 E1
Close The. Sud 12 C4
Close The. T Gr 78 C3
Clough Rd. Colch 50 B3
Clova Rd. South 189 F1
Clovelly Gdns. Runw 174 B4
Clover Cl. Basil 185 F2
Clover Ct. Sud 13 E3
Clover Dr. Thor 89 D3
Clover Way. Ard 51 D3
Clover Way. Basil 185 F2
Cloverlands. Colch 50 B1
Cluanie Orch. Cav 1 C1
Cluny Sq. South 191 E2
Clyde Cres. Chelm 126 B2
Clyde Cres. Rayl 188 B4
Clydesdale Rd. Brain 59 F1
Coach La. Mald 131 F2
Coach Rd. Alres 88 A4
Coach Rd. Gt Hor 49 D4
Coan Ave. Clact 109 E1
Coast Rd. W Mers 121 D3
Coats Hutton Rd. Colch 67 D2
Cobbins Chase. Burn 170 A4
Cobbins Cl. Burn 170 A4
Cobbins The. Burn 170 A4
Cobbs Pl. Sprin 127 E2
Cobden Wlk. Basil 186 B4
Cobham Rd. South 199 E4
Coburb Pl. S Woo F 165 E3
Cock and Bell La. L Mel 7 E3
Cock Rd. Lit Map 17 D1
Cockaynes La. Alres 88 A4
Cockerell Cl. Basil 174 A1
Cockethurst Cl. South 190 A2
Cockett Wick La. St O 108 B1
Cockrell's Rd. Worm 30 A2
Codenham Green. Basil 185 D2
Codenham Straight. Basil 185 D2
Codham Little Park Dr. Weth .. 41 E3
Coggeshall Rd (Feering). Cogg 81 E4
Coggeshall Rd. Ard 33 F1
Coggeshall Rd. Bradw 61 E2
Coggeshall Rd. Brain 60 B2
Coggeshall Rd. Cogg 62 C3
Coggeshall Rd. Ea Col 45 D2
Coggeshall Rd. Gt T 64 A4
Coggeshall Rd. Kelv 81 D3
Coggeshall Rd. Mks T 64 B2
Coggeshall Rd. Stis 60 B2
Coggeshall Way. Hals 26 A1
Coke St. Harw 40 B3
Cokefield Ave. South 191 E2
Coker Rd. Canv 196 B1
Cokers Cl. Bl Not 78 B3
Colam La. Lit Bad 129 E2
Colbert Ave. South 200 C4
Colchester Cl. South 190 C1
Colchester Rd. Ard 51 D2
Colchester Rd. Ard 51 F4

Colchester Rd. Bore 128 A3
Colchester Rd. Bures 28 C4
Colchester Rd. Clact 110 B3
Colchester Rd. Cogg 63 E1
Colchester Rd. Ded 33 F3
Colchester Rd. Ea Col 45 F3
Colchester Rd. Elmst M 69 F3
Colchester Rd. Gt Ben 71 E2
Colchester Rd. Gt Bro 52 A2
Colchester Rd. Gt Oak 55 D3
Colchester Rd. Gt Tot 116 B3
Colchester Rd. Hals 26 A1
Colchester Rd. Lang 104 A3
Colchester Rd. Lawf 35 D2
Colchester Rd. M Bure 29 D3
Colchester Rd. Mald 132 A3
Colchester Rd. South 190 C1
Colchester Rd. St O 108 A3
Colchester Rd. Tend 72 B1
Colchester Rd. Th L S 73 E1
Colchester Rd. Tipt 100 B4
Colchester Rd. Tolle 119 D3
Colchester Rd. Virl 102 A1
Colchester Rd. W Berg 30 A1
Colchester Rd. W Berg 48 C2
Colchester Rd. W Mers 121 E4
Colchester Rd. Wa Col 46 C3
Colchester Rd. Weel 72 B1
Colchester Rd. With 98 B2
Colchester Rd. Wiv 69 E2
Colchester Rd. Wix 55 D3
Cold Hall Chase. Gt Bro 70 C3
Coldnailhurst Ave. Brain 59 F3
Cole Green. Bel S P 5 D1
Cole Hill. Gt Le 95 D3
Coleman St. South 191 D1
Colemans Ave. South 190 B2
Colemans La. Dan 142 B4
Coleridge Rd. Mald 132 A1
Coles Brook Rd. Gt Ben 89 F2
Coles La. Walt 76 A1
Coles Oak La. Ded 33 E3
College Ct. Lawf 35 E2
College Rd. Brain 59 F1
College Rd. Clact 110 A3
College Way. South 199 F4
Coller Rd. Rams 39 F3
Colletts Chase. Worm 29 F3
Colley Rd. Gt Bad 141 D3
Colliers The. Mald 132 C2
Collindale Gdns. Clact 110 B3
Collingdale Cl. Canv 197 E2
Collingwood Cl. Brain 60 B3
Collingwood Rd. Basil 185 E2
Collingwood Rd. Clact 109 E1
Collingwood Rd. Colch 66 C3
Collingwood Rd. S Woo F 165 F3
Collingwood Rd. With 98 A1
Collingwood Terr. Basil 185 E3
Collingwood Wlk. Basil 185 E3
Collingwood. S Ben 187 F2
Collins Cl. Brain 59 F1
Collins Rd. Lit Map 17 E1
Collins Way. South 190 A3
Colne Bank Ave. Colch 49 F1
Colne Bank Ave. Colch 67 E4
Colne Chase. With 97 F1
Colne Cl. S Woo F 165 F4
Colne Dr. South 192 C1
Colne Park Rd. Ea Col 45 E4
Colne Pl. Basil 185 E2
Colne Rd. Bures 28 C4
Colne Rd. Clact 109 F1
Colne Rd. Cogg 63 D3
Colne Rd. Hals 26 A1
Colne Rd. Si Hed 24 C4
Colne Rise. Rowh 86 C4
Colne Springs. Ridge 8 A3
Colne St. Brigh 106 C3
Colne Valley Cl. Hals 25 E1
Colne View. St O 107 D1
Colne Way. St O 106 C2
Colneford Hill. Ea Col 45 E4
Colneys Cl. Sud 7 E1
Colthorpe Rd. Clact 109 F4
Coltishall Cl. Wick 175 D3
Columbine Gdns. Walt 94 A4
Columbine Mews. Stanw 66 B4
Columbines The. Cav 1 C1
Colvin Chase. Chelm 140 A1
Colvin Cl. Colch 66 C4
Colworth Cl. Hadl 188 B2
Colyers Reach. Sprin 128 A1
Comet Way. South 190 A3
Commerce Park. Colch 68 B2
Commerce Way. Colch 68 B2
Commercial Rd. South 190 B2
Common App. Thund 188 A4
Common Cl. Lit Bad 129 F1
Common La. Thund 188 A4
Common La. Woo Wa 130 A2
Common. Gt Wak 193 D2
Common St. Cla 4 A4
Common The. Dan 142 C3
Common The. E Han 153 D4
Common The. Thund 188 A4
Commonhall La. Hadl 188 B2
Commons The. Colch 67 D3
Compasses Rd. Bradw 61 F3

Compton Ct. Canv 197 E1
Compton Rd. Colch 68 B4
Comyns Pl. Writ 126 A1
Con Way. S Ben 187 E2
Conan Doyle Cl. Brain 78 A4
Concord Ave. Canv 196 C3
Conder Way. Colch 68 B2
Conduit La. Woo Mor 143 F3
Conduit St. Chelm 127 D1
Conies Rd. Hals 43 E4
Conifer Cl. Alres 87 F4
Conifer Cl. Colch 68 B4
Conifers. Hadl 188 C2
Coniston Cl. Bl Not 77 E3
Coniston Cl. Rayl 176 C1
Coniston Rd. Canv 197 D2
Coniston Rd. Thund 187 F4
Coniston. South 190 A4
Connaught Ave. Frin 93 F2
Connaught Cl. Clact 110 A2
Connaught Dr. S Woo F 165 E4
Connaught Gdns E. Clact 110 A2
Connaught Gdns W. Clact 110 A2
Connaught Gdns. Brain 60 A2
Connaught Gdns. South 201 E3
Connaught Rd. Lit Cla 91 E3
Connaught Rd. Rayl 189 D4
Connaught Wlk. Rayl 189 D4
Conquerors Cl. Hat Pev 114 A2
Conrad Rd. With 97 F3
Constable Ave. Clact 109 E2
Constable Cl. Colch 49 F2
Constable Cl. Lawf 35 D2
Constable Cl. W Mers 121 E4
Constable Rd. Sud 12 C4
Constable View. Sprin 127 F3
Constable Way. South 202 A4
Constance Cl. With 115 D4
Constantine Rd. Colch 67 E3
Constantine Rd. With 114 C4
Constitution Hill. S Ben 187 E2
Constitution Hill. Sud 12 C4
Convent Hill. Brain 60 A3
Convent La. Brain 60 A3
Convent Rd. Canv 197 D2
Conway Ave. Gt Wak 193 D2
Conway Cl. Elmst M 87 E4
Conway Cl. Hals 43 E4
Cook La. Harw 39 F1
Cook Cres. Colch 68 C4
Cook Pl. Sprin 127 F2
Cook's Hall Rd. W Berg 48 B2
Cook's La. Colch 66 C4
Cookham Ct. South 192 C1
Cooks Cl. Hals 43 F4
Cooks Green. Basil 174 B1
Cooks Hill. Box 32 A3
Coolyne Way. Clact 110 A4
Coombe Rd. Soum 159 E2
Coombe Rise. Chelm 127 D4
Coombes Gr. Roch 179 D1
Coombewood Dr. Thund 187 F3
Cooper Wlk. Colch 68 B4
Cooper's La. Ded 33 F3
Cooper's Row. Chelm 127 D3
Coopers Ave. Mald 132 B3
Coopers La. Clact 109 E2
Coopers Way. South 191 D3
Copdoek. Basil 185 E4
Copelands. Hawk 178 B3
Copford Ave. Rayl 176 C1
Copland Cl. Gt Bad 140 C4
Coppens Green. Wick 174 C3
Copper Beeches. Stanw 66 B3
Copper Beeches. Thund 188 A4
Copperas Rd. Brigh 106 C3
Copperfield Rd. Chelm 126 C4
Coppice End. Colch 50 A2
Coppice Rd. Alres 88 A4
Coppins Cl. Sprin 127 F2
Coppins Rd. Clact 109 E2
Copt Hall La. Gt Wig 103 E2
Copt Hill. Dan 142 C3
Coptfold Cl. South 191 F1
Coral Cl. S Woo F 165 E4
Coralin Wlk. Stanw 66 B3
Corasway. Thund 188 A4
Cordelia Cres. Rayl 176 B2
Cordell Pl. L Mel 7 E4
Cordell Rd. L Mel 7 E4
Cordwainers The. South 191 D3
Coriander Rd. Tipt 100 B2
Cormorant Wlk. Chelm 140 B3
Cornard Rd. Sud 12 C4
Cornec Ave. Rayl 189 D3
Cornec Chase. Rayl 189 E3
Cornel Cl. With 97 E2
Cornerth Cres. Sud 13 D3
Cornfields. S Woo F 165 E4
Cornflower Cl. Stanw 66 B4
Cornflower Dr. Sprin 127 F3
Cornflower Rd. Clact 125 D4
Cornford Way. Lawf 35 D2
Cornhill Ave. Hock 177 F4
Cornhill. Chelm 127 D1
Cornish Gr. S Woo F 165 F3
Cornwall Cl. Lawf 35 D2
Cornwall Cres. Chelm 127 D4
Cornwall Gdns. Brain 60 A2

Cornwall Gdns. Hawk 178 B3
Cornwall Rd. Basil 186 C4
Cornwallis Dr. S Woo F 165 F4
Cornwalls Dri. Mks T 64 C2
Cornworthy. South 201 E4
Corona Rd. Canv 197 E3
Coronation Ave. Brain 59 F1
Coronation Ave. Colch 68 A1
Coronation Cl. Gt Wak 192 C2
Coronation Rd. Burn 170 A2
Coronation Rd. Clact 109 E2
Coronation Way. T Gr 78 B3
Corporation Rd. Chelm 127 D2
Corsel Rd. Canv 197 F2
Cortoncroft Cl. Walt 93 F4
Cosgrove Ave. Hadl 189 D2
Cossington Rd. South 199 F4
Cotelands. Basil 185 F2
Cotman Ave. Lawf 35 D3
Cotman Rd. Clact 109 E3
Cotman Rd. Colch 67 D3
Cotswold Ave. Rayl 176 B2
Cotswold Cres. Chelm 126 B3
Cotswold Ct. Colch 50 B2
Cotswold Dr. L Mel 7 E3
Cotswold Rd. Clact 109 F3
Cotswold Rd. South 190 B1
Cottage Dr. Colch 68 B2
Cottage Gr. Clact 109 E3
Cottage Green. Clact 109 E3
Cottage Pl. Chelm 127 D2
Cottage Wlk. Clact 109 E3
Cottesmore Cl. Canv 197 D1
Cottesmore Gdns. Hadl 189 D1
Cottonwood Cl. Clact 67 E1
Coulde Dennis. E Han 153 D4
Coulsdon Cl. Clact 109 E3
Court St. Nay 20 A1
Courtauld Cl. Hals 25 F1
Courtauld Homes. Hals 25 F2
Courtauld Rd. Basil 174 B1
Courtauld Rd. Brain 60 A2
Courtenay Cl. Sud 7 E1
Courtland Mews. Mald 144 C4
Courtland Pl. Mald 144 C4
Courtlands. Chelm 127 D3
Courtlands. Hals 43 F4
Courts The. Rayl 176 C2
Coval Ave. Chelm 127 D2
Coval La. Chelm 127 D2
Coventry Cl. Colch 68 A4
Coventry Cl. Hull 165 F1
Coventry Hill. Hull 165 F1
Coverts The. W Mers 121 E4
Coverts The. Writ 126 A1
Cow La. St O 107 E2
Cowdray Ave. Colch 50 A1
Cowdray Cres. Colch 67 F4
Cowell Ave. Chelm 126 C3
Cowpar Mews. Brain 78 A4
Cowslip Ct. Stanw 66 B4
Cowslip Mead. Basil 185 D3
Cox Rd. Alres 88 A4
Cox's Hill. Lawf 35 D2
Coxs Cl. S Woo F 165 F4
Crabb's Hill. Hat Pev 113 F2
Crabtree La. Lit Hor 30 B1
Crabtree. Walt 93 E4
Cracknell Cl. Wiv 69 D1
Craftsmans Sq. South 191 D3
Craig's Hill. Bures 28 C3
Craigfield Ave. Clact 110 A3
Craigs La. M Bure 28 C3
Craiston Way. Gt Bad 140 C3
Cramphorn Wlk. Chelm 126 C2
Cranbrook Ave. Thund 188 B2
Crane's La. Kelv 80 C1
Crane's La. Kelv 99 D4
Cranes Ct. Basil 185 E4
Cranes Farm Rd. Basil 185 D4
Cranes La. Basil 185 E4
Cranfield Ct. Runw 174 B4
Cranfield Park Rd. Wick 174 C2
Cranford Cl. Frin 93 F3
Cranleigh Cl. Clact 109 D3
Cranleigh Dr. South 189 F1
Cranleigh Gdns. Hull 165 E1
Cranley Ave. South 190 B1
Cranley Gdns. South 201 E3
Cranley Rd. South 190 B1
Cranmoregreen La. Glems 2 C2
Cranston Ave. South 190 B3
Craven Ave. Canv 197 D2
Craven Cl. Hawk 178 B3
Craven Dr. Colch 50 B2
Craylands. Basil 185 F4
Credon Cl. Clact 109 E3
Credon Dr. Clact 109 F4
Creek Rd. Canv 197 E2
Creek View Ave. Hull 165 E1
Creek View. Basil 185 F2
Creekhurst Cl. Brigh 107 D3
Creeksea La. Burn 169 F3
Creeksea Rd. Cane 169 E1
Creekview Rd. S Woo F 165 F4
Creephedge La. S Woo F 153 F2
Creffield Rd. Colch 67 E3
Crescent Rd. Canv 197 E2
Crescent Rd. Gt Bad 141 D4

Crescent Rd. Hadl 189 D1
Crescent Rd. Mald 131 F3
Crescent Rd. S Ben 187 E1
Crescent Rd. Tolle 119 F1
Crescent Rd. Walt 94 B4
Crescent The. Clact 110 A4
Crescent The. Colch 50 B3
Crescent The. Frin 93 D2
Crescent The. Frin 93 F2
Crescent The. Gt Hor 31 D1
Crescent The. Hadl 188 C2
Crescent The. Mks T 65 D2
Crescent The. Th L S 73 F1
Crescent The. W Berg 48 B3
Cress Croft. Brain 60 B1
Cressing Rd. Brain 60 B1
Cressing Rd. With 97 F3
Crest Ave. Basil 186 B3
Crest The. South 189 E3
Crestlands. Alres 88 B4
Creswick Ave. Rayl 176 B2
Cricketers Cl. Sud 12 C3
Cricketers Cl. South 174 A1
Cricketfield Gr. South 189 F1
Crickhollow. S Woo F 165 E3
Crina Wlk. Basil 185 F3
Cringle Lock. S Woo F 165 F3
Cripplegate. Soum 159 F3
Crispin Ct. Colch 67 F4
Crittall Dr. Brain 59 E2
Crittall Rd. With 98 A1
Crocklands. Hals 44 A3
Crockford Hill. Ard 51 D1
Crockleford Rd. Elmst M 69 F3
Crocus Cl. Clact 109 E2
Crocus Way. Sprin 127 F4
Croft Cl. Brain 60 A2
Croft Cl. S Ben 187 D3
Croft Cl. South 189 F2
Croft Cl. Sprin 127 F4
Croft Rd. Clact 109 E2
Croft Rd. Kelv 81 D1
Croft Rd. S Ben 187 E3
Croft Rd. Sud 12 C4
Croft The. Bures 19 F1
Croft The. Ea Col 45 D3
Croft The. Glems 2 B2
Croft The. Gt Y 9 D1
Croft The. Rayl 188 C4
Crofts The. Barl 192 C2
Crome Cl. Colch 67 D3
Crome Rd. Clact 109 E3
Cromer Rd. South 200 A4
Crompton St. Chelm 126 C1
Cromwell Hill. Mald 131 F2
Cromwell La. Mald 131 F2
Cromwell Rd. Colch 67 F3
Cromwell Rd. Hock 177 F3
Cromwell Rd. South 191 D2
Cromwell Way. With 97 F1
Cropenburg Wlk. Canv 197 D3
Crosby Rd. South 199 E4
Cross Ave. Wick 174 B3
Cross Hill. Gt Oak 56 B1
Cross La. W Mers 121 F4
Cross Park Rd. Wick 174 B2
Cross Rd. Basil 186 C4
Cross Rd. Mald 132 A1
Cross Rd. S Ben 188 A2
Cross Rd. With 97 F3
Cross St. Sud 12 C4
Cross Way. W Mers 121 F4
Crossfield Rd. Clact 109 F2
Crossfield Rd. Thund 187 F4
Crossfield Rd. South 191 E1
Crossfield Way. Walt 93 D3
Crossfields. Nay 20 B3
Crossley Ave. Clact 124 C4
Crosstree Wlk. Colch 68 A2
Crossways Hill. Woo Wa 130 A2
Crossways The. South 199 D4
Crossways. Canv 196 C2
Crossways. Chelm 140 A4
Crossways. Clact 125 D4
Crossways. Col En 26 C1
Crouch Ave. Hull 165 F1
Crouch Beck. S Woo F 165 F4
Crouch Dr. Wick 174 B4
Crouch Dr. With 97 F1
Crouch Meadow. Hull 165 F1
Crouch Rd. Burn 170 B3
Crouch St. Colch 67 F3
Crouch View Cotts. Rett 164 B3
Crouch View Gr. Hull 165 F1
Crouch Way. South 201 F4
Crouchman's Farm Rd. Ult 130 B4
Crouchmans Ave. Gt Wak 193 D2
Crouchview Cl. Wick 175 D4
Crow La. Tend 73 D2
Crow Pond Rd. Terl 96 B2
Crowborough Rd. South 190 C1
Crowhall La. Brad 36 C3
Crowhurst Ct. Colch 67 F4
Crowhurst Rd. Colch 67 F4
Crown Ave. Basil 186 B4
Crown Bay Rd. Colch 68 B4
Crown Gdns. Rayl 176 B1
Crown Hill. Rayl 176 B1
Crown La N. Ard 50 C4

Crown La S. Ard 51 D2
Crown La. Tend 72 B2
Crown Rd. Clact 109 E1
Crown Rd. Col N 155 F3
Crown Rd. Hock 177 D3
Crown St. Ca Hed 15 F2
Crown St. Ded 33 F3
Crown Way. Soum 159 E2
Crownfield Rd. Glems 2 B3
Crows La. S Woo F 154 B3
Crowstone Ave. South 199 E4
Crowstone Cl. South 190 B1
Crowstone Rd. South 199 E4
Croxon Way. Burn 170 A4
Cruce Way. St O 106 C2
Crummock Cl. Bl Not 77 E3
Cuckoo Cnr. South 190 C2
Cuckoo Hill. Bures 19 F1
Cuckoo Hill. Si Hed 24 A4
Culver Par. Colch 67 F4
Culver Rise. S Woo F 165 F4
Culver Sq. Colch 67 F4
Culver St E. Colch 67 F4
Culver St N. Colch 67 F4
Culver Wlk. Colch 67 F4
Culverdown. Basil 185 D3
Culvert Cl. Cogg 62 C1
Cumberland Ave. Mald 131 F1
Cumberland Ave. S Ben 187 E2
Cumberland Ave. South 191 E1
Cumberland Cl. Brain 60 A2
Cumberland Cres. Chelm 127 D4
Cumming Rd. S Han 163 D1
Cunningham Cl. South 201 F4
Cunnington Rd. Brain 60 B2
Cuppers Cl. With 97 F1
Curds Rd. Ea Col 45 D2
Curlew Ave. May 158 A4
Curlew Cl. Clact 109 F3
Curlew Cl. Kelv 81 E1
Curlew Cl. Mald 132 B3
Curlew Cres. Basil 185 D2
Curlew Dr. S Ben 187 E1
Curling Tye La. Woo Wa 131 D2
Curling Tye. Basil 185 E4
Curling Wlk. Basil 185 E4
Currants Farm Rd. Brain 59 F3
Current's La. Harw 40 C3
Curtisway. Rayl 176 C2
Curzon Rd. Sud 13 D4
Curzon Way. Sprin 128 A1
Curzon Wlk. Basil 186 A3
Cusak Rd. Sprin 127 F1
Custom Hall La. Harw 40 B3
Cut The. Tipt 100 B3
Cut Throat La. With 98 A2
Cut-a-thwart La. Mald 131 E2
Cuthedge La. Cogg 80 B4
Cutlers Rd. S Woo F 165 F4
Cutmore Pl. Chelm 139 F4
Cuton Hall La. Bore 128 A3
Cutting Dr. Hals 25 F1
Cymbeline Way. Colch 67 D4
Cypress Cl. Clact 109 F4
Cypress Dr. Chelm 140 B3
Cypress Gr. Colch 68 C4
Cypress Mews. W Mers 121 D4
Cypress Rd. With 98 A2
Cyril Child Cl. Colch 68 C4

D'Archy Rd. Tipt 100 C1
D'arcy Ave. Mald 132 A1
D'Arcy Cl. Burn 170 B3
D'Arcy Cl. Walt 93 F3
D'arcy Rd. Colch 68 B2
D'Arcy Rd. St O 108 A3
D'arcy Way. Brigh 106 C4
D'Arcy Way. Toll D 118 C2
Daarle Ave. Canv 197 D2
Daen Ingas. Dan 142 B4
Daffodil Way. Sprin 127 F4
Dagnets La. Gt Le 77 E1
Dahlia Cl. Clact 109 E2
Dahlia Cl. Sprin 127 F3
Dahlia Wlk. Colch 68 B4
Daimler Ave. Clact 124 B3
Daines Cl. South 201 D4
Daines Way. South 201 D4
Dairy Farm Rd. May 158 B2
Dairy Rd. Sprin 127 F2
Dairyhouse La. Brad 54 C4
Daisleys La. Gt Le 95 D1
Daisy Ct. Bore 128 A3
Dale Cl. Stanw 66 A4
Dale Rd. Hadl 189 D1
Dale The. S Ben 188 A2
Dale The. Wiv 87 E4
Dalen Ave. Canv 197 D2
Dales The. Harw 39 F1
Dales The. Hawk 178 B2
Daleview Ave. Wix 55 E3
Dallwood Way. Brain 60 A2
Dalmatia Rd. South 200 B4
Dalrymple Cl. Sprin 127 D2
Daltes La. St O 108 B2
Daltons Fen. Basil 186 B4
Dalwood Gdns. Hadl 188 C2
Dalwood. South 192 B1
Dalys Rd. Roch 178 C1

Damant's Farm La. Th L S 74 A2
Damases La. Bore 113 D1
Damask Rd. Stanw 66 B4
Dampier Rd. Cogg 62 C2
Danbury Cl. Mks T 64 C2
Danbury Cl. South 189 F2
Danbury Down. Basil 185 F4
Danbury Rd. Rayl 176 A2
Danbury Vale. Dan 143 D3
Dancing Dick's La. With 97 D1
Dandies Chase. South 189 F4
Dandies Cl. South 189 E4
Dandies Dr. South 189 F4
Dane Rd. Chelm 126 C1
Dane St. South 202 A3
Dane's Ave. South 201 F3
Danes Ct. Sud 13 D2
Danescroft Cl. South 189 F2
Danescroft Dr. South 189 E2
Danesfield. S Ben 187 E1
Danesleigh Gdns. South 189 E2
Daneum Holt. Cla 4 A3
Daniel Cole Rd. Colch 67 F2
Daniel Dr. Colch 67 D1
Daniel Way. Silv E 79 F2
Daniell Cl. Clact 109 E3
Darcy Rise. Lit Bad 129 F1
Darenth Rd. Hadl 189 D1
Dark La. Thund 188 A3
Darkhouse La. Rowh 87 D4
Darlinghurst Gr. South 190 A1
Darnay Rise. Chelm 126 B3
Darnel Way. Stanw 66 A4
Darnet Rd. Tolle 119 F1
Darrell Cl. Chelm 127 D3
Dart Cl. With 97 F1
Dartmouth Cl. Rayl 176 B3
Dartmouth Rd. Sprin 127 F3
Darwin Cl. Brain 59 F1
Darwin Cl. Colch 68 A1
Datchet Dr. South 192 C1
Davall Cl. Lit Oak 39 E1
Davenants. Basil 174 A1
Davey Cl. Colch 68 B3
David Ave. Runw 163 E4
Davidson Cl. Sud 13 E2
Dawes La. W Mers 121 F4
Dawlish Cres. Rayl 176 B3
Dawlish Dr. South 189 F1
Dawnford Cl. Stanw 66 B4
Dawnings The. S Woo F 165 E4
Daws Heath Rd. Hadl 188 C3
Daws Heath Rd. Rayl 188 C4
Days Cl. Chelm 127 D4
Dazeley's La. Str S M 34 C4
De Burgh Rd. Colch 66 C3
De Greys Cl. Sud 13 E3
De Staunton Cl. Alres 88 A4
De Vere Ave. Mald 132 A1
De Vere Cl. Hat Pev 114 A2
De Vere Cl. Wiv 87 D4
De Vere Estate. Gt Ben 89 E4
De Vere La. Wiv 87 D4
De Vere Rd. Colch 67 D3
De Vere Rd. Ea Col 44 C4
De Vere Way. Harw 39 F1
De Veres Rd. Hals 25 E1
Dead La. Ard 51 D4
Dead La. Gt Ben 89 F1
Dead La. Lawf 35 E1
Dead La. Lit Cla 91 D1
Deadman's La. Gt Bad 140 B2
Deal Cl. Brain 59 F3
Deal Cl. Clact 125 E4
Deal Way. Brigh 106 C4
Dean Rogers Pl. Brain 59 F4
Dean St. Brigh 106 C4
Dean Way. Chelm 126 C1
Deane's Cl. Harw 40 A1
Deanery Gdns. Brain 59 F4
Deanery Hill. Brain 59 F4
Deanhill Ave. Clact 110 A3
Debden Way. Burn 170 A3
Deben Cl. With 97 F1
Deben Dr. Sud 13 D4
Deben Rd. Colch 50 C1
Dedham Ave. Clact 109 D3
Dedham Meade. Ded 33 F2
Dedham Rd. Ard 33 E1
Dedham Rd. Box 32 A3
Dedham Rd. Lawf 34 C2
Dedham Rd. Str S M 22 C1
Deepdale Rd. Harw 40 A2
Deepdale. Thund 187 F3
Deepdene Ave. Rayl 176 B2
Deepdene. Basil 185 D3
Deeping Wlk. St O 108 A3
Deeping. South 200 A4
Deepwater Rd. Canv 196 C2
Deer Park Cl. Ca Hed 15 F2
Deerhurst Chase. S Woo F 142 C1
Deerhurst Cl. Thund 188 A4
Deerhurst. Thund 188 A4
Deerleap Way. Brain 60 B2
Defoe Cres. Colch 49 F2
Deford Rd. With 114 B4
Deirdre Ave. Wick 174 A4
Deirdre Cl. Wick 174 A4

Delamere Rd. Chelm 126 C1
Delamere Rd. Colch 50 B2
Delaware Cres. South 201 E4
Delaware Rd. South 201 E4
Delder Ave. Canv 197 E1
Delft Rd. Canv 197 D2
Delfzul Rd. Canv 197 D2
Delgada Rd. Canv 197 E2
Delhi Rd. Basil 186 B3
Dell The. Basil 185 E4
Dell The. Gt Bad 140 C3
Dell The. Sud 13 D3
Dell The. Wick 174 C4
Delmar Gdns. Runw 163 E1
Delview. Canv 196 C3
Delvins. Basil 186 A4
Delvyn's La. Gest 16 B4
Dencourt Cres. Basil 185 F3
Dene Cl. Rayl 176 B2
Dene Ct. Chelm 126 B3
Dene Gdns. Rayl 176 B2
Dene Gdns. Rayl 176 B2
Denesmere. S Ben 187 E2
Deneway. Basil 185 E1
Dengayne. Basil 185 E3
Dengie Cl. With 114 C4
Denham Cl. Elmst M 87 F4
Denham Rd. Canv 197 D2
Denmark St. Colch 67 F3
Denten Cl. With 115 D4
Denton App. South 190 A4
Denton Ave. South 190 B3
Denton Cl. South 190 B3
Denver Dr. Basil 174 B1
Derby Cl. May 146 C1
Derby Cl. Steep 147 D1
Derbydale. Hawk 178 B3
Derek Gdns. South 190 C3
Dering Cres. South 189 E4
Derventer Ave. Canv 197 D3
Derwent Ave. Rayl 176 C1
Derwent Gdns. Clact 110 B3
Derwent Rd. Colch 50 B2
Derwent Way. Bl Not 77 E4
Derwent Way. Chelm 126 B2
Devereaux Cl. Walt 93 F4
Devereox Rd. South 200 A4
Devon Gdns. Hawk 178 B3
Devon Rd. Colch 67 D2
Devon Way. Canv 197 D3
Devon Way. Clact 110 C4
Devon Way. Harw 39 E1
Devonshire Gdns. Brain 60 A2
Devonshire Rd. Burn 170 B3
Devonshire Rd. Soum 159 E2
Dewlands. Basil 185 D4
Dewsgreen. Basil 185 E3
Dewyk Rd. Canv 197 E3
Dial Rd. Gt Ben 89 F2
Diana Way. Clact 109 E1
Dickens Cl. Brain 78 A4
Dickens Cl. South 191 D1
Dickens Pl. Chelm 126 B4
Dickett's Hill. Gt Y 15 D3
Digby Mews. W Mers 121 E3
Dilbridge Rd. Colch 68 B4
Dilston. Dan 143 D3
Dinant Ave. Canv 196 C2
Dinants Cres. Mks T 64 C2
Dinsdale Cl. Colch 68 B4
Dismals The. Terl 96 A1
Disraeli Rd. Rayl 189 D4
Distillery La. Colch 68 B2
Ditton Court Rd. South 199 E4
Dixon Ave. Chelm 126 C2
Dixon Ave. Clact 109 E3
Dixon Cl. Lawf 35 D2
Dixon Way. Wiv 69 D1
Dobbies La. Mks T 64 C2
Dock La. Gt Oak 57 D2
Dock Rd. May 147 D1
Dockfield Ave. Harw 39 F2
Dockwra La. Dan 143 D4
Doctor's La. Ashe 3 E1
Docwra Rd. Kelv 81 E1
Doeshill Dr. Wick 174 C4
Doggetts Chase. Roch 178 C3
Doggetts Cl. Roch 178 C2
Doghouse Rd. Bradw 61 F2
Dolby Rise. Sprin 127 F1
Dollant Ave. Canv 197 D2
Dolphins. South 190 B2
Dombey Cl. Chelm 126 C4
Doms La. Terl 96 A1
Domsey Bank. Mks T 64 C2
Domsey Chase. Fee 82 B4
Don Ct. With 97 E1
Donald Thorn Cl. Wick 174 B3
Donald Way. Chelm 140 B4
Donard Dr. W Berg 48 B2
Doney Chase. Lit Brx 115 F3
Donkey La. Str S M 22 C1
Donne Dr. Clact 125 D4
Donyland Way. Rowh 86 C4
Dooley Rd. Hals 25 E1
Dorchester End. Colch 68 A2
Dorewards Ave. Brain 59 D4
Doric Ave. Hawk 178 B3
Dorking Cres. Clact 109 E3

Dorothy Curtice Ct. Copf 65 F3
Dorothy Farm Rd. Rayl 177 D1
Dorothy Gdns. Thund 187 F3
Dorothy Sayers Dr. With 98 A3
Dorset Ave. Gt Bad 140 C3
Dorset Cl. Clact 110 C3
Dorset Cl. Gt Bad 140 C3
Dorset Gdns. Hawk 178 B3
Dorset Rd. Burn 170 B2
Dorset Rd. Mald 144 C4
Dorset Way. Canv 197 D3
Douglas Cl. Chelm 140 B2
Douglas Dr. Wick 174 B3
Douglas Gr. With 97 E1
Douglas Rd. Clact 109 E2
Douglas Rd. Hadl 188 C2
Douglas Rd. Harw 40 A2
Douglas Wlk. Chelm 140 A4
Doulton Way. Hawk 178 B3
Dove Cres. Harw 39 E1
Dove Dr. S Ben 187 D1
Dove La. Chelm 140 A3
Dovecote. South 192 C1
Dovedale Gdns. Clact 110 B3
Dovedale. Canv 197 E3
Dover Cl. Brain 59 F3
Dover Cl. Clact 125 E4
Dover Rd. Brigh 106 C4
Dovercliff Rd. Canv 197 F1
Dovervelt Rd. Canv 197 E3
Dovesgate. S Ben 187 D2
Dow Ct. Soum 159 E2
Dowches Dr. Kelv 81 E2
Dowches Gdns. Kelv 81 E2
Dowling Rd. M Bure 28 C2
Down Hall Rd. Rayl 176 B2
Downer Rd N. Thund 187 F3
Downer Rd S Ben 187 E3
Downesway. S Ben 187 E2
Downey Cl. Basil 185 E4
Downhall Cl. Rayl 176 B2
Downhall Park Way. Rayl 176 B3
Downham Rd. Hawk 178 A3
Downham Rd. Runw 163 E2
Downleaze. S Woo F 165 F4
Downs Gr. Basil 185 F2
Downs Rd. Mald 132 A2
Downs The. Nay 20 B3
Downsway. Sprin 127 E3
Downton Wlk. Tipt 100 B3
Dragon Cl. Burn 170 A3
Drake Ave. May 158 A4
Drake Cl. Thund 188 B3
Drake Gdns. Basil 60 B2
Drake Rd. South 190 B1
Drakes App. Clact 109 D1
Drakes La. Lit Wal 112 A4
Drakes The. South 201 F4
Drakes Way. Rayl 176 C2
Drapers Chase. Mald 132 B2
Drapers Rd. S Woo F 165 F4
Drapery Comm. Glems 2 A2
Drays The. L Mel 7 D3
Drayton Cl. Mald 132 A1
Drewsteignton. South 201 E4
Driberg Way. Brain 60 A1
Driffield Cl. Fee 81 E2
Drift The. Sud 13 E3
Driftway. Basil 185 F2
Drive The. Chelm 127 D3
Drive The. Clact 110 A4
Drive The. Harw 40 A1
Drive The. Hull 165 E2
Drive The. May 157 F4
Drive The. Rayl 189 D4
Drive The. Roch 178 C2
Drive The. South 199 D4
Driveway The. Canv 197 D2
Droitwich Ave. South 191 E1
Drood Cl. Chelm 126 C4
Drum Field. Str S M 22 B1
Drury La. Brain 59 F2
Drury La. Ridge 8 A3
Drury Rd. Colch 67 E3
Dryden Ave. South 191 D1
Dryden Cl. Mald 145 D4
Drywoods. S Woo F 165 E3
Du Cane Pl. With 98 A1
Dubarry Cl. Thund 187 F3
Duck La. Ded 33 F2
Ducketts Mead. Cane 168 B1
Dudley Cl. Colch 68 A2
Dudley Rd. Clact 109 E2
Dudley Rd. Ea Col 44 C4
Dudley Rd. Fing 86 C2
Duffield Dr. Colch 68 C4
Duffield Rd. Gt Bad 140 B3
Duffs Hill. Glems 2 A3
Dugard Ave. Colch 66 C2
Duggers La. Brain 60 A1
Dugmore Ave. Walt 93 E4
Duke St. Brigh 106 C3
Duke St. Chelm 127 D2
Dukes Ave. Soum 159 E2
Dukes La. Sprin 127 F2
Dukes Park Ind Est. Sprin 127 F2
Dukes Rd. Brain 59 F3
Dulverton Ave. South 190 A4
Dulverton Cl. South 190 A3

Dulwich Rd. Clact 110 B3
Dumont Ave. St O 107 D1
Duncan Ave. Colch 67 D2
Duncan Rise. Gt Y 8 C1
Dundee Ave. Hadl 189 D1
Dundee Cl. Hadl 189 E1
Dundonald Dr. South 189 F1
Dungannon Chase. South 201 D3
Dungannon Dr. South 201 D3
Dunkirk Rd. Burn 170 B3
Dunlin Cl. Mald 132 B3
Dunlin Cl. S Woo F 154 B1
Dunlin Ct. Kelv 81 E1
Dunmore Rd. Sprin 128 A2
Dunnock Way. Colch 69 D4
Dunoon Cl. Brain 60 B2
Dunster Ave. South 190 A3
Dunthorne Rd. Colch 50 C1
Dunthorpe Rd. Clact 109 E3
Dupont Cl. Clact 109 E3
Durants Wlk. Wick 174 B3
Durham Rd. Hawk 178 A3
Durham Rd. South 191 E1
Durham Sq. Colch 68 A4
Durham Way. Rayl 176 B3
Durley Cl. S Ben 187 F2
Durrington Cl. Basil 185 E3
Duxford. Wick 175 D3
Dyer's Rd. Mald 132 A1
Dyer's Rd. Stanw 66 B2
Dyke Cres. Canv 196 B2
Dykes Chase. Mald 131 F2
Dyne's Hall Rd. Gt Map 25 E4
Dynevor Gdns. Hadl 189 D1

Eagle Ave. Walt 76 B1
Eagle La. Brain 59 F3
Eagle Way. South 201 F4
Earlhams Cl. Harw 39 F1
Earls Colne Rd. Gt T 46 A1
Earls Hall Ave. South 190 C2
Earls Hall Dr. Clact 108 C3
Earls Hall Par. South 190 C2
Earlsfield Dr. Sprin 127 F2
Earlsmead. With 97 F2
Earlswood Way. Colch 67 E1
Earlswood. S Ben 187 E2
East Bay. Colch 68 A4
East Bridge Rd. S Woo F 165 F4
East Cres. Canv 196 C3
East Dock Rd. Rams 39 F3
East Gores Rd. Gt T 63 F3
East Hanningfield Rd. Rett 153 E1
East Hanningfield Rd. Sand 142 A1
East Hill. Colch 68 A4
East La. Ded 34 A3
East Mayne. Basil 174 A1
East Mersea Rd. W Mers 104 C1
East Mill. Hals 25 F1
East Rd. E Mers 105 F1
East Rd. W Mers 121 F4
East Sq. Basil 185 D3
East St. Brain 60 A2
East St. Cogg 63 D1
East St. Colch 68 A4
East St. Gold 134 A1
East St. Harw 40 B2
East St. Roch 178 C1
East St. South 190 C1
East St. Sud 12 C4
East St. Tolle 119 E1
East St. Wiv 87 D4
East Stockwell St. Colch 67 F4
East Terr. Walt 76 B1
East Thorpe. Basil 185 E3
East Wlk. Basil 185 D3
Eastbourne Gr. South 190 B2
Eastbrooks Mews. Basil 186 A4
Eastbrooks Pl. Basil 186 A4
Eastbrooks. Basil 186 A4
Eastbury Ave. Hawk 178 B2
Eastcheap. Rayl 176 B2
Eastcliff Ave. Clact 110 A2
Eastcote Gr. South 191 E2
Eastend Rd. Brad O S 137 E2
Easterford Rd. Kelv 81 E1
Easterling Cl. Harw 40 A2
Eastern App. Sprin 127 F3
Eastern Ave. S Ben 187 E3
Eastern Ave. South 191 D2
Eastern Cl. South 191 D2
Eastern Cres. Chelm 126 C3
Eastern Espl. Canv 197 E1
Eastern Espl. South 200 B3
Eastern Prom. St O 106 C2
Eastern Rd. Brigh 106 C3
Eastern Rd. Burn 170 B3
Eastern Rd. Rayl 176 A1
Eastfield Rd. Canv 197 E3
Eastgate St. Harw 40 B3
Eastgate. Basil 185 D3
Easthorpe Rd. Copf 82 B4
Eastleigh Rd. S Ben 187 F1
Easton Rd. With 98 A2
Easton Way. Frin 94 A3
Eastview Dr. Rayl 176 B3
Eastways. Canv 196 C3
Eastways. With 98 A2

Eastwood Bvd. South 190 A2
Eastwood Dr. Colch 50 A2
Eastwood La S. South 190 A1
Eastwood Old Rd. Hadl 189 D3
Eastwood Old Rd. South 189 D3
Eastwood Park Cl. South 189 F3
Eastwood Park Dr. South 189 F4
Eastwood Rd N. South 189 F2
Eastwood Rd. Rayl 188 C4
Eastwood Rd. South 189 E1
Eastwood Rise. Rayl 189 E4
Eastwoodbury Cl. South 190 C3
Eastwoodbury La. South 190 B3
Eaton Mews. Colch 68 A2
Eaton Rd. Hadl 189 E1
Eaton Way. Gt Tot 116 C4
Ebenezer Cl. With 97 F3
Ebony Cl. Colch 67 E1
Eckersley Rd. Chelm 127 E2
Eden Cl. With 97 F2
Eden Way. Chelm 126 B3
Edenside. Walt 93 F4
Edgefield Ave. Lawf 35 D2
Edgware Rd. Clact 109 E3
Edgworth Rd. Sud 12 C4
Edinburgh Ave. Hadl 189 D1
Edinburgh Cl. With 115 D4
Edinburgh Gdns. Brain 60 B2
Edison Cl. Brain 59 F1
Edison Gdns. Colch 50 B1
Edison Rd. Clact 110 C3
Edith Cl. Canv 196 C2
Edith Rd. Canv 196 B2
Edith Rd. Clact 109 F1
Edith Rd. South 190 C1
Edith Rd. Walt 93 E4
Edmund Green. Gos 42 C4
Edmund Rd. With 114 C4
Edward Ave. Brigh 106 C4
Edward Cl. Ashi 178 B3
Edward Cl. Lit Cla 91 F3
Edward Dr. Chelm 140 B4
Edward Gdns. Runw 174 B4
Edward Rd. Th L S 91 F4
Edward St. Rams 39 F3
Edwin Hall View. S Woo F 154 B1
Edwin's Hall La. S Woo F 154 B2
Egbert Gdns. Runw 163 E1
Egerton-Green Rd. Colch 67 D2
Egremont St. Glems 2 A1
Egremont Way. Stanw 66 B2
Egret Cres. Colch 69 D4
Eight Acre La. Colch 67 E1
Eld La. Colch 67 F4
Eldbert Cl. South 191 F1
Elder Ave. Wick 174 B3
Elder Tree Rd. Canv 197 E2
Elder Way. Wick 174 B3
Elderberry Gdns. With 98 A2
Elderstep Ave. Canv 197 F2
Elderton Rd. South 190 B1
Eldon Cl. Colch 50 C1
Eldon Way. Hock 177 F3
Eldred Ave. Colch 67 D2
Eldred Dr. Sud 13 E2
Eleanor Chase. Wick 174 B4
Eleanor Cl. Tipt 100 B3
Eleanor Wlk. Tipt 100 B3
Electric Ave. South 190 B1
Elgar Cl. Thund 187 D3
Elgin Ave. Chelm 127 D1
Elham Dr. Basil 186 B3
Elianore Rd. Colch 67 D4
Eliot Cl. Wick 174 B3
Eliot Mews. South 191 D1
Eliot Way. Mald 132 A1
Elizabeth Ave. Rayl 176 B1
Elizabeth Ave. With 115 D4
Elizabeth Cl. Colch 50 B2
Elizabeth Cl. Hawk 177 F2
Elizabeth Dr. Wick 174 A4
Elizabeth Rd. Harw 40 A2
Elizabeth Rd. South 200 B3
Elizabeth Way. Brigh 106 C3
Elizabeth Way. Hals 25 F1
Elizabeth Way. Hat Pev 114 A2
Elizabeth Way. Mald 132 A3
Elizabeth Way. Sud 12 B3
Elizabeth Way. Thund 188 B2
Elizabeth Way. Wiv 69 E2
Ellen Way. Bl Not 77 E4
Ellenbrook Cl. South 189 F2
Ellesmere Rd. Ashi 167 E1
Ellesmere Rd. Canv 196 C2
Elliot Cl. S Woo F 165 F3
Elliots Dr. Walt 94 A4
Ellis Rd. Box 31 F2
Ellis Rd. Brad 54 B4
Ellis Rd. Clact 109 F1
Ellistons Yd. Sud 12 B3
Elm Ave. Mald 132 B3
Elm Bungalows. Brain 59 E2
Elm Cl. Alres 88 A4
Elm Cl. Broom 127 D4
Elm Cl. Gt Bad 140 C3
Elm Cl. Rayl 176 B2
Elm Cl. Si Hed 15 E1
Elm Cl. South 201 F4
Elm Cl. Tipt 100 B4

Elm Cres. Colch 68 B4
Elm Dr. Hals 25 F1
Elm Dr. Rayl 176 B2
Elm Drive. Brigh 106 B4
Elm Gr. Clact 109 F3
Elm Gr. Hull 165 E1
Elm Gr. South 201 D4
Elm Gr. Walt 93 E3
Elm Gr. Wiv 69 D1
Elm Green La. Dan 142 B4
Elm Green. Basil 186 A3
Elm La. Fee 64 A1
Elm Rd. Basil 174 C1
Elm Rd. Canv 197 E2
Elm Rd. Chelm 140 A4
Elm Rd. Hadl 188 B1
Elm Rd. Lit Cla 91 E2
Elm Rd. Runw 174 B4
Elm Rd. S Woo F 165 E4
Elm Rd. South 189 F1
Elm Rd. South 201 F4
Elm Rd. Sud 13 D4
Elm Rise. With 98 A3
Elm Tree Ave. Walt 93 F4
Elm Tree Cl. Walt 93 F4
Elm View Rd. S Ben 187 D2
Elm Way. Bore 112 C1
Elmden Ct. Clact 109 F3
Elmer App. South 200 A4
Elmer Ave. South 200 A4
Elmfield Cl. Clact 110 C4
Elmhurst Ave. S Ben 187 D2
Elmhurst Rd. Harw 40 B2
Elms Dr. Chelm 127 D2
Elms Hall Rd. Col En 44 C4
Elmsleigh Dr. South 189 F2
Elmstead Rd. Colch 68 C3
Elmstead Rd. Wiv 69 E2
Elmtree Rd. Basil 186 A2
Elmwood Ave. Colch 67 E1
Elmwood Ave. Hawk 177 F3
Elmwood Dr. W Mers 121 E4
Elounda Ct. S Ben 187 E2
Elronds Rest. S Woo F 165 E3
Elsden Chase. Soum 159 E2
Elsenham Cres. Basil 185 F3
Elsinor Ave. Canv 196 C3
Elthorne Park. Clact 109 E2
Elton Wlk. Tipt 100 B3
Elwes Cl. Colch 50 B1
Elwin Rd. Tipt 100 B3
Ely Cl. Soum 159 E2
Ely Rd. South 191 D1
Elyslan Gdns. Tolle 119 E1
Ember Way. Burn 170 A3
Emberson Ct. Sprin 127 F2
Empire Rd. Harw 40 B2
Empress Ave. W Mers 121 F3
Endean Ct. Wiv 69 D1
Endeavour Ct. Tolle 119 E1
Endsleigh Ct. Colch 67 E4
Endway The. May 158 B1
Endway. Hadl 188 C1
Enfield Rd. Wick 175 E4
Englefield Cl. Hawk 178 A2
Enid Way. Colch 49 E1
Ennerdale Ave. Bl Not 77 E3
Ennismore Gdns. South 191 D2
Enterprise Ct. Brain 60 A1
Enterprise Way. Wick 174 C3
Enville Way. Colch 50 A2
Epping Cl. Chelm 126 C1
Epping Cl. Clact 109 F4
Epping Cl. South 189 F4
Epsom Cl. Clact 109 E3
Erbury Pl. Cla 4 A4
Eric Rd. Basil 186 C3
Erica Wlk. Colch 68 C4
Erick Ave. Chelm 127 D4
Eridge Cl. Brain 127 E4
Erle Havard Rd. W Berg 48 C2
Ernalds Cl. Ea Col 45 D4
Ernest Rd. Wiv 69 E1
Ernulph Wlk. Colch 68 A4
Errington Rd. Colch 67 E3
Esplanade Gdns. South 199 D4
Esplanade The. Clact 111 D3
Esplanade The. Hull 165 E2
Esplanade. Frin 93 F2
Esplanade. Harw 40 C3
Esplanade. May 146 C1
Essex Ave. Chelm 127 D4
Essex Ave. Clact 124 C3
Essex Ave. Sud 7 F1
Essex Cl. Canv 197 D1
Essex Cl. Rayl 176 C1
Essex Gdns. South 189 F2
Essex Hall Rd. Colch 49 F1
Essex Knowle. Bures 19 F1
Essex Rd. Brain 60 A2
Essex Rd. Burn 170 B3
Essex Rd. Canv 197 E2
Essex Rd. Mald 144 C4
Essex Regiment Way. Broom 101 B1
Essex St. South 200 A4
Essex Way. S Ben 187 F1
Essex Yeomanry Way. Colch 66 A3
Estate Rd. Hadl 188 C2

Estella Mead. Chelm	126	C4
Estuary Cres. Sho G	40	A4
Estuary Gdns. Gt Wak	193	E1
Estuary Mews. Tolle	119	E1
Estuary Park Rd. W Mers	121	F3
Estuary Rd. Sho G	40	A4
Ethel Rd. Rayl	189	D4
Ethelbert Rd. Ashi	167	E1
Etheldore Ave. Hock	177	F4
Ethelred Gdns. Runw	163	E1
Eton Cl. Canv	197	D3
Eton Rd. Clact	109	F2
Eton Rd. Frin	94	A3
Eton Wlk. South	192	C1
Eudo Rd. Colch	67	E2
Europa Way. Rams	39	F2
Evelyn Rd. Hock	177	F3
Evelyn Wood Rd. T Gr	78	C3
Everard Rd. Basil	186	A4
Everest Way. Mald	132	A3
Everest. Rayl	176	B3
Evergreen Dr. Colch	50	B2
Everitt Way. Si Hed	15	F1
Eversley Rd. Basil	186	B3
Eversley Rd. Thund	187	E4
Eves Cnr. Burn	170	A4
Eves Cres. Chelm	127	D3
Eves Ct. Harw	39	E1
Ewan Cl. Hadl	189	D2
Ewan Cl. Stanw	66	B3
Ewan Way. Hadl	189	D2
Ewan Way. Stanw	66	B4
Ewell Hall Chase. Kelv	81	E1
Exchange Way. Chelm	127	D1
Exeter Cl. Basil	185	F4
Exeter Cl. Brain	60	A3
Exeter Cl. Gt Hor	49	D4
Exeter Cl. South	192	C1
Exeter Dr. Colch	68	A4
Exeter Rd. Sprin	127	F3
Exford Ave. South	190	A2
Exhibition La. Gt Wak	192	C2
Exmoor Cl. Chelm	126	B1
Exmouth Dr. Rayl	176	B3
Eynesham Way. Basil	174	A1
Faber Rd. With	114	C4
Fabians Cl. Cogg	63	D2
Factory Hill. Tipt	100	C2
Factory La E. Hals	25	F1
Factory La W. Hals	25	F1
Factory Terr. Hals	25	F1
Faggots Yd. Brain	59	F3
Fair Cl. Brigh	107	D3
Fair Green. Glems	2	A3
Fair Mead. Basil	185	E4
Fairfax Ave. Basil	186	B4
Fairfax Dr. South	190	B1
Fairfax Mead. Sprin	127	F1
Fairfax Rd. Colch	67	F3
Fairfield Cres. South	189	F3
Fairfield Gdns. South	189	F3
Fairfield Rd. Brain	59	F1
Fairfield Rd. Chelm	127	D2
Fairfield Rd. Clact	109	F2
Fairfield Rd. South	189	F4
Fairfield. Gt Wak	193	D2
Fairhaven Ave. W Mers	121	F3
Fairhead Rd. Colch	68	B4
Fairhouse Ct. Basil	185	E3
Fairland Cl. Rayl	176	C3
Fairlawn Gdns. South	190	C3
Fairleads. Dan	142	C4
Fairleigh Ave. Basil	186	B3
Fairleigh Dr. South	189	E1
Fairleigh Rd. Basil	186	B3
Fairlight Rd. S Ben	188	B2
Fairlop Cl. Clact	109	F4
Fairlop Cres. Canv	197	D2
Fairlop Gdns. Basil	185	E3
Fairmead Ave. Hadl	188	C3
Fairmead Ave. South	190	B1
Fairmead. Rayl	176	A2
Fairstead Hall Rd. Fair	96	A3
Fairstead Rd. Fair	96	B3
Fairstead Rd. Terl	96	B2
Fairstead. Basil	185	D3
Fairview Cl. Thund	187	E4
Fairview Cres. Thund	187	E4
Fairview Dr. South	190	B2
Fairview Gdns. Hadl	189	E1
Fairview Rd. Basil	185	F3
Fairview Wlk. Thund	187	E4
Fairview. Canv	196	C3
Fairway Dr. Burn	170	A3
Fairway Gdns Cl. South	189	E3
Fairway Gdns. South	189	E3
Fairway The. South	189	E3
Fairway The. Thund	187	E4
Fairway. Gt Bad	140	B4
Fairway. Wick	174	B2
Fairways The. Col N	155	F3
Fairy Hall La. Ray	59	D1
Fal Dr. With	97	F1
Falbro Cres. Hadl	188	B2
Falcon Cl. South	189	F3
Falcon Cres. Colch	68	A3
Falcon Fields. Mald	144	C4
Falcon Mews. Mald	144	C4
Falcon Rd. Soum	159	E2
Falcon Sq. Ca Hed	15	F2
Falcon Way. Basil	185	E2
Falcon Way. Chelm	140	A3
Falcon Way. Clact	109	F3
Falcon Way. South	192	C1
Falcon Yd. Wiv	87	D4
Falkenham End. Basil	185	E4
Falkenham Path. Basil	185	E4
Falkenham Rise. Basil	185	E4
Falkenham Row. Basil	185	E4
Falkland Cl. Bore	128	C4
Falklands Dr. Mann	35	E2
Falklands Rd. Burn	170	A3
Fallowfield Cl. Harw	39	F2
Fallowfield Rd. Colch	67	E1
Fallows The. Canv	196	C3
Falmouth Rd. Sprin	127	F3
Fambridge Chase. Wh Not	78	C1
Fambridge Cl. Mald	132	A1
Fambridge Dr. Wick	174	C3
Fambridge Rd. Alth	157	F1
Fambridge Rd. Ashi	167	E2
Fambridge Rd. Col N	156	A2
Fambridge Rd. Mald	156	A2
Fambridge Rd. N Fam	156	A2
Fambridge Rd. Purl	156	A2
Fane Rd. Thund	187	E4
Fanny's La. St O	90	B1
Fanton Ave. Wick	174	C2
Fanton Chase. Wick	175	D3
Fanton Wlk. Wick	175	D3
Faraday Cl. Brain	59	F1
Faraday Cl. Clact	110	A4
Faraday Rd. South	189	E3
Farford Field. Sud	13	E3
Farm Cres. Rett	164	C2
Farm Rd. Canv	197	D3
Farm View. Rayl	176	B3
Farm Way. Thund	188	A3
Farm Wlk. Brigh	106	C4
Farmers Way. Clact	109	D2
Farmfield Rd. Gt T	46	A1
Farmleigh Ave. Clact	109	F4
Farnes Ave. Wick	174	B4
Farriers End. Stanw	66	B3
Farriers Way. South	190	C3
Farrington Way. Lawf	35	D2
Farrow Rd. Chelm	139	F4
Farthing Centre The. Chelm	127	D1
Fastnet. South	190	A4
Faulkbourne Rd. Faulk	97	E2
Faulkbourne Rd. With	97	E2
Fauners. Basil	185	D3
Fawkner Cl. Sprin	127	F1
Featherby Way. Roch	179	D1
Feeches Rd. South	190	B3
Feedhams Cl. Wiv	69	E2
Feering Dr. Basil	185	F3
Feering Green. Basil	185	F3
Feering Hill. Fee	81	E2
Feering Rd. Fee	63	D1
Feering Row. Basil	185	F3
Felixstowe Cl. Clact	109	D2
Fellcroft. Basil	186	B3
Felmores. Basil	186	A4
Felstead Cl. Colch	86	A4
Felstead Cl. S Ben	187	E2
Felstead Rd. S Ben	187	E3
Fen La. Ard	33	E1
Fen St. Nay	20	A1
Fenn Cl. S Woo F	165	E4
Fenn Rd. Hals	26	A1
Fennell Cl. Tipt	100	B3
Fennes Rd. Brain	41	F1
Fennfields Rd. S Woo F	165	D4
Fennings Chase. Colch	68	A4
Fenno Cl. Colch	66	C2
Fenwick Way. Canv	197	D3
Ferdinand Wlk. Colch	68	C4
Fermoy Rd. South	201	D4
Fern Hill. Glems	2	A4
Fern Way. Clact	124	C4
Fernbrook Ave. South	200	B4
Ferndale Cl. Clact	109	F4
Ferndale Cres. Canv	197	D1
Ferndale Rd. Harw	40	B3
Ferndale Rd. Rayl	176	C3
Ferndale Rd. South	191	E1
Ferndown Rd. Frin	93	F3
Ferndown Way. Hat Pev	114	A2
Fernie Rd. Brain	59	E1
Fernlea Rd. Burn	170	A3
Fernlea Rd. Harw	40	B3
Fernlea Rd. S Ben	187	F2
Fernlea. Colch	49	E1
Fernleigh Dr. South	190	A1
Fernwood Ave. Clact	110	C3
Fernwood. Hadl	188	C2
Ferrers Rd. S Woo F	165	E3
Ferris Ave. Col N	155	F3
Ferry Rd. Burn	169	F3
Ferry Rd. Canv	196	B4
Ferry Rd. Fing	87	D3
Ferry Rd. Hull	165	E1
Ferry Rd. N Fam	157	D3
Ferrymead. Canv	196	C3
Festival Gdns. Toll D	118	B2
Feverills Rd. Lit Cla	91	E2
Fiat Ave. Clact	124	B3
Fiddlers Folly. E A Gr	47	F1
Fiddlers Hill. E A Gr	47	F1
Field Way. Wiv	69	E1
Field Wlk. Walt	94	A4
Fields Cl. Weel	90	C3
Fields Farm Rd. Lay H	85	D2
Fieldway. Basil	186	B2
Fieldway. Wick	174	B2
Fifth Ave. Canv	196	C2
Fifth Ave. Chelm	127	D3
Fifth Ave. Frin	93	F3
Fifth Ave. Wick	175	D3
Filey Rd. Soum	159	D2
Fillebrook Ave. South	190	A1
Filliol Cl. E Han	153	D3
Finch Dr. Gt Ben	71	E1
Finch Hill. Bul	12	A4
Finch's. Lit Brx	115	F3
Finchdale. Clact	109	F3
Finches The. Thund	188	A4
Finchfield. Rayl	176	B1
Finchingfield Way. Colch	86	A4
Finchingfield Way. Wick	174	B3
Finchland View. S Woo F	165	E3
Finchley Ave. Chelm	140	A4
Finchley Rd. South	199	E4
Finer Cl. Clact	109	E3
Fingringhoe Rd. Colch	68	B1
Fingringhoe Rd. Lang	86	A2
Finham Cl. Colch	68	C4
Fir Tree Cl. Colch	50	A2
Fir Tree La. Lit Bad	129	F1
Fir Tree Rise. Chelm	140	A3
Fir Tree Wlk. Mald	132	B3
Fir Way. Clact	125	D3
Fir Wlk. Canv	196	C3
Firecrest Rd. Chelm	140	A3
Firecrest Rd. Gt Bad	140	B3
Firfield Rd. Thund	188	B3
Firlie Wlk. Colch	68	A1
Firmins Ct. W Berg	48	B2
Firs Chase. W Mers	121	D3
Firs Dr. Writ	126	A1
Firs Hamlet. W Mers	121	D3
Firs Rd. Tipt	100	B2
Firs Rd. W Mers	121	D4
Firs The. Canv	196	C3
Firs The. Lay H	85	D3
First Ave. Canv	196	C2
First Ave. Chelm	127	D3
First Ave. Clact	110	A2
First Ave. Frin	93	F2
First Ave. Glems	2	B3
First Ave. Hals	26	A1
First Ave. Harw	40	B2
First Ave. Hull	165	F1
First Ave. South	199	D4
First Ave. Walt	76	B2
First Ave. Weel	72	C1
First Ave. Wick	175	D3
Firstore Dr. Colch	66	C4
Firwood's Rd. Hals	43	F4
Fish St. Gold	133	F3
Fisher Way. Brain	60	B2
Fishponds Hill. Lit Hor	30	C2
Fisin Wlk. Colch	66	C2
Fitch's Cres. Mald	132	A1
Fitzgerald Cl. Lawf	35	D2
Fitzgilbert Rd. Colch	67	E2
Fitzwalter La. Dan	142	B3
Fitzwalter Pl. Chelm	126	C2
Fitzwalter Rd. Bore	128	C4
Fitzwalter Rd. Colch	67	D3
Fitzwarren. South	192	B1
Fitzwilliam Rd. Colch	67	D4
Five Acres. S Woo F	142	C2
Five Acres. Walt	94	A4
Fiveash La. Bradw	61	F1
Flag Hill. St O	89	F1
Flagstaff Rd. Colch	67	F3
Flail Cl. Elmst M	69	F3
Flambird's Chase. Purl	154	C4
Flamboro Cl. South	189	E3
Flamboro Wlk. South	189	E3
Flanders Cl. Brain	59	F3
Flanders Field. Colch	68	A2
Flatford Dr. Clact	109	D3
Flatford Rd. Str S M	34	B4
Flax La. Glems	2	B2
Fleet Rd. S Ben	187	E1
Fleetway. Basil	185	F2
Fleetwood Ave. Clact	110	C4
Fleetwood Ave. South	190	B1
Fleetwood Cl. Clact	110	C4
Fleming Cl. Brain	59	F1
Flemings Farm Rd. Rayl	189	E4
Flemming Ave. South	189	E1
Flemming Cres. South	189	E1
Fletchers Sq. South	191	D3
Flintwich Manor. Chelm	126	C4
Flixton Cl. Clact	109	D2
Flora Rd. With	97	E2
Florence Cl. Hadl	188	B2
Florence Gdns. Hadl	188	B2
Florence Neale House. Canv	197	D2
Florence Rd. Canv	197	E2
Florence Rd. Walt	76	C1
Florie's Rd. Gt T	63	F4
Flowers Way. Clact	125	D4
Fobbing Farm Cl. Basil	185	D2
Fodderwick. Basil	185	D3
Foksville Rd. Canv	197	E2
Fold The. Basil	185	D3
Folkards La. Brigh	106	C4
Folley The. Lay H	85	D3
Folley The. Stanw	66	B3
Folly Chase. Hock	177	D3
Folly La. Hock	177	D3
Folly The. Toll K	100	C1
Folly The. Wiv	87	D4
Ford La. Alres	88	A3
Ford La. Colch	49	E3
Ford Rd. Clact	109	E2
Ford St. Ald	47	E1
Fordham Rd. Ford	29	F1
Fordham Rd. M Bure	28	C1
Fordham Rd. Worm	29	F1
Fordson Rd. Bore	128	A3
Fordstreet Hill. Ald	47	E1
Fordwich Rd. Brigh	88	C1
Forefield Green. Sprin	127	F4
Foresight Rd. Colch	68	B1
Forest Dr. Chelm	126	C1
Forest Park Ave. Clact	109	F4
Forest Rd. Colch	68	B4
Forest Rd. With	98	A3
Forest View Dr. Hadl	189	D2
Forfar Cl. Hadl	189	E1
Forfields Way. T Gr	78	C3
Forge Cres. Bradw	61	E2
Forge St. Ded	34	A3
Forrest Cl. S Woo F	165	E4
Forsythia Cl. Sprin	127	F4
Fort William Rd. Basil	185	D1
Fortescue Chase. South	191	F1
Fortune Cl. Gt Le	95	D4
Fossetts La. Ford	47	F2
Fostal Cl. South	189	F2
Foster Rd. Canv	197	E2
Foster Rd. Gt Tot	116	A2
Foster Rd. Rams	39	F3
Foulgar Cl. S Woo F	165	F4
Foundry La. Burn	170	A3
Foundry La. Copf	65	E3
Foundry La. Ea Col	45	D3
Fountain La. Copf	83	F4
Fountain La. Hock	177	D3
Fourth Ave. Canv	196	C2
Fourth Ave. Chelm	127	D3
Fourth Ave. Clact	110	B2
Fourth Ave. Frin	93	F2
Fourth Ave. Glems	2	A3
Fourth Ave. Hals	26	A1
Fourth Ave. Wick	175	D3
Fox Burrows La. Writ	126	A1
Fox Cl. Thund	187	F3
Fox Cres. Chelm	126	C2
Fox's Rd. Ashe	3	F1
Foxden. With	98	B3
Foxes La. E A Gr	47	E1
Foxfield Cl. Hock	178	A3
Foxglove Cl. With	97	E2
Foxglove Way. Sprin	127	F3
Foxhall Rd. Steep	159	D4
Foxhatch. Wick	174	C3
Foxholes Rd. Gt Bad	140	C3
Foxmead. With	98	B3
Foxmeadows. Thund	187	F3
Foxwood Pl. Hadl	189	E1
Frampton Rd. Basil	174	A1
Frances Cl. Wiv	69	D1
Francis Cl. Tipt	100	B2
Francis Ct. Silv E	79	E3
Francis Mews. Mald	145	D4
Francis Rd. Brain	59	E1
Francis Rd. Sud	12	C4
Francis St. Brigh	106	C3
Francis Way. Colch	50	B1
Francis Way. Silv E	79	E2
Francis Wlk. Rayl	176	B1
Frank Clater Cl. Colch	68	A4
Franklin Rd. N Fam	167	D4
Franklins Way. Wick	174	C4
Fraser Cl. Chelm	140	B4
Fraser Cl. South	201	F4
Frating Hill. Frat	70	B2
Frating Rd. Ard	52	A2
Frating Rd. Frat	89	D4
Frating Rd. Gt Bro	70	C3
Fratting Abbey Farm Rd. Thor	89	E3
Freebournes Rd. With	98	A1
Freeland Rd. Clact	109	F1
Freelands. Brigh	107	D3
Fremantle Cl. S Woo F	154	B1
Fremantle Rd. Colch	68	A1
Fremantle. South	201	E3
Fremnells The. Basil	185	E4
French Rd. Stow M	155	F1
Frensham Cl. Stanw	66	B4
Frere Way. Fing	87	D3
Freshwater Dr. Basil	185	F2
Frettons. Basil	185	F3
Friars Cl. Clact	109	F3
Friars Cl. Colch	50	B1
Friars Cl. Elmst M	87	E4
Friars Ct. Colch	68	B2
Friars La. Brain	60	A2
Friars La. Mald	131	F1
Friars St. South	201	F4
Friars St. Sud	12	C4
Friars Wlk. Chelm	127	D1
Friday Wood Green. Colch	85	F4
Friends Field. Bures	19	F1
Friern Gdns. Wick	174	A4
Friern Pl. Wick	174	A3
Friern Wlk. Wick	174	A4
Frietuna Rd. Walt	93	F3
Frinton Rd. Clact	110	B3
Frinton Rd. Th L S	92	B4
Frinton Rd. Walt	93	E3
Frobisher Dr. Clact	108	C1
Frobisher Rd. Harw	39	F1
Frobisher Way. Brain	60	B2
Frobisher Way. South	192	C1
Frog Hall Cl. Fing	87	D3
Fronk's Ave. Harw	40	B1
Fronk's Rd. Harw	40	A1
Frowick La. St O	90	A1
Fryatt Ave. Harw	40	A2
Fryth The. Basil	185	F4
Fulford Dr. South	190	A3
Fullbridge. Mald	132	A2
Fuller's Cl. Kelv	81	D1
Fuller's Rd. Colch	68	B1
Fulmar Cl. Colch	69	D4
Fulmar Way. Wick	175	D3
Fulton Rd. Thund	187	E4
Furlongs. Basil	185	E2
Furrow Cl. Colch	66	C3
Furrowfelde. Basil	185	D2
Further Meadow. Writ	139	D4
Furtherwick Rd. Canv	197	D2
Furze Cres. Alres	88	A4
Furze Cl. Gt Bro	71	D3
Fyfield Ave. Wick	174	B3
Fyfield Path. Rayl	176	A2
Fyfields. Basil	186	B4
Gablefields. Sand	141	E3
Gables The. Basil	186	A4
Gables The. Hadl	189	D3
Gadwall Reach. Kelv	81	E1
Gafzelle Dr. Canv	197	F1
Gage's Rd. Bel S P	4	C1
Gager Dr. Tipt	100	C3
Gaiger Cl. Sprin	127	E4
Gains Cl. Canv	197	F2
Gainsborough Ave. Canv	197	F2
Gainsborough Cl. Clact	109	D3
Gainsborough Cl. W Mers	121	E3
Gainsborough Cres. Sprin	127	F2
Gainsborough Dr. Lawf	35	D2
Gainsborough Dr. South	190	C1
Gainsborough Rd. Colch	67	D3
Gainsborough Rd. Sud	12	C4
Gainsborough St. Sud	12	C4
Gainsford Ave. Clact	110	A2
Gainsford End Rd. Topp	14	A3
Galahad Cl. Burn	170	A3
Galleydene Ave. Chelm	140	B2
Galleydene. Hadl	188	B2
Galleywood Rd. Chelm	140	A3
Galleywood Rd. Gt Bad	140	C3
Galliford Rd. Mald	132	A2
Galloway Dr. Lit Cla	91	E2
Galsworthy Cl. Brain	78	A4
Galton Rd. South	199	E4
Gambleside. Basil	185	F2
Gandalf's Ride. S Woo F	165	E3
Ganges Rd. Sho G	40	A4
Gaol La. Sud	12	C4
Gap The. Clact	111	D3
Garden Cl. Alth	157	F2
Garden Farm. W Mers	121	E4
Garden Field. Hat Pev	113	F2
Garden Fields. Gt T	64	B4
Garden Fields. Steep	147	F2
Garden Pl. Sud	12	B4
Garden Rd. Clact	125	D4
Garden Rd. Walt	94	A4
Gardeners La. Cane	168	C1
Gardeners Rd. Hals	25	F1
Gardeners. Gt Bad	140	B3
Gardenia Pl. Clact	109	D2
Gardenia Wlk. Colch	68	C4
Garland Rd. Rams	39	F3
Garners The. Roch	178	C1
Garnons Chase. Worm	30	A3
Garrettlands. Sand	141	F3
Garrod Ct. Rowh	86	A4
Garthwood Cl. W Berg	48	C2
Gascoigne Rd. Colch	68	B4
Gate St. Mald	131	F2
Gatefield Cl. Walt	93	F4
Gateway. Basil	185	D3
Gatscombe Cl. Hock	177	E3
Gattens The. Rayl	176	C2
Gauden Rd. Brain	59	F4
Gay Bowers La. Dan	142	C3
Gay Bowers Rd. Dan	142	C2
Gay Bowers Way. With	115	D4
Gay Bowers. Basil	185	E4
Gay Bowers. Hock	177	D3
Gay Links. Basil	185	D4
Gayleighs. Rayl	176	B2

Gays La. Cane 168 C1
Gayton Rd. South 191 D1
Gazelle Ct. Colch 50 B2
Geesh Rd. Canv 197 E3
Generals La. Bore 112 A1
Genesta Cl. Tolle 119 E1
Genesta Rd. South 199 E4
Genk Cl. Canv 197 D3
Gennep Rd. Canv 197 D3
George Ave. Brigh 106 C4
George Cardnell Way. May ... 146 C1
George Cl. Clact 109 E1
George Cut. Brigh 106 C3
George La. Glems 2 A2
George Rd. Brain 59 E1
George St. Chelm 127 D1
George St. Colch 67 F4
George St. Harw 40 B3
George St. South 202 A3
George Yd. Brain 59 F2
Geranium Cl. Clact 109 E2
Geranium Wlk. Colch 68 B4
Gerard Rd. Clact 109 E2
Gernon Rd. Ard 51 F4
Gestingthorpe Rd. Bel W ... 10 C3
Geylen Rd. Canv 197 F2
Ghyllgrove. Basil 185 D4
Gibcracks. Basil 185 F3
Gibson Rd. Si Hed 24 B4
Giffins Cl. Brain 59 F1
Gifford Green. Basil 186 A3
Gifford Rd. S Ben 187 E3
Gifhorn Rd. Canv 197 F2
Gilberd Rd. Colch 68 A2
Gilbert Cl. Rayl 176 C1
Gilbert Rd. Cla 4 A4
Gilbert Way. Brain 60 B3
Gilchrist Way. Brain 59 F2
Gilda Terr. Brain 59 D1
Gilderdale Cl. Colch 50 B2
Gilders Way. Clact 109 E3
Gill The. Hadl 188 B3
Gills Ave. Canv 197 E2
Gilman Dr. South 201 E4
Gilmore Way. Gt Bad 141 D3
Gilpin Way. Bl Not 77 E4
Gilson Cl. Sprin 127 F1
Gilwell Park Cl. Colch 67 D2
Gimson Cl. With 97 F1
Gippeswyck. Basil 185 E4
Gipson Park Cl. South 189 E3
Girling St. Sud 12 B4
Gladden Fields. S Woo F ... 165 E3
Glade The. Basil 185 E2
Glade The. Colch 50 C1
Gladeview. Clact 109 F4
Gladstone Ct. Chelm 127 D1
Gladstone Gdns. Rayl 176 B1
Gladstone Rd. Colch 68 A3
Gladstone Rd. Hock 177 F3
Gladstone Rd. Tipt 100 B3
Gladwin Rd. Colch 67 E2
Glasseys La. Rayl 188 B4
Glastonbury Chase. South ... 190 A3
Glebe Ave. Brain 59 F3
Glebe Cl. Elmst M 70 A3
Glebe Cl. Gt Wak 193 E2
Glebe Cl. Rayl 176 B2
Glebe Cl. South 200 C4
Glebe Cl. Wix 55 E3
Glebe Cres. With 97 F2
Glebe Dr. Rayl 176 B2
Glebe Field. Basil 185 E4
Glebe Gdns. Fee 81 F3
Glebe La. Deng 149 E1
Glebe Rd. Chelm 127 D2
Glebe Rd. Colch 67 E1
Glebe Rd. Kelv 81 D1
Glebe Rd. Mald 132 B3
Glebe Rd. Tipt 100 B3
Glebe Rd. Wick 174 C4
Glebe The. Purl 144 B1
Glebe Way. Burn 170 B3
Glebe Way. Clact 125 D4
Glebe Way. Frin 93 F3
Glebe Way. Hadl 188 C2
Glebefield Rd. Hat Pev 114 A2
Glebelands. Thund 187 D4
Glen Ave. Colch 67 D4
Glen Rd. Basil 185 F2
Glen Rd. S Ben 187 F3
Glen Rd. South 199 D4
Glen The. Rayl 188 C4
Glenbervie Dr. South 189 F1
Glencoe Dr. Wick 175 D4
Glendale Gdns. South 189 E1
Glendale Gr. Colch 50 B2
Glendale Rd. Burn 170 B3
Glendale. S Woo F 154 C1
Gleneagles Rd. South 189 E3
Gleneagles Way. Hat Pev ... 114 A2
Gleneagles. S Ben 187 D3
Glenhurst Rd. South 191 D1
Glenmere Park Ave. S Ben ... 188 A2
Glenmere. Basil 185 E1
Glenmore St. South 191 E1
Glenridding. S Ben 187 E3
Glenside. Sud 13 D3
Glentress Cl. Colch 50 B2

Glenwood Ave. Hawk 177 F3
Glenwood Ave. Rayl 189 D4
Glenwood Ave. South 190 B1
Glenwood. Canv 196 C3
Glisson Sq. Colch 67 D2
Globe Cl. Tipt 100 B3
Globe Wlk. Tipt 100 B3
Gloucester Ave. Chelm ... 140 B3
Gloucester Ave. Colch 67 E2
Gloucester Ave. Mald 131 F1
Gloucester Ave. Rayl 189 D4
Gloucester Cres. Chelm ... 127 D3
Gloucester Gdns. Brain 60 A2
Gloucester Terr. South 201 D3
Gloucester Way. Sud 7 E1
Glyders The. S Ben 187 F1
Glynde Way. South 191 F1
Goat Hall La. Chelm 140 A2
Goat House La. Haze 143 F2
Goat House La. Purl 143 F2
Goat Lodge Rd. Gt Tot 116 A3
Gobions. Basil 185 D2
Goda Cl. With 114 C4
Goddard Way. Sprin 127 F1
Godfrey's Mews. Chelm ... 127 D1
Godlings Way. Brain 59 F1
Godmans La. Mks T 64 C2
Godric Rd. With 114 C4
Godwin Cl. Hals 25 E1
Godwit Ct. Kelv 81 E1
Goff's La. Beau 73 F4
Goings La. W Mers 121 E3
Goirle Ave. Canv 197 E2
Goldberry Mead. S Woo F ... 165 E3
Goldcrest Cl. Colch 69 D4
Golden Cross Rd. Ashi 178 B3
Golden Dawn Way. Colch ... 49 F1
Golden La. Th L S 73 F2
Golden Lion La. Harw 40 C3
Golden Manor Dr. Thund ... 187 F3
Golden Noble Hill. Colch ... 68 A3
Goldenacres. Sprin 127 F4
Goldenlond. Nay 20 B3
Goldfinch Cl. Colch 69 D4
Goldfinch La. Thund 188 A4
Goldhanger Cl. Rayl 176 A2
Goldhanger Cross. Basil ... 185 F4
Goldhanger Ct. Brain 78 B4
Goldhanger Rd. Gold 132 B2
Goldhanger Rd. Mald 132 B2
Golding Thoroughfare. Sprin ... 127 F2
Golding Way. St O 108 A3
Goldingham Dr. Brain 78 A4
Goldings Cres. Basil 185 F2
Goldings Way. Glems 2 A2
Goldlay Ave. Chelm 127 E1
Goldlay Gdns. Chelm 127 E1
Goldlay Rd. Chelm 127 E1
Goldmer Cl. South 201 E4
Goldsands Rd. Soum 159 F1
Goldsmith Dr. Rayl 176 B4
Goldsworthy Dr. Gt Wak ... 193 E1
Golf Green Rd. Clact 125 D4
Goodchild Way. Gt Y 9 D1
Goodey Cl. Colch 68 A3
Goodlake Cl. Harw 39 F1
Goodmayes Wlk. Wick 174 B3
Goodwood Cl. Thund 188 A4
Goojerat Ct. Colch 67 E3
Goor Ave. Canv 197 E2
Goose Cotts. Rayl 164 C1
Gordon Pl. South 199 F4
Gordon Rd. Basil 185 E3
Gordon Rd. Chelm 140 A3
Gordon Rd. Hadl 189 D1
Gordon Rd. Harw 40 A1
Gordon Rd. South 199 F4
Gordon Way. Harw 40 A1
Gordons. Basil 186 A3
Gore La. Brain 59 D1
Gore The. Basil 185 D4
Goring Rd. Colch 50 B1
Gorse La. Clact 110 A4
Gorse La. Tipt 100 B2
Gorse Way. Clact 124 C4
Gorse Way. Stanw 66 B2
Gorse Wlk. Colch 68 B4
Gosbecks Rd. Colch 67 D1
Gosfield Rd. Rayl 176 A2
Gosfield Hall Dr. Gos 42 B4
Gosfield Rd. Colch 86 A4
Gosfield Rd. Gos 42 B2
Gosford Cl. Cla 4 A4
Goshawk Dr. Chelm 140 A3
Goslings The. Silv E 79 E3
Goslings The. South 202 A4
Gouldings Ave. Walt 94 A4
Goulds Rd. Alph 18 C1
Gowan Brae. S Ben 187 D3
Gowan Cl. S Ben 187 D3
Gowers Ave. Gt Bad 140 C3
Gowers End. Glems 2 B3
Goya Rise. South 202 A4
Graces Cl. With 115 D4
Graces La. Lit Bad 129 D3
Graces Wlk. Frin 94 A3
Grafton Pl. Sprin 128 A2
Grafton Rd. Canv 197 E1
Grafton Rd. Harw 40 B2

Graham Cl. Hock 177 F4
Grainger Cl. South 191 D1
Grainger Rd. South 191 D1
Grampian Gr. Chelm 126 B3
Granary Cl. Latch 157 D3
Grand Dr. South 198 C4
Grand Par. South 198 C4
Grandview Rd. Thund 187 F4
Grange Ave. Hadl 189 D3
Grange Ave. May 158 B4
Grange Ave. Wick 174 B3
Grange Cl. Hals 43 F4
Grange Cl. South 189 F2
Grange Cl. Walt 94 A4
Grange Farm Rd. Colch ... 68 B2
Grange Gdns. Rayl 176 A2
Grange Gdns. South 200 A4
Grange Hill. Cogg 62 C1
Grange Park Dr. South 189 F1
Grange Rd. Basil 186 C4
Grange Rd. Gt Hor 49 D4
Grange Rd. Harw 40 A2
Grange Rd. Lane 52 C4
Grange Rd. Runw 163 E1
Grange Rd. South 189 E1
Grange Rd. Thund 187 F4
Grange Rd. Till 150 A1
Grange Rd. Tipt 99 F2
Grange Rd. Wic Bis 115 F2
Grange Way. Colch 68 B2
Granger Ave. Mald 131 F1
Grangeway. Thund 188 A3
Grantham Ct. Colch 68 A4
Grantham Rd. Gt Hor 49 D4
Grantley Cl. Copf 65 E3
Granville Cl. S Ben 187 F2
Granville Cl. W Berg 48 C2
Granville Rd. Ashi 166 C1
Granville Rd. Clact 109 F2
Granville Rd. Colch 68 A3
Granville Terr. Brain 170 B2
Granville Way. Brigh 107 D4
Grapnells. Basil 185 F2
Grasby Cl. Wiv 69 D1
Grasmead Ave. South 189 F1
Grasmere Ave. Hull 165 E4
Grasmere Cl. Bl Not 77 E3
Grasmere Gdns. Walt 93 F4
Grasmere Rd. Canv 196 C2
Grasmere Rd. Thund 187 F3
Grassfields. Walt 93 F3
Grassmere. Colch 50 A3
Gratmore Green. Basil 185 F2
Gravel Hill Way. Harw 39 F1
Gravel Hill. Nay 20 A1
Gravel Rd. Rayl 189 E4
Gravel The. Cogg 62 C1
Gray Rd. Colch 67 E3
Gray's Cotts. Colch 68 A4
Grayling Dr. Colch 50 C1
Grays Cl. W Mers 121 E3
Grays Mead. Si Hed 15 E1
Graysons Cl. Rayl 176 C1
Great Bentley Rd. Frat 71 D1
Great Burches Rd. Thund ... 188 A4
Great Cob. Sprin 127 F3
Great Eastern Ave. South ... 191 D1
Great Eastern Rd. Hock ... 177 F3
Great Eastern Rd. Sud 12 C4
Great Gibcracks Chase. Sand 142 A1
Great Harrods. Walt 94 A4
Great Hays. South 189 E3
Great Holland Common Rd.
    Clact 92 B1
Great Leighs Way. Basil ... 174 B1
Great Mistley. Basil 185 E3
Great Oaks. Basil 185 D3
Great Ranton. Basil 186 B4
Great Saling. Wick 175 D3
Great Smials. S Woo F 165 E3
Great Spenders. Basil 185 E4
Great Sq. Brain 59 F2
Great Tey Rd. Ald 64 B2
Great Totham Rd. Lit Brx ... 115 F3
Great Wheatley Rd. Rayl ... 176 A1
Great Yd. Hals 43 F4
Great Yeldham Rd. Topp ... 14 B4
Greate House Farm Rd. Lay H 85 D3
Grebe Cl. May 158 A4
Green Acres Rd. Lay H 85 D3
Green Ave. Canv 196 C2
Green Cl. Hat Pev 114 B2
Green Cl. Sprin 127 E2
Green Cl. Writ 126 A1
Green End La. Frin 93 D3
Green Farm Rd. Col En 27 D1
Green La. Ald 47 E1
Green La. Ard 51 E1
Green La. Ard 51 E1
Green La. Box 31 E3
Green La. Burn 170 A4
Green La. Canv 196 C2
Green La. Colch 50 B2
Green La. Gt Hor 31 E3
Green La. Gt Hor 49 E3
Green La. High 22 B2
Green La. Latch 158 A3
Green La. Lit Tot 117 E2
Green La. S Woo F 165 E4

Green La. South 189 F4
Green La. T Gr 78 A1
Green La. Tipt 100 B3
Green La. Walt 76 B1
Green La. Weel 91 D3
Green Man La. Lit Brx 115 F4
Green Mead. S Woo F 165 E4
Green Meadows. Dan 143 D3
Green Oaks Cl. S Ben 187 F2
Green Rd. S Ben 187 E1
Green The. Chelm 126 C2
Green The. Cla 3 E2
Green The. Clact 109 D1
Green The. Mist 35 F2
Green The. South 189 F4
Green The. Writ 126 A1
Green Trees Ave. Col N ... 155 F3
Green Way. Col En 27 D1
Green's Yd. Colch 67 F4
Greenacre Mews. South ... 189 E1
Greenacres. Clact 110 A3
Greenacres. Cogg 62 C1
Greenacres. Colch 49 F2
Greenacres. Hadl 188 C2
Greenbanks. South 190 A1
Greendyke. Canv 196 C3
Greenfield Dr. Gt T 46 B1
Greenfield. With 98 A1
Greenfields. Chelm 140 B1
Greenfields. Gos 42 C4
Greenfinch End. Colch 68 C4
Greenford Rd. Clact 109 E2
Greenhurst Rd. Brigh 107 D3
Greenland Gr. St O 107 E2
Greenlands. Hawk 178 B2
Greenleas. Thund 188 A3
Greensmill. Lawf 35 E3
Greenstead Ct. Colch 68 B3
Greenstead Rd. Colch 68 B4
Greensted The. Basil 185 F3
Greensward La. Hock 177 F4
Greenview. Canv 196 C3
Greenway Cl. Clact 110 A4
Greenway Gdns. Bl Not 77 E4
Greenway The. Clact 110 A4
Greenway The. Runw 163 E2
Greenway. Frin 93 F3
Greenways The. Cogg 63 D2
Greenways. Canv 196 C3
Greenways. Chelm 127 D3
Greenways. Fee 81 E2
Greenways. Gos 42 C4
Greenways. Mald 131 F1
Greenways. Roch 178 C1
Greenways. S Ben 187 E1
Greenways. South 200 C4
Greenwood Ave. S Ben ... 187 F1
Greenwood Gr. Colch 50 B2
Gregory Cl. Hawk 177 F2
Gregory St. Sud 12 C4
Grendel Way. Clact 110 C3
Grenfell Ave. Clact 110 C3
Grenfell Cl. Colch 50 B1
Grenville Cl. Walt 76 C1
Grenville Rd. Brain 59 F1
Grey Ladys. Chelm 140 A1
Grey's Paddock. Kelv 81 E1
Greyhound Hill. Langh 32 C3
Greyhound Rd. Glems 2 A2
Greyhound Way. South ... 191 D1
Greys Cl. Cav 1 B1
Greystones Cl. Colch 67 D2
Grieves Ct. Stanw 66 B2
Griffin Ave. Canv 197 E3
Grimston Rd. Colch 68 A2
Grimston Way. Walt 94 A4
Groom Pk. Clact 109 F2
Grooms La. Silv E 79 F2
Grosvenor Cl. Gt Bad 140 B4
Grosvenor Cl. Tipt 100 B3
Grosvenor Mews. South ... 199 E4
Grosvenor Rd. S Ben 196 C4
Grosvenor Rd. South 199 E4
Grove Ave. W Mers 121 E3
Grove Ave. Walt 94 A4
Grove Cl. Rayl 176 C1
Grove Ct. Rayl 177 D1
Grove Farm Rd. Toll D 117 D4
Grove Field. Brain 42 B1
Grove Hill. Ded 33 E2
Grove Hill. Langh 32 C3
Grove Hill. Rayl 189 D4
Grove Orch. Brain 42 B1
Grove Rd. Canv 197 E2
Grove Rd. Catt 35 E4
Grove Rd. Chelm 127 D1
Grove Rd. Lit Cla 91 E3
Grove Rd. Rayl 176 C1
Grove Rd. S Ben 187 E2
Grove Rd. Tipt 100 C3
Grove Terr. South 200 A4
Grove The. Clact 109 F1
Grove The. Ea Col 45 D3
Grove The. S Woo F 129 F2
Grove The. South 191 E1
Grove The. With 98 A1
Grove Wlk. South 201 F3
Grovelands Rd. Wick 174 B3
Grover St. South 200 A4

Grovewood Ave. Rayl 189 D4
Grovewood Cl. Rayl 189 D4
Gryme's Dyke Way. Stanw ... 66 C2
Guernsey Ct. Mald 131 F1
Guernsey Gdns. Runw 163 E1
Guernsey Way. Brain 59 E1
Guild Way. S Woo F 165 F4
Guildford Rd. Colch 68 A4
Guildford Rd. South 191 D1
Guithavon Rd. With 97 F1
Guithavon Rise. With 97 F1
Guithavon St. With 97 F1
Guithavon Valley. With 97 F1
Gun Hill Pl. Basil 185 E3
Gun Hill. Langh 33 D4
Gunfleet Cl. W Mers 121 D4
Gunfleet. South 201 E4
Gunners Rd. South 202 A4
Gurdon Rd. Colch 67 F2
Gurney Benham Cl. Colch ... 67 D2
Gurton Rd. Cogg 63 D2
Gustedhall La. Roch 177 F2
Gutteridge Hall La. Weel ... 90 C4
Gutters La. Chelm 127 D4
Guy Cook Cl. Sud 13 E3
Guys Farm Rd. S Woo F ... 165 E4
Gwendalen Ave. Canv 197 E2
Gwyn Cl. Bore 112 C1
Gwynne Rd. Harw 40 B2
Gypsy La. Copf 82 B3

Haarle Rd. Canv 197 E1
Haarlem Rd. Canv 196 B2
Hackamore. Thund 188 A3
Hackmans La. Col N 155 D4
Hackmans La. Purl 155 D4
Hacks Dr. Thund 188 A4
Haddon Cl. Rayl 176 A2
Haddon Mead. S Woo F ... 165 E3
Hadfelda Sq. Hat Pev 114 A2
Hadleigh Park Ave. S Ben ... 188 B2
Hadleigh Rd. Clact 109 D2
Hadleigh Rd. Frin 94 A3
Hadleigh Rd. High 22 A3
Hadleigh Rd. South 189 E1
Hadleigh Rd. South 199 F4
Hadley Cl. Brain 42 A1
Hadrians Cl. With 114 C4
Haggars La. Frat 70 C2
Haig Ct. Chelm 127 D1
Hainault Ave. Hawk 178 B2
Hainault Ave. South 190 B1
Hainault Cl. Hadl 188 C2
Hainault Gr. Chelm 126 C1
Hainault Rd. N Fam 156 A1
Halfacres. With 115 D4
Halks Rd. With 97 F2
Hall Chase. Mks T 65 D2
Hall Cl. Gt Bad 141 D3
Hall Cres. Clact 110 C3
Hall Cres. Hadl 188 B2
Hall Cut. Brigh 106 C3
Hall Estate. Gold 133 F4
Hall Farm Cl. Fee 81 F2
Hall Farm Cl. S Ben 187 E1
Hall Farm Rd. S Ben 187 E1
Hall La. Harw 40 A1
Hall La. Ridge 8 A3
Hall La. Sand 141 E3
Hall La. Th L S 74 A1
Hall La. Walt 76 B1
Hall Park Ave. South 199 D4
Hall Park Way. South 199 D4
Hall Rd. Ashel 160 B4
Hall Rd. Bel W 11 D3
Hall Rd. Copf 65 F2
Hall Rd. Deng 160 B4
Hall Rd. Ford 47 E3
Hall Rd. Fox 7 D2
Hall Rd. Gt Bro 52 B1
Hall Rd. Gt Tot 116 A2
Hall Rd. M Bure 28 C3
Hall Rd. Mald 132 A2
Hall Rd. Pan 59 D3
Hall Rd. Roch 178 B1
Hall Rd. Soum 159 F2
Hall Rd. Tipt 100 B2
Hall Rd. Tolle 119 E1
Hall Rd. W Berg 48 B3
Hall Rise. Sud 12 B3
Hall Rise. With 114 C4
Hall St. Chelm 127 D1
Hall St. L Mel 7 E4
Hall View Rd. Gt Ben 89 F4
Hallet Rd. Canv 197 F2
Hallowell Down. S Woo F ... 165 F3
Halstead Ct. Wick 174 B3
Halstead Rd. E A Gr 47 F1
Halstead Rd. Ea Col 45 D3
Halstead Rd. Ford 47 D2
Halstead Rd. Gos 24 C1
Halstead Rd. Gos 42 C2
Halstead Rd. Si Hed 25 D3
Halstead Rd. Stanw 66 B4
Halstead Rd. Walt 93 D4
Halstow Way. Basil 186 B3
Haltwhistle Rd. S Woo F ... 165 E4
Halyard Reach. S Woo F ... 165 F3
Hamberts Rd. S Woo F ... 154 C1

Hamble Cl. With

Hamble Cl. With 97 F1
Hamble Way. Burn 170 A3
Hamboro Gdns. Hadl 189 D1
Hambro Cl. Rayl 176 C2
Hambro Hill. Rayl 176 C2
Hambro' Ave. Rayl 176 B2
Hamford Cl. Walt 76 B1
Hamford Dr. Gt Oak 56 B2
Hamilton Cl. Hadl 189 D1
Hamilton Gdns. Hock 177 F4
Hamilton Rd. Basil 186 C4
Hamilton Rd. Colch 67 E3
Hamilton Rd. Frin 93 D3
Hamilton Rd. Sud 12 C4
Hamilton Rd. Wiv 87 D4
Hamilton St. Rams 39 F3
Hamlet Court Rd. South 199 E4
Hamlet Ct. Bures 28 C4
Hamlet Dr. Colch 68 C4
Hamlet Rd. Chelm 127 D1
Hamlet Rd. South 199 F4
Hamley Cl. Thund 187 D3
Hammonds Rd. Lit Bad 128 C2
Hammonds Rd. Sand 128 C2
Hampstead Ave. Clact 109 E3
Hampstead Gdns. Hock 177 F4
Hampton Cl. South 190 C2
Hampton Ct. Hock 177 E3
Hampton Gdns. South 190 C2
Hampton Rd. Gt Bad 140 C3
Hamstel Rd. South 191 E1
Hanbury Gdns. Colch 50 A3
Hanbury Rd. Chelm 139 F4
Handel Rd. Canv 197 E1
Handley's La. Lit Brx 115 F3
Hankin Ave. Harw 39 E1
Hannah Cl. Canv 197 D3
Hannett Rd. Canv 197 F2
Hanningfield Cl. Rayl 176 A2
Hanover Cl. Basil 185 F3
Hanover Ct. Walt 94 A4
Hanover Dr. Basil 185 F3
Hanover Mews. Hock 177 E3
Hanwell Cl. Clact 109 E3
Harborough Hall Rd. Mess 82 C1
Harcourt Ave. Harw 40 A2
Harcourt Ave. South 190 C1
Hardings Reach. Burn 170 B2
Hardwick Cl. Rayl 176 B1
Hardy Cl. Brain 78 A4
Hardy Cl. Catt 35 E4
Hardys Way. Canv 196 C3
Harebell Cl. Colch 50 A2
Harebell Dr. With 97 F2
Haresland Cl. Hadl 188 C3
Harewood Ave. Hawk 178 B3
Harewood Rd. Chelm 126 C1
Harfred Ave. Mald 132 C2
Harkilees Way. Brain 59 F3
Harley St. Hadl 189 E1
Harley Wlk. Basil 186 A3
Harlings Gr. Chelm 127 E2
Harman Wlk. Clact 109 E3
Harness Cl. Sprin 127 F4
Harold Gdns. Runw 163 F1
Harold Gr. Frin 93 F2
Harold Rd. Brain 59 F1
Harold Rd. Clact 109 F1
Harold Rd. Frin 93 F2
Harold Way. Frin 93 F2
Haron Cl. Canv 197 D2
Harpclose Rd. Sud 12 C4
Harper Way. Rayl 176 B2
Harpur's Rd. Glems 2 A2
Harridge Cl. South 189 F2
Harridge Rd. South 189 F2
Harrison Dr. Brain 60 A1
Harrison Gdns. Hull 165 E1
Harrison Rd. Colch 67 E2
Harrogate Dr. Hock 177 F4
Harrogate Rd. Hock 177 F4
Harrow Cl. Hawk 178 A3
Harrow Gdns. Hawk 178 A3
Harrow Rd. Basil 175 D1
Harrow Rd. Canv 197 D3
Harrow Rd. Clact 109 F2
Harrow Way. Gt Bad 141 D3
Harsnett Rd. Colch 68 A3
Hart Cl. Thund 188 A3
Hart Rd. Thund 188 A3
Hart St. Chelm 127 D1
Hart's La. Ard 33 D1
Hartest Way. Sud 13 D3
Hartford Cl. Rayl 176 A2
Hartford End. Basil 186 A3
Hartington Pl. South 200 A4
Hartington Rd. South 200 A4
Hartland Rd. South 189 E4
Hartley Cl. Sprin 128 A2
Harvard Ct. Colch 50 A2
Harvest Cl. S Woo F 165 E4
Harvest End. Stanw 66 B3
Harvest Rd. Canv 197 D3
Harvest Way. Elmst M 69 F3
Harvesters' Way. Gt T 64 A4
Harvey Cl. Lawf 35 E2
Harvey Cres. Stanw 66 B2
Harvey Rd. Basil 174 B1

Harvey Rd. Colch 67 D1
Harvey Rd. Gt Tot 116 A2
Harvey Rd. Wiv 69 E1
Harvey St. Hals 25 F1
Harwich Rd. Ard 51 E3
Harwich Rd. Ard 51 F4
Harwich Rd. Beau 74 A4
Harwich Rd. Brad 36 C1
Harwich Rd. Colch 68 B4
Harwich Rd. Gt Bro 70 C3
Harwich Rd. Gt Oak 56 B2
Harwich rd. Lawf 34 B1
Harwich Rd. Lit Ben 53 F2
Harwich Rd. Lit Ben 71 E4
Harwich Rd. Lit Cla 91 F3
Harwich Rd. Lit Oak 57 E4
Harwich Rd. Mist 36 A2
Harwich Rd. Rams 56 A4
Harwich Rd. Wix 37 E1
Harwich Rd. Wix 55 F3
Harwich Rd. Wrab 37 E1
Haselfoot Rd. Bore 128 C4
Haskell Mews. Brain 78 A4
Haslemere Gdns. Walt 93 F4
Haslemere Rd. Runw 163 E1
Hasler Rd. Tolle 119 E1
Hassel Rd. Canv 197 E2
Hastings Ave. Clact 125 E4
Hastings Pl. Brigh 106 C4
Hastings Rd. Colch 67 D2
Hastings Rd. South 200 A4
Hastings The. Runw 163 E1
Hatchcroft Gdns. Elmst M 70 A3
Hatfield Gr. Chelm 126 B1
Hatfield Rd. Hat Pev 114 C2
Hatfield Rd. Langf 131 D4
Hatfield Rd. Rayl 176 A2
Hatfield Rd. Terl 96 B1
Hatfield Rd. With 114 C4
Hatherley The. Basil 185 E4
Hatley Gdns. S Ben 187 E3
Havanna Dr. Rayl 176 A4
Haven Ave. Clact 111 D3
Haven Cl. Basil 185 F2
Haven Cl. Canv 196 C2
Haven Cl. Canv 196 B1
Haven Rd. Colch 68 B2
Haven The. Harw 39 F2
Havengore. Basil 186 B4
Havengore. Sprin 127 F3
Havenside. Barl 192 C3
Havering Cl. Clact 109 F4
Havering Cl. Colch 50 A1
Havering Cl. Gt Wak 193 D2
Havisham Way. Chelm 126 C4
Hawbush Green. T Gr 78 C3
Hawfinch Rd. Lay H 85 D3
Hawfinch Wlk. Chelm 140 A3
Hawk Hill. Rett 164 B1
Hawk La. Runw 164 B1
Hawkbush Green. Basil 174 A1
Hawkendon Rd. Clact 109 D2
Hawkes Rd. Cogg 62 C2
Hawkesbury Bush La. Basil 185 D1
Hawkesbury Cl. Canv 196 C1
Hawkesbury Rd. Canv 196 C1
Hawkesway. Clact 109 F3
Hawkhurst Cl. Chelm 126 C1
Hawkins Cl. Purl 143 F1
Hawkins Rd. Alres 88 A4
Hawkins Rd. Colch 68 B3
Hawkins Way. Brain 60 B2
Hawkridge. South 201 E4
Hawks Cl. Dan 143 D3
Hawksway. Basil 185 D2
Hawkswood Rd. S Han 163 D3
Hawkwell Chase. Hawk 177 F2
Hawkwell Park Dr. Hawk 177 F3
Hawkwell Rd. Hock 177 F3
Hawkwood Cl. S Woo F 154 C1
Hawkwood Rd. Si Hed 24 B4
Hawlmark End. Mks T 64 C2
Hawthorn Ave. Colch 68 C4
Hawthorn Cl. Chelm 140 B3
Hawthorn Cl. Hawk 177 F3
Hawthorn Rd. Canv 197 E2
Hawthorn Rd. Clact 109 F3
Hawthorn Rd. Hat Pev 114 A3
Hawthorn Rd. Sud 13 D4
Hawthorn Rise. With 98 A3
Hawthorn Way. Rayl 176 C1
Hawthorn Wlk. S Woo F 154 C1
Hawthorne Gdns. Hock 177 D3
Hawthornes. Purl 144 B1
Hawthorns The. Dan 143 D4
Hawthorns. S Ben 187 E2
Hawthorns. Si Hed 15 E1
Hawthorns. South 189 F2
Hawthorns. Walt 93 F4
Hawtree Cl. South 200 B4
Hay Green. Dan 142 C4
Hay La. Brain 60 B2
Haycocks La. W Mers 104 C1
Haye La. Fing 86 B2
Hayes Barton. South 201 E4
Hayes Chase. Rett 164 C3
Hayes Cl. Chelm 127 D1
Hayes La. Canv 196 C2
Hayes Rd. Clact 109 F2

Hayhouse Rd. Ea Col 45 D3
Haynes Green Rd. Lay M 101 D4
Haytor Cl. Brain 60 B1
Haywain The. Stanw 66 B3
Hayward Ct. Colch 68 B4
Haze Park Rd. Walt 76 C1
Hazel Cl. Hadl 188 C2
Hazel Cl. South 189 E1
Hazel Cl. Thor 89 D3
Hazel Cl. With 98 A2
Hazel Gr. Brain 59 F1
Hazeldene. Rayl 176 B2
Hazeleigh Hall La. Haze 144 B3
Hazell Ave. Colch 67 D1
Hazelmere Rd. Thund 187 E3
Hazelmere. Basil 186 A2
Hazelton Rd. Colch 50 B1
Hazelville Cl. Harw 39 F1
Hazelwood Cres. Lit Cla 91 E1
Hazelwood Gr. South 189 F3
Hazelwood. Hawk 177 F2
Hazelwood. Thund 187 D4
Hazlemere Rd. Clact 110 B2
Head La. Sud 13 D3
Head St. Gold 133 F3
Head St. Hals 25 F1
Head St. Rowh 86 C4
Headcorn Cl. Basil 186 B3
Headgate Ct. Colch 67 F4
Headgate. Colch 67 F3
Hearsall Ave. Chelm 127 D4
Heath Dr. Chelm 140 A3
Heath Rd. Alres 88 A4
Heath Rd. Brad 54 B4
Heath Rd. Colch 66 C3
Heath Rd. E A Gr 48 A1
Heath Rd. Mist 36 A1
Heath Rd. Rowh 86 C4
Heath Rd. St O 90 C1
Heath Rd. Stanw 66 B2
Heath Rd. Tend 54 B1
Heath Rd. Tend 72 C4
Heath Rd. Wiv 69 D1
Heath The. Ded 33 F2
Heath The. Lay H 85 D3
Heather Cl. Clact 110 A4
Heather Cl. Lay H 84 C3
Heather Ct. Sprin 127 F3
Heather Dr. Colch 66 C3
Heather Dr. Hadl 189 D1
Heathercroft Rd. Wick 175 D3
Heathfield Rd. Chelm 127 D4
Heathfield. Rayl 176 B1
Heathfield. Thund 188 B3
Heathfields. E A Gr 66 A4
Heathgate. Wic Bis 115 E3
Heathlands. Thor 89 D3
Heaton Way. Tipt 100 B3
Heckfords Rd. Gt Ben 71 F1
Hedge Dr. Colch 67 D2
Hedge La. Hadl 188 B2
Hedge Lands. Copf 65 E3
Hedgehope Ave. Rayl 176 B2
Hedgerow The. Basil 185 F2
Hedgerows. Bore 128 A3
Hedingham Rd. Bul 11 E1
Hedingham Rd. Gos 24 C1
Hedingham Rd. Hals 25 F2
Hedingham Rd. Wic S P 17 D4
Heeswyk Rd. Canv 197 E3
Heideburg Rd. Canv 197 E3
Heights The. Dan 142 B4
Heilsburg Rd. Canv 197 E3
Helden Ave. Canv 197 D3
Helena Cl. Hawk 177 F3
Helena Ct. S Woo F 165 E3
Helena Rd. Rayl 176 C2
Helford Ct. With 97 E1
Hellendoorn Rd. Canv 197 E1
Helm Cl. Gt Hor 49 E4
Helmons La. W Han 152 A2
Helmsdale. Canv 196 C3
Helpeston. Basil 185 E3
Helston Rd. Sprin 127 F3
Hemingway Rd. With 97 F3
Hemlock Cl. With 98 A2
Hemmings Ct. Mald 144 C4
Hendon Cl. Clact 109 E3
Hendon Cl. Wick 174 B3
Hengist Gdns. Runw 163 E1
Henley Cres. South 190 B2
Henley Ct. Colch 66 C4
Henniker Gate. Sprin 128 A2
Henny Back Rd. Alph 18 C2
Henny Rd. Lam 19 D3
Henrietta Cl. Wiv 69 E2
Henry Dixon Rd. With 98 B3
Henry Dr. Hadl 189 D1
Henry Rd. Chelm 127 D2
Henson Ave. Canv 197 F2
Heralds Way. S Woo F 165 F4
Herbage Park Rd. Woo Wa .. 130 B1
Herbert Gr. South 200 A4
Herbert Rd. Canv 197 E2
Herbert Rd. Clact 109 F2
Herbert Rd. South 201 E3
Herberts Way. Rayl 176 B3
Hereford Rd. Clact 110 C3
Hereford Rd. Colch 68 A4

Hereford Wlk. Basil 185 F4
Hereward Cl. Wiv 69 E2
Hereward Gdns. Runw 163 E1
Hermes Dr. Burn 170 A3
Hermes Way. South 201 F4
Hermitage Ave. S Ben 188 A2
Hermitage Cl. S Ben 188 A2
Hermitage Rd. South 199 F4
Hernen Rd. Canv 197 E3
Heron Dale. Basil 185 E3
Heron Glade. Clact 109 F4
Heron Rd. Kelv 81 E1
Heron Way. Mald 132 B3
Heron Way. May 158 A4
Herongate. S Ben 187 D2
Herongate. South 201 F4
Heronsgate. Walt 93 F3
Herrick Cl. Colch 67 D3
Herring's Way. Ford 47 E3
Herschell Rd. Hadl 189 E1
Hertford Dr. Basil 185 E1
Hertford Rd. Canv 196 C2
Hervilly Way. Walt 94 A4
Hester Pl. Burn 170 B3
Hetherington Cl. Colch 86 A4
Hetzand Rd. Canv 197 F2
Hever Cl. Hock 177 E3
Hewes Cl. Colch 68 C4
Hewitt Rd. Lit Oak 39 E1
Heybridge Dr. Wick 174 C4
Heybridge House Ind Est. Mald 132 A2
Heybridge St. Mald 132 A3
Heycroft Dr. T Gr 78 C3
Heycroft Rd. Hawk 177 F3
Heycroft Rd. South 189 F3
Heycroft Way. Gt Bad 140 C3
Heycroft Way. Tipt 100 B3
Heygate Ave. South 200 A4
Heythrop The. Sprin 127 E2
Heywood Way. Mald 132 A3
Hickford Hill. Bel S P 4 C3
Hickling Cl. South 189 D3
Hickory Ave. Colch 68 B4
High Barrets. Basil 186 A3
High Beeches. S Ben 187 D2
High Bridge Rd. Sprin 127 E1
High Chelmer. Chelm 127 D1
High Cliff Dr. South 198 C4
High Croft. Col En 27 D1
High Elms Rd. Hull 165 F1
High Garrett. Brain 42 B1
High Lift Villas. Box 32 B4
High Mead. Hawk 177 F3
High Pasture. Lit Bad 129 E2
High Rd. Basil 186 A3
High Rd. Hock 177 D3
High Rd. Lay H 85 D3
High Rd. Rayl 176 B1
High Rd. S Ben 187 E2
High Ridge. Gt Brx 116 B4
High St N. W Mers 121 E4
High St. Brad O S 137 D1
High St. Brain 59 F1
High St. Brigh 106 C3
High St. Bures 19 F1
High St. Burn 170 B2
High St. Cane 168 B1
High St. Canv 197 E2
High St. Cav 1 B1
High St. Chelm 127 D1
High St. Cla 4 A4
High St. Clact 109 F1
High St. Colch 67 F4
High St. Ded 33 F4
High St. Ea Col 45 D3
High St. Gt Bad 140 C4
High St. Gt Oak 56 B2
High St. Gt Wak 193 D2
High St. Gt Y 9 D1
High St. Hadl 188 B2
High St. Hadl 198 B4
High St. Hals 25 F1
High St. harw 40 B2
High St. Kelv 81 E1
High St. Langh 32 B2
High St. Mald 132 A1
High St. Mann 35 E2
High St. Mist 35 F2
High St. Nay 20 A1
High St. Rayl 176 B1
High St. Rowh 87 D4
High St. S Ben 187 E1
High St. Soum 159 E2
High St. South 200 A4
High St. South 202 A4
High St. Th L S 73 F1
High St. Tolle 119 E1
High St. W Mers 121 D3
High St. Walt 94 B4
High St. Wick 174 B4
High St. Wiv 87 D4
High Tree La. Walt 76 B1
High View Ave. Clact 109 F3
High View Cl. Clact 109 F3
High View. St L 148 B4
Higham Hill. High 22 A4
Higham Rd. High 22 B2
Higham Rd. Str S M 22 B2
Highams Chase. Gold 134 A4

Highams Rd. Hock 177 F3
Highbank Cl. South 189 F3
Highbirch Rd. St O 90 B2
Highbury Terr. Hals 25 F1
Highbury Way. Sud 13 D3
Highclere Rd. Colch 50 A2
Highcliff Cres. Ashi 178 B4
Highcliff Rd. S Ben 196 C4
Highcliffe Cl. Wick 174 C4
Highcliffe Rd. Wick 174 C4
Highcliffe Way. Wick 174 C4
Highfield Ave. Harw 40 A2
Highfield Ave. S Ben 188 B2
Highfield Cl. Brain 60 A3
Highfield Cl. Dan 142 B3
Highfield Cl. South 190 B1
Highfield Cres. Rayl 176 B1
Highfield Cres. South 190 B1
Highfield Dr. Colch 67 E4
Highfield Dr. South 190 B1
Highfield Gdns. South 190 B2
Highfield Gr. South 190 B2
Highfield Mead. E Ham 153 D4
Highfield Rd. Chelm 126 C2
Highfield Rise. Alth 158 A2
Highfield Stile Rd. Brain 60 A3
Highfield Way. South 190 B2
Highfield. Cla 4 B4
Highfields La. Mess 99 F4
Highfields Rd. With 97 F1
Highfields. Gt Y 9 D1
Highfields. Hals 43 F4
Highland Rd. Corr 185 D1
Highlands Ave. Basil 185 E2
Highlands Blvd. Hadl 189 D1
Highlands Chalet Pk. Clact .. 110 A4
Highlands Cres. Basil 186 C3
Highlands Dr. Mald 131 F1
Highlands Hill. May 158 B3
Highlands Rd. Basil 186 C3
Highlands Rd. Rayl 165 D1
Highlands. Gos 24 C1
Highmead Ct. Rayl 176 B1
Highmead. Rayl 176 B1
Highview Cl. Sud 7 F1
Highview Rd. Thund 188 A4
Highwood Cl. South 189 F2
Highwoods App. Colch 50 B2
Highwoods Sq. Colch 50 A2
Hilary Cl. Roch 178 C3
Hilary Cres. Rayl 176 C1
Hilbery Rd. Canv 197 E2
Hildaville Dr. South 190 B1
Hill Ave. Wick 174 C4
Hill Cl. L Mel 7 E4
Hill Cl. S Ben 187 F2
Hill Cotts. Gt Ben 89 F1
Hill Cres. Chelm 127 E1
Hill Ct. Basil 185 E3
Hill La. Hawk 177 F3
Hill Rd. Chelm 127 E1
Hill Rd. Clact 109 F3
Hill Rd. Cogg 63 D1
Hill Rd. Harw 40 B2
Hill Rd. S Ben 187 F2
Hill Rd. South 190 C1
Hill Top Ave. S Ben 187 F1
Hill View Rd. Sprin 127 E2
Hill View. S Woo F 142 C1
Hillary Cl. Mald 132 A3
Hillary Cl. Sprin 127 E2
Hillborough Rd. South 190 B2
Hillcrest Cotts. Langh 32 C3
Hillcrest Rd. Hock 177 F3
Hillcrest Rd. S Woo F 165 E4
Hillcrest Rd. South 200 A4
Hillcrest Rd. Sud 7 F1
Hillcrest View. Basil 185 E2
Hillcrest. Clact 110 A3
Hillcrest. Steep 147 D1
Hillcrest. Walt 93 E4
Hillhouse La. Tend 73 D2
Hillhouse La. Th L S 73 D2
Hilliards Rd. Gt Bro 53 E1
Hillie Bunnies. Ea Col 45 D4
Hillman Ave. Clact 124 C3
Hillridge. Colch 50 A2
Hills Cl. Brain 59 F2
Hills Cres. Colch 67 D3
Hills Rd. Si Hed 24 B4
Hillside Ave. Hawk 177 F3
Hillside Cres. Clact 110 B3
Hillside Cres. South 199 D4
Hillside Gdns. Brain 59 F1
Hillside Gr. Chelm 140 A4
Hillside Mews. Chelm 140 A4
Hillside Rd. Burn 170 A3
Hillside Rd. Hock 177 D3
Hillside Rd. Rayl 189 E4
Hillside Rd. S Ben 187 E1
Hillside Rd. Soum 159 E2
Hillside Rd. South 198 C4
Hillside Rd. Sud 13 D4
Hillside. Frin 93 F2
Hillston Cl. Colch 68 A1
Hilltop Ave. Hull 165 F1
Hilltop Cl. Rayl 176 B1
Hilltop Cres. Weel 72 C1
Hilltop Rise. Weel 72 C1

Hilltop Rise. Weel

Hillview Cl. Rowh	86	C4
Hillview Rd. Rayl	176	B2
Hillway. South	199	D4
Hillwood Gr. Wick	174	C4
Hilton Cl. Mann	35	E2
Hilton Rd. Canv	197	D3
Hilton Way. Si Hed	24	C4
Hilton Wlk. Canv	197	D3
Hilversum Wlk. Canv	197	D3
Hindles Rd. Canv	197	E2
Hines Cl. Ald	65	D4
Hinguar St. South	201	F3
Hitcham Rd. Cogg	62	C2
Hitchcock Pl. Sud	7	F1
Hitchin Mews. Brain	78	A4
Hither Blakers. S Woo F	165	E4
Hitherwood Rd. Colch	67	E1
Hobart Cl. Chelm	126	C3
Hobbiton Hill. S Woo F	165	E3
Hobbs Dr. Box	32	A3
Hobbs La. Glems	2	B1
Hobleythick La. South	190	B2
Hockley Cl. Basil	185	E3
Hockley Cl. Brad O S	137	E1
Hockley Green. Basil	185	F3
Hockley Rd. Basil	185	E3
Hockley Rd. Brad O S	137	E1
Hockley Rd. Rayl	176	C2
Hockley Rise. Hock	177	F3
Hodges Holt. With	115	D4
Hodgson Ct. Wick	175	D3
Hodgson Way. Wick	175	D3
Hoe Dr. Colch	67	D3
Hoe La. Pent	5	F4
Hoe La. Rett	164	A3
Hoe Mill Rd. Woo Wa	130	C2
Hog's La. Str S M	34	C4
Hogarth Cl. W Mers	121	E3
Hogarth Dr. South	202	A4
Hogarth End. Walt	93	F4
Hogwell Chase. Stow M	166	A4
Holbech Rd. Basil	185	F4
Holbek Rd. Canv	197	F2
Holborough Cl. Colch	68	C4
Holbrook Cl. Clact	109	D2
Holbrook Cl. S Woo F	165	E4
Holdsworth Cl. Glems	2	A2
Holgate. Basil	186	B4
Holkham Ave. S Woo F	165	E3
Holland Ave. Canv	196	B3
Holland Park. Clact	110	A2
Holland Rd. Clact	110	A2
Holland Rd. Frin	93	F2
Holland Rd. Lit Cla	91	F1
Holland Rd. South	199	E4
Holland Rd. Walt	93	D3
Hollands Wlk. Basil	185	E1
Holledge Cres. Walt	93	F3
Hollies Rd. Bradw	61	D1
Holliland Croft. Gt T	64	B4
Hollis Lock. Sprin	128	A2
Hollow La. Broom	126	C4
Hollow La. Bures	19	F2
Hollow Rd. Ashe	3	F2
Hollow Rd. Kelv	80	C1
Holloway Rd. Mald	132	A3
Holly Bank. With	97	F1
Holly Cl. Burn	170	A3
Holly Cl. Colch	67	E1
Holly La. Gt Hor	31	E2
Holly Oaks. Worm	29	F2
Holly Rd. Stanw	66	B3
Holly View Cl. Tend	72	C3
Holly Way. Chelm	140	B4
Holly Way. Elmst M	70	A4
Holly Way. Tipt	100	B3
Holly Wlk. Canv	196	C2
Holly Wlk. With	98	A3
Hollybush Hill. Gt Ben	89	F1
Hollymead Cl. Colch	49	F2
Hollytree Gdns. Rayl	188	B4
Hollywood Cl. Gt Bad	140	C3
Holm Oak. Colch	68	A2
Holman Cres. Colch	67	D2
Holman Rd. Hals	43	F4
Holmbrook Way. Frin	93	F3
Holmes Rd. Hals	43	F4
Holmsdale Cl	190	B2
Holmswood. Canv	197	F3
Holmwood Cl. South	109	D3
Holsworthy. South	201	E4
Holt Dr. Rowh	86	A4
Holt Dr. Wic Bis	115	F3
Holt Farm Way. Hawk	178	B2
Holt's Cl. Lit Hor	30	A2
Holton Rd. Canv	197	F2
Holton Rd. Rayl	177	D1
Holtynge. S Ben	187	E2
Holybread La. Lit Bad	129	E2
Holyoak La. Hawk	177	F2
Holyrood Dr. South	190	A1
Holyrood. Harw	39	F1
Home Farm Rd. Gt Wak	193	D2
Home Farm La. Ard	52	A4
Home Mead. Chelm	140	B1
Home Mead. Writ	126	A1
Homefield Cl. Chelm	126	B3
Homefield Rd. Colch	67	E1

Homefield Rd. With	98	A2
Homefield Way. Ea Col	45	D4
Homefield Way. T Gr	78	B4
Homefield. Soum	159	F3
Homefields Ave. S Ben	187	D3
Homerton Cl. Clact	109	F4
Homestead Gdns. Hadl	188	B1
Homestead Rd. Basil	186	C4
Homestead Rd. Hadl	188	B1
Homestead Way. Hadl	188	B2
Homestead. Sprin	127	D4
Homing Rd. Lit Cla	91	E2
Honey Bridge Rd. Nay	20	B4
Honey Cl. Gt Bad	140	B3
Honey Pot La. Stow M	155	E2
Honeypot La. Basil	185	D4
Honeypot La. St O	91	D2
Honeypot La. Toll K	101	D1
Honeypot La. Wix	54	C2
Honeysuckle Way. Colch	68	C4
Honeysuckle Way. Thor	89	D3
Honeysuckle Way. With	97	E2
Honeywood Ave. Cogg	63	D2
Honeywood Rd. Hals	26	A2
Honiley Ave. Wick	174	B2
Honington Cl. Wick	175	D3
Honiton Rd. South	200	B4
Honywood Cl. Mks T	64	C2
Honywood Rd. Colch	67	E3
Honywood Way. Walt	93	F4
Hood Gdns. Brain	60	B2
Hooley Dr. Rayl	176	B4
Hop Gardens La. Woo Wa	130	C2
Hope Rd. Canv	197	E2
Hope Rd. S Ben	187	E1
Hopkin's La. Harw	40	B3
Hopkins Cl. Walt	93	F3
Hopkins Mead. Sprin	128	A1
Hopkirk Cl. Dan	142	C4
Hopper Wlk. Colch	68	B3
Hopping Jacks La. Dan	142	C4
Hoppit Mead. Brain	59	F1
Horace Rd. South	200	A4
Hordle Pl. Harw	40	B2
Hordle St. Harw	40	B2
Horkesley Hill. Gt Hor	31	D4
Horkesley Rd. Box	49	F4
Horkesley Way. Wick	174	C3
Horley Cl. Clact	109	E3
Horn La. Cogg	63	D1
Hornbeam Cl. Chelm	140	A3
Hornbeam Cl. Colch	67	E1
Hornbeam Wlk. With	98	A2
Hornbeams The. Lit Oak	57	D4
Hornbeams. Thund	187	D4
Hornby Ave. South	190	B3
Hornby Cl. South	190	B3
Hornchurch Cl. Wick	175	D3
Horne Row. Dan	142	B3
Horner Pl. With	98	A1
Hornet Way. Burn	170	A3
Hornsland Rd. Canv	197	F2
Horrocks Cl. Colch	68	A2
Horse and Groom La. Chelm	140	A2
Horsey Rd. Walt	93	E4
Horsley Cross. Basil	185	D4
Hospital La. Colch	67	E3
Hospital Rd. Colch	67	E3
Hospital Rd. South	201	F3
Houblon Dr. Chelm	140	B1
Houchin's La. Cogg	63	D2
Hovefields Ave. Wick	174	B2
Hovefields Dr. Wick	174	B2
Howard Ave. Harw	39	F1
Howard Chase. Basil	185	D4
Howard Cl. Brain	60	B2
Howard Cres. Basil	186	B3
Howard Dr. Sprin	128	A1
Howard Pl. Canv	197	D1
Howard Rd. Clact	110	B2
Howard Vyse Ct. Clact	109	F3
Howards Chase. South	190	C1
Howards Cl. Bore	128	C4
Howbridge Hall Rd. With	114	C4
Howbridge Rd. With	114	C4
Howe Chase. Hals	25	F2
Howe Cl. Colch	68	B4
Howe Green Rd. Purl	155	F4
Hoxton Cl. Clact	109	E2
Hoyners. Dan	143	D4
Hubbards Chase. Walt	94	A4
Hubert Rd. Colch	67	D4
Hucklesbury Ave. Clact	110	C4
Hudson Cl. Clact	109	E3
Hudson Cl. Harw	40	A1
Hudson Cres. South	189	F3
Hudson Rd. South	189	E3
Hudson Way. Canv	197	D3
Hudsons La. High	21	D3
Hugh Dickson Rd. Colch	49	F1
Hughes Stanton Way. Lawf	35	D2
Hull La. Terl	96	A1
Hull's La. Sand	141	F4
Hullbridge Rd. Rayl	176	B4
Hullbridge Rd. S Woo F	154	B1
Hullbridge Rd. S Woo F	165	E4
Hulton Cl. Bore	128	C4
Humber Ave. Clact	124	C3
Humber Cl. Rayl	176	B1

Humber Rd. Sprin	127	E3
Humber Rd. With	97	E1
Humphry Rd. Sud	12	C4
Hundred La. Box	32	B2
Hundred La. Langh	32	B2
Hungerdown La. Lawf	34	C1
Hunnable Rd. Brain	59	F1
Hunt Ave. Mald	132	A3
Hunt Cl. Fee	81	E2
Hunt Dr. Clact	109	E3
Hunt Rd. Ea Col	45	D3
Hunt Way. Walt	93	F3
Hunt's Cl. Writ	139	D4
Hunt's Dr. Writ	139	D4
Hunter Dr. Lawf	35	D2
Hunter Rd. Brain	60	B1
Hunter's Chase. Ard	33	F1
Hunters Ridge. Colch	50	A2
Hunters Way. Sprin	127	F4
Huntingdon Rd. South	200	B4
Huntingdon Way. Clact	109	F3
Hunts Farm Cl. Tolle	119	E1
Hunts Hill. Glems	2	A2
Hunwicke Rd. Colch	68	C4
Hurnard Dr. Colch	67	D4
Hurrell Down. Bore	112	C1
Hurrell Down. Colch	50	A2
Hurrells La. Lit Bad	128	C2
Hurricane Way. Wick	175	D3
Hurst Cl. Brigh	107	D3
Hurst Way. South	189	F2
Hurst Way. Sprin	127	F1
Hyacinth Cl. Clact	109	E2
Hyacinth Cl. Tolle	119	D1
Hyacinth Cl. Sprin	127	F4
Hyde Chase. Purl	143	E2
Hyde Farm Chase. Dan	143	D2
Hyde Green. Dan	143	D4
Hyde La. Dan	143	D3
Hyde Rd. Sud	12	C4
Hyde Way. Wick	174	B3
Hyde Wood La. Ashi	178	C4
Hydeway. Thund	187	F3
Hydewood Rd. Lit Y	9	D2
Hylands The. Hock	177	E3
Hythe Cl. Brain	59	F3
Hythe Cl. Clact	125	E4
Hythe Gr. Brigh	88	C1
Hythe Hill. Colch	68	B3
Hythe Quay. Colch	68	B3
Hythe Station Rd. Colch	68	B3
Hythe The. Mald	132	A1
Iceni Way. Colch	67	D2
Ilfracombe Ave. South	200	B4
Ilex Cl. Colch	67	E1
Ilfracombe Ave. Basil	186	B3
Ilfracombe Rd. South	191	E1
Ilgars Rd. Runw	163	F1
Ilmington Dr. Basil	174	A1
Imogen Cl. Colch	68	C4
Imperial Ave. May	146	C1
Imperial Ave. South	190	B1
Imphal Cl. Colch	67	E1
Inchbonnie Rd. S Woo F	165	F3
Ingarfield Rd. Clact	110	C3
Ingelrica Ave. Hat Pev	114	A2
Ingestre St. Harw	40	B3
Inglenook. Clact	110	A4
Inglis Rd. Colch	67	E3
Ingram Mews. Brain	78	A4
Ingram's Piece. Ard	51	F4
Ingram's Well Rd. Sud	12	C4
Ingrave Cl. Wick	174	C3
Inkerpole Pl. Sprin	127	F2
Inverness Ave. South	190	B1
Inverness Cl. Colch	68	A4
Inworth La. Wa Col	28	B1
Inworth Rd. Fee	81	F2
Inworth Wlk. Colch	68	A1
Inworth Wlk. Wick	175	D4
Ipswich Rd. Clact	110	B3
Ipswich Rd. Colch	50	B2
Ipswich Rd. Langh	32	C1
Ipswich Rd. Str S M	22	C2
Ireton Rd. Colch	67	E3
Iris Cl. Sprin	127	F3
Iron Latch La. E A Gr	66	B4
Iron Latch La. Stanw	66	B4
Ironwell La. Hawk	178	B2
Ironwell La. Roch	178	B2
Irvine Rd. Colch	67	E3
Irvington Cl. South	189	E2
Irvon Hill Rd. Wick	174	B4
Isbourne Rd. Colch	68	C4
Ishams Chase. With	115	E4
Island La. Walt	75	F1
Island Rd. Walt	75	F1
Ivy La. E Mers	106	A2
Ivy Lodge Rd. Gt Hor	49	E4
Ivy Rd. Thund	187	D3
Ivy Wlk. Canv	196	C2
Jacaranda Cl. Sprin	127	F3
Jack Hatch Way. Wiv	69	D2
Jackdaw Cl. South	201	F4
Jacks Cl. Wick	174	C4
Jackson Pl. Gt Bad	140	B3
Jackson Rd. Clact	109	F1

Jaggards Rd. Cogg	63	D2
James Carter Rd. Colch	66	C2
James Cl. Wiv	69	E2
James Gdns. St O	108	A3
James Rd. Clact	109	E1
James St. Brigh	106	C3
James St. Colch	68	A3
Jameson Pl. Sud	12	C4
Jameson Rd. Clact	109	E2
Jameson Rd. Sud	12	C4
Janette Ave. Canv	196	C2
Janmead. With	98	A2
Jaques Cl. Glems	2	B3
Jardine Rd. Basil	186	B4
Jarmin Rd. Colch	67	F4
Jarvis Field. Lit Bad	129	E3
Jarvis Rd. Canv	197	D3
Jarvis Rd. S Ben	187	F2
Jasmine Cl. Colch	68	C4
Jasmine Cl. Sprin	127	F4
Jasmine Way. Clact	125	D4
Jason Cl. Canv	197	D3
Jays La. Mks T	64	C2
Jays The. Colch	50	A2
Jaywick La. Clact	109	D1
Jeffcut Rd. Sprin	127	F1
Jefferson Cl. Colch	66	C3
Jeffery Rd. Gt Bad	141	F4
Jeffrey Cl. Colch	66	C3
Jeffrey's Rd. T Gr	78	C3
Jellicoe Way. Brain	60	B2
Jenkin's Hill. Brad	36	B2
Jenner Cl. Brain	59	F1
Jenner Mead. Sprin	128	A2
Jersey Gdns. Runw	174	B4
Jersey Rd. Mald	132	A1
Jersey Way. Brain	59	E1
Jesmond Rd. Canv	197	D1
Jessica Cl. Colch	68	C4
Joes Rd. Sud	13	F4
John Ball Wlk. Colch	67	F4
John English Ave. Brain	59	F2
John Harper St. Colch	67	F4
John Henry Keene Meml Hms.		
Chelm	127	D2
John Kent Ave. Colch	67	D1
John Raven Ct. Fee	81	E2
John Ray Gdns. Bl Not	78	A3
John Ray St. Brain	60	A2
John St. Brigh	106	C3
John St. South	202	A3
Johnson Cl. Brain	78	A4
Johnson Cl. Roch	178	B3
Johnson Rd. Gt Bad	141	D3
Johnson Rd. St O	108	A2
Johnson's Dr. Elmst M	70	A3
Johnston Cl. Clact	110	C3
Johnston Cl. Hals	43	F4
Johnstone Rd. South	201	D4
Jones Cl. South	190	C2
Jonquil Way. Colch	49	E1
Joseph Gdns. Silv E	79	F2
Josselin Cl. Ea Col	45	D4
Josselin Ct. Basil	174	B1
Josselin Rd. Basil	174	B1
Jotmans La. S Ben	187	D2
Journeymans Way. South	191	D3
Joyce's Chase. Gold	134	A4
Jubilee Ave. Clact	109	F4
Jubilee Cl. Harw	39	F1
Jubilee Cotts. Pag Ch	180	B3
Jubilee Ct. Si Hed	24	C4
Jubilee Dr. Runw	174	B4
Jubilee End. Lawf	35	E3
Jubilee La. Ard	51	E2
Jubilee Rd. Rayl	176	C1
Jubilee Rd. Sud	12	C4
Jubilee Rise. Dan	143	D3
Jubilee Way. Walt	93	F3
Julien Court Rd. Brain	60	A2
Juliers Cl. Canv	197	E2
Juliers Rd. Canv	197	E2
Junction Rd. Basil	186	A2
Junction Rd. Col N	156	A3
Juniper Cl. Hals	43	E4
Juniper Cres. With	98	A2
Juniper Dr. Chelm	140	A3
Juniper Rd. Bore	128	C4
Juniper Rd. South	189	F2
Juniper Rd. Stanw	66	B3
Juniper Way. Colch	68	B4
Jupe's Hill. Wa Col	28	B1
Jupes Hill. Ded	34	B2
Juvina Cl. With	114	C4
Kale Croft. Stanw	66	B3
Kale Rd. S Ben	187	F2
Kamerwyk Ave. Canv	197	E2
Karen Cl. S Ben	196	C4
Karen Cl. Wick	174	B3
Katherine Cl. Rayl	177	D1
Katherine Rd. Basil	186	D1
Kathleen Dr. South	189	F1
Katonia Ave. May	146	C1
Kay Cl. Gt Le	95	D4
Keable Rd. Mks T	64	C2
Keating Cl. Lawf	35	D2
Keats Ave. Brain	77	F4
Keats Cl. Mald	145	D4

Keats Rd. Colch	66	C3
Keats Sq. S Woo F	165	F3
Keats Way. Wick	174	B4
Kebbles. Glems	2	A3
Keble Cl. Colch	67	E3
Keddington Hill. Sud	13	D1
Keeble Cl. Tipt	100	C3
Keeble Park. Mald	144	C4
Keegan Pl. Canv	197	E2
Keelars La. Elmst M	69	F1
Keelers Way. Gt Hor	49	D4
Keelings La. Deng	160	C4
Keelings Rd. Deng	160	C4
Keene Way. Chelm	140	A2
Keer Ave. Canv	197	E1
Keighley Mews. South	192	B1
Keith Ave. Runw	163	E1
Keith Cl. Clact	110	A4
Keith Way. South	190	C3
Kellington Rd. Canv	197	E2
Kelly Rd. Basil	186	C3
Kelredon Rd. Mess	82	B1
Kelso Cl. Gt Hor	49	E3
Kelvedon Cl. Chelm	127	D3
Kelvedon Cl. Rayl	176	A2
Kelvedon Hall La. Gt Brx	99	F2
Kelvedon Rd. Cogg	81	D4
Kelvedon Rd. Lit Brx	115	F3
Kelvedon Rd. Toll D	100	A4
Kelvedon Rd. Toll D	118	B3
Kembles. Rayl	176	C2
Kempson Dr. Sud	13	E3
Kempton Cl. Thund	188	A4
Kemsley Rd. Ea Col	45	D3
Ken Cooke Ct. Colch	67	F4
Kendal Cl. Hull	165	F1
Kendal Cl. Rayl	176	C1
Kendal Ct. Wick	175	D3
Kendal Rd. Colch	68	A3
Kendal Road Folley. Colch	68	A3
Kendal Way. South	189	F4
Kenholme. South	189	F2
Kenilworth Gdns. Rayl	176	B2
Kenilworth Gdns. South	190	A2
Kenilworth Gr. Th L S	74	A1
Kenilworth Rd. Clact	110	C3
Kenley Cl. Wick	175	D3
Kenmore Cl. Canv	197	F1
Kennedy Cl. Rayl	189	D4
Kennedy Cl. Thund	187	D4
Kennedy Way. Clact	110	A3
Kennet Way. Chelm	126	B3
Kenneth Rd. Basil	186	B4
Kenneth Rd. Thund	187	E3
Kennington Ave. Thund	187	E3
Kensington Rd. South	200	B4
Kensington Way. Hock	177	E3
Kent Ave. Canv	197	D3
Kent Ave. South	189	F1
Kent Cl. Brigh	106	C4
Kent Elms Cl. South	189	F3
Kent Gdns. Brain	60	A2
Kent Green Cl. Hock	177	F3
Kent View Ave. South	199	D4
Kent View Rd. Basil	185	F2
Kent Way. Rayl	189	D4
Kent's Ave. Clact	110	C3
Kentings The. Brain	59	F1
Kents Grass. Tolle	119	E1
Kents Hill Rd N. Thund	187	E3
Kents Hill Rd. S Ben	187	E2
Kenway. South	191	D1
Kenworthy Rd. Brain	59	F1
Kenyon Cl. Str S M	22	B1
Kerby Rise. Sprin	127	F1
Kerridge's Cut. Mist	36	A2
Kerry Ct. Colch	68	B4
Kersey Ave. Sud	13	D3
Kersey Dr. Clact	109	D3
Kestrel Way. Clact	109	F3
Kestrel Wlk. Chelm	140	A2
Keswick Ave. Clact	110	B3
Keswick Ave. Hull	165	F1
Keswick Cl. Rayl	176	C1
Keswick Cl. Walt	93	F4
Keswick Rd. Thund	187	F4
Ketleys View. Pan	59	D4
Ketleys. Chelm	140	B2
Kew La. Frin	93	D2
Key Rd. Clact	109	F2
Keyes Way. Brain	60	B2
Keymer Way. Colch	66	C2
Keynes Way. Harw	39	F1
Keysland. Thund	188	A3
Kilburn Gdns. Clact	109	E3
Kildermorie Cl. Colch	50	B2
Kilmaine Rd. Harw	39	F1
Kiln Barn Ave. Clact	109	F4
Kiln Dr. Sud	13	D3
Kiln Rd. Thund	188	A2
Kilns Hill. Cogg	62	C3
Kilnwood Ave. Hock	177	E3
Kilworth Ave. South	200	A4
Kimberley Rd. Barl	192	C3
Kimberley Rd. Colch	68	A3
Kimberley Rd. S Ben	187	E2
Kincaid Rd. St O	108	A2
King Charles Rd. W Mers	121	E3

King Coel Rd. Colch 66 B4
King Edward Ave. Burn 170 A3
King Edward Quay. Colch 68 B3
King Edward VII Dr. Sho G 40 A4
King Edward Way. With 114 C4
King Edward's Rd. S Woo F . 165 E4
King George Rd. Colch 67 F2
King George's Ave. Harw 40 A2
King George's Cl. Rayl 176 B1
King Harold Rd. Colch 67 D2
King Henry's Dr. Roch 190 C4
King St. Brad 54 B4
King St. Ca Hed 15 F2
King St. Mald 132 A1
King St. Sud 12 C4
King Stephen Rd. Colch 68 A3
King's Cl. St O 108 A2
King's Head St. Harw 40 C3
King's La. L Mel 7 E4
King's Quay St. Harw 40 C3
King's Rd. Brain 59 F3
King's Rd. Burn 170 A2
King's Rd. Clact 109 E1
King's Rd. Harw 40 A2
King's Rd. S Ben 187 F1
King's Rd. South 190 A1
Kingfisher Cl. Colch 68 C4
Kingfisher Cl. Mald 132 B3
Kingfisher Cl. South 201 F4
Kingfisher Dr. S Ben 187 E1
Kingfisher Way. Kelv 81 E1
Kingfishers. Basil 185 E2
Kingfishers. Clact 109 F3
Kingley Cl. Wick 174 A4
Kingley Dr. Wick 174 A4
Kings Ave. Clact 110 B3
Kings Chase. With 98 A1
Kings Cl. Canv 196 B2
Kings Cl. Lawf 35 E2
Kings Cl. Rayl 176 C1
Kings Ct. Burn 170 A2
Kings Ct. Harw 40 A2
Kings Farm. Rayl 176 C3
Kings Head Ct. Colch 67 F4
Kings Hill. Sud 13 D3
Kings La. Stis 60 C2
Kings Mead. Peb 27 D4
Kings Meadow Rd. Colch 67 F4
Kings Meadow. Sud 13 D3
Kings Mews. Wiv 69 E2
Kings Par. Clact 110 C3
Kings Park. Thund 187 F3
Kings Rd. Canv 196 B2
Kings Rd. Chelm 126 C2
Kings Rd. Glems 2 B3
Kings Rd. Gt Tot 116 B4
Kings Rd. Hals 25 F1
Kings Rd. Rayl 176 C1
Kings Rd. Soum 159 E2
Kings Way. S Woo F 154 B1
Kings Wlk. Tolle 119 F1
Kingsbridge Cl. Brain 59 F4
Kingsbury Cl. Mks T 64 C2
Kingsbury Wlk. Sud 13 E3
Kingsdown Cl. Basil 186 B3
Kingsdown Wlk. Canv 197 D3
Kingshawes. Thund 188 A3
Kingsland Beach. W Mers 121 E3
Kingsland Cl. W Mers 121 E3
Kingsland Rd. W Mers 121 E3
Kingsley Cres. Thund 188 B4
Kingsley La. Thund 188 A4
Kingsman Dr. Clact 109 E3
Kingsmans Farm Rd. Hull ... 166 A2
Kingsmere Cl. W Mers 121 E4
Kingsmere. Thund 188 A3
Kingsteignton. South 201 E4
Kingston Ave. Sprin 127 F2
Kingston Cres. Sprin 127 F2
Kingston Way. Thund 187 F3
Kingsway. Colch 67 F4
Kingsway. Harw 40 B2
Kingsway. Hull 165 E1
Kingsway. South 190 A1
Kingsway. Tipt 100 B3
Kingswood Chase. South 189 E1
Kingswood Cres. Rayl 176 A1
Kingswood Ct. Basil 185 F3
Kingswood Rd. Basil 185 E3
Kingswood Rd. Colch 49 F2
Kingwell Ave. Clact 109 F3
Kinlett Gdns. Colch 50 A2
Kinloch Chase. With 114 C4
Kino Rd. Walt 94 B4
Kipling Cl. Chelm 127 D3
Kipling Mews. South 191 D1
Kipling Way. Brain 78 A4
Kirby Hall Rd. Ca Hed 15 E4
Kirby Rd. Basil 185 F3
Kirby Rd. Walt 94 A4
Kirk Pl. Sprin 127 F2
Kirkbaye. Walt 93 F3
Kirkby Rd. Frin 93 D3
Kirkhurst Cl. Brigh 107 D3
Kirklees. Chelm 127 D2
Kirkmans Rd. Chelm 140 B2
Kirkton Cl. Sho G 40 A4
Kitchen Hill. Bul 12 A3
Kitchener Rd. N Fam 156 A1

Kitchener Way. Sho G 40 A4
Kitkatts Rd. Canv 197 D2
Kittiwake Dr. Mald 132 B3
Klondyke Ave. Rayl 176 A2
Knapton Cl. Sprin 127 E4
Knight St. S Woo F 165 E4
Knights Cl. Lawf 35 E2
Knights Cl. Tipt 100 C2
Knights Rd. Brain 60 B1
Knights Rd. Cogg 62 C1
Knightsbridge Cl. Colch 67 E2
Knightswick Rd. Canv 197 D2
Knivet Cl. Rayl 176 C1
Knoll The. Rayl 176 B1
Knollcroft. South 201 E3
Knowle The. Basil 185 E2
Knowles Cl. Hals 25 F1
Knox Gdns. Clact 109 F3
Knox Rd. Clact 109 F3
Kohima Rd. Colch 67 D1
Kolburg Rd. Canv 197 E1
Kollum Rd. Canv 197 E2
Koln Cl. Canv 196 B2
Komberg Cres. Canv 197 E3
Konnybrook. Thund 188 A2
Korndyk Ave. Canv 197 E2
Kreswell Gr. Harw 40 A1
Kursaal Way. South 200 B4
Kynaston Pl. With 98 A1
Kynaston Rd. Pan 59 D4

Laars Ave. Canv 197 E3
Laburnum Ave. Wick 174 B3
Laburnum Cl. Clact 109 E2
Laburnum Cl. Gt Ben 89 F4
Laburnum Cl. Hock 177 E3
Laburnum Cl. Wick 174 B4
Laburnum Cres. Walt 93 E3
Laburnum Dr. Chelm 140 B3
Laburnum Gr. Canv 196 B2
Laburnum Gr. Colch 68 C4
Laburnum Gr. Hock 177 D3
Laburnum Way. Hat Pev 114 A2
Laburnum Way. With 98 A3
Labworth Cl. Canv 197 E1
Labworth Rd. Canv 197 E1
Ladbroke Dr. Colch 68 A2
Ladbrooke Rd. Clact 109 E3
Ladell Cl. Colch 66 C2
Ladram Cl. South 201 E4
Ladram Rd. South 201 E4
Ladram Way. South 201 D4
Lady La. Chelm 140 B4
Ladygate Centre. Wick 174 B4
Ladysmith Ave. Brigh 106 C4
Laing Rd. Colch 68 C3
Lake Ave. Clact 109 E2
Lake Dri. Thund 187 F3
Lake Way. Clact 124 C3
Lake Wlk. Clact 109 E2
Lakeside Cres. Canv 197 E3
Lakeside. Rayl 176 B2
Lakeview. Canv 197 D3
Lakin Cl. Sprin 128 A2
Lamarsh Hill. Bures 19 F1
Lamarsh Hill. Gt H 19 D3
Lamarsh Rd. Alph 19 D2
Lamb La. Si Hed 24 B4
Lambert's Rd. Gt T 45 F1
Lambeth Mews. Hock 177 E3
Lambeth Rd. South 189 F3
Lambeth Rd. Thund 187 E3
Lambeth Wlk. Clact 109 F3
Lambourne Cl. Clact 109 F4
Lambourne Cl. Stanw 66 B2
Lambourne Cres. Basil 185 F3
Lambourne Gr. Mald 144 C4
Lambourne Hall Rd. Cane ... 168 C1
Lammas Way. Wiv 69 E1
Lancaster Gdns E. Clact 110 A2
Lancaster Gdns W. Clact 110 A2
Lancaster Gdns. Rayl 189 D4
Lancaster Gdns. South 200 A4
Lancaster Rd. Rayl 189 D4
Lancaster Rd. Sud 7 E1
Lancaster Way. Brain 59 F2
Lancaster Way. Ea Col 44 C1
Lanchester Ave. Clact 124 B3
Lancia Ave. Clact 124 B3
Land Cl. Clact 109 E3
Land La. Colch 68 A4
Landale Dr. Colch 50 A2
Landermere Rd. Th L S 74 A3
Landermere. Basil 185 D4
Landsburg Rd. Canv 197 E3
Landsdown Rd. Sud 13 D4
Landseer Rd. Colch 67 D3
Landwick La. Deng 160 C4
Lane The. Rd. Wa Col 46 B4
Lane The. Clact 109 E2
Lane The. Mist 35 F2
Lane The. W Mers 121 D4
Langdale Gdns. Chelm 140 B4
Langdale. Bl Not 77 E4
Langdon Rd. Rayl 176 A2
Langenhoe Hall La. Lang 104 B3
Langenhoe. Wick 174 C3
Langford Cres. Thund 187 F3
Langford Gr. Basil 186 B4

Langford Rd. Mald 131 F3
Langford Rd. Wic Bis 115 E1
Langham Dr. Clact 109 D2
Langham Dr. Rayl 175 F2
Langham Dr. Rayl 176 A2
Langham La. Langh 32 B1
Langham Rd. Box 31 F1
Langley Cl. Rayl 189 D4
Langley Hill. Lam 19 E2
Langleys. Basil 185 D2
Langport Dr. South 190 A2
Langton Ave. Chelm 126 C3
Langwood. W Mers 121 E4
Lanham Green Rd. T Gr 79 D4
Lanhams. Basil 186 B4
Lanisdale. Dan 143 D4
Lansdown Ave. Hadl 188 C3
Lansdowne Ave. South 190 A1
Lansdowne Cl. Tipt 100 B3
Lansdowne Dr. Rayl 176 B2
Lanvalley Rd. Colch 66 C3
Lappmark Rd. Canv 197 E2
Lapwater Cl. South 189 E1
Lapwing Dr. Kelv 81 E1
Lapwing Dr. Mald 132 B3
Lapwing Rd. Runw 163 E1
Larch Cl. Colch 68 B4
Larch Gr. Chelm 140 B3
Larch Gr. Nay 20 A1
Larch Gr. With 98 A3
Larch Wlk. Hat Pev 114 A3
Larch Wlk. Mald 132 B3
Larches The. Bore 128 C4
Larches The. Thund 187 E4
Larchwood Cl. Hadl 189 D3
Lark Hill Rd. Cane 168 A1
Lark Rise. Sud 12 B3
Larkfield Cl. Hawk 178 B2
Larkfield Rd. Gt Ben 71 E1
Larksfield Cres. Harw 40 A2
Larkspur Cl. With 97 F2
Larkswood Wlk. Wick 174 B3
Larkway. Walt 93 F4
Larneys The. Walt 93 F4
Larup Ave. Canv 197 E2
Larup Gdns. Canv 197 E2
Lascelles Gdns. Hawk 178 B3
Latchetts Shaw. Basil 185 D2
Latchingdon Cl. Rayl 176 A2
Latchingdon Rd. Col N 156 B3
Latchingdon Rd. Latch 156 B3
Latchingdon Rd. Purl 156 B3
Lathcoates Cres. Gt Bad 140 C4
Launceston Cl. Colch 68 A1
Laundry Gdns. Sud 12 B3
Laurel Ave. Harw 39 F1
Laurel Ave. Wick 174 B4
Laurel Cl. Clact 110 A4
Laurel Cl. South 198 B4
Laurel Dr. L Mel 7 E4
Laurel Gr. Chelm 140 A4
Laurels The. Rayl 188 C4
Laurels The. S Woo F 165 E4
Laurence Ave. With 115 D4
Laurence Cl. Elmst M 69 F3
Laurence Croft. Writ 126 A1
Lavender Cl. Tipt 100 B2
Lavender Cl. With 97 F2
Lavender Ct. Sprin 127 F3
Lavender Gr. South 190 B2
Lavender Way. Colch 49 E1
Lavender Way. Wick 174 B4
Lavender Wlk. Clact 125 D4
Lavenham Cl. Clact 109 D2
Laver Ct. Colch 67 E2
Lawford La. Writ 126 B1
Lawling Ave. Mald 132 B3
Lawlinge Rd. Latch 157 D3
Lawn Ave. South 191 D1
Lawn Chase. With 97 F1
Lawn La. Sprin 127 E3
Lawns Cl. W Mers 121 E4
Lawns The. Sprin 127 E3
Lawns The. Thund 187 E4
Lawnscourt. Thund 187 D4
Lawrence Rd. Basil 186 C4
Lawshall's Hill. Wa Col 27 E1
Laxton Ct. Colch 67 D2
Laxton Gr. Frin 93 D2
Laxton Rd. Alres 88 A4
Laxtons The. Hawk 178 B3
Layer Breton Hill. Lay Br 84 A1
Layer Rd. Colch 67 E2
Layer Rd. Gt Wig 102 C3
Layer Rd. Lang 85 F2
Layer Rd. Lay H 85 D4
Layer Rd. Stanw 85 D4
Layzell Croft. Sud 13 E2
Le Cateau Rd. Colch 67 F3
Lea Cl. Brain 60 B1
Lea Gr. Hat Pev 114 C1
Lea La. Gt Brx 98 C1
Lea Rd. S Ben 187 E3
Leach Cl. Gt Bad 141 D4
Leam Cl. Colch 68 C4
Leamington Rd. Hock 177 F4
Leamington Rd. South 200 B4
Leapingwell Cl. Sprin 128 A2
Leas Cl. South 199 D4
Lime Ave. Colch 68 B4

Leas Gdns. South 199 D4
Leas Rd. Clact 109 E1
Leas Rd. Colch 67 E1
Leas The. Burn 170 B3
Leas The. Frin 94 A3
Leas The. South 199 E4
Leaside. Thund 187 D3
Leasway The. South 199 D4
Leasway. Rayl 176 B1
Leasway. Wick 174 A3
Leather La. Brain 59 F2
Leather La. Gt Y 9 D1
Leather La. South 200 A4
Lede Rd. Canv 197 D2
Lee Rd. Basil 186 C3
Lee Lotts. Gt Wak 193 D2
Lee Rd. Harw 40 B2
Lee Wick La. St O 107 E1
Lee Woottens La. Basil 185 D2
Leech's La. Colch 49 E2
Leecon Way. Hawk 178 B2
Leeward Rd. S Woo F 165 F3
Leeway The. Dan 142 C4
Legerton Cotts. Wa Col 28 B1
Legg St. Chelm 127 D2
Leicester Ave. Roch 190 C4
Leicester Cl. Clact 108 C1
Leicester Cl. Colch 68 A4
Leicester Ct. Silv E 79 E2
Leige Ave. Canv 197 D3
Leigh Beck La. Canv 197 F1
Leigh Beck Rd. Canv 197 F2
Leigh Cliff Rd. South 198 C4
Leigh Dr. Wic Bis 115 E3
Leigh Fells. Basil 186 B3
Leigh Gdns. Hadl 189 E1
Leigh Hall Rd. South 189 F1
Leigh Hill Cl. South 198 C4
Leigh Hill. South 198 B4
Leigh Hts. Hadl 188 C2
Leigh Park Cl. South 189 E1
Leigh Park Rd. South 198 B4
Leigh Rd. Canv 197 D1
Leigh Rd. South 190 A1
Leigh View Dr. South 189 E1
Leigham Court Dr. South 189 F1
Leighams Rd. E Han 153 F4
Leighcroft Gdns. South 189 E2
Leighfields Ave. South 189 E3
Leighfields Rd. South 189 E3
Leighfields. Thund 188 A3
Leighlands Rd. S Woo F 165 E4
Leighton Ave. South 189 F1
Leighton Rd. Thund 187 E4
Leighville Gr. South 189 E1
Leighwood Ave. South 189 F3
Leitrim Ave. South 201 E3
Lekoe Rd. Canv 196 C3
Lenham Way. Basil 186 B3
Leon Dr. Basil 185 E2
Leonard Dr. Rayl 176 A2
Leonard Mews. Brain 78 A4
Leonard Rd. Basil 185 D1
Leonard Rd. South 199 E4
Les Bois. Lay H 85 D3
Leslie Cl. South 189 E3
Leslie Dr. South 189 E3
Leslie Gdns. Rayl 176 C1
Leslie Park. Burn 170 B2
Leslie Rd. Rayl 176 C1
Lesney Gdns. Hawk 178 B2
Lethe Grove. Colch 85 F4
Lettons Chase. S Woo F 165 E3
Letzen Rd. Canv 197 D2
Levens Way. Bl Not 77 E3
Lever La. Roch 178 C1
Lewes Rd. South 191 E2
Lewes Way. Thund 188 A4
Lewis Dr. Chelm 140 A3
Lexden Ct. Colch 67 E4
Lexden Gr. Colch 66 C4
Lexden Rd. Colch 67 E3
Lexden Rd. W Berg 48 B2
Ley Field. Mks T 64 C2
Ley The. Brain 60 B1
Leybourne Dr. Sprin 127 F4
Leys Dr. Lit Cla 91 E1
Leys Rd. Wiv 69 E2
Leys The. Basil 185 E2
Leys The. Sprin 127 F3
Leyton Ct. Clact 109 F4
Leywood Cl. Brain 60 B1
Licac Ct. Wiv 69 D1
Lichfield Cl. Chelm 126 C2
Lichfield Cl. Colch 68 A4
Lichfields The. Basil 185 F4
Lifchild Cl. With 115 D4
Lifstan Way. South 200 C4
Lilac Ave. Canv 197 D3
Lilac Ave. Wick 174 B4
Lilac Cl. Chelm 140 B3
Lilian Rd. Burn 170 B3
Lilies The. Brain 42 A1
Lilley's La. Gt Bro 52 B2
Lillies The. Brain 42 A1
Lillyville Wlk. Rayl 177 D1
Lily Cl. Sprin 127 F3
Limbourne Dr. Mald 132 B3
Limburg Rd. Canv 196 B2
Lime Ave. Colch 68 B4

Lime Ave. Hadl 189 E1
Lime Ave. Harw 40 A2
Lime Cl. Clact 109 E2
Lime Cl. With 98 A3
Lime Gr. Sud 12 B3
Lime Rd. S Ben 187 F2
Lime St. Brigh 106 C3
Lime Way. Burn 170 A3
Lime Wlk. Chelm 140 B3
Limebrook Way. Mald 144 C4
Limes The. Chelm 140 A1
Limes The. Gos 42 C4
Limes The. L Mel 7 E4
Limes The. Rayl 176 C1
Limetree Ave. S Ben 187 D2
Limetree Rd. Canv 197 F2
Lincoln Ave. Clact 124 B3
Lincoln Chase. South 191 F2
Lincoln La. Gt Hor 31 E1
Lincoln Rd. Basil 185 E4
Lincoln Rd. Hawk 178 A3
Lincoln Way. Canv 196 C2
Lincoln Way. Colch 68 A4
Lincoln Way. Rayl 176 B3
Linde Rd. Canv 197 D2
Linden Cl. Chelm 185 B4
Linden Cl. Colch 50 C1
Linden Cl. Lawf 35 D2
Linden Cl. Rayl 176 C1
Linden Dr. Clact 109 E4
Linden Leas. Thund 187 E3
Linden Rd. Thund 187 E3
Linden Way. Canv 196 C2
Lindens The. Brain 60 A1
Lindford Dr. Basil 185 F3
Lindisfarne Ave. South 190 A1
Lindisfarne Ct. Mald 144 C4
Lindon Rd. Runw 163 E2
Lindsell Green. Basil 185 F3
Lindsell La. Basil 185 F3
Lindsey Ave. Sud 13 D3
Lindsey Rd. Gt Wak 193 D2
Lingcroft. Basil 185 D2
Lingfield Dr. Roch 179 D3
Lingwood Cl. Dan 142 C4
Link Cl. Colch 49 F2
Link Rd. Brigh 107 D3
Link Rd. Canv 196 C2
Link Rd. Clact 109 E1
Link Rd. Hals 43 E4
Link Rd. Rayl 176 B2
Links Dr. Chelm 139 F4
Links Rd. Bradw 79 E4
Links Way. Hadl 188 C2
Linksway. Hadl 189 E3
Linkway. Basil 185 D3
Linley Gdns. Clact 109 E1
Linne Rd. Canv 197 E3
Linnet Cl. South 201 F4
Linnet Dr. Chelm 140 A3
Linnet Dr. S Ben 187 E1
Linnet Way. Gt Ben 89 E4
Linnets. Basil 185 D2
Linnets. Clact 109 F3
Linroping Ave. Canv 197 E2
Linstead Cl. Clact 109 D2
Lion Rd. Glems 2 A3
Lion Wlk. Colch 67 F4
Lionel Hurst Cl. Sud 13 E3
Lionel Rd. Canv 197 D2
Lionfield Terr. Sprin 127 E2
Lisle Rd. Colch 68 A3
Lister Rd. Brain 77 F4
Liston La. Fox 7 D4
Liston La. L Mel 7 E4
Listonhall Chase. Si Hed 24 A3
Litchfield Cl. Clact 109 F3
Litchfield. Harw 39 F1
Littell Tweed. Sprin 128 A2
Little and Great Sir Hughes La.
  W Han 141 D1
Little Baddow Rd. Dan 142 C4
Little Baddow Rd. Woo Wa . 130 B2
Little Bakers. Walt 94 A4
Little Bentley Rd. Tend 54 A1
Little Bentley. Basil 185 D4
Little Braxted La. With 98 B2
Little Bromley Rd. Ard 52 A4
Little Bromley Rd. Gt Bro 52 C2
Little Bromley Rd. Lit Ben 53 F1
Little Charlton. Basil 186 B3
Little Chittock. Basil 185 F3
Little Church St. Harw 40 B3
Little Clacton Rd. Frin 92 C1
Little Clacton Rd. Lit Cla 109 D4
Little Dorrit. Chelm 126 C4
Little Fields. Dan 143 D4
Little Fretches. South 189 F2
Little Garth. Basil 186 A3
Little Gypps Cl. Canv 196 C2
Little Gypps Rd. Canv 196 C2
Little Harrods. Walt 94 B4
Little Hayes Chase. Stow 155 E1
Little Hays. South 189 D3
Little Horkesley Rd. Worm ... 30 A2
Little Hyde Cl. Gt Y 9 D1
Little Hyde Rd. Gt Y 9 D1
Little London La. Woo Wa ... 130 B2

Little Meadow. Writ 126 A1
Little Nell. Chelm 126 C4
Little Oaks. Basil 185 D3
Little Searles. Basil 186 A4
Little Spenders. Basil 185 E2
Little Sq. Brain 59 F2
Little St Mary's. L Mel 7 E4
Little Stambridge Hall Rd.
  Gt Stam..........................179 E2
Little Stile. Writ 139 D4
Little Tey Rd. Fee 81 F3
Little Thorpe. South 192 A1
Little Totham Rd. Gold 117 E1
Little Totham Rd. Lit Tot 117 E1
Little Wakering Hall La. Gt Wak193D2
Little Wakering Rd. Barl 192 C3
Little Wheatley Chase. Rayl .. 176 A2
Little Wood. Walt 93 F3
Little Yeldham Rd. Lit Y 9 E2
Littlebury Ct. Basil 186 A4
Littlebury Gdns. Colch 68 B2
Littlebury Green. Basil 186 A4
Littlecotes. Colch 49 E2
Littlecroft. S Woo F 165 E3
Littlefield Rd. Colch 67 E1
Littlethorpe. Basil 185 F2
Llewellyn Cl. Sprin 127 E2
Lloyd Rd. Sho G 40 A4
Lloyd Wise Cl. South 191 E2
Loamy Hill Rd. Toll M 117 D4
Lobelia Cl. Bore 128 A3
Locarno Ave. Runw 163 F1
Lock Rd. Hals 43 F4
Lockhart Ave. Colch 67 E4
Lockram La. With 97 F1
Lockram La. With 98 A1
Locks Hill. Roch 178 C1
Lodge Ave. Gt Bad 140 C4
Lodge Cl. Clact 109 F2
Lodge Cl. Lit Oak 57 E4
Lodge Cl. Rayl 176 C1
Lodge Cl. Thund 188 A3
Lodge Cres. Bore 128 C4
Lodge Ct. W Berg 48 C2
Lodge Farm Cl. South 189 E3
Lodge Farm La. St O 108 B2
Lodge La. Glems 2 B2
Lodge La. Ard 51 D3
Lodge La. Ard 51 E3
Lodge La. Brigh 106 C4
Lodge La. Lang 86 B1
Lodge La. Langh 50 B4
Lodge La. Peld 103 E4
Lodge La. Purl 144 B1
Lodge La. Tend 72 C3
Lodge Rd. Brain 59 F1
Lodge Rd. Haze 144 A3
Lodge Rd. Lit Cla 92 A2
Lodge Rd. Lit Oak 57 E4
Lodge Rd. Mald 131 F2
Lodge Rd. Mess 82 B2
Lodge Rd. S Woo F 153 F3
Lodge Rd. Writ 139 D4
Lodgelands Cl. Rayl 176 C1
Lodwick. South 201 E4
Loftin Way. Gt Bad 140 B4
Lombardy Cl. Basil 186 B3
Lombardy Pl. Chelm 127 D2
London Hill. Chelm 139 F1
London Hill. Rayl 176 B2
London Land Cotts. Worm 29 F2
London Rd. Basil 185 E2
London Rd. Basil 187 D3
London Rd. Bl Not 77 E3
London Rd. Brain 59 F1
London Rd. Chelm 139 F4
London Rd. Clact 109 F4
London Rd. Copf 65 E2
London Rd. Fee 81 F2
London Rd. Gt Hor 30 C2
London Rd. Gt Le 77 E3
London Rd. Hadl 189 E1
London Rd. Kelv 81 D1
London Rd. Mald 131 E2
London Rd. Mks T 64 C1
London Rd. Rayl 176 A2
London Rd. South 190 B1
London Rd. Stanw 66 C4
London Rd. Thund 187 D3
London Rd. Wick 174 A4
London Rd. Wick 174 A4
London Rd. Wick 175 E3
Long Acres. Fee 81 F3
Long Brandocks. Writ 126 A1
Long Green. T Gr 78 C4
Long La. Frin 93 D2
Long La. Hull 165 F1
Long Meadow Dr. Wick 174 A4
Long Meadows. Harw 39 F1
Long Melford By-Ps. L Mel 7 F3
Long Pastures. Glems 2 B2
Long Rd W. Ded 33 F2
Long Rd. Canv 196 C2
Long Rd. Lawf 35 D2
Long Rd. Mist 35 D2
Long Riding. Basil 185 E3
Long Wyre St. Colch 67 F4
Longacre. Basil 185 E4

Longacre. Chelm 139 E4
Longacres Rd. T Gr 78 C3
Longacres. Brain 60 A1
Longbarn Hill. Brad 37 D1
Longborough Cl. Basil 174 A1
Longcroft Rd. Colch 68 B4
Longfellow Rd. Mald 132 A1
Longfield Cl. Wick 175 D4
Longfield Rd. Gt Bad 140 C4
Longfield Rd. S Woo F 165 E4
Longfield Rd. Wick 175 D4
Longfield. With 97 F3
Longfields. St O 108 A2
Longhams Dr. S Woo F 165 E4
Longleaf Dr. Brain 77 F4
Longleat Cl. Chelm 126 C4
Longmead Ave. Gt Bad 140 C4
Longmeads Cl. Writ 126 A1
Longmeads. Wic Bis 115 F3
Longmore Ave. Gt Bad 140 C4
Longridge. Colch 68 C4
Longsands. South 201 E4
Longship Way. Mald 144 C4
Longstomps Ave. Chelm 140 A4
Lonsdale Rd. South 191 E1
Lord Holland Rd. Colch 67 F2
Lord Roberts Ave. South 189 F1
Lordship Rd. Writ 126 A1
Lordswood Rd. Colch 67 E1
Lorien Gdns. S Woo F 165 E3
Lorkin's La. Twin 18 B2
Lornes Cl. South 191 E2
Loten Rd. S Ben 187 D1
Lott's La. Brad 54 B4
Lott's Rd. Clact 91 D2
Lottem Rd. Canv 197 E1
Lotts Yd. Colch 68 A3
Louis Dr E. Rayl 176 A2
Louis Dr W. Rayl 176 A2
Louisa Ave. Thund 187 D3
Louisa Cl. Walt 76 C2
Louise Rd. Rayl 176 C1
Louvaine Ave. Wick 174 A4
Love La. Brigh 106 C4
Love La. Rayl 176 B1
Love Way. Clact 109 E3
Lovelace Ave. South 200 B4
Lovelace Gdns. South 191 E1
Lovell Rise. South 190 A3
Lovens Cl. Canv 197 E1
Lover's La. Gt Ben 90 A4
Loves Wlk. Gt Bad 140 C4
Loves Wlk. Writ 139 D4
Lovibond Pl. Sprin 127 F2
Low Rd. Harw 39 F1
Low Rd. South 201 F3
Low St. Glems 2 B3
Lowe Chase. Walt 94 A4
Lowefields. Ea Col 45 E3
Lower Anchor St. Chelm 127 D1
Lower Ave. Basil 186 C4
Lower Burnham Rd. Purl 156 B1
Lower Chase. Alth 157 F2
Lower Church Rd. Thund 187 D3
Lower Farm Rd. Box 21 D1
Lower Green. Chelm 140 B1
Lower Green. Wa Col 28 B1
Lower Harlings. Sho G 40 A4
Lower Holt St. Ea Col 45 E3
Lower Lambricks. Rayl 176 B2
Lower Langley. Gt T 46 B1
Lower Marine Par. Harw 40 B1
Lower Park Rd. Brigh 106 C4
Lower Park Rd. Wick 174 B2
Lower Rd. Ashi 166 B1
Lower Rd. Ashi 167 D1
Lower Rd. Birch 84 A3
Lower Rd. Fox 7 D2
Lower Rd. Hull 166 B1
Lower Rd. Lay Br 102 A4
Lower Rd. M Bure 29 D3
Lower Rd. Peld 103 E3
Lower Southend Rd. Wick 174 B4
Lower St. Cav 1 B1
Lower St. Glems 2 C3
Lower St. Str S M 33 E4
Loxford. Basil 186 A4
Luard Way. Birch 84 A2
Luard Way. With 97 F1
Lubbards Cl. Rayl 176 B3
Lucas Ave. Chelm 140 B3
Lucas Ave. Ford 47 E3
Lucas Rd. Colch 67 F3
Lucas Rd. Sud 12 C4
Lucas's La. Beau 73 E3
Lucerne Dr. Wick 175 D4
Lucerne Rd. Elmst M 70 A3
Lucerne Wlk. Wick 175 D4
Luces La. Ca Hed 15 F2
Lucksfield Way. Gt Bad 140 C3
Lucy Cl. Stanw 66 B3
Lucy La N. Stanw 66 A4
Lucy La S. Stanw 66 B4
Lucy Rd. South 200 A4
Ludgores La. Dan 142 B3
Ludgrove. Latch 157 D3
Ludham Hall La. Bl Not 77 D4
Luff Way. Walt 93 F4
Lufkin Rd. Colch 49 F2

Lugar Cl. Colch 68 C3
Luker Rd. South 200 A4
Lumber Leys. Walt 94 A4
Luncies Rd. Basil 185 F3
Lundy Cl. South 190 A3
Lunnish Hill. Rams 38 C1
Lupin Dr. Sprin 127 F3
Lupin Mews. Sprin 127 F3
Lupin Way. Clact 109 E2
Lushington Ave. Walt 93 F3
Lushington Rd. Lawf 35 E2
Lutus Cl. Cla 4 A3
Lydford Rd. South 199 F4
Lydgate Cl. Lawf 35 D2
Lydia Dr. St O 107 D1
Lylt Rd. Canv 197 D2
Lyme Rd. South 191 E1
Lymington Ave. Clact 110 A4
Lymington Ave. South 189 F1
Lympstone Cl. South 190 A3
Lyndale Ave. South 191 D1
Lyndene. Thund 187 D3
Lyndhurst Dr. S Woo F 142 C1
Lyndhurst Rd. Ashi 167 E1
Lyndhurst Rd. Clact 110 B2
Lynfords Ave. Runw 164 A2
Lynfords Dr. Runw 163 F1
Lynfords Dr. Runw 164 A2
Lynmouth Ave. Chelm 140 B4
Lynmouth Gdns. Chelm 127 E1
Lynn View Cl. S Ben 187 E3
Lynne Cl. Walt 93 E3
Lynstede. Basil 186 A3
Lynton Cl. Harw 40 A2
Lynton Dr. Sprin 127 F3
Lynton Rd. S Ben 188 B2
Lynwood Green. Rayl 189 D4
Lyon Cl. Chelm 140 A2
Lyon Cl. Clact 110 A2
Lyons Hall Rd. Brain 60 B4
Lyster Ave. Gt Bad 141 D4
Lyth Ave. South 201 E4

Macbeth Cl. Colch 68 C4
Macdonald Ave. South 190 C1
Macintyres Wlk. Hawk 178 B3
Mackay Ct. Colch 68 A1
Maclarens. Gt Tot 116 A3
Macmurdo Cl. South 189 E4
Macmurdo Rd. South 189 E4
Madeira Ave. South 189 F1
Madeira Rd. Clact 110 B2
Madeline Pl. Chelm 126 C3
Madgements Rd. Stis 61 D4
Madrid Ave. Rayl 176 A4
Magazine Farm Way. Colch 67 D3
Magazine Rd. South 201 F3
Magdalen Cl. Clact 109 F2
Magdalen Rd. Clact 109 F2
Magdalen St. Colch 68 A3
Magdalene Cres. Silv E 79 E2
Magna Mead. Barl 192 B4
Magnolia Cl. Chelm 140 A3
Magnolia Dr. Colch 68 C4
Magnolia Rd. Hawk 178 A3
Magnolia Way. Roch 191 D4
Magwitch Cl. Chelm 126 C4
Maidenburgh St. Colch 67 F4
Maidment Cres. With 114 C4
Main Rd. Alth 157 F2
Main Rd. Bore 128 B4
Main Rd. Dun 142 B4
Main Rd. E Han 153 E3
Main Rd. Frat 70 C2
Main Rd. Frin 93 D2
Main Rd. Harw 40 A2
Main Rd. Harw 40 C3
Main Rd. Hawk 177 F2
Main Rd. Hock 177 E3
Main Rd. Rams 39 D1
Main Rd. Rett 164 A3
Main Rd. S Woo F 154 A3
Main Rd. St L 148 B4
Main Rd. Worm 29 F2
Maine Cres. Rayl 176 A2
Maitland Pl. South 192 C1
Makins Rd. Rams 39 F3
Malard Cl. Tolle 119 E1
Maldon Ct. Sud 13 D4
Maldon Rd. Birch 83 F2
Maldon Rd. Brad O S 149 E4
Maldon Rd. Burn 169 F4
Maldon Rd. Colch 67 E3
Maldon Rd. Dan 143 D3
Maldon Rd. Dan 143 D4
Maldon Rd. Gold 133 E3
Maldon Rd. Gt Bad 141 E4
Maldon Rd. Gt Brx 99 F1
Maldon Rd. Gt Tot 116 A2
Maldon Rd. Gt Wig 102 C1
Maldon Rd. Hat Pev 114 B1
Maldon Rd. Kelv 81 E1
Maldon Rd. Langf 131 E3
Maldon Rd. Latch 156 C3
Maldon Rd. Marg 139 E1
Maldon Rd. Sand 141 E4
Maldon Rd. South 191 D1
Maldon Rd. Stanw 66 B1

Maldon Rd. Steep 147 E1
Maldon Rd. Tipt 100 B2
Maldon Rd. Toll D 118 B1
Maldon Rd. Toll M 118 B1
Maldon Rd. With 115 D4
Maldon Rd. Woo Mor 144 A4
Maldon Way. Clact 109 D2
Malgraves Pl. Basil 186 A4
Malgraves. Basil 186 A4
Mallard Cl. Kelv 81 E2
Mallard Cl. Lay H 85 D3
Mallard Rd. Chelm 140 A3
Mallard Way. Sud 13 E3
Mallards. May 158 A4
Mallards. South 192 C1
Mallow Field. Hals 25 F1
Malmsmead. South 201 E4
Malrose Rd. Chelm 127 D2
Malthouse Rd. Mann 35 E2
Malting Green Rd. Lay H 85 D3
Malting La. Cla 4 A4
Malting La. Walt 75 E1
Malting Rd. Colch 67 E1
Malting Rd. Peld 103 F3
Malting Villas Rd. Roch 178 C1
Malting Wlk. Wiv 87 D4
Maltings Cl. Bures 19 F1
Maltings Ct. With 114 C4
Maltings La. With 114 C4
Maltings Rd. Brigh 88 C1
Maltings Rd. Gt Bad 141 D3
Maltings Rd. Rett 164 C1
Maltings The. Ray 59 D1
Maltings The. Soum 159 F2
Malvern Ave. Canv 196 B2
Malvern Cl. Chelm 126 B3
Malvern Cl. Rayl 176 B2
Malvern Rd. Hock 177 F4
Malvern Way. Gt Hor 49 D4
Malwood Dr. S Ben 187 D3
Malwood Rd. S Ben 187 D3
Malyon Court Cl. S Ben 188 A2
Malyon Rd. With 114 C4
Malyons Cl. Basil 186 A4
Malyons La. Hull 165 E1
Malyons Mews. Basil 186 A4
Malyons Pl. Basil 186 A4
Malyons The. S Ben 188 A2
Malyons. Basil 186 A4
Manchester Dr. South 189 E1
Manchester Dr. South 189 F1
Manchester Rd. Clact 110 C3
Mandeville Rd. Mks T 64 C2
Mandeville Way. Thund 187 E4
Mandeville Way. Walt 93 F3
Manfield Gdns. St O 108 A3
Manfield. Hals 25 F1
Mangapp Chase. Burn 170 A4
Manilla Rd. South 200 B4
Mannering Gdns. South 190 A2
Manners Way. South 190 C3
Manningtree Rd. Ded 34 A3
Manningtree Rd. Lit Ben 71 F4
Manningtree Rd. Str S M 35 D4
Manns Way. Rayl 176 B3
Manor Ave. Basil 186 B3
Manor Cl. Cav 1 B1
Manor Cl. Gt Hor 49 E4
Manor Cl. Rayl 188 B4
Manor Dr. Gt Bad 140 C4
Manor House Way. Brigh 106 C4
Manor La. Harw 40 A1
Manor Rd. Chelm 127 E1
Manor Rd. Colch 67 F4
Manor Rd. Deng 149 E1
Manor Rd. Frin 93 D2
Manor Rd. Harw 40 A2
Manor Rd. Hat Pev 114 B1
Manor Rd. Hock 177 E3
Manor Rd. S Woo F 165 E4
Manor Rd. South 199 E4
Manor Rd. Sud 7 F1
Manor Rd. Thund 187 E3
Manor Rd. W Berg 48 C3
Manor Rd. Wiv 69 E1
Manor St. Brain 59 F2
Manor Way. Clact 111 D3
Manors Way. Silv E 79 E2
Manse Chase. Mald 132 A1
Mansel Cl. South 189 F3
Mansted Gdns. Hawk 178 B3
Maple Ave. Brain 59 E1
Maple Ave. Mald 132 B3
Maple Ave. South 198 C4
Maple Cl. Clact 109 E2
Maple Cl. Hals 26 A1
Maple Cl. Harw 40 A2
Maple Cl. Chelm 140 A3
Maple Dr. Rayl 176 B4
Maple Dr. Walt 93 E3
Maple Dr. With 98 A3
Maple Leaf. Tipt 100 B4
Maple Rd. Sud 13 D3
Maple Sq. South 191 D1
Maple Way. Burn 170 A3
Maple Way. Canv 196 C2

Maple Way. Colch 68 A2
Mapledene Ave. Hull 165 F1
Mapleford Sweep. Basil 185 E2
Mapleleaf Cl. Hock 177 F4
Mapleleaf Gdns. Wick 174 A3
Maples The. Wick 174 B3
Maplesfield. Hadl 188 B2
Maplestead. Basil 185 E4
Maplin Cl. Thund 187 E4
Maplin Gdns. Basil 185 F3
Maplin Way N. South 192 B1
Maplin Way. South 201 E3
Marasca End. Rowh 86 A4
Maraschino Cres. Rowh 86 A4
Marconi Rd. Chelm 127 D1
Marcos Rd. Canv 197 E2
Marcus Ave. South 201 D4
Marcus Chase. South 201 D4
Marcus Gdns. South 201 D4
Marennes Cres. Brigh 106 C4
Mareth Rd. Colch 67 E1
Margaret Cl. Brigh 106 C3
Margaret Rd. Colch 67 F4
Margaretting Rd. Chelm 139 F1
Margaretting Rd. Writ 139 D1
Margarite Way. Wick 174 A4
Margraten Ave. Canv 197 E1
Marguerite Dr. South 189 F1
Maria St. Harw 40 B3
Marigold Ave. Clact 109 E3
Marigold Cl. Colch 68 C4
Marigold Cl. Sprin 127 F3
Marina Ave. Rayl 176 B2
Marina Cl. South 190 C2
Marina Gdns. Clact 110 B3
Marina Mews. Walt 94 B3
Marina Rd. Hat Pev 114 A2
Marine App. Canv 197 D1
Marine Ave. Canv 197 E1
Marine Ave. South 199 E4
Marine Cl. Hadl 188 D1
Marine Par E. Clact 110 A2
Marine Par W. Clact 109 F1
Marine Par. Canv 197 F1
Marine Par. Hadl 198 B4
Marine Par. Harw 40 B2
Marine Par. May 146 C1
Marine Par. South 200 A4
Mariners Ct. Gt Wak 193 E2
Mariners Way. Mald 145 D4
Marion Ave. Clact 109 F3
Mariskals. Basil 186 A3
Mark Rd. Till 149 F3
Market End. Cogg 62 C1
Market Hill. Cla 4 A4
Market Hill. Cogg 63 D2
Market Hill. Hals 25 F1
Market Hill. Mald 132 A2
Market Hill. Sud 12 C4
Market Pavement. Basil 185 D4
Market Pl. Brain 59 F2
Market Pl. Mald 131 F1
Market Pl. South 200 A4
Market Rd. Chelm 127 D1
Market Rd. Wick 174 A4
Market Sq. Basil 185 D3
Market Sq. S Woo F 165 E4
Market St. Brain 59 F2
Market St. Harw 40 C3
Markland Cl. Chelm 140 B2
Marklay Dr. S Woo F 165 E4
Marks Gdns. Brain 60 B1
Marks Hall Rd. Cogg 62 C3
Marks La. Rett 163 F4
Marland Dr. Mald 131 F1
Marlborough Ave. Till 149 E4
Marlborough Cl. Clact 109 E2
Marlborough Cl. Thund 187 E4
Marlborough Dr. Sud 12 C4
Marlborough Rd. Brain 60 A2
Marlborough Rd. Chelm 127 D1
Marlborough Rd. South 200 B4
Marlborough Wlk. Hock 177 E3
Marlin Cl. Hadl 188 C3
Marlow Gdns. South 190 C2
Marlowe Cl. Brain 78 A4
Marlowe Cl. Mald 145 D4
Marlowe Rd. Clact 109 D1
Marlowe Way. Colch 66 C3
Marlpits Rd. Purl 143 F2
Marmaduke Ave. Rayl 176 A2
Marne Rd. Colch 67 F2
Marney Cl. Gt Bad 140 C4
Marney Dr. Basil 185 F3
Marney Way. Frin 94 A3
Marram Cl. Colch 66 A3
Marsh Cres. Rown 87 D4
Marsh Farm La. Thor 89 E1
Marsh Farm Rd. S Woo F 165 E3
Marsh Rd. Burn 171 E3
Marsh Rd. High 21 F3
Marsh Rd. South 201 F3
Marsh Rd. Till 150 A2
Marsh Way. Brigh 106 C3
Marshall Cl. Fee 81 E2
Marshall Cl. Hadl 189 D2
Marshalls Cl. Rayl 176 C1

Marshalls Rd. Brain

Marshalls Rd. Brain 59 F1
Marshalls. Hawk 178 B2
Marston Beck. Sprin 128 A1
Martello Rd. Walt 94 B4
Marten's La. Nay 20 C4
Martin End. Lay H 85 D3
Martin Mews. S Ben 187 E2
Martin Mews. S Woo F 165 F4
Martin Wlk. Hawk 177 F2
Martin's Rd. Hals 25 F1
Martingale Dr. Sprin 127 F4
Martingale. Thund 188 A3
Martinsdale. Clact 109 F3
Martock Ave. South 190 A3
Martyns Gr. South 190 A1
Martyns Rise. L Mel 7 E3
Marvens. Chelm 140 B2
Maryborough Gr. Colch 68 A1
Marylands Ave. Hock 177 E4
Mascalls The. Gt Bad 140 C4
Mascalls Way. Gt Bad 140 C4
Masefield Dr. Colch 66 C3
Masefield Rd. Basil 78 A4
Masefield Rd. Mald 145 D4
Mashey Rd. Lit Y 9 E3
Mason Cl. Colch 67 D2
Mason Rd. Clact 109 D2
Mason Rd. Colch 49 F1
Matching Green. Basil 185 E4
Matfield Cl. Sprin 127 E4
Mathews Cl. Str S M 22 B1
Matlock Rd. Canv 196 C2
Matthews Cl. Hals 26 A2
Maugham Cl. Wick 174 A3
Maurice Rd. Canv 197 E2
May Ave. Canv 197 E1
May Ave. Canv 197 E2
May Wlk. Chelm 140 C4
May's La. Ded 33 F2
Mayberry Wlk. Colch 68 A2
Maybury Cl. Mks T 64 C2
Mayda Cl. Hals 25 E1
Maydells. Basil 186 A3
Maydene. S Woo F 165 E4
Mayes La. Dan 142 C4
Mayes La. Lit Oak 39 E1
Mayes La. Sand 141 F3
Mayfair Ave. Basil 186 B4
Mayfield Ave. Hull 165 F1
Mayfield Ave. South 190 C2
Mayfield Cl. Colch 50 B1
Mayfield Rd. Writ 126 A1
Mayflower Ave. Harw 40 C3
Mayflower Cl. South 190 A3
Mayflowers. Thund 187 D4
Mayford Way. Clact 109 D3
Mayland Ave. Canv 197 D1
Mayland Cl. Mald 132 B2
Mayland Cl. May 158 A4
Mayland Green. May 158 A4
Mayland Hill. May 158 B3
Mayland Rd. With 98 A1
Maylands Dr. Bl Not 77 E4
Mayling Rd. Brain 59 E1
Mayne Crest. Sprin 127 F3
Mayors Wlk. Colch 67 F4
Maypole Dr. St O 108 A2
Maypole Green Rd. Colch 67 E1
Maypole Rd. Gt Tot 131 F4
Maypole Rd. Tipt 100 B4
Maysent Ave. Brain 59 F3
Maytree Wlk. Thund 187 E3
Maze The. South 189 E4
McCalmont Dr. Rayl 176 B4
McDivitt Wlk. South 190 A3
Mead Pastures. Woo Wa 130 B2
Mead Path. Chelm 139 F4
Mead The. Sud 13 D2
Meadgate Ave. Gt Bad 140 C4
Meadgate. Basil 186 B4
Meadow Cl. Clact 110 A4
Meadow Cl. Gt Bro 71 D3
Meadow Cl. Hals 43 F4
Meadow Cl. Pan 59 D4
Meadow Cl. Wick 174 C4
Meadow Dr. South 200 C4
Meadow Grass Cl. Colch 66 A3
Meadow La. Runw 163 F2
Meadow La. Sud 12 C4
Meadow La. W Mers 121 E3
Meadow Mews. S Woo F 165 D4
Meadow Rd. Colch 67 E1
Meadow Rd. Hadl 188 C1
Meadow Rd. Hull 165 F1
Meadow Rd. Rett 164 B3
Meadow Side. Chelm 127 D2
Meadow View Cl. Colch 66 C3
Meadow View Rd. Sud 12 B3
Meadow View Wlk. Canv 196 C2
Meadow Way. Bl Not 78 B3
Meadow Way. Clact 125 D4
Meadow Way. Hock 177 F3
Meadow Way. Lang 86 A1
Meadow Way. Latch 157 D3
Meadow Way. Wick 174 B2
Meadowclose. Thund 188 A3

Meadowcroft Way. Walt 93 F4
Meadowland Rd. Wick 175 D3
Meadowside. Brain 59 F3
Meadowside. Chelm 127 E2
Meadowside. Rayl 176 B1
Meads The. Basil 186 A2
Meadway The. South 199 D4
Meadway. Canv 197 E1
Meadway. Gos 42 C4
Meadway. Lawf 35 D2
Meadway. Mald 132 A1
Meadway. Rayl 176 C1
Meadway. Thund 187 E4
Meakins Cl. South 189 F4
Mearns Pl. Sprin 127 F2
Mede Way. Wiv 69 E2
Medlar Cl. With 98 A2
Medoc Cl. Basil 186 B4
Medway Ave. With 97 E1
Medway Cl. Chelm 126 B2
Medway Cres. Hadl 189 D1
Medway. Burn 170 A3
Meekings Rd. Sud 13 D4
Meers The. Walt 93 F3
Meesons Mead. Hawk 178 B2
Meesons Meadows. Mald 144 C4
Meeting Field. L Mel 7 E4
Meeting La. E Mers 105 E1
Meeting La. Ridge 8 A4
Meggison Way. S Ben 187 E2
Melba St. Writ 126 B1
Melbourne Ave. Chelm 126 C3
Melbourne Chase. Colch 68 A1
Melbourne Rd. Clact 109 F2
Melcombe Rd. S Ben 187 E2
Melford Rd. Cav 1 C1
Melford Rd. Sud 7 E1
Mell Rd. Tolle 119 F1
Mellor Chase. Colch 66 C4
Melrose Gdns. Clact 110 B3
Melrose Rd. W Mers 121 E3
Melton Cl. Clact 109 D2
Melville Heath. S Woo F 165 F3
Mendip Cl. Rayl 176 C2
Mendip Cres. South 190 A2
Mendip Rd. Chelm 126 B3
Mendip Rd. South 190 A2
Mendlesham Cl. Clact 109 D2
Menin Rd. Colch 67 E2
Menish Way. Sprin 128 A2
Meon Cl. Sprin 127 E3
Meppel Ave. Canv 197 D3
Mercer Ave. Gt Wak 193 D2
Mercers Way. Colch 67 F4
Merchant St. S Woo F 165 F4
Mercia Cl. Gt Bad 141 D3
Mercury Cl. Wick 174 C4
Meredene. Basil 185 F3
Meredith Rd. Clact 109 F2
Meriadoc Dr. S Woo F 165 E3
Merilies Cl. South 190 A2
Merilies Gdns. South 190 A2
Merivale Cl. Lawf 35 E2
Merivale Rd. Lawf 35 D2
Merlin Ct. Canv 197 D2
Merlin End. Colch 50 C1
Merlin Pl. Chelm 126 C3
Merlin Way. Runw 163 E1
Merriam Cl. Catt 35 E4
Merricks La. Basil 185 F1
Merrilees Cres. Clact 110 B3
Merrivale. S Ben 187 E1
Merryfield App. South 189 F2
Merryfields Ave. Hock 177 E4
Merrymount Gdns. Clact 110 A3
Mersea Ave. W Mers 121 D3
Mersea Rd. Colch 68 A2
Mersea Rd. Peld 103 F3
Mersea Rd. Rowh 86 B3
Mersea View. St O 107 D2
Mersey Fleet Way. Brain 60 B1
Mersey Rd. With 97 F1
Mersey Way. Chelm 126 B3
Merstham Dr. Clact 109 E3
Merton Ct. Rowh 86 A4
Merton Pl. S Woo F 165 F3
Merton Rd. Hock 177 D4
Merton Rd. S Ben 187 E2
Mess Rd. South 201 F3
Messines Rd. Colch 67 E2
Meteor Rd. South 199 E4
Methersgate. Basil 185 E4
Metz Ave. Canv 197 D2
Mews Ct. Chelm 127 D1
Mews The. Frin 93 D1
Mews The. Hock 177 E3
Mey Wlk. Hock 177 E3
Meyel Ave. Canv 197 E3
Meynell Ave. Canv 197 E1
Meyrick Cres. Colch 67 F3
Micawber Way. Chelm 126 B4
Michaelstowe Cl. Harw 39 E1
Michaelstowe Dr. Harw 39 E1
Mid Colne. Basil 185 E2
Middle Crockerford. Basil 185 F2
Middle Green. Wa Col 28 B1
Middle King. Brain 60 B1
Middle Mead. Roch 178 C1
Middle Mead. Wick 174 C4

Middle Mill Rd. Colch 67 F4
Middle Way. L Mel 7 E4
Middleborough. Colch 67 F4
Middleburg Rd. Canv 196 C3
Middlefield Rd. Mist 36 A2
Middlefield. Hals 25 F1
Middlemead. S Han 152 B2
Middlemead. W Han 152 B2
Middlesex Ave. South 189 F2
Middleton Cl. Clact 109 E3
Middleton Rd. Sud 12 B3
Middleton Row. S Woo F 165 F3
Middlewick Cl. Colch 68 A1
Midguard Way. Mald 144 C4
Midhurst Ave. South 190 B2
Midland Cl. Colch 67 F2
Midsummer Meadow. South . 192 C1
Midway Rd. Colch 67 E1
Midway. Clact 124 C3
Milburn Cres. Chelm 126 B1
Mildmay Rd. Burn 170 B3
Mildmay Rd. Chelm 127 D1
Mildmays. Dan 142 B4
Mile End Rd. Colch 49 F2
Miles Cl. Stanw 66 B3
Milford Cl. Elmst M 69 E1
Military Rd. Colch 68 A3
Mill Chase. Hals 25 F1
Mill Cl. Till 149 F2
Mill Cl. Tipt 100 B3
Mill Fields. Dan 143 D3
Mill Green Ct. Basil 186 A4
Mill Green Pl. Basil 186 A4
Mill Green. Basil 186 A4
Mill Green. Burn 170 A2
Mill Hill. Brain 60 A1
Mill Hill. Chelm 139 F1
Mill Hill. Lawf 34 B2
Mill Hill. Mann 35 E2
Mill Hill. Purl 144 B1
Mill Hill. S Ben 196 C4
Mill Hill. Sud 12 B4
Mill Hill. Worm 29 F3
Mill La. Ard 52 A2
Mill La. Birch 83 F2
Mill La. Brad 36 B1
Mill La. Cav 5 D4
Mill La. Col En 45 D4
Mill La. Dan 143 D3
Mill La. Ded 33 F4
Mill La. Frin 92 C2
Mill La. Gt Le 95 D4
Mill La. Gt Map 25 F4
Mill La. Gt Stam 179 D1
Mill La. Gt Y 9 D2
Mill La. Harw 40 B2
Mill La. Lay H 85 D3
Mill La. Lit Bad 129 F2
Mill La. Mald 132 A2
Mill La. Nay 20 B4
Mill La. Peb 27 D4
Mill La. Sud 12 B4
Mill La. T Gr 78 B3
Mill La. Terl 96 A1
Mill La. Th L S 73 F1
Mill La. Toll M 117 F2
Mill La. Virl 119 D4
Mill La. Walt 94 B4
Mill La. Weel 91 D3
Mill La. With 97 F1
Mill Lane Cl. Weel 91 D3
Mill Rd. Box 31 F2
Mill Rd. Burn 170 B4
Mill Rd. Cla 4 B4
Mill Rd. Colch 49 F3
Mill Rd. Ford 47 E2
Mill Rd. Fox 6 B3
Mill Rd. Gt Tot 116 B4
Mill Rd. Mald 132 A1
Mill Rd. May 158 A4
Mill Rd. Mks T 65 E2
Mill Rd. Ridge 8 A3
Mill Rd. Till 149 F2
Mill Rd. W Mers 121 E4
Mill St. Colch 68 A3
Mill St. Nay 20 A1
Mill St. Nay 20 B4
Mill St. St O 107 F2
Mill Tye. Sud 13 D2
Mill Vue Rd. Sprin 127 F1
Mill Wlk. Tipt 100 B3
Millars Cl. S Woo F 165 F4
Millbridge Rd. With 97 F1
Miller's Barn Rd. Clact 109 D1
Millers Cl. Brain 60 A4
Millers Cl. Gt Hor 49 D4
Millers Cl. Stanw 66 B3
Millers Croft. Gt Bad 140 C3
Millers Gdns. Kelv 81 D1
Millers La. Stanw 66 B3
Millers Mead. Fee 81 F2
Millfield. Burn 170 A2
Millfields. Writ 126 A1
Milligans Chase. Chelm 140 A1
Mills La. L Mel 7 E2
Millson Bank. Sprin 128 A2
Millview Meadows. Roch 178 C1
Millways. Gt Tot 116 A2

Millwrights. Tipt 100 B3
Milner Rd. Sud 13 D4
Milton Ave. Brain 78 A4
Milton Ave. South 199 F4
Milton Cl. Colch 66 C3
Milton Cl. Rayl 177 D1
Milton Pl. Chelm 127 D3
Milton Pl. South 199 F4
Milton Rd. Harw 40 B2
Milton Rd. Lawf 35 D1
Milton Rd. Mald 145 D4
Milton Rd. South 199 E4
Milton Rd. With 97 F3
Milton St. South 191 D1
Miltsin Ave. Canv 197 E3
Mimosa Cl. Sprin 127 F3
Minden Rd. Sud 12 C4
Minerva Cl. Harw 39 F1
Minsmere Way. Sud 13 E3
Minster Cl. Rayl 177 D1
Minster Way. Mald 144 C4
Minton Hts. Hawk 178 B3
Miramar Ave. Canv 196 C2
Mistley End. Basil 185 E3
Mistley Path. Basil 185 E3
Mistley Side. Basil 185 E3
Mitchell Ave. Hals 25 F1
Mitchell Way. S Woo F 165 E4
Mitchells Ave. Canv 197 E2
Mitton Vale. Sprin 127 F1
Moat End. South 192 A1
Moat Farm Chase. With 97 F2
Moat Field. Basil 185 E4
Moat La. Alph 19 D2
Moat Rd. Ford 47 E3
Moat Rise. Rayl 176 B1
Modlen Rd. Walt 94 A4
Mollands. Basil 185 F2
Molrams La. Gt Bad 141 D3
Monk's La. Ded 33 E3
Monkdowns Rd. Cogg 63 D2
Monklands Ct. Hals 25 E1
Monks Ct. With 97 F2
Monks Lodge Rd. Gt Map 16 B2
Monks Mead. S Woo F 142 C1
Monks Rd. Ea Col 45 D4
Monksford Dr. Hull 165 E1
Monkside. Basil 185 E4
Monkwick Ave. Colch 67 F1
Mons Rd. Colch 67 E2
Montague Ave. Hadl 189 D1
Montague Pl. Canv 196 C2
Montbretia Cl. Stanw 66 B3
Montbretia Ct. Clact 109 E2
Montefiore Ave. Rayl 176 B4
Montgomery Cl. Colch 68 A2
Montgomery Ct. Sprin 127 F4
Montgomery Ct. South 192 C1
Montrose Rd. Sprin 127 F2
Montsale. Basil 186 B4
Moons Cl. Ashi 178 B4
Moor Hall La. S Woo F 142 C2
Moor Park Cl. South 189 E3
Moor Park Gdns. South 189 E3
Moor Rd. Gt T 64 A4
Moor Rd. Langh 32 B2
Moor's Farm Chase. Lit Tot . 117 D2
Moor's La. Gt Ben 71 F1
Moorcroft Ave. Hadl 188 C3
Moorcroft. Hawk 178 B3
Moores Ave. Basil 185 E1
Moorhen Ave. St L 148 B4
Moors Cl. Fee 81 F3
Moors Cl. Gt Ben 71 F1
Moorsfield. Sud 13 D2
Mooreside. Colch 68 A4
Mope La. Wic Bis 115 E3
Moran Ave. Chelm 127 E1
Morant Rd. Colch 68 A3
Morebarn Rd. Gt Bro 52 C1
Moreland Ave. Thund 187 E4
Moreland Cl. Gt Wak 193 D2
Moreland Cl. Thund 187 E3
Moreland Rd. Runw 163 E1
Morella Cl. Gt Ben 89 F4
Morello Ct. Rowh 86 A4
Moretons. Basil 186 A3
Moretons. Chelm 140 A1
Morley Rd. Hals 25 F1
Morley Rd. Tipt 100 B2
Morleys Rd. Ea Col 45 D3
Mornington Ave. Roch 179 D1
Mornington Cres. Canv 197 E2
Mornington Cres. Hadl 188 C2
Mornington Rd. Canv 197 E2
Morrins Cl. Gt Wak 193 E2
Morris Ave. Clact 124 C4
Morris Rd. Chelm 127 E1
Morrow La. Ard 52 A3
Mors End. Str S M 22 B1
Morses La. Brigh 88 C1
Morten Rd. Colch 67 F4
Mortimer Rd. Hat Pev 114 A2
Mortimer Rd. Rayl 176 C3
Morton Rd. Gt Tot 116 A2
Morton Way. Hals 26 A2
Moss Cl. Basil 185 F2
Moss Dr. Basil 185 F2
Moss Path. Chelm 140 B2

Moss Rd. Stanw 66 C2
Moss Rd. With 98 A2
Moss Way. W Berg 48 C2
Moss Wlk. Chelm 140 A3
Mossfield Cl. Colch 67 E3
Mott's La. Mks T 64 B2
Motts La. With 98 A2
Moulsham Chase. Chelm 140 B4
Moulsham Dr. Chelm 140 A4
Moulsham St. Chelm 127 D1
Moulsham Thrift. Chelm 140 A3
Mount Ave. Hock 177 E3
Mount Ave. Rayl 176 B2
Mount Ave. South 199 D4
Mount Bovers La. Hawk 177 F2
Mount Cl. Rayl 176 B1
Mount Cl. Wick 174 C4
Mount Cres. Hock 177 E3
Mount Cres. S Ben 187 F2
Mount Hill. Hals 25 E1
Mount Lodge Chase. Gt Tot . 116 B3
Mount Pleasant Est. Gt Tot .. 116 C3
Mount Pleasant Rd. S Woo F 165 E4
Mount Pleasant. Hals 25 F1
Mount Pleasant. Mald 131 F1
Mount Rd. Brain 60 A2
Mount Rd. Cogg 63 D1
Mount Rd. S Ben 187 F2
Mount Rd. Wick 174 C4
Mount Rise. Hals 25 E1
Mount The. Colch 66 C3
Mount The. Tolle 119 E1
Mount Way. Wick 174 C4
Mountain Ash Ave. South 189 D3
Mountain Ash Cl. Colch 50 B1
Mountain Ash Cl. South 189 D3
Mountains Rd. Gt Tot 116 B4
Mountbatten Cl. Sud 7 F1
Mountbatten Dr. Colch 68 A2
Mountbatten Dr. South 192 C1
Mountbatten Rd. Brain 60 B3
Mountbatten Rd. Sud 7 F1
Mountbatten Way. Sprin 127 F4
Mountdale Gdns. South 189 F2
Mountfields. Basil 186 B2
Mounthill Ave. Sprin 127 E2
Mountnessing. Hadl 188 B1
Mountview Cres. St L 148 B4
Mountview Rd. Clact 110 A3
Moverons La. Brigh 88 B1
Mowden Hall La. Hat Pev 113 F1
Moy Rd. Colch 68 A1
Mucking Hall Rd. Barl 192 B4
Muirway. Thund 187 D4
Mulberry Ave. Colch 68 A2
Mulberry Gdns. With 98 A2
Mulberry Rd. Canv 196 B2
Mulberry Way. Sprin 127 E3
Mullins Rd. Brain 59 F3
Mumford Cl. W Berg 48 C2
Mumford Rd. W Berg 48 B2
Mundon Rd. Brain 60 B1
Mundon Rd. Mald 145 E4
Munnings Dr. Clact 109 E3
Munnings Rd. Colch 67 D3
Munnings Way. Lawf 35 D3
Munro Rd. With 97 F3
Munsons Alley. Soum 159 E2
Munsterburg Rd. Canv 197 E3
Murchison Cl. Chelm 126 C3
Murray Cl. Brain 59 F3
Murrell Lock. Sprin 128 A2
Murrels La. Hock 177 D4
Muscade Cl. Tipt 100 B3
Museum St. Colch 67 F4
Musk Cl. Stanw 66 B4
Musket Gr. Rayl 189 D4
Muswell Wlk. Clact 109 E3
Mychett Cl. Clact 109 D3
Myland Hall Chase. Colch 50 B2
Myrtle Gr. Colch 68 A3

Nabbott Rd. Chelm 126 C1
Nalla Gdns. Chelm 127 D4
Namur Ave. Canv 197 E3
Nancy Smith Cl. Colch 67 F3
Nansen Ave. Ashi 178 B3
Nansen Rd. Clact 110 B3
Napier Ave. Clact 124 B3
Napier Ave. South 200 A4
Napier Ct. Chelm 126 C3
Napier Gdns. Thund 188 B3
Napier Rd. Colch 67 F3
Napier Rd. Rayl 176 C2
Narvik Cl. Mald 144 C4
Nash Cl. Colch 67 D3
Nash Cl. Lawf 35 D3
Nassau Rd. St O 108 A2
Navestock Cl. Rayl 176 A2
Navestock Gdns. South 191 F1
Navigation Rd. Chelm 127 E1
Nayland Cl. Wick 174 C4
Nayland Dr. Clact 109 D2
Nayland Rd. Bures 28 C4
Nayland Rd. Colch 49 E3
Nayland Rd. Gt Hor 31 D2
Nayland Rd. Gt Hor 49 E3
Nayland Rd. Lit Hor 30 C3
Nayland Rd. W Berg 48 B4

Nayland Rd. W Berg

Nayling Rd. Brain 59 E1
Naze Park Rd. Walt 76 C2
Nazeing The. Basil 185 F3
Neale Rd. Hals 25 F1
Neasden Ave. Clact 109 E3
Neil Armstrong Way. South ...190 A3
Nelson Cl. Rayl 176 C2
Nelson Ct. Burn 170 B2
Nelson Gdns. Brain 60 B2
Nelson Gdns. Rayl 176 C2
Nelson Mews. South 200 A4
Nelson Pl. S Woo F 165 F3
Nelson Rd. Ashi 178 B3
Nelson Rd. Basil 185 F3
Nelson Rd. Clact 109 F1
Nelson Rd. Colch 66 C3
Nelson Rd. Harw 40 B2
Nelson Rd. Rayl 176 C2
Nelson Rd. South 190 A1
Nelson St. Brigh 106 C3
Nelson St. South 200 A4
Ness Rd. South 201 F3
Ness Wlk. With 97 E1
Nether Ct. Hals 26 A1
Nether Hill. Gest 10 C2
Nether Mayne. Basil 185 D2
Nether Priors. Basil 185 E3
Nether Rd. Cav 1 B1
Netherfield. S Ben 188 A2
Nethergate St. Cla 4 A4
Nevada Rd. Canv 197 E3
Nevendon Rd. Basil 174 A1
Nevendon Rd. Wick 174 B3
Nevern Cl. Rayl 188 C4
Nevern Rd. Rayl 188 C4
Neville Shaw. Basil 185 D3
New Bowers Way. Sprin 127 F3
New Captains Rd. W Mers 121 D3
New Cut. Bures 28 C4
New Cut. Glems 2 A2
New Cut. Gt Ben 89 F4
New Cut. Lay H 84 C3
New Dukes Way. Sprin 127 F3
New England Cres. Gt Wak ...193 E1
New Farm Rd. Stanw 66 B3
New Hall La. Mund 145 F2
New Hall Rd. Ashi 167 D1
New Kiln Rd. Colch 67 E4
New La. Fee 81 F3
New Lodge Chase. Lit Bad 129 D1
New London Rd. Chelm 127 D2
New Meadgate Terr. Gt Bad ..140 B4
New Moor Cl. Soum 159 F2
New Moor Cres. Soum 159 F2
New Nabbots Way. Sprin 127 F4
New Park Rd. Ashi 167 D1
New Park Rd. S Ben 187 E3
New Park St. Colch 68 A3
New Park. Ca Hed 15 F2
New Pier St. Walt 94 B4
New Queens Rd. Sud 7 F1
New Rd. Ald 47 D1
New Rd. Burn 170 B3
New Rd. Canv 196 C2
New Rd. Gos 42 C3
New Rd. Gt Bad 141 D3
New Rd. Gt Wak 193 E2
New Rd. Hadl 188 B2
New Rd. Hat Pev 114 A2
New Rd. Kelv 81 E1
New Rd. L Mel 7 D4
New Rd. Mann 35 E2
New Rd. Mess 82 B1
New Rd. Mist 35 F2
New Rd. Stanw 66 B3
New Rd. Terl 96 B2
New Rd. Tipt 100 B3
New Rd. Tolle 119 E1
New St. Brain 59 F1
New St. Brigh 106 C3
New St. Chelm 127 D2
New St. Glems 2 A3
New St. Hals 25 F1
New St. Mald 131 F1
New St. Sud 12 C4
New Thorpe Ave. Th L S 74 A1
New Town Rd. Colch 68 A3
New Town Rd. Th L S 73 F1
New Village. Catt 35 E4
New Way. St O 106 C2
New Writtle St. Chelm 127 D1
Newbarn Rd. Gt T 46 A1
Newbridge Hill. W Berg 48 B2
Newbridge Rd. Tipt 100 C3
Newcastle Ave. Colch 66 C2
Newcomen Way. Colch 50 B3
Newcourt Rd. Sprin 127 E2
Newell Ave. South 202 A4
Newgate St. Walt 94 B4
Newhall. Hawk 178 B3
Newhaven La. Harw 40 B3
Newhouse Rd. Ea Col 44 C2
Newington Ave. South 191 F1
Newington Cl. South 191 F1
Newington Gdns. Clact 109 F4
Newland Pl. With 98 A1
Newland Precinct. With 98 A1
Newland St. With 98 A1
Newlands Dr. With 98 A1

Newlands La. Nay 20 A1
Newlands Rd. Canv 197 E3
Newlands Rd. Wick 174 B2
Newman's Rd. Sud 12 C4
Newmill La. Catt 36 A4
Newnham Cl. Brain 59 F1
Newnham Green. Mald 131 F2
Newport Ave. Col N 156 A3
Newport Cl. Gt Bad 141 D3
Newport Cl. Harw 40 A1
Newport Dr. Clact 110 A4
Newport Way. Walt 94 A3
Newpots Cl. Peld 103 E3
Newpots La. Peld 103 F2
Newstead Rd. Gt Wak 193 D2
Newsum Gdns. Rayl 176 A2
Newton Cl. Brain 59 F1
Newton Croft. Sud 13 D4
Newton Hall Gdns. Ashi 178 B3
Newton Park Rd. Thund 188 A4
Newton Rd. Harw 40 A2
Newton Rd. Sud 13 D4
Newton Way. St O 108 A3
Nicholas Cl. Writ 126 A1
Nicholas Ct. Chelm 126 C3
Nicholas St. With 97 F1
Nichols Cl. Lawf 35 D2
Nicholson Cres. S Ben 188 A2
Nicholson Pl. E Han 153 D4
Nicholson Rd. S Ben 188 A2
Nicholsons Gr. Colch 68 A3
Nickleby Rd. Chelm 126 B3
Nien - Oord. Clact 109 E2
Nightingale Cl. Clact 109 F3
Nightingale Cl. Colch 69 D4
Nightingale Cl. Harw 39 F1
Nightingale Cl. South 190 C3
Nightingale Hill. Langh 32 C3
Nightingale Rd. Canv 197 E2
Nightingale Way. Clact 109 F3
Nineacres. Brain 60 A1
Nipsells Chase. May 147 D1
Nipsells Chase. Steep 147 D1
Noakes Ave. Gt Bad 140 C3
Noaks Rd. High 22 B4
Nobel Sq. Basil 174 B1
Nobles Green Cl. South 189 F4
Nobles Green Rd. South 189 F4
Nook The. Wiv 87 E4
Norbury Cl. Mks T 64 C2
Nordland Rd. Canv 197 E2
Nore Rd. Rayl 189 E4
Noredale. South 201 E3
Norfolk Ave. Clact 110 C4
Norfolk Ave. South 189 F4
Norfolk Ave. W Mers 121 E4
Norfolk Cl. Canv 197 D3
Norfolk Cl. Mald 131 F1
Norfolk Cres. Colch 50 A1
Norfolk Dr. Chelm 127 D4
Norfolk Gdns. Brain 60 A2
Norfolk Rd. Mald 131 F1
Norfolk Way. Canv 196 C3
Norman Cl. Mks T 64 C2
Norman Cl. St O 108 A2
Norman Cres. Rayl 176 C2
Norman Hill. Terl 96 A1
Norman Rd. Clact 110 C3
Norman Rd. Mann 35 E2
Norman Way. Colch 67 D2
Norman Way. St O 106 C2
Normandie Way. Bures 28 C4
Normandy Ave. Burn 170 B3
Normandy Ave. Colch 68 A2
Normans Rd. Canv 197 E2
Norris Cl. Brain 60 B3
North Ave. Canv 196 C2
North Ave. Chelm 126 C3
North Ave. South 191 E1
North Benfleet Hall Rd. Wick ..174 C1
North Colne. Basil 185 E2
North Cres. South 190 B3
North Cres. Wick 174 B4
North Crockerford. Basil 185 F2
North Dell. Sprin 127 F4
North Dr. Gt Bad 140 C4
North Dr. May 146 C1
North End Rd. Gest 10 B1
North End Rd. Lit Y 9 F2
North End. Soum 159 F2
North Gunnels. Basil 185 D3
North Hill. Colch 67 F4
North Hill. Lit Bad 129 E3
North La. Copf 65 D3
North Rd. Bel W 10 C3
North Rd. Brigh 106 C4
North Rd. Clact 109 F3
North Rd. Gt Y 9 D1
North Rd. South 190 C1
North Rise. Sud 13 D3
North Shoebury Rd. South 192 B1
North St. Gt Wak 193 D2
North St. Mald 132 A1
North St. Mann 35 E2
North St. Roch 178 C1
North St. Soum 159 E2
North St. South 198 C4
North St. Sud 12 C4
North St: Till 149 F2

North St. Toll D 118 C3
North St. Tolle 119 E1
North St. Walt 76 B1
North St. Walt 94 B4
North Station Rd. Colch 67 F4
Northbourne Rd. Clact 109 F2
Northcroft. Sud 12 C4
Northern Ave. S Ben 187 E3
Northern Rd. Sud 13 D4
Northfield Cres. Gt Wak 193 D2
Northfield Gdns. Colch 50 A2
Northgate St. Colch 67 F4
Northlands Pavement. Basil ..186 A3
Northumberland Ave. South ..200 B4
Northumberland Cl. Brain 60 A2
Northumberland Cres. South .200 B4
Northumberland Ct. Sprin 127 F2
Northview Dr. South 190 B1
Northville Dr. South 190 B2
Northwick Rd. Canv 196 A2
Norton Ave. Canv 197 F2
Norton Rd. Chelm 127 D2
Norway Cres. Harw 39 E2
Norwich Ave. South 191 E1
Norwich Cl. Colch 68 A4
Norwich Cl. South 191 E1
Norwich Cres. Rayl 176 B3
Norwich Wlk. Basil 185 F4
Norwood Ave. Clact 110 A3
Norwood Dr. S Ben 187 F1
Norwood End. Basil 185 E4
Norwood Way. Walt 94 A4
Notley Rd. Brain 59 F1
Nottingham Rd. Clact 110 C3
Nounsley Rd. Hat Pev 114 A1
Nunn's Rd. Colch 67 F4
Nunnery St. Ca Hed 15 E2
Nuns Meadow. Gos 42 C4
Nunty's La. Cogg 44 A1
Nursery Cl. Rayl 176 B1
Nursery Cl. Stanw 66 B3
Nursery Dr. Brain 60 A3
Nursery La. Dan 142 C4
Nursery Rd. Chelm 140 A4
Nursery Rd. Sud 13 D3
Nutcombe Cres. Hawk 178 B2

Oak Ave. Wick 175 E4
Oak Bungalows. Brain 59 F2
Oak Chase. Wick 174 A4
Oak Cl. Th L S 74 A1
Oak Cl. W Berg 48 C2
Oak Fall. With 98 A3
Oak Farm Rd. Woo Wa 130 C1
Oak Hill. Weth 41 D4
Oak Lodge Tye. Bore 128 A3
Oak Rd N. Hadl 188 C1
Oak Rd S. Hadl 188 C1
Oak Rd. Canv 197 E2
Oak Rd. Hals 43 E4
Oak Rd. Lit Map 26 A4
Oak Rd. Mald 132 B3
Oak Rd. Peb 26 C4
Oak Rd. Roch 178 C1
Oak Rd. Sud 13 D3
Oak Rd. Tipt 100 B4
Oak Rd. Wa Col 46 A2
Oak Rd. With 98 B3
Oak Ridge. Lit Oak 57 D4
Oak Tree Rd. Alres 88 A4
Oak Wlk. Hock 177 F4
Oak Wlk. Si Hed 15 E1
Oak Wlk. Thund 187 D4
Oak Wlk. Thund 187 E4
Oak Wood Gr. Basil 186 A3
Oakapple Cl. Colch 67 E1
Oakdene Rd. Basil 186 B4
Oaken Grange Dr. South 190 C3
Oakfield Cl. S Ben 187 E2
Oakfield Rd. Ashi 167 D1
Oakfield Rd. S Ben 187 E2
Oakhurst Cl. Wick 174 B3
Oakhurst Dr. Wick 174 B3
Oakhurst Rd. Rayl 188 C4
Oakhurst Rd. South 191 D1
Oakland Rd. Harw 40 B2
Oakland Way. Lit Bad 129 F1
Oaklands Ave. Colch 66 C3
Oaklands Cl. Bl Not 77 E4
Oaklands Cres. Chelm 140 A4
Oaklea Ave. Sprin 127 F2
Oakleigh Ave. Hull 165 F1
Oakleigh Ave. South 200 B4
Oakleigh Park Dr. South 189 F1
Oakleigh Rd. Clact 109 F4
Oakleighs. S Ben 187 E2
Oakley Ave. Rayl 175 F2
Oakley Rd. Brain 59 F4
Oakley Rd. Harw 39 E1
Oakley Rd. Wix 55 F3
Oakmead Rd. St O 107 D2
Oaks Dr. Colch 67 E4
Oaks Pl. Colch 49 F2
Oaks The. Walt 93 F3
Oakview. Harw 39 F1
Oakwood Ave. Clact 110 C4
Oakwood Ave. South 189 F3
Oakwood Ave. W Mers 121 E4

Oakwood Cl. S Ben 187 D3
Oakwood Cl. Walt 93 F3
Oakwood Ct. Alth 158 A2
Oakwood Dr. W Mers 121 E4
Oakwood Gdns. W Mers 121 E4
Oakwood Rd. Rayl 176 B2
Oast Way. Roch 178 C1
Oatfield Cl. Stanw 66 B3
Oatlands. Elmst M 69 F3
Oban Cl. Walt 175 D3
Oban Rd. South 191 E1
Oberon Cl. Colch 68 C4
Observer Way. Kelv 81 E2
Ockelford Ave. Chelm 126 C3
Ockendon Way. Walt 94 A4
Octavia Dr. With 114 C4
Oddcroft. Col En 26 C1
Odessa Rd. Canv 197 E2
Office La. Lit Tot 117 D2
Old Barn Rd. M Bure 29 D3
Old Bell La. Rett 153 D1
Old Church La. Bul 11 F1
Old Church La. W Berg 48 B3
Old Church Rd. Basil 186 C3
Old Church Rd. E Han 153 D3
Old Coach Rd. Colch 68 A4
Old Court Rd. Chelm 127 E2
Old Court. L Mel 7 E4
Old Forge Rd. Bore 128 C4
Old Forge Rd. Lay H 85 D3
Old Hall La. Tolle 119 E3
Old Hall La. Walt 76 B2
Old Heath Rd. Colch 68 B2
Old Heath Rd. Soum 159 D1
Old House La. Box 32 A1
Old House Rd. Gt Hor 49 D4
Old La. Bradw 61 E3
Old Leigh Rd. South 190 A1
Old London Rd. Wick 175 E3
Old London Rd. Woo Wa 130 C1
Old Market Pl. Sud 12 C4
Old Mead. South 190 A4
Old Mill La. Cogg 81 E4
Old Parsonage Way. Frin 93 F3
Old Pier St. Walt 94 B4
Old Rd. Bradw 61 E3
Old Rd. Clact 109 F2
Old Rd. Cogg 63 E1
Old Rd. Fee 81 F4
Old Rd. Frin 93 F2
Old Rd. Wic S P 17 E3
Old Rose Gdn. Colch 49 E2
Old School La. Elmst M 70 A3
Old School Meadow. Gt Wak ..192 C2
Old Ship La. Roch 178 C1
Old Southend Rd. Sand 152 B4
Old Southend Rd. South 200 A4
Old Vicarage Rd. Harw 40 A2
Old Way. Frin 93 F2
Old Wickford Rd. S Woo F 165 D4
Oldbury Ave. Gt Bad 140 C4
Olde Forge. Brigh 88 C1
Oldwyk. Basil 185 F2
Olive Ave. Hadl 189 D1
Olive Gr. Colch 67 E1
Oliver Pl. With 98 A1
Oliver Way. Chelm 126 C4
Olivers Cl. Clact 109 F2
Olivers Cl. L Mel 7 E4
Olivers Cres. Gt Wak 193 D2
Olivers Dr. With 115 D4
Olivers La. Colch 67 D1
Olivers Rd. Clact 109 F2
Olivia Dr. South 189 F1
Ongar Cl. Clact 109 D2
Onslow Cres. Colch 68 A1
Ophir Rd. Brigh 106 C3
Orange Rd. Canv 197 E2
Orange Tree Cl. Chelm 140 B3
Orchard Ave. Hals 25 E1
Orchard Ave. Hock 177 F4
Orchard Ave. Rayl 188 B4
Orchard Ave. With 97 E1
Orchard Cl. Clact 109 E3
Orchard Cl. Copf 65 E1
Orchard Cl. Gt Bad 140 B3
Orchard Cl. Gt Oak 56 B2
Orchard Cl. Gt Wak 193 D2
Orchard Cl. Hat Pev 114 A2
Orchard Cl. Hock 177 F4
Orchard Cl. Mald 131 F1
Orchard Cl. Rams 39 D1
Orchard Cl. Ridge 8 A3
Orchard Cl. Soum 159 E2
Orchard Cl. Tolle 119 F1
Orchard Cl. Writ 126 A1
Orchard Dr. Brain 60 A1
Orchard Dr. Frin 93 D2
Orchard Dr. Steep 147 D1
Orchard Gdns. Colch 68 A4
Orchard Gr. South 189 F3
Orchard Mead. South 189 F3
Orchard Rd. Alres 88 A4
Orchard Rd. Burn 170 B2
Orchard Rd. Colch 67 F4
Orchard Rd. Kelv 81 E2
Orchard Rd. Mald 131 F1
Orchard Rd. Soum 159 E2
Orchard Rd. Thund 187 D4

Orchard Side. South 189 F3
Orchard St. Chelm 127 D1
Orchard The. Wick 174 A4
Orchard Way. Glems 2 A2
Orchards. With 97 F1
Orchid Pl. S Woo F 165 E4
Orchill Dr. Hadl 188 C2
Orford Cres. Sprin 127 E3
Oriel Cl. Sud 13 D3
Orion Ct. Basil 174 A1
Orion Way. Brain 60 A2
Orlando Cl. Walt 94 B4
Orlando Dr. Basil 174 B1
Ormesby Chine. S Woo F 165 E3
Ormonde Ave. Hadl 189 D1
Ormonde Ave. Roch 178 C2
Ormonde Gdns. Hadl 189 D1
Ormonds Cl. S Woo F 154 A2
Ormsby Rd. Canv 196 B2
Orpen Cl. W Berg 48 B2
Orpen's Hill. Birch 84 A3
Orrmo Rd. Canv 197 E2
Orsett Ave. Hadl 189 E3
Orsett End. Basil 185 E4
Orsino Wlk. Colch 68 C4
Orvis La. Str S M 34 C4
Orwell Cl. Colch 50 C1
Orwell Ct. Wick 175 D3
Orwell Rd. Clact 109 F1
Orwell Rd. Harw 40 B2
Orwell Way. Burn 170 A3
Orwell Wlk. With 97 F2
Osbert Rd. With 114 C4
Osborne Ave. Hock 177 E3
Osborne Cl. Clact 110 A4
Osborne Rd. Basil 185 E3
Osborne Rd. Basil 186 C4
Osborne Rd. South 190 C1
Osborne Rd. W Mers 121 F3
Osborne St. Colch 67 F3
Osea Rd. Gold 133 D2
Osier Cl. Basil 174 A1
Osprey Cl. South 192 C1
Osprey Way. Chelm 140 A3
Ospreys. Clact 109 F3
Osterley Pl. S Woo F 165 E3
Othello Cl. Colch 68 C4
Otten Rd. Bel S P 5 D1
Ottershaw Way. Clact 109 D3
Ouida Rd. Canv 197 D2
Oulton Ave. Canv 196 C3
Oulton Cl. Harw 39 F2
Ouse Chase. With 97 E3
Outing Cl. South 200 B4
Outpart Eastward. Harw 40 C3
Overhall Hill. Col En 27 E1
Overmead Dr. S Woo F 165 F4
Overton Cl. Thund 187 E3
Overton Dr. Thund 187 E3
Overton Rd. Thund 187 E3
Overton Way. Thund 187 D3
Owen Ward Cl. Colch 67 D2
Owl's Hill. Terl 96 A2
Owls Retreat. Colch 68 C4
Oxenford Cl. Harw 39 F1
Oxford Cl. Sud 13 D3
Oxford Cres. Clact 109 F2
Oxford Ct. Ea Col 45 D3
Oxford Ct. Sprin 127 E3
Oxford Meadow. Si Hed 15 E1
Oxford Rd. Canv 197 E2
Oxford Rd. Clact 109 F2
Oxford Rd. Colch 67 E3
Oxford Rd. Frin 94 A3
Oxford Rd. Hals 25 E1
Oxford Rd. Mann 35 E2
Oxford Rd. Roch 178 C2
Oxley Hill. Lang 85 F2
Oxley Hill. Toll D 118 A4
Oxlip Rd. With 97 F2
Oyster Pl. Sprin 127 F2
Oyster Tank Rd. Brigh 106 C3
Ozonia Ave. Wick 174 A3
Ozonia Cl. Wick 174 A3
Ozonia Way. Wick 174 B3
Ozonia Wlk. Wick 174 B3

Paarl Rd. Canv 197 D2
Packards La. Ford 29 F1
Packe Cl. Fee 81 E2
Paddock Cl. Harw 40 B2
Paddock Cl. South 189 F4
Paddock Dr. Sprin 127 F4
Paddock Way. Wiv 69 E2
Paddocks The. Bures 28 C4
Paddocks The. Gt Ben 89 F3
Paddocks The. Gt Tot 116 A2
Paddocks The. Rayl 176 C1
Paddocks The. With 98 A1
Padgetts Way. Hull 165 E2
Page Cl. With 114 B4
Page Rd. Basil 186 C4
Page Rd. Clact 109 F2
Pagel Mead. Basil 185 D3
Pages La. Toll D 99 F1
Paget Rd. Rowh 86 C4
Paget Rd. Wiv 87 E4
Paglesham Rd. Pag Ch 180 B3
Paignton Ave. Sprin 127 E3

Paignton Cl. Rayl 176 B3
Palfrey Hts. Catt 35 E4
Pall Mall. South 189 F1
Pallister Rd. Clact 109 F1
Palm Cl. Chelm 140 B3
Palm Cl. With 98 A4
Palm Rd. Corr 185 D1
Palmeira Ave. South 199 E4
Palmers Croft. Sprin 128 A1
Palmerston Rd. South 199 E4
Palmerston Rd. Th L S 74 A1
Palmerstone Rd. Canv 196 B2
Pampas Cl. Colch 50 A2
Pan La. E Han 152 C3
Pan La. E Han 153 D3
Pan Wlk. Chelm 126 B3
Panfield La. Brain 59 F3
Pannels Cl. Glems 2 A2
Pantile Ave. South 191 E2
Pantile Hill. Soum 159 E2
Pantling's La. Kelv 81 D3
Panton Cres. Colch 68 C4
Panton Mews. Brain 78 A4
Papenburg Rd. Canv 197 D3
Papillon Rd. Colch 67 F4
Parade The. Walt 94 B4
Paradise Rd. Writ 139 D4
Pargat Dr. Rayl 189 E4
Pargetters Hyam. Hock 177 F3
Park Ave. Canv 197 F1
Park Ave. Chelm 126 C2
Park Ave. South 189 F3
Park Boulevard. Clact 110 C3
Park Chase. Hadl 188 C1
Park Chase. St O 108 B3
Park Cl. Sud 13 D4
Park Cl. Wick 174 B3
Park Cotts. Gos 42 C4
Park Dr. Brain 78 A4
Park Dr. Brigh 106 C4
Park Dr. Hals 25 F1
Park Dr. Mald 132 A1
Park Dr. Wick 174 B3
Park Drive Par. Brigh 106 C4
Park Gdns. Hawk 177 F3
Park La. Bul 11 F1
Park La. Canv 197 F2
Park La. Ea Col 45 D3
Park La. Glems 2 B2
Park La. Gos 42 C4
Park La. Langh 32 C2
Park La. South 199 F4
Park La. South 200 B4
Park La. Toll K 101 D2
Park La. Topp 14 A4
Park Lane Cl. Ea Col 45 D3
Park Rd. Ard 51 F2
Park Rd. Burn 170 A3
Park Rd. Canv 197 F1
Park Rd. Chelm 127 D1
Park Rd. Clact 109 E1
Park Rd. Colch 67 E3
Park Rd. Colch 69 D2
Park Rd. Gt Bro 71 E4
Park Rd. Gt Hor 31 D4
Park Rd. Hadl 189 D1
Park Rd. Harw 40 B2
Park Rd. Mald 131 F1
Park Rd. Nay 20 C2
Park Rd. Silv E 80 A1
Park Rd. South 199 F4
Park Rd. Sud 13 D4
Park Rd. Thund 187 F3
Park Rd. Wiv 87 E4
Park Side. Basil 186 A4
Park Side. South 190 A1
Park Sq E. Clact 125 D4
Park Sq W. Clact 124 C4
Park St. Nay 20 B3
Park St. South 199 F4
Park Terr. South 199 F4
Park The. Mann 35 E2
Park Vale Rd. Ca Hed 15 F2
Park View Cres. Gt Bad 140 C3
Park View Dr. Hadl 189 D3
Park Way. Clact 109 E1
Park Wood La. Lit Tot 117 D2
Parkanaur Ave. South 201 D4
Parkdale. Dan 142 B4
Parker Ct. Brad O S 136 C2
Parker Rd. Chelm 127 E1
Parker Way. Hals 43 F4
Parker's Way. Nay 20 A1
Parkeston Rd. Harw 40 A2
Parkeston Rd. Rams 39 F3
Parkfield St. Rowh 86 C4
Parkfields. Si Hed 15 E1
Parkfields. Thund 188 B2
Parkgate Rd. Silv E 80 A2
Parkgate. Canv 199 F4
Parkhall Rd. Gos 41 F4
Parkhurst Dr. Rayl 176 B4
Parkhurst Rd. Basil 186 A4
Parklands Ave. Rayl 176 C1
Parklands Cl. Glems 2 B2
Parklands Dr. Sprin 127 E2
Parklands. Brain 78 A4
Parklands. Canv 197 D3
Parklands. Hawk 178 B2

Parklards Way. Chelm 140 B1
Parkstone Ave. S Ben 188 A2
Parkstone Dr. South 190 C2
Parkway Cl. South 189 F4
Parkway The. Canv 197 D1
Parkway. Chelm 127 D1
Parkway. Rayl 188 C4
Parkwood Ave. Wiv 69 D1
Parkwood Dr. Sud 7 F1
Parmenter Dr. Sud 13 E3
Parnell Cl. Colch 68 A1
Parr Dr. Colch 66 C2
Parry Dr. Clact 109 E3
Parson's Field. Ded 34 A3
Parson's Heath. Colch 50 C1
Parson's Hill. Colch 67 D3
Parsonage La. Lit Bad 129 E1
Parsonage La. Rams 38 A1
Parsonage La. Tend 72 C4
Parsonage St. Hals 25 F1
Parsons Hill. Gt Bro 70 C4
Parsons La. Colch 68 B3
Parsons Lawn. South 192 B1
Parsons Rd. Thund 187 E4
Parsonson Wlk. Colch 68 C3
Partridge Ave. Chelm 126 C3
Partridge Cl. Gt Oak 56 B2
Partridge Dr. Ford 47 E3
Partridge Green. Basil 186 A3
Paschal Way. Gt Bad 140 C4
Paslowes. Basil 185 F2
Paston Cl. S Woo F 154 C1
Patching Hall La. Chelm 127 D4
Paternoster Row. Walt 94 B4
Path The. Gt Ben 89 F4
Pathfields Rd. Clact 109 E2
Pathway The. Walt 93 F3
Pathways. Basil 185 F3
Patmore Rd. Colch 50 B1
Patten Cl. Mks T 64 C2
Patterdale. Thund 187 D4
Pattern Bush Cl. Catt 35 E4
Patticroft. Glems 2 A3
Pattison Cl. With 115 D4
Pattiswick Cnr. Basil 185 F4
Pattiswick Sq. Basil 185 F4
Pattock's La. Gt T 46 B1
Pattocks. Basil 185 F3
Pattrick's La. Harw 40 B2
Pauline Cl. Clact 110 A3
Pauls Cres. Elmst M 69 F3
Pauls Ct. Canv 197 D3
Pauls Way. Clact 109 D1
Pavilion Cl. South 191 F1
Pavilion Dr. South 189 F1
Pawle Cl. Gt Bad 141 D4
Paxman Ave. Colch 67 D2
Paycocke Way. Cogg 63 D2
Payne Pl. E Han 153 D3
Payne's La. Lit Bro 53 E2
Paynters Hill. Basil 185 F2
Paynters Mead. Basil 185 F2
Peace Rd. Stanw 66 B4
Peach Ave. Hock 177 F4
Peacocks Cl. Cav 1 B1
Peacocks Rd. Cav 1 B1
Peakes Cl. Tipt 100 A2
Pear Trees. Thund 187 F2
Pearce Manor. Chelm 139 F4
Pearmain Cl. Runw 163 E1
Pearmain Way. Stanw 66 B2
Pearsons Ave. Rayl 176 B2
Peartree Bsns Centre. Stanw .. 66 C2
Peartree Cl. South 191 E2
Peartree Cl. Brain 60 A1
Peartree Hill. M Bure 29 D3
Peartree La. S Woo F 142 C2
Peartree Rd. Stanw 66 C2
Peartree Way. Lit Cla 91 E1
Pease Pl. E Han 153 D3
Pebmarsh Cl. Colch 86 A4
Pebmarsh Dr. Wick 174 C3
Pebmarsh Rd. Alph 18 C1
Pebmarsh Rd. Col En 26 C1
Pebmarsh Rd. Peb 18 C1
Pecockes Cl. Sud 13 E3
Pedder's Cl. Colch 66 C2
Pedlars Cl. Dan 143 D3
Pedlars Path. Dan 143 D3
Peel Ave. South 202 A4
Peel Cres. Brain 59 F3
Peel Rd. Sprin 127 F2
Peerswood Rd. Colch 67 E4
Peg Millar's La. Fair 96 C3
Peg Millar's La. Terl 96 C3
Pegasus Way. Brain 59 F3
Pegasus Way. Colch 50 B1
Peggotty Cl. Chelm 126 C3
Peldon Pavement. Basil 185 E4
Peldon Rd. Gt Wig 103 D2
Peldon Rd. Lang 86 A1
Peldon Rd. Peld 103 F4
Pelham Cl. Harw 39 F1
Pelham Rd. South 191 F1
Pelham's La. Colch 67 F4
Pelly Ave. With 115 D4
Pembroke Ave. Mald 131 F1
Pembroke Cl. Colch 68 B2

Pembroke Gdns. Clact 110 C3
Pembroke Mews. Basil 186 B4
Pembroke Pl. Chelm 127 D4
Pembury Rd. South 199 E4
Pendle Cl. Basil 174 A1
Pendlestone. Thund 188 B2
Pendower. Rayl 176 A1
Penfold Rd. Clact 109 F1
Penhurst Ave. South 190 C1
Penlan Hall La. Ford 47 D3
Penn Mews. Brain 78 A4
Pennial Rd. Canv 197 D2
Pennine Rd. Chelm 126 B3
Pennsylvania La. Tipt 100 B3
Penny Royal Rd. Dan 142 C3
Pennyroyal Cres. With 97 F2
Penrice Cl. Colch 68 C3
Penshurst Dr. S Woo F 165 E3
Penticton Rd. Brain 59 E1
Pentland Ave. Chelm 127 D3
Pentland Ave. South 201 E3
Pentlow Dr. Cav 1 C1
Pentlow Hill. Pent 6 A4
Pentlow La. Cav 1 C1
Penzance Cl. Sprin 127 F3
Pepper's Rd. Box 31 F1
Pepys St. Harw 40 B3
Percival Rd. Walt 75 E1
Percival Rd. Walt 76 B1
Percy Cottis Rd. Roch 178 C2
Percy Rd. South 189 E1
Percys. Basil 186 A3
Peregrine Cl. Basil 185 D2
Peregrine Cl. Clact 109 F4
Peregrine Ct. Colch 68 C4
Peregrine Dr. Chelm 140 A2
Peregrine Dr. S Ben 187 E1
Perriclose. Sprin 127 E4
Perrin Pl. Chelm 127 D1
Perry Green. Basil 185 D4
Perry Hill. Sprin 127 E2
Perry La. Langh 33 D2
Perry Rd. S Ben 187 D2
Perry Rd. Tipt 100 B3
Perry Rd. With 98 A1
Perry Spring. Basil 185 E3
Perry Way. With 98 A1
Perryfield. Sud 13 D2
Persardi Ct. Rowh 86 A4
Pershore End. Colch 66 C3
Perth Cl. Colch 68 A1
Pertwee Cl. Brigh 106 C4
Pertwee Dr. Gt Bad 140 C3
Pertwee Dr. S Woo F 165 E4
Pesthouse La. Gt Oak 56 B2
Peter Bruff Ave. Clact 109 E3
Peterborough Way. Basil 185 F4
Peterfield's La. Gos 42 C3
Petersfield. Chelm 127 D4
Petrebrook. Sprin 128 A2
Petrel Way. Chelm 140 B3
Pettit La. T Gr 79 D2
Petunia Cres. Sprin 127 F3
Petworth Cl. Elmst M 87 E4
Petworth Gdns. South 191 F1
Pevensey Gdns. Hull 165 F1
Peverel Ave. Hat Pev 114 B1
Pharos La. W Mers 121 E3
Philbrick Cres E. Rayl 176 B2
Philbrick Cres W. Rayl 176 B2
Philip Cl. Walt 94 A4
Philip Rd. With 114 C4
Phillip Rd. Wiv 87 D4
Phillips Chase. Brain 60 A3
Phillips Field Rd. Sud 13 D3
Philmead Rd. S Ben 187 D1
Philpott Ave. South 191 F1
Phoenix Gr. Chelm 140 A4
Phoenix Way. Hadl 188 B4
Picasso Way. South 193 D1
Pickers Way. Clact 110 C4
Picketts Ave. South 189 F2
Picketts Cl. South 189 F2
Picketts. Canv 196 B2
Pickford Wlk. Colch 68 C3
Pickwick Ave. Chelm 126 B3
Picton Cl. Rayl 176 C1
Picton Gdns. Rayl 176 C1
Pier App. Walt 94 B4
Pier Ave. Clact 109 F1
Pier Gap. Clact 109 F1
Pier Hill. South 200 A4
Pierce Glade. Tipt 100 B3
Pierrefitte Way. Brain 59 F2
Pightle Way. Walt 94 A4
Pilborough Way. Colch 66 C2
Pilcox Hall La. Tend 72 B4
Pilgrim Cl. Brain 59 F3
Pilgrims Cl. South 191 F1
Pilgrims Way. Hadl 188 C2
Pine Cl. Canv 196 C2
Pine Cl. Catt 35 E4
Pine Cl. Gt Ben 89 F4
Pine Cl. Hadl 189 D3
Pine Cl. Wick 174 B3
Pine Gr. W Mers 121 D4
Pine Gr. With 98 A3
Pine Rd. Hadl 188 B1
Pinecroft Gdns. Colch 50 A2

Pinecroft Rise. Sud 12 B3
Pines Rd. Chelm 126 B3
Pines The. Hat Pev 114 A3
Pinetrees. S Ben 188 B2
Pinewood Ave. South 189 E3
Pinewood Cl. Clact 109 F4
Pinewood Cl. Hull 165 F1
Pinewood Cl. Walt 93 E3
Pinkham Dr. With 114 C4
Pinmill. Basil 185 E3
Pinners Cl. Burn 169 F4
Pintails. Basil 186 B3
Pintolls. S Woo F 165 E3
Piper Rd. Colch 67 D4
Piper's Tye. Chelm 140 B2
Pippins Rd. Burn 170 B3
Pippins The. Glems 2 B3
Pirie Rd. W Berg 48 C2
Pit La. Tipt 100 B3
Pitmans Cl. South 200 A4
Pitmire Cl. Lam 19 D3
Pitsea Rd. Basil 186 A3
Pitseaville Gr. Basil 185 F3
Pitt Ave. With 115 D4
Pitt Chase. Gt Bad 140 C3
Pitt Green. With 115 D4
Plains Farm Cl. Colch 50 B3
Plains Rd. Gt Tot 116 C3
Plains Rd. Lit Tot 116 C3
Plaistow Green Rd. Hals 43 E3
Plane Tree Cl. Burn 170 A3
Plane Tree Cl. Chelm 140 A3
Plantation Rd. Bore 112 C1
Planton Way. Brigh 106 B4
Plas Newydd Cl. South 200 C3
Plas Newydd. South 200 C3
Plashetts. Basil 185 E4
Playle Chase. Gt Tot 116 A2
Pleasant Rd. South 200 A4
Pleshey Cl. South 200 C4
Pleshey Cl. Wick 174 C3
Plough Dr. Colch 67 D3
Plough Green. Bul 11 F1
Plough La. Sud 12 B4
Plough Rd. Gt Ben 89 F2
Ploughmans Headland. Stanw .. 66 B3
Plover Wlk. Chelm 140 A2
Plovers The. St L 148 B4
Plowmans. Rayl 176 C2
Plum St. Glems 2 A3
Plumberow Ave. Hock 177 F4
Plumberow Mount Ave. Hock .. 177 F4
Plume Ave. Colch 67 D2
Plume Ave. Mald 131 F1
Plumleys. Basil 186 A4
Plummers Rd. Ford 47 F4
Plumptre La. Dan 142 B3
Plumtree Ave. Gt Bad 140 C3
Plymouth Rd. Clact 125 E4
Plymouth Rd. Sprin 127 F3
Plymtree. South 192 B1
Pocklington Cl. Sprin 128 A2
Point Cl. Canv 197 F2
Point Clear Rd. St O 107 E2
Point Rd. Canv 197 F2
Pointer Pl. Walt 93 F4
Pointwell La. Cogg 81 D4
Pole Barn La. Frin 94 A3
Pole La. Wh Not 78 B2
Polecat Rd. T Gr 79 D3
Pollard Wlk. Clact 109 E3
Pollards Green. Sprin 127 F1
Polley Cl. Walt 93 F4
Polstead St. Nay 20 B3
Polstead Way. Clact 109 D2
Polsteads. Basil 185 F2
Pomfret Mead. Basil 185 D3
Pond Chase. Colch 67 D2
Ponders Rd. Ford 47 E2
Pondfield Rd. Colch 50 B1
Pondholton Dr. With 115 D4
Ponds Rd. Chelm 140 A1
Poole St. Cav 1 B1
Poole St. Gt Y 15 D4
Pooles La. S Woo F 165 F2
Poondfield Cl. Alres 88 A4
Poors La N. Hadl 189 D3
Poors La. Hadl 188 C2
Pope's La. Colch 67 F4
Pope's Rd. Wa Col 46 B2
Poperinghe Rd. Colch 67 F2
Popes Cres. Basil 186 A3
Popes Wlk. Rayl 177 D1
Poplar Cl. Clact 109 D1
Poplar Cl. Gt Y 9 D1
Poplar Cl. Hals 43 F4
Poplar Cl. S Woo F 165 E4
Poplar Cl. With 98 A4
Poplar Gr. Burn 170 A3
Poplar Rd. Canv 197 E2
Poplar Rd. Rayl 188 C4
Poplar Rd. Sud 13 D4
Poplar Way. Walt 93 E3
Poplars Ave. Hawk 177 F2
Poplars Cl. Alres 88 A4

Poppy Gdns. Colch 68 B2
Poppy Green. Bore 128 A3
Poppyfield Cl. South 189 E3
Pork Hall La. Gt Le 95 D3
Pork La. Frin 92 C3
Porlock Ave. South 190 A2
Port La. Colch 68 A3
Porter Way. Clact 109 D2
Porter's La. E A Gr 47 F1
Porters Brook Wlk. Colch 50 B1
Porters Cl. E A Gr 47 F1
Porters Cotts. E A Gr 47 F1
Porters Pk. Bore 113 D1
Porters. Basil 186 B4
Portland Ave. Harw 40 B2
Portland Ave. South 200 A4
Portland Cl. Brain 60 A2
Portland Cres. Harw 40 B2
Portland Rd. Colch 67 F3
Portlight Cl. Mist 36 A2
Portobello Rd. Walt 94 B4
Portreath Pl. Chelm 127 D4
Portsmouth Rd. Clact 125 E4
Portway Ct. Hals 25 F2
Post Office La. Glems 2 A3
Post Office La. Lit Tot 117 D2
Post Office Rd. Chelm 127 D4
Post Office Rd. Woo Mor 143 F3
Postman's La. Lit Bad 129 F1
Pot Kiln Chase. Gest 10 C1
Pot Kiln Rd. Sud 13 D3
Pot Kilns The. Sud 13 E3
Potter St. Si Hed 24 C4
Potters Way. South 190 C3
Pottery La. Ca Hed 15 F2
Pottery La. Chelm 127 D3
Pound Farm Dr. Harw 40 A2
Pound Fields. Writ 139 D4
Pound La. Basil 186 C4
Powers Hall End. With 97 F2
Pownall Cres. Colch 67 F2
Poynings Ave. South 191 F1
Poyntens. Rayl 176 B1
Poynters La. Gt Wak 192 C1
Poynters La. South 192 C1
Prentice Cl. Roch 178 C1
President Rd. Colch 66 C3
Preston Gdns. Rayl 176 B2
Preston Rd. Clact 110 B3
Preston Rd. South 199 E4
Prestwood Cl. Thund 188 A4
Prestwood Dr. Thund 188 A3
Pretoria Rd. Hals 25 F1
Prettygate Rd. Colch 67 D2
Prettygate Rd. Colch 67 D3
Pricries The. Hull 165 E1
Primrose Cl. Canv 197 D3
Primrose Hill. Chelm 126 C2
Primrose La. Rams 56 A4
Primrose La. Tipt 100 B3
Primrose Pl. With 97 F2
Primrose Rd. Clact 110 C3
Primrose Wlk. Colch 68 C4
Primrose Wlk. Mald 132 A1
Primula Cl. Clact 109 E2
Primula Way. Bore 128 A3
Prince Albert Rd. W Mers 121 E3
Prince Ave. South 190 B2
Prince Charles Cl. Clact 109 E1
Prince Charles Cl. Sud 12 C4
Prince Charles Rd. Colch 68 A1
Prince Cl. South 190 B3
Prince Philip Ave. Clact 109 E1
Prince Philip Rd. Colch 68 A1
Prince St. Sud 12 C4
Prince William Ave. Canv 196 C3
Prince's Espl. Walt 76 B1
Princel La. Ded 33 F4
Princes Ave. May 158 A4
Princes Ave. South 159 E2
Princes Ave. Thund 187 F3
Princes Rd. Burn 170 B3
Princes Rd. Canv 196 C2
Princes Rd. Chelm 140 A4
Princes Rd. Clact 110 B3
Princes Rd. Harw 40 A2
Princes Rd. Mald 132 A1
Princes St. Mald 131 F2
Princes St. South 199 F4
Princess Anne Cl. Clact 109 E1
Princess Ct. Wick 175 D4
Princess Dr. Colch 50 B2
Princess Gdns. Hawk 178 B3
Princess Rd. Rayl 176 C1
Princess St. Rams 39 F3
Princeton Mews. Colch 50 A2
Prior Cl. Hals 43 F4
Prior Way. Colch 49 F1
Prior's Green. Stis 61 E4
Priors Cl. Basil 185 E3
Priors East. Basil 185 E3
Priory Ave. South 190 C2
Priory Cl. Chelm 126 C1
Priory Cl. Hat Pev 114 A1
Priory Cotts. Birch 83 F3

Priory Cres. South

Priory Cres. South 190 C2
Priory Ct. Hat Pev 114 A2
Priory Farm Rd. Hat Pev 114 A1
Priory La. S Woo F 142 C1
Priory Mews. Hat Pev 114 B1
Priory Rd. Clact 109 F2
Priory Rd. Sud 7 F1
Priory Rd. Tipt 99 F1
Priory Rd. Wa Col 46 A2
Priory St. Colch 68 A4
Priory St. Ea Col 45 D4
Priory The. Writ 126 A1
Priory View Rd. South 189 F3
Priory Way. Soum 159 F2
Priory Wlk. Sud 12 C3
Priory Wood Cres. South 189 F3
Priorywood Dr. South 189 F3
Prittle Cl. Thund 188 B3
Prittlewell Chase. South 190 B2
Prittlewell Sq. South 199 F4
Prittlewell St. South 191 D1
Proctor Way. Mks T 64 C2
Progress Ct. Brain 59 F2
Progress Rd. South 189 E3
Promenade The. Burn 170 B2
Promenade The. South 201 E3
Promenade Way. Brigh 106 C3
Promenade. Harw 40 B2
Promenade. May 146 C1
Promenade. Walt 76 C1
Prospect Cl. Hat Pev 114 A2
Prospect Cl. South 200 B4
Prospect Park. Frin 93 D3
Prospero Cl. Colch 68 C4
Provence Cl. Stanw 66 B4
Providence. Burn 170 B2
Provident Sq. Chelm 127 E1
Prunus Ct. Rowh 86 A4
Prykes Dr. Chelm 127 D1
Pryor Cl. With 98 A1
Pryors Rd. Chelm 140 B1
Pudding La. Birch 84 A2
Pudsey Hall La. Cane 168 A1
Puffin Cl. South 192 C1
Puffinsdale. Clact 109 F3
Pulpitfield Cl. Walt 94 A4
Pulpits Cl. Hock 177 F4
Pump Hill. Gt Bad 140 C4
Pump Hill. St O 108 B2
Pump La. Dan 142 B3
Pump La. Sprin 127 F3
Pump Mead Cl. Soum 159 E2
Pump Rd. Purl 144 B1
Purbeck Cl. Gt Bad 140 C3
Purcell Cl. Colch 68 C3
Purcell Cole. Writ 126 A1
Purdeys Way. Roch 191 D4
Purleigh Cl. Basil 174 B1
Purleigh Gr. Col N 156 A3
Purleigh Rd. Rayl 176 A2
Purleigh St. Purl 144 C1
Purley Way. Clact 109 D3
Purley Way. South 190 B3
Pye Cnr. Ca Hed 15 F2
Pyefleet Cl. Brigh 106 C4
Pyefleet Cl. Fing 87 E3
Pyefleet View. Lang 86 A2
Pyesand. Walt 93 E4
Pygot Pl. Brain 59 F2
Pyms Rd. Chelm 140 A2
Pyne Gate. Chelm 140 A1

Quakers' Alley. Colch 67 F4
Quarter Gate. S Woo F 165 F3
Quay La. Beau 74 A3
Quay La. Sud 12 C3
Quay La. Walt 75 E1
Quay St. Mann 35 E2
Quay The. Burn 170 B2
Quay The. Harw 40 C3
Quebec Ave. South 200 A4
Queech La. Catt 36 A4
Queen Anne Dr. W Mers 121 E3
Queen Anne Gdns. W Mers .. 121 E3
Queen Anne Rd. W Mers 121 E3
Queen Anne's Dr. South 190 B2
Queen Anns Gr. Hull 176 B4
Queen Elizabeth Ave. Clact .. 109 E1
Queen Elizabeth Chase. Roch190 C4
Queen Elizabeth II Sq.
  S Woo F ....
Queen Elizabeth Way. Colch .. 68 A1
Queen Mary Ave. Colch 67 F2
Queen St. Brigh 106 C3
Queen St. Ca Hed 15 F2
Queen St. Chelm 127 D1
Queen St. Cogg 63 D2
Queen St. Colch 67 F4
Queen St. Gt Oak 56 B2
Queen St. Mald 132 A1
Queen St. Si Hed 24 C3
Queen St. Soum 159 E2
Queen Victoria Dr. Sho G 40 A4
Queen's Ave. Mald 132 A1
Queen's Ave. South 189 F1
Queen's Cnr. W Mers 121 E4
Queen's Gdns. Pan 59 D4
Queen's Head Rd. Box 31 F2
Queen's Rd. Chelm 127 E1

Queen's Rd. Clact 109 E1
Queen's Rd. Colch 67 E3
Queen's Rd. Ea Col 45 D4
Queen's Rd. Frin 93 F2
Queen's Rd. Harw 40 A1
Queen's Rd. S Ben 187 E1
Queen's Rd. South 198 C4
Queen's Rd. South 199 F4
Queen's Rd. W Berg 48 B2
Queen's Rd. Wiv 87 E4
Queenborough La. Brain 77 E4
Queenborough Rd. Soum 159 E2
Queenbury Cl. W Mers 121 F3
Queens Cl. Sud 12 C4
Queens Ct. Burn 170 A2
Queens Mews. W Mers 121 D3
Queens Rd. Brain 59 F3
Queens Rd. Burn 170 B3
Queens Rd. Rayl 176 B4
Queens Rd. Sud 12 C4
Queensbury Ave. Copf 65 E3
Queensland Ave. Roch 190 C4
Queensland Cres. Chelm 126 C3
Queensland Dr. Colch 68 A1
Queensmere. Thund 188 A3
Queensway. Clact 110 B3
Queensway. Lawf 35 E2
Queensway. South 200 A4
Queensway. Sud 13 D3
Queensway. Tipt 100 B3
Quendon Rd. Basil 185 F4
Quendon Way. Frin 94 A3
Quilp Dr. Chelm 126 C4
Quilters Cl. Basil 185 E4
Quilters Cl. Clact 110 C3
Quilters Straight. Basil 185 E4
Quinion Cl. Chelm 126 B4
Quorn Gdns. Hadl 189 D1

Rachael Gdns. Silv E 79 F2
Rackenford. South 201 E4
Radiator Rd. Sud 13 D3
Radnor Rd. Ashi 167 E1
Radwinter Ave. Wick 174 B3
Raeburn Cl. Walt 93 F4
Raglan Rd. Frin 94 A3
Raile Wlk. L Mel 7 E4
Railway Sq. Chelm 127 D2
Railway St. Brain 60 A2
Railway St. Chelm 127 D2
Railway St. Mann 35 E2
Railway Terr. Clact 109 F2
Railway Terr. South 191 D2
Rainbow Ave. Canv 197 E2
Rainbow Mead. Hat Pev 114 A3
Rainbow Rd. Canv 197 E2
Rainbow Way. Col En 26 C1
Rainham Way. Frin 94 A3
Rainsborowe Rd. Colch 67 E2
Rainsford Ave. Chelm 126 C2
Rainsford La. Chelm 126 C1
Rainsford Rd. Chelm 126 C2
Rambler Cl. Stanw 66 B4
Ramblers Way. Burn 170 B2
Rampart Cl. South 202 A3
Rampart Terr. South 202 A3
Ramparts Cl. Gt Hor 49 D4
Ramparts Ct. Colch 49 D1
Ramparts The. Rayl 176 C1
Ramplings Ave. Clact 109 F3
Ramsay Dr. Basil 185 F2
Ramsey Chase. Latch 157 D3
Ramsey Cl. Mald 132 B2
Ramsey Rd. Hals 43 E4
Ramsey Rd. Harw 39 E1
Ramshaw Dr. Sprin 127 F2
Ramuz Dr. South 190 B1
Rana Ct. Brain 59 F2
Rana Dr. Brain 59 F2
Randolph Cl. South 189 F2
Randulph Terr. Sprin 127 E2
Randway. Rayl 176 B1
Ranger Wlk. Colch 68 A2
Rangoon Cl. Colch 67 D1
Ransom Rd. Tipt 100 B3
Ranulph Way. Hat Pev 114 A2
Raphael Dr. South 193 D1
Raphael Dr. Sprin 127 F4
Rat La. Hadl 188 B4
Ratcliffe Rd. Colch 66 C3
Ratsborough Chase. Soum .. 159 E1
Rattwick Dr. Canv 197 F2
Raven Dr. S Ben 187 E1
Raven Way. Colch 49 D1
Ravendale Way. South 192 B1
Ravens Ave. Hals 43 F4
Ravensbourne Dr. Chelm 126 C1
Ravenscourt Dr. Basil 185 F3
Ravensdale. Basil 185 D2
Ravensdale. Clact 109 F3
Ravensfield. Basil 185 F3
Ravenswood Chase. Roch ... 190 C4
Rawden Cl. Harw 40 A2
Rawreth La. Rayl 176 A3
Rawstorn Rd. Colch 67 F4
Ray Ave. Harw 40 A2
Ray Cl. Canv 197 D1
Ray Cl. Hadl 189 D1

Ray La. Rams 39 D2
Ray The. Sprin 127 F3
Ray Wlk. Hadl 189 D1
Raycliff Ave. Clact 109 F4
Raydon Way. Sud 13 E3
Rayleigh Ave. Rayl 189 E4
Rayleigh Ave. South 190 C1
Rayleigh Cl. Brain 60 B2
Rayleigh Cl. Colch 50 A1
Rayleigh Downs Rd. Ray 189 D4
Rayleigh Dr. South 189 E2
Rayleigh Rd. Rayl 189 E3
Rayleigh Rd. South 189 E3
Rayleigh Rd. Thund 188 A3
Rayment Ave. Canv 197 E2
Raymonds Cl. S Woo F 165 E4
Raymonds Dr. Thund 187 F3
Rayne Rd. Brain 59 E2
Rayner Rd. Colch 67 D2
Rayner Way. Hals 25 F1
Rayside. Basil 185 E3
Read Cl. Hawk 178 A2
Readers Cl. Gt Bad 140 C3
Reaper Rd. Colch 67 D3
Rebecca Gdns. Silv E 79 F2
Rebels La. Barl 191 F2
Rebow Rd. Harw 40 A1
Rebow Rd. Wiv 87 D4
Rebow St. Colch 68 A3
Recreation Ave. South 189 F1
Recreation Cl. Clact 109 F2
Recreation Rd. Colch 68 A3
Recreation Rd. Si Hed 24 B4
Recreation Way. Brigh 106 C4
Recreation Wlk. Sud 13 D3
Rectory Ave. Hawk 178 B3
Rectory Cl. Colch 49 F1
Rectory Cl. Glems 2 A3
Rectory Cl. Hadl 188 C2
Rectory Cl. Basil 186 B4
Rectory Garth. Rayl 176 B1
Rectory Gdns. Basil 186 B3
Rectory Gr. South 198 B4
Rectory Gr. Walt 174 C4
Rectory Hill. Nay 20 B4
Rectory Hill. Wiv 69 E1
Rectory La. Chelm 127 D2
Rectory La. Lang 86 A2
Rectory La. Latch 157 D2
Rectory La. Rams 39 D1
Rectory La. Rett 164 C3
Rectory La. Wic S P 17 E3
Rectory La. With 98 A4
Rectory La. Woo Mor 143 F3
Rectory Meadow. Bradw 61 E1
Rectory Park Dr. Basil 186 A3
Rectory Rd. Ald 64 C4
Rectory Rd. Basil 186 B3
Rectory Rd. Copf 65 E1
Rectory Rd. Frat 70 C1
Rectory Rd. Frin 93 D2
Rectory Rd. Hadl 188 C2
Rectory Rd. Hawk 178 A2
Rectory Rd. Langh 32 C4
Rectory Rd. Lit Ben 71 F4
Rectory Rd. Midd 12 C2
Rectory Rd. N Fam 166 C4
Rectory Rd. Rams 56 C3
Rectory Rd. Rowh 86 C4
Rectory Rd. Si Hed 15 E1
Rectory Rd. St O 90 C2
Rectory Rd. Stis 61 D4
Rectory Rd. Tipt 100 B3
Rectory Rd. Toil K 101 E1
Rectory Rd. Weel 91 D3
Rectory Rd. Wiv 69 E1
Rectory Rd. Woo Wa 130 B2
Rectory Rd. Wrab 38 A2
Rectory Rd. Writ 139 D4
Rectory Terr. Hawk 178 A2
Red Barn La. Gt Oak 56 A1
Red Barn Rd. Brigh 106 C4
Red House La. Sud 13 D2
Red Lion Yd. Colch 67 F4
Redbridge Rd. Clact 109 F4
Redcliff Dr. South 198 C4
Redcliff Rd. Chelm 127 D1
Reddings La. Till 149 E2
Rede Way. Sud 13 E3
Redgate Cl. Wick 175 D4
Redgates Pl. Sprin 127 F2
Redgrave Rd. Basil 185 F2
Redhills Rd. S Woo F 165 F4
Redhouse La. Box 31 E1
Redmayne Dr. Chelm 140 A4
Redmayne Dr. Chelm 139 F4
Redmill. Colch 67 D2
Redrose Wlk. Clact 109 E2
Redruth Cl. Sprin 127 F3
Redshank Cres. S Woo F 154 B1
Redshank Dr. Mald 132 B3
Redstock Rd. South 191 D1
Redwood Cl. Colch 68 C4
Redwood Cl. With 98 A4
Reed Cl. Clact 109 E3
Reed Hall Ave. Colch 67 E2
Reeds Way. Wick 174 B4
Reeves Way. S Woo F 165 F4
Refinery Rd. Rams 39 F3

Regency Cl. Runw 163 E1
Regency Cl. Sprin 127 E2
Regency Green. Colch 67 D2
Regency Green. South 190 C2
Regent Cl. Runw 106 C4
Regent Cl. Rayl 176 A2
Regent Rd. Brigh 106 C4
Regent St. Mann 35 E2
Regent St. Rowh 87 D4
Regents Ct. Burn 170 A2
Regina Rd. Chelm 127 E2
Reigate Ave. Clact 109 E3
Rembrandt Cl. South 202 A4
Rembrandt Gr. Sprin 127 F3
Rembrandt Way. Colch 67 D3
Remembrance Ave. Burn 170 A2
Remembrance. Hat Pev 114 A2
Remercie Rd. Mist 36 A2
Remus Cl. Colch 49 F3
Rennie Rd. Chelm 127 E1
Renoir Pl. Sprin 127 F4
Repton Cl. Basil 174 A1
Repton Gr. South 190 A4
Retreat Rd. Hock 177 F3
Retreat Rd. South 199 F4
Retreat The. With 98 A1
Rettendon Cl. Rayl 176 A2
Rettendon Gdns. Runw 163 F1
Rettendon Turnpike. Rett 164 B2
Rettendon View. Wick 174 C4
Reymead Cl. W Mers 121 E4
Reynard Ct. Gt Bad 140 C3
Reynards Cl. Walt 93 E3
Reynards Copse. Colch 50 A2
Reynolds Ave. Colch 67 D3
Reynolds Gate. S Woo F 165 F3
Rhoda Rd N. Thund 187 F3
Rhoda Rd. S Ben 187 F2
Richard Ave. Brigh 106 C3
Richard Ave. Wiv 69 E2
Richards Wlk. Clact 109 F3
Richardson Wlk. Colch 66 C3
Richmond Ave. S Ben 187 E1
Richmond Ave. South 199 F4
Richmond Ave. South 200 A4
Richmond Ave. South 201 E3
Richmond Cres. Harw 40 A1
Richmond Dr. Clact 109 D1
Richmond Dr. Rayl 188 B4
Richmond Dr. South 190 B2
Richmond Rd. Runw 163 E1
Richmond Rd. Sprin 128 A2
Richmond Rd. W Mers 121 E3
Richmond St. South 191 E1
Rickling. Basil 185 F2
Rickstones Rd. With 98 A3
Ridge The. Lit Bad 129 F1
Ridge The. Walt 94 A4
Ridgemount. S Ben 187 F2
Ridgeway Gdns. South 199 D4
Ridgeway The. Brain 60 A1
Ridgeway The. Harw 40 A2
Ridgeway The. South 199 D4
Ridgeway. Colch 50 A2
Ridgeway. Rayl 176 B1
Ridgewell Rd. Gt Y 8 C2
Ridgewell Way. Colch 67 F1
Ridings The. Canv 197 D3
Ridings The. Gt Bad 140 B4
Ridings The. Roch 178 C1
Ridlands Cl. T Gr 78 C3
Ridley Rd. Basil 174 B1
Ridley Rd. Chelm 127 D4
Riffams Ct. Basil 186 B4
Riffams Dr. Basil 186 B4
Riffams Chase. Lit Bad 129 E1
Riffams Dr. Gt Bad 141 D4
Riffams La. Dan 142 B4
Rifle Hill. Brain 59 F1
Rigby Ave. Mist 36 A2
Rigby Rd. Mist 36 A2
Rignals La. Chelm 140 B2
Riley Ave. Clact 124 C3
Rimini Cl. Basil 174 A1
Ringwood Dr. Rayl 189 E4
Ripley Cl. Clact 109 D3
Ripple Way. Colch 50 A1
Rippleside. Basil 185 F3
Risby Cl. Clact 109 D2
Rise The. E A Gr 66 A4
Rivendell Vale. S Woo F 165 E3
Rivenhall. Wick 175 D3
River Cl. Hals 25 F1
River Cotts. Bore 128 C4
River Hill. Terl 96 A2
River View Rd. S Ben 187 F1
River View. Brain 59 F1
River View. With 115 D4
Riverbank Cl. Cla 4 B4
Riverdale. South 189 E4
Rivermead. Chelm 127 D2
Riverside Ave E. Lawf 35 E2
Riverside Ave W. Lawf 35 E3
Riverside Ind Est. Roch 178 C1
Riverside Rd. Burn 170 B2
Riverside Way. Kelv 81 E1
Riverside Wlk. Colch 67 F4
Riverside Wlk. Wick 174 A4

Regency Cl. Runw 163 E1
Riverside. Bradw 61 E2
Riverton Dr. St L 135 D1
Rivertons. Basil 185 F2
Riverview Ct. Basil 185 F2
Riverview Gdns. Hull 165 E2
Riverview. Basil 186 A2
Riverview. Lawf 35 E2
Riviera Dr. South 200 B4
Rivish La. L Mel 7 E1
Roach Ave. Rayl 176 B1
Roach Vale. Colch 50 C1
Roach Vale. South 189 F4
Robert Way. Wick 174 C3
Robert Way. Wiv 69 E2
Robert's Hill. M Bure 28 C2
Roberts Rd. Colch 68 A3
Roberts Rd. N Fam 167 D4
Robin Cl. Gt Ben 89 E4
Robin Way. Chelm 140 A3
Robin Way. Sud 12 B3
Robinsbridge Rd. Cogg 62 C1
Robinsdale. Clact 109 F3
Robinson Rd. Brigh 107 D4
Robjohns Rd. Chelm 139 F4
Robletts Way. Worm 29 F2
Rochdale Way. Colch 68 C3
Roche Ave. Hawk 178 C1
Rochefort Dr. Roch 190 C4
Rochehall Way. Roch 191 D4
Rochester Dr. South 190 B2
Rochester Mews. South 190 B2
Rochester Way. Basil 185 F4
Rochester Way. Sud 7 E1
Rocheway. Roch 179 D1
Rochford Ave. South 190 C1
Rochford Cl. Wick 174 C3
Rochford Garden Way. Roch 178 C2
Rochford Hall Cl. Roch 178 C1
Rochford Rd. Canv 197 E2
Rochford Rd. Chelm 127 E1
Rochford Rd. South 190 B3
Rochford Rd. St O 108 A2
Rochford Way. Walt 94 A4
Rockall. South 190 A4
Rockingham Cl. Colch 50 B2
Rockleigh Ave. South 190 A1
Rodbridge Dr. South 200 C4
Rodbridge Hill. L Mel 7 D3
Roddam Cl. Colch 67 E3
Roding Cl. Gt Wak 193 D2
Roding Leigh. S Woo F 165 F4
Roding Way. Wick 174 C3
Rodings The. South 189 E4
Rodney Gdns. Brain 60 B2
Rodney Pl. Sud 7 F1
Rodney Way. Chelm 139 F4
Roedean Cl. South 191 F1
Roedean Gdns. South 191 F1
Rogation Cl. Stanw 66 B3
Roggel Rd. Canv 197 E1
Rokell Way. Walt 93 F3
Rokells. Basil 185 D4
Rokescroft. Basil 186 A3
Roland La. Canv 197 D2
Rolands Cl. Chelm 127 D4
Rolley La. Kelv 81 E1
Rolph Cl. Th L S 74 A1
Romainville Way. Canv 196 B2
Roman Hill. Rowh 86 A4
Roman Rd. Chelm 127 D1
Roman Rd. Colch 68 A4
Roman Way. L Mel 7 E3
Roman Way. St O 107 D2
Romans Pl. Writ 126 A1
Romans Way. Writ 126 A1
Romford Cl. Colch 68 A4
Romney Cl. Brain 59 F3
Romney Cl. Brigh 88 C1
Romney Cl. Clact 109 E3
Romney Cl. Walt 93 F4
Romsey Cl. Hock 177 E3
Romsey Cres. S Ben 187 D3
Romsey Dr. S Ben 187 D3
Romsey Rd. S Ben 187 D3
Romsey Way. S Ben 187 D3
Romulus Cl. Colch 49 F3
Ronald Dr. Rayl 189 A2
Ronald Hill Gr. South 189 D1
Ronald Park Ave. South 190 B1
Ronald Rd. Hals 43 F4
Roodegate. Basil 185 D3
Rookeries The. Mks T 65 D2
Rookery Chase. Ard 33 F1
Rookery Cl. Hat Pev 114 A3
Rookery Cl. Rayl 176 B1
Rookery La. Gt Tot 116 C4
Rookery La. Tipt 100 C3
Rookery Mead. S Woo F 165 E4
Rookery The. Lawf 35 E2
Rookwood Cl. Clact 109 E4
Rookyards. Basil 185 F3
Roosevel Ave. Canv 197 D3
Roosevelt Way. Colch 68 A2
Roothings The. Mald 132 A3
Roots Hall Ave. South 190 C1
Roots La. Wic Bis 115 F3
Rope Wlk. Brigh 107 D3
Rope Wlk. Mald 132 A1
Roper's Chase. Writ 139 D4

Roper's Chase. Writ

225
Ropers La. L Mel
School St. Nay

Ropers La. L Mel 7 D2
Rosabelle Ave. Wiv 69 D1
Rosalind Cl. Colch 68 C4
Rosary Gdns. South 190 A2
Rosbach Rd. Canv 197 E2
Rosberg Rd. Canv 197 F2
Rose Acre. Basil 185 F3
Rose Acre. High 22 C3
Rose Ave. Stanw 66 B2
Rose Cres. Colch 49 E1
Rose Glen. Chelm 140 B4
Rose Hill. Brain 60 A1
Rose La. Virl 119 D4
Rose La. Wiv 87 D4
Rose Rd. Canv 197 D2
Rose Way. Roch 191 D4
Rosebank Rd. W Mers 121 D3
Rosebank. Harw 40 A2
Rosebay Cl. With 97 E2
Roseberry Ave. Thund 187 E4
Rosebery Ave. Colch 68 A4
Rosebery Rd. Chelm 140 A4
Rosecroft Cl. Clact 109 F3
Roselaine. Basil 185 D4
Rosemary Ave. Brain 59 F2
Rosemary Cres. Clact 109 F1
Rosemary Cres. Tipt 100 B3
Rosemary La. Ca Hed 16 A3
Rosemary La. Hals 25 F1
Rosemary La. Thor 89 D3
Rosemary Rd W. Clact 109 F1
Rosemary Rd. Clact 109 F1
Rosemary Way. Clact 125 D4
Rosemead. Thund 187 E4
Roserna Rd. Canv 197 E2
Rosewood Cl. Colch 50 A2
Rosewood La. South 201 F3
Rosilian Dr. Hull 166 B1
Roslings Cl. Chelm 126 B3
Rossendale Cl. Colch 50 B2
Rossendale. Chelm 126 C1
Rossetta Cl. Wiv 69 D1
Rosshill Ind Park. Stobr 191 D2
Rossiter Rd. South 202 A4
Rosslyn Cl. Hock 177 F4
Rosslyn Rd. Hock 177 F4
Rothbury Rd. Chelm 126 B1
Rothchilds Ave. Rayl 176 B2
Rothesay Ave. Chelm 140 A4
Rothmans Ave. Gt Bad 140 C3
Rothwell Cl. Hadl 189 E3
Roughtons. Chelm 140 B2
Round Bush Corner. Birch 83 E2
Round Cl. Colch 67 D4
Round Hill Rd. S Ben 188 A1
Roundacre. Basil 185 D3
Roundacre. Hals 43 F4
Roundbush Rd. Lay M 83 E1
Roundbush Rd. Purl 156 A4
Rous Chase. Chelm 140 A1
Rouses La. Clact 108 C2
Rover Ave. Clact 124 C4
Row The. Str S M 22 B1
Rowallan Cl. Colch 67 D2
Rowan Chase. Tipt 100 B3
Rowan Cl. Clact 109 E2
Rowan Cl. Gt Ben 89 F4
Rowan Cl. Harw 40 A2
Rowan Cl. Stanw 66 B2
Rowan Dr. Mald 132 B3
Rowan Way. Cane 168 C1
Rowan Way. Hat Pev 114 A2
Rowan Way. With 98 A3
Rowan Wlk. South 189 E3
Rowhedge Cl. Basil 174 B1
Rowhedge Ferry Rd. Wiv 87 D4
Rowhedge Rd. Colch 68 C1
Rowherns La. Lit Ben 71 F2
Rowland's Yd. Harw 39 F1
Rowlands The. S Ben 187 F2
Rowley Cl. Catt 35 E4
Roxburghe Rd. Weel 90 C3
Roxwell Ave. Chelm 126 B2
Roxwell Rd. Chelm 126 B2
Roxwell Rd. Writ 126 B2
Royal Cl. Hawk 178 B3
Royal Mews. South 200 A4
Royal Oak Dr. Wick 175 D4
Royal Sq. Ded 33 F4
Royal Terr. South 200 A4
Roydon Bridge. Basil 185 E4
Roydon Way. Walt 93 F3
Royer Cl. Hawk 178 A2
Royston Ave. South 191 D2
Ruaton Dr. Clact 109 E2
Rubens Cl. South 202 A4
Rubens Gate. Sprin 127 F4
Rubicon Ave. Wick 174 C4
Rudd Ct. Colch 50 C1
Rudkin Rd. Colch 49 F3
Rudsdale Way. Colch 66 C3
Ruffles Cl. Rayl 176 C2
Rugby Rd. Sud 13 D2
Rugosa Cl. Stanw 66 B4
Rumseys Fields. Dan 142 C4
Rundells Wlk. Basil 185 F4
Rundels The. Thund 188 A3
Runnacles St. Silv E 79 E3
Running Mare La. Chelm 140 A2
Runnymeade Rd. Canv 197 D2
Runnymede Chase. Thund 188 A3
Runsell La. Dan 143 D4
Runsell View. Dan 143 D4
Runwell Gdns. Runw 163 E1
Runwell Rd. Runw 163 F1
Runwell Rd. Runw 164 A2
Runwell Terr. South 199 F4
Runwood Rd. Canv 196 B2
Rupert Rd. Soum 159 E2
Rurik Ct. Mald 144 C4
Rush Cl. Thund 187 D3
Rush Green Rd. Clact 109 D2
Rushbottom La. Basil 175 D1
Rushes La. Ashel 149 D1
Rushley Cl. Gt Wak 193 D2
Rushley. Basil 174 B1
Rushleydale. Sprin 127 F3
Rushmere Cl. W Mers 121 E3
Ruskin Ave. South 191 D1
Ruskin Cl. Walt 93 F4
Ruskin Path. Wick 174 B3
Ruskin Rd. Chelm 127 F1
Ruskoi Rd. Canv 196 C3
Russell Gdns. Chelm 140 A2
Russell Gdns. Wick 174 C4
Russell Gr. Roch 179 D1
Russell Rd. Clact 110 A2
Russell Rd. N Fam 156 A1
Russell Way. Chelm 139 F4
Russell's Rd. Hals 43 D4
Russet Cl. Brain 60 A1
Russet Way. Burn 170 B3
Russet Way. Hock 177 F4
Russets. Clelm 140 B2
Russets The. Hawk 178 B3
Rutherford Cl. Rayl 189 E3
Rutland Ave. Colch 67 D2
Rutland Ave. South 200 C4
Rutland Dr. Rayl 176 A4
Rutland Gdns. Brain 60 A2
Rutland Gdns. Hawk 178 B3
Rutland Rd. Chelm 127 D4
Rutland Rd. N Fam 167 D4
Rydal Cl. Hull 165 E2
Rydal Cl. Rayl 176 C1
Rydal Way. Bl Not 77 E3
Ryde Ave. Clact 110 A4
Ryde Cl. Hadl 189 D3
Ryde The. Hadl 189 D3
Ryder Way. Basil 174 B1
Rye Cl. Brigh 88 C1
Rye Cl. Colch 66 C3
Rye Cl. Hat Pev 114 A2
Rye Field The. Lit Bad 129 E2
Rye La. Lay H 85 D2
Rye Mill La. Fee 81 F2
Ryedene Cl. Basil 185 F2
Ryedene Pl. Basil 185 F2
Ryedene. Basil 185 F2
Ryegate Rd. Colch 67 F4
Ryes La. Bul 12 A1
Rylands Rd. South 191 E1
Ryle The. Writ 139 D4
Rysley. Lit Bad 129 E2

Sackville Cl. Chelm 126 C2
Sackville Rd. South 191 F1
Sackville Way. W Berg 48 B2
Saddle Rise. Sprin 127 F4
Sadler Cl. Colch 68 A2
Sadlers Cl. Walt 93 E3
Sadlers. Thund 187 D3
Saffory Cl. Rayl 189 E4
Saffron Way. Tipt 100 B2
Sage Rd. Colch 68 A1
Sage Wlk. Tipt 100 B2
St Agnes Dr. Canv 196 B2
St Alban's Rd. Clact 110 A2
St Alban's Rd. Colch 67 E4
St Andrew's Ave. Colch 68 B3
St Andrew's Gdns. Colch 68 B4
St Andrew's Rd. Clact 109 F2
St Andrew's Rd. Hat Pev 114 A2
St Andrew's Rd. Roch 178 C1
St Andrew's Rd. Weel 72 C1
St Andrew's Rise. Bul 11 F3
St Andrews Cl. Alres 88 A4
St Andrews Cl. Canv 196 B2
St Andrews Pl. Brigh 88 C1
St Andrews Rd. Bore 112 C1
St Andrews Rd. Hals 25 F1
St Andrews Rd. South 201 E3
St Andrews Rd. Sud 13 D3
St Ann's Rd. South 191 D1
St Anne's Rd. Colch 68 B4
St Annes Cl. Cogg 63 D1
St Annes Rd. Canv 197 F2
St Anns Rd. Clact 109 F2
St Anthony's Dr. Chelm 140 B4
St Augustine's Ave. South 201 D3
St Austell Rd. Colch 50 B1
St Austin's La. Harw 40 C3
St Barbara's Rd. Colch 67 E2
St Bartholomew Cl. Colch 50 B2
St Bartholomews La. Sud 7 E1
St Benet's Rd. South 190 C1
St Bernard Rd. Colch 50 B1
St Botolph's Circus. Colch 67 F3
St Botolph's St. Colch 67 F3
St Botolph's Terr. Walt 94 B4
St Botolphs Church Wlk. Colch 67 F3
St Bridge Ct. Colch 50 B1
St Catharines Cl. Colch 67 E1
St Catherine Rd. L Mel 7 E4
St Catherine's Rd. Chelm 126 C1
St Catherines Cl. Wick 174 C4
St Charles Dr. Wick 174 C4
St Christopher Rd. Colch 50 B1
St Christophers Cl. Canv 196 B2
St Christophers Way. Clact 125 D4
St Clair Cl. Clact 109 F4
St Clair's Dr. St O 108 A3
St Clair's Rd. St O 108 A3
St Clare Dr. Colch 67 D4
St Clare Meadow. Roch 178 C2
St Clare Rd. Colch 67 D3
St Clement Rd. Colch 50 B1
St Clement's Ave. South 189 F1
St Clement's Cl. S Ben 187 E3
St Clement's Cres. S Ben 187 E3
St Clement's Dr. South 189 F2
St Clement's Rd. S Ben 187 E3
St Clements Cl. Hawk 178 A2
St Clere's Hall La. St O 108 A2
St Cleres Cres. Wick 174 C4
St Cleres Way. Dan 142 B4
St Columb Ct. Colch 50 B1
St Cyrus Rd. Colch 50 B2
St David's Cl. Colch 68 B4
St David's Way. Wick 174 C4
St Davids Dr. Hadl 189 D2
St Davids Terr. Hadl 189 D2
St Davids Wlk. Canv 196 B2
St Dominic Rd. Colch 50 B1
St Edmund's Cl. South 191 E2
St Edmund's Ct. Colch 68 B4
St Edmund's Hill. Bures 19 E3
St Edmund's Hill. Sud 19 E3
St Edmunds La. Bures 19 F1
St Fabian's Dr. Chelm 126 C2
St Faith Rd. Colch 50 B1
St Fillan Rd. Colch 50 B1
St Gabriels Ct. Basil 186 A3
St George's Ave. Harw 40 B1
St George's Dr. South 190 C2
St George's La. South 201 F3
St George's Park Ave. South 190 A1
St Georges Cl. Gt Bro 52 C1
St Georges Wlk. Canv 196 B2
St Georges Wlk. Thund 187 D3
St Giles Cl. Mald 131 F1
St Giles Cres. Mald 131 F1
St Gregory's Ct. Sud 12 B4
St Guiberts Rd. Canv 196 C3
St Helen's Green. Harw 40 C3
St Helen's La. Colch 67 F4
St Helen's Rd. South 199 F4
St Helena Rd. Colch 67 E3
St Helens Ave. Clact 110 A4
St Ives Cl. Clact 109 D2
St Ives Rd. Peld 103 F3
St Jame's St. Ca Hed 15 F2
St James Ave. South 201 D4
St James Cl. Canv 196 B2
St James Cl. South 190 A2
St James Gdns. South 190 A2
St James Park. Chelm 126 B2
St James Rd. Basil 185 E3
St James Rd. Brain 59 F3
St James's Wlk. Hock 177 E3
St Jean Wlk. Tipt 100 B3
St John Ave. Brain 59 F1
St John's Ave. Chelm 140 A4
St John's Ave. Colch 67 F3
St John's Cres. Gt Hor 49 D4
St John's Ct. Tolle 119 E1
St John's Green. Colch 67 F3
St John's Green. Writ 126 A1
St John's Rd. Chelm 140 A4
St John's Rd. Clact 109 D3
St John's Rd. Colch 50 B2
St John's Rd. Gt Wak 193 D2
St John's Rd. S Ben 188 B2
St John's Rd. South 199 F4
St John's Rd. Wiv 87 E4
St John's Rd. Writ 126 A1
St John's St. Colch 67 F3
St Johns Cl. Gt Wak 193 D2
St Johns Cres. Canv 196 B2
St Johns Dr. Rayl 175 F2
St Joseph Rd. Colch 50 B2
St Jude Gdns. Colch 50 B1
St Judes Cl. Colch 50 B1
St Julian Gr. Colch 68 A3
St Lawrence Dr. St L 135 D1
St Lawrence Gdns. South 189 F3
St Lawrence Hill. St L 148 C3
St Lawrence Rd. Colch 50 B1
St Lawrence Rd. Till 149 E3
St Leonard's Rd. South 200 A4
St Leonards Rd. Colch 68 B3
St Luke's Chase. Tipt 100 B3
St Luke's Cl. Colch 50 B1
St Luke's Rd. South 191 E1
St Lukes Cl. Canv 196 B2
St Margaret's Rd. Sprin 127 F2
St Mark Dr. Colch 50 B1
St Mark's Rd. S Ben 188 B2
St Marks Rd. Canv 196 B2
St Marks Rd. Clact 109 F2
St Martin's Cl. Rayl 188 B4
St Martin's Cl. Thund 187 D4
St Martins Cl. Clact 109 F2
St Mary's Cl. Gt Bad 140 C3
St Mary's Cl. Pan 59 D4
St Mary's Cl. S Ben 187 E1
St Mary's Cres. Basil 186 B3
St Mary's Dr. S Ben 187 F1
St Mary's La. Mald 132 A1
St Mary's Path. Basil 186 B4
St Mary's Rd. Brain 60 A2
St Mary's Rd. Burn 170 B3
St Mary's Rd. Clact 109 F2
St Mary's Rd. Frin 94 A3
St Mary's Rd. Gt Ben 89 F3
St Mary's Rd. Kelv 81 E1
St Mary's Rd. S Ben 196 C4
St Mary's Rd. South 190 C1
St Mary's Rd. With 98 A4
St Marys Cl. South 192 B1
St Marys Mews. Tolle 119 E1
St Michael's La. Brain 59 F1
St Michael's Rd. Brain 59 F1
St Michael's Rd. Chelm 140 A4
St Michael's Rd. Harw 40 A1
St Michael's Rd. Rayl 188 C4
St Michael's Rd. Th L S 73 F1
St Michaels Ave. Basil 186 B2
St Michaels Cl. Latch 157 D3
St Michaels Ct. Mann 35 E2
St Michaels Rd. Canv 196 B2
St Michaels Rd. Colch 67 E1
St Michaels Wlk. Chelm 140 B1
St Mildreds Rd. Chelm 140 A4
St Monance Way. Colch 50 B1
St Nazaire Rd. Chelm 126 C3
St Neots Cl. Colch 50 B1
St Nicholas Cl. With 97 F2
St Nicholas Pass. Colch 67 F4
St Nicholas Rd. Till 149 F2
St Nicholas Rd. With 97 F2
St Nicholas St. Colch 67 F4
St Nicholas Way. Cogg 63 D2
St Osyth Rd. Alres 88 B4
St Osyth Rd. Clact 109 E2
St Osyth Rd. Lit Cla 91 E1
St Paul's Rd. Clact 110 A2
St Paul's Rd. Colch 67 F4
St Pauls Rd. Canv 196 B2
St Peter's Ave. Mald 131 F1
St Peter's Cl. Brain 59 F2
St Peter's Rd. Brain 59 F2
St Peter's Rd. Chelm 126 C1
St Peter's Rd. Cogg 63 D1
St Peter's Rd. W Mers 121 D3
St Peter's St. Colch 67 F4
St Peter's Terr. Wick 174 B4
St Peter's Wlk. Brain 59 F2
St Peters Ct. Sud 12 C4
St Peters Field. Burn 170 A3
St Peters Rd. Canv 196 B2
St Peters Rd. Hock 177 D4
St Peters's-in-the-Fields. Brain 59 F2
St Runwald St. Colch 67 F4
St Saviour Cl. Colch 50 B1
St Stephens Rd. Col N 156 A2
St Thomas Cl. Colch 50 C1
St Thomas Rd. Ashi 167 D2
St Vincent Chase. Brain 60 A3
St Vincent Rd. Clact 109 E1
St Vincent's Rd. South 199 F4
St Vincents Rd. Chelm 140 A4
Sairard Cl. South 189 E4
Sairard Gdns. South 189 E4
Salary Cl. Colch 50 C1
Salcombe Rd. Brain 60 B1
Salcott Cres. Wick 174 C3
Salem Wlk. Rayl 176 A2
Salerno Cres. Colch 67 E1
Salerno Way. Chelm 126 C3
Salforal Cl. Rett 153 D1
Salisbury Ave. Colch 67 F3
Salisbury Ave. South 190 C1
Salisbury Rd. Clact 110 B3
Salisbury Rd. South 189 E1
Salmon Cl. Colch 66 C2
Salmon's La. Gt T 64 A2
Saltcoats Hill. Stow M 155 D1
Saltcoats. S Woo F 165 E4
Salter Pl. Sprin 127 F1
Salter's Meadow. Toll D 118 B2
Saltings The. Hadl 188 B2
Salvia Cl. Clact 109 E2
Samphire Cl. With 97 E2
Sampson's La. Peld 103 F2
Samson's Rd. Brigh 88 C1
Samsons Cl. Brigh 106 C4
Samuel Manor. Sprin 127 F2
Samuels Dr. South 201 D4
San Remo Par. South 199 F4
San Remo Rd. Canv 197 E2
Sanctuary Rd. Hadl 189 D2
Sandbanks. Hadl 188 B1
Sanderling Gdns. Mald 132 B3
Sanderlings. S Ben 187 E1
Sanders Dr. Colch 67 D4
Sanders Rd. Canv 197 D3
Sanderson Ct. Colch 67 F4
Sandford Cl. Wiv 87 E4
Sandford Mill Rd. Sprin 127 F1
Sandford Mill Rd. Sprin 128 A1
Sandford Rd. Chelm 127 F2
Sandhill Rd. Rayl 189 E4
Sandhurst Cl. South 189 F2
Sandhurst Cres. South 189 F2
Sandhurst. Canv 196 B2
Sandleigh Rd. South 190 A1
Sandon Cl. Gt Hor 49 E4
Sandon Cl. Hawk 178 B2
Sandon Hall Bridleway. Sand 141 E2
Sandon Rd. Basil 185 F3
Sandown Ave. South 190 A1
Sandown Cl. Clact 110 A4
Sandown Cl. Wick 175 D4
Sandown Rd. Thund 188 A4
Sandown Rd. Wick 175 D4
Sandpiper Cl. Colch 69 D4
Sandpiper Cl. Mald 132 B3
Sandpiper Cl. South 201 F4
Sandpiper Wlk. Chelm 140 B3
Sandpit La. Burn 170 B3
Sandpit Rd. Brain 59 F2
Sandpit Rd. South 202 A4
Sandringham Ave. Hock 177 E3
Sandringham Ct. Sud 13 D4
Sandringham Rd. South 200 B4
Sandwich Cl. Brain 59 F3
Sandwich Rd. Brigh 106 C4
Sandwich Rd. Clact 125 E4
Sandy Hill. M Bure 29 E3
Sandy La. Bul 12 A3
Sandy La. Sud 12 A3
Santour Rd. Canv 196 C3
Saran Ct. Wiv 69 D1
Sarcel. Stis 61 E3
Sargeant Cl. Colch 68 A2
Sarre Way. Brigh 106 C4
Sassoon Way. Mald 145 D4
Satanita Rd. South 199 E4
Saul's Ave. With 115 D4
Sauls Bridge Cl. With 115 D4
Saunders Ave. Brain 59 F2
Savill Rd. Colch 68 B1
Saville St. Walt 76 B1
Sawkins Ave. Gt Bad 140 B3
Sawkins Cl. Gt Bad 140 B3
Sawkins Gdns. Gt Bad 140 B3
Sawney Brook. Writ 126 A1
Sawyer's Rd. Toll D 117 E3
Saxmunden Way. Clact 109 D2
Saxon Cl. Colch 66 C2
Saxon Cl. Rayl 176 C3
Saxon Cl. Runw 163 F1
Saxon Dr. With 97 F2
Saxon Way. Chelm 127 D4
Saxon Way. Clact 110 C3
Saxon Way. Mald 132 A1
Saxon Way. S Ben 187 E1
Saxonville. S Ben 187 D2
Saxted Dr. Clact 109 D2
Sayers. Thund 188 A3
Saywell Brook. Sprin 128 A1
Scalby Rd. Soum 159 D2
Scaldhurst. Basil 186 B4
Scarborough Dr. South 189 F1
Scarborough Rd. Soum 159 D2
Scarfe Way. Colch 68 C3
Scarletts Cl. With 115 D4
Scarletts Rd. Colch 68 B3
Scarletts. Basil 185 E4
Sceptre Rd. Tolle 119 E1
School Chase. Hals 43 F4
School Hill. Birch 84 A2
School La. Basil 175 D1
School La. Birch 84 A2
School La. Ded 33 F4
School La. Frat 71 D1
School La. Gt Hor 31 D1
School La. Gt Wig 102 C2
School La. Lawf 35 D1
School La. Lit Hor 30 B3
School La. Mist 35 F2
School La. S Ben 196 B4
School La. Str S M 22 B1
School La. W Berg 48 C2
School Rd. Colch 68 A1
School Rd. Copf 65 E2
School Rd. Elmst M 70 A2
School Rd. Frin 93 F3
School Rd. Gt Oak 56 B2
School Rd. Gt Tot 116 A2
School Rd. Langh 32 C2
School Rd. Lit Hor 30 B2
School Rd. Lit Map 26 A4
School Rd. Lit Tot 117 D2
School Rd. Lit Y 9 E2
School Rd. Mess 82 B1
School Rd. Pent 5 F3
School Rd. Sho G 40 A4
School Rd. Si Hed 24 B4
School Rd. Silv E 79 F2
School Rd. Tend 72 C3
School Rd. Wic Bis 115 F3
School Rd. Wic S P 17 E3
School St. Nay 20 B3

School St. Sud 12 C4
School View Rd. Chelm 126 C2
School Way. South 189 F2
School Wlk. Brain 59 F2
Schoolfield. Glems 2 A3
Scofield Ct. Sud 13 D3
Scotland St. Nay 20 C3
Scott Cl. Brain 78 A4
Scott Dr. Colch 66 C3
Scotts Hall Cotts. Cane 179 E4
Scotts Hall Rd. Cane 179 E4
Scotts Hill. South 159 D2
Scotts Wlk. Chelm 126 B3
Scotts Wlk. Rayl 177 D1
Scraley Rd. Gt Tot 132 B3
Scraley Rd. Mald 132 B3
Scratton Rd. South 199 F4
Scrip's Rd. Cogg 81 D4
Scrub La. Hadl 188 C2
Scylla Cl. Mald 132 B3
Scythe Way. Colch 66 C2
Scythe Way. Colch 67 D2
Sea Cornflower Way. Clact .. 125 D4
Sea Cres. Clact 124 C3
Sea Flowers Way. Clact 125 D4
Sea Glebe Way. Clact 125 D4
Sea Holly Way. Clact 125 D3
Sea King Cres. Colch 50 A2
Sea Lavender Way. Clact 125 D4
Sea Pink Way. Clact 125 D3
Sea Reach. South 198 C4
Sea Rosemary Way. Clact ... 125 D4
Sea Shell Way. Clact 125 D3
Sea Thistle Way. Clact 125 D4
Sea View Par. May 146 C1
Sea View Par. St L 135 E1
Sea View Prom. Tolle 135 D1
Sea Way. Clact 124 C3
Seabrook Gdns. Bore 112 C1
Seabrook Rd. Gt Bad 141 D3
Seaden Ct. Clact 110 A4
Seafield Ave. Mist 36 A2
Seafield Rd. Harw 40 A1
Seafields Gdns. Clact 110 B3
Seafields Rd. Clact 110 B3
Seaforth Ave. South 191 E1
Seaforth Gr. South 191 E1
Seaforth Rd. South 199 E4
Seagers. Gt Tot 116 A2
Seamer Rd. Soum 159 D2
Seamore Ave. Thund 187 E4
Seamore Cl. Thund 187 E3
Seamore Wlk. Thund 187 E4
Seaton Cl. Lawf 35 D2
Seaview Ave. Basil 185 E2
Seaview Ave. Lit Oak 57 E4
Seaview Ave. W Mers 121 F3
Seaview Dr. Gt Wak 193 E2
Seaview Hts. Walt 94 B4
Seaview Rd. Brigh 106 C4
Seaview Rd. Canv 197 F1
Seaview Rd. South 198 C4
Seaview Rd. St O 201 F3
Seaview Rd. St O 124 A4
Seaview Terr. Hadl 188 B1
Seaview Terr. St O 107 D2
Seaway. Canv 197 D1
Seaway. St L 148 B4
Seawick Rd. St O 124 A3
Sebastian Cl. Colch 68 C4
Second Ave. Canv 196 C2
Second Ave. Chelm 127 D3
Second Ave. Clact 110 A2
Second Ave. Frin 93 F2
Second Ave. Glems 2 B3
Second Ave. Hals 26 A1
Second Ave. Harw 40 B2
Second Ave. Hull 165 F1
Second Ave. South 199 D4
Second Ave. Sud 7 F1
Second Ave. Walt 76 B2
Second Ave. Weel 90 C4
Second Ave. Wick 175 D3
Seddons Wlk. Hock 177 F3
Seden Ct. Clact 92 A1
Sedgemoor. South 192 B1
Selbourne Rd. Hock 177 F3
Selbourne Rd. South 191 E2
Selbourne Rd. Thund 187 E3
Seldon Cl. South 190 A2
Seldon Rd. Tipt 100 B3
Selsey Ave. Clact 125 E4
Selwyn Rd. South 191 E1
Serpentine Wlk. Colch 49 F1
Seven Acres. Wick 174 C4
Seven Ash Green. Sprin 127 E3
Seventh Ave. Canv 196 C2
Seventh Ave. Chelm 127 D3
Severalls La. Colch 50 B3
Severn Rd. Clact 109 F3
Sewards End. Wick 174 C3
Sewell's La. Bel S P 5 D1
Sexton Cl. Rowh 86 A4
Seymour Rd. Clact 108 C1
Seymour Rd. Hadl 188 C2
Seymour Rd. South 190 B1
Seymour St. Chelm 127 D1
Shackleton Cl. Harw 39 F1
Shaftesbury Ave. Harw 40 A2

Shaftesbury Ave. South 200 C3
Shair La. Tend 72 A1
Shakespeare Ave. Rayl 177 D1
Shakespeare Ave. South 190 C1
Shakespeare Cl. Brain 78 A4
Shakespeare Dr. Mald 132 A1
Shakespeare Dr. South 190 C1
Shakespeare Rd. Colch 66 C3
Shakeston Cl. Writ 139 D4
Shamrock Cl. Tolle 119 E1
Shanklin Cl. Clact 110 A4
Shanklin Dr. South 190 A1
Shannon Ave. Rayl 176 B1
Shannon Cl. South 189 F2
Shannon Way. Canv 196 B2
Sharlands Cl. Wick 174 C4
Sharnbrook. South 192 B1
Sharpington Cl. Chelm 140 B2
Shatters Rd. Lay Br 84 A1
Shaw Cl. Walt 93 F4
Shaw Rd. L Mel 7 E4
Shaw Rd. With 97 F3
Shearers Way. Bore 112 C1
Shears Cres. W Mers 121 F3
Sheepcoates La. Gt Tot 116 C1
Sheepcot Rd. Ca Hed 15 F2
Sheepcotes La. Silv E 79 F3
Sheepcotes La. Soum 159 E3
Sheepen Pl. Colch 67 F4
Sheepen Rd. Colch 67 E4
Sheepgate La. Cla 4 A4
Sheepshead Hill. Sud 13 E3
Sheering Wlk. Colch 67 F1
Sheerwater Mews. Colch 69 D4
Sheldon Rd. Canv 197 F2
Shellbeach Rd. Canv 197 E1
Shellcroft. Col En 26 C1
Shelley Ave. Sud 13 D3
Shelley Cl. Mald 145 D4
Shelley Rd. Chelm 127 E1
Shelley Rd. Colch 66 C3
Shelley Sq. South 191 D1
Shelley Wlk. Brain 78 A4
Shelleys La. T Gr 78 C4
Shepard Cl. South 190 A3
Shepherds Cl. Hadl 188 C2
Shepherds Croft. Stanw 66 B3
Shepherds La. Glems 2 A3
Shepherds Wlk. Hadl 188 C2
Sheppard Cl. Clact 109 E3
Sheppard Dr. Sprin 128 A2
Sherborne Cl. Roch 190 C3
Sherbourne Cl. Walt 93 F4
Sherbourne Dr. Basil 174 A1
Sherbourne Gdns. Roch 190 C3
Sherbourne Rd. Colch 68 C4
Sheridan Ave. S Ben 188 A2
Sheridan Cl. Rayl 176 C1
Sheridan Wlk. Colch 66 C3
Sheriffs Way. Clact 109 F4
Sheriton Sq. Rayl 176 B2
Sherry Way. Hadl 188 C3
Sherwood Cl. Colch 68 C4
Sherwood Cres. Hadl 188 C2
Sherwood Dr. Chelm 126 B1
Sherwood Dr. Clact 109 F3
Sherwood Way. Fee 81 E2
Sherwood Way. South 191 F1
Shewell Wlk. Colch 67 F4
Shewsbury Dri. Thund 187 E4
Shillingstone. South 192 B1
Shillito Cl. Colch 66 C2
Ship Hill. Brad 36 C2
Ship Rd. Burn 170 B2
Shipwrights Cl. S Ben 188 A1
Shipwrights Dr. S Ben 188 A2
Shire Cl. Sprin 127 F4
Shirebourn Vale. S Woo F ... 165 E3
Shirley Ct. Clact 109 D1
Shirley Gdns. Basil 186 B4
Shirley Rd. South 189 F3
Shoebridge's Hill. Ded 33 F3
Shoebury Ave. South 201 F4
Shoebury Common Rd. South 201 F4
Shoebury Rd. Gt Wak 193 E2
Shoebury Rd. South 192 A1
Shop La. E Mers 105 F2
Shop Rd. Lit Bro 53 D3
Shopland Hall Rd. Stobr 191 E3
Shopland Rd. Stobr 191 E4
Shore La. Brad 36 C2
Shore Rd. Burn 170 B2
Shorefield Gdns. South 199 F4
Shorefield Rd. South 199 E4
Shorefield. S Ben 187 D2
Short Cut Rd. Colch 67 F4
Short Cut Rd. Colch 67 F4
Short Rd. Hadl 188 B1
Short St. South 191 D1
Short Wyre St. Colch 67 F4
Shortacre. Basil 185 E3
Shortlands. Basil 185 D3
Shortridge Ct. With 114 C4
Shrub End Rd. Colch 67 D2
Shrubland Cl. Clact 110 A3
Shrubland Rd. Colch 68 A3
Shrubland Rd. Mist 36 A2
Shrublands Cl. Chelm 127 E1

Shums Hill. Walt 93 E4
Shut La. Ea Col 45 D3
Siam Pl. Sud 12 C4
Sidmouth Ave. South 190 B3
Sidmouth Rd. Sprin 127 F3
Sidwell Ave. S Ben 187 F1
Sidwell Chase. S Ben 187 F1
Sidwell La. S Ben 187 F1
Sidwell Park. S Ben 187 F1
Siena Mews. Colch 68 A2
Silcock Cl. Colch 50 B1
Silcott St. Brigh 106 C3
Sillett Cl. Clact 109 E3
Silvanus Cl. Colch 67 E3
Silver Rd. Burn 170 B2
Silver St. Mald 131 F2
Silver St. Silv E 79 E2
Silver Way. Runw 174 B4
Silversea Dr. South 190 A1
Silverdale Ave. South 190 C1
Silverdale. Rayl 188 C4
Silverdale. Thund 187 F4
Silverpoint Marine. South 198 A2
Silverthorn Cl. Hawk 178 B2
Silverthorne. Canv 196 C2
Silvertree Cl. Hock 177 D3
Simmonds La. Purl 145 D1
Simmonds Way. Dan 142 C4
Simons La. Colch 68 A3
Simpsons La. Tipt 100 A2
Sims Cl. Ea Col 45 D4
Singer Ave. Clact 124 C4
Singleton Ct. Sud 13 D3
Sinnington End. Colch 50 B2
Sioux Cl. Colch 50 B2
Sir Isaac's Wlk. Colch 67 F4
Sir Walter Raleigh Dr. Rayl ... 176 B3
Sirdar Rd. Rayl 188 B4
Siskin Cl. Colch 68 C4
Sittang Cl. Colch 67 E1
Sitwell Cl. Lawf 35 D2
Siward Rd. With 114 B4
Six Bells Ct. Brain 59 F3
Sixth Ave. Canv 196 C2
Sixth Ave. Chelm 127 D3
Skate's Hill. Glems 2 A1
Skelmersdale Rd. Clact 109 F2
Skerry Rise. Chelm 127 D4
Skiddaw Cl. Bl Not 77 E4
Skinner's La. Chelm 140 A2
Skitts Hill. Brain 60 A1
Skreens Ct. Chelm 126 B2
Sky Hall Hill. Box 32 B4
Skylark Wlk. Chelm 140 A3
Skyrmans Fee. Walt 93 F3
Sladbury's La. Clact 110 B4
Slade Rd. Clact 110 B3
Slade's La. Chelm 140 A2
Slades Cl. Glems 2 B3
Slades The. Basil 185 F2
Sloe Hill. Hals 25 E1
Slough Farm Rd. Hals 25 E1
Slough Cl. Ard 51 E3
Slough La. Purl 143 E2
Slough La. Wiv 69 D3
Slough Rd. Dan 143 E2
Smaley La. L Mel 7 E4
Smallbridge Entry. Bures 29 E4
Smallgains Ave. Canv 197 F2
Smallwood Rd. Colch 67 D2
Smart Ave. Canv 197 D2
Smeaton Cl. Colch 50 B3
Smeetham Hall La. Bul 11 F4
Smith St. South 201 F3
Smither's Chase. Stobr 191 D3
Smithers Dr. Gt Bad 141 D3
Smiths Ave. May 158 A4
Smiths Field. Colch 68 B3
Smythe Cl. Clact 109 E3
Smythies Ave. Colch 68 A4
Snakes La. South 190 A3
Snape Cl. Clact 109 D2
Snape Way. Walt 93 F4
Sneating Hall La. Th L S 92 C4
Snelling Gr. Gt Bad 140 C3
Sniveller's La. Kelv 80 B2
Snoreham Gdns. Latch 157 D3
Snowberry Gr. Colch 68 A2
Snowdonia Cl. Basil 186 B4
Snowdrop Cl. Sprin 127 F4
Snowdrop Cl. With 97 F2
Soane St. Ipswich ? ...

Spurgeon St. Colch 68 B3
Square The. Colch 67 D2
Square The. Mald 132 A3
Square The. Till 149 F2
Squire St. S Woo F 165 F4
Squirrells Ct. Chelm 126 C3
Squirrels Field. Colch 49 F3
Stabbings Ct. Burn 170 B2
Stable Cl. Colch 66 C3
Stable Ct. W Mers 121 F4
Stablecroft. Sprin 127 F4
Stablefield Rd. Walt 94 A4
Stadium Rd. South 191 D1
Stadium Way. Hadl 188 B4
Stafford Cl. South 190 A3
Stafford Cl. Walt 93 F3
Stafford Wlk. Canv 197 D3
Stagden Cross. Basil 185 F3
Stairs Rd. Gt Wak 193 F2
Stalin Rd. Colch 68 A2
Stallards Cres. Walt 93 F3
Stambourne Rd. Gt Y 8 B2
Stambourne Rd. Topp 14 A4
Stambridge Rd. Clact 109 E2
Stambridge Rd. Gt Stam ... 179 E1
Stammers Rd. Colch 49 F2
Standard Ave. Clact 124 B3
Standard Rd. Colch 68 B3
Standley Rd. Walt 76 B1
Stane Field. Mks T 64 C2
Stanes Rd. Brain 59 F3
Stanfield Cl. Stanw 66 C2
Stanfield Rd. South 191 D1
Stanford Rd. Canv 197 D2
Stanley Ave. Brigh 107 D4
Stanley Rd. Ashi 178 B4
Stanley Rd. Canv 197 E2
Stanley Rd. Clact 109 E1
Stanley Rd. Hals 25 E1
Stanley Rd. South 200 A4
Stanley Rd. Sud 12 C4
Stanley Rd. Thund 187 D4
Stanley Rd. Wiv 69 E1
Stanley Rise. Sprin 127 F2
Stanley Wood Ave. Sud 7 F1
Stanley Wooster Way. Colch ..68 C4
Stanmore Cl. Clact 109 E4
Stanmore Rd. Wick 175 D3
Stanmore Way. St O 108 A2
Stannard Way. Sud 13 D3
Stansfield Rd. Thund 187 D4
Stansgate Rd. Steep 147 F3
Stanstead Rd. Hals 43 F4
Stansted Cl. Chelm 126 C1
Stansted Rd. Colch 68 A1
Stansted Way. Walt 94 A3
Stanway Cl. Glems 2 B3
Stanway Rd. S Ben 187 E3
Stanwell St. Colch 67 F3
Stanwyn Ave. Clact 109 F2
Stapleford End. Wick 175 D3
Staplegrove. South 201 E4
Staplers Heath. Gt Tot 116 A2
Star La. Gt Wak 192 C2
Starboard View. S Woo F .. 165 F3
Starling's Hill. Si Hed 24 C2
Station App. Basil 186 A2
Station App. Brain 60 A1
Station App. Canv 196 B3
Station App. Frin 93 F3
Station App. Hock 177 F3
Station App. Runw 174 B4
Station App. S Woo F 165 E4
Station App. South 190 C2
Station App. South 200 A4
Station Ave. Rayl 176 B2
Station Ave. Runw 174 B4
Station Ave. South 191 D2
Station Cres. Col N 155 F3
Station Cres. Rayl 176 B2
Station Hill. Bures 19 F1
Station La. Basil 186 A2
Station La. Harw 40 B2
Station Rd. Alres 88 A4
Station Rd. Alth 157 F1
Station Rd. Ard 51 F4
Station Rd. Brad 36 C1
Station Rd. Brain 59 F1
Station Rd. Brigh 106 C3
Station Rd. Burn 170 A2
Station Rd. Canv 197 F1
Station Rd. Cla 4 B4
Station Rd. Clact 109 F1
Station Rd. Col En 26 C1
Station Rd. Col N 156 A3
Station Rd. Ea Col 45 D4
Station Rd. Frat 89 D4
Station Rd. Gt Ben 89 F4
Station Rd. Harw 40 B2
Station Rd. Harw 40 C3
Station Rd. Hat Pev 113 D4
Station Rd. Hock 177 F3
Station Rd. Kelv 81 E2
Station Rd. L Mel 7 E3
Station Rd. Lawf 35 E3
Station Rd. Mald 132 A2
Station Rd. Mks T 65 D2
Station Rd. Rams 39 F3
Station Rd. Rayl 176 B2

Station Rd. Runw 163 E1
Station Rd. S Ben 196 B4
Station Rd. Si Hed 15 F1
Station Rd. Soum 159 E2
Station Rd. South 189 F1
Station Rd. South 189 F2
Station Rd. South 199 E4
Station Rd. South 201 D4
Station Rd. Sud 12 C4
Station Rd. Sud 12 C4
Station Rd. Th L S 91 F4
Station Rd. Thor 89 D3
Station Rd. Tipt 100 B2
Station Rd. Toll D 118 C3
Station Rd. Tolle 119 E1
Station Rd. Wa Col 45 F4
Station Rd. Wa Col 46 B3
Station Rd. Walt 93 D3
Station Rd. Wh Not 78 C1
Station Rd. Wic Bis 115 D2
Station Rd. With 98 A2
Station Rd. Wiv 87 D4
Station Rd. Wrab 37 F2
Station St. Walt 94 B4
Station Way. Basil 185 D3
Steam Mill Rd. Brad 54 A4
Steele Cl. Mks T 64 C2
Steeple Cl. Hawk 178 B2
Steeple Cl. Mald 132 B3
Steeple Hts. Thund 187 D3
Steeple Rd. Latch 157 E3
Steeple Rd. Soum 159 D3
Steeple Rd. St L 148 B2
Steeplefield. South 189 F3
Steeplehall. Basil 186 A3
Steerforth Rd. Chelm 126 B4
Steli Ave. Canv 196 C3
Stella Maris Cl. Canv 197 F2
Stepfield. With 98 A1
Stephan Cranfield Cl. Rowh ... 87 D4
Stephen Cl. L Mel 7 D3
Stephenson Rd W. Clact 92 A1
Stephenson Rd. Brain 60 A1
Stephenson Rd. Clact 110 A4
Stephenson Rd. Colch 50 B3
Stephenson Rd. N Fam 167 D4
Stephenson Rd. South 189 E3
Sterling Cl. Colch 66 C3
Stevens Cl. Canv 197 E2
Stevens Rd. With 97 F1
Stevens Wlk. Colch 68 C4
Stevenson Way. Wick 174 B3
Stewards Cl. Walt 93 F4
Stewart Rd. Chelm 140 A4
Steyning Ave. South 191 F1
Stile La. Rayl 176 B1
Stilemans. Wick 174 B4
Stiles The. Mald 132 C2
Stirling Ave. Hadl 189 D1
Stirling Pl. Basil 186 A4
Stirrup Cl. Sprin 127 F4
Stivvy's Rd. Woo Wa 130 B2
Stock Chase. Mald 132 A3
Stock Cl. South 190 C2
Stock Rd. South 190 C2
Stock Terr. Mald 132 A3
Stockhouse Cl. Toll K 101 D1
Stockhouse Rd. Lay M 101 D4
Stockwell. Colch 67 F4
Stockwood. Thund 188 A4
Stoke Ash Cl. Clact 109 D2
Stoke Rd. Cla 4 A3
Stoke Rd. Nay 20 A1
Stokefelde. Basil 186 A4
Stokes The. Walt 94 A4
Stone Green Rd. Gt Oak 55 F1
Stone La. Wrab 37 F3
Stone Path Dr. Hat Pev 113 F2
Stone Rd. Gt Bro 53 D1
Stonebridge Hill. Col En 44 C4
Stonebridge Wlk. Chelm 127 D1
Stonecrop. Colch 49 E1
Stonehall Dr. Lit Cla 91 E1
Stonehall La. Gt Oak 55 D1
Stoneham Ave. Clact 109 D2
Stoneham St. Cogg 62 C1
Stonehill Cl. South 189 F2
Stonehill Rd. South 189 F2
Stonehill Way. W Mers 121 D3
Stoneleigh Park. Colch 66 C2
Stoneleighs. Thund 187 F3
Stoney Hills. Burn 170 B4
Stoney La. Brigh 107 D4
Stores La. Tipt 100 B3
Stornoway Rd. South 191 E1
Stour Cl. Glems 2 B1
Stour Cl. Harw 39 E1
Stour Gdns. Cla 13 D2
Stour Green. Cla 4 A3
Stour Rd. Harw 40 B3
Stour St. Cav 5 E4
Stour St. Mann 35 E2
Stour St. Sud 12 C4
Stour Vale. Cla 4 A3
Stourdale Cl. Lawf 35 D2
Stourside. Sho G 40 A4
Stourton Rd. With 97 F2
Stourview Ave. Mist 36 A2
Stourview Cl. Mist 36 A2

Stow Rd. Col N 155 E3
Stowe's La. Till 149 E2
Straight Rd. Box 31 F1
Straight Rd. Brad 36 B1
Straight Rd. Colch 66 C3
Straight Rd. Gt Ben 90 A2
Straight Way. Birch 84 A1
Stranger's Chr. Brigh 88 C1
Strangman Ave. Brain 188 A2
Strasbourg Rd. Canv 197 E3
Stratford Pl. Walt 94 B4
Stratford Rd. Clact 110 B3
Stratford Rd. Ded 33 E3
Strathmore Rd. N Fam 167 D4
Straw La. Sud 12 C4
Strawberry Cl. Brain 60 A1
Strawberry La. Tipt 100 C2
Street The. Ard 51 F4
Street The. Ashe 3 E1
Street The. Brad 36 C1
Street The. Bradw 61 E2
Street The. Bul 11 F3
Street The. Chelm 140 A1
Street The. Cla 3 E2
Street The. Fee 81 F3
Street The. Gos 42 C4
Street The. Gt T 64 A4
Street The. Hat Pev 114 A2
Street The. Latch 157 D3
Street The. Lit Cla 91 E2
Street The. Mess 82 B1
Street The. Midd 12 C2
Street The. Peb 27 D4
Street The. Rams 39 D1
Street The. S Woo F 154 A2
Street The. Steep 147 F1
Street The. Stis 61 D3
Street The. Stow M 155 E2
Street The. T Gr 79 D3
Street The. Tend 72 C3
Street The. Terl 96 B2
Street The. Toll M 117 D3
Street The. Topp 14 A4
Street The. Viri 119 D4
Street The. Wa Col 46 B3
Street The. Walt 75 D1
Street The. Weel 72 C1
Street The. Wh Not 78 C1
Street The. Wic Bis 115 F3
Street The. Woo Wa 130 B1
Stretford Cl. Silv E 79 E2
Strickmere. Str S M 22 B1
Stroma Ave. Canv 196 C3
Stroma Gdns. South 201 E3
Stromburg Rd. Canv 196 C3
Stromness Pl. South 191 E1
Stromness Rd. South 191 E1
Strood Cl. W Mers 121 D4
Strood The. W Mers 104 B2
Strudwick Cl. Brain 59 F1
Strutt Cl. Hat Pev 114 A2
Stuart Cl. Canv 197 D2
Stuart Cl. Gt Bad 141 D4
Stuart Cl. Gt Wak 192 C2
Stuart Cl. South 191 D1
Stuart Rd. South 191 D1
Stuarts Way. Brain 60 A1
Stubbs Cl. Walt 93 F4
Stubbs La. Brain 60 B1
Stublands. Basil 185 F3
Studd's La. Colch 49 E2
Stump La. Sprin 127 E2
Sturrick La. Gt Ben 89 E4
Sturrocks. Basil 185 F2
Sudbourne Ave. Clact 109 D2
Sudbrook Cl. Wick 174 B3
Sudbury Cl. Hawk 177 F2
Sudbury Hill. Ca Hed 15 F2
Sudbury Rd. Bul 11 F3
Sudbury Rd. Bures 19 F1
Sudbury Rd. Ca Hed 16 A2
Sudbury Rd. Canv 196 C3
Sudbury Rd. Gest 10 C1
Sudbury Rd. Hals 25 F2
Sudbury Rd. L Mel 7 E2
Sudbury Rd. Lit Map 17 E1
Sudbury Rd. Nay 20 B3
Sudbury Rd. S Han 163 D3
Sudeley Gdns. Hock 177 E3
Suffolk Ave. South 189 F2
Suffolk Ave. W Mers 121 E4
Suffolk Cl. Clact 110 C4
Suffolk Cl. Colch 50 A1
Suffolk Dr. Sprin 128 A2
Suffolk Knowle. Bures 19 F1
Suffolk Rd. Mald 131 F1
Suffolk Rd. Sud 12 C4
Suffolk Sq. Sud 12 C4
Suffolk St. Walt 94 B4
Suffolk Way. Canv 196 C2
Suffolk Wlk. Canv 196 C2
Sugar La. Si Hed 23 F4
Sugden Ave. Wick 174 A4
Sulleys Hill. High 22 A4
Sullivan Cl. Colch 68 C3
Summercourt Rd. South 199 F4
Summerdale. Alth 158 A2
Summerfields. Si Hed 15 F1

Summerhill. Alth 157 F2
Sumpters Way. South 190 C3
Sunbeam Ave. Clact 124 C3
Sunbury Ct. South 192 C1
Sundale Cl. Clact 110 C3
Sunflower Cl. Sprin 127 F3
Sunnedon. Basil 185 E3
Sunningdale Ave. South 190 A1
Sunningdale Fall. Hat Pev . 114 A2
Sunningdale Rd. Alth 157 F1
Sunningdale Rd. Chelm 126 C2
Sunningdale Way. Walt 93 F4
Sunningdale. Canv 197 E2
Sunny Point. Walt 76 B2
Sunny Rd. Hawk 177 F3
Sunnybank Cl. South 189 F3
Sunnyfield Gdns. Hock 177 D3
Sunnyfields Rd. Brain 42 B1
Sunnymede Cl. Thund 188 A3
Sunnyside Ave. Basil 186 B3
Sunnyside Rd. Ford 47 E3
Sunnyside. Brain 59 F2
Sunnyway. St L 148 B4
Sunrise Ave. Chelm 127 D3
Surbiton Ave. South 200 B4
Surbiton Rd. South 191 E1
Surig Rd. Canv 197 D2
Surrey Ave. South 189 F2
Surrey La. Tipt 100 B2
Sussex Cl. Bore 128 C4
Sussex Cl. Canv 197 D3
Sussex Gdns. Clact 110 C3
Sussex Rd. Colch 67 E4
Sussex Way. Canv 197 D3
Sutcliffe Cl. Wick 174 B3
Sutherland Bvd. Hadl 189 D1
Sutherland Pl. Wick 174 B3
Sutor Cl. With 97 F1
Sutton Court Dr. Roch 190 C4
Sutton Mead. Sprin 128 A2
Sutton Park Ave. Colch 67 D2
Sutton Rd. Roch 190 C4
Sutton Rd. South 191 D1
Sutton Rd. Stobr 191 D3
Suttons Rd. Gt Wak 193 E1
Swale Rd. Thund 188 A3
Swallow Cl. Lay H 85 D3
Swallow Dale. Basil 185 E2
Swallow Dr. S Ben 187 E1
Swallow Field. Ea Col 45 D3
Swallow Path. Chelm 140 A2
Swallow Rd. Runw 163 E1
Swallow's Row. Gt Ben 72 A1
Swallowcliffe. South 192 B1
Swallowdale. Clact 109 F4
Swallowdale. Colch 68 B2
Swan Chase. Si Hed 24 C4
Swan Cl. Hat Pev 114 A2
Swan Dale. Clact 109 F4
Swan Gr. Wa Col 46 B3
Swan La. Runw 163 E1
Swan Mead. Basil 185 E2
Swan Pass. Colch 67 F4
Swan Rd. Beau 73 E3
Swan Side. Brain 59 F2
Swan St. Kelv 81 E2
Swan St. Si Hed 15 F1
Swan St. Wa Col 46 B2
Swan Yd. Cogg 63 D1
Swanage Rd. South 191 D1
Swanfield. L Mel 7 E4
Swans Green Cl. Thund 188 A3
Swanscomb Rd. Wa Col 45 F2
Swanstead. Basil 185 F2
Swaynes. Str S M 22 B1
Sweden Cl. Harw 39 F2
Sweet Briar Ave. S Ben 187 E1
Sweet Briar Rd. Stanw 66 B4
Sweetbriar Lodge. Canv 196 C2
Sweyne Ave. Hawk 178 A2
Sweyne Ave. South 190 C1
Sweyne Cl. Rayl 176 A2
Swift Ave. Clact 124 C3
Swift Cl. Brain 78 A4
Swinborne Ct. Basil 174 A1
Swinborne Rd. Basil 174 B1
Swinbourne Dr. Brain 59 E2
Swiss Ave. Chelm 127 D2
Sycamore Cl. Canv 196 C2
Sycamore Cl. With 98 A4
Sycamore Gr. Brain 59 E1
Sycamore Gr. South 191 D1
Sycamore Pl. Gt Ben 89 F4
Sycamore Rd. Colch 68 B4
Sycamore Rd. Mald 132 B3
Sycamore Rd. Sud 13 D4
Sycamore Way. Cane 168 B1
Sycamore Way. Catt 35 E4
Sycamore Way. Chelm 140 B3
Sycamore Way. Clact 109 E2
Sycamore Way. Walt 93 E3
Sycamores The. Basil 186 B3
Sydervelt Rd. Canv 197 D2
Sydner Cl. Gt Bad 141 D3
Sydney Rd. Hadl 189 D1
Sydney Rd. S Ben 187 E2
Sydney St. Brigh 106 C3
Sydney St. Colch 68 A1

Syers Field. Weth 23 D1
Sykes Mead. Rayl 176 B1
Sylvan Cl. Canv 197 D1
Sylvan Cl. Chelm 140 A3
Sylvan Way. Hadl 189 D2
Symons Ave. South 189 F4

Tabor Ave. Brain 59 F2
Tabor Cl. Brigh 106 C4
Tabor Rd. Colch 68 B4
Tabor's Hill. Gt Bad 140 C4
Tabora Ave. Canv 196 C3
Tabors Ave. Gt Bad 140 C3
Tabrum's La. Rett 165 D3
Tabrums The. 154 B1
Taffrail Gdns. Hadl 165 F3
Tailors Way. South 190 C3
Takely End. Basil 185 D3
Takely Ride. Basil 185 D3
Talbot Ave. Clact 124 C3
Talbot Ave. Rayl 176 B2
Talbot Rd. Lit Cla 91 E1
Talbot Rd. Sud 7 F1
Talbot St. Harw 40 B3
Talcott Rd. Colch 68 A1
Talisman Cl. Tipt 100 B3
Talisman Wlk. Tipt 100 B3
Tall Trees. Colch 49 F2
Tallow Gate. S Woo F 165 F3
Tally Ho. Colch 50 A2
Tallyho Cnr. Str S M 22 B1
Tamar Ave. With 97 F1
Tamar Rise. Sprin 127 E3
Tamarisk Way. Clact 124 C3
Tamarisk Way. Colch 68 C4
Tambour Cl. Gt T 64 B4
Tamworth Cha. Colch 68 A1
Tan La. Lit Cla 91 F2
Tangerine Cl. Colch 68 B3
Tangmere Cl. Wick 175 D3
Tankerville Dr. South 189 E1
Tanner Cl. Clact 109 D2
Tanners Way. S Woo F 165 E4
Tanswell Ave. Basil 186 A3
Tanswell Cl. Basil 186 A3
Tantelen Rd. Canv 196 C3
Tapley Rd. Chelm 126 C4
Tapsworth Cl. Clact 109 E3
Tapwoods. Colch 67 D4
Tara Cl. Colch 50 B1
Taragona Mews. Colch 68 A2
Taranto Rd. Canv 197 D3
Tarragon Cl. Tipt 100 B2
Tasman Ct. Chelm 126 C3
Tattersal Gdns. Hadl 189 D1
Tattersall Way. Chelm 139 F4
Tattersalls Chase. Soum ... 159 F2
Taunton Dr. South 190 A2
Taunton Rd. Sprin 127 E3
Taverners Green Pl. Wick . 174 C3
Taverners Wlk. With 97 F2
Tavistock Rd. Sprin 127 F3
Tawney's Ride. Bures 29 D4
Taylor Ave. Chelm 126 C3
Taylor Ct. Colch 67 F4
Taylor Dr. Mann 35 E2
Taylor's Rd. Rowh 86 C4
Teak Wlk. With 98 A2
Teal Ave. May 158 A4
Teal Way. Kelv 81 E1
Tees Cl. With 97 F1
Tees Rd. Sprin 127 E3
Teign Dr. With 97 E1
Teigngrace. South 201 E4
Teignmouth Dr. Rayl 176 B3
Telese Ave. Canv 197 E2
Telford Rd. Brain 60 A1
Telford Rd. Clact 110 B4
Telford Way. Colch 50 B3
Temperance Yd. Ea Col 45 D3
Templars Cl. With 97 F2
Temple Cl. Hadl 188 C2
Temple Cl. Walt 94 A3
Temple Cl. Colch 50 B1
Temple La. Silv E 79 E2
Temple La. T Gr 79 E2
Temple Pattle. Catt 35 E4
Templewood Ct. Hadl 188 B2
Templewood Rd. Basil 186 A3
Templewood Rd. Colch 50 C1
Templewood Rd. Hadl 188 B2
Temptin Ave. Canv 197 D3
Tendring Ave. Rayl 176 A2
Tendring Rd. Tend 54 C1
Tendring Rd. Tend 72 A4
Tendring Rd. Th L S 73 E2
Tennyson Ave. South 191 D1
Tennyson Cl. Brain 77 F4
Tennyson Cl. Hadl 189 D1
Tennyson Dr. Basil 186 A3
Tennyson Rd. Chelm 126 C3
Tennyson Rd. Mald 145 D4
Tenpenny Hill. Alres 88 C3
Tenter Field. Str S M 22 B1
Tenterfield Rd. Mald 132 A1
Tenterfields. Basil 186 B4
Teramo Rd. Canv 197 E2
Terling Cl. Colch 68 A1
Terling Hall Rd. Hat Pev ... 113 E3

Terling Rd. Hat Pev

Terling Rd. Hat Pev 113 F3
Terling Rd. With 97 E2
Terling. Basil 185 D3
Terminal Cl. South 201 F4
Terminus Dr. Basil 186 A2
Termitts Chase. Hat Pev 113 F4
Terms Ave. Canv 197 D3
Tern Cl. Kelv 81 E2
Terndale. Clact 109 F3
Terni Rd. Canv 197 E2
Terra-Cotta Pl. Glems 2 C4
Terrace Hall Chase. Gt Hor ... 49 E3
Terrace The. South 201 F3
Tewkes Rd. Canv 197 E3
Tewkesbury Rd. Clact 109 F2
Tey Rd Cl. Ea Col 45 E3
Tey Rd. Ald 64 C4
Tey Rd. Ald 65 D4
Tey Rd. Cogg 63 D3
Tey Rd. Ea Col 45 E2
Thackeray Cl. Brain 78 A4
Thackeray Row. Wick 174 B3
Thames Ave. Chelm 126 B2
Thames Cl. Brain 60 B1
Thames Cl. Hadl 189 D1
Thames Cl. Rayl 176 B1
Thames Dr. Hadl 189 D1
Thames Rd. Canv 196 C2
Thames Way. Burn 170 A3
Thameside Cres. Canv 196 C2
Thatchers Croft. Lach 156 C3
Thatchers Dr. Elmst M 69 F3
Thaxted Wlk. Colch 86 A4
Thear Cl. South 190 B2
Thelma Ave. Canv 197 D2
Thelsford Wlk. Colch 68 C4
Theobalds Rd. Hadl 189 E1
Thielen Rd. Canv 197 D2
Third Ave. Canv 196 C2
Third Ave. Chelm 127 D3
Third Ave. Clact 110 B2
Third Ave. Frin 93 F2
Third Ave. Glems 2 B3
Third Ave. Hals 26 A1
Third Ave. Harw 40 B2
Third Ave. Walt 76 B2
Third Ave. Wick 175 D3
Third Wlk. Canv 196 C2
Thirlmere Cl. Bl Not 77 E4
Thirlmere Rd. Thund 187 F4
Thirslet Dr. Mald 132 B2
Thirtle Cl. Clact 109 E3
Thisselt Rd. Canv 197 D2
Thistledown Cl. Basil 185 E3
Thistledown. Basil 185 E3
Thistledown. Colch 50 A2
Thistledown. Pan 59 D4
Thistley Cl. Gold 133 F3
Thistley Cl. South 189 F2
Thistley Green Rd. Brain 60 A4
Thomas Bell Rd. Ea Col 45 D3
Thomas Dr. Canv 196 C3
Thomas Rd. Basil 186 C4
Thomas Rd. Clact 109 E2
Thomas St. Brigh 106 C3
Thomas Wakley Cl. Colch 49 F3
Thomasin Rd. Basil 174 B1
Thompson Ave. Canv 197 F2
Thompson Ave. Colch 66 C3
Thorin's Gate. S Woo F 165 E3
Thorington Ave. Hadl 188 B3
Thorington Rd. Rayl 177 D1
Thornberry Ave. Weel 72 C1
Thornborough Ave. S Woo F 165 F4
Thornbury Rd. Clact 109 F2
Thorndale. Thund 188 A4
Thorndon Cl. Clact 109 D2
Thorndon Park Cl. Hadl 189 E3
Thorndon Park Cres. Hadl .. 189 D3
Thorndon Park Dr. Hadl 189 D3
Thorne Rd. Kelv 81 D1
Thorney Bay Rd. Canv 197 D1
Thornford Gdns. South 190 C3
Thornhill Cl. Walt 93 F4
Thornhill. Purl 144 B1
Thornhill. South 189 F2
Thorns Way. Walt 94 A4
Thornwood Cl. W Mers 121 E3
Thornwood. Colch 49 F2
Thorolds. Basil 185 F2
Thoroughgood Rd. Clact ... 109 F2
Thorp Leas. Canv 197 D1
Thorpe Bay Gdns. South ... 201 D3
Thorpe Cl. Hawk 177 F2
Thorpe Espl. South 201 D3
Thorpe Hall Ave. South 201 D4
Thorpe Hall Cl. South 201 D4
Thorpe Park La. Th L S 92 B4
Thorpe Rd. Beau 74 A3
Thorpe Rd. Clact 109 F4
Thorpe Rd. Hawk 177 F2
Thorpe Rd. Th L S 92 C4
Thorpe Rd. Walt 92 C4
Thorpe Rd. Weel 73 D1
Thorpedene Ave. Hull 165 F1
Thorpedene Gdns. South ... 201 E3
Thorrington Cross. Basil ... 185 E3
Thorrington Rd. Gt Ben 89 E4
Thorrington Rd. Lit Cla 91 E2

Threadneedle St. Ded 33 F4
Three Crowns Rd. Colch 49 F1
Three Gates Cl. Hals 43 E4
Three Mile Hill. Chelm 139 E1
Thrift Wood. S Woo F 142 C1
Throwley Cl. Basil 186 B3
Thrushdale. Clact 109 F3
Thundersley Church Rd.
  Thund. 187 F3
Thundersley Gr. Thund 187 F3
Thundersley Park Rd. S Ben 187 F2
Thurlow Dr. South 200 C4
Thurlston Cl. Colch 50 B1
Thurlstone. Thund 188 B3
Thurstable Cl. Tolle 119 F1
Thurstable Rd. Tolle 119 E1
Thurstable Way. Tolle 119 F1
Thurston Ave. South 191 F1
Thyme Mews. With 97 F2
Thyme Mews. With 97 F2
Thyme Rd. Tipt 100 B3
Tiberius Gdns. With 114 C4
Tickfield Ave. South 190 C1
Tidings Hill. Hals 43 F4
Tidworth Ave. Runw 163 F1
Tighfield Wlk. S Woo F 165 E3
Tilburg Rd. Canv 197 D2
Tilbury Rd. Gt Y 9 D2
Tilbury Rd. Ridge 8 B4
Tile Barn La. Lawf 34 B1
Tile House Rd. Gt Hor 49 D4
Tilkey Rd. Cogg 62 C2
Tillingham Rd. Ashel 160 A4
Tillingham Rd. Soum 159 F3
Tillingham Rd. Till 149 E1
Tillingham Way. Rayl 176 A2
Tillwicks Cl. Ea Col 45 D4
Tilney Turn. Basil 185 F2
Timberlog Cl. Basil 185 F3
Timberlog La. Basil 185 F3
Timbermans View. Basil 185 F2
Timpsons La. Sprin 127 F2
Tindal Sq. Chelm 127 D1
Tindal St. Chelm 127 D1
Tinker St. Rams 56 B4
Tinker's La. Roch 178 C1
Tinkler Side. Basil 185 D3
Tinnocks La. St L 135 D1
Tintagel Way. Mald 144 C4
Tintern Ave. South 190 B1
Tippersfield. S Ben 187 F2
Tippett Cl. Colch 68 C3
Tiptree Cl. South 189 F2
Tiptree Gr. Wick 174 B4
Tiptree Hall La. Tipt 100 A1
Tiptree Rd. Gt Brx 99 E1
Tiptree Rd. Lit Brx 115 F3
Titania Cl. Colch 68 C4
Tithe Cl. With 97 F2
Tithe The. Wick 174 A3
Tobruk Rd. Chelm 126 C3
Tobruk Rd. Colch 67 E2
Tofts Chase. Lit Bad 129 F3
Tog La. Gt Hor 31 D2
Toledo Cl. South 200 A4
Toledo Rd. South 200 A4
Tollesbury Cl. Wick 174 C3
Tollesbury Rd. Toll D 118 C1
Tollesbury Rd. Tolle 118 C1
Tolleshunt D'arcy Rd. Toll M 117 F2
Tollgate Dr. Stanw 66 B4
Tollgate East. Stanw 66 B3
Tollgate Rd. Stanw 66 B3
Tollgate W. Stanw 66 B3
Tollgate. Thund 188 B3
Tolliday Cl. Wiv 69 D1
Tom Tit La. Woo Mor 143 F4
Tonbridge Rd. Hock 177 F4
Tongres Rd. Canv 197 D2
Tony Webb Cl. Colch 50 B2
Took Dr. S Woo F 165 E3
Top Rd. Toll K 101 D1
Top Rd. Woo Wa 130 B1
Toppesfield Ave. Wick 174 B3
Toppesfield Rd. Gt Y 14 C4
Toppesfield Rd. Gt Y 15 D4
Torquay Cl. Rayl 176 B3
Torquay Dr. South 189 F1
Torquay Rd. Sprin 127 E3
Torrington Cl. Sprin 127 F3
Torrington. South 201 E4
Torsi Rd. Canv 197 E2
Tortose Cl. Colch 68 A2
Torver Cl. Bl Not 77 E3
Totham Hill Green. Gt Tot .. 116 C3
Totlands Dr. Clact 110 A4
Totman Cl. Rayl 188 B4
Totman Cres. Rayl 188 B4
Totnes Wlk. Sprin 127 F3
Totteridge Cl. Clact 109 E3
Toucan Way. Basil 185 D2
Toucan Way. Clact 109 F3
Toulmin Rd. Hat Pev 114 A2
Tower Ave. Chelm 126 C2
Tower Court Mews. South . 199 F4
Tower Cut. Brigh 106 C3
Tower Rd. Clact 109 F1
Tower Rd. Wiv 69 D1
Tower St. Brigh 106 C3

Towerfield Cl. South 201 F4
Towerfield Rd. South 201 F4
Towers Rd. Mald 132 B3
Town Croft. Chelm 127 D3
Town End Field. With 114 C4
Town Sq. Basil 185 D3
Townfield Rd. Roch 178 C1
Townfield St. Chelm 127 D2
Townfield Wlk. Gt Wak 192 C2
Towngate. Basil 185 D3
Townsend Rd. Tipt 100 B4
Towse Cl. Clact 109 E3
Traddles Ct. Chelm 126 C3
Trafalgar Rd. Colch 66 C3
Trafalgar Rd. South 201 E4
Trafalgar Way. Brain 60 A2
Travers Way. Basil 186 A3
Tree Cl. Clact 109 F4
Treecot Dr. South 190 A4
Treelawn Dr. South 189 F2
Treelawn Gdns. South 189 F2
Trenchard Cres. Sprin 127 E4
Trenders Ave. Rayl 176 A4
Trenham Ave. Basil 186 B4
Trent Cl. Burn 170 A3
Trent Cl. Wick 174 B3
Trent Rd. Chelm 126 B3
Trews Gdns. Kelv 81 E2
Trimley Cl. Basil 185 E4
Trimley Cl. Clact 109 D2
Trinder Way. South 174 A3
Trinity Ave. South 199 F4
Trinity Cl. Chelm 127 E2
Trinity Cl. Elmst M 69 E1
Trinity Cl. Mann 35 E2
Trinity Cl. Rayl 176 C1
Trinity Cl. W Mers 121 E4
Trinity Rd. Chelm 127 E1
Trinity Rd. Hals 25 E1
Trinity Rd. Mann 35 E2
Trinity Rd. Rayl 176 C1
Trinity Rd. South 191 E1
Trinity Row. S Woo F 165 F4
Trinity Sq. Colch 67 F4
Trinity Sq. S Woo F 165 F4
Trinity St. Colch 67 F4
Trinity St. Hals 25 F1
Trinity Wood Rd. Hock 178 A4
Triton Way. Thund 188 A3
Triumph Ave. Clact 124 C4
Trotters Field. Brain 60 A2
Trotwood Cl. Chelm 126 C4
Troubridge Cl. S Woo F 165 F4
Trunette Rd. Clact 109 E2
Trunnions The. Roch 178 C1
Truro Cres. Rayl 176 B3
Trusses Rd. Brad O S 136 C2
Tryon Ct. Hals 25 E1
Tudor Cl. Brigh 106 C4
Tudor Cl. Clact 109 D1
Tudor Cl. Rayl 176 C1
Tudor Cl. Rayl 189 E4
Tudor Cl. Sud 7 F1
Tudor Cl. Thund 187 F3
Tudor Cl. Walt 76 B1
Tudor Cl. With 97 F1
Tudor Gdns. South 189 E2
Tudor Gdns. South 201 E3
Tudor Green. Clact 124 C4
Tudor Green. Sud 7 F1
Tudor Rd. Canv 196 B2
Tudor Rd. Rayl 189 E4
Tudor Rd. South 190 C1
Tudor Rd. Sud 7 F1
Tudor Way. Hawk 177 F2
Tudor Way. Wick 174 A4
Tudwick Rd. Tipt 100 C1
Tudwick Rd. Toll D 117 F3
Tudwick Rd. Toll M 117 F3
Tufnell Way. Colch 49 E1
Tugby Pl. Chelm 126 C3
Tulip Cl. Sprin 127 F4
Tulip Way. Clact 109 E2
Tulip Wlk. Colch 68 B4
Tumbler's Green. Stis 61 E4
Tunbridge Rd. South 190 C1
Tunstall Cl. Basil 186 B3
Tunstall Cl. St O 108 A3
Tupman Cl. Chelm 126 B3
Turkentine. Sud 13 E3
Turkey Cock La. E A Gr 65 F4
Turkey Oaks. Chelm 127 E2
Turner Ave. Lawf 35 D3
Turner Cl. South 201 F4
Turner Cl. Wiv 69 E1
Turner Rd. Colch 49 F2
Turnstone End. Colch 68 C4
Turpins Ave. Clact 110 B3
Turpins Cl. Clact 110 B3
Turpins La. Walt 93 F3
Turpins The. Basil 185 E4
Turstan Rd. With 114 C4
Tusser Cl. With 98 A4
Tusser Ct. Gt Bad 140 B4
Tusset Mews. Colch 66 C4
Tutors Way. S Woo F 165 F4
Twain Terr. Wick 174 B3

Tweed Cl. Hals 43 E4
Twining Rd. Colch 66 C2
Twitten La. Chelm 140 A1
Twyford Ave.Gt Wak 193 D2
Twyzel Rd. Canv 197 E3
Tyburn Hill. Wa Col 46 A3
Tydeman Cl. Stanw 66 B2
Tye Green. Glems 2 A3
Tye Hill. Lawf 34 C2
Tye La. Elmst M 69 F2
Tye Rd The. Gt Ben 90 A4
Tye Rd. Elmst M 69 A4
Tye The. E Han 153 E4
Tyefields. Basil 186 B4
Tyehurst Cres. Colch 50 B1
Tyler Ave. Clact 109 D2
Tylers Ave. South 200 A4
Tylers Cl. Chelm 140 A3
Tylers Ride. S Woo F 165 F4
Tylewood. S Ben 188 B1
Tylney Ave. Roch 178 C2
Tylneys Rd. Hals 26 A2
Tyms Way. Rayl 176 C2
Tyndale Cl. Hull 165 E2
Tyndale Dr. Clact 109 D1
Tyndales La. Dan 143 D3
Tyne Way. Chelm 126 B3
Tynedale Ct. Colch 50 A2
Tynedale Sq. Colch 50 A2
Tyrel Dr. South 200 A4
Tyrells Cl. Sprin 127 F2
Tyrells Way. Gt Bad 140 C4
Tyrells. Hawk 177 E3
Tyrone Rd. South 201 D4
Tyrrell Ct. Basil 186 B3
Tyrrell Rd. S Ben 187 D1
Tythe Barn Way. S Woo F .. 165 E4
Tythe Cl. Sprin 127 F4
Tythings The. Hals 43 E4

Ullswater Cl. Bl Not 77 E3
Ullswater Rd. Thund 187 F4
Ulster Ave. South 201 E3
Ulting Hall Rd. Ult 130 C4
Ulting La. Langf 130 C3
Ulting La. Ult 130 C3
Ulting Rd. Hat Pev 114 B1
Ulting Way. Wick 175 D4
Ulverston Rd. Ashi 167 E1
Una Rd. Basil 186 C3
Una Rd. Rams 39 F3
Undercliffe Gdns. South ... 198 C4
Underhill Rd. S Ben 187 F2
Underwood Squ. Hadl 189 E1
Union La. Roch 178 C1
Union Rd. Clact 125 D4
Unity Cl. Colch 68 A2
Upland Cres. W Mers 121 E4
Upland Dr. South 50 B1
Upland Rd. South 199 D4
Upland Rd. W Mers 121 E4
Uplands Cl. Hawk 177 F3
Uplands Cl. S Ben 187 D2
Uplands Cres. Sud 7 F1
Uplands Ct. Clact 109 E1
Uplands Dr. Sprin 127 E4
Uplands Park Rd. Rayl 176 B2
Uplands Rd. Clact 109 E1
Uplands Rd. Hawk 177 F3
Uplands Rd. S Ben 187 D2
Uplands Rd. Sud 7 F1
Upp Hall La. Gt T 64 B3
Upper Ave. Basil 186 C4
Upper Branston Rd. Clact . 109 E2
Upper Bridge Rd. Chelm ... 127 D1
Upper Chapel St. Hals 25 F1
Upper Chase. Alth 157 F2
Upper Chase. Chelm 140 A4
Upper East St. Sud 12 C4
Upper Farm Rd. Ashe 8 B4
Upper Fenn Rd. Hals 26 A1
Upper Holt St. Ea Col 45 E3
Upper Lambricks. Rayl 176 C2
Upper Market Rd. Runw 174 B4
Upper Park Rd. Brigh 106 C4
Upper Park Rd. Clact 109 E2
Upper Park Rd. Wick 174 B2
Upper Rd. Sud 19 F4
Upper Roman Rd. Chelm .. 127 D1
Upper Second Ave. Frin 93 F3
Upper St. Glems 2 C4
Upper St. Str S M 22 B1
Upper Third Ave. Frin 93 F3
Upper Trinity Rd. Hals 25 F1
Upton Cl. W Berg 48 B2
Upway The. Basil 185 E4
Upway. Rayl 176 B2
Urmond Rd. Canv 197 D2
Uttons Ave. South 198 B4
Uxbridge Cl. Wick 174 C3

Vaagen Rd. Canv 197 D2
Vale Ave. South 191 D1
Vale Cl. Colch 50 C1
Vale End. Chelm 140 B2
Vale The. Basil 185 E2

Victoria Rd. Mald

Valentine Way. Silv E 79 E4
Valentines Dr. Colch 50 B1
Valentines. Wick 174 B3
Valfreda Way. Wiv 69 D1
Valkyrie Cl. Tolle 119 E1
Valkyrie Rd. South 199 E4
Vallance Cl. South 191 F2
Valletta Cl. Chelm 127 D2
Valley Bridge. Chelm 127 D3
Valley Cl. Stanw 66 C2
Valley Cres. W Berg 48 C2
Valley Rd. Brain 60 A2
Valley Rd. Clact 110 A3
Valley Rd. Colch 68 C2
Valley Rd. Harw 39 E1
Valley Rd. Sud 13 F4
Valley Rd. Wiv 87 E4
Valley View Cl. Colch 50 A2
Valley View. Glems 2 C4
Valleybridge Rd. Clact 110 A3
Van Dieman's La. Chelm ... 140 B4
Van Dieman's Rd. Chelm .. 140 B4
Van Diemens Pass. Canv .. 197 F2
Van Dyck Rd. Colch 67 D3
Vanderbilt Ave. Rayl 176 B4
Vanderwalt Ave. Canv 197 E2
Vane La. Cogg 63 D3
Vanessa Dr. Wiv 69 D1
Vange Corner Dr. Corr 185 D1
Vange Hill Dr. Basil 185 F2
Vange Park Rd. Basil 185 D1
Vanguard Way. Brain 60 A2
Vanguard Way. South 201 F4
Vansittart St. Harw 40 B3
Varden Cl. Chelm 126 C3
Vardon Dr. Hadl 189 D2
Vaughan Ave. South 191 F1
Vaughan Cl. Roch 178 C3
Vaulx Rd. Canv 197 D3
Vauxhall Ave. Clact 124 C3
Vauxhall Dr. Brain 59 E1
Vellacotts. Chelm 127 D4
Venables Cl. Canv 197 E2
Venlo Rd. Canv 197 D3
Ventnor Dr. Clact 110 A4
Vera Rd. S Han 163 D1
Verlander Dr. Rayl 176 A4
Vermeer Cres. South 202 A4
Vermeer Ride. Sprin 127 F4
Vermont Cl. Basil 186 B4
Vermont Cl. Clact 110 A2
Vernon Ave. Rayl 176 A2
Vernon Rd. Hadl 189 E1
Vernon Rd. N Fam 156 A1
Vernon Way. Brain 60 B3
Vernons Rd. Wa Col 46 C3
Vernons Wlk. Basil 174 A1
Veronica Wlk. Colch 68 C4
Vesta Cl. Cogg 62 C1
Veyses End. Str S M 22 B1
Viaduct Rd. Chelm 127 D1
Viborg Gdns. Mald 144 C4
Vicarage Ave. Wh Not 78 C1
Vicarage Cl. Canv 196 B4
Vicarage Cl. Toll D 118 B2
Vicarage Cres. Hat Pev 114 A2
Vicarage Gdns. Clact 109 F1
Vicarage Hill. S Ben 187 F1
Vicarage La. Gt Bad 140 C3
Vicarage La. Mund 145 F1
Vicarage La. Th L S 73 F1
Vicarage La. Till 149 F2
Vicarage La. Walt 94 B4
Vicarage Meadow. Hals 25 F1
Vicarage Meadow. Soum ... 159 E2
Vicarage Mews. Gt Bad 140 C3
Vicarage Rd. Bel S P 5 D1
Vicarage Rd. Chelm 140 A4
Vicars Orchard. Bul 11 F3
Viceroy Cl. Colch 68 A2
Vickers Rd. South 190 B3
Victor Ave. Basil 186 B3
Victor Dri. South 198 C4
Victor Gdns. Hawk 177 F3
Victor Rd. Colch 68 A3
Victoria Ave. Rayl 176 A2
Victoria Ave. South 190 C1
Victoria Ave. Walt 93 E4
Victoria Ave. Wick 174 B4
Victoria Chase. Colch 67 F4
Victoria Circus. South 200 A4
Victoria Cl. Wiv 69 D1
Victoria Cres. Chelm 127 D2
Victoria Cres. Lawf 35 E2
Victoria Cres. Wick 174 A4
Victoria Dr. Gt Wak 193 E1
Victoria Dr. South 189 F1
Victoria Espl. W Mers 121 F3
Victoria Gdns. Colch 50 A2
Victoria Pl. Brigh 106 C3
Victoria Pl. Colch 67 F4
Victoria Pl. Colch 68 A3
Victoria Rd S. Chelm 127 D1
Victoria Rd. Basil 185 E1
Victoria Rd. Chelm 127 D2
Victoria Rd. Clact 110 A2
Victoria Rd. Col N 155 F3
Victoria Rd. Colch 67 F4
Victoria Rd. Mald 132 A1

Victoria Rd. Rayl 176 C2
Victoria Rd. S Woo F 165 E3
Victoria Rd. South 198 C4
Victoria Rd. South 200 B4
Victoria Rd. Walt 94 B4
Victoria Rd. Weel 91 D3
Victoria St. Brain 60 A1
Victoria St. Harw 40 B2
Victory Cl. Clact 109 E2
Victory Rd. W Mers 121 D3
Viking Rd. Mald 131 F1
Viking Way. Clact 110 C3
Viking Way. Runw 163 E1
Vikings Way. Canv 196 B2
Villa Rd. S Ben 187 E2
Villa Rd. Stanw 66 B3
Village Cl. Walt 93 E4
Village Dr. Canv 196 C2
Village Gate. Sprin 128 A2
Village Hall Cl. Canv 196 B2
Village Way. Walt 93 E3
Villiers Pl. Bore 112 C1
Villiers Way. Thund 187 F3
Vince Cl. W Mers 121 E3
Vincent Cres. South 201 F4
Vincent Rd. Ashi 167 D1
Vine Dr. Wiv 69 E2
Vine Farm Rd. Wiv 69 E2
Vine Rd. Tipt 100 B3
Vinesse Rd. Lit Hor 30 B2
Vineway The. Harw 40 A2
Vineyard Gate. Colch 67 F3
Vineyard St. Colch 67 F3
Vineyards The. Gt Bad 140 C4
Vint Cres. Colch 67 E3
Vintners The. South 190 C3
Viola Wlk. Colch 68 C4
Violet Cl. Sprin 127 F4
Virgil Rd. With 97 F3
Virginia Cl. Clact 109 D1
Virginia Cl. Thund 187 D4
Virley Cl. Mald 132 B2
Vista Ave. Walt 75 E1
Vista Rd. Clact 110 A2
Vista Rd. Wick 174 C4
Vivian Ct. Walt 94 B4
Volwycke Ave. Mald 144 C4
Voorburg Ave. Canv 197 E2
Voorne Ave. Canv 197 E1
Voysey Gdns. Basil 174 A1

Waalwyk Dr. Canv 197 E2
Waarden Rd. Canv 197 D2
Waarem Ave. Canv 197 D2
Waddesdon Rd. Harw 40 B2
Wade Rd. Clact 110 A4
Wade Reach. Walt 94 A4
Wadham Park Ave. Hock 177 D4
Wagtail Dr. Mald 132 B3
Wagtail Pl. Kelv 81 E1
Wakefield Cl. Colch 68 A4
Wakelin Way. With 98 A1
Wakering Ave. South 202 A4
Wakering Rd. Gt Wak 193 D1
Wakering Rd. South 192 A1
Wakes St. Wa Col 46 B3
Wakescolne. Wick 175 D3
Wakeshall La. Bel S P 9 E4
Waldegrave Cl. Lawf 35 D2
Waldegrave Way. Lawf 35 E2
Waldegrave. Basil 185 D2
Waldegraves La. W Mers 122 A4
Walden Cl. Gt Tot 116 A2
Walden House Rd. Gt Tot 116 A2
Walden Way. Walt 94 A3
Waldingfield Rd. Sud 12 C4
Waldringfield. Basil 185 D4
Walford Cl. Cogg 63 D2
Walford Pl. Sprin 127 F1
Walford Way. Cogg 63 D2
Walk The. E A Gr 66 A4
Walk The. Hull 165 E2
Walker Dr. Hadl 189 D1
Walkers Cl. Sprin 127 E4
Walkey Way. South 202 A4
Walkways. Canv 196 C3
Wall La. Wrab 37 F3
Wall Rd. Canv 197 F2
Wall St. St O 123 E3
Wallace Cl. Hull 165 E2
Wallace Cres. Chelm 140 B4
Wallace St. South 201 F4
Wallace's La. Bore 112 C2
Wallasea Gdns. Sprin 127 F3
Wallflower Ct. Sprin 127 F3
Wallis Ave. South 190 C1
Wallis Ct. Colch 66 C2
Walls The. Mist 35 F3
Walnut Ct. Hock 177 F4
Walnut Dr. With 98 A4
Walnut Gr. Brain 59 F1
Walnut Tree La. Sud 12 B4
Walnut Tree Way. Colch 67 D2
Walnut Tree Way. Tipt 100 B4
Walnut Way. Brigh 106 C4
Walnut Way. Clact 109 E1
Walpole Wlk. Rayl 177 D1
Walsingham Rd. Sud 13 E3
Walsingham Rd. Colch 67 F1

Walsingham Rd. South 191 D1
Walter Way. Silv E 79 E2
Walters Cl. Chelm 140 B2
Walters Cl. South 189 F3
Walters Yd. Colch 67 F4
Waltham Cres. South 191 D2
Waltham Glen. Chelm 140 B4
Waltham Rd. Bore 112 C3
Waltham Rd. Rayl 176 A2
Waltham Way. Terl 95 F1
Waltham Way. Frin 94 A3
Walthams Pl. Basil 186 A4
Walthams. Basil 186 A4
Walton Rd. Clact 110 A2
Walton Rd. South 200 C3
Walton Rd. Th L S 74 B1
Walton Rd. Walt 93 E4
Walton Rd. Walt 94 A4
Wambrook. South 192 B1
Wamburg Rd. Canv 197 F2
Wansfell Gdns. South 200 C4
Wantz Chase. Mald 132 A1
Wantz Haven. Mald 132 A1
Wantz Rd. Mald 132 A1
Warburton Ave. Si Hed 24 B4
Warde Chase. Walt 94 A4
Wargrave Rd. Clact 109 E2
Warham Rd. Harw 39 F1
Warley Way. Frin 94 A3
Warner Dr. Brain 59 E2
Warners Gdns. South 190 C3
Warnham Cl. Clact 109 D3
Warren Chase. Thund 188 A2
Warren Cl. Rayl 188 B4
Warren Dr. Wick 175 D4
Warren La. Stanw 66 B2
Warren La. Writ 126 B2
Warren Rd. Brain 60 B1
Warren Rd. Hadl 189 D1
Warren Rd. Hals 25 E1
Warren Rd. S Han 163 E4
Warrens The. Walt 93 F3
Warrens The. Wic Bis 115 F3
Warrenside. Brain 78 A4
Warrior Sq E. South 200 A4
Warrior Sq N. South 200 A4
Warrior Square Rd. South 201 F3
Warwick Cl. Canv 197 D3
Warwick Cl. Mald 132 A1
Warwick Cl. Rayl 176 C1
Warwick Cl. Thund 187 E4
Warwick Cres. Clact 109 F2
Warwick Cres. Mald 132 A1
Warwick Dr. Mald 132 A1
Warwick Dr. Roch 190 C4
Warwick Gdns. Rayl 176 C1
Warwick Green. Rayl 177 D1
Warwick Rd. Clact 109 F2
Warwick Rd. Rayl 176 C1
Warwick Rd. Rayl 189 D4
Warwick Rd. South 200 C3
Warwick Sq. Chelm 126 C2
Wash La. Clact 109 E1
Wash La. Gold 133 D4
Wash La. Lit Tot 133 D4
Washford Gdns. Clact 109 E1
Washington Cl. Mald 131 F1
Washington Rd. Harw 40 A1
Washington Rd. Mald 131 F1
Wat Tyler Way. Basil 186 A1
Wat Tyler Wlk. Colch 67 F4
Watchfield La. Rayl 176 B1
Watchouse Rd. Chelm 140 B1
Water La. Bures 19 F1
Water La. Cav 1 B1
Water La. Colch 67 E4
Water La. Lit Hor 30 C4
Water La. Nay 20 C4
Water La. Peb 27 D4
Water La. Stis 61 E3
Waterdene. Canv 196 C3
Waterford Rd. South 201 E3
Waterhale. South 192 A1
Waterhouse La. Ard 52 B3
Waterhouse La. Chelm 126 C1
Waterhouse St. Chelm 126 C1
Waterloo La. Chelm 127 E1
Waterloo Rd. South 201 E4
Watermill Rd. Fee 81 F2
Waterside Rd. Brad O S 136 C2
Waterside Rd. Pag Ch 181 D3
Waterside. Brigh 106 C3
Waterville Rd. Basil 186 A2
Waterworks Dr. Clact 109 D3
Waterworks Rd. Tolle 119 E1
Watery La. Bradw 62 A1
Watery La. Rayl 165 E1
Watkins Way. South 192 C1
Watlington Rd. S Ben 187 D1
Watson Cl. South 201 E4
Watson Rd. Clact 109 F2
Watt's La. Roch 178 C1
Watts Rd. Colch 67 D1
Wavell Ave. Colch 67 E4
Wavell Cl. South 127 E4
Waveney Dr. Sprin 127 E4
Waverley Cres. Runw 163 E2
Waverley Rd. Thund 187 E3
Wavertree Rd. S Ben 187 D2

Wavring Ave. Walt 93 F4
Waxwell Rd. Hull 165 F1
Wayfarer Gdns. Burn 170 A3
Wayletts. Hadl 189 D3
Wayside. Dan 142 C4
Weald The. Canv 196 C2
Wear Dr. Sprin 127 E3
Weare Gifford. South 201 E4
Weaver's Ct. Sud 12 C4
Weaverdale. South 192 C1
Weavers Cl. Colch 66 C3
Weavers Dr. Glems 2 A2
Weavers La. Sud 12 C4
Weavers Row. Hals 25 F1
Weavers. Basil 185 F2
Weaversfield. Silv E 79 E3
Webster Cl. Si Hed 24 B4
Websters Way. Rayl 176 B3
Wedgewood Way. Hawk 178 B3
Weel Rd. Canv 197 E1
Weeley By-Ps Rd. Weel 72 C1
Weeley Rd. Gt Ben 89 F4
Weeley Rd. Lit Cla 91 E2
Weggs Willow. Colch 68 B4
Weight Rd. Chelm 127 E1
Weir Farm Rd. Rayl 188 B4
Weir Gdns. Rayl 176 B1
Weir La. Rowh 86 B4
Weir Pond Rd. Roch 178 C1
Welbeck Ave. Rayl 176 A2
Welbeck Cl. Hawk 177 F3
Welbeck Rd. Canv 197 D2
Welch Cl. South 191 F1
Well Field. Writ 126 A1
Well La. Birch 83 D3
Well La. Chelm 140 A1
Well La. Cla 4 A4
Well La. Copf 83 D3
Well La. Dan 142 B4
Well Side. Mks T 64 C2
Well St. Brigh 106 C4
Well Terr. Mald 132 A3
Well's St. Chelm 127 D2
Welland Ave. Chelm 126 B3
Welland Rd. Burn 170 A3
Wellands Cl. Wic Bis 115 E3
Wellands. Wic Bis 115 F3
Weller Gr. Chelm 126 C4
Wellesley Rd. Clact 109 F2
Wellesley Rd. Colch 67 F3
Wellfield Way. Walt 93 E3
Wellington Ave. Hull 176 B4
Wellington Ave. South 190 A1
Wellington Cl. Brain 60 B2
Wellington Cl. Chelm 126 B3
Wellington Rd. Ashi 166 C1
Wellington Rd. Harw 40 C3
Wellington Rd. Mald 131 F1
Wellington Rd. Rayl 176 C2
Wellington St. Brigh 106 C3
Wellington St. Colch 67 F3
Wellmeads. Chelm 140 A4
Wells Ave. South 190 B3
Wells Ct. Sprin 127 E3
Wells Gdns. Basil 185 F4
Wells Hall Rd. Sud 13 E2
Wells Rd. Colch 68 A4
Wellsfield. Rayl 176 C2
Wellstead Gdns. South 190 A2
Wellstye Green. Basil 185 F4
Welshwood Park Rd. Colch 50 C1
Wembley Ave. May 158 A4
Wendene. Basil 185 F2
Wendon Cl. Hawk 178 B2
Wenham Dr. South 190 C1
Wenlock Rd. Weel 90 C3
Wensley Rd. Thund 188 A3
Wents Cl. Gt Ben 71 F1
Wentworth Cl. Hat Pev 114 A2
Wentworth Cres. Brain 59 F3
Wentworth Meadows. Mald .. 131 F1
Wentworth Rd. South 191 D2
Wesley Ave. Colch 68 B4
Wesley Rd. South 200 A4
Wessem Rd. Canv 197 D3
West Ave. Chelm 126 C3
West Ave. Clact 109 F1
West Ave. Hull 165 E2
West Ave. May 146 C1
West Beech Ave. Wick 174 C4
West Beech Cl. Wick 174 C4
West Belvedere. Dan 142 C4
West Bowers Rd. Woo Wa ... 130 B2
West Chase. Mald 131 F2
West Chase. Mald 145 D4
West Cres. Canv 196 C2
West Dock Rd. Rams 39 F3
West End Rd. Tipt 100 A2
West Green. S Ben 187 D3
West Hanningfield Rd. Sand . 140 C1
West Hanningfield Rd. W Han 140 C1
West House Estate. South 159 E2
West Lawn. Chelm 140 B1
West Ley. Burn 170 B3
West Lodge Rd. Colch 67 E3
West Point Pl. Canv 196 B2
West Rd. Clact 125 E4
West Rd. Hals 25 F1
West Rd. South 190 C1

West Rd. South 201 E3
West Sq. Chelm 127 D1
West Sq. Mald 131 F2
West St. Cogg 62 C1
West St. Colch 67 F3
West St. Harw 40 C3
West St. Roch 178 C1
West St. Rowh 86 C4
West St. South 190 C1
West St. South 198 C4
West St. Tolle 119 E1
West St. Walt 94 B4
West St. Wiv 87 D4
West Station Yd. Mald 131 F1
West Stockwell St. Colch 67 F4
West Thorpe. Basil 185 E3
West View Cl. Colch 50 A2
West View Dr. Rayl 176 A1
West Wood Cl. Thund 188 B2
Westborough Rd. South 190 B1
Westbourne Cl. Hadl 188 B3
Westbourne Cl. Hock 178 A4
Westbourne Gr. Gt Bad 140 B4
Westbourne Gr. South 190 A2
Westbourne Gr. South 190 A2
Westbury Cl. Copf 65 E3
Westbury Rd. Frin 93 D3
Westbury Rd. South 191 E1
Westbury. Hawk 178 B2
Westcliff Ave. South 199 F4
Westcliff Dr. South 189 F1
Westcliff Par. South 199 F4
Westcliff Park Dr. South 190 B1
Westcliffe Gdns. Canv 197 F1
Westcott Cl. Clact 109 F3
Westerdale. Sprin 127 E4
Westergreen Meadow. Brain ..59 F1
Westerings The. Gt Bad 140 C3
Westerings The. Hawk 177 F3
Westerings. Purl 144 B1
Westerings. S Woo F 142 C1
Westerland Ave. Canv 197 E2
Westerlings The. T Gr 78 C3
Western Apps. South 190 A4
Western Cl. Silv E 79 F2
Western Espl. Canv 197 D1
Western Espl. South 199 F4
Western La. Silv E 79 F2
Western Prom. Brigh 106 B3
Western Prom. St O 106 C2
Western Rd. Brigh 106 C3
Western Rd. Burn 170 B2
Western Rd. Hadl 188 C3
Western Rd. Hadl 189 D1
Western Rd. Rayl 176 A1
Western Rd. Silv E 79 F2
Western's End. Catt 35 E4
Westfield Ave. Chelm 127 D2
Westfield Cl. Wick 174 C4
Westfield Dri. Cogg 63 D2
Westfield. Cla 4 A3
Westgate. South 201 F3
Westlake Ave. Basil 186 C3
Westlake Cres. Wiv 69 D1
Westleigh Ave. South 189 E1
Westman Rd. Canv 197 F2
Westmarch. S Woo F 165 E3
Westminster Dr. Hock 177 E3
Westminster Dr. South 190 A1
Westminster Gdns. Brain 60 A2
Westmorland Cl. Mist 36 A2
Weston Rd. Colch 68 A2
Weston Rd. South 200 A4
Westridge Rd. Clact 110 A3
Westropps. L Mel 7 E3
Westwater. S Ben 187 D2
Westway. Chelm 139 F4
Westway. Colch 67 F4
Westway. S Woo F 165 E4
Westwood Dr. W Mers 121 F3
Westwood Gdns. Hadl 188 B3
Westwood Hill. Colch 49 D2
Westwood Rd. Canv 197 D2
Wet La. Box 31 F3
Wetherfield Cl. Rayl 176 A2
Wetherfield Rd. Colch 86 A4
Wetherfield Rd. Si Hed 15 E1
Wetherfield Way. Wick 175 D3
Wetzlar Cl. Colch 68 A2
Weybourne Cl. South 191 D2
Weybourne Gdns. South 191 D2
Weybridge Wlk. South 192 C1
Weymouth Cl. Clact 125 E4
Weymouth Rd. Sprin 127 F3
Whaley Rd. Colch 68 B4
Wharf La. Bures 28 C4
Wharf Rd. Chelm 127 E1
Wharf Rd. Mald 132 C2
Wharfe Cl. With 97 F1
Wheatfield Rd. Stanw 66 B3
Wheatley Way. Chelm 126 C2
Wheatlands. Elmst M 69 F3
Wheatley Ave. Brain 60 B2
Wheatley Cl. Hawk 178 B2
Wheaton Rd. With 98 A1
Wheatsheaf Cl. Wrab 37 F3
Wheatsheaf La. Wrab 37 E2
Wheeler Cl. Colch 68 C3
Wheelwrights The. South 191 D3

Whernside Ave. Canv 197 E3
Whist Ave. Runw 163 F1
Whistler Rise. South 202 A4
Whitby Rd. Soum 159 D2
White Cotts. Fair 95 E2
White Elm Rd. S Woo F 143 D1
White Hall Rd. Gt Wak 193 D2
White Hart La. Hock 177 F3
White Hart La. South 127 F4
White Hart La. W Berg 48 C3
White Horse Ave. Hals 43 E4
White Horse La. Mald 131 F1
White Horse La. With 97 F2
White House Chase. Rayl 176 C1
White House Rd. South 189 F3
White Lodge Cres. Th L S 74 B1
White Rd. Canv 196 B3
White Trees Cl. S Woo F 165 D3
Whitefriars Cres. South 199 E4
Whitefriars Way. Colch 67 D3
Whitegate Rd. Brigh 107 D3
Whitegate Rd. South 200 A4
Whitehall Cl. Colch 68 B2
Whitehall La. Th L S 73 E1
Whitehall Rd. Colch 68 B2
Whitehouse Cres. Gt Bad 140 B4
Whitehouse Hill. Virl 119 D4
Whitehouse La. Bel S P 5 D1
Whitehouse La. W Berg 48 B2
Whitehouse Meadows. South 190 A3
Whitehouse Rd. S Woo F 165 E4
Whitelands Cl. Runw 163 F1
Whiteshott. Basil 185 D2
Whitethorn Gdns. Chelm 140 B4
Whiteways Ct. With 97 F2
Whiteways. Canv 197 E1
Whiteways. South 189 F3
Whitewell Rd. Colch 67 F3
Whitlands. Glems 2 A3
Whitmore Ct. Basil 185 F4
Whitmore Way. Basil 185 E4
Whittaker Way. W Mers 121 F4
Whittingham Ave. South 191 F1
Whytewaters. Basil 185 F2
Whyverne Cl. Sprin 127 F3
Wick Beech Ave. Wick 174 C4
Wick Chase. South 191 F1
Wick Cres. Wick 174 C3
Wick Dr. Wick 174 B4
Wick Dr. Wick 174 C3
Wick Farm Rd. St L 148 B4
Wick La. Ard 51 D4
Wick La. Fing 87 E2
Wick La. Harw 40 A1
Wick La. St O 90 B2
Wick La. Wick 174 C4
Wick Rd. Burn 170 B2
Wick Rd. Colch 68 B1
Wick Rd. Gt Ben 90 A3
Wick Rd. High 21 F1
Wick Rd. Langh 32 C2
Wickfield Ash. Chelm 126 B3
Wickham Bishops. Wic Bis .. 115 E2
Wickham Pl. Basil 185 E3
Wickham Rd. Colch 67 E3
Wickham Rd. With 97 F2
Wickham's Chase. S Woo F . 143 E1
Wicklow Ave. Chelm 126 B3
Wickmead Cl. South 191 F1
Wicks Cl. Brain 59 E2
Widford Chase. Chelm 139 F4
Widford Cl. Chelm 139 F4
Widford Gr. Chelm 139 F4
Widford Park Pl. Chelm 139 F4
Widford Rd. Chelm 139 F4
Widgeon Pl. Kelv 81 E1
Widgeons. Basil 186 B3
Wigboro Wick La. St O 107 F1
Wigborough Rd. Lay H 84 C1
Wigborough Rd. Peld 103 D2
Wignall St. Lawf 34 C2
Wilbye Cl. Colch 67 D2
Wilkin Ct. Colch 67 D2
Wilkinsons Mead. Sprin 128 A2
Willett Rd. Colch 67 D2
William Boys Cl. Colch 68 B4
William Cl. Wiv 69 E2
William Dr. Clact 109 E1
William Groom Ave. Harw 40 A1
William Rd. Basil 186 C3
William's Wlk. Colch 67 F4
Willingale Ave. Rayl 176 A2
Willingale Way. South 192 C1
Willingham Way. Colch 68 C4
Willmott Rd. South 190 B3
Willoughby Ave. W Mers 121 E3
Willoughby Dr. Sprin 127 F1
Willoughby's La. Brain 60 B4
Willow Ave. Walt 93 E3
Willow Cl. Brigh 106 B3
Willow Cl. Burn 170 A3
Willow Cl. Canv 196 C3
Willow Cl. Hock 177 F3
Willow Cl. Rayl 176 B2
Willow Cl. South 189 F3

Willow Cres. Hat Pev 114 A2
Willow Dene. Si Hed 15 E1
Willow Dr. Rayl 176 B2
Willow Gr. S Woo F 154 A1
Willow Hall La. Wix 55 E4
Willow Meadows. Si Hed 24 C4
Willow Rise. With 98 A3
Willow Tree Way. Ea Col 45 D3
Willow Way. Clact 125 D4
Willow Way. Harw 39 F1
Willow Wlk. Cane 168 B1
Willow Wlk. Hadl 188 B2
Willow Wlk. Hock 177 F3
Willow Wlk. Tipt 100 B4
Willow Wlk. Weel 90 C4
Willowbank. Chelm 140 A2
Willowdale Centre. Runw 174 B4
Willows The. Basil 186 B3
Willows The. Bore 128 C4
Willows The. Colch 68 A2
Willows The. S Ben 187 D2
Willows The. South 192 A1
Wilmington Rd. Colch 50 B1
Wilmslowe. Canv 197 F3
Wilrich Ave. Canv 197 E2
Wilshire Ave. Sprin 127 F2
Wilsner. Basil 186 B4
Wilson Cl. Wiv 69 D1
Wilson Marriage Rd. Colch 50 B1
Wilson Rd. South 199 F4
Wilson's La. Mks T 64 C2
Wimarc Cres. Rayl 176 A2
Wimborne Rd. South 191 D1
Wimbourne Gdns. Walt 93 F4
Wimbush Ct. Basil 186 A4
Wimbush End. Basil 186 A3
Wimbush Mews. Basil 186 A4
Wimhurst Cl. Hock 177 F4
Wimpole Rd. Colch 68 A3
Winbrook Cl. Rayl 188 C4
Winbrook Rd. Rayl 188 C4
Winchcombe Cl. South 189 F2
Winchelsea Dr. Gt Bad 140 C4
Winchelsea Pl. Brigh 106 C4
Winchester Cl. South 189 F4
Winchester Dr. Rayl 176 A3
Winchester Rd. Colch 68 A3
Winchester Rd. Frin 94 A3
Wincoat Cl. S Ben 187 E2
Wincoat Dr. S Ben 187 E2
Windermere Ave. Hull 165 E1
Windermere Dr. Bl Not 77 E3
Windermere Rd. Clact 110 B3
Windermere Rd. South 200 B4
Windermere Rd. Sud 13 D4
Windermere Rd. Thund 187 F4
Windham Rd. Sud 13 D4
Windmill Fields. Cogg 62 C2
Windmill Gdns. Brain 60 A4
Windmill Park. Clact 109 F3
Windmill Rd. Brad 36 B1
Windmill Rd. Hals 25 E1
Windmill Row. Glems 2 B3
Windmill View. Tipt 100 B3
Windrush Dr. Sprin 127 D3
Windsor Ave. Clact 109 E2
Windsor Cl. Canv 197 D2
Windsor Cl. Colch 68 A1
Windsor Ct. Brigh 106 C3

Windsor Gdns. Brain 60 A2
Windsor Gdns. Hawk 178 A2
Windsor Gdns. Runw 163 E1
Windsor Gdns. Thund 188 B2
Windsor Pl. Sud 13 D4
Windsor Rd. Basil 186 C4
Windsor Rd. South 190 C1
Windsor Rd. W Mers 121 E4
Windsor Way. Chelm 126 C1
Windsor Way. Rayl 176 C1
Windward Way. S Woo F 165 F3
Winfields. Basil 186 B4
Wingate Cl. Brain 59 F2
Winifred Rd. Basil 186 A3
Winnock Rd. Colch 68 A3
Winsford Gdns. South 190 A2
Winsley Rd. Colch 68 A2
Winsley Sq. Colch 68 A2
Winston Ave. Colch 67 D2
Winston Ave. Tipt 100 C3
Winston Way. Hals 26 A2
Winstree Cl. Lay H 84 C3
Winstree Rd. Burn 170 A3
Winstree Rd. Stanw 66 B3
Winstree. Basil 186 A4
Winter's Hill. Lay B 83 F1
Winter's Rd. Lay B 83 F1
Winterbournes. Walt 94 A4
Winterswyk Ave. Canv 197 F2
Winton Ave. South 199 F4
Winton Ave. Wick 174 A4
Wisdoms Green. Cogg 63 D2
Wistaria Pl. Clact 109 E3
Wiston Rd. Bures 30 B4
Witch Elm. Harw 39 F1
Witch La. Cogg 63 D4
Witchards. Basil 185 D3
Witham Lodge. With 114 C4
Witham Rd. Bl Not 78 A3
Witham Rd. Langf 131 E4
Witham Rd. Lit Brx 115 F3
Witham Rd. T Gr 79 D2
Witham Rd. Terl 96 C1
Witham Rd. Toll M 117 E3
Witham Rd. Wh Not 78 A3
Withrick Wlk. St O 108 A3
Withypool. South 192 B1
Withywindle The. S Woo F 165 E3
Witney Rd. Basil 170 B2
Wittem Rd. Canv 197 D3
Witterings The. Canv 197 D3
Witting Cl. Clact 109 E3
Witton Wood Rd. Frin 93 F3
Wivenhoe Cross. Wiv 69 E1
Wivenhoe Park Cnr. Colch 69 D3
Wivenhoe Rd. Alres 88 A4
Wivenhoe Rd. Ard 51 E1
Wix By-Ps. Lit Ben 53 F1
Wix Rd. Brad 36 C1
Wix Rd. Gt Oak 55 E2
Wix Rd. Gt Oak 56 A2
Wix Rd. Rams 38 C1
Woburn Ave. Walt 93 E4
Wolfe Ave. Colch 68 A3
Wollards Gdns. L Mel 7 E4
Wollaston Cres. Basil 174 B1
Wollaston Way. Basil 174 B1
Wolseley Ave. Clact 124 C3
Wolseley Rd. Chelm 127 D1

Wolton Rd. Colch 67 D1
Wolves Hall La. Tend 54 C1
Wonston Rd. Soum 159 E2
Wood Ave. Hock 177 F4
Wood Dale. Gt Bad 140 C3
Wood End. Hawk 177 E3
Wood Farm Cl. South 189 E2
Wood Field End. Lay H 85 D3
Wood Green. Basil 174 A1
Wood La. E A Gr 47 F1
Wood La. Mald 132 A3
Wood Rd. Mald 132 A3
Wood St. Chelm 140 A4
Woodberry Cl. Canv 197 D3
Woodberry Cl. Hadl 189 E3
Woodberry Rd. Wick 175 D3
Woodberry Way. Walt 94 A4
Woodbridge Gr. Clact 109 D2
Woodburn Cl. Thund 188 A2
Woodbury Cres. South 190 C3
Woodcock Cl. Colch 68 C3
Woodcote Cres. Basil 186 B3
Woodcote Rd. South 190 A1
Woodcote Way. Thund 187 D4
Woodcotes. South 192 C1
Woodcroft Cl. Thund 188 B2
Woodcutters Ave. South 189 E3
Woodend Cl. Thund 188 B2
Woodfield Cl. Walt 94 A4
Woodfield Cotts. Mald 132 B3
Woodfield Dr. W Mers 121 D4
Woodfield Gdns. South 198 C4
Woodfield Park Dr. South 190 A1
Woodfield Rd. Brain 60 A2
Woodfield Rd. Hadl 189 D2
Woodfield Rd. South 199 D4
Woodfield Way. Hat Pev 114 A2
Woodfield. Wick 174 B3
Woodford Cl. Clact 109 F4
Woodgrange Cl. South 200 C4
Woodhall Cl. Sud 7 F1
Woodhall Rd. Chelm 127 D4
Woodhall Rd. Sud 7 F1
Woodham Dr. Hat Pev 114 A2
Woodham Halt. S Woo F 165 E4
Woodham Mortimer Rd.
  Woo Wa 143 F4
Woodham Park Dr. S Ben 187 E1
Woodham Rd. Rett 164 C3
Woodham Rd. S Ben 187 D1
Woodham Rd. S Woo F 155 D2
Woodham Rd. Stow M 155 D2
Woodhays. Basil 186 B4
Woodhill Rd. Dan 142 A3
Woodhill Rd. Sand 142 A3
Woodhurst Rd. Canv 196 C2
Woodland Cl. Hadl 188 C2
Woodland Rd. Chelm 127 D2
Woodland Rise. Weel 72 C1
Woodland Way. Gos 42 C4
Woodland Way. Wiv 69 D1
Woodlands Ave. Rayl 188 C4
Woodlands Cl. Basil 185 F2
Woodlands Cl. Clact 110 A4
Woodlands Cl. Hock 177 E3
Woodlands Cl. Rayl 188 B4
Woodlands Dr. Basil 185 E1
Woodlands Park. Hadl 189 D2

Woodlands Rd. Hock 177 E3
Woodlands Rd. Wick 174 B4
Woodlands The. Brigh 106 C4
Woodlands The. South 201 F4
Woodlands. Alth 158 A2
Woodlands. Brain 60 B2
Woodlands. Colch 50 C1
Woodlands. Gt Oak 56 A1
Woodleigh Ave. South 189 E2
Woodlow. Thund 188 A3
Woodpecker Cl. Colch 68 C4
Woodpond Ave. Hock 177 F3
Woodroffe Cl. Sprin 128 A2
Woodrolfe Farm La. Tolle 119 F1
Woodrolfe Park. Tolle 119 F1
Woodrolfe Rd. Tolle 119 F1
Woodrow Way. Colch 68 C4
Woodrows La. Clact 109 D3
Woodrush End. Colch 66 A3
Woods The. Hadl 188 C2
Woodside Ave. Thund 187 E4
Woodside Chase. Hawk 177 F2
Woodside Cl. Colch 50 C1
Woodside Cl. South 189 D3
Woodside Rd. Ashi 198 C3
Woodside Rd. Hock 177 D3
Woodside View. Thund 187 E4
Woodside. Hadl 189 D3
Woodside. Lit Bad 129 F1
Woodside. Mund 145 E1
Woodside. Walt 94 A3
Woodstock Cres. Hock 177 E3
Woodstock. W Mers 121 E4
Woodview Cl. Colch 50 B2
Woodview Dr. Gt Le 95 D4
Woodville Cl. Hawk 178 B2
Woodville Rd. Canv 197 E2
Woodyards. Brad O S 136 C2
Woolards Way. S Woo F 165 E4
Woolner Rd. Clact 109 E3
Woolpack La. Brain 59 F3
Woolpack. South 201 E4
Woolwich Rd. Clact 109 E3
Worcester Cl. Brain 60 A1
Worcester Cl. Colch 68 A4
Worcester Cl. Steep 147 D1
Worcester Cres. Alres 88 A4
Worcester Ct. Gt Bad 141 D3
Worcester Dr. Rayl 176 C1
Worcester Rd. Burn 170 B3
Wordsworth Ave. Mald 145 D4
Wordsworth Cl. South 191 D1
Wordsworth Ct. Chelm 127 D3
Wordsworth Rd. Brain 59 F4
Wordsworth Rd. Colch 66 C3
Workhouse Hill. Box 31 F2
Workhouse La. S Woo F 154 A1
Workhouse Rd. Lit Hor 30 B1
Worlds End La. Fee 81 E2
Worthington Way. Colch 66 C2
Wrabness Rd. Rams 38 B2
Wrabness Rd. Rams 39 D1
Wren Ave. Rayl 189 E4
Wren Ave. South 189 E4
Wren Cl. Gt Ben 71 E1
Wren Cl. South 189 E4
Wren Cl. Thund 187 D3
Wrendale. Clact 109 F3
Wright's Ave. T Gr 78 C3

Writtle Cl. Clact 109 D2
Writtle Rd. Chelm 139 F4
Writtle Wlk. Basil 185 F4
Wroxham Cl. Colch 67 D3
Wroxham Cl. South 189 D3
Wryneck Cl. Colch 49 F2
Wulvesford. With 114 B4
Wyatts Dr. South 200 C4
Wyatts La. Sud 19 E4
Wyburn Rd. Hadl 188 C3
Wyburns Ave E. Rayl 188 C4
Wyburns Ave. Rayl 188 C4
Wych Elm. Colch 68 A2
Wycke Hill. Mald 144 B4
Wycke La. Tolle 119 F1
Wycliffe Cl. Colch 49 F1
Wycombe Ave. Thund 187 D3
Wyedale Dr. Colch 66 C3
Wykeham Rd. Writ 126 A1
Wykes Green. Basil 185 E4
Wyncolls Rd. Colch 50 B3
Wyndham Cl. Colch 86 A4
Wyndham Cres. Clact 110 A3
Wynters. Basil 185 D2
Wythams. Basil 186 B4
Wythefield. Basil 186 A3

Yale Mews. Colch 50 A2
Yamburg Rd. Canv 197 E2
Yare Ave. With 97 E1
Yarnacott. South 201 E4
Yarwood Rd. Chelm 127 F1
Yeldham Lock. Sprin 128 A1
Yeldham Rd. Ca Hed 15 E2
Yeldham Rd. Si Hed 15 E2
Yeovil Chase. South 190 A2
Yew Cl. With 98 A3
Yew Tree Cl. Colch 68 C4
Yew Tree Cl. Hat Pev 114 A3
Yew Tree Gdns. Chelm 140 B3
Yew Way. Clact 124 C3
Yorick Ave. W Mers 121 E3
Yorick Rd. W Mers 121 E3
York Cl. Rayl 189 D4
York Cl. Sud 12 C4
York Gdns. Brain 60 A2
York Pl. Colch 68 A4
York Rd. Ashi 178 B4
York Rd. Brigh 106 C3
York Rd. Burn 170 B2
York Rd. Chelm 140 A4
York Rd. Clact 110 C3
York Rd. Ea Col 45 D3
York Rd. Rayl 189 D4
York Rd. South 200 C4
York Rd. Sud 12 C4
York Rise. Rayl 189 D4
York St. Mann 35 E2
Young Cl. Clact 109 E3
Young Cl. South 190 A4
Ypres Rd. Colch 67 F2

Zandi Rd. Canv 197 E1
Zealand Dr. Canv 197 F2
Zelham Dr. Canv 197 F2
Zider Pass. Canv 197 F2

STREET ATLASES ORDER FORM

The Street Atlases are available from all good bookshops or by mail order direct from the publisher. Orders can be made in the following ways. **By phone** Ring our special Credit Card Hotline on **01933 443863** during office hours (9am to 5pm) or leave a message on the answering machine, quoting your full credit card number plus expiry date and your full name and address. **By post or fax** Fill out the order form below (you may photocopy it) and post it to: **Philip's Direct, 27 Sanders Road, Wellingborough, Northants NN8 4NL** or fax it to: **01933 443849**. Before placing an order by post, by fax or on the answering machine, please telephone to check availability and prices.

COLOUR TOWN AND CITY EDITIONS

	PAPERBACK	
	Quantity @ £3.50 each	£ Total
WARRINGTON, WIDNES, RUNCORN	☐ 0 540 07588 4	➤ ☐
NORTHWICH, WINSFORD, MIDDLEWICH	☐ 0 540 07589 2	➤ ☐
DERBY	☐ 0 540 07608 2	➤ ☐
PEAK DISTRICT TOWNS	☐ 0 540 07609 0	➤ ☐

COLOUR EDITIONS

	HARDBACK	SPIRAL	POCKET	
	Quantity @ £10.99 each	Quantity @ £8.99 each	Quantity @ £4.99 each	£ Total
BERKSHIRE	☐ 0 540 06170 0	☐ 0 540 06172 7	☐ 0 540 06173 5	➤ ☐
MERSEYSIDE	☐ 0 540 06480 7	☐ 0 540 06481 5	☐ 0 540 06482 3	➤ ☐
	Quantity @ £12.99 each	Quantity @ £8.99 each	Quantity @ £4.99 each	£ Total
SURREY	☐ 0 540 06435 1	☐ 0 540 06436 X	☐ 0 540 06438 6	➤ ☐
	Quantity @ £12.99 each	Quantity @ £9.99 each	Quantity @ £4.99 each	£ Total
BUCKINGHAMSHIRE	☐ 0 540 07466 7	☐ 0 540 07467 5	☐ 0 540 07468 3	➤ ☐
DURHAM	☐ 0 540 06365 7	☐ 0 540 06366 5	☐ 0 540 06367 3	➤ ☐
HERTFORDSHIRE	☐ 0 540 06174 3	☐ 0 540 06175 1	☐ 0 540 06176 X	➤ ☐
EAST KENT	☐ 0 540 07483 7	☐ 0 540 07276 1	☐ 0 540 07287 7	➤ ☐
WEST KENT	☐ 0 540 07366 0	☐ 0 540 07367 9	☐ 0 540 07369 5	➤ ☐
EAST SUSSEX	☐ 0 540 07306 7	☐ 0 540 07307 5	☐ 0 540 07312 1	➤ ☐
WEST SUSSEX	☐ 0 540 07319 9	☐ 0 540 07323 7	☐ 0 540 07327 X	➤ ☐
TYNE AND WEAR	☐ 0 540 06370 3	☐ 0 540 06371 1	☐ 0 540 06372 X	➤ ☐
SOUTH YORKSHIRE	☐ 0 540 06330 4	☐ 0 540 06331 2	☐ 0 540 06332 0	➤ ☐
	Quantity @ £12.99 each	Quantity @ £9.99 each	Quantity @ £5.50 each	£ Total
GREATER MANCHESTER	☐ 0 540 06485 8	☐ 0 540 06486 6	☐ 0 540 06487 4	➤ ☐
	Quantity @ £12.99 each	Quantity @ £9.99 each	Quantity @ £5.99 each	£ Total
CHESHIRE	☐ 0 540 07507 8	☐ 0 540 07508 6	☐ 0 540 07509 4	➤ ☐
DERBYSHIRE	☐ 0 540 07531 0	☐ 0 540 07532 9	☐ 0 540 07533 7	➤ ☐

STREET ATLASES ORDER FORM

COLOUR EDITIONS

	HARDBACK	SPIRAL	POCKET	£ Total
	Quantity @ £12.99 each	Quantity @ £9.99 each	Quantity @ £5.99 each	
SOUTH HAMPSHIRE	☐ 0 540 07476 4	☐ 0 540 07477 2	☐ 0 540 07478 0	➤ ☐
NORTH HAMPSHIRE	☐ 0 540 07471 3	☐ 0 540 07472 1	☐ 0 540 07473 X	➤ ☐
OXFORDSHIRE	☐ 0 540 07512 4	☐ 0 540 07513 2	☐ 0 540 07514 0	➤ ☐
WEST YORKSHIRE	☐ 0 540 06329 0	☐ 0 540 06327 4	☐ 0 540 06328 2	➤ ☐
	Quantity @ £14.99 each	Quantity @ £9.99 each	Quantity @ £5.99 each	£ Total
LANCASHIRE	☐ 0 540 06440 8	☐ 0 540 06441 6	☐ 0 540 06443 2	➤ ☐

BLACK AND WHITE EDITIONS

	HARDBACK	SOFTBACK	POCKET	£ Total
	Quantity @ £10.99 each			
WARWICKSHIRE	☐ 0 540 05642 1	—	—	➤ ☐
	Quantity @ £12.99 each	Quantity @ £9.99 each	Quantity @ £4.99 each	Total
BRISTOL AND AVON	☐ 0 540 06140 9	☐ 0 540 06141 7	☐ 0 540 06142 5	➤ ☐
CARDIFF, SWANSEA & GLAMORGAN	☐ 0 540 06186 7	☐ 0 540 06187 5	☐ 0 540 06207 3	➤ ☐
EDINBURGH & East Central Scotland	☐ 0 540 06180 8	☐ 0 540 06181 6	☐ 0 540 06182 4	➤ ☐
EAST ESSEX	☐ 0 540 05848 3	☐ 0 540 05866 1	☐ 0 540 05850 5	➤ ☐
WEST ESSEX	☐ 0 540 05849 1	☐ 0 540 05867 X	☐ 0 540 05851 3	➤ ☐
NOTTINGHAMSHIRE	—	☐ 0 540 05859 9	☐ 0 540 05860 2	➤ ☐
STAFFORDSHIRE	☐ 0 540 06134 4	☐ 0 540 06135 2	☐ 0 540 06136 0	➤ ☐
	Quantity @ £12.99 each	Quantity @ £9.99 each	Quantity @ £5.99 each	£ Total
GLASGOW & West Central Scotland	☐ 0 540 06183 2	☐ 0 540 06184 0	☐ 0 540 06185 9	➤ ☐

➡

Post to: Philip's Direct, 27 Sanders Road, Wellingborough, Northants NN8 4NL

◆ Free postage and packing

◆ All available titles will normally be dispatched within 5 working days of receipt of order but please allow up to 28 days for delivery

☐ Please tick this box if you do not wish your name to be used by other carefully selected organisations that may wish to send you information about other products and services

Registered Office: 25 Victoria Street, London SW1H 0EX

Registered in England number: 3396524

I enclose a cheque / postal order, for a **total** of ☐ made payable to *Reed Book Services*, or please debit my

☐ Access ☐ American Express ☐ Visa ☐ Diners

account by ☐

Account no
☐☐☐☐ ☐☐☐☐ ☐☐☐☐ ☐☐☐☐

Expiry date ☐☐ ☐☐

Signature...

Name...

Address...

....

....

....POSTCODE

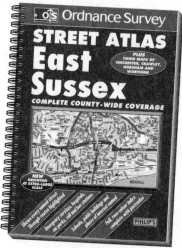